Representative Plays by American Dramatists

Edited with
Historical and Critical Introductions

By Montrose J. Moses

In Three Volumes
Volume   I   1765–1819
Volume II   1815–1858
Volume III   1856–1911

ROOTS AND SOURCES OF THE AMERICAN THEATRE

SONNECK, Oscar ....Early Opera in America

CARSON, William, G.B. ......Managers In Distress:
The St. Louis Stage, 1840-1844

LUDLOW, Noah Miller ......Dramatic Life as I Found It.
*With a lengthy introduction by Prof. Francis Hodge
(Univ. of Texas) and new index by Prof. Napier Wilt
(Univ. of Texas)*

MOSES, Montrose, J. (ed.) ....Representative Plays By American Dramatists, 3 vols.
Vol. 1, 1765-1819
Vol. 2, 1815-1858
Vol. 3, 1856-1917

BROWN, Thomas Allston ....History of the New York Stage
*From The First Performance In 1732 To 1901.
Three Volumes.*

MOSES, Montrose, J. ....The American Dramatist. Revised edition.

Representative Plays by American Dramatists

From 1765 to the Present Day

Edited, with an Introduction to Each Play

By MONTROSE J. MOSES

1815-1858

* *

BENJAMIN BLOM, INC.

New York

First published by E. P. Dutton & Co. Inc., 1925,
Copyright renewed by Mrs. Leah H. Moses, 1953
Reissued by Benjamin Blom, Inc. 1964 by arrangement with Mrs. L. H. Moses.

Printed in U.S.A. by
NOBLE OFFSET PRINTERS, INC.
NEW YORK 3, N. Y.

To
DANIEL FROHMAN
whose name is so excellently associated with the
AMERICAN THEATRE

Table of Contents

PREFACE

In August, 1917, this volume was made ready for the press, but the stress of war, and the consequent rise in cost of manufacture, necessitated its delay. Following this, it was found advisable to issue the third volume of "Representative Plays", inasmuch as contracts with certain living playwrights prohibited the postponement of the final volume in the series any longer. Thus it is that the second volume has been postponed beyond the allotted seven years. It has not been found necessary in any way to change its plan or scope, which aims to complete a cycle of dramas illustrating the successive progresses or changes in play writing in this country. It may be said of this second volume that it is more consciously *American* than the first, representing in its effort after type, a purely native product. Not that the playwrights were so much after the *American* type as they were after a vehicle for a certain type of acting which dominated the thirties, forties and fifties, and which in its most excessive expression resulted in the American minstrel.

It has been the effort on the part of the present editor to select for this volume examples of plays which have had interesting stage histories, and which have been called forth by a special type of acting. They are not marked by the propaganda spirit which is to be seen in many of the plays in Volume I. But they illustrate the fashion of a period, they are models of what was generally acceptable to the theatregoers of the time. The technique is imitative, and the inventiveness of plot meagre. Character grew in the hands of the actor after it had been suggested in slim and crude outline by the dramatist. Whatever life many of the plays of this genre had, centred in the strength of its character.

I have to thank the Public Libraries of New York and Boston for their courtesy to me, as well as the Library Com-

1

pany of Philadelphia and the Columbia University Library. I
have consulted with Dr. F. W. Atkinson, late of the Brooklyn
Polytechnic, and Miss Sydney Cowell has supplied me with
materials relating to the career of Mrs. Bateman. Data of
this kind are indispensable. Hardly a page in this book but
bears the impress of a guiding hand. Memory recalls how
closely companionship may mean collaboration, and without
such close companionship this work would never have been
done.

MONTROSE J. MOSES.

New Hartford, Conn.
September 17, 1925.

INDIVIDUAL BIBLIOGRAPHIES FOR PLAYS

Only essential references are given, and wherever possible the author's name is·indicated, rather than the title. In such cases the full title of the reference may be had by consulting the General Bibliography, Vol. I and Vol. III.

JOSEPH HUTTON

Allibone; the Reminiscences of James H. Caldwell; Drake, "Dictionary of American Biography"; Durang; The Newbern *Sentinel;* Rees, "Dramatic Authors"; Wegelin; Winter, William, "The Jeffersons" (Boston, James R. Osgood & Co., 1882).

JOHN HOWARD PAYNE

Allibone; Brown; Clapp, 101–112; Dunlap, 2:256; Duyckinck; Ireland; Rees, 113; Harrison, Gabriel, "John Howard Payne, Dramatist, Poet, Actor. And Author of 'Home, Sweet Home'" (Philadelphia, Lippincott, 1885); Brainard, Charles H., "John Howard Payne: A Biographical Sketch, with Narrative of Removal of Remains from Tunis to Washington"; Wegelin, Oscar, "Writings of John Howard Payne", *Literary Collector,* March, 1905, pp. 94–100, Bibliography (see also Wegelin's "Early American Plays"); Correspondence of Washington Irving and John Howard Payne, *Scribner,* 48:461–82 (October, 1910)—48:597–616 (November, 1910)—Edited by Payne's grand-nephew, Thatcher T. Payne Luquer; Hanson, Willis T., "Early Life of Payne; with Contemporary Letters and Bibliography"; Sanborn, F. B., "Romance of Mary W. Shelley, John Howard Payne, and Washington Irving"; "Home, Sweet Home", When Payne Wrote.—Letters from Paris, 1822–23. Edited by his grand-nephew, Thatcher T. Payne Luquer.— *Scribner,* 58:742–54 (December, 1915); Fry, Theodore S.,

3

Memoir of John Howard Payne. Pt. 1. "Mr. Payne in America" (November 24, 1832, p. 161). Pt. 2. "Mr. Payne in England" (p. 169); Hutton and Matthews, "Actors and Actresses of Great Britain and the United States"; Edwin Booth's Prompt Book of "Brutus", edited by William Winter (Boston: Charles H. Thayer, 1878); Genest, Rev. John, "Some Account of the English Stage from the Restoration in 1660 to 1830" (Vol. 8, p. 677, an analysis of "Brutus," with sources); Washington Irving, Life and Letters; Lamb, Charles, Life and Letters, edited by E. V. Lucas; Francis, J. W., "Old New York" (p. 213); Bernard, John, "Retrospections of America (1797–1811)". Edited by Mrs. Bayle Bernard. With Introduction and Notes by Hutton and Matthews (New York: Harper, 1887); Jefferson, Joseph, "Autobiography"; Phelps, "Players of a Century"; Hawkins, F. W., "The Life of Edmund Kean, from Published and Original Sources" (London, Tinsley Brothers, 1869, 2 vols.); Molloy, J. Fitzgerald, "Life and Adventures of Edmund Kean, Tragedian, 1787–1833" (London: Ward & Downey, 1888, 2 vols.); Alger, "Life of Edwin Forrest"; Winter, William, "Life and Art of Edwin Booth" (New York, Macmillan, 1894); Wilson, James Grant, "Bryant and His Friends". Other book sources are Clark, Susie C., "John McCullough"; Harrison, Frederick G., "Preëminent Americans", vol. ii; Stone, Herbert S. "First Editions of American Authors"; Wyndham, H. Saxe, "Annals of Covent Garden" (London, 1906, 2 vols.); Catalogue of Payne Papers Sold at Auction; A. L. A. Portrait Catalogue. Among the many magazine references may be mentioned: *Historical Magazine,* 1860, 371—1861, 184; *Living Age,* 1:250; London *Athenæum,* 1835, 13—1836, 129; *Harper's Monthly,* May, 1858, 786. General articles on Payne: *Cath. World,* 37:82; *Critic,* 2:223; *Ev. Sat.,* 10:505, 515; *Irish Monthly,* 17:520; *Literary World* (Boston), 14; 192—16:95; *Magazine Am. Hist.,* 9:335 (L. Hutton); *Munsey,* 7:694; *Potter Am. Mo.,* 19:88; *Theatre,* '85, 2:211; Last Days of John Howard Payne, *Amer.,* 9:460; Southern Sweetheart of Payne, *New England Mag.,* n. s. 5:355; Payne's Homestead, *Country Life,* 26:69–72; Mary Shelley's Suitors, *Fortnightly Rev.* (Gribble), 96:652–63; J. H. Payne's "Brutus", *Portfolio,* 22:23. Articles on "Home, Sweet Home": American Homes (Gillespie),

10: 231–36; *Musician,* (Bullard) 18: 227—(Maguire) 18: 268. Alfred Bates, in his "The Drama", vols. xix, xx, has an account of Payne, and publishes his "Thérèse".

DAVID PAUL BROWN

Dunlap; Wemyss; Wood; Rees; National Cyclopedia of American Biog.; Wegelin; Brown, D. P., "The Forum; or, Forty Years Full Practise at the Philadelphia Bar". With Biographical Memoir (2 vols.); Oberholtzer; Clarke, Asa Booth, "The Elder and the Younger Booth" (Osgood & Co., 1882); Durang (Anecdotal); Wegelin; *American Hist. Regis.,* 1896, 3:622; *Christian Rev.,* July, 1858; *So. Lit. Mess.,* July, 1858.

NATHANIEL PARKER WILLIS

A very large bibliography could be compiled. The following is sufficient for the reader: Brown; Ireland; Rees, 132; Bates, "Drama," xx: 52; files of the New York *Mirror;* Griswold, "Prose Writers of America"; the Works of E. A. Poe (Virginia Edition), consult indices; Diaries of Macready; Moses, M. J., "Famous Actor-Families", (Wallack); Morrell, Thomas H., "A Sketch of the Life of James William Wallack" (1865); Wilson, James Grant, "Bryant and His Friends". The dramas of Willis are discussed in an article by C. C. Felton, in the *No. Am. Rev.,* 51: 141. The authentic biography of Willis is that by H. A. Beers, in the *American Men of Letters Series* (Houghton Mifflin).

JOSEPH S. JONES

Appleton's Cyclopedia; Clapp; Ireland, 2: 388; Rees; Phelps; Woods. An Obituary Notice appears in the New York *Herald,* December 31, 1877; and in Boston papers as referred to in the text. Among the biographies with references to Jones: Falconbridge, *pseud.* of Jonathan F. Kelley, "Dan Marble: A Biographical Sketch" (1851); Hill, George Handel, "Scenes from the Life of An Actor" (1853); Ludlow, "Dramatic Life as I Found It"; Moses, M. J., "Famous Actor-Families" (under Hackett); Owens, Mrs. Mary C. (Stevens), "Memories of the Professional and Social Life of John E. Owens". By His Wife (Baltimore, 1892); Winsor's "Memorial History of Boston" (Chap. v); Wemyss; Winter, William, "The Wallet of Time", i: 149; also Winter's "John Gilbert" (*Dunlap Soc. Pub.*, 11, 1890). Alfred Bates, in his "The Drama," vol. xix, publishes "The People's Lawyer". Some of Jones's plays are listed in the Library Catalogues of the Boston Athenæum and of the Baltimore Peabody Institute. For a suggestive article on "Our Humble Dramatic Origins", by Walter P. Eaton, see the condensation in *The Literary Digest,* March 11, 1916.

Robert T. Conrad

Allibone; Brown; Duyckinck; Wegelin; Wemyss; Oberholtzer; Morris, "Makers of Philadelphia"; Simpson, Henry, "Eminent Philadelphians"; Rees, 39; Lives of Edwin Forrest by Alger and Rees; Murdoch, James E., "Impressions"; Winter, William, "Wallet of Time"; Moses, M. J., "Actor-Families" (Davenport); Edgett, "E. L. Davenport" (Dunlap Society). Alfred Bates refers to Conrad in "The Drama", xix, 25, 37.

Anna Cora Mowatt

Mowatt, A. C., "Autobiography of an Actress"; "Mimic Life; or, Before and Behind the Curtain". Biographical accounts of Mrs. Mowatt: Mary Howitt in *Howitt,* 3: 146, 167, 181; Antobiography of A. C. M., as reviewed by Dr. Walker, *Evang. R.,* 8: 546; "Personal Recollections of a Christian Actress" (Marion Harland), *Our Continent,* March 15, 1882; Hutton and Matthews, "Actors and Actresses of Great Britain and the United States", vol. 4, 155–70; "Visit to Mrs. Anna Cora Mowatt" (Mrs. B. Harrison), *Bookman,* 1: 164. Short accounts of Mrs. Mowatt are also to be found in Mrs. Hale's "Records of Women", in Griswold's "Female Poets", in Read's "Female Poets", and in May's "American Female Poets". For general references consult Allibone; Adams, "Dictionary of the Drama" (under "Fashion"); Clapp, 430–34; Duyckinck; Ludlow; Phelps, 268; Rees, 99. Much critical material on the plays is contained in the Works of E. A. Poe (Virginia Edition), consult indices; Harrison, J. A., "The Life and Letters of E. A. Poe" (Crowell);

Living Age, 41:33; London *Athenæum,* 1854, 175; *No. Am. Rev.,* April, 1854, 544—April, 1856, 580. References to Mrs. Mowatt are also contained in Edgett, "E. L. Davenport" (Dunlap Soc., n. s. 14); Winter, William, "Brief Chronicles" (Dunlap Soc., 1889, Pt. 2, No. 8); Wallack, Lester, "Memories"; Moses, M. J., "Famous Actor-Families" (Davenport). Mrs. Ritchie wrote an article on Frances Anne Kemble, *Macmillan,* 68:190. Alfred Bates, in "The Drama", xx:60, gives the prologue and epilogue of "Fashion."

UNCLE TOM'S CABIN

Brown; Phelps; Wemyss; Stowe, Charles Edward, "Life of Harriet Beecher Stowe"; Fields, Annie, "The Life and Letters of Harriet Beecher Stowe"; Maclean, Grace Edith, "Uncle Tom's Cabin in Germany"; Stowe, Lyman Beecher, Biography of H. B. S.; McCray, F. Y., "The Life of the Author of Uncle Tom's Cabin" (New York, Funk & Wagnalls Co., 1889); a synopsis of an article on Uncle Tom's Cabin, by the Rev. Charles Edward Stowe, "Dramatization and Production of", *The Literary Digest,* 42:1151, June 10, 1911; Ames, Edgar W., "First Presentation of Uncle Tom's Cabin", *Americana,* 6:1045–52, November, 1911; Stockbridge, Frank P., "The Most Popular American Drama", *Green Book,* 9:80–87, January, 1913; "What's Become of Uncle Tom's Cabin?" *Am. Playwright,* 3:264–66, August, 1914; "Uncle Tom's Cabin in Liverpool" (H. T. Peck), *Bookman,* 6:310, December, 1897. References to the play may also be found in the "History of the Boston Theatre", in Bates's "The Drama", xx:74, in Mrs. Owens's Memoirs of John E. Owens. Many casts are given in French's Acting Edition of the play. The different prompt-copies in the New York Public Library are evidence of the way in which every stage-manager wrote in new scenes and eliminated old ones at will.

MRS. SIDNEY F. BATEMAN

Annual Register, 1881, p. 460; London *Academy,* No. 455, pp. 70–71; London *Athenæum,* No. 2779, p. 173; London *Era,* January 15, 22, 1881, p. 8, p. 14; London *Era Almanack,* 1882, 1883, Obituary Notices; London *Times,* January 14, 1881,

p. 10; *Dictionary of National Biography* (under Mr. and Mrs. Bateman); New York *Times,* October 28, 1856 (the New York *Tribune* of the same date gives the cast of "Self" in the advertisements); Cowell, Joseph, "Thirty Years Among the Players" (New York: Harper); Winter, William, "Brief Chronicles" (Dunlap Soc., Pt. 1, No. 7, 1889, p. 7; Memories of John E. Owens; Pascoe, "Dramatic List"; Adams, Davenport, "Dictionary of the Drama" (Vol. 1, Philadelphia, Lippincott, 1904); Ireland, ii: 552; Keese, W. L., "W. E. Burton: Actor, Author, and Manager" (New York, Putnam, 1885.); Phelps, "Players of a Century"; Scott, Clement, "The Drama of Yesterday and To-day" (London, Macmillan, 1899, 2 vols.); Hutton, Laurence, "Curiosities of the American Stage." Consult also the various standard biographies of Sir Henry Irving, like those by Brereton, Fitzgerald, and Bram Stoker.

HORSESHOE ROBINSON

Brown; Dunlap, i: 163; Ireland; Phelps; Wegelin (Mr. Wegelin has in preparation a complete bibliography of Paulding); New York *Herald* as referred to in text; Scharf, Col. J. Thomas, "Chronicles of Baltimore" (Baltimore, 1874); Hackett, James H., "Recollections"; Moses, M. J., "Famous Actor-Families" (under Hackett); Winter, William, "Wallet of Time"; Bates, Alfred, "The Drama", xx: 56. Paulding comments on the National Drama in No. 2, *The American Quarterly Review.* There is a life of Paulding by his son, William I. Paulding (Scribner, 1867), and one of John Pendleton Kennedy, by Henry T. Tuckerman (Putnam, 1871). "Horseshoe Robinson" was issued as by the author of "Swallow Barn", Philadelphia, 2 vols., Carey, Lea, and Blanchard, 1835. The book was dedicated to Washington Irving.

FASHIONABLE FOLLIES

By JOSEPH HUTTON

JOSEPH HUTTON

(1787–1828)

Local history in the American Theatre is just beginning
to demand the attention of students. There is ample material
for a foundation; and the pioneer historians, like Dunlap,
Durang, and Seilhamer, have blazed the trail. But many
names have yet to be reinstated in theatrical annals, and
their reinstatement will probably bring to light many evi-
dences of the drama's activity in heretofore neglected
places. Dr. Archibald Henderson's thorough investigations,
connected with the life of Thomas Godfrey, Jr., have proven
that the culture of Wilmington, North Carolina, was pledged
to the support of drama in pre-Revolutionary days; and, were
one to verify carefully the claims of such itinerant theatrical
managers as Smith, Ludlow, and Cowell, other sources, so
long neglected, would be established.

Despite Clapp, Boston has yet to prepare a systematic
record of its local theatres from earliest times; despite
Ireland and Brown, New York dramatic history still needs
to be clarified.* Seilhamer's plan was a commendable one,
and is invaluable as far as it goes, but it could be followed
further, for the local history of Philadelphia, since 1800, thus
reinforcing Durang. In other words, some Philadelphia
student—and by analogy students in other localities—would
render an invaluable service by tracing the careers of the
Prune Street Theatre, the Olympic and others, mentioned
casually in the biographies of managers and actors, but not
fully recorded.

Were such data, systematically compiled, made available,
it would be an easy matter to account for the different
activities of Joseph Hutton, actor and dramatist. Historians
have contented themselves with the bare mention of his

* Professor Odell, of Columbia University, has in process such a documentary
history of the New York stage.

name, giving his dates and a list of his literary works.
Dunlap refers to three of his plays, and remains satisfied
with that. Drake's "Dictionary of American Biography"
places him in a line or two, as does Allibone. But here and
there, in American theatrical biography, we find traces of
Hutton, indicating that his experiences as an itinerant player
were wide, and, were they known, would be full of color.

This much we do know, to begin with, that he was born
in Philadelphia, on February 25, 1787. His play, "The School
for Prodigals," was given at the Chestnut Street Theatre, in
1808; and in the cast were Warren, Wood, Jefferson and
Blissett. Hutton's next essayal was a musical afterpiece,
"The Wounded Hussar; or, Rightful Heir", presented the
next season at the same house. Then followed "Fashionable
Follies", in 1809, and "The Orphan of Prague", in 1810. A
long poem, "The Field of Orleans", inspired by the historical
events of the moment, and dedicated to the hero of the hour,
General Andrew Jackson, was his next effusion.

But by this time Hutton was thoroughly established as a
successful devotee of the Muse. In 1811, his poems were
published in a volume entitled "Leisure Hours". In some
stray record I find a casual critical estimate of his poetry,
which points to Hutton's being a disciple of Scott. In 1823,
dramatic biographical sources indicate that he moved to Newbern, North Carolina, where, evidently tired of the road, he
settled down with his family, and devoted himself to teaching; he also became a regular contributor to the Newbern
Sentinel. It was here that he died, on January 31, 1828.

These slight records of fact give little or nothing of his
career, either as dramatist or as actor. But they are outlines
upon which further investigation should be based. Rees,
whose slim volume, "The Dramatic Authors of America",
is a pioneer effort at chronological statement, declares that
Hutton was much more successful as a dramatist than as an
actor. "His 'Cuffee and Duffee' was highly applauded", he
writes; "its allusion to a duel in high life was truly ludi-
crous, and the characters most admirably drawn." Then,
with that delightful disregard of accuracy, which marks
even the most faithful of theatrical historians—see Seilhamer's strictures against Dunlap—Rees adds that Hutton
died in the far West. Again, from the same source, a letter

from the manager, Caldwell, is found, wherein he claims to have been the true instrument in bringing the legitimate drama to the South and West. "For my first company", he writes, "in New Orleans, numbered among it Mr. and Mrs. Hutton, Mr. and Mrs. Entwhistle, etc."

In his record of the Jefferson family, William Winter refers to Caldwell's company at Petersburgh, Virginia, of which Mr. Jefferson,—probably Thomas—was a member. Among his associates there were Mr. and Mrs. Hutton. In view of the fact that Hutton wrote a play entitled "Fashionable Follies," and was a member of the same company as was Jefferson, it is interesting to note, as a matter of dramatic coincidence, that Jefferson, the second, appeared in a comedy by Leonard McNally, entitled "The Follies of Fashion," which, when it was given at Covent Garden, in 1785, bore as its original title, "Fashionable Levities."

Durang, in his "History of the Philadelphia Stage". refers to Hutton in the following manner:

"It will be perceived that some changes, too, had taken place at the Prune Street Theatre. The Williamses and Mrs. Williams, Misses Durang and Herbert, did not continue there during the season. The Misses Durang were engaged at the Park, in January, 1822, after their engagement expired with Stanislas. Where the others were engaged we do not remember. As we are not particularly conversant with the movements of this house, we shall here give a few of its bills of that day, which will afford the reader a general idea of the company and their relative positions, the more particularly so, as several of the performers, whose names therein appear, arrived subsequently to be distinguished members of the profession. Two were well-known authors, Joseph Hutton and Mr. Stone, the latter especially, as author of the far-famed 'Metamora'."

The parts taken by Mr. Hutton were—

Prune Street Theatre
Mr. Mass's Benefit
On Tuesday Evening, March 12th, 1822
"The Wanderer; or, the
Rights of Hospitality."
Mr. Hutton took the part of *Ramsay*.

At the end of the drama a Daylight scene was given, and then followed a "Recitation", written for the occasion, and to be spoken by Mr. Hutton.

Recitation—"Death of Marmion"—
By a young Gentleman of this City.

. . . . .

Prune Street Theatre
First Night of "Montrano"
For the Benefit of Mr. Stone
The author of "Metamora"
On Saturday Evening, April 20th, 1822
"Montrano; or, Who's the Traitor."
Mr. Hutton took the part of *Jean Latouch*.
The entertainment concluded with the cel-
ebrated melo-drama, in three acts, of
"The Snow Storm."
Mr. Hutton took the part of *Brant*.

The Historical Society of Pennsylvania adds to our knowledge of Hutton by saying that he lived near the South Street
Theatre, in Philadelphia, and was a teacher and accountant.
It may be that in the latter capacity he served whatever
theatrical organization he was with.

Of his career in Newbern, North Carolina, the same
unsatisfactory results followed my investigations. At the
suggestion of the North Carolina Historical Society, I wrote
to a citizen of Newbern, regarding Hutton's death certifi-
cate, or any records to be gleaned from the local paper there.
He replied:

"I have been unable to find any trace of Hutton up to
this time. The file of the *Sentinel,* which I have been able
to get hold of, only goes back to 1831. We have no public
records of deaths covering that period. The records here
do not show the name, either as grantor or grantee, devisor
or devisee, nor in any way. It may possibly be that his
grave could be located in the cemetery, but it would require
some search. . . . I have heard the name in some connection."

Fortunately the Library of Congress has a file of the Newbern *Sentinel* for the year of Hutton's death, and from it the

following obituary notice of the paper's literary contributor is culled. It is from the *Carolina Sentinel,* the issue for Saturday, February 2, 1828.

DIED,

On Thursday morning last, Mr. Joseph Hutton, formerly resident of the City of Philadelphia, where he was born on the 25th day of February, 1787.—His funeral obsequies were attended yesterday afternoon with masonic honors.

In the sudden and lamented death of this Gentleman, a bereaved Wife and amiable Daughter sustain a severe and irreparable loss—but the privation is not limited to the lonely domestic circle. Society, and especially Newbern and its vicinity, have cause to feel deep regret at the unexpected event. To a mind of no ordinary capacity, Mr. Hutton added the advantages of an excellent education, and highly and variously cultivated and enriched intellect. As an instructor of youth, few have given more general satisfaction, or been more successful in the art of teaching and in school discipline. As an Orator, he was eloquent and impressive; and as a writer, prompt, chaste, glowing and argumentative. As a votary to the "tuneful nine", he was highly favoured, and long will be remembered the perennial feast which his prolific muse has afforded the readers of the Newbern *Sentinel.* During the residence of five years amongst us, he was in his deportment courteous, affable and unobtrusive —as a member of Society, moral and exemplary.

"The place that knew him, shall know him no more forever."

From Hutton's plays we have selected for inclusion in the present volume, "Fashionable Follies", because after a manner it is of an interesting social caste. Though its invention may be more or less imitative of the comedy of the period, and very evident in its solution, its characters are sharply defined, and exhibit that quality of argumentation for which evidently Hutton was noted. Though written ostensibly for the stage, the play has little dramatic action. For that reason it was probably stopped in rehearsal by the manager who had accepted it. Certain it is, as the title-page bears evidence, it was cast at the Olympic Theatre, and its dedication, when published, to Thomas Hope, records the fact of that gentleman's encouragement through hours of anguish and disputation which Hutton must have gone through with the management.

The satirical preface, written for the first edition, tells of Mr. Pepin's presenting "Fashionable Follies" to Mrs. Wilmot for her benefit. It would seem that Mr. Dwyer, of the Olympic Company, was chiefly instrumental in discouraging continuance with rehearsals. There must have been personal as well as critical reasons for his attitude, because he was given an ample part, in the rôle of *Delany*. For three years the fate of "Fashionable Follies" hung fire. A prologue had been written for it by one Joseph M'Coy, and Hutton had prepared the epilogue. But no persuasiveness on the author's part could procure for his play a production. So it was that, in vindication, he published the play, determined that the public should judge for itself the injustice to which he had been subjected. He not only poured forth the bitterness of his feelings in his preface, but he included the program as it had been originally assigned.

Interesting as the piece may be as a document influenced by the spirit of the time, whatever excellences "Fashionable Follies" may contain are better realized in the reading than in the acting. For the intrigue is too palpable. It is not even lightened by that mirth which Rees claims inspirited Hutton's "Cuffee and Duffee".

TO

THOMAS HOPE, Esǫ.

THE FOLLOWING PAGES ARE RESPECTFULLY

offered,

AS A SMALL TRIBUTE OF RESPECT,

FOR HIS

LIBERAL & UNSOLICITED ENCOURAGEMENT

OF THE WORK,

By the Author.

PREFACE

The profound alchymists, in the reign of Charles the First, swore they had discovered a wonderful elixir, which was an absolute antidote to mortality: and I have the honour to assure the gentlemen, interested in this sublime epistle, that had they no other merit, the notice which I have taken of them, is alone sufficient to save their fame from perishing. Unconscious of the honour I have long intended them, they are ranging through the western hemisphere, bellowing forth the ravings of a deranged imagination, which the author has mistaken for wit; or reciting a *lecture on heads,* in the Arcadian, herio-comico-tragico-pastoral stuff of prose titupping on a Parnassian pony. Nevertheless, wherever they may be, the unqualified panegyric of this preface will reach them, and tickle their ears, like—umph! no matter for the likeness, as my friend, old lawyer Quillet would say. But to *leave these damnable faces and begin:*

First, To that sagacious arenaut, Donald M'Kenzie, Esq.—hush! I can hear you quite hither—No passion—I am not going to give an account of your journey to the moon, in that famous balloon,

> Made with vast labour and a vast of thread!

Nor am I going to say, how you visited Vulcan—that's all moonshine!—Nor inform the world that you beheld the limping deity forging lightning,

> And beauteous Venus, O! disastrous lot!
> Mixing up thunder in an earthen pot!

Nor how you procured a pot of thunder and a flash of lightning, which you found so far superior to the common bullet and rosin, long in vogue, as to preserve them in the histrionic Olympus, and use them, ever since, in the theatrical thunder gust!—I won't mention a word of this—therefore, be com-

17

posed; be calm; don't put yourself in a passion. "What!"
methinks I hear you say—"what! my name fixed to a
preface, and be calm!"

Not so loud, sir; if you please; of what are you so apprehensive? Of compliments and commendations! O! fie!—I
despise flattery. Heaven help the while!—your superiority
of genius and talent begets you admirers—let them praise
you!

"But why mention me at all!" Peace, and I will tell you.
To give you a proof of my *affectionate, most affectionate
friendship!!* Pray, sir, don't you remember, how handsomely Mr. Pepin treated Mrs. Wilmot, about the year 1812,
concerning her benefit, both in Baltimore and Philadelphia?
—By the by, that is nothing to either you or I—but, my very
dear friend, you know, that Mrs. Wilmot determined upon
taking a benefit in this city—that upon making known her
intention to your *very dear friend,*—myself, he presented her
with FASHIONABLE FOLLIES, believing that it might assist
in the accomplishment of her hopes. You took your
part—made me a promise that you would exercise all your
abilities as an actor, to do justice to the cast; and your power,
as acting manager, to bring the piece out in the best manner
possible. Very well—this was an exercise of that *urbanity,*
which the world knows to be your peculiar characteristic!—
But, sir, why did you, afterwards, return your part to Mrs.
Wilmot, and flatly refuse to suffer the performance of the
play?—Was this conduct compatible with that gentlemanly
character, which you once offered to establish on the *Jersey
shore?*—Not exactly—It is true, you told me, in extenuation,
that your company could not do justice to my play!—Admirable flatterer!—But it is equally true, that you told others,
that your reason was, a want of merit in the piece!!—Candid
judge! Monument of veracity! Modern Longinus! But,
sir, let me whisper in your ear, the absolute *why and wherefore* FASHIONABLE FOLLIES was not represented. You had
all *missed a benefit,* and you determined, Mrs. Wilmot should
have no chance!

There was the rub, and so you bore your point!

As to the merits of the play, no one will accuse you of being
a judge; but the public will now have an opportunity of

forming an opinion for themselves, and this is another *why and wherefore* I publish it. A few more words, and with *you* I have done; without hoping that, what I have said, can possibly affect you; because you have so often spoken the prologue of old New Castle Burr.

> Equal to me is praise or blame,
> I acts for fun and not for fame!
> And though the stage I loves as life,
> She is my mistress, not my vife!

Sir, you have committed a rape upon my play—by endeavouring to rob Mrs. Wilmot of any service it might have been to her in the advancing of her benefit, and the author of those advantages he might have received from its appearance. I shall therefore divide this *rape of the play* into four distinct heads, "to let you know my thoughts!"

> The rape indecent,
> The rape dormant,
> The rape abortive,
> The rape desired.

The rape indecent;—because you committed it upon a lady's pecuniary resources. For which you claim my—*admiration!!*

The rape dormant;—because beneath the most specious appearance, to me, slumbered your intention to commit it. For this you have my—*esteem!*

The rape abortive;—because you did not succeed in your intention—Mrs. Wilmot gaining a benefit, and I all the advantages I expected from the piece. For this you have my—*pity!*

The rape desired;—because the most ardent wishes of your heart were for the destruction of the play. For this accept my—*contempt!* And so, with all due deference, I take my leave of your attempts.

To Mr. Dwyer—Nay, start not, as I have done at one of your heavenly faces!—I'll be mild and gentle—"and brief, for *you're* in haste." I consider your conduct in this affair, far less reprehensible, than your managerical colossus. Though you and the company did follow his example—

So I have seen—the similie is fine,
  And wonderfully pat, though rather old;
When rising Phœbus shoots his rays benign,
  A flock of sheep come skipping from the fold:—
One restless sheep cries, baa! and all the throng,
  Lambs, ewes, and wethers, bellowing, pour along.

As an actor, sir, you stand pre-eminent among the meritorious; and as a *lecturer upon heads.* George Steevens himself, on hearing you, would stand like

Laughter holding both his sides.

Yet I have some fault to find with you. The reader of the play who has seen you act, will not believe that the part of Delany is unsuited to your talents. You acknowledged the truth yourself. You took the Prologue from my hands— promised to study both it and the above part, and yet the labour of study was so burdensome to an actor, who had studied—Reader, would you believe it—EIGHT whole parts in the entire range of the drama!! Wonderful! You gave up your part—and why, forsooth!—Was a man, that had starred it all over America—"who had travelled from London to Kamschatka—had ching-chinged to a Chinaman's joss —smoked the calumet of peace with the descendants of Powhatan, and danced the war dance with the Catabaws," to submit to the "stale, flat, and unprofitable" drudgery of studying a new part?—No! though he had made a previous promise!—The underlings of the theatre, following your example, threw up their parts, and this is the principal *why and wherefore* FASHIONABLE FOLLIES was not performed. Though you are, by no means, so censurable as the acting manager, yet to you, in a great measure, may be attributed the non-appearance of my play. Had you declined studying the part of Delany, when first presented to you, which by the by, as an actor under engagements with a manager, you could have no right to do, I should have been content; but as it was, you stand accused—And so, with Mr. Dwyer, I have done. As to the proprietors of the house, since they were mere pipes played upon by every Rosencrantz and Guildenstern about them, I shall let them rest in peaceful obscurity, not leaping over any ribands to come at them.

To the public, I would observe, that this play, after a delay of three years, is brought before them, that they may judge of its claims to representation; and say, whether the *why and the wherefore* convinces them that I have been unfairly dealt with. What I have declared is correct to the minutiæ, and every promise stated to have been made by the gentlemen, before mentioned, was absolutely given. To their decision I trust the fate of my FASHIONABLE FOLLIES, convinced that they ever will be

> Well pleased to praise; and not afraid to blame,
> Averse alike to flatter or offend.

THE AUTHOR.

PROLOGUE

Written by Joseph M'Coy, Esq.

Prompt to protect, with bounty even profuse,
The motley brood of every foreign muse;
Will you turn churls to-night and judge severe,
Because the author sits amongst you here?
What! will your easy goodness rest content
With worn-out plots and hacknied sentiment;
With scenes, a hundred times daubed o'er and o'er,
When daubed anew, they come from foreign shore!
To distant authors courteous welcome give,
And bid exotics in this garden thrive?
Prone to indulge, forgive the burlesque rage,
And monstrous mumm'ry of the German stage?
And yet will you, when here a native bard,
Timid and anxious, seeks your fond regard,
Sharpen your wits and watch him, close as chaste,
Lest he has some design to spoil your taste?
No, let it ne'er be said in future times,
The muses found no favour in these climes!
Let not a cold neglect of taste and art,
Check the free pulse of genius' throbbing heart:
But fire the enthusiast with your kind applause,
And he is armed to conflict in your cause:
Bold to repel the slander, dealt severe,
That blasted genius droops and withers here,
Prove you can prize his liberal toils to-night,
And strike one blow to do Columbia right.

DRAMATIS PERSONÆ

Peregrine Positive...........................Mr. M'Kenzine.
Dorriville................................ Tyler.
Captain Dorriville........................ Webster.
Delany.................................... Dwyer.
Edward Positive........................... Foster.
Ploughby.................................. Hogg.
Grenouille................................ Southey.
Solomon................................... Wilmot.
Robert.................................... Robinson.
Fixum..................................... Legg.
Chambers..................................
Keeper of the Prison......................

Miss Charlotte Positive................... Mrs. Melmoth.
Maria Dorriville.......................... Wilmot.
Fanny..................................... Miss White.
Dame Ploughby............................. Bradley.

The scene lies on the borders of LAKE CHAMPLAIN, in NEW YORK; and a few miles of the surrounding country.

FASHIONABLE FOLLIES

ACT I.

SCENE I.—*A room in the mansion of* PEREGRINE POSITIVE.

Enter MISS POSITIVE *and* MARIA.

MISS POSITIVE. But let me tell you, Miss Prate-a-pace, Miss Maria Dorriville, your impertinence is insufferable to a lady of my superior parts and respectability. Surely, girl, you must have forgotten yourself!

MARIA. Girl! ha, ha, ha, my dear Miss Positive, I did not, indeed, I did not think it improper, or that it could rouse your anger, to ask a simple question, what your age was?

MISS POSITIVE. Girl, girl, do you know what you are about? this is too much. Do you know who I am?

MARIA. Yes, Madam, the sister of my best friend, the generous Mr. Positive.

MISS POSITIVE. Yes, his beloved, his——

MARIA. Elder sister, Madam.

MISS POSITIVE. Very well, Miss, very well. [*With great vexation.*]

MARIA. Nay, nay, my dear——

MISS POSITIVE. It is no matter, Miss, but I shall acquaint my brother with your impertinence. This is always the way when people of quality stoop so low as to extend their protection to the reduced. Yes, Miss, this comes of it.

MARIA. Madam!

MISS POSITIVE. Had you been left to follow the follies and broken fortunes of your mad father, the daughter of

the delinquent Dorriville would not now have had the opportunity of insulting the sister of her benefactor.

MARIA. Insult you, Madam!—Had that sister a heart,
warmed by the genial current of sympathy, she would scorn
to wound the feelings of the unfortunate.

MISS POSITIVE. Very well, lecture me, too! I hope I know
my duty.

MARIA. Indeed you do not.

MISS POSITIVE. How!

MARIA. I say you do not, Madam, for your first and
greatest duty is humanity.

MISS POSITIVE. Very fine, Miss, very fine: this is very
fine rodomontade to a lady of my standing in the city, and
my wealth and respectability in the country.

MARIA. You touched upon a chord, Miss Positive, that
aroused all the feelings of a daughter's soul, and must seek
the cause within your own bosom, if my words offend. And
let me say, Madam, that Charles Delany's father was the
villain who ruined mine. Nay, more, that the man who pays
his adoration [scornfully] at the shrine of Miss Positive's
charms, is he who at this very moment holds those very
bonds which were obtained by robbery.

MISS POSITIVE. Robbery!

MARIA. Yes, by the vilest robbery! not by the midnight
thief, who seeks the solitary spot where undefended wealth
affords an easy prey; but by the smiling villain, by whom
the unsuspecting victim is lured from the paths of virtue,
who seizes the moment when his insidious wiles have lulled
the admonitions of reason, to lead him to the gaming table,
where all is staked upon one fatal throw, and in a moment
lost forever! Such a robber was Delany's father, such a
hapless victim to his artifices, mine.

MISS POSITIVE. You can talk very finely, Miss, but my
brother shall be made acquainted with your unbecoming
pride. If I am to be insulted by your rudeness, I shall
reside no longer in the house of an abandoned brother.

MARIA. Miss Positive, I intended no insult, nor did I
expect you would wound my feelings by touching on the
misfortunes of my father.

MISS POSITIVE. Nor would I, if I had not been provoked
beyond all sufferance: suppose that the charming Charles

Delany has sagacity enough to discover, in spite of your insulting beauty, the merit that lies concealed beneath this garb of maiden modesty, must you take upon you to be jealous?

MARIA. My dear Miss Positive, for mercy's sake, don't be afraid, I'll never be jealous of *you*.

MISS POSITIVE. That's right, my dear child.

MARIA. Besides, 'twould be absurd to think of rivalling you; no, Madam, your superior qualifications come between Delany's eyes and my beauty, by which the latter suffers a total eclipse.

MISS POSITIVE. I did not suppose—no, no, not absolutely rival me—the man who seeks my love——

MARIA. Is unworthy mine. [*Aside.*] You need be under no apprehension.

MISS POSITIVE. O! no. But I hope you do not mean to try your charms upon Delany! not from any fear of your success, but I should be sorry to see you meet with a disappointment. My feelings won't permit it, indeed.

MARIA. Indeed, I believe you, and now shall we retire?

MISS POSITIVE. Yes, my dear, and depend upon it, you shall partake of my happiness as the fair enslaver of the universally admired, Charles Delany. O! how the disappointed fair ones will cast their envious eyes upon me, as I ride, the admiration of the throng, with the first and only object of my affections. "Happy dog!" cries one, to my husband. "O! the malicious creature," cry the women, "how she now displays her long concealed charms!" Ha, ha, ha, how I shall triumph. Won't it be enchanting?

MARIA. O! certainly.

MISS POSITIVE. Pray, Maria, my dear, what colour would you have our curricle?

MARIA. Green, I think.

MISS POSITIVE. Green! why child, you are absolutely mad! green, what, why that means jealousy, as the immortal Shakspeare says, "'tis a green-eyed monster."

MARIA. What think you then of red?

MISS POSITIVE. [*Screaming.*] That's worse still, wantonness, fie, fie, fie!

MARIA. That would never do, indeed, for you, my dear Miss Positive. [*Then aside.*] As I live, the very thing.

MISS POSITIVE. No, no, let me see, I'll have it blue and white, the true emblems, my dear Miss Dorriville, of chastity and innocence. [*Exit.*

MARIA. Poor Miss Charlotte, how I pity her, for I am certain, in spite of all his promises, he never means to marry her; yet her silly vanity would not only strive to make her appear years younger than she really is, but absolutely persuades her that Delany loves her. This is a "fashionable folly" of all others the most despicable. And yet, I am as much in love as poor Charlotte. O! Edward, Edward, if you knew how tenderly I love, I fear you would despise me. [*Exit.*

SCENE II.—*A room in a country inn; a table, pen, ink and paper.*

CHARLES DELANY *enters, fashionably dressed, boots, spurs and a riding whip.*

DELANY. Holloa! house, demme, have you all gone out? I say, Chambers, where the devil are you? here I whisked to the country upon my Canada paddle, as hot with love as an eel in the sun. Why, Chambers.

CHAMBERS. Coming, sir.

DELANY. Come along then, you crab. If I succeed in this scheme, I shall be the happiest dog in America. I'll take her from the old fox, Positive, drive like the devil to Brighton, thence to New York, take lodgings. Yes, it will do,—but what will the old ones say? No matter, it's a fashionable folly, and fashion justifies any thing,* Chambers!

Enter CHAMBERS.

CHAMBERS. Here, sir.

DELANY. Quick, quick, get me a lobster, pickles, bread, butter, and turnips, or I'll heave the garret into the cellar.

CHAMBERS. The lobster shall be boiled in an instant.

DELANY. Sooner, sooner.

CHAMBERS. It shall, sir. [*Going.*]

DELANY. Here, Chambers, come back; let it be roasted.

CHAMBERS. Roasted, sir!

---

* This is not written by the author as a maxim of truth; but is intended as the false reasoning of a deluded imagination.

DELANY. Roasted, you crab-nose looking craw-fish, roasted.

CHAMBERS. Why, sir, I never heard of such a thing.

DELANY. How should you hear any thing, so far from the city?

CHAMBERS. But do you really mean that I shall cook the lobster in this manner?

DELANY. To be sure I do.

CHAMBERS. Very well, sir.

DELANY. Let it be immediately done.

CHAMBERS. It shall be done directly; but, sir, this is, as a body may say, changing the course of nature.

DELANY. Huzza! I have done it. Do you know, Chambers, that's just what I'm after? It runs in my blood.

CHAMBERS. Indeed!

DELANY. What's a man good for in this world if he's not deaf to the calls of nature? Why I should have been as poor as a travelling priest, if my father had let nature take her course.

CHAMBERS. Why, that's all remarkably true, sir. If I were to let nature take her course, sir, my heart would melt at every body's misfortunes, and I should give away all my substance.

DELANY. That would never do; but, my lean publican, to look at your body, one would think all your substance was gone already; ha, ha, ha.

CHAMBERS. To say the truth, I am not overburthened with flesh.

DELANY. However, you are right, never let such an ancient feeling as pity enter your heart; it's an unfashionable folly, I never heard of since the days of John Howard. Pity! every man of mettle would laugh at you, you would be hooted out of civilized society.

CHAMBERS. That is remarkably true, sir.

DELANY. I mean to overturn nature entirely. My father did so before me, for curse me if ever I saw a dollar of his money until nature overturned and cheated him. He died.

CHAMBERS. That was strange, that nature should cheat him.

DELANY. Yes, considering how cursedly it was in his nature to——

CHAMBERS. Why was it, sir?

DELANY. Yes, it was a way of his, a fashionable folly. He always lent his friends money to play, and then with loaded dice, heh! Chambers, he won it again, and more, too. He did it genteelly; they never suspected him, and curse me if they didn't call him the Hon. Charles Delany. But I never had any of it until his death.

CHAMBERS. How happened that, sir?

DELANY. He kept it in trade.

CHAMBERS. What, sir, a merchant?

DELANY. A merchant, sir! do you mean to insult me? do you suppose that my father would waste his time in making out invoices, filling up bills of lading, or calculating duties! No, sir, no such dishonourable employment. He kept two farobanks and three billiard tables, sir.

CHAMBERS. Wheugh!

DELANY. But, Chambers, get what I ordered.

CHAMBERS. Instantly, sir. [*Then aside.*] Two faro-banks and three billiard tables! these may be follies now-a-days, but when I was young they punished them as crimes.

[*Exit.*

DELANY. I have got clear of that infernal, musty hole, my study. Why should I study, when nature has already made me a lawyer, by giving me the most material qualification, impudence? Now for old Peregrine. I know Maria's his daughter, although he's positive she is not. Now there he's wrong, for it's impossible for a man to say, it's a wise father that knows his own children. I've heard my dad say, he often met his children ragged in the street and did not know them. Can Maria be the delinquent's daughter! Poh! old Dorriville took her with him. I'll marry her—no, I won't, but I'll bilk old Perry—get a pair of Canada ponies for the mammoth curricle, and Maria shall be mistress of myself and fortune. It's fashionable. Chambers.

Enter CHAMBERS.

CHAMBERS. Did you call?

DELANY. Is the lobster ready?

CHAMBERS. No, sir.

DELANY. Has my servant arrived?

CHAMBERS. No, sir.

DELANY. When he comes, send him to me. [*Exit* CHAM-
BERS.] What's all this?

Enter CAPT. DORRIVILLE.

CAPT. DORRIVILLE. If a fellow had a heart as hard as a
howitzer or the breech of a nine pounder, he could not be
cruel to those coaxing chambermaids. Curse me if Diogenes
could scarcely resist them. Here I am at last, within a few
miles of the spot. My sweet Fanny——

DELANY. Who the devil's this? Sir, I have the honour
of being your servant.

CAPT. DORRIVILLE. Thank you, sir, it's the first time I
ever had the honour of having one. But zounds, I don't
intrude—I don't presume——

DELANY. Yes, you do, but I pardon you, because it's fashionable to be impudent. Doubtless you've some end in it.

CAPT. DORRIVILLE. [*Aside.*] I think I have seen that face
before. By heaven, sir, I have a noble end in view. To bring
to chastisement the base traducer of a father's fame, and
press a beloved sister to my bosom!

DELANY. [*Aside.*] It looks much like him. Sir, you are
a wonder; who the devil are you?

CAPT. DORRIVILLE. A wonder, sir, as you have just now
assured me; but no more a wonder than that I am a man. A
villain deluded my father to the gaming table, bewailed his
losses, lent him money to regain what he had lost, and styled
himself his friend, while practising to undo him. Should
not this, sir, rouse me to revenge? [*Deeply affected.*]

DELANY. What's the matter with me! [*Aside.*] Revenge! no, sir, your father is not the only one that has been
ruined by gambling and such like fashionable follies.

CAPT. DORRIVILLE. Follies! I should have styled them
vices.

DELANY. That's not the style now-a-days. Formerly indeed, they were called vices, by some silly old puts, but the
word has been expunged from the modern vocabulary. If a
blood, sir, was not to frequent the billiard table, stake at faro,
keep a girl and ogle with her at the theatre, he would be
hissed out of genteel society.

CAPT. DORRIVILLE. And have our modern bucks no desire
to avoid being stigmatized with the appellation of fools?

DELANY. That depends upon it's being fashionable or otherwise. Now-a-days it's fashionable, and I should thank any man that would call me a fool.

CAPT. DORRIVILLE. Indeed!

DELANY. But you were mentioning your father.

CAPT. DORRIVILLE. My father was obliged to fly; I learnt this from my guardian, some years after, although he would never reveal the villain's name that ruined him.

DELANY. No! that was unfortunate.

CAPT. DORRIVILLE. It was. I entered my country's service, and am returned from a foreign station on furlough, to embrace a sister, and if possible, to discover and chastise the destroyer of my father.

DELANY. My dear fellow, you look very much like a friend of mine.

CAPT. DORRIVILLE. And you like one of mine.

DELANY. Indeed!

CAPT. DORRIVILLE. Charles Delany. [*Taking him cordially by the hand.*]

DELANY. George Dorriville——

CAPT. DORRIVILLE. Hush! no Dorriville; that name is blasted, and until restored to its pristine purity, it belongs not to me. To you, Charles, and to my guardian, I will be known; but I have assumed the name of Risible, and the character of levity, the more effectually to conceal myself from those who formerly knew me.

DELANY. Mum's the word then. But have you seen service, George?

CAPT. DORRIVILLE. I have. I was with the brave unfortunate Decatur, when treachery slew him in the arms of victory; and with the brave fortunate Decatur, when the frigate, in burning ruin, rolled the curling smoke in volumes to the skies! now we are along side—on board—the match is applied—she blazes, a fiery monument to the glory of our tars.

DELANY. By my soul, 'twas gallantly achieved!

CAPT. DORRIVILLE. Left the *Chesapeake* in the Mediterranean—came to the *Chesapeake* in the *Hornet*—arrived at Baltimore—want a passage, says I, to the skipper: What name? Jack Risible—always laughing—ha, ha, ha!

DELANY. Damme, but this is overturning nature entirely. [*Aside.*]

CAPT. DORRIVILLE. Kissed the bar-maid—jumped into the stage coach—turned the turtle with us on the road; yet here I am, arrived safe, after all my dangers.

DELANY. So you've taken this method to deceive your acquaintances, and wish to discover your father's principal creditor?

CAPT. DORRIVILLE. Exactly so.

DELANY. And he's the first to hear of it. [*Aside.*]

CAPT. DORRIVILLE. Yes, Delany, a man may make every witless blockhead believe that he's no fool at all. Poh, says he, looking into himself, I'm a Solomon, there's a very idiot, don't know a pike from a punch-bowl, and so in the folly of another finds an excuse for his own. So much for example. But beneath this garb of levity, I conceal a son seeking the restoration of his father's fame.

DELANY. That's filial gratitude, I don't like that. It's not justified by fashion.

CAPT. DORRIVILLE. Fashion!

DELANY. Yes, there's Billy Sprightly, t'other day, called the old dad, a damned put, because the weight of his purse drew the strings rather tight; and the next day forged his name for a few hundreds. Fan Feather called her mother a fool, because she said a woman was never intended for a corselet; and Dolly Simple ran away with Joe Slang, a beau taylor, because her father said marriage was rather too fashionable. But let me hear, Dorriville, what you intend to do to your father's creditor when you discover him.

CAPT. DORRIVILLE. Demand an ample restoration of my father's fame and property.

DELANY. But if he refuse?

CAPT. DORRIVILLE. Why, then I'll turn Turk and treat him as a Christian.

DELANY. What is your guardian's name?

CAPT. DORRIVILLE. Positive.

DELANY. So then, Maria is his sister. [*Aside.*] And are you going thither immediately?

CAPT. DORRIVILLE. Instantly. I long to embrace my sister, and speak my gratitude to the best of men, for his care of my dear Maria.

DELANY. [*Aside.*] If he goes there, before Maria is in my power, my plans are ruined. How shall I act? ha! I have it. It will do. [*To him.*] George, I believe I have befriended you.

CAPT. DORRIVILLE. You have my note for money lent when I stood in need.

DELANY. Damn the money; but would it give you satisfaction to return the obligation?

CAPT. DORRIVILLE. I have panted for an opportunity.

DELANY. Which offers now. [*Taking his hand.*]

CAPT. DORRIVILLE. I may see Mr. Positive and my sister first?

DELANY. That will never do. If you are once seen there, you can be of no use to me, as it is from Peregrine I'm about stealing the sweetest creature in the world. A few hours' delay to serve a friend, George——

CAPT. DORRIVILLE. I'd forego much gratification to serve you, so let us hear; but in the first place, who is it that has brought you from that tabernacle of knowledge, the city? When I left America, you expected to study law.

DELANY. What is law to love, or the head to the heart? love brought me, you sword-fish, that chubby archer, and Venus, the beautiful handmaid of Hymen.

CAPT. DORRIVILLE. Aye, and now you are going to elope with some round-faced country girl, with black eyes, and cheeks as red as a rose.

DELANY. Zounds! no.

CAPT. DORRIVILLE. With whom then, at this distance from town?

DELANY. With one of the most delightful, delectable girls in the world. An eye like the peepers of genius, and her whole form as much superior to the goddess of beauty, as a bishop is to a village preacher.

CAPT. DORRIVILLE. You have commenced a dangerous voyage; but I cannot blame you, Charles, for I adore my Fanny.

DELANY. Who is she?

CAPT. DORRIVILLE. One whom you seem to despise, a round-faced country girl, with black eyes, and cheeks as red as a rose. But no more, I must not think of her, while dishonour is coupled with the name of Dorriville. But, Charles, before I hear more of your plan, does the lady love you?

DELANY. That she shall herself tell, when she thanks you for your assistance in her flight.

CAPT. DORRIVILLE. Then, Charles, proceed.

DELANY. The lady's name is Julia Danvers.

CAPT. DORRIVILLE. Danvers! our late neighbour's daughter? I never knew he married.

DELANY. Nor did he, but what of that, my dear fellow; you would not have a man a saint because he never married? couldn't he have a daughter, without having a wife, eh, George? It's a fashionable folly.

CAPT. DORRIVILLE. And with her consent you mean to carry her off.

DELANY. Exactly so. I only wish you to keep a look-out in the rear, while I make off with the spoil. The better to conceal my intentions to this daughter, I have pretended to be cursedly smitten with the virgin charms of the old tabby, Miss Positive. She's as vain as a peacock and as ugly as an owl, without a grain of his wisdom. And now, my dear fellow, I am going to whisk her off to parson Grumble's, and all you have to do is to cover our retreat. Then we'll be secure, and call upon Perry for his blessing before supper. Will you assist me?

CAPT. DORRIVILLE. I am astonished that Mr. Positive should refuse your offers.

DELANY. Zounds! he don't refuse; he'd be very glad of the match; but Julia and I are too fashionable to put up with a chimney-corner marriage; we want éclat, and it's fashionable to elope now-a-days, that's all. Refuse me; zounds! I never asked his consent. I'll write to Julia immediately, and here's apparatus, dropped I believe by Cupid himself. [*Seats himself and writes.*]

CAPT. DORRIVILLE. You are an eccentric being, Charles, but noble at heart. I will assist you; but let it be done at once, for I am anxious to embrace my sister and my guardian.

DELANY. Thank you, George, thank you. I'll send my servant before with the letter to Julia, and we will follow him with all possible dispatch. So it's done. [*Folds and seals it.*] And as we go, my dear George, I will inform you at what spot I have appointed to meet the runaway. Chambers.

Enter CHAMBERS.

CHAMBERS. Sir.

DELANY. Has Grenouille arrived?

CHAMBERS. Yes, sir.

DELANY. Where is he?

CHAMBERS. In the kitchen, sir, devouring a piece of cold, tough mutton that has been cooked these three days.

DELANY. The ravenous rascal! send him hither directly. [*Exit* CHAMBERS.] I need not mention, my dear George, what a weighty obligation——

CAPT. DORRIVILLE. Hold, Charles, I am already indebted to you, and an opportunity——

DELANY. Pshaw! damn the money.

Enter GRENOUILLE, a meagre fop, large ruffles and huge neckcloth. Takes snuff immediately.

GRENOUILLE. He bien, my master, que est ce vous voulez! vat you vant, sair, eh?

DELANY. Here, Grenouille, take this letter and deliver it *unseen* into the hands of the person to whom it is directed.

GRENOUILLE. Ah! hah! I entend bien, I understand a you vell.

DELANY. Mind, sirrah, unseen, or I will break every bone in your skin.

GRENOUILLE. By gar, you cannot break the bone of my flesh, parce que I no av de flesh.

CAPT. DORRIVILLE. You look rather lank, Monsieur.

GRENOUILLE. Vous avez raison, by gar, I vill go to Monsieur Perry's avec the grand diligence. Donnez-moi the lettre, [DELANY *gives him the letter*] by gar monsieur quelque chose. [*To* DORRIVILLE.] Suppose you hit moi on de belly, I vill sound all de same as von kettle drum, je suis as hollow as von vind sail, by gar.

DELANY. Well, well, away, Grenouille, and deliver the letter, as I ordered you.

GRENOUILLE. Allons.   [*Exit.*

DELANY. Now, then, George, let us on to the consummation of my wishes.

CAPT. DORRIVILLE. I will prepare and be with you in a
moment.   [*Exit.*

DELANY. So, so, my hot spark, I have you in the toil. He
little thinks that letter was written to his own sister; she
shall be the price of his father's bonds, and if he prove
obstreperous, I'll put him in prison on the note he gave me
for a few hundreds I lent him. I could have done without
him, but it was necessary to keep him from Perry's till I ran
off with Maria. Now I must devise some plan to get rid
of him, ha! say I have altered the hour of meeting; it
will do. How shall I feel, after seducing the sister and
imprisoning her brother? heh! zounds! I must not moralize.
It is a fashionable folly, and fashion justifies anything.

[*Exit after* DORRIVILLE.

ACT II.

SCENE I.—*Outside of* PLOUGHBY'S *cottage, situated on the
borders of Lake Champlain. Extensive view of the
country. The sunbeams are seen upon the lake.*

DORRIVILLE *enters from the cottage.*

DORRIVILLE. Hail! my country; once more I press my
natal soil and breathe thy purer air, America, thou sole abode
of liberty, and peace. Welcome, ye grassy fields, ye shady
arbours, and ye limpid streams that flow meandering through
the winding dell; and thou, pellucid Champlain, whose un-
ruffled bosom reflects the radiance of the morning sun! Welcome: welcome, my country, scene of all my bliss, of all my
misery, and all my wrongs! To these proud scenes for sixteen years I've been a stranger, and toiled beneath the burning suns of India; but nature now resumes her empire irre-
sistibly and must be satisfied. O! my children, dear pledges
of her love, who is now a saint in heaven; how my heart
pants to feel the throb of yours! be still more bounteous,
Providence, let me embrace my boy, kiss off the tear of
rapture from my daughter's cheek, and my remaining days
shall pass in gratitude. I have amassed enough to redeem

my bonds and still have thousands left, yet if my children are no more, my wealth is useless, and my peace is gone forever!

Enter ROBERT *from the cottage.*

ROBERT. Servant, sir; mother have sent I to ax if you'll be so kind as to come and eat your breakfast.

DORRIVILLE. Directly, my good lad.

ROBERT. Very well, sir.

DORRIVILLE. From him, perhaps, I may learn something. [*Aside.*] Come here a moment, Robert. Do you know all the residents around the country?

ROBERT. 'Nan.

DORRIVILLE. Do you know every one about here?

ROBERT. O! yes, sir, from Sam Hub, the carter, to the city ladies. Suke Hub and I were to be married, but my market nag died, and then old man said I were too poor.

DORRIVILLE. And do you love Susan?

ROBERT. Better nor mother's brindle cow.

DORRIVILLE. Well, well, don't despair, Robert, you shall lead your lass to the altar yet.

ROBERT. Sir!

DORRIVILLE. You shall marry Susan.

ROBERT. Shall I, sir?

DORRIVILLE. I will make up the loss, and find whatever else may be wanting.

ROBERT. Will you, sir? I'll run and tell mother. [*Going.*]

DORRIVILLE. Stay a few moments, Robert. Is not the country mansion of Mr. Peregrine Positive, near here?

ROBERT. O! bless you, sir, yes, close by, an' if they weren't so many trees in the way you might a most see it, sir.

DORRIVILLE. Are the family here at present?

ROBERT. Yes, sir, they live here altogether.

DORRIVILLE. And who compose the family now?

ROBERT. Why, there am Mr. Perry, who be certain of everything, and lord, sir, if you were to see how often he be mistaken, you'd laugh. Every body must agree with he, or else he won't agree with any body; and then what an uproar!

DORRIVILLE. Very eccentric, indeed! but has he no good qualities, my honest lad?

ROBERT. O! yes, plenty; he do look for all the poor about,

and send all the *unnatural* children to school but, thank Heaven! I be a *natural* child.

DORRIVILLE. If he does so many charitable actions, how comes it, Robert, that he did not replace your nag?

ROBERT. Somebody told him I got drunk, sir, but it's none of it not true, sir.

DORRIVILLE. Well, who are the other inhabitants of the mansion?

ROBERT. Then, there am Mr. Perry's sister, Miss Charlotte. She am a kind o' sort and kind o' not sort; more not sort, though. She says, green's red if Mr. Perry says so. She am up to the chin in love, and by gom, but her chin be as wrinkled as our Towser's muzzle, and she do want to marry Charles Delany.

DORRIVILLE. Indeed! does *he* live in this part of the country?

ROBERT. There be his plantation. [*Pointing off.*]

DORRIVILE. I know it, for it once was mine. [*Aside.*]

ROBERT. Then there am old man's nephew, master Neddy Positive, who they say be dying in love with Miss Maria.

DORRIVILLE. Indeed!

ROBERT. And they do say, that Miss Maria be dying for him, and so, by gom, as I told father, if that were the case, it were likely to be a dead match, he, he, he.

DORRIVILLE. And, who, who is this Maria,—Edward's cousin?

ROBERT. No, she be only Mr. Perry's ward; but he do love her as if she were his own. Miss Maria Dorriville; her father have left America to live among the copper coloured Indians in Calcut.

DORRIVILLE. [*Aside.*] I thank thee, Heaven, that one at least is safe. [*To him.*] And wherefore did he leave America?

ROBERT. I weren't acquainted with him, for reason, because I were just born; but they do say, that he run in debt and would never pay, and then run away for fear they would make him.

DORRIVILLE. Indeed! how trumpet-tongued is scandal! how fatal is the venom of her breath! like the destructive Upas of the East, she issues deadly poison, and ruins all that come within the compass of her rage! [*Aside.*]

ROBERT. There be sister Fanny, she'll be married if her lover ever come back.

DORRIVILLE. Who is he?

ROBERT. Miss Maria's brother.

DORRIVILLE. Indeed! and where is he?

ROBERT. I don't know, sir. Mr. Perry have sent him away.

DORRIVILLE. And is he engaged to marry your sister?

ROBERT. A while before he went abroad, and old Mr. Perry consented to it, and when master Dorriville went to sea, he tooked Fan for a companion to Miss Maria.

DORRIVILLE. What is the character of young Positive?

ROBERT. Better than all the rest, sir. But will you please to come, the breakfast will be all cold.

DORRIVILLE. I'll come immediately.

ROBERT. Very well, sir.   [*Exit into the cottage.*

DORRIVILLE. So, even in this retired spot has calumny been busy with the name of Dorriville; has been the herald of the vilest falsehood malice ever forged! Ran in debt and *would* not pay! How this child of unsophisticated nature moves me. His language is the mirror to his soul, from which sincerity rises, and the heart's dictates issue from the lips. Heavenly simplicity, 'tis with thee alone that truth and honesty reside. If young Positive has gained my daughter's heart, let them be united, and George shall yet be blessed with the sweet daughter of this humble cottage. Kind Heaven, fulfil my expectations, and all my sufferings will be forgotten!   [*Exit into the cottage.*

SCENE II.—*A room in the cottage.*

Enter DAME *and* ROBERT.

DAME. Well, Robert, where's the gentleman?

ROBERT. He am in the next room, drinking coffee; lord, mother, what a sight he said to I.

DAME. Indeed!

ROBERT. And then I told him all about Suke Hub and I.

DAME. And what did he say to that?

ROBERT. Guess. Why, can't you guess, mother?

DAME. No, sure.

ROBERT. Why, then I'll tell you; he said we should be married.

DAME. Did he, though?

ROBERT. I be shot, if he didn't, and said he'd find all we wanted. And then he ax'd I about Mr. Perry, and so I told him all about it, you know.

DAME. That were right; but I wonder what keeps thee feyther so long in town? I wish he were home to see our lodger. I wonder what he will say to our taking him.

ROBERT. Never fear, mother, feyther's heart am as soft as a rotten turnip, and I be sure, that when he hears the gentleman am misfortunate, he'll be as glad as he never were, that we took him.

PLOUGHBY. [*Within.*] So, my lad, rub the nags well down, and put 'em safe away.

DAME. There he am.

ROBERT. Yes, there he am.

Enter PLOUGHBY.

DAME. So, John.

ROBERT. Well, feyther, how be'est thee? Just come from York?

PLOUGHBY. Yes, lad, I be just come from the land of wickedness. Well, Dame, and how be'est? gi' us a kiss; and Bob, lad, how be'est thee? I be shot, but I loves home best yet. Here, Bob, take my hat and hang it on the horn over the door. [ROBERT *takes it, goes out and returns.*] Well, and how am Fanny, at the mansion?

DAME. She be pure, John.

PLOUGHBY. Better be pure, Dame, in her father's cottage, than foul in the palace of a king; for even bad men do pay a respect to virtue, but vice be treated with scorn by every one. But, heh! Dame, where did thee get that new gown?

ROBERT. She have gotten it honestly, feyther.

DAME. I bought it, John.

PLOUGHBY. Where did thee get the money?

ROBERT. Why, feyther, from the gentleman.

PLOUGHBY. I can't feel 'em.

[*Putting his hands on his head.*

DAME. What be the matter, does thee head ache?

PLOUGHBY. A lazy hawk told me I were the largest steer

o' all the horned cattle, I were driving to market, and by gom, I'm afraid he has told the truth.

DAME. Is thee mad, John: the gentleman lodger that we got yesterday be a real gentleman.

PLOUGHBY. What! has thee got a lodger?

DAME. Yes, and he have paid a week's board before hand.

PLOUGHBY. Well.

ROBERT. And he says, feyther, that I and Suke Hub shall be one.

DAME. Two, Robert, one and one makes two.

PLOUGHBY. Yes, Dame, and sometimes, when folks am married, one and one makes three, and being poor, you know——

ROBERT. Yes, but feyther, the gentleman says he will make us both rich.

PLOUGHBY. Why, will he though? well, well, I give my consent, and be very glad you took the lodger.

DAME. But he be main misfortunate.

PLOUGHBY. Am he though? then he am the more welcome; I be none of those who do entertain prosperity and spurn adversity from the door; and I trust, Dame, that our country, which am the only soil where true liberty and peace do grow, will ever cultivate that sweet plant which be more fragrant than a rose, charity! Poor soul, mayhap he's lost a most every thing.

DAME. No, John, he do pay well——

PLOUGHBY. No, Dame, he don't pay at all. I should feel my heart thumping against my ribs, when ever I looked at the dollar which I had taken from a poor *creter* in distress, though I could well spare what he wanted for nothing. Well, did thee give him the best room?

DAME. Thee knows, John, I couldn't give him the best room, for thee weren't here.

PLOUGHBY. Couldn't! mercy! and where did'st put him?

DAME. In the little thatched chamber.

PLOUGHBY. What, Dame!

ROBERT. Feyther, don't thee get angry.

PLOUGHBY. Fie, fie, fie! run, Robert, and put his bed in the best chamber, before he goes into the thatched room again.

ROBERT. Very well. [*Exit.*

PLOUGHBY. Dame, Dame, how could thee use the misfortunate so? thee hast treated him so badly, Dame, I'll be shot if I sha'n't be ashamed to look him in the face. Do I look shameless? heh!

DAME. No, John, thee face be as red as our turkey cock. Now, don't be angry, John, I'm sure I feels for the misfortunate, but I couldn't let him have your chamber without you consented.

PLOUGHBY. Well, well, Dame, there. [*Embraces her.*] Thee am a good, kind hearted sort of a soul, but remember this, Dame, whenever thee axes who's at the gate, and am answered, misforten, let her in, and if thee husband be such a brute as to find fault, thee'lt have this for thy consolation, that when thee knock'st at the door of mercy for admission, thee will not find it barred.

DAME. Ah! John, thee am always doing all the good thee can.

PLOUGHBY. I only do my duty, Dame, that's what we be sent for. What's he that won't help a fellow creter in distress? he be like—I don't know what—but Dame, when my waggon and horses be stalled, I do all I can to get 'em out, and he am a bigger brute than a horse, that won't lend a hand to get another out of the slough of misfortune!

DAME. That be all as true as our sun dial.

PLOUGHBY. But where am the gentleman?

DAME. He be in the next room, drinking coffee.

PLOUGHBY. Come along then, Dame, and let I make him welcome, if I can look him in his face, after thee has treated him so bad.   [*Exeunt.*

SCENE III.—*The hall of* POSITIVE *mansion.* SOLOMON *snoring in a chair, a bottle held fast in his hand.*

GRENOUILLE. [*Within.*] Monsieur Solomon, by gar, where are a you? monsieur Solomon, you no ave'a in de pantry.

SOLOMON. [*Waking and gaping.*] Who the devil calls? [*Gets up, but being very drunk, he sinks again into the chair.*] So! not got over it yet.

GRENOUILLE. [*Within.*] Monsieur Solomon.

SOLOMON. Who the devil [*Hiccoughs*] disturbs me so early in the morning? it's so dark that positively I can't see

the length of my [*Hic.*] nose. Heh! [*Rubbing his eyes.*]—
What time o'day is it? Let me see, I believe I must have had
my dinner; yes, I have had my dinner, but, as my master
says, I'm positive I've had nothing to drink since—[*Drinks
largely.*] Ha, a drop of *bony spree,* as mounseer Greenowl
used to call it, is a most excellent thing. It enlivens the
[*Hic.*] spirits so, and above all, it makes a man sleep so
comfortable, that it is a very desirable companion. To be
sure, I have got rather too much in the habit of using it, but
then it's all my master's fault; for in the morning he'll go
out with master Edward [*Hic.*] upon charity, and leave me
all alone in this huge house, and of course I must hold intercourse with *bony spree,* merely to keep away the blue devils.
[*Staggering off.*]

Enter GRENOUILLE, *on the opposite side.*

GRENOUILLE.　Ah! ha! monsieur Solomon, venez ici, come
back, if you please, I was chercher for you.

SOLOMON.　Mounseer Greenowl, I'm glad to see you in the
country again—[*Hic.*]

GRENOUILLE.　Je vous remercie, I thank a you. Ah, ha!
monsieur, you 'ave a lit drunk, a!

SOLOMON.　A little upon the staggering order; but it's all
my master's fault.

GRENOUILLE.　Comment? how?

SOLOMON.　You know, mounseer, I'm not over [*Hic.*] fond
of liquor, but, [*drinks*] but when Mr. Perry went out, he was
so positive that I would be intoxicated before he came back,
that I put myself into this helpless situation, merely to keep
him from telling a falsehood. Nothing more.

GRENOUILLE.　Ha, ha, ha.

SOLOMON.　Don't laugh, mounseer; but where did you
leave your master?

GRENOUILLE.　I leave a him, at de—de maison de liquer.

SOLOMON.　Amazing in liquor! you're wrong, mounseer,
you should never [*Hic.*] leave your master in liquor; I never
leave Mr. Perry when he is intoxicated; fie! mounseer, fie!

GRENOUILLE.　Ha, ha, ha, you are ver merry, monsieur
Solomon; ven ever I come pour vous voir, to see a you, you
are always de bon esprit, by gar.

SOLOMON.　Yes, mounseer, *bony spree* is my best friend, I

always [*Hic.*] keep a bottle in my pocket. I'll take a drop now; will you drink, mounseer? [*Drinks largely.*]

GRENOUILLE. No, monsieur, parceque, I want something more substantial. You have always bon humeur, you are alvay in good spirit, by gar.

SOLOMON. Yes, I am always in good spirits, only when I drink *bony spree,* and then I have [*Hic.*] good spirits in me, heh! mounseer?

GRENOUILLE. Le diable, I 'ave forgot de lettre. [*Taking it out of his pocket.*] Monsieur Solomon, voulez vous avoir la bonté, vill you 'ave de goodness to deliver a votre mistress——

SOLOMON. My mistress!——

GRENOUILLE. By gar, you no un, understand a me, monsieur. Will you give this lettre to mademoiselle Maria Dorriville?

SOLOMON. O! deliver a letter! to be sure I will: [*Hic.*] but don't believe, mounseer, that I am drunk, if any body was to tell you so. O! no, this innocent, harmless cordial [*drinks*] never made any body drunk. Give me the letter, mounseer.

GRENOUILLE. There it is. [*Gives it to him.*] And now for de pantry. I feel all over in *de stomach,* I am ver hungry; by gar, I vill eat von goose, von turkey, von——

SOLOMON. Wheugh! why mounseer, to hear you talk, [*Hic.*] one would suppose that you invented eating.

GRENOUILLE. Ha, ha, ha! you are de wit; no eating 'ave beaucoup d'âge, it be so old as Adam.

SOLOMON. Did Adam invent eating?

GRENOUILLE. Oui, yes, you know, monsieur, Adam de first man, and——

SOLOMON. Yes, but not the first animal that eat, [*Hic.*] you know, mounseer.

GRENOUILLE. No! ma foi!

SOLOMON. First, you know, the world was made.

GRENOUILLE. Oui, vell.

SOLOMON. Well, [*Hic.*] Adam was not made until the sixth day; now, mounseer, what the fishes, beasts, and birds did to live until Adam come to learn them how to eat, [*Hic.*] is very wonderful.

GRENOUILLE. Vous avez raison, dat is ver true; allons,

come for de pantry; I no vant any body to teach me for eat; I eat a by instinct, by gar.

SOLOMON. Then you eat by the only rule that ever taught fish, flesh, and fowl. Come along, mounseer. [*Hiccough.*]

GRENOUILLE. Allons. [*Exeunt.*

ACT III.

SCENE I.—*A room in the cottage of* FARMER PLOUGHBY. DORRIVILLE, PLOUGHBY, *and his wife discovered at dinner.*

PLOUGHBY. Come, sir, don't be shy, you am kindly welcome, and you may eat hearty, for we got more in the closet, a'n't we, Dame?

DAME. Yes, John, and I hope the gentleman will eat what he wants.

DORRIVILLE. My good friends, I am grateful for your hospitality, but am plentifully supplied. I have learned to trust to myself for some years past, and your attentions are as welcome as they were unexpected.

PLOUGHBY. I am glad you be satisfied, sir. [*They rise.*]

DORRIVILLE. I have intruded, farmer, into your humble dwelling——

PLOUGHBY. I beg pardon, sir, but I be far from considering your stay an intrusion. I hope you am comfortable and happy?——

DORRIVILLE. Happy! O! no, 'tis more than sixteen years since I could say that I was happy.

PLOUGHBY. Poor soul, poor soul, how I do pity him! [*Aside.*] I be sorry for your mishaps, and as far as an American farmer's means do go, you am welcome.

DORRIVILLE. Thank you, thank you. I have proved your kindness, and will not fail hereafter to requite it.

PLOUGHBY. Thank you, sir, but I don't think you will.

DORRIVILLE. Be assured.

PLOUGHBY. Yes, sir, but I won't be rewarded; the seeing you pleased be more satisfaction than if you were to give me all your wealth. I hope my wife have been agreeable, since you have been here, sir?

DORRIVILLE. Yes, I do assure you.

DAME. Yes, I love to be agreeable to the gentlemen.

DORRIVILLE. I wish, if it were possible, to have a few moment's private conversation with you, farmer.

PLOUGHBY. To be sure, sir, certainly; Dame, didn't thee hear what the gentleman said? He wants to be private, so thee must go away directly.

DAME. Well, well, I be going. I wish I could hear what he want to say. [*Aside, and exit.*]

PLOUGHBY. There, sir, the woman have gone, and now you know you may speak without disguisement, for I be one that do never blab.

DORRIVILLE. I wish to have a private interview with Mr. Peregrine Positive, whose family mansion is not far distant from the cottage.

PLOUGHBY. That be right, sir, if you am misfortunate, Mr. Perry's the man that will be glad to see you.

DORRIVILLE. I do not wish to see him on pecuniary matters, O! no, I am not in want of money.

PLOUGHBY. I know that, sir; but do you know Mr. Perry?

DORRIVILLE. Formerly, he was my most intimate, my most affectionate and well tried friend.

PLOUGHBY. Then I'll be shot, sir, but you may easily see him, for he am always trying to find out new friends, and I'll be certain he'll remember an old one.

DORRIVILLE. I understand he is very charitable.

PLOUGHBY. Always at it, sir.

DORRIVILLE. I would not have him know me, or that I am rich; and in procuring me an interview, you can be of service.

PLOUGHBY. I am very glad, sir; but be sure not to tell him you am rich; or he'll be sure not to see you.

DORRIVILLE. I only wish you to see Mr. Positive, and tell him you have sheltered in your cottage a person from abroad, who is in great distress, and wishes to see him alone.

PLOUGHBY. Yes, sir, I be very willing to oblige, but am one who do love the whole truth, and that, you know, he, he, he, would be a swinger.

DORRIVILLE. You would but say the truth, my good friend, for although I am rich, yet still am I in great distress. A father's feelings tremble at my heart,—a father, separated for sixteen tedious years from all his heart holds dear on earth, a darling son, a beloved daughter——

PLOUGHBY.   That's enough, sir—say no more—sixteen! mercy on me! [*Tears.*] I'll go, sir, if I tell a bouncer as big as my barn.

DORRIVILLE.   Good farmer, your feelings are indeed honourable; accept this purse as the prelude to my future bounty.

PLOUGHBY.   Sir! I beg pardon, sir, [*putting it away from him*] but I have got a heavier purse than that.

DORRIVILLE.   Indeed!

PLOUGHBY.   What be worth all the gold in the world, sir; and will weigh heavier than gold, when all come before the Great Judge; it be a quiet conscience. I be thankful to you, sir, but I won't be paid for doing my duty. That would make kindness no kindness at all. I do think, sir, that he who does good for pay, would do bad for pay, and am a bartering slave that would sell his honour for a paltry guinea!

DORRIVILLE.   Noble, generous, and humane! [*Taking his hand affectionately.*] O! as you value peace on earth and happiness hereafter, preserve a quiet conscience! I have known the horrors of a troubled one! that can make the gelid dungeon floor as soft and peaceful as a bed of down, this makes a bed of down more terrible than even a dungeon's gloom!

PLOUGHBY.   That be all very true, indeed, sir; therefore do you keep the gold and let me keep my conscience quiet. Good day, sir; but won't it do if I send my son, Bob? he am a cute lad, and will tell Mr. Perry, just as well as I.

DORRIVILLE.   It will be the same; only let it be said, I wish to see Mr. Positive alone.

PLOUGHBY. Very well, sir.   [*Exit.*

DORRIVILLE.   Who will now say that virtue and greatness live alone with birth and fortune? Who will now despise the humble peasant, when he can boast such qualities as these? Education may varnish hypocrisy; but nature only could mould a heart like this! simple, god-like virtue! I will see Peregrine, and inquire how my bonds are held, and what is the real destiny of my children, before I openly proclaim my unexpected return, and if my hopes are answered, the sun of prosperity and peace may yet gild the evening of my life.   [*Exit.*

SCENE II.—*A room in* POSITIVE *mansion.*

Enter PEREGRINE *and* EDWARD.

PEREGRINE. But I tell you, my impertinent nephew, I am positive——

EDWARD. So you always are, uncle.

PEREGRINE. Zounds! sir, and so I always shall be. Haven't I seen the world? haven't I ching-chinged to joss with a Chinaman, lived in the palace of a nabob, and combed the tails of the greatest bashaw in Barbary? Haven't I danced with the flat-headed Hottentot, and smoaked the calumet with the descendants of Powhatan? And yet I don't know better than my downy-chinned nephew! I'll disinherit you—I'm positive.

EDWARD. Yes, my dear uncle, and when you went out to-day, you were positive you'd put Scroggins in prison for stealing the parson's nag: instead of which, you imprisoned the preacher for debt, and gave Scroggins enough money to buy two.

PEREGRINE. You know, you impudent dog, as well as you do you're alive, that Scroggins was not guilty.

EDWARD. But you were positive he was, uncle.

PEREGRINE. Hem! had I not cause to be so? did not the parson declare he stole it, and upon investigation, didn't I find that he lied?

EDWARD. But you were positive he did not: however, let me be positive this once——

PEREGRINE. You! you be positive? what unparalleled effrontery! In all my travels I never heard any thing to equal it! Ah! you are not like my dear sister, Charlotte; she coincides with me in every thing.

EDWARD. Yes, she thinks, with you, that Charles De-lany——

PEREGRINE. Yes, sirrah, and I too am positive that Charles Delany is completely fettered by the silken chains, woven by the beauty of my elder sister, Miss Charlotte Positive.

EDWARD. Ha, ha, ha.

PEREGRINE. Zounds! sir, what do you laugh at?

EDWARD. At the idea of Delany's loving my aunt, and that you should be deceived so easily, who have travelled from Kamschatka to Cape Horn, and from the Philippines to Acapulco.

PEREGRINE.   Why, do you think he don't?

EDWARD.   I'm convinced he don't.   Take my word for it, he only affects to love my aunt in order to cover his designs upon my dear, beloved Maria.

PEREGRINE.   Boy, boy, you are mad, I'm positive: and I don't know, but your disease is contagious!   If I thought he could be such a damned scoundrel——

EDWARD.   Could be!   recollect, is he not the son of him who robbed and ruined Mr. Dorriville?

PEREGRINE.   Poor Dorriville!   But now I know you wrong Delany; for has he not promised to make the delinquent an ample restitution, if ever he returns, or in case he does not, to bestow the bonds upon his children?

EDWARD.   He has promised.

PEREGRINE.   And will perform.

EDWARD.   Time will determine.

PEREGRINE.   Zounds!   I tell you I'm positive he will!   and why?   because my sister, Charlotte, condescends to honour him with her hand in marriage.

EDWARD.   Remember, uncle, what I say, he'll neither marry my aunt, nor repay the injured Dorriville, except by the ruin of his lovely and innocent daughter, Maria.

PEREGRINE.   How!

EDWARD.   I have watched him closely, and am not mistaken.   But let him beware my vengeance, if he dares but speak a word that may call the blush of modesty into that virgin cheek.

PEREGRINE.   I admire your spirit, Edward, but you may rest satisfied that you accuse Delany wrongfully.

EDWARD.   No, uncle.

PEREGRINE.   You do, indeed.

EDWARD.   You may depend, it——

PEREGRINE.   Zounds!   I'll tell you, you are too fiery!   I am positive you wrong him.

Enter SOLOMON.

SOLOMON.   And I am [*Hic.*] positive that *bony spree* is my best friend.

PEREGRINE.   How now, scoundrel!

EDWARD. As usual, Solomon, drunk.

SOLOMON. O! bless you, no, master Edward, only a little comfortable or so.

PEREGRINE. Did I not say you would be drunk before I returned?

SOLOMON. Yes, sir, there, [*Hic.*] there's the thing, it's all your fault, sir.

PEREGRINE. Mine! sirrah.

SOLOMON. Yes, sir, you will force me to drink against my inclinations. [*Drinks.*]

PEREGRINE. I! why, haven't I declared a thousand times that I would turn you out of doors for your inebriety? the sotting Hollander is a fool to you.

SOLOMON. But you haven't turned me out yet. Whenever you go out, you are positive I will be drunk before you get back, and then I am obliged to get so, to prevent you from telling a lie.

PEREGRINE. Begone, scoundrel, nor make my lenity an excuse for the crime.

SOLOMON. Crime! I beg you, sir, [*Hic.*] if you've any respect for my feelings, don't call a fashionable folly by so harsh a name. Yes, sir, I'm a buck of the first class, who think it as necessary to get drunk in order to be gentlemen, [*Hic.*] as it is to live in, or—I mean, to eat in order to live. Come, lord, sir, how could a man of your travel be so mistaken. But I had forgot what brought me here; farmer Ploughby's *sober* son wants you.

PEREGRINE. Didn't I tell that fellow I'd put him in prison, if ever he dared——

SOLOMON. I told him so, but he said you threatened him fifty times, and he never smelt [*Hic.*] confined air yet.

PEREGRINE. Send him here. [*Exit* SOLOMON.] I don't know what I shall do with that drunken fool; if I turn him away, he'll starve, and that charity forbids.

Enter ROBERT.

ROBERT. Servant, sir.

PEREGRINE. Didn't I tell you, sirrah, that if ever I clapped eyes on you again, I'd send you to the county jail as a vagrant,—and how dare you come here after it?

ROBERT. So I told father, but he said, Mr. Perry am one

who do say a great many things and never does any; so I
thought I might venter, because I know you loves charity,
and that am my business here.

PEREGRINE. You scoundrel, I'll imprison you for that!
Answer me, sirrah, [*taking his hand affectionately*] what
have you to do with charity, who can scarcely buy a pole
for a hen roost?

ROBERT. It be no fault o' mine, sir; if my heart will feel
for the misfortunate, I can't help it.

PEREGRINE. And have you dared to feel for the unfortunate? [*Shaking him cordially by the hand, and speaking
with seeming anger.*] I don't know, my good Robert, whether
you get drunk or no.

EDWARD. I told you he did not, uncle, but you were
positive he did.

PEREGRINE. I am told your market nag is dead, Robert;
take this and buy another. [*Offering him a purse.*]

ROBERT. Thank you, sir; [*refusing* it] at any other
time I be willing to receive it, but I can't take pay for my
duty.

PEREGRINE. Heh! [*Much affected.*] What a treasure
have I refused in this youth! come to my arms, you dog,
and let me feel your honest heart beating against mine.
[*Embraces him.*] My dear boy, you shall buy all the nags
in the country.

ROBERT. Thank you, sir, but I ha' got another nag.

PEREGRINE. You have! and who has dared to give you
another horse?

ROBERT. The gentleman.

EDWARD. What gentleman?

ROBERT. The gentleman for whom I be come after charity.

PEREGRINE. Why, is he not poor?

ROBERT. He told father he were in distress, but I think
it be all flummery like, for he am going to marry Suke Hub
and I, and give us a cottage and cattle and every thing.

EDWARD. This is very strange! how long has he been at
your house, Robert?

ROBERT. Only yesterday, sir.

PEREGRINE. Why, Edward, what does this mean? I never
saw any thing like this abroad. Zounds! have I travelled
round the world, to have my duty monopolized under my

very nose? I must inquire into this affa'r. Where can I
see this strange man?

ROBERT. That be just what brought me here; he do want
to see you all alone by yourself at our cottage.

PEREGRINE. Lead the way; I am positive you don't get
as drunk as I heard. [*Exeunt* PEREGRINE *and* ROBERT.]

EDWARD. Why should I conceal from her the fervour of
my affection? I know this Charles Delany; he's a fashionable gentleman. 'Sdeath, fashionable! 'tis fashionable to
ruin unsuspecting virtue, attend the orgies of the brothel,
squander thousands at the gaming table, and he's the most
fashionable who can present the longest list of the follies
and vices to which he is addicted. I will seek Maria, confess
my love, and if she denies my suit, I will protect her from
Delany's arts. [*Exit.*

SCENE III.—*The garden.*

Enter MARIA.

MARIA. Poor lady Charlotte, she is so confident of her
own charms, and yet so jealous of every body else, that she's
continually unhappy. She dreads, poor ancient maid, Delany's being in love with me; and, indeed, though his attention is most evident to her, yet he has often poured his
rude and fulsome flattery into my ears. But a worthier
object has fortified my heart against his insidious arts, the
good and noble Edward. My walk has somewhat fatigued
me. [*Seats herself upon a bank.*]

Enter SOLOMON.

SOLOMON. A pretty chase Miss Maria Dorriville has led
me; if it hadn't been for my constant companion, [*Hic.*]
bony spree, I should have been excessively fatigued. Ha!
Miss, have I found you at last?

MARIA. And now you have found me, master steward,
what is the urgent business that led you to seek me? what
do you want?

SOLOMON. Why, [*Hic.*] as for myself, Miss, I don't
want much; only I think you have led me a pretty chase in
order to deliver my message.

MARIA. A message for me! from my guardian, I suppose.

SOLOMON. No, not from him.

MARIA. Well, deliver it.

SOLOMON. Yes, Miss, with all imaginable speed; but I don't know whether I didn't leave it in the pantry.

MARIA. Leave a message in the pantry!

SOLOMON. Yes, for mounseer Greenowl—[Hic.]

MARIA. Who! why has Delany come back from the city?

SOLOMON. Yes, to-day. Master Greenowl kept eating so [Hic.] enormously that two or three times he snapped at the letter——

MARIA. A letter! what letter?

SOLOMON. A letter which I have in my pocket for you. [Hic.]

MARIA. For me! why, you blockhead, why did you not give it to me before? Come, deliver it.

SOLOMON. With all imaginable speed. Here, Miss Maria, here—[pulls out the bottle] no, that's not it; this is bony spree, and so as long [Hic.] as it's in the way, I'll just take a small drop, by way of postage. [Drinks largely.]

MARIA. You tedious old sot, why do you not give me the letter?

SOLOMON. With all imaginable speed. [Puts the bottle carefully in his pocket and takes out the letter.] Ah! here it is. [Gives it.]

MARIA. Here it is, and now, master Solomon, be good enough to leave me.

SOLOMON. With [Hic.] all imaginable speed; but you'll not be able to see among the trees, so you'd better let me read it, for, I assure you, just now I can see double. [Staggers off.]

MARIA. Who can it be from? I know not any one that could write to me, except my brother; or perhaps 'tis from my father! O! no, there is no such happiness in store for me! I tremble to part the seal. [Opens it and reads.]

"Madam,

Meet me at six o'clock this evening in the wood that separates Delany's estate from your guardian's. I am one who can give you information of Capt. Dorriville; nay more, can lead you to the only means that can obtain the restoration of your father's bonds! You must be unattended, for I am incog and do not wish to be seen."

[*She drops the letter.*]

Just Heaven! thou hast heard a daughter's prayers, and I shall restore my father's fame! yes, I will meet this mysterious messenger. It must be near the hour. Who is this? It is Edward.

Enter EDWARD.

EDWARD. Maria—good Heaven! what has been the matter? your face is so dejected; there is so much anxiety depicted in it—Ah! could I attribute it to the same which makes me sad. I have been seeking you, my lovely friend.

MARIA. For what?

EDWARD. It is a cause on which my happiness and peace depend.

MARIA. Indeed! [*Confused.*]

EDWARD. And fills my bosom with such hopes and fears.

MARIA. Your words are unintelligible—I do not understand them.

EDWARD. Rather, dear Maria, say you will not. Would you not pity the man who, kneeling at the shrine of happiness, was still uncertain that she smiled upon him? Ah! my fair friend, you cannot be ignorant of the love which your virtues and your charms have inspired me with.

MARIA. Edward.

EDWARD. I have sought you to disclose that love and hear from you my doom. At your feet I kneel and pray you to pronounce it.

MARIA. I cannot speak, you confuse me so; but why should I disguise it? Know then, Edward, before I thought you loved me, this heart was yours. [*Sinks into his arms.*]

EDWARD. Did I hear right? This is such an unexpected happiness, that I almost doubt its reality. But tell me, what was it clothed your face with such anxiety?

MARIA. This letter; by this I am led to believe that I shall hear from, perhaps see, my brother, and obtain the means of restoring my father's fame. Peruse it. [EDWARD *reads it.*]

EDWARD. At the wood and alone! That must not be.

MARIA. There can be no danger at such an hour, and

should any one attend me, the object of my going may be defeated. Consider too, perhaps my father, unwilling to be publicly recognized, has returned and waits to see me.

EDWARD. It may be so, indeed. I shall say no more, beloved Maria, to prevent your going. But who brought this letter?

MARIA. Solomon delivered it to me, but I did not enquire from whom he received it.

EDWARD. I'll seek him and endeavour to learn. [*Exeunt.*

SCENE IV.—*The wood.*

Enter CAPTAIN DORRIVILLE.

CAPT. DORRIVILLE. Delayed their elopement until to-morrow! Delany, I hope you have not deceived me. An irresistible impulse has impelled me to this spot, where I hope my strong suspicions may meet disappointment. Delany is a thoughtless votary of fashion, and may be led into vices which his heart abhors. I'll linger here until the hour has passed; then hasten to Mr. Positive's. Destruction! can it be possible? yes, here comes the man I least, at this moment, wished to see. I'll retire and observe him. [*He withdraws.*]

Enter DELANY.

DELANY. So, all is secure: Dorriville swallowed the bait, and ere to-morrow arrives, Maria will be in my power. I have managed this business like an experienced one. It's true I shall be censured, but it's a fashionable folly, and I shall be thought more of at the faro. By all the darts in Cupid's quiver, here comes the lovely angel! Venus, assist me with thy soft persuasion. [*Retires.*]

Enter MARIA.

MARIA. This is the spot where he requested me to meet him; where is this most mysterious friend? Not here? 'tis past the hour, and I begin to tremble with apprehension! I'll return to the mansion. [*Going.*]

DELANY. Stay, Maria. [*Advancing.*]

MARIA. Ha! should Edward's fears prove true! Delany here! I think, sir, ere this that Miss Charlotte should have been favoured with your company.

DELANY. Charlotte! my angel, don't let us waste a moment upon the old tabby. I should be afraid Cupid would strike me blind, if I glanced at the daughter of Erebus while the favourite of Elysium was by.

MARIA. I understand you not, nor came I here to be insulted. [*Here* CAPT. DORRIVILLE *appears behind.*] I came to meet a friend, of course, sir;—your presence is offensive.

DELANY. Yet stay, Maria, and hear what I have to say to you. I love you to madness.

MARIA. How!

DELANY. I have merely flattered Miss Positive, in order to deceive Peregrine. My heart ever has been, ever shall be—yours.

MARIA. Is this your honour, this the promised restoration of my father's property, upon your marriage with Miss Positive? Away, and let me pass.

DELANY. My dear Maria, I cannot.

MARIA. No!

DELANY. Will not.

MARIA. How!

DELANY. My love forbids it. Listen to me while I declare the letter you received was written by me to lure you here, that I might tell you how I love.

CAPT. DORRIVILLE. Villain! [*Aside*]

MARIA. I stand confounded at your insolence, your villainy! You have stooped to delude me: led me to hope my brother would meet me here; nay, that I should even see my father; and now insult me with your detested love!

CAPT. DORRIVILLE. Four years have strangely altered her, but it must be my sister. [*Aside.*]

DELANY. Be calm, my fair trembler, I've servants in waiting that shall whisk you off in a twinkling, if you refuse my offers; and Maria Dorriville shall be mine, by persuasion or by force.

CAPT. DORRIVILLE. Can this be Charles Delany? [*Aside.*]

MARIA. You dare not be such a villain!

DELANY. Villain! you forget 'tis fashionable, my dear;

but let us argue this subject. In that letter I told you the truth.

MARIA. Indeed!

DELANY. Yes, for once I have been so unfashionable as to speak the truth; but, my dear girl, if you regard my reputation, never mention it again, for I shall be hooted out of civilized society if you do. I can give you information of your brother.

MARIA. I could listen now forever. For four years I have not seen him. Yet tell me, Delany——

DELANY. Nay, more, I both can and will lead you in the only way that can regain your father's bonds.

MARIA. Will you?

DELANY. On one condition.

MARIA. Name it.

DELANY. Consent instantly to elope with me, and to-morrow I will lay your father's bonds at your feet.

MARIA. Monster!

CAPT. DORRIVILLE. [*Aside.*] Execrable villain!

DELANY. I'll take lodgings for you in the city; you shall have me all to yourself, without the nonsensical and unfashionable ceremony of marriage. You'll be the admiration of the town; all the men will adore you, all the women envy you; and I shall be the happiest devil in the world.

MARIA. Devil you would be, indeed. O! monstrous, you would recompense my father by his daughter's ruin, and make her eternal misery the price of those bonds which were obtained by robbery!

CAPT. DORRIVILLE. [*Aside.*] This shall not go unpunished.

DELANY. It is immaterial to me how they were obtained; it is sufficient that they are mine; and the only way for you to recover them, Maria, is——

MARIA. To lose myself! ignoble and ungen'rous dastard! away, and let me pass.

DELANY. By Heaven, you stir not.

CAPT. DORRIVILLE. [*Aside.*] I burn with indignation!

MARIA. Villain, villain! is this your justice? An unprotected woman you can brave, but were that brother here, you led me to expect, your coward soul would shrink to meet his vengeance. O! George, why are you not here to save me! Away, Delany, and let me pass, or dread the vengeance of an injured brother!

DELANY. As to your brother, my coy maid, were he present, I should not dread his interference, but he is far from hence, and in spite of everything, his sister shall be mine.

MARIA. Merciful Heaven!

DELANY. By Jove, but I have gone too far to retreat now, and if you are not mine willingly, I'll whisk you off into Delany manor, and force shall obtain those favours for which love sues in vain.

MARIA. You are not such a villain!

DELANY. Villain! ha, ha, ha, you know very little of fashionable life, if you call it villainy. But I'll introduce you to all the fashionable follies of the day; you shall soon know how to enjoy the world.

MARIA. Are there no angels to protect me?

DELANY. Time admits of no delay; you must be mine, Maria; therefore submit. Why should I hesitate? No friend is nigh—it shall be so; though your heart recoiled in horror from me, still would I hold you to my bosom! the only man I fear'd is——

CAPT. DORRIVILLE. At your side, my honourable friend. [*Advancing between* DELANY *and* MARIA.]

MARIA. Just Heaven!

DELANY. Damnation! foiled at last. [*Aside; then assuming courage.*] Your appearance here is untimely. Begone, you are in livery.

CAPT. DORRIVILLE. I am, my fashionable gentleman; but it is the livery of my country, and while I wear it, it shall never be sullied by my suffering the brutal violence of a scoundrel towards an unprotected woman.

MARIA. Brave and generous man.

DELANY. Scoundrel! this shall not pass unpunished, my game cock of honour. You have run into the toil, and it shall hold you. [*Exit.*

MARIA. Sir.

CAPT. DORRIVILLE. What did the villain mean? does he mean to arrest me for the sums I borrowed of him before I left America? It cannot be possible!

MARIA. How shall I thank you, sir, for your timely interference to protect me?

CAPT. DORRIVILLE.   Thank me!

MARIA.   But for you, I shudder while I think what might have been my fate.

CAPT. DORRIVILLE.   Do you not know me, Maria?

MARIA.   Powers of bliss! meant you my brother?

CAPT. DORRIVILLE.   Sister!

MARIA.   O! extacy!   [*Sinks into his arms.*]

CAPT. DORRIVILLE.   This is indeed an unexpected happiness.   But I know it all, Maria, Delany holds my father's bonds!

MARIA.   He does, indeed.

CAPT. DORRIVILLE.   Villain! deceitful, treacherous villain! But come, my sister, let us to your friend, our father, Mr. Positive, and on the way, I will inform you of Delany's infamous behavior towards me.   [*Exeunt.*

ACT IV.

SCENE I.—*A room in the house of* CHARLES DELANY, *who is seated at a table.*

DELANY.   I never dreamt that he suspected me, but by Heaven, my high mettled spark, I'll repay you for my disappointment.   So, so, she's gone, and all my fashionable hopes of boasting I had ruined a virtuous woman are blasted. 'Sdeath! how curst unlucky it was that she should slip, as it were, through my fingers!   But for that damned *mal apropos* appearance of her brother, whom I supposed safe in Ploughby's cottage, she would, ere this, have been snug in the next chamber.   Damnation! to be foiled after such a daring attempt, is too bad.   But I will have vengeance.   I must be speedy, though, for if he gets to Peregrine's, he will be safe, and I laughed at too soon.   Grenouille.

Enter GRENOUILLE.

GRENOUILLE.   Ici, mon maître, que est ce que voulez?   Vat would you 'ave avec moi?

DELANY.   Did you tell the bailiff I sent you for to attend me immediately?

GRENOUILLE.   Oui, I 'ave tell him.

DELANY. Is he at hand?

GRENOUILLE. He is in de house.

DELANY. Send him to me.

GRENOUILLE. Oui, avec le grand diligence. [*Exit.*

DELANY. I am out of humour with myself and all the world. If it is so troublesome to become a fashionable gentleman, I shall soon abandon the race. Damme, if I think I'd take Maria, if she were to rush into my arms. No, but I will have vengeance, if possible, upon Dorriville. So, Mr. Fixum.

Enter BAILIFF.

BAILIFF. Mr. Delany, your most obedient, dutiful servant; your man——

DELANY. My man; there you are mistaken, Mr. Fixum.

BAILIFF. Well, sir, it's the first time I ever mistook my man, Mr. Delany.

DELANY. No, sir, for once *mis-took* me.

BAILIFF. There I *mistook* a man, indeed.

DELANY. Well, well, a truce to your imprisoned wit.

BAILIFF. My wit, sir, is never in prison; it always flies free.

DELANY. Then let it fly to the devil.

BAILIFF. That's too long a journey.

DELANY. But, zounds! let us have no more of this; it would do to sport over wine and cards, and such like fashionable amusements of the gentlemen of the debtors' apartment; but while we delay, my man may escape. I sent for you, Mr. Fixum, to intrust you with the most important action. Here is a note of hand, payable on demand; speed with it to the wood which separates my estate from Positive's. Do you take me?

BAILIFF. It isn't the first time I have *taken* you, Mr. Delany, he, he, he.

DELANY. Hem! there you will, or at least near there, if you speed, find a gentleman and a lady.

BAILIFF. Which must I take?

DELANY. Heh! by my hopes, but that is well thought of. If he will let you, take her, and bring her here with all speed; if not,—take him and—don't bring him here.

BAILIFF. Very well, sir.

DELANY. You will know him by his being in uniform, and calling himself Risible; but his real name is George Dorriville.

BAILIFF. What! the delinquent I had such a chase after, about sixteen years ago?

DELANY. No, his son. But have you been a scoundrel so long?

BAILIFF. Four years to the back of it.

DELANY. What a conscience of rascality you must have.

BAILIFF. Faith, sir, a bailiff should have no conscience, and no feeling, or the scenes he sometimes witnesses, would ruin him in his occupation. Yet I have done some good actions in my life.

DELANY. When did such a miracle occur?

BAILIFF. The time I routed your father's last faro bank was one.

DELANY. Why, you—but come, I have had young Dorriville's note for some time; he has just returned from the Mediterranean, and——

BAILIFF. I don't like this job, sir.

DELANY. Why?

BAILIFF. Because, it's disagreeable, even to a bailiff, to tell a man he must go to prison, when he has returned from fighting the battles of his country.

DELANY. Pshaw! Take the note and do your duty.

BAILIFF. I dare not refuse. [*Takes it.*] If he refuses the lady——

DELANY. Demand the money.

BAILIFF. If he refuses the money——

DELANY. Demand himself.

BAILIFF. If he refuses himself——

DELANY. Get along, you booby! take him and give him a close lodging, in one of your closest chambers.

BAILIFF. I shall do my duty.

DELANY. Very well, away then. [*Exit* BAILIFF.] Then, my dear friend, a long adieu. Now, if Fixum should find him alone, he will lie snug, and every one but myself be ignorant of his fate. But there is something villainous, as Fixum says, in imprisoning a brave fellow, who has just escaped from the enemies of his country! But he would have it so. Maria must be mine, if it's only because I bet

Dick Splutter I'd have her in town in a week. Besides, its fashionable, and fashion has no more to do with feeling, than a priest with a punch bowl. [*Exit.*]

SCENE II.—*Another part of the wood.*

Enter CAPT. DORRIVILLE *and* MARIA.

CAPT. DORRIVILLE. My dear sister, are we not near the house?

MARIA. I am afraid, my dear George, that we have taken the longest way.

CAPT. DORRIVILLE. Then let us hasten forward; for I must see my guardian as soon as possible. I am in Delany's power, and as he left us he threatened vengeance on me.

MARIA. Good Heaven! let us fly. Yet hold, our guardian is at the cottage of farmer Ploughby.

CAPT. DORRIVILLE. My Fanny's father.

MARIA. But she, George, has resided with me ever since your departure. The cottage is close by, and let us seek Mr. Positive there.

CAPT. DORRIVILLE. There, Maria, I have reason for not yet being known.

MARIA. Then I will fly and bring my guardian to you.

CAPT. DORRIVILLE. Is there no danger?

MARIA. None, none.

CAPT. DORRIVILLE. Then speed, my dear Maria, and I'll loiter here, till your return.

MARIA. I fly to save you. [*Exit.*]

CAPT. DORRIVILLE. No, my beloved Fanny, we will never be united to depend upon the bounty of a friend, and I would scorn to marry you to indigence. Who comes here? As I live, 'tis her, it is my charming Fanny! I'll avoid her! avoid her, I'll perish first! what, after four years' absence, to avoid? no, no. [*Retires.*]

Enter FANNY.

FANNY. What hopes and fears alternate fill my bosom. Delany's servant has informed me that my dear George has returned to America! Why have not I seen him?

CAPT. DORRIVILLE. Lovely, affectionate girl. [*Aside.*]

FANNY. Every day has brought some tale of his adventurous intrepidity, and filled this heart, which doats on him, with wonder and apprehension. I will hasten to my father's, and learn if he has indeed arrived.

CAPT. DORRIVILLE. I can hold no longer. [*Advancing towards her.*] Fanny, my love, my life!

FANNY. What noise? [*Discovers* CAPT. DORRIVILLE, *screams and sinks into his arms.*]

CAPT. DORRIVILLE. Look up, my love, and bless me with one word.

FANNY. O! George, is it indeed true; do I behold you once again?

CAPT. DORRIVILLE. Yes, my dear Fanny, and now, in spite of envious fortune, we will part no more.

FANNY. But how is it that I find you here?

CAPT. DORRIVILLE. You shall know that anon; Delany is a villain, and I am in his power.

FANNY. O! Heaven!

CAPT. DORRIVILLE. My sister has flown to the cottage to find my guardian, and now, my love, we'll follow her. Let me once reach Mr. Positive, and Delany's malice will be disappointed.

As he is leading FANNY *off,* FIXUM *enters.*

BAILIFF. Sir, your servant.

CAPT. DORRIVILLE. Sir, yours.

BAILIFF. Your name is Risible.

CAPT. DORRIVILLE. You are mistaken, friend.

BAILIFF. Then it is Dorriville.

CAPT. DORRIVILLE. It is, indeed.

BAILIFF. Then, Mr. Dorriville, *alias* Mr. Risible, a word with you. This is your note.

CAPT. DORRIVILLE. Well, it is.

BAILIFF. Then, according to my instructions, I have a few civil questions to ask. Will you let this lady go with me?

CAPT. DORRIVILLE. Whither?

BAILIFF. To Charles Delany's.

CAPT. DORRIVILLE. Scoundrel! [*Striking him.*]

BAILIFF. Assault and battery, Mr. Dorriville.

FANNY. Pray, dear George, be calm.

BAILIFF. Will you pay the money?

CAPT. DORRIVILLE. I cannot, now.

BAILIFF. Then you must deliver up yourself.

FANNY. O! Heaven! 'tis as I thought.

CAPT. DORRIVILLE. Can Delany, indeed, be such a villain?

BAILIFF. The maid, the money, or yourself.

CAPT. DORRIVILLE. Wait, but a few short moments, and it shall be paid.

BAILIFF. Delays are dangerous.

CAPT. DORRIVILLE. Then go with me; I will discharge it and——

BAILIFF. That is contrary to orders. If you can immediately discharge the debt, well: if not, you must instantly go along with me.

FANNY. O! George, George.

CAPT. DORRIVILLE. Must I then leave her?

BAILIFF. I wait, sir.

CAPT. DORRIVILLE. No, I will first place her in safety and then—villain, stand back! [*Partly draws his sword: the* BAILIFF *retreats.*] No, no, that will not do. This sword, which ever has been drawn to enforce my country's laws, shall not now be used to violate them.

BAILIFF. I must do my duty, sir.

CAPT. DORRIVILLE. I am ready.

FANNY. O! George, must you so soon be taken from your friends?

CAPT. DORRIVILLE. Bear up, my dear Fanny, and though we now part, we soon shall meet again. Fly and inform Mr. Positive of my disaster, and I shall not be long in this scoundrel's custody.

FANNY. Let me hasten, on the wings of love, to snatch you from the power of Delany. [CAPT. DORRIVILLE *embraces her and exit with the* BAILIFF. FANNY *contrary.*]

SCENE III.—*A room in the cottage of* FARMER PLOUGHBY.

Enter PEREGRINE *and* PLOUGHBY.

PEREGRINE. But tell me, candidly, farmer.

PLOUGHBY. Yes, sir.

PEREGRINE. Well, then, are you positive that he is miserably poor?

PLOUGHBY. I don't know for that, sir, but I be certain he do seem main misfortunate, and as to his being poorish or so, I have not told you so, sir, have I?

PEREGRINE. No, indeed, farmer, you did not. That's true, and it's just as I said. I'm positive he is some spy from Europe, or some impostor.

PLOUGHBY. Postor, sir!

PEREGRINE. Yes, an impostor, farmer. You have been swallowing the smoke of your chimney all your life, and may be easily deceived by appearances; but I have seen the world, and a great many such deceptions; he'll find it hard to impose upon me, farmer. But I am positive you know him. Who the devil is he?

PLOUGHBY. I don't, sir.

PEREGRINE. Are you positive?

PLOUGHBY. No, sir.

PEREGRINE. No!

PLOUGHBY. You am positive, sir, an one or t'other must be wrong.

PEREGRINE. Pshaw! nonsense. This man appears more eccentric than field-marshal Suwarrow, and I'm afraid, like his, it's all feigned. A rich, unfortunate, poor and liberal-hearted gentleman. Zounds! who can he be? In all my travels, I never came across such a person. Tell him, farmer, that I wait his leisure. He's some ordinary fellow in disguise, I'm positive.

PLOUGHBY. Very well, sir, I'll tell him all your worship says.

PEREGRINE. No, farmer, not all; only tell him that I wish to see him.

PLOUGHBY. Very well, sir.

PEREGRINE. Do you hear, farmer, no more. Whatever we may think, we should not hurt the feelings of any one.

PLOUGHBY. That be very true, sir. [*Exit.*

PEREGRINE. Of all our curiosities, this is the greatest. Here's a man comes into my neighbourhood, and usurps my prerogative of doing all the good he can, and yet, he says he's poor! It's all a lie, I'm positive; but he's here.

Enter DORRIVILLE.

PEREGRINE. Sir, your servant.

DORRIVILLE. Sir, yours. [*Then aside.*]. He does not know me, I perceive.

PEREGRINE. Damn it, he looks unhappy, very unhappy! and misfortune seems to have placed her hoary emblems on a head, a life of peace would not so soon have whitened. I long to hear his story and to thrust my purse into his pocket. I wonder what's the reason he don't speak to me? [*Aside.*]

DORRIVILLE. Having heard of your charitable disposition, sir, I requested to see you——

PEREGRINE. Never mind my charitable disposition. Zounds! have I travelled over the habitable and uninhabited world, to have my actions continually thrown into my teeth? I am positive, sir, that I am not a charitable man! My dear sir, you look unfortunate and in distress; let this tribute of sympathy ease the torturing fangs of poverty. [*Offering his purse.*]

DORRIVILLE. You are not charitable! [*Seizing his hand.*] But you mistake the nature of my sorrows.

PEREGRINE. Why, are you not poor?

DORRIVILLE. By no means; I am immensely rich.

PEREGRINE. Indeed!

DORRIVILLE. Sixteen years of honest industry have enabled me to provide against pecuniary difficulties.

PEREGRINE. There it is; I was positive he was some impostor or other; but I'll pay him for endeavouring to deceive me. [*Aside.*] And how dare you, sir, have the impudence to send for me, if you are not poor? heh——

DORRIVILLE. Sir!

PEREGRINE. That is—damn it, sir, who the devil are you? —what was your motive in sending for me?

DORRIVILLE. O! sir, the greatest, the most tender motive that could actuate the breast! the fond, the long lost father, anxious for his children's safety. [*Much affected.*]

PEREGRINE. Your words are unintelligible to me, but why did you do this? a father—but I cannot speak—damn it, sir, how am I to give you tidings of them?

DORRIVILLE. 'Tis only you that can.

PEREGRINE. I! still more incomprehensible. But I am positive I know nothing concerning your children.

DORRIVILLE. My story is not long, nor will I be prolix in the recital. Will your patience indulge me a few moments, while I relate the circumstances which have brought me to the condition you behold?

PEREGRINE. Zounds! if your preface thus affects me, I am positive I cannot hear your tale out: yet, if I can alleviate your sufferings, though my heart should break, still I would attend. Proceed.

DORRIVILLE. Thirty years have passed since cruel fate deprived me of the best of fathers.

PEREGRINE. That loss was irreparable!

DORRIVILLE. To me it was particularly so: but let me pursue my tale. I, of course, as his only child, fell heir to all his rich estates. Though reared in the nursery of affluence, this sudden acquisition of immense wealth did not elevate my pride.

PEREGRINE. Then you deserved to have it all. What a noble field for the exercise of benevolence. How happy you must have been.

DORRIVILLE. I trust I was not unmindful of that sacred duty. Never came a face of sorrow to my door, but that the grateful smile of joy illuminated its departure.

PEREGRINE. That was noble.

DORRIVILLE. 'Twas but the fulfilment of my duty. For what are riches give us, if not to make the wretched happy?

PEREGRINE. Certainly.

DORRIVILLE. Yet, sir, unsuspecting those, who styled themselves my friends, while basking in the sunshine of my prosperity, and sucked my substance, like the voracious leech, I was lured into the lap of fashion and of sensual pleasure, from which the transition is rapid to destructive dissipation.

PEREGRINE. That was unfortunate.

DORRIVILLE. While reason was asleep and reposed upon the bosom of the fury, chance introduced me to a lady, whose beauty charmed my soul, and whose virtues awed me to respect and veneration.

PEREGRINE. Zounds! sir, did you find virtue in the train of dissipation?

DORRIVILLE. No, sir, no; she turned aside as she saw the harlot advancing, and though compelled, by necessity, to live near the orgies of debauch and ebriety, she lived retired and untainted by them.

PEREGRINE. I never heard any thing like this before.

DORRIVILLE. In short, sir, I woo'd, I won, and upon promising to retire from the thoughtless votaries of sensual pleasure, I wedded with Amelia.

PEREGRINE. Amelia! why, zounds! sir, I had a friend, a faithful friend who married an Amelia.

DORRIVILLE. Indeed!

PEREGRINE. Yes, sir; but I was always confident she would be the ruin of him.

DORRIVILLE. And were you not mistaken in your supposition, sir?

PEREGRINE. Why, to say the truth, I was a little out in my guess for that once.

DORRIVILLE. The marriage rites performed, we left the world and returned to my paternal mansion, where, some years, we lived in happiness and peace, during which time, my wife blest me with a son and daughter. What were the follies of the world to the delights of domestic life? as my infants would lisp the tender names of mother, father, and the tear of rapture stood trembling in Amelia's eyes, I would not have exchanged my feelings for the world's empire.

PEREGRINE. Sir, this must, indeed, have been felicity, although, being an old bachelor, I never experienced such an earthly paradise.

DORRIVILLE. Into this paradise a serpent crept, but, unlike our progenitors, I was deceived by him. This fiend, this leviathan in infamy, styled himself my friend and gained my confidence entirely. Often did my Amelia warn me to beware of him, but so completely had he coiled himself about my heart, that even she could not persuade me to suspect him.

PEREGRINE. 'Twas a strange infatuation!

DORRIVILLE. It was a fatal one!

PEREGRINE. Indeed?

DORRIVILLE. Step by step the villain led me to that dissipation from which I had so long withdrawn myself, and at last, O! horrible! at the faro bank, which too late I learned he had instituted, he himself, my friend, for my destruction, I staked and lost my all!

PEREGRINE. Why, sir, this is exactly the story of my friend!

DORRIVILLE. Your patience, sir. I flew home, and disclosed the fatal truth to my Amelia. No upbraidings passed her lips; a settled melancholy preyed upon her soul, and in three weeks, I followed the best of women to the grave. [*Much affected.*]

PEREGRINE. 'Twas terrible, indeed!

DORRIVILLE. Soon after, the villain produced my bonds against me, and as they embraced more than all my property, I was obliged to fly, although a friend offered to advance the surplus, which I refused, since it would have left him penny-less. Under the protection of this real friend, I placed the pledges of Amelia's love, and fled to India, where, by sixteen years of honest industry, I have amassed four times the wealth my treacherous friend despoiled me of.

PEREGRINE. Why, this was the situation of my friend! [*Gazing steadfastly at* DORRIVILLE.] He placed his children under my protection, when he fled.

DORRIVILLE. And have you carefully protected the dear pledges entrusted to your care?

PEREGRINE. What do you take me for?

DORRIVILLE. For one who makes humanity an occupation; for a friend to the unfortunate.

PEREGRINE. I am positive, sir, that I am not; but if you could inform me where I could find this afflicted father——

DORRIVILLE. Well, sir, if I could—— [*Anxiously.*]

PEREGRINE. Then, sir, I would grasp his hand, would hold him to my heart and whisper in his ear, that twelve years after his departure, I procured his son a warrant in his country's service, which his good conduct has since changed to a commission.

DORRIVILLE. Indeed! and his daughter——

PEREGRINE. Resides secure and happy at my house hard by.

DORRIVILLE. And yet you would tell the world that you are not charitable.

PEREGRINE. Certainly I would. Do you call a duty being charitable? Dorriville was my friend, lent me the very money which has since increased to a clumsy fortune. Nay, more, were Dorriville here, I would tell him that the son of his false friend, who has gone to his account, through my persuasion, has consented to return his bonds and estate whenever he appears.

DORRIVILLE. All-seeing Providence, thy ways are just!
[*Kneels.*]

PEREGRINE. What means this fervour?

DORRIVILLE. Do you not know me, Peregrine? [*Rising.*]

PEREGRINE. No, indeed; yet now, methinks, I can perceive some traces——

DORRIVILLE. How must I be changed!

PEREGRINE. Can you be—— [*Becomes affected.*]

DORRIVILLE. The delinquent Dorriville? I am.

PEREGRINE. Are you—Charles Dorriville? let me see. [*He takes both DORRIVILLE's hands in his and gazes in his face, much affected.*] Charles, how grief has changed you! so much, that even I did not know you! [*Tears.*] But I know you now; yes, you are Charles Dorriville, I feel it here, as my heart flies to your embrace. Closer, my first, my only friend! [*They sink into each others arms.*]

DORRIVILLE. O! Peregrine, how shall I repay you for your kindness to my children?

PEREGRINE. Can you, Charles, ask such a question? I thought you knew that one embrace would overpay me for all. But come, you must to my house. Young Delany, though curse me if I can see for what, has taken a fancy to my sister, Charlotte.

DORRIVILLE. Indeed? ·

PEREGRINE. And when she honours him with her hand, he'll restore your bonds. These are the conditions.

DORRIVILLE. This is joyful news, indeed, for though I am prepared to redeem them, it will be a noble retribution on Delany's part. I will just step in and inform my humble friends, and follow you immediately. [*Exeunt contrary.*]

ACT V.

SCENE I.—*The hall of* POSITIVE *mansion.*

Enter EDWARD, *driving in* SOLOMON.

EDWARD. Tell me, directly, Solomon.

SOLOMON. Why, sir, [*Hic.*] you will not let me speak a single word, although I feel so much inclined to talk. Lord, sir, you can't think how suddenly *bony spree* will convert a man's tongue into [*Hic.*] a woman's.

EDWARD. Will you answer me?

SOLOMON. You keep calling, tell me directly, Solomon, but, sir, you don't let [*Hic.*] me know what it is I am to tell you.

EDWARD. 'Tis false, you drunken sot; have I not asked you fifty times, where you got that letter?

SOLOMON. What letter?

EDWARD. There again. What letter?

SOLOMON. I have got no letter. [*Hic.*]

EDWARD. No, sirrah, but you had one.

SOLOMON. Lord bless you, master Edward, I have [*Hic.*] had many a one.

EDWARD. I shrewdly suspect, Solomon, that you have been bribed by Delany.

SOLOMON. No such good luck.

EDWARD. How! why, would you take one?

SOLOMON. Certainly. [*Hic.*]

EDWARD. And betray your master?

SOLOMON. No, keep the bribe and betray Delany. [*Hic.*]

EDWARD. Honest fellow. Why, then, do you prevaricate, Solomon, when I ask you concerning the letter?

SOLOMON. Not I, master Edward, I speak as plain as our stuttering parson. [*Hic.*]

EDWARD. Answer me, then. Where did you get the letter, which a few hours ago you gave to Miss Dorriville?

SOLOMON. I bought it.

EDWARD. Bought it!

SOLOMON. Yes, sir, at a confounded dear rate, I [*Hic.*] assure you, for I gave a goose, a duck, a turkey——

EDWARD. I must take a different course. Well, Solomon, who did you buy it of?

SOLOMON. Can't you guess?

EDWARD. No, surely.

SOLOMON. Only think, sir, of somebody of [*Hic.*] your acquaintance, that loves eating most ravenously.

EDWARD. What a tedious, drunken old fool! Maria may be murdered before I can get a word to the purpose from him. Will you disclose?

SOLOMON. Why, can't you guess, sir? [*Hic.*]

EDWARD. You old villain, if you don't instantly tell me

what man gave you that letter, I'll tear the secret from your heart? [*Seizing him.*]

SOLOMON. It was no man. [*Hic.*]

EDWARD. What woman, then?

SOLOMON. No woman, sir. [*Hic.*]

EDWARD. Who then?

SOLOMON. He's only about half a man, sir. [*Hic.*]

EDWARD. Who?

SOLOMON. Mounseer Greenoul. [*Hic.*]

EDWARD. Did you get it from Grenouille?

SOLOMON. Yes, sir.

EDWARD. And where is his master; has he also returned to the country?

SOLOMON. I don't know, sir. [*Hic.*] He said he left him amazing in liquor. I gave him some sober advice——

EDWARD. It may have been from Delany, to decoy her to the wood for the worst of purposes! At that thought, my brain grows wild! I'll away to the wood; perhaps I am too late! If I am, by Heaven, I'll—stand away, fellow. [*Exit, pushing* SOLOMON *down.*]

SOLOMON. So, so, this comes of love; it turns every man inside out. I wouldn't be in love, if I could roll [*Hic.*] in *bony spree*. Wheugh! how dry he has made me. [*Drinks, and exit.*]

SCENE II.—*Outside of the cottage.*

Enter DELANY.

DELANY. I long to know how my tool of vengeance has succeeded. If he caught Dorriville before he reached Peregrine's, he is safe within my custody. I don't know how I feel, but I begin to think that a fashionable life, as I understand the term, must disturb a quiet conscience. I'll away to Peregrine's—Who the devil's this! the most unfortunate sight for a repentant scoundrel, that possibly could be! Maria, and alone! Now she will be mine, in spite of Dorriville. No, damn it, she is not alone; an aged and venerable looking man supports her; but who, I know not. I'll retire and observe them. [*Withdraws.*]

Enter DORRIVILLE, *conducting* MARIA.

MARIA. I am greatly indebted to your kindness, sir; but I think I must be near the cottage of farmer Ploughby.

DORRIVILLE. 'Tis here, my lovely maid.

MARIA. What happy chance, sir, brought you to my aid? I fainted with terror at the sight of the reptile so near me, and on recovering, I found you supporting me.

DORRIVILLE. I was following a friend who had some time before left this cottage, and am happy that the delay, which I chided, made me the instrument of your preservation. And now, may I ask what brought you, thus alone, into the wood?

MARIA. O! sir, I was lured there for the worst of purposes. Under the specious garb of friendship, an ungenerous villain deceived me.

DORRIVILLE. That was cruel!

MARIA. His purpose was, indeed, most base, but I pardon all, since Providence sent a long lost brother to my rescue!

DORRIVILLE. A brother!

MARIA. Just returned, after an absence of four years.

DORRIVILLE. Powers of hope! [*Aside.*]

MARIA. When he left us, the villain threatened vengeance, and I left my brother in the wood, and was hastening hither for his rescue, when the accident occurred which placed me under your protection. Let me hasten to Mr. Positive——

DORRIVILLE. Mr. Positive!

MARIA. Yes, the generous Mr. Positive, my guardian.

DORRIVILLE. O! my prophetic heart! Tell me, maid—why need I ask it? my fervent feelings cannot err! Nature, to my heart, resistlessly impels the dear, delightful truth!

MARIA. Said you?——

DORRIVILLE. And bids me spring with joy to clasp a long lost daughter.

MARIA. Daughter!

DORRIVILLE. Your father's name?

MARIA. Dorriville.

DORRIVILE. My child, my child! [MARIA *sinks into his arms.*]

MARIA. Never before have my ears drunk in so sweet a sound. My child! O! father! father!

DORRIVILLE. My dear, beloved Maria! [*Embraces her again.*]

MARIA. Ah! my father, how misery has laid her withered hand upon you, and scattered her hoary emblems upon your head!

DORRIVILLE. This tender interview o'erpays me for all my sufferings; but come, let us hasten for your brother, and follow Mr. Positive. Delany——

MARIA. O! name him not; it was Delany that decoyed me to the wood.

DORRIVILLE. Indeed! Then Peregrine must be deceived! But come.

PLOUGHBY. Now do ye, Dame, let me give her a bit of air. [*Within the cottage.*]

DORRIVILLE. How is this?

Enter from the cottage, PLOUGHBY *and his wife, supporting*
FANNY.

PLOUGHBY. Now, don't 'ee do so, Fanny.

DAME. She am dead.

MARIA. Fanny!

DORRIVILLE. What's the matter, farmer?

PLOUGHBY. O! be you here, sir? I told you we should have some bad luck, cause you made Dame take that great big purse! What did thee take it for, Dame?

DAME. Why, sure, John, I——

PLOUGHBY. Hold thee tongue: here be datur Fanny, sir, after you and Mr. Perry went away, comed runnin' for dear life, and axed for Mr. Perry, and when I told her he were gone, she falled down on the floor and then, sir, I picked her up in my arms, and she ha'nt spoke since. Now, don't 'ee Fanny.

MARIA. Fanny, my lovely girl, look up.

FANNY. O! [*She revives.*]

DAME. She do speak.

PLOUGHBY. Don't thee make a noise, Dame.

FANNY. O! my dear father, where is he?

PLOUGHBY. Where am who, Fanny?

FANNY. My dear George.

DORRIVILLE. My son!

MARIA. My brother!

FANNY. O! sir, if you are Mr. Dorriville, if you are his father, fly and save him!

PLOUGHBY. Only to think, Dame.

MARIA. What mean you, Fanny?

FANNY. I met my Dorriville in the wood near here, and scarcely had we expressed our mutual surprise and joy, when a bailiff appeared, tore him from me, at the suit of Charles Delany, and hurried him to prison! [*Sinks on her father's bosom.*]

MARIA. To prison?

DORRIVILLE. Horrible sound! to prison? Let me hasten to his rescue. Farmer, conduct your daughter to Mr. Positive's. Come, my dear Maria, I cannot part from you: and you, Fanny, affectionate, lovely girl, I'll soon restore your lover to you, to be separated no more.   [*Exit with* MARIA.

DAME. Come, Fanny.

PLOUGHBY. Don't thee be gloomified, Fanny; don't thee hear Mr. Dorriville do say, you shall ha' him? What do'ee want more than that?   [*Exeunt.*

DELANY *comes forward.*

DELANY. What can be the matter with me, I wonder? I never saw any thing like this in the fashionable world! How the old man hung upon her neck, and when a tear gushed from his eyes upon his furrowed cheek, I felt something knocking about my heart, like that unfashionable commodity, humanity. Now, if I had succeeded in my scheme, what would have been the consequence? Instead of finding her thus, the afflicted father might have found his child, deserted by her profligate seducer, the tenant of some contaminated brothel! Instead of the bloom of purity, the mildew of corruption would have blasted all her beauties! Then what would I have been?—a fashionable gentleman! a fashionable villain! one who had lured her to the lap of infamy, then left her there to brave a hard, unfeeling world! who had bartered his eternal felicity for a momentary gratification! A father mad with agony—a noble brother, too—O! 'twould have been glorious!—It is not too late to prove myself a man.   [*Exit hastily.*

SCENE III.—*A room in a Prison.* CAPTAIN DORRIVILLE
seated at a table; a keeper waiting.

CAPT. DORRIVILLE. Is this the rich reward for all my
services? But hold, nor dare to reprobate my country's laws,
because a villain has abused them! What could have detained my sister? Well, sir, what do you want?

KEEPER. To know if you want any thing.

CAPT. DORRIVILLE. No—Yet stay: a little wine.

KEEPER. Yes, sir.

CAPT. DORRIVILLE. Be speedy.

KEEPER. Yes, sir.

CAPT. DORRIVILLE. Why do you not go then? [*Rises.*]

KEEPER. The money.

CAPT. DORRIVILLE. Money! [*Throws himself down in
agony.*] I have no money. I paid my last dollar to the man
who drove me to the inn.

KEEPER. That's very strange! Most of our prisoners have
plenty, and come here to take care of it.

CAPT. DORRIVILLE. Can it possible?

KEEPER. Fact, I assure you. Though some are as poor
as a pullet in the spring, others and the most of 'em have
purses as plump as a partridge in December. It's fashionable.

CAPT. DORRIVILLE. Well, I have no money.

KEEPER. No money, no wine. [*Exit.*]

CAPT. DORRIVILLE. Unfeeling wretch! Maria may have
fallen into Delany's power——

BAILIFF. Very well, sir, if the money's paid. [*Within.*]

Enter DORRIVILLE.

DORRIVILLE. In every feature I behold my son! How
shall I contain my feelings! [*Aside.*] Sir——

CAPT. DORRIVILLE. Good day, friend. What, have you
grown gray in such a trade as this? But perhaps your heart
is not so flinty! A little wine will refresh me greatly, which
your humanity might bestow, if familiarity with affliction
have not steeled your bosom.

DORRIVILLE. I have, indeed, been long familiar with affliction; but I do not understand you!

CAPT. DORRIVILLE. Are you not the keeper of this prison?

DORRIVILLE. I!

CAPT. DORRIVILLE. Do but accompany me to Mr. Positive's, and I will discharge every demand against 'me.

DORRIVILLE. You mistake my character. I came your friend.

CAPT. DORRIVILLE. Then I beg you to forgive me! But what is your business here?

DORRIVILLE. To tell you, you are free.

CAPT. DORRIVILLE. How! can it be possible! By whom have I been liberated?

DORRIVILLE. By a friend.

CAPT. DORRIVILLE. It was yourself!

DORRIVILLE. It was your father.

CAPT. DORRIVILLE. Who? did you say my father? O! sir, deceive me not; but tell me, where is my father?

DORRIVILLE. George! [Deeply affected.]

CAPT. DORRIVILLE. You cannot mean it!

DORRIVILLE. My son!

CAPT. DORRIVILLE. My father! [Rushes into his arms.]

DORRIVILLE. I hold him to my heart! God of mercy receive my thanks!

CAPT. DORRIVILLE. O! my father, have I found you, indeed! But tell me by what miracle are you here?

DORRIVILLE. By none. But come, leave this place. Your sister waits within, to hasten with us to Mr. Positive's. On the way, all shall be explained.

CAPT. DORRIVILLE. My sister safe! I am indeed rejoiced; but lost in wonder.   [Exeunt.

SCENE IV.—A room in POSITIVE mansion.

Enter PEREGRINE and CHARLOTTE meeting.

CHARLOTTE. So soon returned, brother?

PEREGRINE. Yes; rejoice with me, my dear sister. In my travels, I never met any thing so pleasing.

CHARLOTTE. You know your pleasure is the first wish of my heart.

PEREGRINE. Ah! if Edward were but such an accommodating dog as you are——

CHARLOTTE. Dog as I am, brother!

PEREGRINE. What the devil did I say? But, my dear sister, I am so overjoyed that I forgot myself. Forgive me. Dorriville has returned.

CHARLOTTE. What Dorriville?

PEREGRINE. Charles Dorriville, my friend.

CHARLOTTE. What! the delinquent?

PEREGRINE. The same.

CHARLOTTE. Dear me! I must marry Delany immediately, or poor Dorriville's bonds may be enforced!

PEREGRINE. O! ho! how anxious she is for—Delany, hem! [*Aside.*] But Dorriville's coming here, sister, so we'll marry you to Delany, Maria to Edward, and I'm positive——

CHARLOTTE. Pardon me, brother; but it is so monstrous an affair, I must be consulted.

PEREGRINE. Well, it's all for your sake.

CHARLOTTE. I must express my opinion.

PEREGRINE. What! you an opinion! my dear sister, you are mad!

CHARLOTTE. No, my dear brother.

PEREGRINE. Mad, sister.

CHARLOTTE. Not mad, brother.

PEREGRINE. Stark mad, madam.

CHARLOTTE. I am not, sir. Nor do I think Delany loves me.

PEREGRINE. Not so mad as I thought her! You don't, eh?

CHARLOTTE. No, for I have not seen him since his arrival from town, which is a whole day!

PEREGRINE. Well, sister, if you have failed——

CHARLOTTE. What then?

PEREGRINE. I can offer you no consolation.

CHARLOTTE. Indeed!

PEREGRINE. I'm positive of one thing.

CHARLOTTE. What is that, pray?

PEREGRINE. That Delany loves you now as well as ever he did. [*Then aside.*] There, I believe, I am right for once.

CHARLOTTE. I tell you what, brother; unless you insist upon the fulfilment of Delany's promises, I perceive that I shall die a maid, and get no husband at all!

PEREGRINE. I insist on his promises! Why, zounds! sister, you make me blush! I demand of a young man of one or two and twenty that he shall marry an old woman of sixty? for shame!

CHARLOTTE. Old woman? Very well, brother.

PEREGRINE. Zounds! you women think that if you never get married you never get old. Zounds! sister, I believe you've tumbled into Shakspeare's seventh age, second childhood! Suppose he does not like you, as a husband is all you want, blaze away again. Huggins has plenty of ochre, and I'm positive, with your purse, though you cannot captivate the roving Charles Delany, you'll stand a good chance of shoving yourself off at this age.

CHARLOTTE. Shoving myself off! I never expected this from you, brother. But I know who has lured his affections from me. Your ward, the pert daughter of the hot-headed Dorriville; and to think that you should have joined to deceive me!

PEREGRINE. Poor soul, poor soul!

CHARLOTTE. If I had only got him—— [Sighs.]

PEREGRINE. Aye, if she had only got him—— [Aside, sighs.]

CHARLOTTE. My kindness might have won his heart! he should have reposed in downy slumbers on my bosom, and hushed, in my arms, his loudest griefs to rest! But you, brother, have deprived me of this felicity,—you and your paragon of excellence, Maria Dorriville.

PEREGRINE. Ha! ha! ha! if a handsome young maid comes in contact with an ugly old one, what a whirlwind! I tell you, sister, I never was interested except to forward your views, nor has Delany any designs upon Maria. But here comes the man to make all clear.

CHARLOTTE. Indeed! then he shall feel an injured woman's vengeance! [Walking about, PEREGRINE following her.]

PEREGRINE. O! my dear sister, don't say a word, I pray; let your disdain be his only punishment.

CHARLOTTE. He shall find, brother, I am not to be injured with impunity. Stand back, brother.

PEREGRINE. Then do, my dear Charlotte, retire and practise a little. You'll be better able to express your feelings after a little study.

CHARLOTTE. No, my wrongs shall supply me with words, and he shall tremble at my frowns!

PEREGRINE. Then, for the love of silence, let frowns be all, for if once your tongue gets a going, nothing but miraculous dumbness will stop it.

Enter DELANY, *hastily.*

Delany, I am glad to see you, for two reasons, to clear your promise to Dorriville, and to convince my sister—[*Here* CHARLOTTE *comes down the stage between* PEREGRINE *and* DELANY, *and frowns tremendously upon the latter.* PEREGRINE *laughs.*]

CHARLOTTE. O! you base, cruel, ungenerous man; how could you plant such pangs in a heart that adores you like mine?

PEREGRINE. Why, you're as impudent—— [*Aside to her.*]

CHARLOTTE. But for your sake, barbarous man, I'll forswear the sex, and die a maid. [*Weeps.*]

DELANY. Mr. Positive—I have deceived you—I came here——

PEREGRINE. Deceived me!

CHARLOTTE. Well, that's some comfort, at any rate.

PEREGRINE. But follow me, sir, and explain. Deceived me! I'm positive—but come, sir. [*Exeunt.*

SCENE V.—*The hall of* POSITIVE *mansion.*

Enter FARMER *and* DAME PLOUGHBY, *conducting* FANNY. SOLOMON *showing them in.*

PLOUGHBY. Now, don't 'ee be so solemncolly, Fanny, Mr. Dorriville have said you should ha' him.

DAME. Do'ee be more composed, Fanny.

FANNY. I am perfectly so, now, my dear mother.

SOLOMON. If you feel [*Hic.*] dejected, Miss Fanny, take a drop of this reviving cordial. [*Offering the bottle.*] It's quite innocent. That you may be under no fear, [*Hic.*] I'll take a drop first. [*Drinks.*]

FANNY. I thank you, Solomon; I do not want it.

PLOUGHBY. Heh! who be coming here? Mr. Perry, Madam Charlotte, and Mr. Delany.

Enter PEREGRINE, DELANY *and* CHARLOTTE.

PEREGRINE.   One word more.   Had you any design upon my ward?

DELANY.   I had.

CHARLOTTE.   You base man!

PEREGRINE.   What was your design?

DELANY.   Her ruin!

PEREGRINE.   O!   You damned scoundrel!

DELANY.   I own my guilt and plead for pardon.   All my attentions to this lady, whose love I cannot return, were but to cover my designs upon your ward; but I come——

Enter EDWARD.

EDWARD.   My dear uncle—Delany here!   This is too much.

PEREGRINE.   What mean you, Edward?

CHARLOTTE.   Is that so strange, nephew, while I am here?

EDWARD.   Delany is a villain!   [*All start.*]

DELANY.   Villain!   well, I was one.

EDWARD.   I thought you sooner would have sought some deep, oblivious solitude, where mortal footsteps never trod!   Where is Captain Dorriville?

PEREGRINE.   In the Mediterranean.

EDWARD.   He's in America.

CHARLOTTE.   Why, Edward.

EDWARD.   He *was* in prison!

PEREGRINE.   Prison!   at whose suit?

EDWARD.   His creditor's, the honorable Charles Delany.

PEREGRINE.   Is this true?

DELANY.   It is, indeed.   But, sir, I came here to confess how deeply I had injured him, and to redress the wrongs of Mr. Dorriville!   Where I hoped for pardon, I have met with upbraidings!   I go to prove that I am not a villain!

[*Exit.*

PEREGRINE.   You have touched his feelings keenly, Edward.

EDWARD.   Mr. Dorriville's returned, I've heard!   Nay, I met him, Captain Dorriville and Maria, hastening hither, and from them learned what you have heard.

CHARLOTTE.   What an escape I've had!   But who are these?

EDWARD. 'Tis Mr. Dorriville and my Maria—and Captain Dorriville!

FANNY. My dear George.

PLOUGHBY. Servant, ladies and gentlemen, we be come here, by Mr. Dorriville's commandment.

PEREGRINE. You are welcome, farmer.

Enter DORRIVILLE, CAPT. DORRIVILLE *and* MARIA.

EDWARD. My dear Maria.

CAPT. DORRIVILLE. My dear Fanny, I am yours forever! [*Embraces her.*]

PLOUGHBY. There, Dame.

DORRIVILLE. Peregrine, my friend, rejoice with me. The delinquent Gamester has returned, and has made both his children happy.

PEREGRINE. I do. Come to my heart, my brave lad; welcome once more to your guardian's arms. [*Embraces* CAPT. DORRIVILLE.]

CAPT. DORRIVILLE. My benefactor!

PEREGRINE. Pshaw! but come, take your Fanny, and be happy! And you, Edward—Charles, have I your permission? [DORRIVILLE *bows.*] Well, then, take my dear Maria, and prevent her from eloping with Delany. Zounds! I forgot: Charles, my eldest sister. [*Introducing* CHARLOTTE.]

DORRIVILLE. Madam, I'm rejoiced to see you.

CHARLOTTE. Sir, you are welcome home.

PLOUGHBY. Sir, I be a plain man, but must speak. My dear George, you am welcome to datur Fanny; and I do hope she'll raise a hundred such brave soldiers as you am. That's what I do.

DAME. And I too, sir. [*Curtseying.*]

PEREGRINE. That's a plentiful blessing, at any rate.

SOLOMON. So, as all's now settled, I'll make [*Hic.*] so bold as to drink the health of all. [*Drinks, bowing to the audience.*]

GRENOUILLE. Vous avez raison, by gar. [*Within.*]

PEREGRINE. Who have we here?

SOLOMON. That's mounseer Greenowl.

EDWARD. Delany returned!

CAPT. DORRIVILLE. Indeed! [*With rising indignation.*]

FANNY. My dear George, pray be calm.

Enter DELANY, *followed by* GRENOUILLE, *with papers.*

PEREGRINE. That fellow's mad, I'm positive.

DELANY. No, sir, he has just regained his senses.

DORRIVILLE. You're come, sir, I suppose, for the redemption of my bonds? Present them,—I'm ready.

DELANY. Worlds should not purchase them! Mr. Dorriville, how my father injured you is known to all here; but I am not accountable for his actions, however I regret them. For my own, I come to make atonement, and return those bonds, cancelled, which I held against you! [*Takes the papers and gives them to* DORRIVILLE.]

DORRIVILLE. I'm thunderstruck! [*They all express astonishment and joy.*] For this, accept my hand, and mine and my daughter's pardon.

CAPT. DORRIVILLE. And mine, Charles; and again I hail you, friend.

PEREGRINE. And mine.

CHARLOTTE. And mine.

FANNY. And mine.

PLOUGHBY and DAME. And mine.

SOLOMON. And mine. [*Hic. Drinks.*] Your health, mounseer Greenowl.

EDWARD. Let me crave your pardon for my rash expressions.

DELANY. Your motive, sir, is ample justification.

CHARLOTTE. Mr. Delany, since you have repented and behaved in so handsome a manner to Mr. Dorriville, the virgin charms of her you have so barbarously misused are still at your service. [*All laugh.*]

DELANY. I am grateful, madam, for the honour you intend me; but I never will give my hand where I find it impossible to bestow my heart. [*Bows.*]

PEREGRINE. Bravo! well said.

CHARLOTTE. You are all barbarous brutes; and so I'm at last determined to live single.

PEREGRINE. A wise conclusion, sister, now you can get no one to marry you. Ha, ha, ha.

DELANY. And now, as I feel unfashionably comfortable, let me hope that every one will profit by our example, and learn that fashionable follies are indeed fashionable vices; and that though Fashion may lead a man to the commission of many crimes, she can justify none.

THE END.

EPILOGUE.

Written by the Author.

To be spoken by MARIA.

Well, patrons, how like you our play? 'tis FASHION,
Which many here take great delight to dash in;
Fashion, celestial sound! I hope that you
Have found the *fashion,* which we've shown you, *new.*
Ah! see Miss Damson in yon full crammed box,
In floating ringlets waves—her wig's soft locks;
While Bobby Slyboots, with an anxious mien,
Ogles beside her, and she hopes, unseen.
Dear Susan [*sighs*] sighs,—ah! Bobby, is it you?
I'm squeezed to death! Miss Fretful, how do you do?
Dear me, I'm suffocated; but my dear,
You know it's all the *fashion* to be here.
There's Mr. Easy in that box, od's life!
Talking to every woman—but his wife.
While she, good soul, to advocate the plan,
Except her husband, talks to every man;
Because it's *fashionable.*—Dr. Grumble,
Who looks so pleasant—I'm your very humble: [*Bows.*]
What! has my lady used her tongue again?
Poor soul! no matter, pray dismiss your pain;
Look not so grum, and conquer all your passion,
Because, you know, with us, 'tis all the *fashion.*
Damme, cries Tom, insult me, sir, your name, sir,
Dick Bluster, damme, sir, you'll find I'm game, sir.—
Fashion demands a challenge from the wight,
But *fashion* seldom makes the *heroes* fight.
Mercy! who's that, beside the widow Spangle?
Alas! poor author, it is critic Dangle!

And Monsieur Fluttermore, that ugly elf,
Who thinks of no one, but his odious self:
Hear him, he speaks, eh?   Dangle, vat's de **reason**,
You praise no author or actor all dis season?
Damme, cries Dangle, what is that to you,
Do you pretend to be a critic too?
To praise an actor I would ne'er refuse,
But it is all the *fashion* to *abuse*.
Thus *fashion* leads, and all her vot'ries follow,
Like list'ning hounds that mind the huntsman's halloo:
And here should Fashionable Follies find
Critics indulgent, and our patrons kind;
Now let their hands a native author laud,
And make it all the *fashion* to applaud.

BRUTUS;

OR,

THE FALL OF TARQUIN

By John Howard Payne

JOHN HOWARD PAYNE

1791–1852

It is not always that the American dramatist has made his name and his success on American soil. In recent times we look to Hubert Henry Davies, author of "Cousin Kate" and "The Mollusc", who had to go to London before he became recognized as a playwright, and so, too, to the case of Edward Knoblauch, author of "Kismet", whose London success identified him so completely with English conditions that he has now become a British subject.

John Howard Payne rose into prominence at the time when the picturesque formal acting of the day held ascendency in the great work of Edmund Kean. Born in New York city, on June 9, 1791, Payne developed, at an early age, those two characteristics which were constantly to the fore during his entire life: a love for drama and for journalism. As a school-boy, he edited a little paper, entitled *The Thespian Mirror,* which was published in Wall Street. According to Wegelin, Payne made his literary début in a juvenile sheet called *The Fly,* edited by Samuel Woodworth, whose fame, like Payne's, was to be bound up both in drama and a song. For Woodworth was the author of "Forest Rose" and "The Old Oaken Bucket".

Even when Payne went to Union College, Schenectady, New York (1806), he could not refrain from starting another periodical, which he designated *The Pastime,* and in which he probably received the encouragement of Charles Brockden Brown, with whom he had travelled to Albany on his way to college.

Despite the fact that Payne's father disliked the idea of his son being connected with the professional stage, the boy's talent in this direction began to show itself at an early age. Yet, strange to say, Payne's father, a schoolmaster by occupation, was also an elocution teacher of no mean distinction, and was so regarded by those who knew him when he was head master of an Academy at Easthampton, Long Island, where the family lived for some time. However much Payne's family may have tried to divert his interest away from the stage by putting him in a commercial house, where one of his brothers was a partner, the boy still persisted in his inclination to become an actor, inspired, no doubt, by the phenomenal success of "Young Master Betty", who was then the talk of London.

So it was that, on February 24, 1809, Payne made his professional appearance in the rôle of *Young Norval,* at the New York Park Theatre, and the press heralded him as a veritable "American Roscius". Family prejudice had by this time abated somewhat on account of family reverses, and it is recorded that during this first year of his professional work, Payne made an income of over ten thousand dollars. As long as his very striking appearance and his youthfulness lasted, so long did the public interest in him exist.

But there arrived a moment when, even though Payne made a considerable livelihood, he found that for him there was little hope of future advancement. So despairing did he become that he even listened once more to the uttered prejudices of members of his family, who were ever loath to recognize the theatre, and for a time he retired from the stage. He then tried to ingratiate himself into the profession of librarian. But George Frederick Cooke arrived in America just at this moment, and an opportunity was given Payne to play *Edgar* opposite the great actor's *Lear,* and it was then that Cooke began suggesting to Payne that success awaited him across seas. So he sailed on a packet-ship for London, on January 17, 1813, to be gone many years.

He arrived on the other side at a time when the theatres were in a very upset condition. Drury Lane and Covent Garden were both in precarious circumstances, and were continually at odds with each other. This was the period of Edmund Kean, and the theatrical history which swirled around Kean was one of wild living, as well as of definite riots on the part of the theatrical public, prone, on the slightest provocation, to take sides, and even to come to physical blows during an evening's performance. Amidst such an atmosphere of uncertain competition, Payne made his first appearance at Drury Lane, as *Norval,* on June 4, 1813. He immediately received an engagement, and supported the famous Miss O'Neil, at the same time meeting, in a social way, such men as Roscoe, John Philip Kemble, the poet, Campbell, Coleridge, Southey, and Charles Lamb.

Here again, however, he soon came to realize that there was little hope of his advancing as an actor beyond a certain position, which did not content him. And he found it necessary to turn his hand to literary labor which would bring him an additional income. The fashion of the times was for the "patent" houses to utilize whatever dramatic material seemed most favorable in the Continental playhouses. A season's offerings by both Drury Lane and Covent Garden consisted largely of adaptations and translations from the French.

This demand attracted Payne's attention while he was in Paris. Through the influence of Hobhouse, a friend of Lord Byron, he was employed by Drury Lane to remain in Paris, and to send to the Theatre Royal as many adaptations as could be secured by him, and whipped into shape for English consumption. This led to his adapting a piece entitled "Maid and Magpie". In a way it was an exercise in a foreign language. But his first *official* commission was "Accusation; or, The Family of d'Anglade". From now on Payne was continually wide-awake in regard to the material he could procure for his ever-ready pen to adapt. All during his stay abroad he was invoking the aid of his friends in the securing of manuscripts as soon as plays were produced in Paris with any appreciable success.

But it would seem that, however much Payne's ambition may have been along original lines, and however much necessity may have forced him to do the amount of translating he did do, he was in no sense of the word a business man. The managers always got the better of him. And the biographical records of this period of his career show him to have been the catspaw of Kinnaird, of Drury Lane, and of Harris, of Covent Garden. He literally sacrificed himself for their profit.

Payne's friends were much cleverer in their attitude. One only has to read the correspondence which exists between Washington Irving and Payne, and between Charles Lamb

and Payne, to recognize not only their own cordial aid, which
was ever at Payne's disposal, but also their very keen advice
regarding contracts and regarding Payne's own temper,
which was ever tried and highly strung, by reason of some
existing or imagined injustice done him. Because, it would
appear that, circumstances working against him inside and
outside of the theatre, Payne was ever prone to think there
was a clique plotting against him, not realizing that the general spirit of the theatrical times was one of jealousy and of
irritation. Irving says, in 1824: "I am sorry to find you
writing in dumpiest mood; but don't let yourself be cast
down. Gad, man, you've made a lump of money since last
autumn; and if it has been rather sopped up by old debts,
what's to prevent your making more?"

Nevertheless, Payne, even though he was underpaid for
what he did, succeeded in keeping very closely in touch with
the French and English theatres, now writing for Drury
Lane, then being bribed over to Covent Garden, and again
returning to Drury Lane. It was in such manner that Kean
was kept trotting back and forth, until he himself became the
dictator. After his treatment in regard to "Brutus", Payne
was sorely tempted into the managerial field, and actually
gave several productions at Sadler's Wells (1819), at a time
when that theatre was run down in locality and reputation,—
a venture which led him into further debt.

But notwithstanding his perturbations of mind, he was of
great service to the theatrical managers of the day, Drury
Lane often courted his favor. Harris, of Covent Garden,
tried to outdo his rivals by offering a more tempting contract.
Stephen Price, of New York, looking for foreign material
through the recommendation of Washington Irving, employed Payne as an agent, and there was an additional source
of income in this direction. But even here Payne's feelings
forced him into suspecting that he was being unjustly treated.
It is interesting to find him airing his grievances before
Mary Godwin (Mrs. Shelley), and to find, in a letter from
Washington Irving, a very just warning that it is not always
well for a dramatist thus to parade his grievances broadcast.

"Brutus" is probably John Howard Payne's most widely
remembered piece. It was during one of the precarious
moments in the history of Drury Lane that Payne went to

the management and suggested that, inasmuch as Kean desired to regain the favor of the English public—a favor which had, in a way, been waning—he would write for the great actor a piece suitable for his talents—talents which unfortunately were being slightly overshadowed by the tremendous success of Talma in the same tragic field. Just before "Brutus" was given, Kean had appeared in Racine's "Andromache", and had failed, thus calling from him a curse upon the whole "damn'd theatre population of London".

"Brutus; or, The Fall of Tarquin", therefore, came at a moment when, if it were a success, it would improve not only the treasury of Drury Lane, but the temper of Kean himself. According to Payne's introduction to the published drama:

> Seven plays upon the subject of Brutus are before the public. Only two have been thought capable of representation, and those two did not long retain possession of the stage. In the present play, I have had no hesitation in adopting the conceptions and language of my predecessors wherever they seemed likely to suit the plan which I had prescribed. This has been so done as to allow of no injury to personal feelings or private property; such obligations to be culpable must be secret, but it may be observed that no assistance of other writers may be available without an effort almost, if not altogether, as laborious as original composition.

Payne's sources have been zealously analyzed by Genest, in his invaluable account of "The English Stage from the Restoration in 1660 to 1830". He has measured the indebtedness to Plutarch's "Life of Poplicola", and to Shakespeare's "Julius Cæsar". He has mapped out the passages which show the influence of Nathaniel Lee's "Lucius Junius Brutus, the Father of His Country"; of Richard Cumberland's "The Sibyl; or, The Elder Brutus"; of Hugh Downman's "Lucius Junius Brutus; or, The Expulsion of the Tarquins"; and of William Duncombe's tragedy, "Junius Brutus". And, after calling attention to Payne's historical inaccuracies, he arrives at the conclusion that the merits of the piece are negligible. His comparative analysis, however, is interesting to the student who wishes to make an intensive study of the play.

The statement of Payne regarding his indebtedness to the seven plays is open to several interpretations. One may question how far he drew upon his sources without credit; how just was the accusation of plagiarism which quickly followed the presentation of the piece, and brought interesting comment in defence of Payne from both Irving and the poet, Tom Moore. To the latter, Irving wrote: "Payne has given credit for his play to six authors from whom he has taken hints; but, because he has included a seventh, from whom he has borrowed nothing, they have raised against him a hue and cry for plagiarism."

There was even some talk of suppressing the play because certain democratic expressions therein were thought inimical to the spirit of the government of the Georges. Duyckinck claims that "one of the very proprietors who were making money out of the piece told him that the owners of Cumberland's play of the Sybil, one of the seven predecessors of Brutus, intended to bring action for the invasion of the copyright, and that an injunction on the performance of the play by the government, on the ground of the dangerous democratic sentiments it contained, was anticipated."

However that may be, we know that great preparations were made for the first performance of "Brutus", and, according to Molloy, the biographer of Edmund Kean, Payne himself was allowed a day's grace from Fleet Street, where he was imprisoned for debt, in order to "communicate his ideas regarding the characters to the performers and especially to Kean; though it often happened when he had walked to Drury Lane to meet the tragedian by appointment, the latter was not to be found, or, pitiful to relate, was not in a condition to be seen."

The play was produced on Tuesday evening, December 3, 1818, and ran for twenty-three consecutive nights. Due to previous holiday arrangements, it had to be put aside until January 13, 1819, when it ran for fifty-three consecutive nights. The prologue was penned by the Rev. George Croly, sedate author of the religious novel of the second coming of Christ, entitled "Salathiel", and the epilogue, spoken by Mrs. Glover, was written by a friend.

So instantaneous was the success of the play that the printer of the theatre hastened to buy the copyright of the

piece from Payne, and proceeded then and there to set the
text in type. Theodore S. Fry, in his chatty estimate of the
poet and dramatist, written for the New York *Mirror*, just
at the time of Payne's return to America, gives the following pen picture of the scene:

> It was wished to publish it so instantaneously, that
> the manuscript was taken from the prompter during the
> performance, as fast as it was done with, to the printing
> office in the cellar under the stage. We have heard
> descriptions repeated from Mr. Payne himself, of his
> astonishment when going down to correct a proof, at
> finding the whole Roman senate, with their togas thrown
> over their shoulders, busy, by grim torch light, setting
> types! During this hurry, it was thought expedient that
> the preface should be as brief as possible. There was no
> time for a distinct enumeration of the passages from
> other authors.

This was one of the explanations given by Payne for the
lack of explicit credit to his seven sources.

According to the criticisms of the day, there is no doubt
that it was the wonder of Kean's acting which brought the
play to such success, and drew for it such extended literary
notice. It would seem that every one profited from its success but Payne. After the opening night, fifty pounds were
added to Kean's salary, and during the run the treasury was
enriched to the extent of ten thousand pounds. However,
out of all this prosperity, the dramatist received only one
hundred and eighty-three pounds and six shillings. There
was a tremendous undercurrent of feeling against Payne.
Even the "committee" to whom he appealed did not find it
in their power to give him any additional sum of money, and
Payne had once more to turn his attention to some quick
translation.

All this time he thought it most probable that there was a
secret plot against him. If thinking makes it so, his attitude
must have had some effect upon Kean, whose whole life
was marked by vagary, by quick friendships, and by equally
as rapid enmities. Evidently, on the first flush of the reading
of "Brutus," Kean had thought Payne was just the man to

write a play for him on the subject of "Virginius", and the perverse actor commissioned him to do so. But, while he was playing in "Brutus", his feeling for Payne began to abate, and, when the manuscript of "Virginius" was brought to him, he tossed it aside nonchalantly, and would have nothing to do with it. A part of it was published in the *London Magazine;* that is all we know of a subject which was later treated by James Sheridan Knowles. This indifference of Kean's was given public expression when he presented a gold-topped snuff-box to the stage-manager, Kemble, brother of Sarah Siddons and Charles Kemble, and had engraved upon it a scene from "Brutus". He ignored showing any appreciation for what the dramatist himself had done.

To those who have read Shakespeare's "Coriolanus" and "Julius Cæsar," "Brutus; or, The Fall of Tarquin" will not pass as any very great original work. Yet even the reading of it shows the tremendous opportunity the almost bombastic poetry would afford an actor of rotund style. It is small wonder that the rôle should have appealed so strongly to Edwin Forrest, whose style was of that florid kind. There are some who contend that in no way did the piece merit the success it had. Yet it stands forth, according to William Archer, as one of only two American plays presented by Samuel Phelps, during his distinctive régime at Sadler's Wells—the other piece being George Henry Boker's "Calaynos".

"Brutus" also graced the repertories of Macready, Edwin Booth, and John McCullough.* I have used a copy of the text, now owned by the New York Public Library, wherein the "cuts" were evidently made by J. W. Wallack; his signature on the fly-leaf and the notes on the margins of the play are in the same hand.

From printed accounts it is easy to imagine that, whereas Forrest succeeded in bringing forth the intellectual superiority of the character, Kean brought out the spiritual growth of the part, which can very readily be felt in the reading. This supposition is founded on the comparison made by one of Kean's biographers, of the great actor's *Brutus,* in "Julius Cæsar", with the *Brutus* of Kemble. The latter's conception

*A Drury Lane revival of the play was given, in 1845, with Gustavus V. Brooke as *Brutus.*

was "dignity of person, but Kean's seemed the very dignity of soul."

Writing in his "Life and Art of Edwin Booth", William Winter makes this excellent comparative suggestion:

> Edmund Kean gave the curse on *Sextus* in a gasping whisper, all the while clutching convulsively at his throat, as though strangling with passion; and the effect must have been terrific. Booth subdued the tumult of the situation, and augmented its power, by intense concentration, and a low, restrained, but incisive and righteously vindictive utterance, withering, ominous, dreadful, and set off by action that fully conveyed the delirious ecstasy of implacable vengeance. . . . The supremely fine part of Booth's *Brutus* was the judgment scene. . . . The address to the populace, in act third, was an extraordinary example of passionate eloquence. . . . During the judgment scene, the strained excitement of the actor became that of painful grief.

It may be that some of this interpretation of the son was gained by watching the work of his father, for some years before, when the two were in Washington, Edwin Booth had played *Titus* to the *Brutus* of the elder Booth.

"Brutus; or, The Fall of Tarquin" is not a drama that could be revived easily at the present moment in America, because the style of acting it demands is no longer the theatrical tradition—the acting of picturesque gesture and rounded utterance has given way to more quiet and more realistic and intensive methods. When the piece was first given in the United States, for the Benefit of Manager Simpson, at the Park Theatre, New York, on March 15, 1820, the rôle of *Brutus* was played by Mr. Pritchard. Forrest first appeared in the part, November 29, 1832, on the evening when the performance was given in honor of Payne's return home—a celebration brought to successful consummation through the efforts of George P. Morris.

When Payne reached New York, on July 25, 1832, critics called attention to the fact that almost his entire dramatic career had been confined to the stage history of London. His immortal "Home, Sweet Home", with music by Sir

Henry Bishop, and based on a Sicilian song which Payne had heard a peasant girl sing, appeared in an opera, "Clari", which brought Payne into some notoriety, and made both fortune and reputation for Charles Kemble, now become manager of Covent Garden, and Miss M. Tree, the first to sing the famous song. Payne came out the heavy loser in the financial arrangements, as he did with "Charles the Second", which he was forced to sell for one quarter the accustomed sum usually paid for the copyright of a play.

So we might go through Payne's entire dramatic career, which was one of unceasing trouble, partly brought about by his own temperament, and outline the numerous adaptations which he made for the different theatres, with small profit as to the literary measurement of his genius, but with excellent profit as a reflection of the spirit of the theatrical times in London.

Payne's friendship with Washington Irving, which resulted in their writing "Charles the Second", and several other compositions done either in consultation or under the kindly and valuable supervision of Irving, brings the author of "Bracebridge Hall" into American dramatic history, even though Irving never allowed his name to appear on the title-pages or the programs as co-author, and never wanted it to be known the actual proportion of the work he did. The comedy of "Charles the Second", dedicated to Kemble, was similar in incident and situation to "La Jeunesse de Henri V." When it was produced, in 1824, Harrison writes that the accuracy of the production was so maintained throughout that "the costumes too were as if cut out of the frames of old pictures, down to the veriest trifle." Thus was it with Kemble, as manager, and as percursor of Henry Irving and Beerbohm Tree—all three upholders of that type of theatrical scene akin to a Royal Academy canvas. Payne dedicated his "Richelieu" to Washington Irving. In the interesting correspondence, which is preserved, of their friendly association, one notes the amount of editing and polishing Irving did to the manuscripts submitted to him by Payne. Their friendship was such that Irving often weathered Payne over financial difficulties.

But all during his exile, Payne was homesick, and it is most in consonance with his feeling that he should have been

the author of "Home, Sweet Home". He wrote to one of his
brothers, from Paris, in 1822:

> I feel the want of some of you—parts of myself—in
> this strange world, for though I am naturalized to vaga-
> bondism, still it is but vagabondism. I long for a home
> about me.

Not only was Payne lonely, but he was also unhappy.
Neither his work nor his associations seemed to have brought
him any abiding pleasure. His correspondence is mostly
concerned with business, even though his friends tried to cheer
him up, and show him wherein he was progressing in his
work. He was not ungrateful for all this. His love and appreciation of what Washington Irving did for him was shown
on many occasions. He was continually forwarding bundles
of manuscripts to his friends, asking their aid in seeing, for
example, that they reached Elliston, who was then the manager of Drury Lane, or Charles Kemble, or any other member of the dramatic hierarchy of the time. In his preface to
"Thérèse; or, The Orphan of Geneva", a play written for
J. W. Wallack, we find Payne's estimate of theatrical conditions. He writes:

> It is so necessary in the production of the modern
> drama to consult the peculiarities of leading performers,
> and not offend the restive spirit by means of situation
> almost pantomimic and too impatient to pause for
> poetical beauty. Thus it seems almost hopeless to look
> to the stage of the present days for a permanent literary
> distinction. An actable play seems to derive its value
> from what is done more than from what is said, but the
> great power of a literary work consists in what is said,
> and the manner of saying it. He, therefore, who best
> knows the stage, can best tell why, in the present temper
> of the audience, good poets should so often make bad
> dramatists.

Payne had had disconcerting experience with this play,
"Thérèse". A pirated copy of it was taken down in short-
hand during one of the performances, according to Duyck-

inck, and a rival version quickly prepared and presented at Covent Garden. This is another illustration of how misfortune seemed to dog his footsteps.

After Payne came back to this country, he turned his attention toward the channels of political preferment. At first, true to his ever-present inclination for literary work, he issued a prospectus for a most pretentious magazine, the subscription price of which was to be ten dollars. But the scheme advanced no further than the printed announcements. Then he began writing for the *Democratic Review* (1838) and other magazines, and later espoused the cause of the Indians of Alabama and Georgia, in whom he became interested during a trip South. In fact, in 1849, a volume was published by Payne, entitled "Ancient Cherokee Traditions".

In 1838, Payne was living in Washington, and two years afterwards was appointed by President Tyler to the consulship of Tunis. His advocate for the post was Daniel Webster. That he was recalled in 1845, was not due to any illmanagement on his part, but to the fact that our next president was putting into effect his "spoliation policy".

On the election of Fillmore as President, Webster had Payne re-appointed to the consulship. It is interesting to note that on the evening of December 17, 1850, Jenny Lind, appearing in Washington on an occasion when Webster, Clay, Scott and Payne were in the audience, stepped to the footlights and sang "Home, Sweet Home".

While at his post as consul, Payne died on April 9, 1852. It was not until 1883 that his body was transferred to America, with national honor, and he was buried at Oakhill Cemetery, in Washington, on June 9th, of the same year.

BRUTUS: OR, THE FALL OF TARQUIN

Dramatis Personæ and Cast

Park Theatre, New York, November 29, 1832

Brutus.....................................Mr. Forrest.
Titus......................................Mr. Scott.
Sextus Tarquin............................Mr. Clark.
Aruns.....................................Mr. Barry.
Claudius..................................Mr. Kepple.
Collatinus................................Mr. Barrett.
Valerius..................................Mr. Blakeley.
Lucretius.................................Mr. Nexsen.
Horatius..................................Mr. Richings.
Celius....................................Mr. Conway.
Flavius Corunna...........................Mr. Harvey.
Centurion.................................Mr. Povey.
First Plebeian............................
Second Plebeian...........................
Third Plebeian............................
Fourth Plebeian...........................
Fifth Plebeian............................

Tullia....................................Mrs. Barnes.
Tarquinia.................................Mrs. Sharp.
Lucretia..................................Miss Waring.
Lavinia...................................Mrs. Durie.
Priestess.................................Miss Smith.

The costumes are indicated in the acting edition of the play, published by Samuel French.

PREFACE

This tragedy is submitted to the publick with the most grateful sense of the kindness with which it has been honoured. It was originally intended to be published as sent to the Theatre; but the omissions and changes consequent on its being performed, were numerous. The reader will now find it in every respect a copy from the prompt book. The imperfect lines which sometimes occur in the verse have arisen from the determination to make the conformity complete.

Seven plays upon the subject of Brutus are before the publick. Only two have been thought capable of representation, and those two did not long retain possession of the stage. In the present play I have had no hesitation in adopting the conceptions and language of my predecessors wherever they seemed likely to strengthen the plan which I had prescribed. This has been so done as to allow of no injury to personal feelings or private property. Such obligations to be culpable must be secret; but it may be observed that no assistance of other writers can be available without an effort almost, if not altogether, as laborious as original composition.

I am reluctant to select peculiar objects of praise, when I found zeal and politeness so universal.—But I must be permitted to add my gratitude to the publick admiration of Mr. KEAN's most masterly and splendid performance of the principal character.—Mrs. GLOVER, too, has claims on me which must not be forgotten.—The play was introduced by her to the Theatre, and its share of publick favour must be largely attributed to the critical taste of this very amiable and intelligent woman.

To the SUB-COMMITTEE and the MANAGER, I also beg to return my grateful thanks.

4, Southampton-street, Covent Garden,
December 9, 1818.

PERSONS REPRESENTED

Lucius Junius.............................Mr. Kean.
Titus...Mr. D. Fisher.
Sextus Tarquin.........................Mr. H. Kemble
Aruns...Mr. Penley.
Claudius....................................Mr. Coveney.
Collatinus.................................Mr. Bengough.
Valerius.....................................Mr. Holland.
Lucretius...................................Mr. Powell.
Horatius....................................Mr. Yarnold.
Celius..Mr. Carr.
Flavius Corunna.......................Mr. R. Phillips,
Centurion..................................Mr. Ley.
Messenger.................................Mr. Marshall.
First Roman..............................Mr. Ebsworth.
Second Roman..........................Mr. Smith.
Third Roman.............................Mr. Buxton.

Officers.

Messrs. Hope, Mathews, Brown, Appleby, Cooper, Goodman.

Populace.

Messrs. Evans, Wyber, G. Hogg, Williams, Thomas, Pem-
bery, West, T. West, Tutton, Bynam, Billet, Newman,
Tulip, Martin, Bettel, Melvin, H. Hogg, Dean, J. Seymour, Price, Speake, Hay, Hildrow, Tabby, Deakin,
Burn, Sanders, &c., &c.

Senators.

Messrs. Miller, Staples, Seymour, Johnson, Chapple, Read,
Connor, Richardson, &c.

Tullia.....................................Mrs. Glover.
Tarquinia................................. Mrs. W. West.
Lucretia...................................Mrs. Robinson.
Priestess of Rhea's Temple................Mrs. Brereton.
Vestal....................................Miss Cooke.
Lavinia................................... Miss Ivers.

Ladies of the Court.

Mesdms. Coveney, Chatterley, Calvert, Bates, Corri, Parnell.

Vestals.

Mesdms. Carr, Ebsworth, Vials, Smith, M. Bates, Caulfield.

Attendants on Lucretia,

Mesdms. Wilton, Lyon, Scott, Hill.

———

Scene *varies from Rome, to the camp before* Ardea *and to*
Collatia.

Time of the Action, about 2300 years ago.

PROLOGUE.*

Written by a friend, spoken by Mr. H. Kemble.

TIME rushes o'er us; thick as evening clouds
Ages roll back:—what calls them from their shrouds?
What in full vision brings their good and great,
The men whose virtues make the nations' fate,
The far, forgotten stars of human kind?
The STAGE,—the mighty telescope of mind!

If later, luckless arts that stage profane,
The actor pleads—not guilty of the stain:
He, but the shadow flung on fashion's tide—
Yours, the high will that all its waves must guide:
Your voice alone, the great reform secures,
His, but the passing hour—the age is yours.
  Our pledge is kept. Here, *yet*, no chargers wheel,
No foreign slaves on ropes or scaffolds reel,
No gallic amazons, half naked, climb
From pit to gallery,—the low sublime!
In Shakespeare's halls, shall dogs and bears engage?
Where brutes are actors, be a booth the stage!
And we shall triumph yet. The cloud has hung
Darkly above—but day shall spring—*has* sprung—
The tempest has but swept, not shook the shrine;
No lamp that genius lit has ceased to shine!
Still lives its sanctity. Around the spot
Hover high spirits—shapes of burning thought—
Viewless—but call them, on the dazzled eye
Descends their pomp of immortality:
Here, at your voice, Rowe, Otway, Southern, come,
Flashing like meteors thro' the age's gloom.

* [Ed.] This prologue was penned by the Rev. George Croly.

Perpetual *here*—king of th' immortal band,
Sits *Shakespeare* crown'd. He lifts the golden wand,
And all obey;—the visions of the past
Rise as they lived—soft, splendid, regal, vast.
Then Ariel harps along the enchanted wave,
Then the Wierd sisters thunder in their cave,—
The spell is wound. Then shows his mightier art,
The Moor's lost soul; the hell of Richard's heart,
And stamps, in fiery warning to all time,
The deep damnation of a tyrant's crime.

     To-night we take our lesson from the tomb:
'Tis thy sad cenotaph, colossal Rome!
How is thy helmet cleft, thy banner low,
Ashes and dust are all thy glory now!
While o'er thy wreck, a host of monks and slaves,
Totter to "seek dishonourable graves."

     The story is of Brutus: In that name
Tower'd to the sun her eagle's wing of flame!
When sank her liberty, that name of power,
Pour'd hallow'd splendours round its dying hour.
The lesson lived for man—that heavenward blaze
Fixed on the pile the world's eternal gaze.

     Unrivall'd England! to such memories thou,
This hour dost owe the laurel on thy brow;
Those, fixed, when earth was like a grave, thy tread,
Prophet and warrior! 'twixt the quick and dead,—
Those bade thee war for man,—those won the name
That crowns thee—famed above all Roman fame.

     Now, to our scene,—we feel no idle fear,
Sure, of the hearts, the *British* justice here;
If we deserve it, sure of your applause—
Then, hear for Rome, for England, for "our cause!"

BRUTUS

or,

The Fall of Tarquin

ACT I.

SCENE I.—*A Street in Rome.*

Enter VALERIUS *and* LUCRETIUS.

VALERIUS.

Words are too feeble to express the horror
With which my soul revolts against this Tarquin.
By poison he obtain'd his brother's wife,
Then, by a baser murder, grasp'd the crown.
These eyes beheld that aged monarch thrown
Down from the senate house,—his feeble limbs
Bruis'd by the pavement,—his time-honour'd locks
Which, from the very robber would have gain'd
Respect and veneration,—bath'd in blood!
With difficulty rais'd, and tottering homeward,
The murderers follow'd—struck him—and he died!

LUCRETIUS.

Inexpiable crime!

VALERIUS.

High in her regal chariot Tullia came—
The corpse lay in the street. The charioteer
Turn'd back the reins in horror. *"On, slave, on!*
"Shall dead men stop my passage to a throne?"
Exclaim'd the parricide. The gore was dash'd
From the hot wheels up to her diadem!

LUCRETIUS.

And Heaven's avenging lightnings were withheld!
Here rules this Tullia, while the king, her husband,
Wastes our best blood in giddy, guilty war!
Spirit of Marcus Junius!—Would the gods
Deign to diffuse thy daring through the land,
Rome from her trance with giant spirit would start,
Dash off her fetters and amaze the world!

VALERIUS.

Junius, didst say? Oh! tyranny long since
Had sunk—chain'd—buried in its native hell—
But Tarquin, trembling at his virtues, murder'd
Him and his elder son. The younger, Lucius,
Then on his travels, 'scap'd the tyrant's sword,
But lost his reason at their fearful fall.

LUCRETIUS.

Ay, the same Lucius who now dwells with Tarquin,—
The jest, the fool, the laughing stock o' th' court,
Whom the young princes always carry with 'em
To be the butt of their unfeeling mirth.

VALERIUS.

Hold! I hear steps. Great things may yet be done,
If we are men, and faithful to our country.   [*Exeunt.*

SCENE II.—*The Camp before Ardea.*

Enter CLAUDIUS *and* ARUNS, *laughing.*

ARUNS.

There is no doctor for the spleen like Lucius!
What precious scenes of folly did he act
When, lately, through the unknown seas of Greece
He went with us to Delphi!—But behold!
Where, full of business his wise worship comes.

Enter LUCIUS JUNIUS.

CLAUDIUS.

Whither so fast, good Junius, tell us whither?

LUCIUS.

To Rome, to Rome—the queen demands my presence.
The state needs aid and I am called to court.
Am I a fool? If so, you cannot say
I'm the first fool grac'd by a monarch's favour.

ARUNS.

Why, Junius, travel has improv'd thy wit,
Thou speakest shrewdly.

LUCIUS.

Do I so, my lord?
I'm always glad when you and I agree;
You have just such a wit as I should choose.
Would I could purchase such!—though it might split
My head, as confin'd air does—water bubbles!

CLAUDIUS.

How say you? Purchase? Pr'ythee, what would'st give?

LUCIUS.

What would I give?—ten acres of my land!

ARUNS.

Thy land! Where lies it?

LUCIUS.

Ask the king, my cousin:
He knows full well. I thank him, he's my steward,
And takes the trouble off my hands.

CLAUDIUS.

Who told thee so?

LUCIUS.

The king himself.   Now twenty years are past,
Or more,—since he sent for me from my farm.
"Kinsman," said he, with a kind, gracious smile,
"For the black crime of treason which was charg'd
"Against thy father and thy elder brother,
"Their lives have paid: for thee, as I love mercy,
"Live and be happy: simple is thy mind"—

ARUNS.

True, kinsman, true—i'faith, 'tis wondrous simple.

LUCIUS.

"And that simplicity will be a pledge
"That thou wilt never plot against thy sovereign"—

CLAUDIUS.

Indeed, for that, I'll be your bondsman, Junius.

LUCIUS.

"Live in my house, companion of my children.
"As for thy land, to ease thee of all care,
"I'll take it for thy use; all that I ask
"Of thee, is gratitude."

ARUNS.

And art thou not
Grateful for goodness so unmerited?

LUCIUS.

Am I not?   Never, by the holy gods,
Will I forget it!   'Tis my constant pray'r
To heaven, that I may one day have the pow'r
To pay the debt I owe him.   But stay—stay—
I brought a message to you from the king.

ARUNS.

Thank the gods, then, for thy good memory, fool!

LUCIUS.

The king your father sends for you to council,
Where he debates how best to conquer Ardea.
Shall I before, and tell him ye are coming?

CLAUDIUS.

Aye, or behind, or with us, or stay here—
As thy wit prompts—as suits thy lofty pleasure.
[*Exeunt* ARUNS *and* CLAUDIUS, *laughing*.

LUCIUS. [*Alone*.]

Yet, 'tis not that which ruffles me—the gibes
And scornful mockeries of ill-govern'd youth—
Or flouts of dastard sycophants and jesters,
Reptiles, who lay their bellies on the dust
Before the frown of majesty!—All this
I but expect, nor grudge to bear ;—the face
I carry, courts it !—Son of Marcus Junius !
When will the tedious gods permit thy soul
To walk abroad in her own majesty,
And throw this vizor of thy madness from thee?
To avenge my father's and my brother's murder !
(And sweet I must confess would be the draught !)
Had this been all—a thousand opportunities
I've had to strike the blow—and my own life
I had not valued as a rush.—But still—
There's something nobler to be done—my soul !
Enjoy the strong conception. Oh ! 'tis glorious
To free a groaning country—
To see Revenge
Spring like a lion from its den, and tear
These hunters of mankind ! Grant but the time,
Grant but the moment, gods ! If I am wanting,
May I drag out this idiot-feigned life
To late old age, and may posterity
Ne'er hear of Junius but as Tarquin's fool !
[*Exit* LUCIUS JUNIUS.

SCENE III.—*Rome.—A State Apartment in the Palace of* TULLIA.

Enter TULLIA, *preceded by* GUARDS, BANNER BEARERS, LADIES,—*and followed by* VALERIUS. *She appears perturbed, and speaks apart.*

TULLIA. [*Apart.*]

Why should the steady mind to shadows yield?
And yet this vision shakes my frame with horror!
I thought his spirit thunder'd in my ear,
"*Remember, when, with wild ambition's frenzy,*
"*And all Rome's empire in your view, you drove*
"*Your chariot wheels o'er your dead father's body,*
"*Up to the shouting forum!*" Why, my soul,
Dost thou not shun remembrance of that hour?
'Twas but the cause—the cause—For this base clay
How differs it from the dull earth we tread on
When the life's gone?—But, next, the Sibyl came,
Whose mystic book at such a price we bought,
And cried, "*The race of Tarquin shall be kings,*
"*Till a fool drive them hence and set Rome free!*"
Strange prophecy!—What fool?—It cannot be
That poor dolt, the companion of my sons—
—Hark thee, Valerius—Know'st thou that same fool
Now in the camp?

VALERIUS.

I know him well.—A man
Who, when he had a name, was Lucius Junius:—
A braver citizen Rome never boasted,
And wise and learn'd withal; now chang'd, alas!
A spectacle which humbles me to look on!

TULLIA.

But is he harmless in his moody humours?

VALERIUS.

Tame as my horse, which, though devoid of reason,
Shall turn, shall stop, and at my angry bidding

Shall kneel, till I am throned on his back!
And this shall Junius; the like instinct stirs
Junius and him,—no more.

TULLIA.   [*Apart.*]

Hence, idle fears!—
—Yet, when he went to Delphi, 'tis giv'n out
The oracle address'd him with strange portents,
And each night since, my dreams have been disturb'd
By a wild form, too much resembling his,
Leading our soldiers forth with sword and flame,
Revolters from the camp, to storm the palace.
But he is sent from thence and shall be watch'd.

Enter HORATIUS.

HORATIUS.

Your orders are obey'd.   Lucius awaits.

[*Exit* HORATIUS.

TULLIA.

Set him before us.
[*To* VALERIUS.]   Tell me, will he answer
If we do question him?

VALERIUS.

I think he will:
Yet sometimes when the moody fit doth take him,
He will not speak for days; yea, rather starve
Than utter nature's cravings; then anon
He'll prattle shrewdly, with such witty folly
As almost betters reason.

HORATIUS *returns with* LUCIUS JUNIUS.

TULLIA.

Hark thee, fellow,
How art thou call'd?

LUCIUS.

A fool.

TULLIA.

Fool for thy nature:
Thou answer'st well,—but I demand thy name.

Lucius.

Nothing but fool.

Tullia.

His faculties are brutish;—
Brutus shall be thy name.

Brutus.

Thanks to your grace!

Horatius.

Dost like thy new name, gentle brute?

Brutus.

So well,
Who will may take the fool. I care not who—
Your highness, an' it like you.

Horatius.

I the fool!
Sirrah, good words, or I will have thee beaten.

Brutus.

A fool thou wilt not beat—a brute thou dar'st not,
For the dull ass will kick against his striker,
If struck too harshly.

Tullia.

Let me hear no more;
There's mischief in his folly. Send him hence.

                                   [Brutus *going.*
But stay—I'll search him farther.—Hark thee, Brutus,
Thou wast at Delphi, with our sons the princes—
Tell me—what questions put they to Apollo?

Brutus.

Your sons did ask who should be chief in Rome.

Tullia.

Hah! What replied the oracle to that?

BRUTUS.

With pains and strugglings the prophetic dame
This destiny reported from her god—
"Great and most glorious shall that Roman be,
"Who first shall greet his mother with a kiss."

TULLIA.

That is fulfill'd by Sextus.

HORATIUS.

Aye, he straight
Hasten'd from thence, and kissed the queen his mother.

BRUTUS.

Woe for me, I have no mother!—
And yet I kiss'd her first.

TULLIA.

Thou kiss'd her? Thou?

BRUTUS.

Yea, madam, for just then my foot did slip
In the fresh blood of a new-slaughter'd victim,
And, falling, I did kiss my mother—earth.

TULLIA.

Oh, that the earth had swallow'd thee outright
Till thou hadst kiss'd the centre! I perceive,
The gods are leagued with folly to destroy us.
My very blood chills at my heart.—Away.

[*Exeunt* TULLIA, GUARDS *and* LADIES.

HORATIUS.

Hark thee, thou Brutus; I in part suspect
Thou ap'st this folly; if I find thee trifling
Or juggling with the Pythia for predictions,
By all the gods, I'll have thee flay'd, thy skin
Strip'd into thongs, to strangle thee withal,
Dissembling varlet!—   [*Strikes* BRUTUS, *who seizes him.*

VALERIUS.

Shame, my lord! forbear!
Threat'ning a fool, you do but wrong yourself.

HORATIUS.

But that the princes love his son, brave Titus,
My dagger should have pierc'd his throat ere now,
And sent him to his mother earth for ever!
He shall be watch'd.—Come, come with me, Valerius.
                                    [Exit HORATIUS.

VALERIUS.

The gods restore thee, Brutus, to thyself,
And us to thee! Farewell!   [Exit VALERIUS.

BRUTUS. [Alone.]
A little longer,
A little longer yet support me, patience!
The day draws on: it presses to the birth—
I see it in the forming womb of time—
The embryo liberty.—Hah!—'tis my son—
Down, rebel nature, down!—

                    Enter TITUS.

TITUS.

Welcome to Rome!
Would I might welcome thee to reason, too!

BRUTUS.

Give me thy hand—nay, give it me—

TITUS.

What would'st thou?
Speak to thy son.

BRUTUS.

I had a thing to say,
But I have lost it. Let it pass—no matter.

TITUS.

Look not upon me with those eyes, but speak;
What is it that annoys thee? tell thy friend—
How can I serve thee? What dost lack?

BRUTUS.

Preferment.
Thou can'st do much at court.

TITUS.

Ah, this is nothing!

BRUTUS.

So much the fitter for a fool's petition,
And a court promise.

TITUS.

Oh, this trifling racks me.

BRUTUS.

Lend me thine ear: I'll tell a secret to thee
Worth a whole city's ransom. This it is;
Nay, ponder it, and lock it in thy heart—
There are more fools, my son, in this wise world
Than the gods ever made.

TITUS.

Say'st thou, my father?
Expound this riddle. If thy mind doth harbour
Aught that imports a son like me to know,
Or knowing to achieve, declare it.

BRUTUS.

Now, my son,
Should the great gods, who made me what thou see'st,
Repent, and in their vengeance cast upon me
The burden of my senses back again—
What would'st thou say?

TITUS.

Oh, my lamented father,
Would the kind gods restore thee to thy reason—

BRUTUS.

Then, Titus, then I should be mad with reason.
Had I the sense to know myself a Roman,
This hand should tear this heart from out my ribs
Ere it should own allegiance to a tyrant.
If, therefore, thou dost love me, pray the gods
To keep me what I am.   Where all are slaves,
None but the fool is happy,

TITUS.

We are Romans—
Not slaves—

BRUTUS.

Not slaves?   Why, what art thou?

TITUS.

Thy son.
Dost thou not know me?

BRUTUS.

You abuse my folly.
I know thee not.—Wert thou my son, ye gods!
Thou would'st tear off this sycophantic robe,
Tuck up thy tunick, trim these curled locks
To the short warrior-cut, vault on thy steed;
Then, scouring through the city, call to arms,
And shout for liberty—

TITUS.   [Starts.]

Defend me, gods!

BRUTUS.

Hah! does it stagger thee?

TITUS.

For liberty?
Said'st thou for liberty?—It cannot be.

BRUTUS.

Indeed!—'tis well—no more.

TITUS.

What would my father?

BRUTUS.

Begone! you trouble me.

TITUS.

Nay, do not scorn me.

BRUTUS.

Said I for liberty? I said it not:
The awful word breath'd in a coward's ear,
Were sacrilege to utter. Hence, begone!
Said I, you were my son?—'Tis false: I'm foolish;
My brain is weak and wanders; you abuse it.

TITUS.

Ah, do not leave me; not in anger leave me.

BRUTUS.

Anger, what's that? I am content with folly;
Anger is madness, and above my aim.   [*Musick heard.*
Hark! here is musick for thee,—food for love,
And beauty to serve in the rich repast.
Tarquinia comes. Go, worship the bright sun,
And let poor Brutus wither in the shade.   [*Exit* BRUTUS.

TITUS.

Oh, truly said! bright as the golden sun
Tarquinia's beauty beams, and I adore!   [*Soft musick.*

TARQUINIA *enters, preceded by damsels bearing a crown of
gold, some with censers, &c., proper for the ceremonials of
a dedication to Fortune.*

What dedication, or what holy service
Doth the fair client of the gods provide?
In the celestial synod is there one
Who will not listen to Tarquinia's prayer?

TARQUINIA.

I go to Fortune's temple, to suspend
Upon the votive shrine, this golden crown.
While incense fills the fane, and holy hymns
Are chanted for my brother's safe return,
What shall I ask for Titus?

TITUS.

Tho' the goddess,
In her blind bounty should unthrone the world,
To build me one vast empire, my ambition,
If by thy love unblest, would slight the gift:
Therefore of Fortune I have nought to ask—
She hath no interest in Tarquinia's heart,
Nature, not Fortune, must befriend me there.

TARQUINIA.

Thy gentle manners, Titus, have endear'd thee,
Although a subject Roman, to Tarquinia:
My brother Sextus wears thee next his heart;
The queen herself, of all our courtly youth
First in her favour holds the noble Titus:
And though my royal father well may keep
A jealous eye upon thy Junian race,—
A race unfriendly to the name of king,—
Yet, thee he cherishes; with generous joy
The monarch sees thy early virtue shoot,
And with a parent's fondness, rears its growth.

TITUS.

Oh! neither name, nor nature, nor the voice
Of my lost father, could he wake to reason,
Not all the wrongs that tyranny could pile
On my afflicted head,—not all the praise
That patriot gratitude could shower upon me,
Can shake the faithful purpose of my soul
To sever it from love and my Tarquinia.

TARQUINIA.

Approve that firmness in the shock of trials,
And if my love can recompense thy virtue,
Nor tortures, nor temptations, nor the wreck
Of Rome and empire, shall divide me from thee.
To this I pledge my hand. Now to the temple!

[*Exeunt omnes.*

END OF THE FIRST ACT.

ACT II.

SCENE I.—*The Tent of* SEXTUS *in the Camp before Ardea.
A magnificent Banquet.*

SEXTUS, COLLATINUS, CLAUDIUS, *and* ARUNS, *discovered
drinking.*

SEXTUS.

Come, then, here's to the fairest nymph in Italy;
And she's in Rome.

ARUNS.

Here's to the fairest nymph in Italy;
And she is not in Rome.

SEXTUS.

Where is she then?

ARUNS.

Ask Collatine; he'll swear she's at Collatia.

SEXTUS.

His wife!

ARUNS.

Even so.

CLAUDIUS.

Is it so, Collatine?
Well, 'tis praiseworthy in this vicious age
To see a young man true to his own spouse.

Oh, 'tis a vicious age! When I behold
One who is bold enough to steer against
The wind of tide and custom, I behold him
With veneration; 'tis a vicious age.

COLLATINUS.

Laugh on! though I'm the subject! If to love
My wife's ridiculous, I'll join the laugh;
Though I'll not say if I laugh *at,* or *with* you!

ARUNS. [*Ironically.*]

The conscious wood was witness to his sighs,
The conscious Dryads wiped their watery eyes,
For they beheld the wight forlorn, to-day,
And so did I;—but I shall not betray.
Here now he is, however, thanks to me;
That is, his semblance, for his soul dwells hence.
How was it when you parted? [*Mimicking.*] *She,*—"my
    love,
"Fear not, good sooth, I'll very constant prove."
He,—"And so will I,—for, wheresoe'er I steer,
" 'Tis but my mortal clay; my soul is here."   [*All laugh.*

SEXTUS.

And prythee, Collatine, in what array
Did the god Hymen come to thee? How dress'd,
And how equipp'd? I fear me much, he left
His torch behind, so that thou could'st not see
A fault in thy belov'd; or was the blaze
So burning bright, that thy bedazzled eyes
Have since refused their office?

COLLATINUS.

And doth Sextus
Judge by his own experience, then, of others?
To him, I make no doubt, hath Hymen's torch
Discover'd faults enough! what pity 'twas
He had not likewise brought i' th' other hand
A mirror, where the prince might read himself.

SEXTUS.

I like thee now: thou'rt gay, and I'll be grave.
As to those dear, delicious creatures, women,
Hear what my own experience has taught me.
I've ever found 'em fickle, artful, amorous,
Fruitful in schemes to please their changeful fancies,
And fruitful in resources when discover'd.
They love unceasingly—they never change—
Oh, never!—no!—excepting in the object.
Love of new faces is their first great passion,
Then love of riches, grandeur, giddy sway!
Knowing all this, I seek not constancy.
But, to anticipate their wishes, rove,
Humour their darling passion, and am bless'd!

COLLATINUS.

This is the common cant; the stale, gross, idle,
Unmeaning jargon, of all those, who, conscious
Of their own littleness of soul, avoid
With timid eye the face of modest virtue:
Who, mingling only with the base, and flush'd
With triumphs over those they dare attack,
The weak, the forward, or deprav'd, declare,
(And fain would make their shallow notions current)
That womankind are all alike, and hoot
At virtue, wheresoe'er she passes by them.
I have seen sparks like these,—and I have seen
A little worthless village cur, all night
Bay with incessant noise the silver moon,
While she, serene, throned in her pearled car,
Sailed in full state along.—But Sextus' judgment
Owns not his words,—and the resemblance glances
On others, not on him.

SEXTUS.

Let it glance where and upon whom it will,
Sextus is careless of the mighty matter.
Now hear what I have seen. I've seen young men
Who, having fancied they have found perfection—

COLLATINUS.

Sextus, no more—lest I forget myself,
And thee.—I tell thee, prince—

ARUNS.

Sextus, you go too far.

SEXTUS.

Why, pray, good sir, may I not praise the wife
Of this same testy, froward husband here,
But on his cheek offence must quivering sit,
And dream'd of insult?

COLLATINUS.

I heed you not,—jest on; I'll aid your humour;
Let Aruns use me for his princely laughter,
Let Claudius deck me with ironic praise;
But when you touch a nearer, dearer subject,
Perish the man, nay, may he doubly perish,
Who can sit still, and hear, with skulking coolness,
The least abuse, or shadow of a slight,
Cast on the woman whom he loves! though here
Your praise or blame are pointless equally,
Nor really add the least, nor take away
From her true value more than they could add
To th' holy gods, or stain them on their thrones!

ARUNS.

If that a man might dare to ope his lips
When Collatinus frowns, I would presume
To say one word in praise of my own wife;
And I will say, could our eyes stretch to Rome,
In spite of the perfections of Lucretia,
My wife, who loves her fire-side and hates gadding,
Would prove far otherwise employ'd—and better,—
Aye, better, as a woman, than the deity
Residing at Collatia.

SEXTUS. [*Aside.*]

Well timed;—I'll seize th' occasion:
View this Lucretia ere I sleep, and satisfy
My senses whether fame has told the truth.
[*Aloud.*] I'll stake my life on't—Let us mount our horses
And post away this instant towards Rome,—
That we shall find thy wife, and his, and his,
Making the most of this, their liberty.
Why, 'tis the sex: enjoying to the full
The swing of licence which their husbands' absence
Affords. I'll stake my life that this is true:
And that my own, (ill as I may deserve it)—
Knows her state best, keeps best within the bounds
Her matron duties claim; that she's at home
While yours are feasting at their neigbours' houses.
What say'st thou, Collatine?

COLLATINUS.

Had I two lives I'd stake them on the trial,
Nor fear to live both out.
                                SEXTUS.

Let us away then.
Come, come, my Collatinus,—droop not thus—
Be gay.
                        COLLATINUS.

I am not sad.
                        SEXTUS.

But fearful for th' event.

COLLATINUS.

Not in the least.
                        SEXTUS.

A little.
                        COLLATINUS.

Not a whit.
You do not know Lucretia.

SEXTUS.

But we shall.
Let's lose no time. Come, brothers! Let's away.
                                [*Excunt omnes.*

SCENE II.—*Rome.—An Apartment in the Palace.*

Enter BRUTUS.

BRUTUS. [*Alone.*]

Oh, that some light would beam from heav'n to teach me
When to burst forth and how to gain my purpose.
For Rome I would resign all other bonds,
And tear each private tie from my fix'd heart.
—Ha!—Some one comes! It is my son! He seems
Wrapt in Elysium, and elate with joy! [*Retires.*

Enter TITUS.

TITUS.

'Tis done! 'tis done! auspicious are the fates,
Tarquinia's word is pledg'd, and all is brightness!

BRUTUS. [*Coming down.*]

That exclamation was too lofty, boy:
Such raptures ill become the troubled times—
Of such, no more.

TITUS.

Oh, at an hour like this
Who could repress the thrill of grateful joy!

BRUTUS. [*Eagerly.*]

What dost thou mean?

TITUS.

Tarquinia.

BRUTUS.

What of her?

TITUS.

Her vows are pledg'd,
And heaven's propitious smile will make her mine.

BRUTUS.

Thine? What! Thine? Heav'n make Tarquinia thine?
Away! away! Heav'n spurns the race she springs from!

TITUS.

How !—Father, wert thou to thyself restor'd,
Thou would'st exult to see thy son thus blest.
Our vows are past. They cannot be recall'd.
And soon the nuptial altar will behold her
My own for ever.

BRUTUS.

No, Titus, not for ever !
If thou art mine, thou can'st not be Tarquinia's.
Renounce thy father,—or renounce thy love.

TITUS.

Nay, loose me, father, this is frenzy all.
E'en hadst thou spoken the dictates of thy soul,
(For sure thou can'st not know what thou requir'st)
I must not, would not, could not, yield Tarquinia.
Nay—let me go—or my rack'd heart will break.

BRUTUS.

Leave me. Retire. Thine is no Roman heart.
Ere long the moon will change—the moon, my goddess—
And then thou may'st behold a change in Brutus.

TITUS.

'Tis as I thought. Folly resumes its reign.
Look on him, oh ye gods !
Grant him once more the treasure now withheld,
And to his son restore a long lost father !   [*Exit* TITUS.

BRUTUS. [*Alone.*]

I was too sudden. I should have delay'd
And watch'd a surer moment for my purpose.
He must be frighted from this dream of love.
What ! shall the son of Junius wed a Tarquin !
As yet I've been no father to my son,—
I could be none: but, through the cloud that wraps me,
I've watched his mind with all a parent's fondness,
And hail'd, with joy, the Junian glory there.

Could I once burst the chains which now enthral him,
My son would prove the pillar of his country—
Dear to her freedom as he is to me.
The time may come when heaven will heal our wrongs—
To your hands, mighty powers, I yield myself—
I will not doubt heaven's goodness or Rome's virtue—
Then, hence despair! Still, thou and I are twain!

[*Exit* BRUTUS.

SCENE III.—*The house of* COLLATINUS, *at Collatia.—An
apartment, lighted up.*

LUCRETIA *discovered, surrounded by her maids, all employed
in embroidery and other female occupations.—*LAVINIA *is
by the side of* LUCRETIA.

LUCRETIA.

How long is it, Lavinia, since my lord
Hath chang'd his peaceful mansion, for the camp
And restless scenes of war?

LAVINIA.

Why, in my simple estimation, madam,
'Tis some ten days, or thereabout, for time
Runs as it should with me,—in yours, it may be
Perhaps ten years.

LUCRETIA.

I do not understand thee.
Say'st thou, with me time runs not as it should?
Explain thy meaning—what should make thee think so?

LAVINIA.

All that I mean is, that if I were married,
And that my husband were call'd forth to th' wars,
I should not stray through the grove next my house,
Invoke the pensive solitude, and woo
The dull and silent melancholy,—brood
O'er my own thoughts alone, or keep myself

Within my house mew'd up, a prisoner.
'Tis for philosophers
To love retirement; women were not made
To stand coop'd up like statues in a niche,
Or feed on their own secret contemplations.

LUCRETIA.

Go to; thou knów'st not what thou say'st, Lavinia.
I thank the gods who taught me that the mind,
Possess'd of conscious virtue, is more rich
Than all the sunless hoards which Plutus boasts;
And that the chiefest glory of a woman
Is in retirement,—that her highest comfort
Results from home-born and domestic joys,—
Her noblest treasure, a deserving husband!
—Who, not a prisoner to the eye alone,
A fair complexion or melodious voice,
Shall read her deeper,—nor shall time, which palls
The rage of passion, shake his ardent love,
Increasing by possession. This, (again I thank
The gracious gods)—this husband, too, is mine!
—Soft—I hear footsteps! Hour of rapture! Look!
My life, my love, my Collatinus comes!

Enter COLLATINUS, CLAUDIUS, ARUNS, *and* SEXTUS.
LUCRETIA *rushes into the arms of* COLLATINUS.

My lord, most welcome!

COLLATINUS.

Welcome these, my friends,
Lucretia!—our right royal master's sons;
Passing this way, I have prevail'd with them
To grace our humble mansion.

LUCRETIA.

Welcome yourself!
And doubly welcome, that you bring such friends.
Haste maidens, haste—make ready for our guests!
                              [*Exeunt* ATTENDANTS.
My heart is full of joy!

ARUNS.

Rather, fair lady,
You should be angry, that, unseasonably,
And with abrupt intrusion, we've thus broke
Upon your privacy.

LUCRETIA.

No, my good lord;
Those to whom love and my respect are due,
Can ne'er intrude upon me;—had I known
This visit, you, perhaps, might have been treated
With better cheer,—not a more kind reception.
This evening, little did I think my house
Would have possess'd such lodgers.

CLAUDIUS.

Rather, lady,
Such birds of passage;—we must hence to-night.

LUCRETIA.

To-night? Doth not my lord say no to that?

COLLATINUS.

I would, Lucretia; but it cannot be.
If aught the house affords, my dearest love,
To set before your guests, I pray prepare it:
We must be at the camp ere morning dawn.
An hour or two will be the utmost limit
Allow'd us here.

LUCRETIA.

With all the speed I can,
I'll play the caterer; though I am tempted,
Would that delay your journey, to be tardy
And prove a sluggish housewife.

[*Exit* LUCRETIA.

SEXTUS.

This is indeed a wife! Here the dispute
Must end;—
And, Collatinus, we must yield to thee!

ARUNS.

I will not envy thee,—but 'tis a wife
Of wives—a precious diamond, pick'd
From out the common pebbles.   To have found her
At work among her maids at this late hour,
And not displeas'd at our rude interruption,—
Not to squeeze out a quaint apology,
As, *"I am quite asham'd; so unprepar'd!*
"Who could have thought! Would I had known of it!"
And such like tacit hints, to tell her guests
She wishes them away—thou'rt happy, Collatine.

COLLATINUS.

Enough, enough !
The gods forbid I should affect indifference,
And say you flatter me. I am most happy.—
But Sextus heeds us not. He seems quite lost.

SEXTUS.

Pray pardon me,
My mind was in the camp. How wine could heat us
To such a mad exploit, at such a time,
Is shameful to reflect on ; let us mount,
This instant, and return.

COLLATINUS.

Now we are here,
We shall encroach but little on our time
If we partake the slender fare together
Which will, by this, await us. Pray, my lords,
This way.   [*Exit* COLLATINUS.

SEXTUS.

Along—I'll follow straight.
                         [*Exeunt* ARUNS *and* CLAUDIUS.
[*Apart.*] Had she staid here till now, I should have done
Nothing but gaze. Nymphs, goddesses
Are fables ;—nothing can, in heaven or earth
Be half so fair !—But there's no hope !—Her face,
Her look, her eye, her manners, speak a heart
Unknowing of deceit ; a soul of honour,

Where frozen chastity has fix'd her throne
And unpolluted nuptial sanctity.
—Peace, undigested thoughts!—Down—down! till ripen'd
By further time, ye bloom!   [*Exit.*

END OF ACT THE SECOND.

ACT III.

SCENE I.—*Rome.—The Capitol.—Equestrian Statue of* TAR-
QUINIUS SUPERBUS.—*Night.—Thunder and Lightning.*

Enter BRUTUS.

BRUTUS. [*Alone.*]

Slumber forsakes me, and I court the horrors
Which night and tempest swell on every side.
Launch forth thy thunders, capitolian Jove!
Put fire into the languid souls of men,
Let loose thy ministers of wrath amongst them,
And crush the vile oppressor! Strike him down,
Ye lightnings! Lay his trophies in the dust!
                         [*Storm increases.*
Ha! this is well!—flash, ye blue forked fires!
Loud-bursting thunders, roar! and tremble earth!
   [*A violent crash of thunder, and the statue of* TARQUIN,
      struck by a flash, is shatter'd to pieces.
What! fallen at last, proud idol! struck to earth!
I thank you, gods! I thank you! When you point
Your shafts at human pride, it is not chance,
'Tis wisdom levels the commission'd blow.
But I—a thing of no account—a slave—
I to your forked lightnings bare my bosom
In vain—for what's a slave?—a dastard slave?
A fool, a Brutus? [*Storm increases.*] Hark! the storm
    rides on!
The scolding winds drive through the clattering rain,
And loudly screams the haggard witch of night.
Strange hopes possess my soul. My thoughts grow wild,
Engender with the scene and pant for action.

With your leave, majesty, I'll sit beside you.
                    [*Sits on a fragment of the statue.*
Oh, for a cause! A cause, ye mighty gods!

Enter VALERIUS, *followed by a* MESSENGER.

VALERIUS.

What! Collatinus sent for, didst thou say?

MESSENGER.

Aye, Collatinus, thou, and all her kinsmen,
To come upon the instant to Collatia;
She will take no denial. Time is precious,
And I must hasten forth to bring her husband.
                              [*Exit* MESSENGER.

BRUTUS. [*Apart.*]

Ha! Collatinus and Lucretia's kinsmen!
There's something dark in this—Valerius too
Well met—Now will I put him to the test—
Valerius—Hoa!

VALERIUS.

Who calls me?

BRUTUS.

Brutus.

VALERIUS.

Go,
Get thee to bed !   [VALERIUS *is departing.*

BRUTUS.

Valerius!

VALERIUS.

Peace, I say,
Thou foolish thing! Why dost thou call so loud?

BRUTUS.

Because I will be heard! The time may come
When thou shalt want a fool.

VALERIUS.

Pr'ythee, begone!
I have no time to hear thy prattle now.

BRUTUS.

By Hercules, but you must hear.   *[Seizing his arm.*

VALERIUS.

You'll anger me.

BRUTUS.

Waste not your noble anger on a fool.
'Twere a brave passion in a better cause.

VALERIUS,

Thy folly's cause enough.

BRUTUS.

Rail not at folly—
There's but one wise,
And him the gods have kill'd.

VALERIUS.

Killed?—Whom?

BRUTUS.

Behold!
Oh, sight of pity!—Majesty in ruins!
Down on your knees—down to your kingly idol!

VALERIUS.

Let slaves and sycophants do that; not I.

BRUTUS.

Wilt thou not kneel?

VALERIUS.

Begone; you trouble me.
Valerius kneels not to the living Tarquin.

BRUTUS.

Indeed!—Belike you wish him laid as low.

VALERIUS.

What if I do?

BRUTUS.

Jove tells thee what to do—
Strike!—Oh! the difference 'twixt Jove's wrath and thine!
He, at the crowned tyrant aims his shaft,
Thou, mighty man, would'st frown a fool to silence,
And spurn poor Brutus from thee.

VALERIUS.

What is this?
Let me look nearer at thee. Is thy mind,
That long-lost jewel, found?—and Lucius Junius,
Dear to my heart, restor'd? or art thou Brutus,
The scoff and jest of Rome, and this a fit
Of intermittent reason?

BRUTUS.

I am Brutus!
Folly, be thou my goddess! I am Brutus.
If thou wilt use me, so!—If not, farewell.
Why dost thou pause? Look on me! I have limbs,
Muscles and sinews, shoulders strong to bear,
And hands not slow to strike! What more than Brutus
Could Lucius Junius do?

VALERIUS.

A cause like ours
Asks both the strength of Brutus and the wisdom
Of Lucius Junius.

BRUTUS.

No more. We're interrupted.

VALERIUS.

Farewell. Hereafter we'll discourse
And may the gods confirm the hope you've waken'd.
                                        [*Exit* VALERIUS.
BRUTUS. [*Alone.*]

My soul expands! my spirit swells within me
As if the glorious moment were at hand!

Sure this is Sextus—why has he left the camp?
Alone!—and muffled!—

Enter SEXTUS, *wrapped in a mantle.*

Welcome, gentle prince!

SEXTUS.

Ha! Brutus here!—Unhous'd amid the storm?

BRUTUS.

Whence com'st thou, prince? from battle? from the camp?

SEXTUS.

Not from the camp, good Brutus—from Collatia—
The camp of Venus,—not of Mars, good Brutus.

BRUTUS.

Ha!

SEXTUS.

Why dost thou start?—thy kinswoman, Lucretia—

BRUTUS. [*Eagerly.*]

Well—what of her? speak!

SEXTUS.

Aye, I will speak,—
And I'll speak *that* shall fill thee with more wonder,
Than all the lying oracle declar'd.

BRUTUS.

Nay, prince, not so,—you cannot do a deed
To make me wonder.

SEXTUS.

Indeed! Dost think it?—
Then let me tell thee, Brutus,—wild with passion
For this fam'd matron,—though we met but once,—
Last night I stole in secret from the camp

Where, in security, I left her husband.
She was alone. I said affairs of consequence
Had brought me to Collatia. She receiv'd me
As the king's son, and as her husband's friend—

BRUTUS. [*Apart.*]

Patience, oh heart!—a moment longer, patience!

SEXTUS.

When midnight came, I crept into her chamber—

BRUTUS. [*Apart.*]
Inhuman monster!

SEXTUS.

Alarm'd and frantic
She shriek'd out, "Collatinus! Husband! Help!"
A slave rush'd in—I sprung upon the caitiff,
And drove my dagger through his clamourous throat;
Then, turning to Lucretia, now half dead
With terror, swore, by all the gods at once,
If she resisted, to the heart I'd stab her,
Yoke her fair body to the dying slave,
And fix pollution to her name for ever!

BRUTUS.

And—and—the matron?—

SEXTUS.

Was mine!

BRUTUS. [*With a burst of frenzy.*]

The furies curse you then!—Lash you with snakes!
When forth you walk may the red, flaming sun
Strike you with livid plagues!—
Vipers, that die not slowly, gnaw your heart!
May earth be to you but one wilderness!
May mankind shun you—may you hate yourself—
For death pray hourly, yet be in tortures
Millions of years expiring!

SEXTUS.

Amazement! What can mean this sudden frenzy!

BRUTUS.

What? Violation! Do we dwell in dens,
In cavern'd rocks,—or amongst men in Rome?
        [*Thunder and lightning become very violent.*
Hear the loud curse of heaven! 'Tis not for nothing
The thunderer keeps this coil above your head!
        [*Points to the fragments of the statue.*
Look on that ruin! See your father's statue
Unhors'd and headless! Tremble at the omen!

SEXTUS.

This is not madness. Ha!—my dagger lost!—
Wretch!—thou shalt not escape me!—Ho! a guard!—
The rack shall punish thee!—A guard, I say!
        [*Exit* SEXTUS.

BRUTUS. [*Alone.*]

The blow is struck!—the anxious messages
To Collatinus and his friends explain'd:
And now, Rome's liberty or loss is certain!
I'll hasten to Collatia—join my kinsmen—
To the moon, folly! Vengeance, I embrace thee!
        [*Exit* BRUTUS.

SCENE II.—*An Apartment in the house of* COLLATINUS.

COLLATINUS *enters wildly, a bloody dagger in his hand,
followed by* VALERIUS *and* LUCRETIUS.

COLLATINUS.

* She's dead. Lucretia's dead! I pluck'd this steel
From my Lucretia's heart! This is her blood!
Howl, howl, ye men of Rome! Look! there she lies

---

* The scene which was omitted after the first representation, and for which this intro-
ductory speech of Collantinus is substituted, will be found in a note at the end of the play.

That was your wonder.
Ye mighty gods, where are your thunders now?
Ye men and warriors, have you human hearts?
But who shall dare to mourn her loss like me?

Enter BRUTUS.

BRUTUS.

I dare,—and so dare every honest Roman.

LUCRETIUS.

Whence comes this mad intrusion?   Hence, begone!

BRUTUS.

The noble spirit fled! How died Lucretia?

VALERIUS.

By her own hand she died!

BRUTUS.

Heroic matron!
Now, now the hour is come! By this one blow
Her name's immortal and her country sav'd!
Hail, dawn of glory! [*Snatching the dagger.*]   Hail, thou
        sacred weapon!
Virtue's deliverer, hail! This fatal steel
Empurpled with the purest blood on earth,
Shall cut your chains of slavery asunder!
Hear, Romans, hear! did not the Sibyl tell you
A fool should set Rome free? I am that fool;
Brutus bids Rome be free!

VALERIUS.

What can this mean?

BRUTUS.

It means that Lucius Junius has thrown off
The mask of madness, and his soul rides forth
On the destroying whirlwind, to avenge
The wrongs of that bright excellence and Rome!

LUCRETIUS.

Can this be Lucius Junius?

VALERIUS.

Ha! the voice
Of inspiration speaks!

COLLATINUS.

Oh, glorious Brutus,
Let me in tears adore the bounteous gods
Who have restor'd thee to redress my woes;
And, in my woes, my country!

BRUTUS.

No more of this.
Stand not in wonder. Every instant now
Is precious to your cause. Rise! Snatch your arms!
[BRUTUS *kneels.*

Hear me, great Jove! and thou, paternal Mars,
And spotless Vesta! To the death I swear
My burning vengeance shall pursue these Tarquins!
Ne'er shall my limbs know rest till they are swept
From off the earth, which groans beneath their infamy!
This, from the bottom of my soul I swear! [*He rises.*
Valerius, Collatine, Lucretius,—all—
Here, I adjure ye by this fatal dagger,
All stain'd and reeking with her sacred blood,
Be partners in my oath,—revenge her fall!

ALL.

We swear!

BRUTUS.

Well have ye said: and, oh methinks I see
The hovering spirit of the murder'd matron,
Look down and bow her airy head to bless you!
Summon your slaves, and bear the body hence
High in the view, through all the streets of Rome,
Up to the Forum!—On! The least delay,
May draw down ruin and defeat our glory!
On, Romans, on! The fool shall set you free!
[*Exeunt omnes.*

SCENE III.—*The Palace of* TULLIA.

Enter FLAVIUS CORUNNA, *in haste, meeting* HORATIUS.

CORUNNA.

My lord, my lord! Quick, tell me, where 's the queen?

HORATIUS.

Whence this alarm? what would'st thou?

CORUNNA.

Rebellion rages—

HORATIUS.

Rebellion!

CORUNNA.

Lucretia,
The wife of Collatinus, is no more.
The furious multitude have borne her body
With shouts of vengeance through the streets of Rome,
And "Sextus Tarquin," is the general cry.

HORATIUS.

Where are thy troops? why dost thou dally here,
When thou should'st pay their insolence with death?

CORUNNA.

The soldiers join the throng—the gates are clos'd,
And the mad crowd exclaim, "We banish Tarquin."
Brutus all wild with vengeance leads them on.

HORATIUS.

What miracle is this? How say'st thou, Brutus?

CORUNNA.

Aye, the fool Brutus. Now before the rostrum
The body of Lucretia is expos'd,
And Brutus there harangues assembled Rome.

He waves aloft
The bloody dagger; all the people hear him
With wildest admiration and applause;
He speaks as if he held the souls of men
In his own hand, and moulded them at pleasure.
They look on him as they would view a god,
Who, from a darkness which invested him,
Springs forth, and, knitting his stern brow in frowns,
Proclaims the vengeful will of angry Jove.

HORATIUS.

Fly thro' the city; gather all the force
You can assemble, and straight hasten hither.
I'll to the queen.—Lose not a moment.   Hence!
I tremble for Rome's safety!—haste!—begone!

[*Exeunt at opposite sides.*

SCENE IV.—*The Forum.*

The populace fill the stage. BRUTUS *is discovered upon the
Forum.   The dead body of* LUCRETIA *is on a bier beneath.*
COLLATINUS, LUCRETIUS, *and the* FEMALE ATTENDANTS *of*
LUCRETIA *stand around her corpse.* VALERIUS *and others
are seen.*

BRUTUS.

Thus, thus, my friends, fast as our breaking hearts
Permitted utterance, we have told our story;
And now, to say one word of the imposture,—
The mask necessity has made me wear.
When the ferocious malice of your king,—
King do I call him?—When the monster, Tarquin,
Slew, as you most of you may well remember,
My father Marcus and my elder brother,
Envying at once their virtues and their wealth,
How could I hope a shelter from his power,
But in the false face I have worn so long?

FIRST ROMAN.

Most wonderful!

SECOND ROMAN.

Silence! he speaks again.

BRUTUS.

Would you know why I summon'd you together?
Ask ye what brings me here? Behold this dagger,
Clotted with gore! Behold that frozen corse!
See where the lost Lucretia sleeps in death!
She was the mark and model of the time,
The mould in which each female face was form'd,
The very shrine and sacristy of virtue!
Fairer than ever was a form created
By youthful fancy when the blood strays wild
And never resting thought is all on fire!
The worthiest of the worthy! Not the nymph
Who met old Numa in his hallow'd walks,
And whisper'd in his ear her strains divine,
Can I conceive beyond her;—the young choir
Of vestal virgins bent to her. 'Tis wonderful
Amid the darnel, hemlock, and base weeds
Which now spring rife from the luxurious compost
Spread o'er the realm, how this sweet lily rose,—
How from the shade of those ill neighbouring plants
Her father shelter'd her, that not a leaf
Was blighted, but array'd in purest grace,
She bloom'd unsullied beauty. Such perfections
Might have call'd back the torpid breast of age
To long forgotten rapture; such a mind
Might have abash'd the boldest libertine,
And turn'd desire to reverential love
And holiest affection! Oh, my countrymen!
You all can witness when that she went forth
It was a holiday in Rome; old age
Forgot its crutch, labour its task,—all ran,
And mothers turning to their daughters cried,
"There, there's Lucretia!" Now, look ye where she lies!
That beauteous flower, that innocent sweet rose,
Torn up by ruthless violence—gone! gone!

ALL.

Sextus shall die!

BRUTUS.

But then—the king—his father—

FIRST ROMAN.

What shall be done with him?

SECOND ROMAN.

Speak, Brutus!

THIRD ROMAN.

Tell us!

BRUTUS.

Say, would ye seek instruction? would ye ask
What ye should do? Ask ye yon conscious walls
Which saw his poison'd brother, saw the incest
Committed there, and they will cry, Revenge!
Ask yon deserted street, where Tullia drove
O'er her dead father's corse, 'twill cry, Revenge!
Ask yonder senate house, whose stones are purple
With human blood, and it will cry, Revenge!
Go to the tomb where lies his murder'd wife,
And the poor queen, who lov'd him as her son,
Their unappeased ghosts will shriek, Revenge!
The temples of the gods, the all viewing heavens,
The gods themselves, shall justify the cry
And swell the general sound, Revenge! Revenge!

ALL.

Revenge! Revenge!

BRUTUS.

And we will be reveng'd, my countrymen!
Brutus shall lead you on; Brutus, a name
Which will, when you're reveng'd, be dearer to him
Than all the noblest titles earth can boast. [Shout.

FIRST ROMAN.

Live, Brutus!

SECOND ROMAN.

Valiant Brutus!

THIRD ROMAN.

Down with Tarquin!

SECOND ROMAN.

We'll have no Tarquins!

FIRST ROMAN.

We will have a Brutus!

THIRD ROMAN.

Let's to the Capitol, and shout for Brutus!

BRUTUS.

I, your king?
Brutus your king!—No, fellow-citizens!
If mad ambition in this guilty frame
Had strung one kingly fibre,—yea, but one—
By all the gods, this dagger which I hold
Should rip it out, though it entwin'd my heart.

VALERIUS.

Then I am with thee, noble Brutus!
Brutus, the new restor'd! Brutus, by Sibyl,
By Pythian prophetess foretold, shall lead us!

BRUTUS.

Now take the body up. Bear it before us
To Tarquin's palace; there we'll light our torches,
And, in the blazing conflagration, rear
A pile for these chaste relics, that shall send
Her soul amongst the stars. On! Brutus leads you!
                    [*Exeunt, the mob shouting.*

END OF THE THIRD ACT.

ACT IV.

SCENE I.—*A court belonging to* TARQUIN'S *Palace. In the front, a grand entrance, with folding gates closed.*

Enter TULLIA.

TULLIA. [*Alone.*]

Gods! whither shall a frantic mother fly!
Accursed siege of Ardea! Tarquin, Tarquin,
Where art thou? Save thy wife, thy son, thy city!

Enter TITUS.

TITUS.

Where is the prince? where's Sextus?

TULLIA.

Where? Oh, heavens!
His madness hath undone us! Where is Sextus?
Perhaps ev'n now the barbarous ruffians hurl him
Alive into the flames, or, piece-meal, drag
Along the rebel streets his mangled trunk—

TITUS.

No more! I'll save him, or avenge—
                    [*Going.* HORATIUS *meets and stops him.*

HORATIUS.

Turn, noble Roman, turn;
Set not your life upon a desperate stake!
Hark! they are at the gates!

TULLIA.
Does my son live?
                    HORATIUS.

Furious he sprang upon the rabble throng,
And hew'd his desperate passage: but the time
Admits no further question—Save yourself!

TULLIA.

Let the tide enter;
Let the vile rabble look upon the eyes
Of majesty and tremble. Who leads them on?

HORATIUS.

Your new nam'd fool, your Brutus.

TITUS.

Death! my father?

TULLIA.

Brutus in arms!
Oh, Sibyl! Oh, my fate! farewell to greatness!
I've heard my doom.

TITUS.

Earth, earth, enclose me!

TULLIA.

Hark! it bursts upon us!   [*Shouts are heard.*

HORATIUS.

Ha! nearer yet! Now be propitious, Mars!
Now, nerve my arm with more than mortal fury
Till the dissembler sink beneath its vengeance.
                                   [*Exit* HORATIUS.

TULLIA.

Fly! save my child—save my—save your Tarquinia.

TITUS.

Or die, defending.   [*Exit* TITUS.

    [*Tumult becomes very violent, and the battering at the
    gate and wall commences.*

TULLIA.

Ah! if amidst my legions I might fall,
Death were not then inglorious; but to perish
By the vile scum of Rome—hunted by dogs—
Baited to death by brawling, base mechanics—
Shame insupportable!

[*The gate and wall are shattered down. The palaces
behind are in flames. The soldiers and populace
rush over the ruins.* BRUTUS *appears in the midst
of them, and advances to the front.*

BRUTUS.

Seize the parricade!

[*They advance and surround her.*

TULLIA.

Avaunt! I am your queen.

BRUTUS.

Tarquins! we cast you from us.

TULLIA.

Give me a sword and let me fall like Tullia.

BRUTUS.

No, we reserve our swords for nobler uses
Than to make war with women: To the Tarquins,
To your adulterous son we leave that shame.

TULLIA.

If then 'twill better sate thy cruelty,
Precipitate me quick into those flames,
And with the wreck of empire mix my ashes.

BRUTUS.

Take her to Rhea's temple, take her hence
And lodge her with her ancestors!

TULLIA.

Ye gods!
My father's sepulchre!—I'll not approach it.

BRUTUS.

'Twill furnish wholesome recollection. Hence!

TULLIA.

Not to that fatal place! Send me not thither!

BRUTUS.

'Tis fix'd.

TULLIA.

Choose the most loathsome dungeon—there confine me,
Or give me death instead. My heart recoils
Against that temple.

BRUTUS.

There, and only there,
By your dead father's tomb, you must abide
The judgment of the state.

TULLIA.

Then, by the gods
Whom, for the last time, I invoke,—whose shrines
I've incens'd o'er and o'er, though now forsaken,
Now at my utmost need, if no means else
Of ready death present themselves,
No particle of food shall pass these lips,
Till, in the void of nature, hungry madness
With blank oblivion entering, shall confound
And cancel all perception.   [*Exit* TULLIA, *guarded.*

Enter TITUS, *who meets* BRUTUS *as he is going off.*

TITUS.

Turn, oh my father,
And look upon thy son.

BRUTUS.

What would'st thou? speak!

TITUS.

If thou hast reason, oh, have mercy also!
But if in madness thou hast done this deed—

BRUTUS.

I am not mad but as the lion is
When he breaks down the toils that tyrant craft

Hath spread to catch him. Think not we will suffer
These monsters to profane the air of heaven.
Shall Titus, then, oppose our great design?
Shall Brutus meet a recreant in his son?
Banish this folly!—Have a care!—I know thee—
There is a lurking passion at thy heart
Which leaves but half a soul for Rome and me!

TITUS.

You wrong me. Like a Roman I exult
To see Lucretia's murder thus aveng'd—
And like a son glory in such a father!
Yet hear me through.—Nay, do not frown, but hear me.—

BRUTUS.

Go on; confess thy weakness and dismiss it.

TITUS.

'Twas in the sleep of my dear father's reason,
When Tarquin's freed-man in a saucy mood
Vented vile jests at thy unhappy weakness,
Stung to the quick, I snatch'd a weapon up
And fell'd him to my foot.

BRUTUS.

Why, 'twas well done.
The knave was saucy and you slew him—On!

TITUS.

'Twas on this very spot Tarquinia stood,
And when the wrathful father had denounc'd
Immediate death on this my filial act,
She with the tongue of interceding pity,
And tears that stream'd in concert with her suit,
Implor'd, prevail'd, and gave me life—and love.

BRUTUS.

'Tis well. Behold, I give her life for life:
Rome may be free altho' Tarquinia lives—

This I concede; but more if thou attemptest,—
By all the gods!—Nay, if thou dost not take
Her image, though with smiling cupids deck'd,
And pluck it from thy heart, there to receive
Rome and her glories in without a rival,
Thou art no son of mine, thou art no Roman!

[*Exit* BRUTUS.

Enter TARQUINIA.

TARQUINIA.

Save, save me, Titus! oh, amid the crash
Of falling palaces, preserve Tarquinia!
Or, do I meet in thee a double rebel,
Traitor alike to me and to your king?
Speak, I conjure thee! Will the son of Brutus
Now take me to his pity and protection,
Or stab with perfidy the heart that loves him!

TITUS.

Cruel suspicion! Oh, ador'd Tarquinia,
I live but to preserve you. You are free:
I have my father's sanction for your safety.

TARQUINIA.

I scorn a life that is preserv'd by Brutus!
I scorn to outlive parents, brothers, friends!
I'll die with those
Whom this dire night hath murder'd!

TITUS.

Who are murder'd?
Whom hath the sword of Brutus slain? Not one
Of all thy kindred—

TARQUINIA.

Say'st thou? Lives my mother?

TITUS.

She lives—and Sextus,—even he escapes
The storm which he has rais'd, and flies to Ardea.

TARQUINIA.

Speed him, ye gods, with eagle swiftness thither!
And may those thunders which now shake the walls
Of tottering Ardea, like a whirlwind burst
On this devoted city, 'whelm its towers,
And crush the traitorous hive beneath their ruins.
Now, Titus, where is now thy promis'd faith?
Did'st thou not swear no dangers should divide us?

TITUS.

I did; and, constant to my oath, behold me
Thy faithful guardian in this night of terrors.

TARQUINIA.

Be still my guardian; snatch me from these terrors,
Bear me to Ardea, be the friend of nature,
And give the rescued daughter to the arms
Of her protecting parent; thus you gain
The praise of men, the blessings of the gods,
And all that honour, all that love can grant.

TITUS.

Despair! Distraction! Whither shall I turn me!

TARQUINIA.

Why do you waver? Cast away this weakness;
Be glorious in your cruelty and leave me.
By all the demons who prepare the heart
To rush upon the self-destroying steel,
The same dire moment which gives thee to Brutus,
Gives me to death!

TITUS.

Horror! Tarquinia, hold!

TARQUINIA.

Lo! I am arm'd. Farewell!—How I have lov'd you,
My death shall witness,—how you have deceiv'd me

Let your own conscience tell. Now to your father!
Now go and mingle with the murderers;
Go, teach those fiends what perjury can do,
And shew your hands bath'd in Tarquinia's blood;
The filial deed shall welcome you to Brutus,
And fill his gloomy soul with savage joy.

TITUS.

Take, take me hence for ever! Let me lose
In these dear arms the very name of son,
All claims of nature, every sense but love!

TARQUINIA.

The gods that guard the majesty of Rome,
And that sweet power, whose influence turns thy heart
To pity and compliance, shall reward
And bless thee for the deed!

TITUS.

Can he be blest,
On whom a father's direful curse shall fall?

TARQUINIA.

A madman's imprecation is no curse.
Be a man.

TITUS.

Oh, while thy love upholds me, I can stand
Against the world's contempt; remember, only,
For whose dear sake I am undone; remember
My heart was honour's once.

TARQUINIA.

And shall be ever!
Come, I will show thee where bright honour grows,
Where thou shalt pluck it from the topmost branch,
And wear it in its freshest, fairest bloom.

[*Exeunt* TITUS *and* TARQUINIA.

SCENE II.—*A Street in Rome*.

Enter HORATIUS *and* CELIUS.

HORATIUS.

Brutus and Collatinus are appointed
To sovereign sway, as consuls for the year.
Their self-elected senate meets to-morrow.
Tho' some remain, too honest for their views,
These for security exact conditions—
They ask a chief whose well establish'd fame
May win the hearts of this inconstant people;
A chief so brave, that, should we prove victorious,
He may compel the king to keep his faith;
Or, if we fall, boldly revenge our deaths—
And such a chief I've found.

CELIUS.

Indeed!—In whom?

HORATIUS.

The consul's son—his much lov'd son—young Titus.

CELIUS.

What! to rebel against his father's power?

HORATIUS.

Aye, he is ours. This very night, Tarquinia
Will lead him forth to the Quirinal gate,
Whence they straight hasten to the camp at Ardea.
Impetuous youth is wrought upon with ease.
Though 'tis his father's frown upon his love,
And early vows pledg'd to the fair Tarquinia,
Alone, which prompt him thus to lead our band,
Once in our pow'r, we'll mould him to our ends;
His very name will prove a tower of strength,
And Rome, once more, shall be restor'd to Tarquin.

CELIUS.

Bravely resolv'd! But tell me—where's the queen? *

* In the first American edition, we have, "Where is Tullia?"

HORATIUS.

A captive, and confin'd in Rhea's temple,
Watched by the vestals, who there guard the flame
Upon the tomb where lies her murder'd father.
Unhappy queen! our swords shall soon release thee!
Come! Hence at once! The hour draws near—away—
Ere two days pass these reptiles shall be crush'd,
And humbled Rome sue for its monarch's pardon.

[*Exeunt* HORATIUS *and* CELIUS.

Enter LUCRETIUS *and* VALERIUS.

VALERIUS.

That was Horatius 'parted, was it not?

LUCRETIUS.

The same.

VALERIUS.

Am I deceiv'd? Methinks I heard
Something like discontent and treason mutter'd.

LUCRETIUS.

I fear all is not safe. Assembled groups
Of Tarquin's friends have been seen close in conference
Muttering his name aloud. Aye, and some base,
Degenerate Romans call'd for a surrender,

VALERIUS.

Horatius' arts may justly wake suspicion;—
And Rome, we know, is still disgrac'd by many
Too base, too sordid, to be bravely free.
Let us go forth and double all the guards,
See their steps watch'd and intercept their malice.

LUCRETIUS.

Nay—there's a safer course than that—arrest them!

VALERIUS.

The laws and rights we've sworn to guard, forbid it!
Let them be watch'd. We must not venture farther.
To arrest a Roman upon bare surmise
Would be at once to imitate the tyrant
Whom we renounce, and from his throne have driven!

[*Exeunt* LUCRETIUS *and* VALERIUS.

SCENE III.—*Rome. The Temple of Rhea, with a large central door leading to the Tomb of* SERVIUS TULLIUS, *late King of Rome. On one side of the stage a statue of Rhea, and on the other, a statue of Vesta, with altars and incense burning before each.*

PRIESTESS *of Rhea.* VIRGINS *of the Temple.*

PRIESTESS.

Daughters of Rhea, since the lords of Rome
Have to your holy hands consign'd the charge
Of their now captive queen, inform the Priestess
How your sad prisoner abides her durance.
Is her proud soul yet humbled, or indignant
Doth it still breathe defiance and contempt?

VIRGINS.

Sullen and silent she resolves on death;
She will not taste of nourishment. She comes!

Enter TULLIA.

PRIESTESS.

I pray you, royal lady, be entreated—

TULLIA.

I tell you, no!

PRIESTESS.

Think what a train of weary hours have pass'd
Since you had taste of food.

TULLIA.

'Tis well!
The fewer are to come.

PRIESTESS.

How can you live to meet your royal husband.
To fold your children in your arms again,
If you resist support?

TULLIA.

Hah! well remember'd!
What news from Ardea? Will he march for Rome?
Hark! Do you hear his trumpet? Is he coming?
Aye, this is hope and worth the feeding.
'Tis well. 'Tis well.
But, tell me—doth the king know of this kindness?

PRIESTESS.

What king? we comprehend you not.

TULLIA.

What king?
Brutus, the king of Rome,—knows he of this?

PRIESTESS.

He does.

TULLIA.

And would he I should live?

PRIESTESS.

He would.

TULLIA.

Merciful villain!
Yes, he would have me live to page his triumphs:
I know the utmost of his mercy—
Subtle traitor!
I'll not taste food, tho' immortality
Were grafted to each atom—Hark! What's that?
Heard you that groan?

PRIESTESS.

It is your fancy's coinage.

TULLIA.

Again! 'Tis deep and hollow:
It issues from the vault—Set the door open!
Open, I say.

PRIESTESS.

It is your father's sepulchre.

TULLIA.

My father! righteous gods! I kill'd my father!
Horrible retribution!

PRIESTESS.

Wretched daughter,
If thou hast done this deed, prepare thy spirit
By wholesome meditation for atonement,
And let no passion interrupt the task
Of penitence and prayer.

TULLIA.

I'll pray no more.
There is no mercy in the skies for murder,
Therefore no praying, none.
I have a plea for my impenitence—
Madness!
These groans have made me mad; all the night through
They howl'd distraction to my sleepless brain!
You've shut me up with furies to torment me,
And starv'd me into madness. Hark! again!
Unbar the door! Unbar it! By the gods,
The voice is more than human which I hear!
I'll enter there—I will be satisfied,
Altho' the confirmation should present
His awful form—*

> She rushes forward. The PRIESTESS and VESTALS, in
> confusion and alarm, spring to the bar, which, falling
> with a crash, the door flies open, and discovers a monu-

---

* The first American edition continues with the lines:
> And drive me into worse perdition
> Than hell hath yet a name for.

mental figure of SERVIUS TULLIUS, *with lamps burning on each side of it.* TULLIA *recoils, shrieks,* falls, and expires. The, others group around her, and the curtain falls to soft music.*

END OF THE FOURTH ACT.

ACT V.

SCENE I.—*A Street in Rome, with the Temple of Mars in view.*

Enter BRUTUS *and* COLLATINUS, *as Consuls, with* LICTORS, VALERIUS, LUCRETIUS, *and numerous followers.*

BRUTUS.

You judge me rightly, friends. The purpled robe,
The curule chair, the lictors' keen-edg'd axe,
Rejoice not Brutus;—'tis his country's freedom:
When once that freedom shall be firmly rooted,
Then, with redoubled pleasure, will your Consul
Exchange the splendid miseries of power,
For the calm comforts of a happy home.

Enter a MESSENGER.

MESSENGER.

All health to Rome, her Senate, and her Consuls!

BRUTUS.

Speak on—What message hast thou to impart?

MESSENGER.

I bring intelligence of Sextus Tarquin,
Who, on arriving at a neighbouring village,
Was known, and by the people ston'd to death.

---

* The English edition (1818) has " and exclaims, " 'Tis he! It is my father," followed by remaining stage directions.

BRUTUS.

Now, Lucretia!
Thy ghost may cease to wander o'er the earth,
And rest in peace!

LUCRETIUS.

Heaven's ways are just!

COLLATINUS.

Yet I regret the villain should be slain
By any hand but mine!

Enter a CENTURION.

CENTURION.

Health to Brutus!
Shame and confusion to the foes of Rome!

BRUTUS.

Now, without preface, soldier, to your business.

CENTURION.

As I kept watch at the Quirinal gate
Ere break of day, an armed company
Burst on the sudden through the barrier guard,
Pushing their course for Ardea. Straight alarm'd,
I wheel'd my cohort round, and charg'd 'em home:
Sharp was the conflict for a while, and doubtful,
Till, on the seizure of Tarquinia's person,
A young Patrician—

BRUTUS.

Ha! Patrician?

CENTURION.

Such
His dress bespoke him, though to me unknown.

BRUTUS.

Proceed!—What more?

CENTURION.

The lady being taken,
This youth, the life and leader of the band,
His sword high waving in the act to strike,
Dropt his uplifted weapon, and at once
Yielded himself my prisoner.—Oh, Valerius,
What have I said, that thus the Consul changes?

BRUTUS.

Why do you pause? Go on.

CENTURION.

Their leader seiz'd,
The rest surrender'd. Him, a settled gloom
Possesses wholly, nor, as I believe,
Hath a word pass'd his lips, to all my questions
Still obstinately shut.

BRUTUS.

Set him before us.   [*Exit* CENTURION.

VALERIUS.

Oh, my brave friend, horror invades my heart.

BRUTUS.

Silence. Be calm.

VALERIUS.

I know thy soul
A compound of all excellence, and pray
The mighty gods to put thee to no trial
Beyond a mortal bearing.

BRUTUS.

No, they will not—
Nay, be secure,—they cannot. Pr'ythee, friend,
Look out, and if the worst that can befall me
Be verified, turn back, and give some sign
What thou hast seen—Thou can'st excuse this weakness,
Being thyself a father.   [VALERIUS *gives the sign.*
Ha!—enough:
I understand thee:—Since it must be so,
Do your great pleasure, gods! Now, now it comes!

TITUS *and* TARQUINIA *are brought in, guarded.* TITUS *advances.* TARQUINIA *remains in the background.*

TITUS.

My father!—give me present death, ye powers!

CENTURION.

What have I done!—Art thou the son of Brutus?

TITUS.

No, Brutus scorns to father such a son!
Oh, venerable judge, wilt thou not speak?
Turn not away; hither direct thine eyes,
And look upon this sorrow-stricken form,
Then to thine own great heart remit my plea,
And doom as nature dictates.

VALERIUS.

Peace,—you'll anger him—
Be silent and await! Oh, suffering mercy,
Plead in a father's heart, and speak for nature!
    [BRUTUS *turns away from his son, waves his hand to the*
    CENTURION *to remove him to a farther distance, and*
    then walks forward and calls COLLATINUS *down to him.*

BRUTUS.

Come hither, Collatinus. The deep wound
You suffer'd in the loss of your Lucretia
Demanded more than fortitude to bear;
I saw your agony—I felt your woe—

COLLATINUS.

You more than felt it;—you reveng'd it, too.

BRUTUS.

But, ah! my brother Consul, your Lucretia
Fell nobly, as a Roman spirit should—
She fell, a model of transcendent virtue.

COLLATINUS.

My mind misgives. What dost thou aim at, Brutus?

BRUTUS. [*Almost overpower'd.*]

That youth—my Titus—was my age's hope—
I lov'd him more than language can express—
I thought him born to dignify the world.

COLLATINUS.

My heart bleeds for you—He may yet be sav'd—

BRUTUS. [*Firmly.*]

Consul,—for Rome I live,—not for myself:
I dare not trust my firmness in this crisis,
Warring 'gainst every thing my soul holds dear!
Therefore return without me to the Senate—*
Haply my presence might restrain their justice.
Look that these traitors meet their trial straight,—
And then despatch a messenger to tell me
How the wise fathers have dispos'd of—Go!—

[COLLATINUS *goes out on one side, attended: and as*
  BRUTUS *is departing on the other side,* TARQUINIA
  rushes forward.

TARQUINIA.

Stop,—turn and hear the daughter of your king!
I speak for justice—mercy thou hast none.
For him, your son,
By gratitude and love I drew him off!
I preserv'd his life!
Who shall condemn him for protecting mine?

BRUTUS.

We try the crime; the motive, heaven will judge.
My honour he hath stabb'd—I pardon that.
He hath done more—he hath betray'd his country.

* In the 1818 English edition, this is followed by a line, " I ought not now to take a seat
among them—"

That is a crime which every honest heart
That beats for freedom, every Roman feels,
And the full stream of justice must have way.

TARQUINIA.

Because thy soul was never sway'd by love,
Canst thou not credit what his bosom felt?

BRUTUS.

I can believe that beauty such as thine
May spread a thousand fascinating snares
To lure the wavering and confound the weak;
But what is honour, which a sigh can shake?
What is his virtue, whom a tear can melt?
Truth,—valour,—justice,—constancy of soul,—
These are the attributes of manly natures:—
Be woman e'er so beauteous, man was made
For nobler uses than to be her slave.

TARQUINIA.

Hard, unrelenting man! Are these the fruits
Of filial piety,—and hath thy son
Wearied the gods with pray'rs, till they restor'd
A mind, and gave thee reason? Would to heaven
They'd given thee mercy, too! 'twould more become thee
Than these new ensigns, Brutus; more than all
Thy lictors, haughty Consul,—or thy robes
Dipt in the blood,—oh horror!—of a son!—

BRUTUS.

No more—By all the gods, I'll hear no more!

TITUS.

A word, for pity's sake. Before thy feet,
Humbled in soul, thy son and prisoner kneels.
Love is my plea; a father is my judge;
Nature my advocate!—I can no more:
If these will not appease a parent's heart,
Strike through them all and lodge thy vengeance here!

BRUTUS.

Break off. I will not, cannot hear thee further.
The affliction nature hath impos'd on Brutus,
Brutus will suffer as he may.—Enough
That we enlarge Tarquinia. Go, be free!
Centurion, give her conduct out of Rome!
Lictors, secure your prisoner. Point your axes.
To the Senate—On!   [*Exit* BRUTUS.

CENTURION.

Come, lady, you must part.

TARQUINIA.

Part! Must we part?
You shall not tear him from me; I will die
Embracing the sad ruin I have made.

CENTURION.

You've heard the Consul.

TARQUINIA.

Thou hast heard the king,
Fought for him while he led you on to conquest.
Thou art a soldier, and should'st spurn an office
Which malefactors, though condemn'd for murder,
Would rather die by torture than perform.

TITUS.

If thou dost wish
That I should 'scape the peril of my fate,
I conjure thee to accord
To Brutus, and accept his promis'd safeguard.
Your words, your looks, your beauty, feed his wrath.
In that fair face he reads my guilty love,
And pity flies his heart; let passion pause;
Leave me to solitude, to silence leave me;
Then nature's gentlest whispers may be heard.

TARQUINIA.

Say'st thou? Conduct me to the dreariest waste
That ever melancholy madness trod,

And let my swelling heart in silence burst;
Plunge me in darkness, shroud this fatal form
In everlasting night, I am content!
Lo! I obey! This is the test of love;
This is the sacrifice:—I part to save thee!

TITUS.

See I am warn'd. Farewell, my life's last joy!
When my eyes lose thy image, they may look
On death without dismay. To those blest powers,
Who gave thee every virtue, every grace
That can ensure perfection, I commit thee.

> [*They embrace and are torn asunder.* TITUS *is carried off by the* LICTORS *on one side, and* TARQUINIA *by the* CENTURION *and* GUARDS *on the other.*

SCENE II.—*Rome.—An Apartment in the House of* BRUTUS.

Enter BRUTUS.

BRUTUS. [*Alone.*]

Like a lost, guilty wretch, I look around
And start at every footstep, lest it bring
The fatal news of my poor son's conviction!—
Oh Rome, thou little know'st—No more—It comes.

Enter VALERIUS.

VALERIUS.

My friend, the Senate have to thee transferr'd
The right of judgment on thy son's offence.

BRUTUS.

To me?

VALERIUS.

To thee alone.

BRUTUS.

What of the rest?

VALERIUS.

Their sentence is already pass'd.
Ev'n now, perhaps, the lictor's dreaded hand
Cuts off their forfeit lives.

BRUTUS.

Say'st thou that the Senate have to me **referr'd**
The fate of Titus?

VALERIUS.

Such is their sovereign will.
They think you merit this distinguish'd honour.
A father's grief deserves to be rever'd:
Rome will approve whatever you decree.

BRUTUS.

And is his guilt establish'd beyond doubt?

VALERIUS.

Too clearly.

BRUTUS. [*With a burst of tears.*]

Oh, ye gods! ye gods!
[*Collecting himself.*]   Valerius!

VALERIUS.

What would'st thou, noble Roman?

BRUTUS.

'Tis said thou hast pull'd down thine house, Valerius,
The stately pile that with such cost was rear'd.

VALERIUS.

I have, but what doth Brutus thence infer?

BRUTUS.

It was a goodly structure: I remember
How fondly you survey'd its rising grandeur,—

With what a—fatherly—delight you summon'd
Each grace and ornament, that might enrich
The—child—of your creation,—till it swell'd
To an imperial size, and overpeer'd
The petty citizens, that humbly dwelt
Under its lofty walls, in huts and hovels,
Like emmets at the foot of towering Etna:
Then, noble Roman, then with patriot zeal,
Dear as it was and valued, you condemn'd
And level'd the proud pile: and in return
Were by your grateful countrymen sirnam'd,
And shall, to all posterity descend,—
Poplicola.

VALERIUS.

Yes, Brutus, I conceive
The awful aim and drift of thy discourse—
But I conjure thee, pause! Thou art a father.

BRUTUS.

I am a Roman Consul!—What, my friend,
Shall no one but Valerius love his country
Dearer than house, or property, or children?
Now, follow me;—and in the face of heaven
I'll mount the judgment-seat: there see, if Brutus
Feel not for Rome as warmly as Poplicola.

[*Exeunt* BRUTUS *and* VALERIUS.

SCENE THE LAST.—*Exterior of the Temple of* MARS.—*Senators, Citizens,* COLLATINUS, LUCRETIUS, *discovered. At the left of stage a Tribunal, with a Consular chair upon it.*

BRUTUS *enters, followed by* VALERIUS;—*he bows as he passes, and ascends the Tribunal.*

BRUTUS.

Romans, the blood which hath been shed this day
Hath been shed wisely. Traitors who conspire
Against mature societies, may urge
Their acts as bold and daring; and tho' villains,

Yet they are manly villains—But to stab
The cradled innocent, as these have done,—
To strike their country in the mother-pangs
Of struggling child-birth, and direct the dagger
To freedom's infant throat,—is a deed so black,
That my foil'd tongue refuses it a name.   [*A pause.*
There is one criminal still left for judgment.
Let him approach.

Titus is brought in by the Lictors, *with their axes turn'd edgeways towards him.*

Pris—on—er—[*The voice of* Brutus *falters and is choaked, and he exclaims, with violent emotion.*]
Romans! forgive this agony of grief—
My heart is bursting—Nature must have way—
I will perform all that a Roman should—
I cannot feel less than a father ought!
    [*He becomes more calm. Gives a signal to the* Lictors
       to fall back, and advances from the Judgment-seat to
       the front of the stage, on a line with his son.
Well, Titus, speak—how is it with thee now?
Tell me, my son, art thou prepar'd to die?

TITUS.

Father, I call the powers of heaven to witness
Titus dares die, if so you have decreed.*
The gods will have it so?

BRUTUS.

They will, my Titus:
Nor heav'n, nor earth, can have it otherwise.
The violated genius of thy country
Rears its sad head and passes sentence on thee!
It seems as if thy fate were pre-ordain'd
To fix the reeling spirits of the people,
And settle the loose liberty of Rome.

    * The American edition (1819) reads:
      " Titus dares die, when you have decreed
      The gods will have me."

'Tis fix'd;—oh, therefore, let not fancy cheat thee:
So fix'd thy death, that 'tis not in the power
Of mortal man to save thee from the axe.

TITUS.

The axe!—Oh heaven!—Then must I fall so basely?
What, shall I perish like a common felon?

BRUTUS.

How else do traitors suffer?—Nay, Titus, more—
I must myself ascend yon sad tribunal
And there behold thee meet this shame of death,—
With all thy hopes and all thy youth upon thee,—
See thy head taken by the common axe,—
All,—if the gods can hold me to my purpose,—
Without one groan, without one pitying tear.

TITUS.

Die like a felon?—Ha! a common felon!—
But I deserve it all:—yet here I fail:—
This ignominy quite unmans me!
Oh, Brutus, Brutus! Must I call you father,
Yet have no token of your tenderness,
No sign of mercy? Not even leave to fall
As noble Romans fall, by my own sword?
Father, why should you make my heart suspect
That all your late compassion was dissembled?
How can I think that you did ever love me?

BRUTUS.

Think that I love thee by my present passion,
By these unmanly tears, these earthquakes here,
These sighs that strain the very strings of life,—
Let these convince you that no other cause
Could force a father thus to wrong his nature.

TITUS.

Oh, hold, thou violated majesty!
I now submit with calmness to my fate.

Come forth, ye executioners of justice—
Come, take my life,—and give it to my country!

BRUTUS.

Embrace thy wretched father. May the gods
Arm thee with patience in this awful hour.
The sov'reign magistrate of injur'd Rome
Bound by his high authority, condemns
A crime, thy father's bleeding heart forgives.
Go—meet thy death with a more manly courage
Than grief now suffers me to show in parting,
And, while she punishes, let Rome admire thee!
No more. Farewell! Eternally farewell!—

TITUS.

Oh, Brutus! Oh, my father!—

BRUTUS.

What would'st thou say, my son?

TITUS.

Wilt thou forgive me?—Don't forget Tarquinia
When I shall be no more.

BRUTUS.

Leave her to my care.

TITUS.

Farewell, for ever!

BRUTUS.

For ever!   [BRUTUS *re-ascends the Tribunal.*
Lictors, attend!—conduct your prisoner forth!

VALERIUS. [*Rapidly and anxiously.*]
Whither!

[*All the characters bend forward in great anxiety.*

BRUTUS.

To death!—[*All start.*]   When you do reach the spot,
My hand shall wave, your signal for the act,
Then let the trumpet's sound proclaim it done!

> [TITUS *is conducted out by the* LICTORS.—*A dead march,
> —which gradually dies away as it becomes more dis-
> tant.* BRUTUS *remains seated in a melancholy posture
> on the Tribunal.*

Poor youth!   Thy pilgrimage is at an end!
A few sad steps have brought thee to the brink
Of that tremendous precipice, whose depth
No thought of man can fathom.   Justice now
Demands her victim!   A little moment
And I am childless.—One effort and 'tis past!—

> [*He rises and waves his hand, convuls'd with agitation,
> then drops on his seat and shrouds his face with his
> toga.   Three sounds of the trumpet are heard instantly.
> —All the characters assume attitudes of deep misery.—*
> BRUTUS *starts up wildly, descends to the front in ex-
> treme agitation, looks out on the side by which* TITUS
> *departed, for an instant, then, with an hysterical burst,
> exclaims,*

Justice is satisfy'd and Rome is free!*

> [BRUTUS *falls.—The characters group around him.*

END OF THE TRAGEDY.

EPILOGUE,

Written by a FRIEND, *spoken by Mrs.* GLOVER.

May Mrs. GLOVER venture to appear?
She neither uses nor speaks daggers here;
She comes quite tame, in the old English way,
To hope you all have—wept at our new play.

Tullia no more, I tread on English ground;
There's pride, hope, courage, in the very sound;

* This line is not in the American (1819) edition.

Myself your debtor, many a changeful year
For generous kindness—never changing here,
I come to ask that kindness now for one
Unknown,—or but by this night's fortunes known,
To cheer a trembling votary of the Nine,
And fill his heart with gratitude—like *mine*.

Aye, this *is* England—well its signs I know!
Beauty above, around me, and below:
Such cheeks of rose, such bright bewitching eyes!
Well may the kneeling world give you the prize!
Where, where on earth does woman wear a smile
Like yours, ye glory of "THE GLORIOUS ISLE".

But bless me—what two nondescripts together!
The *she*—a pile of ribband, straw, and feather;
Her back a pillion, all above and on it
A church-bell? cradle? tower?—No, faith, a bonnet!
Aye, and an actual woman in it, able—
Rouse but her tongue, to make that tower a Babel!

Now for the *he*, the fellow nondescript,
Whence has that mockery of man been shipt?
Have ROSS or BUCHAN, brought him to console
The quidnuncs for the passage to the pole?
While, on her icebergs, howls some Greenland squaw
Robbed of her pretty monster till next thaw!
No, Paris has the honour. *"Ah que oui."*—
"Voilà"—the air, grace, shrug,—smell of *Paris!*
France gave his step its trip, his tongue its phrase,
His head its peruke, and his waist its stays!
The thing is contraband.—Let's crush the trade,
Ladies, insist on't—*all* is best *home made*—
All British, from your shoe-tye or your fan,
Down to that tantalizing wretch—call'd—man!

Now for the compound creature—first, the wig,
With every frizzle struggling to look big;
On the roug'd-cheek the fresh dyed whisker spread,
The thousandth way of dressing a calf's head.
The neckcloth next, where starch and whalebone vie

To make the slave a walking pillory.
The bolster'd bosom—ah, ye envying fair,
How little dream you of the stuff that's there!
What straps, ropes, steel, the aching ribs compress,
To make the Dandy "beautifully less."
Thus fools, their final stake of folly cast,
By instinct, to *strait waistcoats* come at last.
Misjudging Shakspeare! this escaped thine eye,
For tho' the brains *are* out, the thing *won't* die.

And now, farewell! But one word for the Bard,—
The smile of Beauty is his best reward;
Then smile upon him, you, and you, and you!
I see the poet's cause is won. Adieu!

NOTE.

*The following scene in the third act was omitted after the
first representation, in compliance with the wishes of many,
who thought it injurious to the general effect of the play.
As, however, there was some difference of opinion upon
this point, the scene is here inserted as it originally stood.
LUCRETIA is supposed to be surrounded by her relations,—
COLLATINUS and LUCRETIUS by her side,—her hair dishevelled,—wild in her attire;—and all the other characters in
attitudes of deep grief.*

LUCRETIA.

Bear witness, then, Lucretia's mind is guiltless,—
Yet never can Lucretia smile again!
Lost to herself, her husband and her child,
Lost to the world, her country and her friends,
The arms of love can pillow her no more,
And the sweet smile of her dear innocent babe
Would but awaken her to deeper anguish!
And shall she live, bereft of all life's treasures,
The spectre of the past for ever rising
To fright her into madness? Think not, countrymen,
Indignant virtue can survive pollution!

By her own hand a Roman wife can fall.   [*Stabs herself.*
'Tis to the heart!   Tarquin, the blow was thine! [*She falls.*

COLLATINUS.

Belov'd unhappy wife!   What hast thou done?

LUCRETIA.

A deed of glory.   Now, my husband, now—
With transport can I press thee to my bosom.
Father and kinsmen, ye can own me now!
My pure soul springs from its detested prison!
Virtue exults!   The gods applaud my daring!
And, to our dear, lov'd babe, I can bequeath
A mother's noblest gift,—a spotless name!   [*Dies.*

LUCRETIUS.

Staff of my age!   Gone, gone, for ever gone!
A wretched father's last and only joy!
Come, death, strike here!   Your shaft were welcome now!
Snatch me from earth to my poor, lost, lov'd child!

COLLATINUS.

My wife! my wife!   Dear, dear, wrong'd, murder'd wife!
Let me be rooted here in endless sorrow—
Who, who shall dare to mourn her loss like me!

Enter BRUTUS.

BRUTUS.

I dare, and so dare every honest Roman.

The scene then proceeds as printed in the preceding pages.

SERTORIUS;

OR,

THE ROMAN PATRIOT

By DAVID PAUL BROWN

DAVID PAUL BROWN

(1795–1875)

It is not difficult to account for the development of the closet drama as a type distinctive in itself. The American dramatist interpreted it as meaning a form wherein a classical subject or a romantic tale was clothed in poetry imitative of Elizabethan models. The plays were all cut after the same fashion, and, whenever one of them got across the footlights through the sheer brilliancy of the actor's genius, that was a signal for the defenders of closet drama to come to the fore with their theories as to stage technique.

This middle period of the American theatre, typified by the Philadelphia school of playwrights, is illustrative of the mistaken notion that sonorous lines meant poetry, and that impassioned declamation meant drama. There is a long list of plays of this character, no better exemplified than by "Sertorius."

The type was fostered by the culture of the times. David Paul Brown's attitude toward his own work, and toward Shakespeare, was the attitude of well-educated "gentlemen" of the North and South during ante-bellum days. The education of the professional lawyer or doctor was cut and dried, —classical in its scope. And he who did not know his Shakespeare backward, argued himself unknown. In my reading of American drama, I have found "Julius Cæsar" and "Coriolanus" inspiration for a great number of American closet dramas. Speeches like Cæsar's swimming of the Tiber occur with frequency, told with the same stress of narrative, and for the same illustrative purpose.

So retentive was the memory of these casual dramatists that, unconsciously, the imitative process asserted itself. Even such a poet as George Henry Boker fell into the rut which such imitation encourages. However excellent his "Francesca da Rimini" may be, as an acted drama, there are lines therein whose counterpart may be easily located in Shakespeare.

It is not surprising, therefore, that such a Shakespearian appreciator as Dr. Brown was, should in the same manner become a slavish devotee of the bard. In diverse ways, his "Sertorius" is a poor writing of "Julius Cæsar". Like many of his contemporaries, Brown allowed his appreciation of "the bard" to overflow in a treatise on his works. The student will find a ponderous row of such treatises, from John Quincy Adams, James H. Hackett, and others, to the present. That is in itself sufficient to show the closeness with which the Elizabethan drama was followed at this period— with none of the authoritative evidence of the modern scholar, but with the conviction of one who knew his poet well. Such an aggressive student of Shakespeare was William Gilmore Simms. Therefore, Brown's "Sketches of the Life and Genius of Shakespeare" is typical.

The author of "Sertorius" was born in Philadelphia, on September 28, 1795, and his education was marked by the classical thoroughness of the time. He was descended from a line of Friends. At the early age of seventeen, he began the study of medicine, under Dr. Benjamin Rush, but the death of the latter was a rude termination of his ambitions in that direction, and it was not long before he was reading law with William Rawle, impressions of whom he has left in his "The Forum; or, Forty Years Full Practise at the Philadelphia Bar."

In September, 1816, he passed his examinations, and there followed a long legal career, during which he occupied important posts in the Supreme Court of his native State, as well as of the United States. His forensic ability won him a reputation far and near, and a large proportion of his literary work is illustrative of how often, as a public speaker, he was called to officiate on important occasions. His speeches were gathered together in a volume by his son, Robert Edward, in 1873.

Brown married Emmeline Catharine Handy in 1824. By that time he had gained fame as an easy and graceful writer. And people thought it only fitting that, when Lafayette visited Philadelphia in 1824, he should be presented with an address from the pen of one of their most gifted literary sons.

Brown's busy activity as a lawyer was punctuated by his taste for play writing; and to his credit there are recorded four dramatic contributions: his tragedy "Sertorius; or, The Roman Patriot"; his melodrama, "The Prophet of St. Paul's;" another tragedy, "The Trial"; and, finally, a farce entitled "Love and Honour; or, The Generous Soldier." The latter two were never acted, and probably were never published.

Writing was an easy accomplishment with Brown; in fact, casualness of composition is a characteristic which marks American literature of this period. Oberholtzer claims that "Sertorius" was written while Brown took evening horse-back rides to Yellow Springs, the popular spa of the day, situated in the hills of northern Chester County. In two weeks he had finished the manuscript; and the same speed marked the evolution of "The Prophet of St. Paul's", completed inside of a month.

With his increasing practise as a lawyer we have no concern here; though, by the evidence left us of his bearing as a special pleader, we can gain some idea of the manner in which he delivered his lecture, when he gave it, on Shakespeare's "Hamlet". "He possesses in an eminent degree those qualities which acquire and secure favour. His manners are frank and courteous; his conversation is sparkling and vivacious; and his temper is amiable and benevolent. As an advocate he has few superiors. . . . His declamation is bold and empassioned; his diction uncommonly free and felicitous; and he possesses a readiness, self-command, and tact, which never forsake him."

"Sertorius" was written in 1830, and was accepted for presentation by Junius Brutus Booth. I can find no report of the negotiations, not even in Brown's own correspondence as published, but we know from Wemyss that it was produced at the Philadelphia Chestnut Street Theatre on December 14, of that year, although Mrs. Asa Booth Clarke, in her "The Elder and the Younger Booth", gives January, 1832. There are also many anecdotal passages in Durang, descriptive of the preparations for the first performance. It is clear that it was revived several times, and that, whenever Booth essayed the title rôle, he met with unqualified success. In his repertory with "Sertorius" were "Sylla" and "Oronooka".

Wemyss further states: "The beautiful poetry of this play flowed from his lips, and must have gratified the fastidious taste of any author—how, then, must it have delighted the audience! The play wanted action—there was too much declamation." But he gives us to believe that on this initial run of "Sertorius", it was brought to a close merely because Booth's engagement had terminated.

Brown was not by any means flattered by the publicity his play gave him. In fact, nothing could overcloud the position he most coveted in his real profession. A journalist, writing him to secure printed copies of his plays, received from him the following illuminating letter. It reveals the casualness of the cultured "gentleman", who plays at an art, while ably upholding the best traditions of an acknowledged learned profession.

"Dear Sir;—I received your kind letter, dated the first of this month, and hasten to reply. I am, perhaps, unlike most dramatic writers of the present, or any other, day—for although neither of my dramas has met with much success, I think both have met with more than they were entitled to. This impression of mine may be ascribable to my utter indifference to their fate. They were written rather as matters of relief from the cares and toils of an arduous profession, than with any view to their representation upon the stage. And if I may speak frankly, I must say, they derived greater celebrity from their author, than their author will ever derive from them. In other words, it was not so remarkable that, with vast professional engagements, I should have written two bad plays, as that I should have been able to write any at all. 'Sertorius' has been performed nine times, and, with the aid of Mr. Booth, was well received. 'The Prophet of St. Paul's' has been thrice performed, and, by the aid of good luck, has not yet been *damned;* but for my own part, I should be unwilling to run so narrow a chance. In the worst possible result, however, I should have been totally unaffected, as I confess to you; although I have much pleasure in the composition of such matters, I have no interest in their fate. I am an advocate, not a dramatist.

"I have attended to your request, and deposited with Messrs. Carey & Hart, a copy of 'Sertorius' and the 'Prophet', which I hope you will shortly receive.

"Very respectfully yours,
"DAVID PAUL BROWN."

Here is a frank confession, in refutation of the critics who, in their review of "Sertorius", were prone to overpraise it for excellences it did not have. He who wrote that in the play it would be difficult to find a jarring line, had not his ear well trained. And we are pleased to find the unsigned notice in the *American Quarterly Review,* for September, 1830, credited to the discerning pen of James K. Paulding. For his opinion of "Sertorius" was that its blank verse was correct, without being harmonious, handicapped by its stateliness, after the manner of "Cato". And he recommended to Brown, and to others of Brown's school, the closer and better understanding of Elizabethan poetry.

Paulding scored Brown on the lack of voicing the real spirit of the people. He writes: "It should, we think, be one of the characteristics of an American writer to speak respectfully of the people. In this way only lies the right road toward the development of a true national literature." In the reading of the play, that democratic spirit can be readily measured, and an interesting comparison made with the same spirit revealed in "Jack Cade", which is to be found elsewhere in this volume. It must have been this democratic note of appeal which struck the responsive ear of the elder Booth.

"Sertorius" is dedicated to Joseph R. Ingersoll, who penned the Prologue. Its similarity to "Julius Cæsar", already noted, goes so far as to make use of the cobbler pun, and tempers the scene of conspiracy in accord with Shakespeare's handling. The intermingling of prose and poetry follows the convention learned from the Elizabethan drama, while, now and again, there is a striving for the unusual word, like "immarcessible", "diffide", and "jeopard". The poetry has the commonplaceness of the imitator, but the play, as a whole, is evidence of the power in acting required to breathe into declamation the action necessary for the stage. Although by many this play was regarded as "among the choicest productions of the tragic Muse", in the history of American Drama it is only important as illustrative of the closet drama. In that capacity it still has certain holding quality.

Brown's contributions to the magazines, his book reviews which were noted, and his many legal and occasional papers have yet to be recorded in a full bibliography by the student. Dunlap mentions his plays in his "History of the American Theatre", while Rees and Wood make casual comment on them. But what we know of Brown, outside of his legal work, which looms large in the annals of Pennsylvania, is to be gleaned from his reminiscent work, "The Forum", which contains an anecdotal "Memoir".

INSCRIBED
AS A TRIBUTE OF GREAT PROFESSIONAL RESPECT
AND
PERSONAL FRIENDSHIP
TO
JOSEPH R. INGERSOLL, Esq.

Dramatis Personæ and Cast of Characters

Philadelphia Chestnut Street Theatre.

December 14, 1830.

SERTORIUS; or, THE ROMAN PATRIOT.

Sertorius........................... Junius Brutus Booth
Perpenna Vento.................... Mr. W. B. Wood
Aufidius........................... Mr. Charles Young
Pompey............................ Mr. Wemyss
Mucius (a schoolmaster)............Mr. W. Jones
Flavius (a carpenter)............... Mr. J. Mills Brown
Caiphus (a shoemaker)............. Mr. Hart
Metellus........................... Mr. Green
Servilius........................... Mr. Proctor
Marcia (a daughter of Marcellus).... Mrs. Flynn
Timandra..........................Mrs. C. Greene

A full account of rehearsals and anecdotes of Booth are given in Durang's "History of the Philadelphia Stage".

DRAMATIS PERSONÆ

QUINTUS SERTORIUS, *the Roman Patriot.*
MARCELLUS, *friend to* SERTORIUS.
MANLIUS.
PERPENNA VENTO,
AUFIDIUS, } *Conspirators.*
MARCUS ANTONIUS,
LENARIUS.
PHAROS DEMETRIUS, *Ambassador from Mithridates.*
MUCIUS, *a schoolmaster.*
FLAVIUS, *a carpenter.*
CAIPHUS, *a shoemaker.*
SERVILIUS, *bondsman of* SERTORIUS.
METELLUS,
POMPEY, } *Romans.*

MARCIA, *daughter of* MARCELLUS.
TIMANDRA, *gentlewoman of* MARCIA.

Spanish Senators, Soldiers, and Citizens.
Roman Lictors, Ædiles, and Patricians.

Scene:—Throughout the Play, in various parts of SPAIN.

SERTORIUS

ACT I.

SCENE I.—*A Street in front of the Capitol of Lusitania.*

Enter AUFIDIUS. *and* PERPENNA *from opposite sides of the stage.*

AUFIDIUS.

Whither in so much haste, valiant Perpenna?
Have Pompey and Metellus sack'd the town,
That thus with eager step, and anxious eye,
You shun, or seek them?

PERPENNA.

Not so, Aufidius—'Tis to meet our friends,
The Senate, who assemble at this hour
With the Ambassador from Mithridates,
To act upon the proffer'd league with Pontus.
Go you not thither?—we shall lack your counsel.

AUFIDIUS.

The Senate's but one man—Sertorius
Lords it alone o'er all the powers of Spain;
Why should we, then, in empty pageantry,
Swell his proud triumph!—What he wills, is law:
Jove reigns not more supremely.—
Think'st thou he will consent to march 'gainst Rome?

PERPENNA.

If he refuse, his ruin is secure,
And fate forestalls our purpose. Haughty Spain,

187

Brac'd by old feuds for deep and deadly war,
And vain of late success, looks for new conquests—
Rome, her old enemy, her promis'd prey;
And should Sertorius mar these golden prospects,
'Twill only be in peril of his own.
We'll see his boasted faith severely tested:
This is a question, view it as he may,
Between himself and country—accept or not
The proffer'd league, in either he's undone.

AUFIDIUS.

Not so, Perpenna—so ascendant is he,
O'er all the hopes and happiness of Spain,
United with her strongest sympathies,
A union in misfortune and success,
And almost deified by superstition,
They dare not—and they *would* not if they *dare*,
Impugn his high decree.

PERPENNA.

Time shall determine—I have sown the seed,
Ay, sown it in the people's very heart,
That soon shall ripen in a glorious harvest,
And thou, and I, and all shall reap the fruit.
Upon this very subject, shalt thou see,
By bribes and strong allurements have I wrought
The Senate to my purpose. Thou know'st, Aufidius,
With what unceasing zeal,—enduring patience,
I've toiled and plotted 'gainst this hated rival—
Rival in love, and in the lists of war:
To-day the heavens shall hear and crown my pray'rs,
For by himself, or us, Sertorius falls.
—But question me no more—no more delay;
The Senate have assembled, and our absence
May chill their glowing purpose.

AUFIDIUS.

Have with thee, then. But thou shalt see, Perpenna,
Affianced as they may be to our cause,
How every heart shall shrink in his rebuke,

And bow before him. By the mailed Mars,
E'en Pompey's star sheds but a sickly ray,
Beside his spotless and meridian splendour.
Nay, even grant the Senate should stand firm,
Where are the people—the Sertorian band,
Who cling around him with unwavering love,
Like the fond ivy twining round the oak,
Or life's warm eddies circling through the heart—
In conquest and defeat!—Thy own brave cohorts,
Marshall'd and train'd by thee, desert their leader,
And with one voice cry, "March us to Sertorius!
"The victor, who subdues himself and others."
From such devotion what room is left for hope?

PERPENNA.

Say there were none—is hatred too extinct?
Can I forget the loss of those throng'd legions,
Seduc'd by his base arts from my command?
But for my vast supplies of men and means,
This favour'd agent of superior powers,
This lofty idol of an impious worship,
Despite of his bravadoes and their love,
Had long since yielded to Metellus' force,
And grac'd a Roman triumph. But, Aufidius,
Let us not pause and ponder on our griefs,
While the kind fates supply the means of vengeance:
This day decides his doom.

AUFIDIUS.

Then let us in. But mark me now, Perpenna,
Our votes are vain: Sertorius has decided,
And that which he decides, fate's awful fiat
Stamps as irrevocable—It is done.   [*Exeunt.*

SCENE II.

Enter MUCIUS, FLAVIUS, CAIPHUS, *and* CITIZENS.

CITIZENS.

Huzza! huzza! Mithridates and Sertorius—Pontus and
Spain!

FLAVIUS.

Sertorius and Mithridates—Spain and Pontus, say I! Since the alliance was sought from, and not by us—wherefore then, should we kneel and pay tribute?

MUCIUS.

A glorious day—a day of joy to Spain! The wars are over—that is, they will be over; for when Spain joins with Pontus, Rome must yield. Great Mithridates is a match for Rome, and we're a match for him: hence you perceive, when of three foes,—and all of equal strength,—two shall combine, the other is o'erthrown.

CAIPHUS.

'Tis plain—by last, leather, and lapstone, wondrous plain. Why learning is the very sole of this nether world. Here now is Mucius, who has done more in five words to show how old Rome is to be mastered, than all your kings and generals in fifty years.—Well said, bookworm!

FLAVIUS.

Ay, ay, Mucius is a rare one, and not the less so for being commended by thee, who art also a rare one—seeing you are the opposite of each other, or should be, judging from your mysteries.

MUCIUS.

Mystery me no mysteries—come, demonstrate.

FLAVIUS.

Nay, nay, be not impatient, good Mucius, on this day of liberty and triumph; as thou hast most laudably, learnedly, and logically shown it is, or at least *is to be*.

MUCIUS.

What meanest thou by mysteries?—

FLAVIUS.

Why, thy mystery is to supply furniture for the head, being a schoolmaster, or pedagogue; and his, is to furnish the feet, being a shoemaker, or cobbler.

MUCIUS.

And thine to accommodate the neck, being a carpenter or gallows-maker—therefore it is that thou art ever between us twain, as alike an enemy to both head and foot.

FLAVIUS.

Fie on 't, fie! you are only chafed because my trade is the more prescriptive and honourable of the three.

CAIPHUS.

Why more prescriptive?

FLAVIUS.

Because the gallows was in use before schools were taught, or shoes mended; and not before the world required it either—mankind having a natural itch for elevation.

MUCIUS.

But why more honourable?

FLAVIUS.

Because it is the end of guilt and dishonour,—whereas your arts are too frequently the credentials and lures of both. Calf-skin from top to toe, thrives best as the times run;—it is a most vendible commodity.

MUCIUS.

Hang thyself to prove thy *first* position, and I care not to admit the *last* for the sake of the service. But no longer parley; let us to the Capitol to greet the glorious league.

FLAVIUS.

Here is a score of wiseacres for you—walking a *mile* to greet a *league*.—Beshrew me, but this smacks of policy—playing into the shoemaker's hand! sole leather shall pay for this. [*Aside.*]

CITIZEN.

Ay, to the Capitol—to the Capitol!—'tis meet the people should assert their rights, and ratify this treaty. We all approve it!—

CITIZENS.

All!—all!

FLAVIUS.

What if Sertorius should deny your rights?

MUCIUS.

And if he should!—a drachma for his denial. Perpenna is my man; he bends, and bows, and cries "Good Citizens," on all occasions; while Sertorius heeds us not—sees us not—but with his head among the stars, seems to disdain the earth he treads upon, and to spurn us as so many impediments to his advancement.

CAIPHUS.

Right, Mucius. He is parlous proud; but it were better in him never to provoke our anger;—this is no time for antics; we who made, can unmake. We are not to be put off as old leather that has done its best service—we must be satisfied.

CITIZENS.

We will be satisfied! we will have justice. [*Exeunt.*

FLAVIUS.

And if I mistake not, you are in a fair way to require my service, if you are deemed worthy the charge; and should not be strung up summarily upon some native gibbet, for the double purpose of economy, and expedition. [*Exit.*

SCENE III.

Senate Chamber.

SERTORIUS, PERPENNA, AUFIDIUS, AMBASSADOR, SENATORS,
LICTORS, *and* ÆDILES.

SERTORIUS.

Pharos Demetrius, we decline your offer.—
'Tis true that Rome has prov'd a wayward mother,
Proud, cruel, and relentless. Does it follow
That we, her banish'd sons, to mend our fortunes,
Should clasp a stranger to our dear embrace;
Jointly to prey upon a parent's bosom,
And like the pelican, in ruthless famine,
Devour our source of life?

PHAROS.

What binds, or what
Should bind Sertorius to such a parent?
Have you not fought her battles, shed your blood
In her defence, devoted all your life
To the aggrandizement and power of Rome—
And, save those scars engraven on your front
To show how much you dared, and what you suffer'd,
Where's your reward?

SERTORIUS. [*Laying his hand on his heart.*]

'Tis here, Demetrius—
In that immortal casket—where all life's treasure dwells!
Think'st thou unjust requital mars our love,
Or that devotion to our country's cause
Regards past offering whilst 't has aught to offer?
If I am outlaw'd, is not Rome abus'd—
Troubled, and tortur'd by intestine treason?
The weapons of her hope, sheath'd in her heart
By parricidal hands!—why should she then,
Bleeding at every vein from inward faction,
Receive from me the final, fatal blow,
That terminates her glory and her grief?

PHAROS.

In striking her, dost thou not punish them—
Them, who have mounted on thy hopes to empire—
Them, who have exil'd thee from friends and home,
And all that makes life dear, or death deplor'd?
Has then revenge, that balm of injur'd minds,
No cure, no charms for thee?—then let ambition,
Pointing the way to fortune and renown,
Allure thee to those proud, supernal heights,
Which only gods, and men like gods attain.

SERTORIUS.

By heaven! Demetrius, I avow it proudly,
Here in the very centre of the realm—
—My friends, bear with me, nature will have way—
Borne as I am upon the people's love
To power and station, and what else beside
The noblest minds desire—Still I confess,
Far rather would I be the meanest subject
Of mighty Rome, than the wide world's proud master.

PHAROS.

A subject!—thou may'st be her Emperor,
The monarch of the mighty of the earth.

SERTORIUS.

Not so, Demetrius!—Rome expires with freedom;
Were I her monarch, Rome would cease to be,
And leave my sceptre worthless.

PHAROS.

Grant it were so:—even thy humble prayer
To be a private citizen of Rome—it is denied thee!
The intercession of thy mother Rhea—
The recollection of thy great exploits—
Thy hardships—filial love, and loyalty,
All plead for thee in vain.—That men should pause
Between proportion'd, comparable objects
Excites no wonder,—but that a man like thee,

Who scorns to halt when glory bids thee on,
Should hesitate, between conflicting views,
One placing thee upon the neck of Rome,
The other at her foot—the foot that spurns thee!—
Ye gods, 'tis past belief—thou dost but mock me!
Think of great Marcius, and his Volscian bands,
Trampling triumphantly o'er prostrate Rome—
Let that inspire thee.—He sought for aid, while aid
Solicits thee, and monarchs are thy suitors.

SERTORIUS.

Does the time-honour'd page of Roman story
Supply no prouder models for Sertorius,
Than discontented and rebellious traitors?
Men who alike oppos'd, or serv'd the State
To gratify ambition, or revenge!—
What say'st thou to those stainless men of Rome,
Who rose superior to their private wrongs—
Who sacrific'd revenge to public good,
And magnified their nature and the world?
Can I lose sight of their illustrious virtues,
Their services, their sufferings and faith,
Banish'd and branded with the name of traitors,
Yet ever yielding to the hand that smote them!
Where is the Roman that forgets such Romans,
Or scorns their bright example?
Know then, Demetrius, that the patriot heart
Throbs first and last for country. What, shall a pillar,
Howe'er magnificent and richly wrought,
Degrade the temple that its strength sustains?
Or shall they, as in sacred Grecian domes,
Unite in mutual grandeur,—and when time,
With his unsparing, fell, and ravening maw,
Disrobes them of the ornament of youth,
Dissolving and prostrating all their glory,
Sink in one common ruin, and become
More fam'd and cherish'd than in pristine pride?

PHAROS.

The temple of thy faith, proud Rome, must fall!
No pillar can sustain it;—the crimson'd swords

Of factious Sylla and his lawless bands,
Hew down the massy fabric of her fame,
The boast and dread of full five hundred years,
Into its elements,—·why then shouldst thou
Hang round, and perish with this falling ruin?

SERTORIUS.

Now by the gods, you turn my blood to flame,
And mar the traitor you would make of me!
If there be aught more arduous to accomplish,
Than to dissever all my thoughts from Rome,
And change my doating duty into hatred,
'Twere to unite with such a curse as Sylla;
The pamper'd minion of Nicopolis—
Bloated, not sated with patrician blood—
The felon, that purloins his country's glory,
To prostitute it to his country's shame!
Thou say'st Rome's fall will crush me; I submit;
The brave man never should outlive his country:
As clings the infant to its mother's arms,
Blessing and blest—so cleaves the patriot's heart
To the embraces of his native soil,
At once deriving, and imparting life.

PERPENNA. [To AUFIDIUS, aside.]

Not now to speak, were to be dumb for ever:
The crisis has arrived, and on the instant
Hangs life, or death eternal.

PHAROS.

Three thousand talents—forty ships of war,
Great Mithridates offers now to Spain:
When were such offers made, or when rejected?

AUFIDIUS.

What do we hazard for this vast reward?

SERTORIUS.

Talk not of hazard! I dare hazard all
But that, without which all is penury;

The cherish'd, priceless, **peerless** jewel—Honour.
When on the borders of the rapid Rhone,
Arm'd cap-a-pie in massy mail, I stood,
While the huge billows thunder'd for their prey,
I paus'd not to appreciate the peril,
But plung'd, at once, like Curtius, in the gulf,
Haply to live or die. 'Twas for my country!
But when you ask, that to destroy that country
I should shake hands with her inveterate foe,
And sell myself to shame—immortal shame,
I tremble, and profess myself a coward:
I cannot do it—shuddering nature dare not!

PHAROS.

Yet, noble Quintus!—

SERTORIUS.

Urge me no more—my resolution's deaf,
And cannot hear you. Come, your voices, friends.

PERPENNA.

The Senate do concur with Mithridates.

SERTORIUS.

Thou dost concur, Perpenna, not the Senate.

SENATORS.

We ratify the league, and join 'gainst Rome.

SERTORIUS.

Impossible!—
A Roman Senate turn her arms 'gainst Rome!
We, who are bound to magnify her fame—
To stretch her empire to earth's utmost verge,
That glory, like the ever radiant sun,
May rise and set upon her vast horizon!
Is this the voice of all—do none dissent?

SENATORS.

We all unite with him.

SERTORIUS.

Then all unite, to disunite this arm
From Lusitania's cause. Whate'er betides,
No change shall change my steadfastness of soul,
Or make a traitor of me.

PERPENNA.

Remember, Quintus, what we owe to Spain;
Adopted, nurtur'd, cherish'd, honour'd by her.—

SERTORIUS.

I well remember all: but where's the pledge
Ye give to Spain—adopted as ye are
By her affection; grafted on her state;
How shall she trust you, while ye recreants prove
To your first love, in wantonness of vice,
And found the very altar of your faith
On having been foresworn?—
Let me beseech you, weigh this matter nearly;
Oppose your honour to the proffer'd treasure,
And all the gold of Pontus turns to dross.
—What! are ye a hireling tribe,
To be bought out by him that bids the highest?
If the design be noble, grasp it nobly;
And do not, like a band of sordid slaves,
Embrace your bondage, for the golden fetters.

AUFIDIUS. [*To* PERPENNA.]

See how they quake and quail beneath his eye!
A moment longer, and the cause is lost.

SENATORS.

Rome's lost to us—then are we lost to Rome.

SERTORIUS.

Then are you lost to me. These dignities,
The outward ensigns of inherent worth,
Were dearly purchas'd by the name of traitor,
And thus I cast them off for such as *you* are.
                    [*Throws off his scarf and crown.*]

PERPENNA.

Quintus Sertorius, we are constituted,
By public suffrage, and the laws of Spain,
The guardians of the realm; the conservators,
Not of the rights of Rome, but Lusitania.
How shall we answer to ourselves and others,
For the perversion of this sacred trust?

SERTORIUS.

Peace, peace, Perpenna! I will answer it.
Who shares the glory, only, shares the peril:
I stand alone in both. If Mithridates
Demand Bythynia and Cappadocia,
Accustom'd as they are to kingly rule,
And held by conquest only, by the Romans,
It meets with our accordance: but to encroach
Where every foot of ground supports a freeman,
None but a slave could urge it.

SENATORS.

We do not urge it—we submit to this,
Restrain old Rome within her just domain,
Her ancient limits—and Spain rests content.

PERPENNA. [*Aside.*]

Patience, ye gods!—and thou, great Æolus,
That with thy sovereign wand, curb'st and direct'st
The ever changing and rebellious winds,
And gather'st them within thy stormy bosom,—
Teach man fidelity!

PHAROS.

My mission is discharg'd—the terms promulg'd,
Which, and which only, Pontus can accord;
And thus I take my leave.

SERTORIUS.

I here dissolve the Council.
Farewell, Demetrius!—to your king repair;
If he approve the terms we now propose—
The only league that we can ratify,
He may command our service: but from myself,
And from Spain too, while she relies on me,
All other hopes are vain. And so, farewell.
[*Exeunt at opposite sides of stage.*

PERPENNA.

Most noble Senators! pillars of the State!
Why did ye flee from Rome in search of freedom,
To forge new fetters here, and hug your chains?
What evil demon, hot from Tartarus,
Made you intractable to haughty Sylla,
That thus converts you into pliant tools
Of the renown'd Sertorius—a Roman outcast!
His guards—his supple pandars—fawning slaves!—
In birth, in fortune, and in dauntless daring,
Who yields the palm to him?—and yet in power,
His eagle-wing'd ambition soars so high
That we are only left to gaze and wonder
At the proud pinnacle on which he revels,
While grovelling in our lowly sphere beneath him.
Who shares his glory? who divides his council?
Who dares to disobey his stern decree?
Let this day answer! this eventful day,
That dedicates you to perpetual bondage.
How will you e'er presume to face the people,
Whose rights you have abus'd, whose trust betray'd!
Arm'd in their wrongs, and wrought to desperation,
In anxious expectation, thousands wait,
Thronging your public walks—your Senate doors,

To greet the adoption of this glorious league:
And who shall dare proclaim the base result?
None who have ever shar'd in that result;
And all of you have shar'd—for none resisted.
You were o'erborne, forsooth, by great Sertorius!
A mighty Senate—govern'd by a frown!—

SENATOR.

Chide us not, brave Perpenna: did not Quintus
Absolve us from all answer to the people?
The people, who have sanction'd what is done
By the unbounded faith repos'd in him,
Thus rendering opposition to his will
Like vain resistance of the cataract,
Making it rage the more.

PERPENNA.

He did absolve you—'but will *they* absolve you?
Your virtues, they appropriate to *him;*
Your vices are your *own:*—nay, even more—
His vices, also, are ascribed to *you!*
Redeem the past—atone for your disgrace—
Fly through the streets, and publicly proclaim
This outrage on your rights, and those of Spain!
Nought else can save you from deserv'd reproach.

SENATOR.

All earth shall witness that we were coerc'd.
                              [*Exeunt* SENATORS.

AUFIDIUS.

Said I not truly, my confiding friend,
When I foretold this triumph of Sertorius?
Despite of all the rooted hate I bear him,
I almost grow enamour'd of his virtues,
When I behold him, like the baited lion,
With all his hopes reposing on himself,
Surrounded by his hunters and their toils,
Still firm and fearless, ever facing dangers.

PERPENNA.

Reserve thy praises for his monument—
They will improve in marble, and endure;
While he yet lives, they're fulsome flattery:
To give them currency, and weight, and value,
They need the stamp of death.—
To live in glory is the meed of thousands;
But honour never shall become eternal,
Till hallow'd and attested by the grave.
How many mighty and majestic minds,
In after life demolish the proud structure,
Elaborated and adorn'd by youth,
With gems of science—trophies of the war,
Garlands of love, and spoils of great ambition!
Death is the crown, or crucifix of Fame!

AUFIDIUS.

When to immortal Jove we sacrifice,
Who mingles poison in his pure oblations,
We kill, but curse not—nay, the song of joy,
Chaplets of flowers, and temples fill'd with incense,
Surround and soothe the bleeding victim's anguish.
A patriot is the sacrifice you offer—
Shall we do less for him!—

PERPENNA.

No more, Aufidius: if my own heart's blood
Gush'd from the wounds inflicted on your hero,
Mine is the hand should deal the deadly blow,
And mine the eye should look unwavering on.
But hopes destroy'd, endear those which remain:—
The time reproves us—haste thee, then, my friend;
Blow to contagious winds the sickly rumour
Of treachery, of treason, and dishonour,
That every breast may swell with the infection,
And re-infect the pestilential air.—

Exeunt.

ACT II.

Scene I.—*A Hall in the House of* Marcellus.

Marcellus, Marcia *and* Timandra.

Marcia.

Alas, how ruthless is the rage of war!
Defeat, or victory, still onward leads
To wider scenes of bloodshed and disaster.
When shall the conflict end, which thus derives
Fresh vigor from misfortune or success—
Like great Antæus, whose gigantic frame,
From each successive fall, deriv'd new strength?

Marcellus.

It only ends in the extinction of our hapless realm.
Already full two hundred thousand foes,
Beleaguer our possessions. Rome's best gen'rals,
Loaded with laurels, won in other wars,
Unite to overthrow this fated city;
Each moment freighted with some dire event,
Rolls onward to the huge catastrophe
Of hideous and inevitable ruin.

Marcia.

         Oh, my father,
Look not with this despairing, hopeless eye,
Upon Spain's prospects—clouded as they are,
And fraught with grief, is there not yet still one
Undaunted, and devoted to her cause?
Signally favour'd by the pitying Gods?

Marcellus.

Thou mean'st Perpenna—dost thou not, my child?

Marcia.

         Was it Perpenna that
Besieg'd Lauron in face of the great Pompey?

Quell'd the Characitani? and at Sucro,
Melaria—Turia—overcame the Romans,
Led by renown'd Metellus? surely, father,
I err in my remembrance if it was!

MARCELLUS.

Not so, my daughter—You have all by *heart*.
Come hither, fair one, and recount to me,
The conquests of your soldier. What more precious
Than deeds heroic from the lips we love!
Methinks *Sertorius* was the hero's name?

MARCIA.

Recount to you, my father!—you, who taught me
The fam'd exploits of every martial leader?

MARCELLUS.

A hopeful pupil, who so well remembering
The conquests gain'd, forgets by whom achiev'd!
But canst thou teach me nothing in return,
Which thou alone canst teach, and I should learn?
Are those the only triumphs of Sertorius—
Is there no bloodless victory, dearer far
Than the acquirement of the world beside?

MARCIA.

What means my father?

MARCELLUS.

I mean, the conquest of this tender heart—
This citadel, that yielded to a smile,
And pour'd its treasures at the conqueror's feet.—
Ha! little traitor, art thou self condemn'd?
"Was it *Perpenna* that besieg'd Lauron,
In face of the great Pompey?" runs the text so?
Nay, nay! thou art a traitor—come, confess;
And still so guileless, artless, and so fair,
We almost love the treason—for the traitor.

MARCIA.

Forgive this constant and devoted heart
The only fraud it ever practis'd on you;
A fraud long practis'd on its thoughtless self:
I will chastise it, father, if you bid me—
But it is past reclaim—for ever gone.

MARCELLUS.

And thou wouldst follow? thus the sequel reads.
Now, by unspotted Dian, thy young love,
All radiant in bright hope's delusive plumage,
Wings the bold eaglet's unresisted flight
Forthright and upward to the cloudless sun.
Beware, my Marcia, pause—and learn from me
How evanescent and how vain is glory;
A sparkling bubble on life's stormy ocean;
A meteor, that delights—deludes—destroys;
A lamp sepulchral in a charnel house,
Gilding, with flickering ray, the shades of death.
—This idol, who engross'd the hearts of all,
Who reigns in thine with sway so absolute,
And almost shares devotion with the Gods—
Has done a deed to-day, should shake his fame,
Though rooted in earth's centre!—

MARCIA.

What deed, my father? 'tis impossible,
That the preserver and support of Spain,
The faithful, fearless, and resistless soldier,
Could ever act beneath that lofty virtue,
Which wafts its precious incense to the skies,
An offering fit for heaven.

MARCELLUS.

Judge then, when I relate the dire event:
Thou know'st the King of Pontus, Mithridates,
Whose fame is equall'd only by the Romans,
Propos'd a union with the Spanish power,
For the invasion of tyrannic Rome;
On terms most bounteous, and by all approv'd—
By all, save one—Sertorius!—

MARCIA.

Why cast the odium on Sertorius?
Should not the Senate share it?

MARCELLUS.

The Senate, stimulated by Perpenna,
In one acclaim consented to the league;
But stern Sertorius awed them to his purpose,
And clinging to the Romans, spurn'd the compact.
Incens'd and outrag'd by his haughty bearing,
The Senators denounce him to the people,
And all his garner'd glories, by this act,
Are scatter'd to the winds. The common herd,
Urg'd on by master spirits—who, unseen,
Guide and promote the mischief they condemn,—
Besiege him with revilings and complaints,
Proclaim him traitor—and with ruffian hands
Would rob him of his life!

MARCIA.

              Thy arm, Timandra—
His life!—saidst thou his life, my father?
The life of one, who is the life of all!—

MARCELLUS.

Be calm, my child; repose upon this breast,
Thy native pillow—Silence all thy fears.
Thou art of Roman lineage: chide thy heart then,
That thus betrays the weakness it should hide.
—Here, at the sun's decline, Sertorius meets me;
And ever faithful to his pledge, he comes.
Welcome, Sertorius—ever, ever welcome.

Enter SERTORIUS.

SERTORIUS.

Health and high honour to the brave Marcellus.
Ever gentle Marcia! the rude, unsparing blasts

Of savage war, have blanch'd thy maiden cheek;
Cheer up, my fair one—for the spring of peace
Shall pluck the lily from that faded brow,
And plant its roses there; why shouldst thou droop!
No cankerous cares corrode thy youthful heart,
Or trace their channels through these vestal veins.

MARCELLUS.

If flowers fade upon her virgin cheek,
'Tis not for want of dew!—Leave us, my child,
Anon thou shalt return. Comfort and solace her,
My good Timandra, and make her griefs thy own.
                    [*Exeunt* MARCIA *and* TIMANDRA.

SERTORIUS.

Oh, what a treasure hast thou there, Marcellus!
Unlike the miser's wealth, this little jewel
Improves in lustre each succeeding hour,
And lights you on to joy.

MARCELLUS.

                    And yet this jewel,
So rare and lustrous to thy partial eye,
Beams not alone on me—another shares—
Shares, did I say?—monopolizes it;
While all unconscious of this world of beauty,
Like fair Narcissus, he enamour'd grows
Of his own charms, and covets what he has.

SERTORIUS.

Betroth'd to brave Perpenna!—
'Tis the last blow—bear this, my stubborn soul,
And ever after be invulnerable;—[*Aside.*]
No other shaft can pierce thee. Happy pair!
Crown them with joys perennial, ye blest powers,
And guard their hearts 'gainst agonies like mine,
Too grave to bear, too poignant to conceal.

MARCELLUS.

Why, how now, Quintus—dost thou scorn my child,
That thus thou wouldst transfer her to a rival?
Must I be plain? I tell thee she is thine,
By her free choice; and I, her happy father,
Confirm a title which I can't withhold,
And would not if I could. The self-will'd dame
Avoids the gallant, gay, adoring throng
That haunt her walks, and hang upon her accents,
As zephyrs curl around the fragrant rose;
And yields herself to thee—a veteran soldier.

SERTORIUS.

Mine!
Say'st thou? Mine!—the peerless Marcia mine!
Oh fortune, thou dost mock me!—Good Marcellus,
Think'st thou I would transplant that fragile flower
From the gay parterre which it now adorns,
Exhaling odours on the vernal gale,
To pine and perish on this wintry bed?
How much I love her and have ever loved,
And ever shall, avails not now to know;
Let it suffice—I cannot make her wretched.
But yesterday, she was the world to me:
For yesterday—Ambition's mountain wave,
The wildest, proudest, loftiest of the main,
Rich, radiant, sparkling, foaming with delight,
And redolent with hope, its suppliant bosom
Bow'd at my feet, and woo'd me on to glory.
To-day—I am degraded by the State,
Despoil'd of outward honour, and despis'd,
Torn from repose, condemn'd in shame to roam
Through foreign climes, to seek myself a grave!—
Childless, and parentless, and friendless too.

MARCELLUS.

But still not hopeless!—

SERTORIUS.

Ay, hopeless too. Banish'd from cruel Rome,
And worse than banish'd by ungrateful Spain;

Proscrib'd, and stigmatis'd with base dishonour!—
Hunted and haunted by the inconstant rabble!—
Pursued, and baited to thy very door,
By foul mouth'd slander and severe reproach.

[*Noise from without.*]

And, hark! the ruffian rout corrupt the air
With their accursed clamour:—I will forth.

MARCELLUS.

Forbear, my friend! 'twere phrenzy and not courage;
Your life would pay the forfeit of your rashness.

SERTORIUS.

'Tis burthensome!—I long to lay it down!—
My temper cannot brook ingratitude,
That parent sin, from which all vices spring,
To cumber and corrupt and curse the world.   [*Exeunt.*

SCENE II.

A Street in front of MARCELLUS' *House.*

Enter MUCIUS, FLAVIUS, CAIPHUS, CITIZENS, *and* RABBLE.

CAIPHUS.

Peace, peace, let Mucius speak; he is of the Greek school, freshly vamped for the occasion, and waxeth into most eloquent rage; ye shall hear.

FLAVIUS.

And yet he has more *grease* than Greek about him; and by Pluto, less grace than either. And a word in thy ear, Mucius; if Sertorius should grow wrathful, thou shalt see this porcupine shooting his quills as he now does, fried and basted in his own fat! He will be offered up as an atonement for all those, who in opposition to the gods, laugh and grow gross, in spite of worldly learning and lamentation.

CITIZENS.

Hark ye! hark—he speaks.

MUCIUS.

Soldiers and citizens:—The times cry out revenge, and
they must have it. Revenge cries out for blood, and it
will have it. This Quintus has despised our sacred rights,
and sold us to our ancient enemy.—What fate do you award
him for his crimes?

CITIZENS.

A traitor's fate—dishonourable death!

ALL.

Death!—death!—death!

Enter SERTORIUS *and* MARCELLUS.

SERTORIUS.

What mean ye, recreant slaves! Do ye conspire
Against the State or me?—why thus assemble,
Brooding upon imaginary griefs,
And plotting treason which you dare not breathe,
In fear of your own fancy!—What would ye have?

CITIZEN.

Speak to him, Mucius, and unfold our wrongs.

MUCIUS.

We would unite with Pontus—join this league
'Gainst haughty Rome, our deadly enemy,
And drive her armies from our blood-stain'd shores!

SERTORIUS.

You would unite with Pontus?—Brave confederates,
You whom no tie can bind but that of Mammon!
To Mithridates you would lend your aid,

To extirpate old Rome!—A hundred legions
Of veteran troops, with Pompey for their leader,
Encompass you about, and sack your towns—
Yet ye would join with Pontus!—Scarcely able
To save yourselves, and guard your household gods,
You would, forsooth, invade the threat'ning foe—
Nay more, ye would be leaders—shame upon ye!
Leaders, who yet have never learn'd to follow
Where glory mark'd the way! Hence to your homes!
Is this a fit occasion, when Spain's fortunes
Stand nicely equipois'd in Fate's dread balance,
And heaven and earth pause on her destiny,
Thus, by inglorious faction, to provoke
The special vengeance of superior powers?
—But what care you for life's vicissitudes?
The mighty storm drives harmless o'er your heads—
None but the great, the good, the godlike, feel it,
You are below its fury.

MUCIUS.

We are the freemen of the soil, Sertorius.

SERTORIUS.

             Peace, magpie!
Say rather that ye are the soil of freemen—
The rank, foul compost whence sedition springs.
Ye gods! how abject is the tyranny of slaves,
Who forge a sceptre from their servile chains,
And lord it o'er the aristocracy
Which nature form'd—inverting her great laws,
That power should govern, and the weak obey.

MUCIUS.

We claim the privilege to speak our griefs.
Thou hast, by over-wrought authority,
Bow'd down the Senate to thy sovereign will,
And sacrificed our rights to love of Rome.

SERTORIUS.

And is this all?—Can none of you remember
Another outrage practis'd upon Spain?

I found you slaves, in bodies and in mind;
I burst the chains of both and set you free,
And this is my requital: you would fain return
To your old bondage; freedom has grown irksome.
Or would you, disobedient as you are,
Presume to rule the State? First learn to serve;
So shall ye best acquire the power to govern:
First overcome yourselves, before ye seek
To supervise and sway your fellow men.
Think not that honours dignify the wearer;
They have no several value—but reflect
Lustre reciprocal, or combine disgrace.
Say I throw down these trappings of my office;
These envied symbols of authority,
Which, while th'y allure with splendour, crush with weight;
On whom will you confer them, potent sirs,
Whose Atlantean shoulders shall sustain
Your falling empire, undermin'd and curst
By such as you are?—Freemen of the soil!
Disperse, ye knaves—hence to your several homes,
And vent your spleen on those who court your favour!
I do despise the one, abhor the other.

Mucius.

Thou wilt not hear us:
Then in the face of Spain I call thee traitor!
And summon thee to answer to the people,
The charge I thus prefer.

Citizens.

Ay, answer to the people!

Sertorius.

                    Here's *my* Tarpeian rock,
The tow'ring *height* from which Sertorius falls!—
Dost hear, Marcellus, *they* proclaim *me* traitor!
This mighty Areopagus decides my doom,
And hurls me to perdition. Traitors are often made
As felons are, by the foul accusation,

The pride of virtue, being virtue's shield.
By Hercules! 'twere worth a little treason
To purge the country of this rank disease;
It grows plethoric, and its bursting veins
Require the lancet.

Enter MANLIUS.

MANLIUS.

Sertorius! well encounter'd; I am fraught
With direful tidings to thyself and Spain.

SERTORIUS.

Out with the public grief, before the public!
A private sorrow asks a private ear.
The weight that all men share, from sympathy
Is lighten'd; but the thunderbolt, that falls
On one poor heart, scathes, scatters, and destroys it.
Let not the million gloat upon *my* woe!
What has befallen Spain?

MANLIUS.

Our City is besieged—our boldest ranks
Driven to her very gates! victorious Pompey,
Flush'd with success, resistlessly pours down
His veteran troops; and nought is left for hope.

SERTORIUS.

Despair should win, then, what vain hope has lost!
But why despair? here are some scores of leaders,
Burning to match their might with valiant Pompey!
Distinguished men; who would prescribe my duty,
Alike in peace or war.

MANLIUS.

Ah! jest not thus! the frantic populace,
Breathing contagious fear, rush to the forum,
Invoke thy aid, and build their faith on thee.

SERTORIUS.

This may not be: I am a banish'd man,
The sovereign people have proscrib'd my service—
How shall I mitigate their stern decree?
They say I am a traitor—leagued with Rome:
What! will ye trust your armies with a traitor?

MUCIUS.

Pardon us, good Sertorius, pardon, pardon!

SERTORIUS.

You do mistake, 'tis I should sue for pardon,
Since I have been condemn'd. Forgive me, citizens,
The love I bear the State, the blood I've shed,
The days of labour and the nights of pain
I've borne for you; I pray forgive them all!;
I do deplore them deeply, and repent
All such transgressions, and will sin no more.
Have with ye, friends.
[*Exeunt* SERTORIUS, MARCELLUS, *and* MANLIUS.

CITIZENS.

Unlook'd for change—our city is undone.

FLAVIUS.

Now who shall speak for you? Mucius is a good captain
to lead you into battle, but who shall conduct the retreat,
which, as the times run, is likely to be the most necessary
movement?—What sayst thou, my lad of wax?

CAIPHUS.

I am content you should call me anything but *last,* when a
retreat is in vogue—that should be Mucius' fate: I am
satisfied to lead the retreat. Besides, being a cobbler, it is
meet, you know, that I should foot it—So here goes, follow
who may! [*Exit.*

CITIZEN.

Ay, ay! Mucius, thou hast betrayed us into jeopardy, and must answer it—We submitted to thy direction, and thou hast perilled us.

MUCIUS.

You mistake—I submitted to your direction:—spoke I not upon your motion? urged I not your complaint, rather than my own? Now observe the dilemma:—If Sertorius be not restored to Spain, Spain will hang me; and if Sertorius be restored to Spain, *he* will hang me—and all because I said for you, what you were not able to say for yourselves. Such, such, alas! is the *enviable* distinction of superior acquirements—the higher you are, the nearer the gallows.—But let us to the Forum, where all shall be explained! [*Aside.*] That is, I will endeavour to justify myself, for having been such a fool as to attempt justifying you—an Augean task forsooth!

ALL.

To the Forum—the explanation!—to the Forum!
[*Exeunt all but* FLAVIUS.

FLAVIUS.

So, my predictions are all thus far verified; and whichever party succeed, hanging it seems will be rife, and my trade put into requisition. All this comes of ambition: Mucius, forsooth, must translate himself from his desk to a rostrum, and now perforce the rostrum is to be exchanged for a gibbet—unless Quintus should be merciful to him, and protect him from the vengeance of his former friends. In these times, nothing can guard us, but square, rule and compass. But I must also to the Forum:—He who expects to be in at the death, should never give up the chase, much less recede when the boar is at bay.   [*Exit.*

ACT III.

SCENE I.—*A Public Street.*

Enter CITIZENS.

1ST CITIZEN.

Defeated, say'st thou?

2ND CITIZEN.

Ay: as I pass'd the postern, scatter'd troops,
Dejected and dismayed, in wild disorder,
Rush'd through the city's gates; while busy rumour,
Seizing upon the half told tale of woe,
Surrounds it with new terrors, and, appall'd,
Shrinks from her own creation.

1ST CITIZEN.

Who led the army?

2ND CITIZEN.

Perpenna, as 'tis said—a gallant soldier,
Inur'd and practis'd in the arts of war;
Outnumber'd, it is true, by Pompey's forces,
But full of hope, and eager for the conflict.
Sertorius, as thou know'st, incens'd with Spain,
Spurns or contemns all reconciliation—
Impatient, listens to our prayers, and answers,
"Ye who would banish *me,* now *banish* Pompey!"

1ST CITIZEN.

'Tis thought, he still is not inflexible,
But views, with anxious and paternal eye,
The wayward fortunes of deluded Spain,
And fain would crown our hopes.

2ND CITIZEN.

Alas, not so: his wonted spirit's gone.
His mother's death,—the pride of palmy Rome,

His tutelary saint—his heart's dear idol,
Has quite unmann'd him: now whole days he sits,
Wrapt and absorb'd in a consuming grief:—
E'en peerless Marcia, Spain's bright paragon,
Employs her winning witchery in vain,
To mitigate his woe.

LENARIUS hastily passes across the stage.

1ST CITIZEN.

What ho! Lenarius!
What are the latest tidings from the camp?

LENARIUS.

Disaster and defeat! and all the evils
That throng the train of unsuccessful war:—
Perpenna is o'erthrown: the conqu'ring Romans,
Surmounting all resistance, hither come,
Hot with revenge, and thirsting after plunder.
Like a dark torrent, from yon western hill,
In one huge surge they pour their forces down,
And inundate the plain beneath with ruin.
Accustom'd to success, our vanquish'd soldiers
Desert their stations—and grown desperate,
Refuse to fight, unless Sertorius leads them.

1ST CITIZEN.

Unhappy Spain—thy struggle soon must end,
When friends and foes alike conspire against thee.

LENARIUS.

Redeem the time!
Reflection cannot shun the shaft of fate,
Endure it as she may. Thought is too slow,
Resting on past, to meet approaching woe.
Haste to Marcellus—and recount to him
The dire event; a single hope remains,
That hope is in Marcellus and his daughter.
He is the second self of proud Sertorius,

His friend, companion, brother, counsellor;
If he should fail, aided by Marcia's beauty,
Salvation is a dream—this hour's our last.

[*Exeunt.*

SCENE II.

An Apartment in the House of MARCELLUS.

SERTORIUS. [*Solus.*]

Rhea, my mother!—in that hallow'd name,
How many hours of guileless happiness,
Of sportive and unchequer'd innocence,
Roll back upon the ocean of past years,
And burst upon the view!
—Death, the destroyer! from thy potent spell,
Nor sex, nor age, nor strength, nor weakness 'scapes:
Time's hoary locks—the ringlets of gay youth—
The hero's laurel, and the poet's wreath—
Love, honour, health, and beauty, are thy spoil:—
The mitred, and the sceptred yield to thee,—
In deferential horror, all—all submit,
Save virtue, who in radiant smiles beholds
Thy dread approach, and, arm'd in heaven's proof,
Contemns thee and thy retinue of ills,
Alike triumphant o'er the tomb and thee.
Thou canst not rob thy victim—thou mayst slay him,
Tear him from those dear arms that cling around him,
And teach survivors to deplore thy power:—
But, for this temp'ral life—this life of sorrow—
This life of death—thou giv'st him life eternal,
Unfading joy, and everlasting love!—

Enter SERVILIUS, *suddenly.*

How now, Servilius!
Dost thou presume thus to invade my grief?—
Why was I born?—or why do I survive?—
Virtue's extinct! the vicious only live!—

SERVILIUS.

Forgive your slave!—The daughter of Marcellus—

SERTORIUS.

Dead too!—then let the world dissolve,
And night and chaos rule the dark domain!

SERVILIUS.

Not so, my lord——but, overwhelm'd with care,
She craves admittance to your gracious presence,
And will not be refused.

SERTORIUS.

And must not be—attend upon her hither.

[*Exit* SERVILIUS.

Marcia in grief!—this frail and fragile flow'r
Yields to the blast, and bends to earth with sorrow.

Enter MARCIA.

MARCIA.

Pardon me, good my lord, that in my love
I thus o'erstep the outward forms of life,
To join my heart with yours and share your grief!

SERTORIUS.

My gentle Marcia! thou alone canst share it:
Fair counterpart of her for whom I grieve,
Let me enfold thee in this aching breast,
For ever there to dwell—for ever thine,
Gloomy and sad—but warm in its affection
And full of love, of tenderness, and thee.

MARCIA.

Ever noblest!
I fear my tidings shall enhance thy woe:
The Roman legions, o'erbearing all our troops,

Assault our gates! dismay invades each heart—
Thy fam'd Sertorian band desert their leader,
And call aloud for thee!

SERTORIUS.

They call in vain—in vain, my gentle Marcia—
Ambition is extinct within this bosom,
Buried in Rhea's grave!—life has no value,
When all that gave life worth, has past away.

MARCIA.

All, my Sertorius!

SERTORIUS.

Forgive me, Marcia—'twas unkindly said,
Nay more, untruly said, while thou art mine:
Rich in the treasure of thy matchless love!
I live alone for thee—alone in thee!

MARCIA.

Ah, my good lord—indulge your humble suitor,
Who knows not whether she would gain, or lose
The boon she asks—in each event undone!
Your friends, confiding in the tender love
They know I bear you, through me urge their suit,
That you to hapless Spain would lend your aid.
Unsparing havoc, rapine, and destruction,
Urge on their fell career—old age and youth,
Matrons and maidens, weep the vengeful hour!—

SERTORIUS.

Where is Perpenna, and his gallant cohorts,
That thus the crimson tide of bold invasion
Pollutes the very sacristy of Spain,
And bears her household gods from their own altars!

MARCIA.

O'erthrown, my lord—and driven from the field,
With mighty slaughter!—the boldest Spanish hearts

All cower like doves before the Roman eagles,
And Sylla's lurid star sheds pestilence
Upon the hopes of Spain!

SERTORIUS.

O'erthrown, sayst thou?—fled! driven from the field!
Hear this, ye gods! Where sleep your thunderbolts,
That thus the guilty triumph in their guilt,
And bold impiety outfaces heaven!—
—In the decrees of Fate, if there remain
Though but one blessing for the wretched Quintus,
Bestow it now, ye gods! when most I need it,
And ever after pour your quiver on me!
Shall the destroyer of his country's peace
Conceal his blood-stain'd brow with laurel crown,
Pluck'd from Spain's verdant fields?
—What ho! my armour! Let it be proclaim'd
Throughout our host—Sertorius leads them on,
To fall, or flourish, in the cause of Spain!

MARCIA.

Oh, my good lord—

SERTORIUS.

What sayst thou, gentle love?
Thy suit is won—And yet that tearful eye
Betrays an anxious and ill-boding heart:—
What dost thou fear, my fair one?

MARCIA.

Ah, chide me not, lest my full heart should break,
And drown thee in its sorrows!—Oh, my Quintus,
Women were ever made the sport of fortune,
And Roman dames, beneath the icy brow
Of cold reserve, conceal devouring fires,
That prey upon the heart in endless fury!—

SERTORIUS.

Art thou not mine—pledg'd and betroth'd to me?
Am I not thine, beyond the power of fortune,
My first—my blest—my sole remaining blessing?

MARCIA.

Yet, dearest Quintus, mingle not again
In those rude scenes of sanguinary war!
Think of my aged father—think of her
Whose hopes, and happiness, all spring from thee!

SERTORIUS.

Forbear, my Marcia! Every tear thou shed'st
Inflames me more. Should the victorious foe
Subvert our city, thou, my sainted love,
Wilt grace proud Sylla's conquest.

MARCIA.

                    Never! never!
Thy fate is mine—unalterably mine;
With thee I live or die, flourish or perish!
Think not, in Spain's submission I shall yield,
To swell the number of the captive train:—
Think'st thou I shrink from death? rather I fear
To live, unblest by thee.

SERTORIUS.

Nay, talk not thus—I shall return to thee,
To smile upon thee, and enjoy thy smile,
While conscious safety reigns throughout the heart,
And Lusitania triumphs o'er the foe.
Fear nothing, love—why should the innocent
Tremble and quake with fear?—the guilty fear,
For cowardice, and guilt, appall each other;
But virtue ever wears a lion's heart,
Beneath the downy plumage of the dove.

MARCIA.

Yet, O! my Quintus, should thy precious life
Fall sacrifice beneath the Roman sword!

SERTORIUS.

No more, I pray thee: What the gods ordain,
Is circumvolv'd in rayless mystery,

Dark and inscrutable to human eye,
Still ever just—why should the just despair?

MARCIA.

Why should I not despair, my noble Quintus!
Thus having wrought thee to this fierce encounter,
The gods in justice may decree thy death,
To punish Marcia for her impious zeal!

SERTORIUS.

No more, my little Roman—*very little Roman;*
All will be well, confide in the assurance.
Come, let me lead thee in—thy honour'd father
Will join with thine his blessing on Sertorius,
And pour forth prayers for Spain: fear nothing, love,
I will be frugal of my life for thee.   [*Exeunt.*

ACT IV.

SCENE I.—*The Field of Battle.*

SERTORIUS, ANTONIUS, PERPENNA, MANLIUS, LENARIUS, *and*
SOLDIERS.

SERTORIUS.

My gallant soldiers, ye mistake the foe,
He lies before you. Onward then to meet him!
Thou, brave Antonius, with thy trusty band
Maintain this ground, while by the southern gate
I throw myself upon the rear of Pompey,
And teach this hopeful pupil of great Sylla,
A general's duty is to look behind, (1)
Rather than guard his van. When ye shall hear
The clangour of our steel on Roman helmets,
Ope wide your gates, and grapple with the foe.
Courage, my friends—remember that this hour

Shall make your fame eternal as the stars,
Should fortune smile upon ye: should she frown,
Why let her frown—at worst, we can but die,
And dying in defence of virtuous freedom,
Is to subdue the unpropitious gods,
And win those honours, which stern fate denies!
Who is the foe?—a name of warlike note!
The conq'ring Romans! Who are ye, my friends?
Let Tingis, Bactis, and Saguntum answer—
The conquerors of these conquerors. Forward then!
Strike home for life and dearer liberty;
And you, immortal self-devoted band, (2)
Who live and die for me—who die *with* me,
Now witness for me, to the attentive gods,
That never from this scene of mortal strife
Shall we return, if not in victory—
So let us all embrace, and to our posts.
[*Confers with* LENARIUS.] We profit by delay.

                               [*Exit* LENARIUS.

MANLIUS.

Quintus Sertorius—in the hour of danger,
Were it not well provision should be made
To meet the worst result? The old, the feeble,
Our wives—our offspring, they demand our care.

SERTORIUS.

They have your care;
Can they have more than life? and life is theirs—
The husband's, brother's, son's, and father's arm
Shall guard the wife, the sister, parent, child—
Their *only* guard,—who would depute another?
Dream not of mercy—'tis an idle phantom;
The leopard sooner shall become unspotted,
And ravens change their plumage with the swan,
Than barbarous Sylla yield his thirst for blood.
In every blow, let thoughts like these inspire you,
And Lusitania's free.   [*Exeunt omnes.*

SCENE II.

The Roman Camp.

Enter METELLUS *and* POMPEY.

METELLUS.

Reward has been proclaim'd throughout the camp,
To him that shall possess us of the traitor.
The overthrow of Spain, for vet'ran arms,
Is but a sickly triumph—but to subdue
This outlaw, who affects to pity Rome,
While he exults in her calamities—
A crocodile, that mingles with the blood
Of dying victims, his deceitful tears—
One, who has scorn'd our threats, defied our leaders,
Subdued our armies—circumvented us
In our own toils—Ye gods! it were a conquest,
—Though but one man, worth all of Lusitania!

POMPEY.

This hour shall end his glory. Yet Metellus,
Yon golden sun, that soon will bathe in blood,
Views not, in all his wide and bright career,
—Let us do justice to a valiant foe,—
A prouder or more glorious sacrifice!
Æneas, our great ancestor, from Troy
In filial love bore off the old Anchises—
Lo! where, upon the shoulders of one man,
A *nation* rests, and scorns the rage of war!—
Were envy of my nature, by the gods,
I freely now avow, no mortal breathes,
Whose fortitude in danger and defeat,
Whose ceaseless vigilance—surpassing skill
In all the chances, rules, and arts of war
Could sooner move me! What indeed more noble,
Than to redeem the fortunes of a state,
And, seizing fearlessly the wayward helm,
While the whole crew stand trembling and appall'd,

With blanchless cheek, and an undaunted eye,
And the nerv'd arm, fram'd as to rule the trident,
To steer the shatter'd vessel into port,
And, like a rock amid the troubled ocean,
Laugh at the billows, and defy the storm.

METELLUS.

You have grown amorous of the traitor's fame,
And as a lover, with indulgent eye,
Burnish his beauties, and forget his crimes.

Enter a SENTINEL.

SENTINEL.

A herald from the foe.

Enter LENARIUS.

METELLUS.

Declare thy mission!

LENARIUS.

Quintus Sertorius, speaking through my voice,
Proposes, in the view of either camp,
To spare all further carnage, and to end
This cruel war of brother against brother;
In single combat to decide the day
With great Metellus—and, if overthrown,
To bow unmurmuring to the will of Rome.

METELLUS.

Return and bear this answer back with you—
The sentiment of learned Theophrastus:—
It is a general's province, like a general
To live and die:—distinguish'd by his country,
Selected to fulfil her high behests,
'Tis not for him to vent his private spleen,
To sacrifice his office to himself,

And rest a nation's quarrel on his arm!
Nay, more, Sertorius does not meet us fairly;
Driven to his last resort, by hope abandon'd,
Let him surrender, and not stipulate—
Such terms belong to foes on equal ground.
Is Spain prepar'd to bow the knee to Rome?

LENARIUS.

My mission, brave Metellus, is discharg'd:
I come not hither in the State's behalf,
And therefore speak not in her sacred name;
My challenge is from *Quintus,* and to *thee.*

METELLUS.

Thou hast my answer; to your camp repair—
Give him safe conduct:—And remind your hero,
When traitors shall grow weary of their lives,
Fate has supplied them other means of death,
Than staining with their blood an *honest* sword.

[*Exit* LENARIUS.

POMPEY.

Well urg'd, Metellus—worthy of thyself,
My brother of the war!—I almost fear'd thee.
The artful foe grows jealous of thy fame,
And fain would steal what he despairs of winning.

METELLUS.

Not so, my valiant, unsuspicious friend;
This is the harbinger of other wiles,
By which the crafty Quintus would ensnare us.
Look to thy post—the very air breathes mischief.

POMPEY.

Exhaustless man! vanquish'd, but unsubdued—
While victory perches on the Roman banner,
Thou wing'st the falcon's flight to bear her off.

Enter SENTINEL.

SENTINEL.

My lords, the enemy unbars his gates,
And, as is thought, capitulates to Rome.

METELLUS.

Said I not so? See how this Proteus changes—
Threat'ning—inviting—fawning to betray!
Summon each leader to his martial charge}
                            [*Exit* SENTINEL.

The gates of Janus open but in war—
This is but feign'd submission: the lion crouches—
Beware his spring!

Enter a ROMAN SOLDIER.

Why from your post?—What bodes this fearful haste?
How stand the phalanx and the rearmost guard?

SOLDIER.

All driven in, my lord: The treacherous foe,
In serried column, from the western forest,
Sweeps as a whirlwind through our scatter'd ranks.

METELLUS.

The day is lost, and we are all undone!
Surrounded by the foe whom late we baited,
Conquest becomes defeat.   Sound the alarum!
                            [*Exit* SOLDIER.

POMPEY.

Surpris'd, but not dismay'd—
Despair not, brave Metellus.   Ho, my shield!
Almighty Jove, direct and nerve this arm
To deeds of glory! Let the traitor feel
Swift retribution from a Roman sword!
                    [*Flourish of trumpets and clash of arms—*
                            [*Exeunt.*

Scene III.

Another part of the Field.—The Spaniards are beaten in.

Enter Sertorius, Perpenna, *and* Soldiers.

Sertorius.

Come, plant your falchions here.   [*Pointing to his breast.*]
Ye panic stricken hares! Let me not see
The haughty Romans stalk o'er prostrate Spain,
And glut their swords with the defenceless blood
Of unresisting youth, and helpless age.

Perpenna.

The heavens declare against us: 'tis in vain
To militate with gods.

Sertorius.

The gods are ever with the brave, Perpenna,
Till we diffide in them: Our doubts are traitors
To heaven and us, and antedate our doom.
The craven heart, that shuns impending peril,
Expires on its own spear, while dauntless courage
Grapples with death, and rends his terrors from him.
Had I a thousand lives, and each immortal,
I'd jeopard all for the last hour of honour.
Look there—behold!—see where your riven ranks
Bow like the reed before the mighty tempest,
While here you stand, *weighing* the chance of war,
Which lofty minds *control!*—Shrink those who may,
Though not an arm will strike for liberty,
I rush alone to perish or be free!
              [*Flourish of trumpets.*]
                        [*Exit, followed by troops.*

SCENE IV.

A Street in the City.

Enter MUCIUS, CAIPHUS, FLAVIUS, CITIZENS, *and* RABBLE.

MUCIUS.

Victoria! victoria! victoria!—Spain is triumphant! Rome is overthrown!

CITIZEN.

How learn'dst thou that, good Mucius?

MUCIUS.

Lenarius has arrived, all reeking from the field, full freighted with the glorious tidings!—Rome, I tell you, is extinct—Sertorius has won immarcessible fame, and returns in triumph! Here'll be a jubilee for you—a complete saturnalia among the Spaniards. Our rebellion against Quintus, is forgotten in the general joy—success is ever full of forgiveness; and if hereafter you find me, thrusting my head and ears into the political concerns of the realm, may I endure the fate of the Falerian schoolmaster, the only faithless, if not the only foolish pedagogue, on record, and be whipped to death by my own pupils.

FLAVIUS.

Didst thou hear the progress of the fight?

MUCIUS.

In faith, did I—through all its cases, from the nominative to the ablative—and from a practical scholar, I tell you. In the first place, Sertorius challenged Metellus to single combat; but Metellus' stomach was too squeamish to digest such a repast, so he declined—as well he might.

FLAVIUS.

But what said Pompey? he never *declines;*—at least I have heard it said, he seldom is in the *vocative.*

MUCIUS.

Therefore said he nothing. And what should Pompey say? It was no business of his, you know, to fight other men's battles, if he had been ten times Pompey; and to be plain, forsooth, he was not disposed to go out of his way for a cracked crown; for they say, our Quintus, however mild and gentle he may be when petting and fondling on his fawn, is a very demi-devil in war, and thinks nothing of making crow's meat of a whole phalanx of the enemy, when the humour serves.—Only think of this, masters, and ever after remember the ascendency of learning in my person, by which, alone, you were protected from sudden and certain death. Hero or no hero, the recollection of the birch and ferule makes the blood tingle to the fingers' ends. Even that incarnate fiend, Alexander, we are told, always remembered Aristotle, with fear and reverence.

CITIZEN.

Well,—a plague upon your episodes!—after the challenge, how proceeded they?

MUCIUS.

Sertorius, by this time, had reached the forest, whence he forthwith poured a storm upon them; while we assailed them from the east. Pompey, however, for a time made head against Spain, and overthrew Perpenna, who commanded one of the wings.

FLAVIUS.

Ay! he commanded one of the *wings;* that I suppose was the reason of his being among the first to *fly*.

MUCIUS.

Peace, thou deal board, or my lips are closed—as though, in thy own phrase, they were clamped, or dove-tailed.

CAIPHUS.

Proceed, most excellent Mucius.

MUCIUS.

Upon Perpenna's flight, Quintus threw himself into the very centre of the Roman phalanx—Then you may suppose there was hot work. He was so covered with blood, and so surrounded with swords, and shields, and helmets, that he looked for all the world—pardon the figure—like a ruby set in steel. The Sertorian band, whose obligation it is, you know, to die with their general, rushed in upon the foe. They grappled with a brazen wall. For a long time their attempts were fruitless; until, in the last desperate effort from within and without, they broke the Roman ranks, and turned the tide of war:—mighty slaughter ensued, and Pompey and Metellus were both wounded, and narrowly escaped capture. But hark! the hero comes: stand by, and greet him as becometh the magnitude of our repentance, and this day's glory.

[*Flourish of trumpets, and acclamations.*]

Triumphal Entry of SPANIARDS.

SERTORIUS.

Yield offerings to the gods, where they are due—
Not to vain man. The watchful Destinies,
Unmindful of your base ingratitude,
Have bless'd your arms with triumph:
Be wary of success, and bear it wisely,
As best becomes the changing tides of life:
Let not the syren and seductive wiles
Of proud prosperity ensnare your hearts—
Self-conquest is the best and proudest triumph,
And victory, without it, is defeat.
The peril past, forestall its quick return
By circumspective care, and piety;
And let not sloth enervate and destroy
Your martial spirit, and obscure your fame:
Be ever as you are——and ever free.

MANLIUS.

My lord, the brave Marcellus comes to greet you.

Enter MARCELLUS.

SERTORIUS.

My friend, Marcellus!—father, I should say,—
Where lags our little trembler? I have come
At once to chide, and cheer her.

MARCELLUS.

See where she comes—despite of this array
Of martial pomp, and rude report of war—
With blushing garlands, pluck'd by her fair hand,
To grace the victor's brow!

Enter MARCIA.

MARCIA.

O! my dear lord—

SERTORIUS.

Blest **recompence** of toils and dangers past!
Come to this heart, and there for ever reign:
Thou art the victor, Marcia—let me crown thee
With thy own works—chains best become the captive.

MARCIA.

In crowns, or chains, I still divide with thee:
—No, not divide, but rather still unite,
Remaining ever, one—inseparable.

SERTORIUS.

Fair artlessness! how worthless is the pomp
Of the world's flattery, when compar'd with thee,
All chaste and tintless, as the virgin snow.
Come, take me with thee, wheresoe'er thou wilt:
Like the bright cynosure, by thee I steer,
And shun the rocks and shoals of treachery.

[*Music.—Exeunt.*

ACT V.

Scene I.—*The House of* Perpenna.

Enter Perpenna *and* Aufidius.

PERPENNA.

Doubly dishonour'd! overthrown by Pompey,
Then overthrown by Pompey's overthrow!
Defeat was neutraliz'd, while it secur'd
Accumulated woe on Quintus' head;
But changeling Fortune has carv'd out his road
To deathless honour, through my deathless shame,
And twin'd the laurel round that hated brow,
Which cypress should encircle. Marcia, too—
The lovely Marcia, who in banishment
Clung to his beggary, and abjur'd the world—
How will her doting and devoted heart
Revel and riot in his peerless honours!
Now hanging round his neck in sportive smiles,
And now reclining on his rugged bosom—
Spring's not more lovely, when with gentle hand,
And golden tresses deck'd with diamond dew,
And diadem of new-blown violets,
She throws aside the hoary locks of winter,
And melts him, in her glance, to life and love!

AUFIDIUS.

How now, Perpenna? whence this low'ring brow,
While Spain reels to her basis with rejoicing?

PERPENNA.

And why should I rejoice, while fortune's minion
Rends from my brow the sparkling coronet,
Tears from my heart its dear and only solace,
Foiling ambition, and defeating love?
Why should I smile and fawn upon this idol,
Who fells me to the earth, then tramples on me—
Provokes my grief, and then derides my groans?

AUFIDIUS.

Courage, my friend—why should the brave despair?

PERPENNA.

Why should they not, when unremitting torture
Preys with the vulture's fangs upon the heart?
Let those who ever felt Promethean torment,
Probe this torn bosom, and prescribe its cure!—
A maiden, in whose fair and heavenly form
The blended charms of all her sex are centred,
With eye of frost my glowing bosom chills—
While, unsolicited—almost unsought,
She throws herself into a rival's arms—
I'll not endure it! By the mighty Jove,
This hour's his last!

AUFIDIUS.

What, are ye mad? Think you the frantic mob
Will brook this outrage on their demigod,
Whom they yet kneel to worship? 'Twere sacrilege!
Expel the Pythian priestess from her tripod,
Or in prophetic travail strangle her,
And shun the lightnings of the Delphic god—
Then hope to 'scape the vengeful populace.—
Nay, pause a while:
The flood of favour shall abate its height,
And ebb again—Then is the hour of vengeance!

PERPENNA.

I pause no longer: flood, or ebb, in fortune,
He rides the waves triumphant: th' ills of life,
The tests and touchstones of external glory,
By which alone its currency is tried,
And sterling coin distinguish'd from the false,
Increase his weight, and stamp new value on him:
But, over all, he's rich where I am wretched—
In Marcia's love,—who clings more closely to him,
While the world frowns, and friends and fame recede.
Timid and tender as the passion-flower, (3)

There's yet no peril, but she braves for him,
And, skipping like Diana's fawn about him, (4)
Deems all her care rewarded by a smile.

AUFIDIUS.

Why conjure up your wrongs to aid your courage?
Or why endanger life for your revenge?
A few short hours, and you shall wreak your wrath
Securely—in the centre of your friends,
Not 'midst a phrensied and fickle mob. Sertorius
Partakes to-night, within your castle walls,
Your princely cheer—then is the time to strike:—
Select your guests—invite the chosen few
Whose hearts, and hands, and poniards too are yours.

PERPENNA.

Thou art my oracle—So shall it be!
'Tis not in nature to endure this load,
Heap'd up by hate and unrequited love!
Haste to our friends—apprise them of the plot:
Sertorius dead, Spain falls to our allotment,
And Rome is brib'd to peace by feign'd submission.

AUFIDIUS.

Besides, Perpenna, we avoid suspicion
Of preconceiv'd design: a sudden quarrel,
With the excuse which sparkling wine supplies,
Shall look more seemly, than with hate prepense,
And cold deliberation, thus to slay him,
While Io Pæns rend the vaulted heavens,
And men and gods unite to swell his glory.

PERPENNA.

Still—still Aufidius—in my own house—
At my own banquet slaughtered!—'tis horrible!
The empty fancy chills my glowing heart!
Yet die he must! He cannot—shall not live,
Though the same blow that fells him to the earth,

Consign me to hell's torments with Ixion.   (5)
About it straight: let all things be dispos'd
To make our vengeance sure; which consummate,
Nought then remains, but to unite with Pompey
On our own terms.   But should we fail, Aufidius?—

AUFIDIUS.

'Tis but another blow—inflicted here!
Less terrible than the unsated tooth
Of gnawing hate, which feeds upon, and coils
Around the heart, in ceaseless agony.

PERPENNA.

Give me thy hand—

AUFIDIUS.

Ay, grasp it as becomes death's awful compact—
By blood cemented—'twill not shrink from thine.

[*Exeunt.*

SCENE II.

An Apartment in the House of MARCELLUS.

SERTORIUS *and* MARCIA.

MARCIA.

Nay, my dear lord, forgive this anxious heart:
It pines and withers when thou art away,
Like flowers deserted by the genial sun:
Indeed—indeed, you must not leave me thus.
—What, on our marriage day—

SERTORIUS.

But for a time, sweet Marcia—not to leave thee,
For still my spirit hovers where thou art;
But 'twere reproachful, when expectant friends

Unite in gratitude to do me honour,
That we should shun the homage they would pay,
And prove it undeserv'd, or undeserving:
It must not be, my love—it must not be.

MARCIA.

'Tis ever as thou wilt:—but still, my Quintus,
This boding bosom throbs with anxious fear—
Fear undefin'd—but not less terrible:
There is a weight that loads my anxious thoughts,
Which, causeless in the past, precedes its cause.

SERTORIUS.

Fear, gentle love—what scope is there for fear?
'Tis not a fray, but feast, that calls me forth;
All friends of Spain, and all Sertorius' friends.
Shall I, just reeking from the scenes of war,
Scarr'd, and enseam'd by mortal controversy,
Shrink from the warm embrace of courtesy?—
'Tis fancy all!

MARCIA.

My lord,—Perpenna—art thou well assur'd—

SERTORIUS.

Of what, fair dame?—he ever is assur'd,
Whose heart is open to the eye of day—
Who wears no lurking danger in his smiles,
Nor dreams of tigers' hearts beneath the fleece
Of inoffensive flocks. What should I fear?
Shall I imbitter all the joys of life,
To shrink from death, and die in my own fears—
While nought but poison'd bowls, and air-drawn daggers,
And treach'rous friends—or enemies disguis'd,
And snares, and lures, and dark conspiracies,
Flit through the fever'd brain in endless terror—
Beset th' affrighted soul—and prey upon it,
Till nought remains of life, but dread of death,
And all of death is suffer'd, but the *name?*

—But see, my Marcia, where the golden day
Gilds yon sky-helmed mount with purple hues,
Like fabled dolphins, varying as it dies.
Thou dost beguile the time, my dear delight,
And make a laggard of me.

MARCIA.

Nay, my dear lord—if that you are resolv'd,
I do but play the usurer with my love,
Enlarging day, at the expense of night,
And losing what I gain.

SERTORIUS.

One more embrace—and then a short farewell.

MARCIA.

Farewell, my love—but if thou shouldst delay,
In faith, I shall invade your festive rites,
And come to chide, and guard, and win you back
To this lone breast. Farewell, but fail me not!

SERTORIUS.

Never, till life fail me!   [*Exit.*

MARCIA.

"Never till life fail me!"—Art thou then gone?—
His parting words sink like a funeral knell
Into my soul, and freeze my blood with horror.
The fading day—the deathlike sleep of nature—
The treach'rous calm that rests upon creation—
And the deep torpor that invests my brain,
Are the precursors of calamity!
I struggle, but my anxious fears subdue me.
Who waits? Timandra!—Timandra, I say!

Enter TIMANDRA.

TIMANDRA.

What is your pleasure, Madam?

MARCIA.

                              My good Timandra,
We must be gone forthwith. Question me not—
The times admit no pause: mischief's afoot—
My lord, my husband, is begirt with foes.

TIMANDRA.

How—wherefore are you thus alarm'd, my lady?
What should you dread?

MARCIA.

What should I dread? I dread uncertainty,
Through whose vast maze and labyrinths of doubt
The anxious soul, in never-ending grief,
Explores its fate—and, in its devious course,
Oft times creates the perils it would shun.

TIMANDRA.

Would you vouchsafe an ear to my advice,
Faithful, though humble—I beseech you, Madam,
Do not go forth: the night is closing round us,
And the wild tumult of this festive day,
To friends and foes, alike, is fraught with danger.

MARCIA.

Thou then canst fear, without *my cause* of fear!
The harmless revels of triumphant friends,
Thy timid fancy conjures into evil;
Yet when I tell thee that my o'erfraught soul
Predicts—foresees—would shun, impending peril,
Thou cant'st as sadly of the closing night,
As though the sun should never rise again.
—What is, or night, or day, to those who love,
Without love's object! Should my Quintus fall,
With *me* a never-ending darkness reigns—
The darkness of the grave!

TIMANDRA.

Pr'ythee, dear Madam, yield not thus to grief,
Founded in fears, that are themselves *unfounded:*
My Lord will soon return—he will, believe me—
Return to bless you, and dispel your woe.

MARCIA.

Say that he should—which but to *doubt* were death!
Does it befit the daughter of Marcellus,
While her dear husband's fate is pois'd before her,
To watch the wavering scales, nor rush to save him?
To save, or die with him! Thou know'st, Timandra,
The wily, reckless temper of Perpenna—
His deadly rivalry—relentless hate,
His subtle treason in the Pontic league—
His late defeat by Pompey and Metellus,
Chang'd by the prowess of my gallant love
To peals of victory, and shouts of joy—
His persevering and audacious suit
Preferr'd to me, while well he knew my heart
Was wedded to another: think'st thou, then,
There is not falsehood in this fawning friendship,
Professed towards the unsuspecting Quintus?
I would have told my fears, and stay'd my lord,
But that I could not stain his noble nature
With foul mistrust of those *he deems* his friends.
—What say'st thou now? If thou wilt go with me,
Summon our freedmen, and attend me straight—
No earthly power impedes me.

TIMANDRA.

                Dearest lady,
Your will shall be obeyed, whate'er befalls;
I live but in your favour.

MARCIA.

Let us away—abide by my direction,
The winged moments chide this dull delay.   [*Exeunt.*

SCENE III.

Banquet.

PERPENNA, AUFIDIUS, ANTONIUS, LENARIUS, CONSPIRATORS.

PERPENNA.

　　　　　　　　He comes not:—
The setting sun begins to tinge the west
With his departing rays—and still he comes not.
What bodes this strange delay?—

ANTONIUS.

He does mistrust us: since the Pontic league
Was sanction'd by thy voice, and thine, Aufidius,
Quintus has ever worn a guarded eye,
And from the bold, confiding, reckless soldier,
Become reserv'd, diffiding, and suspicious.
Besides, instinctive nature well might warn him,
Not to desert the loving arms of Marcia,
For the embraces of less tender friends.

PERPENNA.

—No more!—If he neglect his plighted word,
I will not forfeit mine—and witness for me,
While this libation to the gods I pour
In token of my faith—this hour he dies,
E'en though my poniard reach his heart—

ANTONIUS.

　　　　　　　　Forbear—he comes—
Subdue that threat'ning brow, and beam with smiles
Like gay Hyperion, when he gilds the storm
In his precedent glory.

Enter SERTORIUS.

PERPENNA.

Welcome, Sertorius—welcome to our banquet,
Where, without thee, festivity expires,
And pensive sadness fills the throne of joy,

SERTORIUS.

Fie, fie, Perpenna—thou, a camp bred soldier,
With tongue untutor'd in the Tyrian school,
Hast thrown aside thy candour with the sword,
And wrapp'd thy sinewy frame in silken folds,
To play the courtier, and the flatterer.

PERPENNA.

Let music speak, and to the heavens proclaim
Spain's deep devotion to her benefactor:—   [*Music.*
Nay, sound again, till the enamour'd spheres
Catch the proud note, and swell the symphony.
                              [*Music, clarion, &c.*

SERTORIUS.

I pray ye, cease, nor thus incense the gods
By impious adulation to a mortal.
The feast invites us—we await our host.

Music strikes up—GUESTS *are seated—music continued, and
dance.*

ANTONIUS.

Why should we talk of war, when wine inspires
Our buoyant hearts with thrilling ecstasy?
Let frigid cynics scoff at Cupid's chains—
No valued trophy that the hero wears,
Clings half so closely to the heart, as love.

AUFIDIUS.

There are no cynics in the art of love:
E'en stern Diogenes, in the amorous list
Bore off voluptuous Lais from his rivals,
And rioted and revell'd in her charms—
Shall the gay soldier, flush'd with rich Falernian,
Play anchorite, and scorn the lip of beauty?

SERTORIUS.

Quote not the vices of philosophy,
To justify indulgence of your own;

But emulate her virtues, if you can.
The love which twines most closely round the heart,
Disdains the use of words, and shuns the eye
Like truth, despising outward ornament,
In native worth: the God you worship, bends
A feeble bow, and dips his shaft in wine— (6)
The wound soon heals.

LENARIUS.

The deities instruct us how to love,
While, glowing in their own celestial fires,
They yield their sov'reignty at Cupid's shrine.
Witness the goddess of the rosy morn,
When, rising from the star bestudded couch
Of great Orion, radiant with delight,
She blushes through the pure and lucid skies
And harbingers the day.

PERPENNA.

Or beauteous Thetis, when from coral caves,
Rob'd in cerulean vesture she appears,
Loose and reclining on the sea-girt shore.

AUFIDIUS.

Or Amphitrite, blushing from the arms
Of mighty Neptune—skimming o'er the waves
In em'rald car, and coronet of pearl,
While sportive Tritons gambol in her train.

ANTONIUS.

Or the gay Queen of love, with zone ungirt,
Free and lascivious as the wanton winds,
That breathe their spices through Idalium's groves,
And melt the soul to joy.

SERTORIUS.

Peace, parasites!
The outraged gods frown on your lewd desires,
To earth disgusting—and a crime to heaven.

PERPENNA.

                    You're grave, Sertorius,
And mar the mirthful vein.   My gallant friends,
Come, twine your garlands round the flowing bowl,
And pledge together in one mingled draught,
The fellest foe, and fastest friend of Rome—
Sertorius, and Sylla.

SERTORIUS.   [*Aside.*]

Feretrian Jove!—what crime does this portend?
The name of Sylla is the current pass,
For broken faith, and violated honour.
I see it all—I am beset—betray'd!
Bear up, my soul—and, worthy of thyself,
Endure approaching peril, as the past—
Dying as all should die, who hope to live
In the proud pages of futurity.
—I am the friend of Spain, not foe of Rome:
While Sylla, is the enemy of both.

PERPENNA.

Thou dost mislike our pledge, valiant Sertorius;
We wait upon thy motion—we quaff the garland (7)
To the sentiment, thine still retains its place.

AUFIDIUS.

We will amend, and make atonement, Quintus,
By adding to this unrequited pledge,
The fair Nicopolis, and beauteous Marcia.   (8)

SERTORIUS.

Audacious villain! thus I greet your pledge!   [*Strikes him.*]
I'll tear that scorpion tongue out of your throat!—
Join spotless Marcia, to a common drab!
'Twere easier to unite thy downward soul,
With elevated and aspiring thoughts!—
—Forgive me, ye chaste heavens, that I smote him!
'Twill make the minion proud.

PERPENNA.

Quintus Sertorius, darest thou thus assail
My peaceful guests? Beware of retribution!

SERTORIUS.

Thy peaceful guests?—thy impious sycophants!
Thy base confederates in projected crime.
I know ye all, and I despise ye all,
And the black purpose of your ribald crew:
But thou, Perpenna—thou, the traitor host,
Supreme in infamy—who prostitut'st
The charms, and smiles, and blandishments of life,
To toils and snares for unsuspicious honour—
Thus I devote thee, 'midst thy parasites,
Upon the altar of polluted faith,
To the infernal gods—thus meet thy fate!

[*Rushes towards* PERPENNA, *whom the* CONSPIRATORS
surround, drawing and brandishing their daggers.]

Ha! valiant traitors! how your weapons blush,
While wielded thus 'gainst a defenceless man,
But dauntless as defenceless! Death to me—
To me, alone, is but repose from toil:
'Tis only for the living that I fear.
[*Aside.*] My gentle love—my ever tender Marcia,
Who shall reveal this damning deed to thee?
—I have no weapon—why then do ye pause?
Come—let me note you for posterity,
Who is the first to strike—I stand alone:
He who is first, shall be the last remember'd—
Immortaliz'd in shame.

[PERPENNA *dashes down his goblet, the signal for assault.*]

ANTONIUS.

My poniard speaks for me!—

PERPENNA.

And mine! [*Stabs him.*]

AUFIDIUS.

Though *last,* the *deepest*—death atones for *blows.*

MARCIA.   [*Speaking from without.*]

What! bar the gates of hospitality!
Lock up the portals to the human heart!

Enter MARCIA.

[SERTORIUS *falls at her feet.*]

Prophetic soul! My lord—my dear Sertorius—

SERTORIUS.

My Marcia! bless'd and blessing, thus I die!   [*Dies.*]

MARCIA.

Not dead!—Oh, no! thou canst not die without me.
Thy own lov'd, loving Marcia calls to thee!
—Bleeding and breathless! Which of ye did this?
Was't thou, Perpenna, or, Antonius, thou?—
Or all of you, whose eyeballs glare upon me,
Like baleful comets, freighted with portents
Of dire mischance, and woe remediless?
'Tis horrible! And see, he beckons to me—
Yes, yes, my love, I come to thee—I come:
Though the whole earth divide us, I am thine .
—Where am I, and why gaze ye on me thus,
With stranger eyes? I am betroth'd to Quintus—
This is my wedding night—behold the banquet:
Ye are my guests—I bid ye welcome all
In my lord's name: my father also greets ye.
—Ha! [*Shrieks.*] Poinards, for bridal feasts!
Crimson'd with blood!—Monsters, ye've slain my **husband!**
Seize upon and bind them!—Alas, I cannot weep,
The fever of my brain drinks up my tears—
My bosom heaves not—it is chang'd to marble—
But I can laugh! Sertorius has return'd—
Return'd in victory, and crown'd with glory!
Oh, my poor throbbing heart—it bursts with joy!
                                        [*Swoons upon the body.*]

PERPENNA.

Look here, Revenge, and sate thyself with blood!
See where the patriot and the hero lies,
Clasp'd in the fond embrace of virtuous love!—
If this be death, who would desire to live?
If what I feel be life, who fear to die?

[*Clamor from without.*]

—What noise is that?—the castle is beset.
Away, my friends! the Roman Camp affords
Our ready refuge, and assured reward. (9)

[*Curtain falls.*]

NOTES

IT will be observed, that in the preceding work, some liberties have been taken, under poetical privileges, and particularly in respect to Lusitania and Spain being considered as the same. This, however, it is presumed, will be excused; as Spain, or Hesperia, originally embraced Lusitania or Portugal,—and both of them, for a time, as would appear by Plutarch, were subject to the government of Sertorius.

SERTORIUS, one of the most distinguished names of antiquity, was the son of Quintus and Rhea. In his youth he served under Marius, in Gaul; where the Romans being routed, his horse was killed, and although wounded, he swam across the Rhone in complete armour, and thus escaped. In the wars between Sylla and Marius, he took part with the latter, and ever bore the most determined hate towards the former, as was presumed, from Sylla having caused him to be disappointed in the contest for the tribuneship. Upon the overthrow of Marius, the influence of Sylla procured the banishment of Sertorius, and that of many other valiant Romans, who sought refuge in Spain; where, in a short

time, Sertorius acquired an almost sovereign control.   He
formed his Senate, and established public schools, wherein
the Spaniards were instructed.   He was not permitted, however, to remain undisturbed: Sylla sent large armies to assail
and to subdue him, but without success.   The Roman armies
were routed, although headed by such commanders as Pompey and Metellus.   The vigilance and skill of Sertorius were
deemed irresistible; so much so, that Mithridates, king of
Pontus, surnamed the Great, sent an ambassador to him,
proposing to pay to Spain three thousand talents, and supply
forty ships of war, if she would consent to unite against
Rome.   Sertorius caused the ambassador to appear before
the Senate, where, notwithstanding the Senators were
unanimous in favour of the treaty, he refused it, as dishonourable and unjust.   In consequence of this refusal,
Perpenna Vento, elated with the vanity of birth, aspired to
the command, and sowed dissension among the Senators and
people.   The conspiracy daily gathered strength, and among
the rest Perpenna drew in Antonius, who had a considerable
command in the army.   They prepared letters for Sertorius,
which imported that a victory was gained by his officers, and
a number of the enemy slain.   Sertorius offered sacrifices for
the tidings, and Perpenna invited him and the conspirators
to supper, which he was prevailed upon to accept..   The
entertainments at which Sertorius was present, had been
always attended with great order and decorum, as he had
ever accustomed his guests to divert themselves in an innocent and irreproachable manner.   But in the midst of the
entertainment, the conspirators sought occasion to quarrel,
giving in to the most dissolute discourse, and pretending
drunkenness as the cause of their ribaldry.   Vexed at their
obscenities, or suspecting their design, he threw himself upon
his couch, as though he neither heard nor regarded them.
Perpenna took a cup of wine, and while drinking, purposely
let it fall out of his hand—which was the signal for them
to fall on.   Antony struck Sertorius with his sword—Sertorius resisted, but was finally despatched with many wounds.
—*Vide Plutarch*, vol. iii, title *Sertorius*.

NOTE (1).—*Page* 223.

"A general's duty is to look behind,
Rather than guard his van."

Pompey, upon one occasion, while besieging Sertorius in Spain, sent word to the Lauronites, that "they might be perfectly easy, and sit securely on their walls:" but when Sertorius was informed of it, he only laughed and said, "I will teach that scholar of Sylla,"—so in ridicule he called Pompey, —"that a general ought to look behind him, rather than before him:"—and at the same time unexpectedly attacked Pompey in the rear, who was compelled quietly to look on, while his allies perished.

NOTE (2).—*Page* 224.

"And you, immortal self-devoted band."

It was the custom in Spain, for the band which fought near the general's person, when he fell, to die with him— which was called a libation. It is said, that when once defeated near the walls of a town, and the enemy were pressing hard upon him, the Sertorian band, to save Sertorius, exposed themselves without any precaution, and passed him upon their shoulders from one to another, till he had gained the walls.—*Vide Plutarch.*

NOTE (3).—*Page* 235.

"Timid and tender as the passion-flower."

I fear this is a slight anachronism—being of the impression that the passion-flower derived its name from the crucifixion, which was one hundred years after the date of Sertorius.

NOTE (4).—*Page 236.*

"And, skipping like Diana's fawn about him."

Spanus, a countryman, of Lusitania, having caught a milk white fawn, presented it to Sertorius. The fawn, in time, became so tractable, as to come when called, follow him where he went, and even to bear the tumults of the camp. By degrees the people were brought to believe, that this fawn was a gift from Diana, and discovered to him secrets of great importance. If, for instance, Sertorius had intelligence of some victory gained by his officers, he used to conceal the messenger, and produce the animal crowned with flowers for its good tidings; bidding the people rejoice, and offer sacrifices, on account of some news they would soon hear. By this invention he caused the barbarians to consider themselves as under the immediate direction of heaven.

NOTE (5).—*Page 237.*

"Consign me to hell's torments with Ixion."

Ixion, for his crimes, was struck with thunder by Jupiter, who ordered Mercury to tie him to a wheel in hell, which was perpetually whirling round—rendering his punishment eternal.

NOTE (6).—*Page 244.*

" . . . the God you worship, bends
A feeble bow, and dips his shaft in wine."

There are, according to some theogonists, two Cupids, one of whom is a lively, ingenuous youth, son of Jupiter and Venus—the other, a son of Nox and Erebus, distinguished only by debauchery and vice.

NOTE (7).—*Page 245.*

"We quaff the garland."

"Drinking the Crown, or Garland," consisted in throwing the chaplets of flowers, with which the Romans were generally crowned at an entertainment, into the cyathus or goblet, before drinking. It is related of Mark Antony and Cleopatra, that the latter being suspected of an intention to destroy the former, Antony drank only from the cup which Cleopatra previously tasted. Upon one occasion, having tasted of his cup, she sportively challenged him "to drink the garland;" whereupon he gallantly snatched hers from her head, and was proceeding to drink, when she stopped him, at the same time apprising him that the flowers of which the crown was composed were poisonous; hereby convincing him of two things: first, that she had no desire to destroy him— and secondly, that if she had, all his precautions would prove fruitless.

NOTE (8).—*Page 245.*

"The fair Nicopolis."

Nicopolis, a famous courtezan—mistress of Sylla—and who, upon her death, bequeathed to him immense wealth.

NOTE (9).—*Page 248.*

Perpenna, to ingratiate himself with Pompey, offered to surrender to him all the papers of Sertorius, and the letters of his correspondents in Rome. Pompey, however, without examining them, commanded the papers to be burnt, and ordered Perpenna to instant death. None escaped but Aufidius: he lived to an old age, in a village of the Barbarians, wretchedly poor, and universally despised.

—*Plutarch.*

TORTESA, THE USURER

By Nathaniel P. Willis

NATHANIEL PARKER WILLIS

(1806–1867)

There was always the touch of the dilettante about Willis and, like the dilettante, he had positive and negative qualities He frittered much of his energy away on a *paragraph attitude* toward the world, but his loyalty in friendship was no better measured than in the case of Edgar Allan Poe. His prose works are illustration of the fashion of the day—the "views afoot" kind of article, in which he revelled when he went abroad.

His association with Morris and Faye, in the editing of The New York *Mirror,* brought him in contact with the literary and artistic activity of the time, and his casual approach toward the drama was probably the result of his theatregoing as an editor. His drama criticisms, in comparison with Poe's, are not as incisive, though they both viewed plays from the standpoint of their literary excellences. So, we must take Willis, not as the professional dramatist, interested in the theatre as a vital medium of expression, but as the *litterateur,* who wrote dramas after a romantic model.

It is not the object of the present editor to dwell on facts concerning a life so easily accessible in biographical form as that of Willis. He was born in Portland, Maine, on January 20, 1806, and graduated from Yale, in the class of 1827. The final years of his life were spent in trying to save a paper, founded by him, called the *Home Journal.* He died on his birthday, 1867.

The character of his style, as a writer, is discernable in such of his works as "Famous Persons and Places", "Hurrygraphs", a "Lecture on Fashion", "People I Have Met" and "Letters from Under a Bridge".

After his return from abroad in 1836, Willis turned his hand to play writing. The result was "Bianca Visconti", written expressly for Josephine Clifton, the rôle of *Pasquali* being consciously shaped for the actor, Harry Placide. In its issue for August 19, 1837, *The Mirror* published, in advance, certain passages from the manuscript. We are told by Willis's biographer, Mr. Beers, whose volume adds to the permanent value of the *American Men of Letters Series,* and who at no time took Willis's dramatic ventures seriously, that Willis was offered by Colman, the play publisher, $300 for an edition of "Bianca", which, according to a letter from Willis, would indicate that this price was not at all bad, inasmuch as Epes Sargent had sold his "Velasco" for only $60.

It may be that Willis first turned his attention to the stage through the action of James William Wallack, who addressed the following letter to George P. Morris, for insertion in *The Mirror,* together with an advertisement. Wallack at the time was on the eve of sailing for Europe:

> Packet Ship *Sheffield.*
> May 28th, 1836.

My dear Sir:

I am most anxious to procure, on my return to the United States, an original play by a native author, and on some striking and powerful American subject. Of course, I am desirous that the principal character should be made prominent, and adapted to me and my dramatick capabilities, such as they may happen to be. Will you be kind enough to offer for such a production the sum of *one thousand dollars,* which I will pay to any writer who will present the best piece of the description alluded to? All manuscripts will be submitted to a committee of literary gentlemen of your city, and to the author of the play selected by them will be adjudged the premium just specified. Be kind enough to insert the enclosed advertisement in *The Mirror;* and with very many thanks for the kind manner in which you have interested yourself in this matter for me, I am, my dear sir, your obliged and faithful servant,

> James Wallack.

The notice which accompanied this letter was addressed "To Native Dramatick Authors", and began, "The subscriber offers the sum of *one thousand dollars* for the best original play upon an attractive and striking subject in American history. The principal part to be adapted to his style of acting."

Although there is no evidence that Willis competed for this prize, he must have thought it a good idea to try his hand at a play for such a distinctive romantic actor as Wallack. Not only that, but his return from abroad had probably inspired him to convert into dramatic form some of the romantic material he had picked up in Italy and elsewhere. In comparison with what Forrest was offering to his Philadelphia group of writers, Wallack's offer was munificent, especially as it carried with it a benefit, worth at least five or seven hundred dollars additional.

"Bianca" was given at the New York Park Theatre, on August 25, 1837, followed soon after by another piece for Miss Clifton, entitled "The Kentucky Heiress", November 29, 1837. We are told that on September 1, 1837, Turner Merrit, of the Park Theatre, thinking Willis a mine of usefulness for his purpose, agreed to pay him one thousand dollars, if, within a year from date, he would write another piece for Miss Clifton. The result was "The Betrothal." Under the impetus of the financial offer, Willis fulfilled his contract in two months' time, and *The Mirror* announced its performance, November 25, 1837. It met with great disfavour from the press and public, and probably was very bad, for Willis never had it published; nor did he print even a part of "Imei, the Jew", which occupied his attention, according to Beers, during January, 1839.

He then turned his attention to a play which he successively called "Dying for Him", "The Usurer Matched", and finally "Tortesa, the Usurer". Not that he began it then, for, early in the spring of 1838, *The Mirror* published four installments of it. But he probably touched it up for the coming production. He and Wallack had come to an agreement, whereby Willis was to receive one-half the proceeds of the 4th, 9th, and 18th nights, it being understood that each night $300 was first to be deducted for expenses. If Wallack took the play to England, which was most likely, then Willis was to have one-third the proceeds of the 4th, 8th, and 12th performances.

These were the financial conditions under which "Tortesa,

the Usurer" was presented at the New York National Theatre, on April 8, 1839. One can imagine that, in the writing of this piece, Willis was under the spell of Wallack's acting, which he himself characterized, after witnessing his "Don Cæsar de Bazan", in London, as marked by "abandon". Be it recorded that the National, which had passed under Wallack's management, on September 4, 1837, was the first of those Wallack theatres, which, in the annals of the American Theatre, were to play such a distinctive part in maintaining a high standard of acting.*

When Wallack took the piece to England, and appeared in it at the Surrey Theatre, August, 1839, he was hard pressed for money, and, in consequence, Willis, according to his own correspondence, suffered.

I gave it up [he wrote] and he pocketed the whole. By the way, I have two more nights at the National, which I authorize you to look after and receive for me. The 13th and 18th representations remain for me. Will you see if you can get Kean or Vandenhoff in for *Angelo* on those nights? I have seen a great deal of Kean since I have been here, and he is truly a good fellow and a great actor. He breakfasted with us a day or two ago, and Mary was very much interested that he should do well in America. I have given Vandenhoff "Bianca" for himself and daughter to play in America. She is a fine, handsome girl, but I have not seen her play.

"Tortesa" was to affect the life of another Wallack. In Lester Wallack's "Memories", I find he mentions the fact that, after his first visit to America, he, now attained to man's estate, assumed the rôle of *Angelo,* originally played by Edmond S. Conner.

It does not take much to recognize in "Tortesa" the influence of "Romeo and Juliet" and "A Winter's Tale"; much more so than of "The Merchant of Venice", which Beers claims Wallack must have had in mind while picturing the main character. That the outlines of his story were taken

* See M. J. Moses' "Actor-Families," chapter on The Wallacks.

from Italian literature is acknowledged by Willis himself, who had turned to the Florentine story of "Genevra d'Amori". A comparative study of the tale, as it occurs in literature, would be of interest. One would have to consider Domenico Maria Manni's "La Sepolta Viva", translated by Thomas Roscoe in his "Italian Novelists" (1825, vol. iv), and also Shelley's "Ginevra", written in 1821.

In his famous essay on the American Drama, published in the *American Whig Review,* for 1845, and earlier in *Burton's Gentleman's Magazine,* for August, 1839, Poe has certain pointed strictures to make about "Tortesa". He says:

Tortesa will afford plentiful examples of . . . irrelevancy of intrigue,—of this misconception of the nature and of the capacities of plot. We have said that our digest of the story is more easy of comprehension than the details of Mr. Willis. . . . As a drama of character, "Tortesa" is by no means open to so many objections as when we view it in the light of its plot; but it is still faulty. The merits are so exceedingly negative, that it is difficult to say anything about them. . . . *Angelo* may be regarded simply as the medium through which Mr. Willis conveys to the reader his own glowing feelings. . . . Having spoken thus of "Tortesa"—in terms of nearly unmitigated censure—our readers may be surprised to hear us say that we think highly of the drama as a whole—and have little hesitation in ranking it before most of the dramas of Sheridan Knowles. Its leading faults are those of the modern drama generally. . . .

And another contemporary critic, writing in the *North American Review* for July, 1840, speaks as relentlessly after his examination. For he says:

It cannot be denied that this piece shows a good deal of dramatic genius; but still, when we look carefully into the plot, we must admit that it is very imperfectly constructed; that the parts are not well harmonized; that it has violent changes of character and transitions of feeling, which may pass unnoticed amidst the hurry of the stage and the display of scenic pomp, but which

stand prominently forward, when the play is subjected to
the reader's unclouded judgment. How, for instance,
when the guards were set around the sanctuary which
held the supposed body of *Isabella,* to prevent *Angelo's*
entrance, could the lady herself escape? how could she
get out, when *Angelo* could not get in? And how could
Tortesa be so wrought upon, first, by the supposed death
of *Isabella,* and, secondly, by her unexpected return to
life, by which it appeared that he had been deceived;
how, under all these circumstances, could he be so
wrought upon as to fall actually in love with the lady,
and, through the influence of this very love, to do a deed
of munificent generosity for the purpose of promoting
her marriage with his rival? It seems to us, that this
is a revolution of character which sets dramatic propriety and probability at defiance.

In this vein we ourselves might analyze "Tortesa, the
Usurer", and every play that consistently groups itself under
the name of "romantic comedy". Whether or not Willis had
high regard for the finished product is nowhere indicated.
He published it, he distinctly states, to save it from piracy.
But this much can be said for "Tortesa, the Usurer": its
poetry is far from mediocre, even though in its feeling and,
often in its expression, it is imitative; and its character of
Tortesa is an excellent vehicle for such an actor as the elder
Wallack, and as his son, Lester,—a picturesque, romantic
type which has disappeared for the time being from our
stage.

TORTESA, THE USURER

Dramatis Personæ and Cast of Characters
As given by Wallack at the New York National Theatre
April 8, 1839

Duke of Florence..................... Mr. Rogers
Count Falcone........................ Mr. T. Matthews
Tortesa, a Usurer.................... Mr. Wallack
Angelo, a young painter.............. Mr. Conner
Tomaso, his servant.................. Mr. Lambert

Isabella de Falcone................... Miss Monier
Zippa, a Glover's daughter........... Mrs. W. Sefton

Other characters—A Counsellor, a page, the Count's secretary, a Tradesman, a Monk, Lords, Ladies, Officers, Soldiers, etc.

PREFACE

The following Drama was produced last year at the NATIONAL THEATRE, NEW YORK, by JAMES H. WALLACK—himself playing *Tortesa*. To his most admirable personation of this character, and the care and skill with which it was brought out under his management, the Author feels that he is indebted for its flattering and signal success in his own country. At the moment of publication, MR. WALLACK is about to appear in it at the SURREY THEATRE; and for its success, as far as the Actor can insure it the Author has no fears. To the later tribunal, of the Reader's judgment, he commits it tremblingly.

London, 12th July, 1839.*

* This preface is not in the American edition. Instead there is the following:

PRESENTATION

To save his country the perpetuation of a wrong, the Author anticipates the law, by presenting this published Play to whomever pleases to perform it for his own benefit.

DRAMATIS PERSONÆ

Duke of Florence.
Count Falcone.
Tortesa—*a usurer.*
Angelo—*a young painter.*
Tomaso—*his servant.*

*　　*　　*

Isabella de Falcone.
Zippa—*a Glover's daughter.*
Other characters—*a Counsellor, a page, the Count's Secretary, a Tradesman, a Monk, Lords, Ladies, Officers, Soldiers, &c.*

TORTESA THE USURER

ACT I.

Scene I.

A drawing-room in Tortesa's *house.* Servant *discovered reading the bill of a tradesman, who is in attendance.*

Servant [*reading*].

"Silk hose, doublet of white satin, twelve shirts of lawn."
He'll not pay it to-day, good mercer!

Tradesman.

How, master Gaspar? When I was assured of the gold on delivery? If it be a *credit* account, look you, there must be a new bill. The charge is for ready money.

Servant.

Tut-tut—man, you know not whom you serve. My master is as likely to overpay you if you are civil, as to keep you a year out of your money if you push him when he is cross'd.

Tradesman.

Why, this is the humor of a spendthrift, not the careful way of a usurer.

Servant.

Usurer! humph. Well, it may be he is—to the rich! But the heart of the Signor Tortesa, let me tell you, is like the bird's wing—the dark side is turned upwards. To those who look up to him he shows neither spot nor stain! Hark! I

263

hear his wheels in the court. Step to the ante-room—for he
has that on his hands to-day which may make him impatient.
Quick! Give way! I'll bring you to him if I can find a
time.

TORTESA [*speaking without*].

What ho! Gaspar!

SERVANT.

Signor!

TORTESA.

My keys! Bring me my keys!

[*Enter* TORTESA, *followed by* COUNT FALCONE.]

Come in, Count.

FALCONE.

You're well lodged.

TORTESA.

The Duke waits for you
To get to horse. So, briefly, there's the deed!
You have your lands back, and your daughter's mine—
So ran the *bargain!*

FALCONE [*coldly*].

She's *betroth'd*, sir, to you!

TORTESA.

Not a half hour since, and you hold the parchment!
A free transaction, see you!—for you're *paid*,
And I'm but *promised!*

FALCONE [*aside*].

(What a slave is this,
To give my daughter to! My daughter! Psha!
I'll think but of my lands, my precious *lands!*)
Sir, the Duke sets forth—

TORTESA.

Use no ceremony!
Yet stay! A word! Our nuptials follow quick
On your return?

FALCONE.

That hour, if it so please you!

TORTESA.

And what's the bargain if her humor change?

FALCONE.

The lands are yours, again—'tis understood so.

TORTESA.

Yet, still a word! You leave her with her maids.
I have a right in her by this betrothal.
Seal your door up till you come back again!
I'd have no foplings tampering with my wife!
None of your painted jackdaws from the court,
Sneering and pitying her! My lord Falcone!
Shall she be private?

FALCONE [aside].

(Patience! for my lands!)
You shall control my door, sir, and my daughter!
Farewell now! [Exit FALCONE.

TORTESA.

Oh, omnipotence of money!
Ha! ha! Why, there's the haughtiest nobleman
That walks in Florence. He!—whom I have bearded—
Checked—made conditions to—shut up his daughter—
And all with *money!* They should pull down **churches**
And worship it! Had I been *poor,* that man
Would see me rot ere give his hand to me.
I—as I stand here—dress'd thus—looking thus—

The same in all—save money in my purse—
He would have scorn'd to let me come so near
That I could breathe on him! Yet, that were little—
For pride sometimes outdoes humility,
And your great man will please to be familiar,
To show how he can stoop. But halt you there!
He *has* a jewel that you may not name!
His *wife's* above you! You're no company
For his most noble *daughter!* You are brave—
'Tis nothing! comely—nothing! honorable—
You are a phœnix of all human virtues—
But, while your blood's mean, there's a frozen bar
Betwixt you and a *lady,* that will melt—
Not with religion—scarcely with the grave—
But like a mist, with *money!*

Enter a SERVANT.

SERVANT.

                Please you, sir!
A tradesman waits to see you!

TORTESA.

                Let him in! [*Exit* SERVANT.
What need have I of forty generations
To build my name up? I have bought with money
The fairest daughter of their haughtiest line!
Bought her! Falcone's daughter for so much!
No wooing in't! Ha! ha! I harp'd on that
Till my lord winced! "My bargain!" still "my *bargain!*"
Nought of my *bride!* Ha! ha! 'Twas excellent!

[*Enter* TRADESMAN.]

What's thy demand?

TRADESMAN.

Ten ducats, please your lordship!

TORTESA.

Out on "your lordship!" There are *twelve* for ten!
Does a lord pay like that? Learn some name sweeter
To my ears than "Your lordship!" I'm no lord!
Give me thy quittance! Now, begone! Who waits?

SERVANT.

The Glover's daughter, please you, sir!

Enter ZIPPA.

TORTESA.

Come in,
My pretty neighbor! What! my bridal gloves!
Are they brought home?

ZIPPA.

The signor pays so well,
He's well served.

TORTESA.

Um! why, pertinently answered!
And yet, my pretty one, the words were sweeter
In any mouth than yours!

ZIPPA.

That's easy true!

TORTESA.

I would 'twere *liking* that had spurr'd your service—
Not *money*, Zippa, sweet! [*She presents her parcel to him,
with a meaning air.*]

ZIPPA.

Your bridal gloves, sir!

TORTESA [*aside*].

(What a fair shrew it is!) My gloves are paid for!
And will be thrown aside when worn a little.

ZIPPA.

What then, sir!

TORTESA.

Why, the bride is paid for, too!
And may be thrown aside, when worn a little!

ZIPPA.

You mock me now!

TORTESA.

         You know Falcone's palace,
And lands, here, by Fiesole? I bought them
For so much money of his creditors,
And gave them to him, in a plain, round bargain,
For his proud daughter! What think you of that?

ZIPPA.

What else but that you loved her!

TORTESA.

         As I love
The thing I give my money for—no more!

ZIPPA.

You *mean* to love her?

TORTESA.

        'Twas not in the bargain!

ZIPPA.

Why, what a monster do you make yourself!
Have you no heart?

TORTESA.

A loving one, for you!
Nay, never frown! I marry this lord's daughter
To please a *devil* that inhabits me!
But there's an *angel* in me—not so strong—
And this last loves you!

ZIPPA.

Thanks for your weak angel!
I'd sooner 'twere the devil!

TORTESA.

Both were yours!
But for the burning fever that I have
To pluck at their proud blood.

ZIPPA.

Why, this poor lady
Cannot have harm'd you!

TORTESA.

Forty thousand times!
She's noble-born—there's one wrong in her cradle!
She's proud—why, that makes every pulse an insult—
Sixty a minute! She's profuse in smiles
On those who are, to *me*, as stars to glow-worms—
So I'm disparaged! I have pass'd her by,
Summer and winter, and she ne'er looked on me!
Her youth has been one tissue of contempt!
Her lovers, and her tutors, and her heart,
Taught her to scorn the low-born—*that am I!*
Would you have more?

ZIPPA.

Why, this is moon-struck madness.

TORTESA.

I'd have her *mine*, for all this—jewell'd, perfumed—
Just as they've worshipped her at court—my slave!

They've mewed her breath up in their silken beds—
Blanch'd her with baths—fed her on delicate food—
Guarded the unsunn'd dew upon her skin—
For some *lord's* pleasure! If I could not get her,
There's a contempt in that, would make my forehead
Hot in my grave!

ZIPPA [*aside*].

　　　　　　(Now heaven forbid *my* fingers
Should make your bridal gloves!) Forgive me, Signor!
I'll take these back, so please you! [*Takes up the parcel
again.*]

TORTESA [*not listening to her*].

　　　　　　But for this—
This devil at my heart, thou shouldst have wedded
The richest commoner in Florence, Zippa!
Tell me thou wouldst!

ZIPPA [*aside*].

　　　　　　(Stay! stay! A thought! If I
Could *feign* to love him, and so work on him
To put this match off, and at last to break it—
'Tis possible—and so befriend this lady,
Whom, from my soul, I pity! Nay, I will!)
Signor Tortesa!

TORTESA.

　　　　　　You've been dreaming now,
How you would brave it in your lady-gear;
Was't not so?

ZIPPA.

No!

TORTESA.

What then?

ZIPPA.

I *had* a thought,

If I dare speak it.

TORTESA.

Nay, nay, speak it out!

ZIPPA.

I had forgot your riches, and I thought
How lost you were!

TORTESA.

How *lost?*

ZIPPA.

Your qualities,
Which far outweigh your treasure, thrown away
On one who does not love you!

TORTESA.

Thrown away?

ZIPPA.

Is it not so to have a gallant shape,
And no eye to be proud on't—to be full
Of all that makes men dangerous to women,
And marry where you're scorned?

TORTESA.

There's reason there!

ZIPPA.

You're wise in meaner riches! You have gold,
'Tis out at interest!—lands, palaces,
They bring in rent. The gifts of nature only,
Worth to you, Signor, more than all your gold,
Lie profitless and idle. Your fine stature—

TORTESA.

Why—so, so!

ZIPPA.

Speaking eyes—

TORTESA.

Ay—passable!

ZIPPA.

Your voice, uncommon musical—

TORTESA.

Nay, *there,*
I think you may be honest!

ZIPPA.

And your look,
In all points lofty, like a gentleman!
[*Aside.*]   (That last must choke him!)

TORTESA.

You've a judgment, Zippa,
That makes me wonder at you! We are both
Above our breeding—I have often thought so—
And lov'd you—but to-day so more than ever,
That my revenge must have drunk up my life,
To still sweep over it. But when I think
Upon that proud lord and his scornful daughter—
I say not you're forgot—*myself am lost*—
And love and memory with me! I must go
And visit her! I'll see you to the door—
Come, Zippa, come!

ZIPPA [*aside*].

(I, too, will visit her!
You're a brave Signor, but against two women
You'll find your wits all wanted!)

TORTESA.

Come away!
I must look on my bargain! my good bargain!
Ha! ha! my *bargain!* [*Exeunt.*

SCENE II.

The Painter's Studio. ANGELO *painting.* TOMASO *in the fore-ground, arranging a meagre repast.*

TOMASO.

A thrice-pick'd bone, a stale crust, and—excellent water!
Will you to breakfast, Master Angelo?

ANGELO.

Look on this touch, good Tomaso, if it be not life itself—
[*Draws him before his easel.*] Now, what think'st thou?

TOMASO.

Um—fair! fair enough!

ANGELO.

No more?

TOMASO.

Till it mend my breakfast, I will never praise it! Fill me
up that *outline,* Master Angelo! [*Takes up the naked bone.*]
Color me that water! To what end dost thou dabble there?

ANGELO.

I am weary of telling thee to what end. Have patience,
Tomaso!

TOMASO [*coaxingly*].

Wouldst thou but paint the goldsmith a sign, now, in good
fair letters!

ANGELO.

Have I no genius for the art, think'st thou?

TOMASO.

Thou! ha! ha!

ANGELO.

By thy laughing, thou wouldst say *no!*

TOMASO.

Thou a genius! Look! Master Angelo! Have I not seen thee every day since thou wert no bigger than thy pencil?

ANGELO.

And if thou hast?

TOMASO.

Do I not know thee from crown to heel? Dost thou not come in at that door as I do?—sit down in that chair as I do? —eat, drink, and sleep, as I do? Dost thou not call me Tomaso, and I thee Angelo?

ANGELO.

Well!

TOMASO.

Then how canst thou have genius? Are there no marks? Would I clap thee on the back, and say good morrow? Nay, look thee! would I stand here telling thee in my wisdom what thou art, if thou wert a genius? Go to, Master Angelo! I love thee well, but thou art comprehensible!

ANGELO.

But think'st thou never of my works, Tomaso?

TOMASO.

Thy works! Do I not grind thy paints? Do I not see thee take up thy palette, place thy foot thus, and dab here, dab there? I tell thee thou hast never done stroke yet, I could not take the same brush and do after thee. Thy works, truly!

ANGELO.

How think'st thou would Donatello paint, if he were here?

TOMASO.

Donatello! I will endeavor to show thee! [*Takes the palette and brush with a mysterious air.*] The picture should be there! His pencil [*throws down* ANGELO'S *pencil, and seizes a broom*], his pencil should be as long as this broom! He should raise it thus—with his eyes rolling thus—and with his body thrown back thus!

ANGELO.

What then?

TOMASO.

Then he should see something in the air—a sort of a hm-ha-r-r-rrr—(you understand). And he first strides off here and looks at it—then he strides off there and looks at it —then he looks at his long brush—then he makes a dab! dash! flash! [*Makes three strokes across* ANGELO'S *picture.*]

ANGELO.

Villain, my picture! Tomaso! [*Seizes his sword.*] With thy accursed broom thou hast spoiled a picture Donatello could ne'er have painted! Say thy prayers, for, by the Virgin!—

TOMASO.

Murder! murder! help! Oh, my good master! **Oh, my** kind master!

ANGELO.

Wilt say thy prayers, or die a sinner? Quick! or thou'rt dead ere 'tis thought on!

TOMASO.

Help! help! mercy! oh mercy!

Enter the DUKE *hastily, followed by* FALCONE *and attendants.*

DUKE.

Who calls so loudly! What! drawn swords at mid-day!
Disarm him! Now, what mad-cap youth art thou [*To*
     ANGELO.]
To fright this peaceful artist from his toil?
Rise up, sir! [*To* TOMASO.]

ANGELO [*aside.*]

(Could my luckless star have brought
The Duke here at no other time!)

DUKE [*looking round on the pictures*].

                          Why, here's
Matter worth stumbling on! By Jove, a picture
Of admirable work! Look here, Falcone!
Did'st think there was a hand unknown in Florence
Could lay on color with a skill like this?

TOMASO [*aside to* ANGELO].

Did'st thou hear that?
     [DUKE *and* FALCONE *admire the pictures in dumb show.*]

ANGELO [*aside to* TOMASO].

(The palette's on thy thumb—
Swear 'tis thy work!)

TOMASO.

Mine, master?

ANGELO.

                     Seest thou not
The shadow of my fault will fall upon it
While I stand here a culprit? The Duke loves thee

As one whom he has chanc'd to serve at need,
And kindness mends the light upon a picture,
I know that well!

FALCONE [*to* TOMASO].

The Duke would know your name, sir!

TOMASO [*as* ANGELO *pulls him by the sleeve*].

Tom—Angelo, my lord!

DUKE [*to* FALCONE].

We've fallen here
Upon a treasure!

FALCONE.

'Twas a lucky chance
That led you in, my lord!

DUKE.

I blush to think
That I might ne'er have found such excellence
But for a chance cry, thus! Yet now 'tis found
I'll cherish it, believe me.

FALCONE.

'Tis a duty
Your Grace is never slow to.

DUKE.

I've a thought—
If you'll consent to it?

FALCONE.

Before 'tis spoken,
My gracious liege!

DUKE.

You know how well my duchess
Loves your fair daughter?   Not as maid of honor
Lost to our service, but as parting child,
We grieve to lose her.

FALCONE.

My good lord!

DUKE.

Nay, nay—
She is betroth'd now, and you needs must wed her!
My thought was, to surprise my grieving duchess
With a resemblance of your daughter, done
By this rare hand, here.   'Tis a thought well found,
You'll say it is?

FALCONE [*hesitatingly*].

Your Grace is bound away
On a brief journey.   Were't not best put off
Till our return?

DUKE [*laughing*].

I see you fear to let
The sun shine on your rose-bud till she bloom
Fairly in wedlock.   But this painter, see you,
Is an old man, of a poor, timid bearing,
And may be trusted to look close upon her.
Come, come!   I'll have my way!   Good Angelo,
[*To* TOMASO.]
A pen and ink.   And you, my lord Falcone!
Write a brief missive to your gentle daughter
I dared not pluck at Fortune.

FALCONE.

I will, Duke.   [*Writes.*

ANGELO [*aside.*]

Now
Shall I go back or forwards? If he writes
Admit this Angelo, why, I am he,
And that rare phœnix, hidden from the world,
Sits to my burning pencil. She's a beauty
Without a parallel, they say, in Florence.
Her picture'll be remembered! Let the Duke
Rend me with horses, it shall ne'er be said
I dared not pluck at Fortune!

TOMASO [*aside to* ANGELO].

Signor!

ANGELO.

(Hush!
Betray me, and I'll kill thee!)

DUKE.

Angelo!

ANGELO [*aside to* TOMASO].

Speak, or thou diest!

TOMASO [*to the* DUKE].

My lord!

DUKE.

Thou hast grown old
In the attainment of an excellence
Well worth thy time and study. The clear touch,
Won only by the patient toil of years,
Is on your fair works yonder.

TOMASO [*astonished*].

Those, my lord!

DUKE.

I shame I never saw them until now,
But here's a new beginning. Take this missive
From Count Falcone to his peerless daughter.
I'd have a picture of her for my palace.
Paint me her beauty as I know you can,
And as you do it well, my favor to you
Shall make up for the past.

TOMASO [*as* ANGELO *pulls his sleeve*],

         Your Grace is kind!

DUKE.

For this rude youth, name you his punishment!

[*Turns to* ANGELO.]

His sword was drawn upon an unarm'd man.
He shall be fined, or, as you please, imprisoned.
Speak!

TOMASO.

If your Grace would bid him pay—

DUKE.

           What sum?

TOMASO.

Some twenty flasks of wine, my gracious liege,
If it so please you. 'Tis a thriftless servant
I keep for love I bore to his dead father.
But all his faults are nothing to a thirst
That sucks my cellar dry!

DUKE.

        He's well let off!
Write out a bond to pay off your first gains
The twenty flasks!

ANGELO.

Most willingly, my liege. [*Writes.*

DUKE [*to* TOMASO].

Are you content?

TOMASO.

Your Grace, I am!

DUKE.

Come then!
Once more to horse! Nay, nay, man, look not black!
Unless your daughter were a wine-flask, trust me
There's no fear of the painter!

FALCONE.

So I think,
And you shall rule me. 'Tis the roughest shell
Hides the good pearl. Adieu, sir! [*To* TOMASO.]
[*Exeunt* DUKE *and* FALCONE.

ANGELO *seizes the missive from* TOMASO, *and strides up and
down the stage, reading it exultingly. After looking at
him a moment,* TOMASO *does the same with the bond ·for
the twenty flasks.*

ANGELO.

Give the letter!
Oh, here is golden opportunity—
The ladder at my foot, the prize above,
And angels beckoning upwards. I will paint
A picture now, that in the eyes of men
Shall live like loving daylight. They shall cease
To praise it for the constant glory of it.
There's not a stone built in the palace wall
But shall let thro' the light of it, and Florence
Shall be a place of pilgrimage for ever
To see the work of low-born Angelo.
Oh that the world were made without a night,

That I could toil while in my fingers play
This dexterous lightning, wasted so in sleep.
I'll out, and muse how I shall paint this beauty,
So, wile the night away.   [*Exit.*

TOMASO [*coming forward with his bond*].

Prejudice aside, that is a pleasant-looking piece of paper!
[*Holds it off, and regards it with a pleased air.*] Your bond
to *pay,* now, is an ill-visaged rascal—you would know him
across a church—nay—with the wind fair, *smell* him a good
league! But this has, in some sort, a smile. It is not like
other paper. It reads mellifluously. Your name is in the
right end of it for music. Let me dwell upon it! [*Unfolds
it, and reads*] "I, Tomaso, promise to pay"—stay! "I
Tomaso—I, Tomaso, promise to pay to Angelo my master
twenty flasks of wine!" [*Rubs his eyes, and turns the note
over and over.*] There's a damnable twist in it that spoils
all. "I, Tomaso"—why, that's I. And "I promise to pay"—
Now, I promise no such thing! [*Turns it upside down, and,
after trying in vain to alter the reading, tears it in two.*]
There are some men that cannot write ten words in their
own language without a blunder. Out, filthy scraps. If the
Glover's daughter have not compassion upon me, I die of
thirst! I'll seek her out! A pest on ignorance! [*Pulls his
hat sulkily over his eyes, and walks off.*]

SCENE III.

An Apartment in the Falcone Palace. ANGELO *discovered
listening.*

ANGELO.

Did I hear footsteps? [*He listens.*] Fancy plays me tricks
In my impatience for this lovely wonder!
That window's to the north! The light falls cool.
I'll set my easel here, and sketch her—Stay!
How shall I do that? Is she proud or sweet?
Will she sit silent, or converse and smile?
Will she be vexed or pleased to have a stranger

Pry through her beauty for the soul that's in it?
Nay, then I heard a footstep—she is here!

Enter ISABELLA, *reading her father's missive.*

ISABELLA.

"The duke would have your picture for the duchess
Done by this rude man, Angelo! Receive him
With modest privacy, and let your kindness
Be measured by his merit, not his garb."

ANGELO.

Fair lady!

ISABELLA.

Who speaks?

ANGELO.

Angelo!

ISABELLA.

You've come, sir,
To paint a dull face, trust me!

ANGELO [*aside.*]

(Beautiful,
Beyond all dreaming!)

ISABELLA.

I've no smiles to show you,
Not ev'n a mock one! Shall I sit?

ANGELO.

No, lady!
I'll steal your beauty while you move, as well!
So you but breathe, the air still brings to me
That which outdoes all pencilling.

ISABELLA [*walking apart*].

His voice
It not a rude one. What a fate is mine,
When ev'n the chance words on a poor youth's tongue,
Contrasted with the voice which I should love,
Seems rich and musical!

ANGELO [*to himself, as he draws*].

How like a swan,
Drooping his small head to a lily-cup,
She curves that neck of pliant ivory!
I'll paint her thus!

ISABELLA [*aside*].

Forgetful where he is,
He thinks aloud. This is, perhaps, the rudeness
My father fear'd might anger me.

ANGELO.

What color
Can match the clear red of those glorious lips?
Say it were possible to trace the arches,
Shaped like the drawn bow of the god of love—
How tint them, after?

ISABELLA.

Still, he thinks not of me
But murmurs to his picture. 'Twere sweet praise,
Were it a lover whispering it. I'll listen,
As I walk, still.

ANGELO.

They say, a cloudy veil
Hangs ever at the crystal-gate of heaven,
To bar the issue of its blinding glory.
So droop those silken lashes to an eye
Mortal could never paint!

ISABELLA.

There's flattery,
Would draw down angels!

ANGELO.

Now, what alchymy
Can mock the rose and lily of her cheek!
I must look closer on't! [*Advancing.*] Fair lady, please you,
I'll venture to your side.

ISABELLA.

Sir!

ANGELO [*examining her cheek*].

There's a mixture
Of white and red here, that defeats my skill.
If you'll forgive me, I'll observe an instant,
How the bright blood and the transparent pearl
Melt to each other!

ISABELLA [*receding from him*].

You're too free, sir!

ANGELO [*with surprise*].
Madam!

ISABELLA [*aside*].

And yet, I think not so. He must look on it,
To paint it well.

ANGELO.

Lady! the daylight's precious!
Pray you, turn to me! In my study, here,
I've tried to fancy how that ivory shoulder
Leads the white light off from your arching neck,
But cannot, for the envious sleeve that hides it.
Please you, displace it! [*Raises his hand to the sleeve.*]

ISABELLA.

Sir, you are too bold!

ANGELO.

Pardon me, lady! Nature's masterpiece
Should be beyond your hiding, or my praise!
Were you less marvellous, I were too bold;
But there's a pure divinity in beauty,
Which the true eye of art looks on with reverence,
Though, like the angels, it were all unclad!
You have no right to hide it!

ISABELLA.

How? No right?

ANGELO.

'Tis the religion of our art, fair madam!
That, by oft looking on the type divine
In which we first were moulded, men remember
The heav'n they're born to! You've an errand here,
To show how look the angels. But, as Vestals
Cherish the sacred fire, yet let the priest
Light his lamp at it for a thousand altars,
So is your beauty unassoiled, though I
Ravish a copy for the shut-out world!

ISABELLA [aside].

Here is the wooing that should win a maid!
Bold, yet respectful—free, yet full of honor!
I never saw a youth with gentler eyes;
I never heard a voice that pleased me more;
Let me look on him!

Enter TORTESA, unperceived.

ANGELO.

In a form like yours,
All parts are perfect, madam! yet, unseen,

Impossible to fancy. With your leave
I'll see your hand unglov'd.

ISABELLA [*removing her glove*].

I have no heart
To keep it from you, signor! There it is!

ANGELO [*taking it in his own*].

Oh, God! how beautiful thy works may be!
Inimitably perfect! Let me look
Close on the tracery of these azure veins!
With what a delicate and fragile thread
They weave their subtle mesh beneath the skin,
And meet, all blushing, in these rosy nails!
How soft the texture of these tapering fingers!
How exquisite the wrist! How perfect all!

TORTESA *rushes forward*.

TORTESA.

Now have I heard enough! Why, what are you,
To palm the hand of my betrothed bride
With this licentious freedom?

[ANGELO *turns composedly to his work*.]

And you, madam!
With a first troth scarce cold upon your lips—
Is this your chastity?

ISABELLA.

My father's roof
Is over me! I'm not your wife!

TORTESA.

Bought! paid for!
The wedding toward—have I no right in you?
Your father, at my wish, bade you be private;
Is this your obedience?

ISABELLA.

　　　　　　　　Count Falcone's will,
Has, to his daughter, ever been a law;
This, in prosperity—and now, when chance
Frowns on his broken fortunes, I were dead
To love and pity, were not soul and body
Spent for his smallest need! I did consent
To wed his ruthless creditor for this!
I would have sprung into the sea, the grave,
As questionless and soon! My *troth* is yours!
But I'm not wedded yet, and, till I am,
The hallowed honor that protects a maid
Is round me, like a circle of bright fire!
A savage would not cross it—nor shall you!
I'm mistress of my presence. Leave me, sir!

TORTESA.

There's a possession of some lordly acres
Sold to Falcone for that lily hand!
The deed's delivered, and the hand's my own!
I'll see that no man looks on't.

ISABELLA.

　　　　　　　Shall a lady
Bid you begone twice?

TORTESA.

　　　　　　　Twenty times, if't please you!

She looks at ANGELO, *who continues tranquilly painting.*

ISABELLA.

Does he not wear a sword! Is he a coward,
That he can hear this man heap insult on me,
And ne'er fall on him?

TORTESA.

　　　　　　　Lady! to your chamber!
I have a touch to give this picture, here,
But want no model for't. Come, come. [*Offers to take her
　　by the arm.*]

ISABELLA.

Stand back!
Now, will he see this wretch lay hands on me,
And never speak? He cannot be a coward!
No, no! some other reason—not a coward!
I could not love a coward!

TORTESA.

If you will,
Stay where you're better miss'd—'tis at your pleasure;
I'll hew your kisses from the saucy lips
Of this bold painter—look on't, if you will!
And first, to mar his picture!

[*He strikes at the canvas, when* ANGELO *suddenly draws,
attacks and disarms him.*]

ANGELO.

Hold! What wouldst thou?
Fool! madman! dog! What wouldst thou with my picture?
Speak—But thy life would not bring back a ray
Of precious daylight, and I cannot waste it!
Begone! begone!

[*Throws* TORTESA'S *sword from the window and returns to
his picture.*]

I'll back to paradise!
'Twas this touch that he marr'd! So! fair again!

TORTESA [*going out*].

I'll find you, sir, when I'm in cooler blood!
And, madam, *you!* or Count Falcone *for* you,
Shall rue this scorn!   [*Exit.*

ISABELLA [*looking at* ANGELO].

Lost in his work once more!
I shall be jealous of my very picture!
Yet one who can forget his passions so—

Peril his life, and, losing scarce a breath,
Turn to his high, ambitious toil again—
Must have a heart for whose belated waking
Queens might keep vigil!

ANGELO.

                    Twilight falls, fair lady!
I must give o'er! Pray heaven, the downy wing
Of its most loving angel guard your beauty!
Good night! [*Goes out with a low reverence.*]

ISABELLA.

Good night!

[*She looks after him a moment, and then walks thoughtfully off the stage.*]

END OF THE FIRST ACT.

ACT II.

SCENE I.

TOMASO *discovered sitting at his supper, with a bottle of water before him.*

TOMASO.

Water! [*Sips a little with a grimace.*] I think, since the world was drowned in it, it has tasted of sinners. The pious throat refuses it. Other habits grow pleasant with use—but the drinking of water lessens the liking of it. Now, why should not some rivers run wine? There are varieties in the *eatables*—will any wise man tell me why there should be but one *drinkable* in nature—and that water? My mind's made up—it's the curse of transgression.

[*A rap at the door.*]

Come in!

Enter ZIPPA, *with a basket and bottle.*

ZIPPA.

Good even, Tomaso!

TOMASO.

Zippa! I had a presentiment—

ZIPPA.

What! of my coming?

TOMASO.

No—of thy bottle! Look! I was stinting myself in water to leave room!

ZIPPA.

The reason is superfluous. There would be room in thee for wine, if thou wert drowned in the sea.

TOMASO.

God forbid!

ZIPPA.

What—that thou shouldst be drowned?

TOMASO.

No—but that being drowned, I should have room for wine.

ZIPPA.

Why, now?—why?

TOMASO.

If I had room for wine, I should want it—and to want wine in the bottom of the sea, were a plague of Sodom.

ZIPPA.

Where's Angelo?

TOMASO.

What's in thy bottle? Show! Show!

ZIPPA.

Tell me where he is—what he has done since yesterday—what thought on—what said—how he has looked, and if he still loves me; and when thou art thirsty with truth-telling—(dry work for such a liar as thou art,)—thou shalt learn what is in my bottle!

TOMASO.

Nay—learning be hanged!

ZIPPA.

So says the fool!

TOMASO.

Speak advisedly! Was not Adam blest till he knew good and evil?

ZIPPA.

Right for once.

TOMASO.

Then he lost Paradise by too much learning.

ZIPPA.

Ha! ha! Hadst thou been consulted, we should still be there!

TOMASO.

Snug! I would have had my inheritance in a small vine-yard!

ZIPPA.

Tell me what I ask of thee.

TOMASO.

Thou shalt have a piece of news for a cup of wine—pay and take—till thy bottle be dry!

ZIPPA.

Come on, then! and if thou must lie, let it be flattery. That's soonest forgiven.

TOMASO.

And last forgotten! Pour out! [*She pours a cup full, and gives him.*] The Duke was here yesterday.—

ZIPPA.

Lie the first!

TOMASO.

And made much of my master's pictures.

ZIPPA.

Nay—that would have made two good lies. Thou'rt prodigal of stuff!

TOMASO.

Pay two glasses, then, and square the reckoning!

ZIPPA.

Come! Lie the third!

TOMASO.

What wilt thou wager it's a lie, that Angelo is painting a court lady for the Duchess?

ZIPPA.

Oh, Lord! Take the bottle! They say there's truth in wine—but as truth is impossible to thee, drink thyself at least, down to probabilities!

TOMASO.

Look you there! When was virtue encouraged? Here have I been telling God's truth, and it goes for a lie. Hang virtue! Produce thy cold chicken, and I'll tell thee a lie for the wings and two for the side-bones and breast. [*Offers to take the chicken.*]

ZIPPA.

Stay! stay! It's for thy master, thou glutton!

TOMASO.

Who's ill a-bed, and forbid meat. [ANGELO *enters.*] I would have told thee so before, but feared to grieve thee. (She *would* have a lie!)

ZIPPA [*starting up*].

Ill! Angelo ill! Is he *very* ill, good Tomaso?

TOMASO.

Very! [*Seizes the chicken, as* ANGELO *claps him on the shoulder.*]

ANGELO.

Will thy tricks never end?

TOMASO.

Ehem! ehem! [*Thrusts the chicken into his pocket.*]

ANGELO.

How art thou, Zippa?

ZIPPA.

Well, dear Angelo! [*Giving him her hand.*] And thou
wert not ill, indeed?

ANGELO.

Never better, by the test of a true hand! I have done
work to-day, I trust will be remembered!

ZIPPA.

Is it true it's a fair lady?

ANGELO.

A lady with a face so angelical, Zippa, that—

ZIPPA.

That thou didst forget mine?

ANGELO.

In truth, I forgot there was such a thing as a world, and so
forgot all in it. I was in heaven!

TOMASO [*aside, as he picks the leg of the chicken*].

(Prosperity is excellent white-wash, and her love is an
old score!)

ZIPPA [*bitterly*].

I am glad thou wert pleased, Angelo!—very glad!

TOMASO [*aside*].

(Glad as an eel to be fried.)

ZIPPA [*aside*].

("In Heaven," was he! If I pay him not that, may my
brains rot! By what right, loving me, is he "in Heaven"
with another?)

TOMASO [*aside*].

(No more wine and cold chicken from that quarter!)

ZIPPA [*aside*].

(Tortesa loves me, and my false game may be played true.
If he wed not Falcone's daughter, he will wed me, and so I
am revenged on this fickle Angelo! I have the heart to
do it!)

ANGELO.

What dost thou muse on, Zippa?

ZIPPA.

On one I love better than thee, Signor!

ANGELO.

What, angry? [*Seizes his pencil.*] Hold there till I sketch
thee! By Jove, thou'rt not half so pretty when thou'rt
pleased!

ZIPPA.

Adieu, Signor! your mockery will have an end! [*Goes
out with an angry air.*]

ANGELO.

What! gone? Nay, I'll come with thee, if thou'rt in
earnest! What whim's this? [*Takes up his hat.*] Ho,
Zippa! [*Follows in pursuit.*]

TOMASO [*pulls the chicken from his pocket*].

Come forth, last of the chickens! She will ne'er forgive
him, and so ends the succession of cold fowl! One glass to
its memory, and then to bed! [*Drinks, and takes up the
candle,*] A woman is generally unsafe—but a jealous one
spoils all confidence in drink. [*Exit, muttering.*

SCENE II.

An Apartment in the Falcone Palace. Enter SERVANT, *showing in* ZIPPA.

SERVANT.

Wait here, if't please you!

ZIPPA.

Thanks! [*Exit* SERVANT.] My heart misgives me!
'Tis a bold errand I am come upon—
And I a stranger to her! Yet, perchance
She needs a friend—the proudest do sometimes—
And mean ones may be welcome. Look! she comes!

ISABELLA.

You wished to speak with me?

ZIPPA.

I *did*—but now
My memory is crept into my eyes;
I cannot think for gazing on your beauty!
Pardon me, lady!

ISABELLA.

You're too fair yourself
To find my face a wonder. Speak! Who are you?

ZIPPA.

Zippa, the Glover's daughter, and your friend!

ISABELLA.

My friend?

ZIPPA.

I said so. You're a noble lady
And I a low-born maid—yet I have come
To offer you my friendship.

ISABELLA.

         This seems strange!

ZIPPA.

I'll make it less so, if you'll give me leave.

ISABELLA.

         You'll please me!

ZIPPA.

   Briefly—for the time is precious
To me as well as you—I have a lover,
A true one, as I think, who yet finds boldness
To seek your hand in marriage.

ISABELLA.

         How? We're rivals!

ZIPPA.

Tortesa loves me, and for that I'd wed him.
Yet I'm not sure I love him more than you—
And you must hate him.

ISABELLA.

         So far freely spoken—
What was your thought in coming to me now?

ZIPPA.

To mar your match with him, and so make mine!

ISABELLA.

Why, free again! Yet, as you love him not
'Tis strange you seek to wed him!

ZIPPA.

         Oh no, madam!
Woman loves once unthinkingly. The heart
Is born with her first love, and, new to joy,

Breathes to the first wind its delicious sweetness,
But gets none back! So comes its bitter wisdom!
When next we think of love, 'tis *who loves us!*
I said Tortesa loved me!

ISABELLA.

You shall have him
With all my heart! See—I'm your friend already!
And friends are equals. So approach, and tell me,
What was this first love like, that you discourse
So prettily upon?

ZIPPA [*aside*].

(Dear Angelo!
'Twill be a happiness to talk of him!)
I loved a youth, kind madam! far beneath
The notice of your eyes, unknown and poor.

ISABELLA.

A handsome youth?

ZIPPA.

Indeed, I thought him so!
But you would not. I loved him out of pity;
No one cared for him.

ISABELLA.

Was he so forlorn?

ZIPPA.

He was our neighbor, and I knew his toil
Was almost profitless; and 'twas a pleasure
To fill my basket from our wasteful table,
And steal, at eve, to sup with him.

ISABELLA [*smiling*].

Why, that
Was charity, indeed! He loved you for it—
Was't not so?

ZIPPA.

He was like a brother to me—
The kindest brother sister ever had.
I built my hopes upon his gentleness:
He had no other quality to love.
Th' ambitious change—so do the fiery-hearted;
The lowly are more constant.

ISABELLA.

                  And yet, he
Was, after all, a false one?

ZIPPA.

                Nay, dear lady!
I'll check my story there! 'Twould end in anger,
Perhaps in tears. If I am not too bold,
Tell me, in turn, of all your worshippers—
Was there ne'er one that pleased you?

ISABELLA [aside].

                (Now could I
Prate to this humble maid, of Angelo,
Till matins rang again!) My gentle Zippa!
I have found all men prompt to talk of love,
Save only one. I will confess to you,
For that one could I die! Yet, so unlike
Your faithless lover must I draw his picture,
That you will wonder how such opposites
Could both be loved of women.

ZIPPA.

                Was he fair,
Or brown?

ISABELLA.

In truth, I marked not his complexion.

ZIPPA.

Tall?

ISABELLA.

That I know not.

ZIPPA.

Well—robust, or slight?

ISABELLA.

I cannot tell, indeed! I heard him speak—
Looked in his eyes, and saw him calm and angered—
And see him now, in fancy, standing there—
Yet know not limb or feature!

ZIPPA.

You but saw

A shadow, lady!

ISABELLA.

Nay—I saw a *soul!*
His eyes were light with it. The forehead lay
Above their fires in calm tranquillity,
As the sky sleeps o'er thunder-clouds. His look
Was mixed of these—earnest, and yet subdued—
Gentle, yet passionate—sometimes half god-like
In its command, then mild and sweet again,
Like a stern angel taught humility!
Oh! when he spoke, my heart stole out to him!
There was a spirit-echo in his voice—
A sound of thought—of under-playing music—
As if, before it ceased in human ears,
The echo was caught up in fairy-land!

ZIPPA.

Was he a courtier, madam?

ISABELLA.

He's as lowly
In birth and fortunes, as your false one, Zippa!
Yet rich in genius, and of that ambition,
That he'll outlast nobility with fame.
Have you seen such a man?

ZIPPA.

Alas! sweet lady!
My life is humble, and such wondrous men
Are far above *my* knowing. I could wish
To *see* one ere I died.

ISABELLA.

You *shall,* believe me!
But while we talk of lovers, we forget
In how brief time you are to win a husband.
Come to my chamber, Zippa, and I'll see
How with your little net you'll snare a bird
Fierce as this rude Tortesa!

ZIPPA.

We will find
A way, dear lady, if we die for it!

ISABELLA.

Shall we? Come with me, then! *[Exeunt.*

SCENE III.

An Apartment in the Falcone Palace. TORTESA *alone waiting for the return of the* COUNT.

TORTESA [*musing*].

There are some luxuries too rich for purchase.
Your *soul,* 'tis said, will buy them, of the devil—
Money's too poor! What would I not give, now,
That I could *scorn* what I can hate and ruin!
Scorn is the priceless luxury! In heaven,
The angels *pity.* They are blest to do so;
For, pitying, they look down. We do't by *scorn!*
There lies the privilege of noble birth!—
The jewel of that bloated toad is *scorn!*
You may take all else from him. You—being mean—

May get his palaces—may wed his daughter—
Sleep in his bed—have all his peacock menials
Watching your least glance, as they did "my lord's;"
And, well-possess'd thus, you may pass him by
On his own horse; and while the vulgar crowd
Gape at your trappings, and scarce look on him—
He, in his rags, and starving for a crust—
You'll feel his *scorn*, through twenty coats of mail,
Hot as a sun-stroke! Yet there's something for us!
Th'archangel fiend, when driven forth from heaven,
Put on the serpent, and found sweet revenge
Trailing his slime through Eden! So will I!

Enter FALCONE, *booted and spurred.*

FALCONE.

Good morrow, Signor.

TORTESA.

Well-arrived, my lord!
How sped your riding?

FALCONE.

Fairly! Has my daughter
Left you alone?

TORTESA.

She knows that I am here.
Nay—she'll come presently! A word in private,
Since we're alone, my lord!

FALCONE.

I listen, Signor!

TORTESA.

Your honor, as I think, outweighs a bond?

FALCONE.

'Twas never questioned.

TORTESA.

On your simple word,
And such more weight as hangs upon the troth
Of a capricious woman, I gave up
A deed of lands to you.

FALCONE.

You did.

TORTESA.

To be
Forfeit, and mine again—the match not made?

FALCONE.

How if *you* marr'd it?

TORTESA.

I? I'm not a boy!
What I would yesterday, I will to-day!
I'm not a lover—

FALCONE.

How? So near **your bridal**
And not a lover? Shame, sir!

TORTESA.

My **lord count,**
You take me for a fool!

FALCONE.

Is't like a fool
To love a high-born lady, and your bride?

TORTESA.

Yes; a thrice-sodden fool—if it were I!
I'm not a mate for her—you know I **am not!**

You know that, in her heart, your haughty daughter
Scorns me—ineffably!

FALCONE.

You seek occasion
To slight her, Signor!

TORTESA.

No! I'll marry her
If all the pride that cast down Lucifer
Lie in her bridal-ring! But, mark me still!
I'm not one of your humble citizens,
To bring my money-bags and make you rich—
That, when we walk together, I may take
Your shadow for my own! These limbs are clay—
Poor, common clay, my lord! And she that weds me,
Comes down to my estate.

FALCONE.

By this you mean not
To shut her from her friends?

TORTESA.

You'll see your daughter
By coming to my house—not else! D'ye think
I'll have a carriage to convey my wife
Where she will hear me laughed at?—buy fine horses
To prance a measure to the mocking jeers
Of fools that ride with her? Nay—keep a table
Where I'm the skeleton that mars the feast?
No, no—no, no!

FALCONE [aside].

(With half the provocation,
I would, ere now, have struck an emperor!
But baser pangs make this endurable.
I'm poor—so patience!) What was it beside
You would have said to me?

TORTESA.

　　　　　　But this: Your daughter
Has, in your absence, covered me with scorn!
We'll not talk of it—if the match goes on,
I care not to remember it! [*Aside.*] (*She* shall—
And bitterly!)

FALCONE [*aside*].

　　　　　　(My poor, poor Isabella!
The task was too much!)

TORTESA.

　　　　　　There's a cost of feeling—
You may not think it much—*I* reckon it
A thousand pounds per day—in playing thus
The suitor to a lady cramm'd with pride!
I've writ you out a bond to pay me for it!
See here!—to pay me for my shame and pains,
If I should lose your daughter for a wife,
A thousand pounds per day—dog cheap at that!
Sign it, my lord, or give me back my deeds,
And *traffic* cease between us!

FALCONE.

　　　　　　Is this earnest,
Or are you mad or trifling? Do I not
Give you my daughter with an open hand?
Are you betroth'd, or no?

Enter a SERVANT.

　　　　　　Who's this?

SERVANT.

　　　　　　A page
Sent from the Duke.

FALCONE.

Admit him.

Enter PAGE, *with a letter.*

PAGE.

For my lord,
The Count Falcone.

TORTESA [*aside*].

(In a moment more
I would have had a bond of such assurance
Her father on his knees should bid me take her.

[*Looking at* FALCONE, *who smiles as he reads.*]

What glads him now?)

FALCONE.

You shall not have the bond!

TORTESA.

No? (*Aside.*) (Here's a change! What hint from Duke or
        devil
Stirs him to this?) My lord, 'twere best the bridal
Took place upon the instant. Is your daughter
Ready within?

FALCONE.

You'll never wed my daughter!

Enter ISABELLA.

TORTESA.

My lord!

FALCONE.

She's fitlier mated! Here she comes!
My lofty Isabella! My fair child!
How dost thou, sweet?

ISABELLA [*embracing him*].

Come home, and I not know it!
Art well? I see thou art! Has ridden hard?
My dear, dear father!

FALCONE.

Give me breath to tell thee
Some better news, my lov'd one!

ISABELLA.

Nay, the joy
To see you back again's enough for now.
There can be no news better, and for this
Let's keep a holiday 'twixt this and sunset!
Shut up your letter, and come see my flowers,
And hear my birds sing, will you?

FALCONE.

Look, my darling,
Upon this first! [Holds up the letter.]

ISABELLA.

No! you shall tell me all
You and the Duke did—where you slept, where ate,
Whether you dream'd of me—and, now I think on't,
Found you no wild-flow'rs as you cross'd the mountain?

FALCONE.

My own bright child! [Looks fondly upon her.]

TORTESA [aside].

('Twill mar your joy, my lord!
To see the Glover's daughter in your palace,
And your proud daughter houseless!)

FALCONE [to ISABELLA].

You'll not hear
The news I have for you!

TORTESA [advancing].

Before you tell it,
I'll take my own again!

ISABELLA [*aside*].

(Tortesa here!)   [*Curtseys.*]
I crave your pardon, sir; I saw you not!
(Oh hateful monster!) [*Aside.*]

FALCONE.

Listen to my news,
Signor Tortesa! It concerns you, trust me!

ISABELLA [*aside*].

(More of this hateful marriage!)

TORTESA.

Tell it briefly,
My time is precious!

FALCONE.

Sir, I'll sum it up
In twenty words. The Duke has information,
By what means yet I know not, that my need
Spurs me to marry an unwilling daughter.
He bars the match!—redeems my lands and palace,
And has enrich'd the young Count Julian,
For whom he bids me keep my daughter's hand!
Kind, royal master! [*Reads the note to himself.*]

ISABELLA [*aside*].

(Never!)

TORTESA [*aside, with suppressed rage*].

('Tis a lie!
He's mad, or plays some trick to gain the time—
Or there's a woman hatching deviltry!
We'll see.) [*Looks at* ISABELLA.]

ISABELLA [*aside*].

(I'll die first! Sold and taken back,
Then thrust upon a husband paid to take me!

To save my father I have weigh'd myself,
Heart, hand, and honor, against so much land!—
I—Isabella! I'm nor hawk nor hound,
And, if I change my master, I will choose him!)

TORTESA [*aside*].

She seems not over-pleased!

PAGE.

Your pardon, Count!
I wait your answer to the Duke!

FALCONE.

My daughter
Shall give it you herself. What sweet phrase have you,
Grateful and eloquent, to bear your thanks?
Speak, Isabella!

ISABELLA [*aside*].

(There's but one way left!
Courage, poor heart, and think on Angelo!)

[*Advances suddenly to* TORTESA.]

Signor Tortesa!

TORTESA.

Madam!

ISABELLA.

There's my hand!
Is't yours, or no?

TORTESA.

There *was* a troth between us!

ISABELLA.

Is't broke?

TORTESA.

I have not broke it!

ISABELLA.

Then why stand **you**
Mute as a statue, when 'tis struck asunder
Without our wish or knowledge?   Would you be
Half so indifferent had you lost a horse?
Am I worth having?

TORTESA.

Is my life worth having?

ISABELLA.

Then are you robb'd!   Look to it!

FALCONE.

Is she mad!

TORTESA.

You'll marry me?

ISABELLA.

will!

FALCONE.

By heaven you shall not!
What, shall my daughter wed a leprosy—
A bloated money-canker?   Leave her hand!
Stand from him, Isabella!

ISABELLA.

Sir! you gave me
This "leper" for a husband, three days gone;
I did not ask my heart if I could love him!
I took him with the meekness of a child,

Trusting my father! I was shut up for him—
Forc'd to receive no other company—
My wedding-clothes made, and the match proclaim'd
Through Florence!

FALCONE.

Do you love him?—tell me quickly!

ISABELLA.

You never ask'd me that when I was bid
To wed him!

FALCONE.

I am dumb!

TORTESA.

Ha! ha! well put!
At him again, 'Bel! Well! I've had misgivings
That there was food in me for ladies' liking.
I've been too modest!

ISABELLA [*aside*].

(Monster of disgust!)

FALCONE.

My daughter! I would speak with you in private!
Signor! you'll pardon me.

ISABELLA.

Go you, dear father!
I'll follow straight.   [*Exit* FALCONE.

TORTESA [*aside*].

(She loiters for a kiss!
They're all alike! The same trick woos them all!)
Come to me, 'Bel!

ISABELLA [*coldly*].

To-morrow at this hour
You'll find the priest here, and the bridesmaids waiting.
Till then, adieu!   [*Exit.*

TORTESA.

              Hola! what, gone? Why, Bella!
Sweetheart, I say! So! She would coy it with me!
Well, well, to-morrow! 'Tis not long, and kisses
Pay interest by seconds! There's a leg!
As she stood there, the calf shewed handsomely.
Faith 'tis a shapely one! I wonder now,
Which of my points she finds most admirable!
Something I never thought on, like as not.
We do not see ourselves as others see us.
'Twould not surprise me now, if 'twere my beard—
My forehead! I've a hand indifferent white!
Nay, I've been told my waist was neatly turn'd.
We do *not* see ourselves as others see us!
How goes the hour? I'll home and fit my hose
To tie trim for the morrow. [*Going out.*] Hem! the door's
Lofty. I like that! I will have mine raised.
Your low door makes one stoop.   [*Exit.*

END OF THE SECOND ACT.

ACT III.

SCENE I.

ANGELO *discovered in his studio, painting upon the picture of*
ISABELLA.

ANGELO.

My soul is drunk with gazing on this face.
I reel and faint with it. In what sweet world
Have I traced all its lineaments before?
I know them. Like a troop of long-lost friends
My pencil wakes them with its eager touch,
And they spring up, rejoicing. Oh, I'll gem
The heaven of Fame with my irradiate pictures,
Like kindling planets—but this glorious one
Shall be their herald, like the evening star,
First-lit, and lending of its fire to all.

The day fades—but the lamp burns on within me.
My bosom has no dark, no sleep, no change
To dream or calm oblivion. I work on
When my hand stops. The light tints fade. Good night,
Fair image of the fairest thing on earth,
Bright Isabella! [*Leans on the rod with which he guides his
hand, and remains looking at his picture.*]

Enter TOMASO, *with two bags of money.*

TOMASO.

For the most excellent painter, Angelo, two hundred
ducats! The genius of my master flashes upon me. The
Duke's greeting and two hundred ducats! If I should not
have died in my blindness but for this eye-water, may I be
hanged. [*Looks at* ANGELO.]   He is studying his picture.
What an air there is about him—lofty, unlike the vulgar!
Two hundred ducats! [*Observes* ANGELO's *hat on the table.*]
It strikes me now that I can see genius in that hat. It is not
like a common hat. Not like a bought hat. The rim turns
to the crown with an intelligence. [*Weighs the ducats in his
hand.*] Good, heavy ducats. What it is to refresh the vision!
I have looked round, ere now, in this very chamber, and
fancied that the furniture expressed a melancholy dulness.
When he hath talked to me of his pictures, I have seen the
chairs smile. Nay, as if shamed to listen, the very table
has looked foolish. Now, all about me expresseth a choice
peculiarity—as you would say, how like a genius to have such
chairs! What a painter-like table! Two hundred ducats!

ANGELO.

What hast thou for supper?

TOMASO.

Two hundred ducats, my great master!

ANGELO [*absently*].

A cup of wine! Wine, Tomaso!   [*Sits down.*

TOMASO.

(So would the great Donatello have sat upon his chair!
His legs thus! His hand falling thus!) [*Aloud.*] There
is nought in the cellar but stale beer, my illustrious master!
(Now, it strikes me that his shadow is unlike another man's
—of a *pink* tinge, somehow—yet that may be fancy.)

ANGELO.

Hast thou no money? Get wine, I say!

TOMASO.

I saw the Duke in the market-place, who called me Angelo,
(we shall rue that trick yet,) and with a gracious smile asked
me if thou hadst paid the twenty flasks.

ANGELO [*not listening*].

Is there no wine?

TOMASO.

I said to his grace, no! Pray mark the sequel: In pity of
my thirst, the Duke sends me two—ahem!—*one* hundred
ducats. Here they are!

ANGELO.

Didst thou say the wine was on the lees?

TOMASO.

With these *fifty* ducats we shall buy nothing but wine.
(He will be rich with fifty.)

ANGELO.

What saidst thou?

TOMASO.

I spoke of *twenty* ducats sent thee by the Duke. Wilt thou
finger them ere one is spent?

ANGELO.

I asked thee for wine—I am parched.

TOMASO.

Of these *ten* ducats, think'st thou we might spend one for a flask of better quality?

ANGELO.

Lend me a ducat, if thou hast one, and buy wine presently. Go!

TOMASO.

I'll lend it thee, willingly, my illustrious master. It is my last, but as much thine as mine.

ANGELO.

Go! Go!

TOMASO.

Yet wait! There's a scrap of news! Falcone's daughter marries Tortesa, the usurer? To-morrow is the bridal.

ANGELO.

How?

TOMASO.

I learned it in the market-place! There will be rare doings!

ANGELO.

Dog! Villain! Thou hast lied? Thou dar'st not say it!

TOMASO.

Hey! Art thou mad? Nay—borrow thy ducat where thou canst! I'll spend that's my own. Adieu, master!

Exit TOMASO, *and enter* TORTESA *with a complacent smile.*

ANGELO.

Ha?—well arrived! [*Draws his sword.*

TORTESA.

Good eve, good Signor Painter.

ANGELO.

You struck me yesterday.

TORTESA.

I harmed your picture—
For which I'm truly sorry—but not you!

ANGELO.

Myself! myself! My picture is myself!
What are my bones that rot? Is this my hand?—
Is this my eye?

TORTESA.

I think so.

ANGELO.

No, I say!
The hand and eye of Angelo are there!
There—there—[*points to his pictures*]—immortal!
Wound me in the flesh,
I will forgive you upon fair excuse.
'Tis the earth round me—'tis my shell—my house;
But in my picture lie my brain and heart—
My soul—my fancy. For a blow at these
There's no cold reparation. Draw, and quickly!
I'm in the mood to fight it to the death.
Stand on your guard!

TORTESA.

I will not fight with you.

ANGELO.

Coward!

TORTESA.

I'm deaf.

ANGELO.

Feel then!

TORTESA *catches the blow as he strikes him, and coldly flings back his hand.*

TORTESA.

Nay, strike me not!
I'll call the guard, and cry out like a woman.

ANGELO [*turning from him contemptuously*].

What scent of dog's meat brought me such a cur!
It is a whip I want, and not a sword.

TORTESA [*folding his arms*].

I have a use for life so far above
The stake you quarrel for, that you may choose
Your words to please yourself. They'll please me, too.
Yet you're in luck. I killed a man on Monday
For spitting on my *shadow*. Thursday's sun
Will dry the insult, though it light on *me!*

ANGELO.

Oh, subtle coward!

TORTESA.

I am what you will,
So I'm alive to marry on the morrow!
'Tis well, by Jupiter! Shall you have power
With half a breath to pluck from me a wife!
Shall I, against a life as poor as yours—
Mine being precious as the keys of heaven—
Set all upon a throw, and no odds neither?
I know what honor is as well as you!

I know the weight and measure of an insult—
What it is worth to take or fling it back.
I have the hand to fight if I've a mind;
And I've a heart to shut my sunshine in,
And lock it from the scowling of the world,
Though all mankind cry "Coward!"

ANGELO.

Mouthing braggart!

TORTESA.

I came to see my bride, my Isabella!
Show me her picture! [*Advances to look for it.*]

ANGELO.

Do but look upon't,
By heaven's fair light, I'll kill you! [*Draws.*

TORTESA.

Soft, she's mine!
She loves me! and with that to make life precious,
I have the nerve to beat back Hercules,
If you were he!

ANGELO [*attacking him*].

Out! Out, thou shameless liar!

TORTESA [*retreating on the defence*].

Thy blows and words fall pointless. Nay, thou'rt mad!
But I'll not harm thee for her picture's sake!

ANGELO.

Liar! she hates thee!

[*Beats him off the stage and returns, closing the door violently.*]

So! once more alone!

[*Takes* ISABELLA'S *picture from the easel, and replaces it with* ZIPPA'S.]

Back to the wall, deceitful loveliness!
And come forth, Zippa, fair in honest truth!
I'll make *thee* beautiful!

[*Takes his pencil and palette to paint.*]

[*A knock is heard.*]

Who knocks! come in!

Enter ISABELLA, *disguised as a monk.*

ISABELLA.

Good morrow, Signor.

ANGELO [*turning sharply to the monk*].

There's a face, old monk,
Might stir your blood—ha? You shall tell me, now,
Which of these heavenly features hides the soul!
There *is* one! I have worked upon the picture
Till *my* brain's thick—I cannot see like you.
Where is't?

ISABELLA [*aside*].

(A picture of the Glover's daughter!
What does he, painting *her?*) Is't for its *beauty*
You paint that face, sir?

ANGELO.

Yes—th' immortal beauty!
Look here! What see you in that face? The skin—

ISABELLA.

Brown as a vintage-girl's!

ANGELO.

The mouth—

ISABELLA.

A good one

To eat and drink withal!

ANGELO.

The eye is—

ISABELLA.

Grey!

You'll buy a hundred like it for a penny!

ANGELO.

A hundred eyes?

ISABELLA.

No.   Hazel-nuts!

ANGELO.

The forehead—

How find you that?

ISABELLA.

Why, made to match the rest!

I'll cut as good a face out of an apple—
For all that's fair in it!

ANGELO.

Oh, heaven, how dim
Were God's most blessed image did all eyes
Look on't like thine! Is't by the red and white—
Is't by the grain and tincture of the skin—
Is't by the hair's gloss, or the forehead's arching,
You know the bright inhabitant? I tell thee
The spark of their divinity in some
Lights up an *inward* face—so radiant,
The outward lineaments are like a veil
Floating before the sanctuary—forgot
In glimpses of the glory streaming through!

ISABELLA [*mournfully*].

Is Zippa's face so radiant?

ANGELO.

Look upon it!
You see thro' all the countenance she's *true!*

ISABELLA.

True to *you*, Signor!

ANGELO.

To herself, old man!
Yet *once*, to *me* too! [*Dejectedly*.]

ISABELLA [*aside*].

(Once to him! Can Zippa
Have dared to love a man like Angelo!
I think she dare not. Yet if he, indeed,
Were the inconstant lover that she told of—
The youth who was "her neighbor!") Please you, Signor!
Was that fair maid your neighbor?

ANGELO.

Ay—the best!
A loving sister were not half so kind!
I never supp'd without her company.
Yet she was modest as an unsunn'd lily,
And bounteous as the constant perfume of it.

ISABELLA [*aside*].

('Twas he indeed! Oh! what a fair outside
Has falsehood there! Yet stay! If it were *I*
Who made him false to her? Alas, for honor,
I must forgive him—tho' my lips are weary
With telling Zippa how I thought him perjured!
I cannot trust her more—I'll plot alone!)

[*Turns and takes her own picture from the wall.*]

What picture's this, turned to the wall, good Signor?

ANGELO.

A painted lie!

ISABELLA.

                    A lie!—nay—pardon me!
I spoke in haste. Methought 'twas like a lady
I'd somewhere seen!—a lady—Isabella!
But she was true!

ANGELO.

                    Then 'tis not she I've drawn.
For that's a likeness of as false a face
As ever devil did his mischief under.

ISABELLA.

And yet methinks 'tis done most lovingly!
You must have thought it fair to dwell so on it.

ANGELO.

Your convent has the picture of a saint
Tempted, while praying, by the shape of woman.
The painter knew that woman was the devil,
Yet drew her like an angel!

ISABELLA [*aside*].

                    (It is true
He praised my beauty as a painter may—
No more—in words. He praised me as he drew—
Feature by feature. But who calls the lip
To answer for a perjured oath in love?
How should love breathe—how not die, choked for utterance,
If *words* were all. He loved me with his eyes.
He breathed it. Upon every word he spoke
Hung an unuttered worship that his tongue

Would spend a life to make articulate.
Did he not take my hand into his own?
And, as his heart sprang o'er that bridge of veins,
Did he not call to mine to pass him on it—
Each to the other's bosom? I have sworn
To love him—wed him—die with him—and yet
He never *heard* me—but he *knows* it well,
And, in his heart holds me to answer for it.
I'll try once more to find this anger out.
If it be jealousy—why—then, indeed,
He'll call me black, and I'll forgive it him!
For then my errand's done, and I'll away
To play the cheat out that shall make him mine.)
[*Turns to* ANGELO.] Fair Signor, by your leave, I've heard
    it said
That in the beauty of a human face
The God of Nature never writ a lie.

ANGELO.

'Tis likely true!

ISABELLA.

    That howso'er the features
Seem fair at first, a blemish on the soul
Has its betraying speck that warns you of it.

ANGELO.

It should be so, indeed!

ISABELLA.

    Nay—here's a face
Will show at once if it be true or no.
At the first glance 'tis fair!

ANGELO.

Most heavenly fair!

ISABELLA.

Yet, in the lip, methinks, there lurks a shadow—
Something—I know not what—but in it lies
The devil you spoke of!

ANGELO.

Ay—but 'tis not there!
Not in her lip! Oh, no! Look elsewhere for it.
Tis passionately bright—but lip more pure
Ne'er passed unchallenged through the gate of heaven.
Believe me, 'tis not there!

ISABELLA.

How falls the light?
I see a gleam not quite angelical
About the eye. Maybe the light falls wrong—

ANGELO [*drawing her to another position*].

Stand here! D'ye see it now?

ISABELLA.

'Tis just so here!

ANGELO [*sweeps the air with his brush*].

There's some curst cobweb hanging from the wall
That blurs your sight. Now, look again!

ISABELLA.

I see it
Just as before.

ANGELO.

What! still? You've turn'd an eyelash
Under the lid. Try how it feels with winking.
Is't clear?

ISABELLA.

'Twas never clearer!

ANGELO.

Then, old man!
You'd best betake you to your prayers apace!
For you've a failing sight, death's sure forerunner—
And cannot pray long. Why, that eye's a star,
Sky-lit as Hesperus, and burns as clear.
If you e'er marked the zenith at high noon,
Or midnight, when the blue lifts up to God—
Her eye's of that far darkness!

ISABELLA [*smiling aside*].

Stay—'tis gone!
A blur was on my sight, which, passing from it,
I see as you do. Yes—the eye is clear.
The forehead only, now I see so well,
Has in its arch a mark infallible
Of a false heart beneath it.

ANGELO.

Show it to me!

ISABELLA.

Between the eyebrows there!

ANGELO.

I see a tablet
Whereon the Saviour's finger might have writ
The new commandment. When I painted it
I plucked a just-blown lotus from the shade,
And shamed the white leaf till it seemed a spot—
The brow was so much fairer! Go! old man,
Thy sight fails fast. Go! go!

ISABELLA.

The nostril's small—
Is't not?

ANGELO.

No!

ISABELLA.

Then the cheek's awry so near it,
It makes it seem so!

ANGELO.

Out! thou cavilling fool!
Thou'rt one of those whose own deformity
Makes all thou seest look monstrous. Go and pray
For a clear sight, and read thy missal with it.
Thou art a priest, and livest by the altar,
Yet dost thou recognize God's imprest seal,
Set on that glorious beauty!

ISABELLA [*aside*].

(Oh, he loves me!
Loves me as genius loves—ransacking earth
And ruffling the forbidden flowers of heaven
To make celestial incense of his praise.
High-thoughted Angelo! He loves me well!
With what a gush of all my soul I thank him—
But he's to win yet, and the time is precious.)
[*To* ANGELO.] Signor, I take my leave.

ANGELO.

Good day, old man!
And, if thou com'st again, bring new eyes with thee,
Or thou wilt find scant welcome.

ISABELLA.

You shall like
These same eyes well enough when next I come! [*Exit.*

ANGELO.

A crabbed monk! [*Turns the picture to the wall again.*]
I'll hide this fatal picture
From sight once more, for till he made me look on't

I did not know my weakness. Once more, Zippa,
I'll dwell on thy dear face, and with my pencil
Make thee more fair than life, and try to love thee!

[*A knock.*]

Come in!

Enter ZIPPA

ZIPPA.

Good day, Signor Angelo!

ANGELO.

Why, Zippa, is't thou? is't thou, indeed!

ZIPPA.

Myself, dear Angelo!

ANGELO.

Art well?

ZIPPA.

Ay!

ANGELO.

Hast been well?

ZIPPA.

Ay!

ANGELO.

Then why, for three long days, hast thou not been near me?

ZIPPA.

Ask thyself, Signor Angelo!

ANGELO.

I have—a hundred times since I saw thee.

ZIPPA.

And there was no answer?

ANGELO.

None!

ZIPPA.

Then shouldst thou have ask'd the picture on **thy easel!**

ANGELO.

Nay—I understand thee not.

ZIPPA.

Did I not find thee feasting thy eyes upon it?

ANGELO.

True—thou didst?

ZIPPA.

And art thou not enamoured of it—wilt tell **me truly?**

ANGELO [*smiling*].

'Tis a fair face!

ZIPPA.

Oh, unkind Angelo!

ANGELO.

Look on't! and, seeing its beauty, if thou dost not **forgive**
me, I will never touch pencil to it more.

ZIPPA.

I'll neither look on't, nor forgive thee. But if **thou wilt**
love the picture of another better than mine, thou shalt paint
a new one!
[*As she rushes up to dash it from the casel,* ANGELO
*catches her arm, and points to the picture. She looks
at it, and, seeing her own portrait, turns and falls on
his bosom.*]

ZIPPA.

My picture! and I thought thee so false! Dear, dear,
Angelo! I could be grieved to have wronged thee, if joy
would give me time. But thou'lt forgive me?

ANGELO.

Willingly!   Willingly!

ZIPPA.

And thou lovest me indeed, indeed! Nay, answer not! I will never doubt thee more! Dear Angelo! Yet—[*Suddenly turns from* ANGELO *with a troubled air.*]

ANGELO.

What ails thee now?
[ZIPPA *takes a rich veil from under her cloak, throws it over her head, and looks on the ground in embarrass'd silence.*]
Dost thou stand there for a picture of Silence?

ZIPPA.

Alas! dear Angelo! When I said I forgave and lov'd thee, I forgot that I was to be married to-morrow!

ANGELO.

Married!   to whom?

ZIPPA.

Tortesa, the usurer!

ANGELO.

Tortesa, saidst thou?

ZIPPA.

Think not ill of me, dear Angelo, till I have told thee all! This rich usurer, as thou knowest, would for *ambition* marry Isabella de Falcone.

ANGELO.

He would, I know.

ZIPPA.

But for *love,* he would marry your poor Zippa.

ANGELO.

Know you that?

ZIPPA.

He told me so the day you anger'd me with the praises of the court lady you were painting. What was her name, Angelo?

ANGELO [*composedly*].

I—I'll tell thee presently! Go on!

ZIPPA.

Well—jealous of this unknown lady, I vow'd, if it broke my heart, to wed Tortesa. He had told me Isabella scorn'd him. I flew to her palace. She heard me, pitied me, agreed to plot with me that I might wed the usurer, and then told me in confidence that there was a poor youth whom she loved and would fain marry.

ANGELO [*in breathless anxiety*].

Heard you his name?

ZIPPA.

No! But as I was to wed the richer and she the poorer, she took my poor veil, and gave me her rich one. Now canst thou read the riddle?

ANGELO [*aside*].

(A "poor youth!" What if it is I. She "loves and will wed him!" Oh, if it were I!)

ZIPPA.

Nay, dear Angelo! be not so angry! I do not love him! Nay—thou know'st I do not!

ANGELO [*aside*].

(It may be—nay—it must! But I will know! If not, I may as well die of that as of this jealous madness.) [*Prepares to go out.*]

ZIPPA.

Angelo! where go you? Forgive me, dear Angelo! I swear to thee I love him not!

ANGELO.

I'll know who that poor youth is, or suspense will kill me!

[*Goes out hastily, without a look at* ZIPPA. *She stands silent and amazed for a moment.*]

ZIPPA.

Why cares he to know who that poor youth is! "Suspense will kill him?" Stay! a light breaks on me! If Isabella were the court lady whom he painted! If it were Angelo whom she loved! He is a poor youth!—The picture! The picture will tell all!

[*Hurriedly turns round several pictures turned to the wall, and, last of all,* ISABELLA'S. *Looks at it an instant, and exclaims*]

Isabella!

[*She drops on her knees, overcome with grief, and the scene closes.*]

SCENE II.

A Lady's dressing-room in the Falcone Palace. ISABELLA *discovered with two phials.*

ISABELLA.

Here is a draught will still the breath so nearly,
The keenest-eyed will think the sleeper dead,—
And *this* kills quite. Lie ready, trusty friends,
Close by my bridal veil! I thought to baffle
My ruffian bridegroom by an easier cheat;
But Zippa's dangerous, and if I fail
In *mocking* death, why *death indeed* be welcome!

Enter ZIPPA *angrily.*

ZIPPA.

Madam!

ISABELLA.

You come rudely!

ZIPPA.

If I offend you more, I still have cause—
Yet as the "friend" to whom you gave a husband,
(So kind you were!)   I *might* come unannounced!

ISABELLA.

What is this anger!

ZIPPA.

I'm not angry, madam!
Oh no!   I'm patient!

ISABELLA.

What's your errand, then?

ZIPPA.

To give you back your costly bridal veil
And take my mean one.

ISABELLA.

'Twas *your* wish to change.
'Twas *you* that plotted we should wed together—
You in my place, and I in yours—was't not?

ZIPPA.

Oh, heaven! you're calm!   Had *you* no plotting, too?
You're noble born, and so your face is marble—
I'm poor, and if my heart aches, 'twill show through.
You've robb'd me, madam!

ISABELLA.

I?

ZIPPA.

Of gold—of jewels!—
Gold that would stretch the fancy but to dream of,
And gems like stars!

ISABELLA.

You're mad!

ZIPPA.

His love was worth them!
Oh, what had you to do with Angelo?

ISABELLA.

Nay—came you not to wed Tortesa freely?
What should *you* do with Angelo?

ZIPPA.

You mock me!
You are a woman, though your brow's a rock,
And know what love is. In a ring of fire
The tortured scorpion stings himself, to die—
But love will turn upon itself, and grow
Of its own fang immortal!

ISABELLA.

Still, you left him
To wed another?

ZIPPA.

'Tis for that he's mine!
What makes a right in any thing, but pain?
The diver's agony beneath the sea
Makes the pearl his—pain gets the miser's gold—

The noble's coronet, won first in battle,
Is his by bleeding for't—and Angelo
Is ten times mine because I gave him up—
Crushing my heart to do so!

ISABELLA.

                    Now you plead
Against yourself. Say it would kill *me* quite,
If you should wed him? Mine's the greater **pain,**
And so the fairer title!

ZIPPA [*falling on her knees*].

                    I implore you
Love him no more! Upon my knees I do!
He's not like you! Look on your snow-white **arms!**
They're form'd to press a noble to your breast—
Not Angelo! He's poor—and fit for mine!
You would not lift a beggar to your lips!—
You would not lean from your proud palace-stairs
To pluck away a heart from a poor girl
Who has no more on earth!

ISABELLA.

I will not answer!

ZIPPA.

Think what it is! Love is to you like music—
Pastime! You think on't when the dance is o'er—
When there's no revel—when your hair's unbound,
And its bright jewels with the daylight pale—
You want a lover to press on the hours
That lag till night again! But I—

ISABELLA.

                    Stop there!
I love him better than you've soul to dream of!

ZIPPA [*rising*].

'Tis false! How can you? He's to you a lamp
That shines amid a thousand just as bright!
What's one amid your crowd of worshippers?
The glow-worm's bright—but oh! 'tis wanton murder
To raise him to the giddy air you breathe,
And leave his mate in darkness!

ISABELLA.

Say the worm
Soar from the earth on his own wing—what then?

ZIPPA.

Fair reasons cannot stay the heart from breaking.
You've stol'n my life, and you can give it back!
Will you—for heaven's sweet pity?

ISABELLA.

Leave my presence.
[*Aside.*] (I pity her—but on this fatal love
Hangs my life, too.) What right have such as you
To look with eyes of love on Angelo?

ZIPPA.

What right?

ISABELLA.

I say so. Where's the miracle
Has made you fit to climb into the sky—
A moth—and look with love upon a star!

ZIPPA [*mournfully*].

I'm lowly born, alas!

ISABELLA.

Your *soul's* low born!
Forget your anger and come near me, Zippa,
For e'er I'm done you'll wonder! Have you ever,
When Angelo was silent, mark'd his eye—

How, of a sudden, as 'twere touch'd with fire,
There glows unnatural light beneath the lid?

ZIPPA.

I have—I've thought it strange!

ISABELLA.

Have you walk'd with him
When he has turn'd his head, as if to list
To music in the air—but you heard none—
And presently a smile stole through his lips,
And some low words, inaudible to you,
Fell from him brokenly?

ZIPPA.

Ay—many times!

ISABELLA.

Tell me once more! Hast never heard him speak
With voice unlike his own—so melancholy,
And yet so sweet a voice, that, were it only
The inarticulate moaning of a bird,
The very tone of it had made you weep?

ZIPPA.

'Tis strangely true, indeed!

ISABELLA.

Oh heaven! You say so—
Yet never dreamt it was a spirit of light
Familiar with you!

ZIPPA.

How?

ISABELLA.

Why, there are seraphs
Who walk this common world, and want, as we do—
Here, in our streets—all seraph, save in wings—

The look, the speech, the forehead like a god—
And he the brightest!

ZIPPA [*incredulously*].

Nay—I've known him long!

ISABELLA.

Why, listen! There are worlds, thou doubting fool!
Farther to flee to than the stars in heaven.
Which Angelo can walk as we do this—
And does—while you look on him!

ZIPPA.

Angelo!

ISABELLA.

He's never at your side one constant minute
Without a thousand messengers from thence!
(O block! to live with him, and never dream on't!)
He plucks the sun's rays open like a thread,
And knows what stains the rose and not the lily—
He never sees a flower but he can tell
Its errand on the earth—(they all have errands—
You knew not that, oh dulness!) He sees shapes
Flush'd with immortal beauty in the clouds—
(You've seen him mock a thousand on his canvas,
And never wonder'd!) Yet you talk of love!
What love you?

ZIPPA.

Angelo—and not a dream!
Take you the dream and give me Angelo!
You may talk of him till my brain is giddy—
But oh, you cannot praise him out of reach
Of my true heart.—He's here, as low as I!—
Shall he not wed a woman, flesh and blood?

ISABELLA.

See here! There was a small, earth-creeping mole,
Born by the low nest of an unfledged lark.

They lived an April youth amid the grass—
The soft mole happy, and the lark no less,
And thought the bent sky leaned upon the flowers.
By early May the fledgling got his wings;
And, eager for the light, one breezy dawn,
Sprang from his nest, and buoyantly away,
Fled forth to meet the morning. Newly born
Seem'd the young lark, as in another world
Of light, and song, and creatures like himself,
He soar'd and dropp'd, and sang unto the sun,
And pitied every thing that had not wings—
But most the mole, that wanted even eyes
To see the light he floated in!

ZIPPA.

                    Yet still
She watch'd his nest, and fed him when he came—
Would it were Angelo and I indeed!

ISABELLA.

Nay, mark! The bird grew lonely in the sky.
There was no echo at the height he flew!
And when the mist lay heavy on his wings
His song broke, and his flights were brief and low—
And the dull mole, that should have sorrowed with him,
Joy'd that he sang at last where she could hear!

ZIPPA.

Why, happy mole again!

ISABELLA.

                    Not long!—for soon
He found a mate that loved him *for his wings!*
One who with feebler flight, but eyes still on him,
Caught up his dropp'd song in the middle air,
And, with the echo, cheered him to the sun!

ZIPPA [*aside*].

(I see! I see! His *soul* was never mine!
I was the blind mole of her hateful story!

No, no! he never loved me! True, we ate,
And laugh'd, and danced together—but no love—
He never told his thought when he was sad!
His folly and his idleness were mine—
No more! The rest was lock'd up in his soul!
I feel my heart grow black!) Fair madam, thank you!
You've told me news! (She shall not have him neither,
If there's a plot in hate to keep him from her!
I must have room to think, and air to breathe—
I choke here!) Madam, the blind mole takes leave!

ISABELLA.

Farewell!   [*Exit* ZIPPA.

[*Takes the phial from the table.*]

                    And now, come forth, sweet comforter!
I'll to my chamber with this drowsy poison,
And from my sleep I wake up Angelo's,
Or wake no more!   [*Exit.*

END OF THE THIRD ACT.

ACT IV.

SCENE I.

*A sumptuous drawing-room in the Falcone Palace. Guests
assembled for the bridal.* LORDS *and* LADIES *promenading,
and a band of musicians in a gallery at the side of the
stage.*

IST. LORD.

Are we before the hour? or does the bridegroom
Affect this tardiness?

2ND. LORD.

                              We're bid at twelve.

1ST. LORD.

'Tis now past one. At least we should have music
To wile the time. [*To the musicians.*] Strike up, good
    fellows!

2ND. LORD.

                Why,
A man who's only drest on holidays
Makes a long toilet. Now, I'll warrant he
Has vex'd his tailor since the break of day,
Hoping to look a gentleman. D'ye know him?

1ST. LORD.

I've never had occasion!

2ND. LORD.

              Poor Falcone!
He'd give the best blood in his veins, I think,
To say as much!

1ST. LORD.

            How's this! I see no stir
Among the instruments. Will they not play?

2ND. LORD.

Not they! I ask'd before you, and they're bid
To strike up when they hear Tortesa's horses
Prance thro' the gateway—not a note till then!

Music plays.

1ST. LORD.

Hé comes!

Enter TORTESA, *dressed over-richly.*

TORTESA.

Good day, my lords!

1ST. LORD.

Good day!

2ND. LORD.

The sky
Smiles on you, Signor! 'Tis a happy omen
They say, to wed in sunshine.

TORTESA.

Why, I think
The sun is not displeased that I should wed.

1ST. LORD.

We're happy, sir, to have you one of us.

TORTESA.

What have I been *till now!* I was a man
Before I saw your faces! Where's the change?
Have I a tail since? Am I grown a monkey?

[LORDS *whisper together, and walk from him.*]

Oh for a mint to coin the world again
And melt the mark of gentleman from clowns!
It puts me out of patience! Here's a fellow
That, by much rubbing against better men,
Has, like a penny in a Jew's close pocket,
Stolen the color of a worthier coin,
And thinks he rings like sterling courtesy!
Yet look! he cannot phrase you a good morrow,
Or say he's sad, or glad, at any thing,
But close beneath it, rank as verdigrease,
Lies an insulting rudeness! He was *"happy"*
That I should now be one of them. *Now!* Now!
As if, *till now,* I'd been a dunghill grub,
And was but just turn'd butterfly!

A LADY *advances.*

LADY.

Fair sir,
I must take leave to say, were you my brother,
You've made the choice that would have pleas'd me best!
Your bride's as good as fair.

TORTESA.

I thank you, Madam!
To be *your* friend, she should be—good and fair!

[*The* LADY *turns, and walks up the stage.*]

How like a drop of oil upon the sea
Falls the apt word of woman! So! her "brother"!
Why, there could be no contumely there!
I might, for all I *look,* have been her brother,
Else her first thought had never coupled us.
I'll pluck some self-contentment out of that!

[*Enter suddenly the* COUNT'S SECRETARY.]

How now!

SECRETARY.

I'm sent, sir, with unwelcome tidings.

TORTESA.

Deliver them the quicker!

SECRETARY.

I shall be
Too sudden at the slowest.

TORTESA.

Pshaw! what is't?
I'm not a girl! Out with your news at once!
Are my ships lost?

SECRETARY [*hesitatingly*].

The lady Isabella—

TORTESA.

What? run away!

SECRETARY.

Alas, good sir! she's dead!

TORTESA.

Bah! just as dead as I! Why, thou dull blockhead!
Cannot a lady faint, but there must be
A trumpeter like thee to make a tale on't?

SECRETARY.

Pardon me, Signor, but—

TORTESA.

Who sent you hither?

SECRETARY.

My lord the Count.

TORTESA [*turning quickly aside*].

He put it in the bond,
That if by any humor of my own,
Or accident that *sprang not from himself*,
Or from his daughter's will, the match were marr'd,
His tenure stood intact. If she *were* dead—
I don't believe she is—but if she were,
By one of those strange chances that do happen—
If she were dead, I say, the silly fish
That swims with safety among hungry sharks
To run upon the pin-hook of a boy,
Might teach me wisdom!

[*The* SECRETARY *comes forward, narrating eagerly to the
company.*]

Now, what says this jackdaw?

SECRETARY.

She had refused to let her bridesmaids in—

LADY.

And died alone?

SECRETARY.

A trusty serving maid
Was with her, and none else. She dropp'd away,
The girl said, in a kind of weary sleep.

IST. LORD.

Was no one told of it?

SECRETARY.

The girl watch'd by her,
And thought she slept still; till, the music sounding,
She shook her by the sleeve, but got no answer;
And so the truth broke on her!

TORTESA [*aside*].

(Oh indeed!
The plot is something shallow!)

2ND. LORD.

Might we go
And see her as she lies?

SECRETARY.

The holy father
Who should have married her, has check'd all comers,
And staying for no shroud but bridal dress,
He bears her presently to lie in state
In the Falcone chapel.

TORTESA [*aside*].

(Worse and worse—
They take me for a fool!)

1ST. LORD.

But why such haste?

SECRETARY.

I know not.

ALL.

Let us to the chapel!

TORTESA.

[*Drawing his sword, and stepping between them and the door.*]

Hold!

Let no one try to pass!

1ST. LORD.

What mean you, sir!

TORTESA.

To keep you here till you have got your story
Pat to the tongue—the truth on't, and no more!

LADY.

Have you a doubt the bride is dead, good Signor?

TORTESA.

A palace, see you, has a tricky air!
When I am told a tradesman's daughter's dead,
I know the coffin holds an honest corse,
Sped, in sad earnest, to eternity.
But were I stranger in the streets to-day,
And heard that an ambitious usurer,
With lands and money having bought a lady
High-born and fair, she died before the bridal,
I would lay odds with him that told me of it
She'd rise again—before the resurrection.
So stand back all! If I'm to fill to-day

The pricking ears of Florence with a lie,
The bridal guests shall tell the tale so truly,
And mournfully, from eyesight of the corse,
That ev'n the shrewdest listener shall believe,
And I myself have no misgiving of it.
Look! where they come!

[*Door opens to funereal music, and the body of* ISABELLA *is
borne in, preceded by a* MONK, *and followed by* FALCONE
and mourners. TORTESA *confronts the* MONK.]

What's this you bear away?

MONK.

Follow the funeral, but stay it not.

TORTESA.

If thereon lie the lady Isabella,
I ask to see her face before she pass!

MONK.

Stand from the way, my son, it cannot be!

TORTESA.

What right have you to take me for a stone?
See what you do! I stand a bridegroom here.
A moment since the joyous music playing
Which promised me a fair and blushing bride.
The flowers are fragrant, and the guests made welcome;
And while my heart beats at the opening door,
And eagerly I look to see her come,—
There enters in her stead a covered corse!
And when I ask to look upon her face—
One look, before my bride is gone for ever,—
You find it in your hearts to say me nay!—
Shame! Shame!

FALCONE [*fiercely*].
Lead on!

TORTESA.

My lord, by covenant—
By contract writ and seal'd—by value rendered—
By her own promise—nay, by all, save taking,
This body's mine! I'll have it set down here
And wait my pleasure! See it done, my lord,
Or I will, for you!

MONK [to the bearers].

Set the body down!

TORTESA [takes the veil from the face].

Come hither all! Nay, father, look not black!
If o'er the azure temper of this blade
There come no mist, when laid upon her lips,
I'll do a penance for irreverence,
And fill your sack with penitential gold!
Look well!

[Puts his sword to ISABELLA's lips, and after watching it with intense interest a moment, drops on his knees beside the bier.]

She's dead indeed! Lead on!

The procession starts again to funereal music, and TORTESA follows last.

SCENE II.

A Street in Florence. The funereal music dying away in the distance. Enter ZIPPA, straining her eyes to look after it.

ZIPPA.

'Tis Angelo that follows close behind,
Laying his forehead almost on her bier!
His heart goes with her to the grave! Oh, heaven!
Will not Tortesa pluck out of his hand
The tassel of that pall?

[*She hears a footstep.*]

Stay, stay, he's here!

Enter TORTESA, *musing.* ZIPPA *stands aside.*

TORTESA.

I've learned to-day a lord may be a Jew,
I've learned to-day that grief may kill a lady;
Which touches me the most I cannot say,
For I could fight Falcone for my loss
Or weep, with all my soul, for Isabella.

ZIPPA *touches him on the shoulder.*

ZIPPA.

How is't the Signor follows not his bride?

TORTESA.

I did—but with their melancholy step
I fell to musing, and so dropp'd behind—
But here's a sight I have not seen to-day!

[*Takes her hand smilingly.*]

ZIPPA.

What's that?

TORTESA.

A friendly face, my honest Zippa!
Art well? What errand brings thee forth?

ZIPPA.

None, Signor!
But passing by the funeral, I stopped,
Wondering to see the bridegroom lag behind,
And give his sacred station next the corse
To an obtrusive stranger.

TORTESA.

Which is he?

ZIPPA [*points after* ANGELO].

Look there!

TORTESA.

His face is buried in his cloak.
Who is't?

ZIPPA.

Not *know* him? Had I half the cause
That *you* have, to see through that mumming cloak,
The shadow of it would speak out his name!

TORTESA.

What mean you?

ZIPPA.

Angelo! What right has he
To weep in public at her funeral?

TORTESA.

The painter?

ZIPPA.

Ay—the peasant Angelo!
Was't not enough to dare to love her living,
But he must fling the insult of his tears
Betwixt her corse and you? Are you not mov'd?
Will you not go and pluck him from your place?

TORTESA.

No, Zippa, for my spirits are more apt
To grief than anger. I've in this half hour
Remember'd much I should have thought on sooner,—
For, had I known her heart was capable
Of breaking for the love of one so low,
I would have done as much to make her his
As I have done, in hate, to make her mine.
She lov'd him, Zippa! [*Walks back in thought.*]

ZIPPA [*aside*].

Oh, to find a way
To pluck that fatal beauty from his eyes!
'Tis twilight, and the lamp is lit above her,
And Angelo will watch the night out there,
Gazing with passionate worship on her face.
But no! he shall not!

TORTESA [*advancing*].

Come! what busy thought
Vexes your brain now?

ZIPPA.

Were your pride as quick
As other men's to see an insult, Signor!
I had been spared the telling of my thought.

TORTESA.

You put it sharply!

ZIPPA.

Listen! you are willing
That there should follow, in your place of mourner,
A youth, who, by the passion of his grief
Shews to the world he's more bereaved than you!

TORTESA.

Humph! well!

ZIPPA.

Still follows he without rebuke;
And in the chapel where she lies to-night,
Her features bared to the funereal lamp,
He'll, like a mourning bridegroom, keep his vigil,
As if all Florence knew she was his own.

TORTESA.

Nay, nay! he may keep vigil if he will!
The door is never lock'd upon the dead
Till bell and mass consign them to the tomb;

And custom gives the privilege to all
To enter in and pray—and so may he.

ZIPPA.

Then learn a secret which I fain had spared
My lips the telling. Question me not how,
But I have chanced to learn, that Angelo,
To-night, will *steal the body from its bier!*

TORTESA.

To-night! What! Angelo? Nay, nay, good Zippa!
If he's enamoured of the corse, 'tis there—
And he may watch it till its shape decay,
And holy church will call it piety.
But he who steals from consecrated ground,
Dies, by the law of Florence. There's no end
To answer in't.

ZIPPA.

                    You know not Angelo!
You think not with what wild, delirious passion
A painter thirsts to tear the veil from beauty.
He painted Isabella as a maid,
Coy as a lily turning from the sun.
Now she is dead, and, like a star that flew
Flashing and hiding thro' some fleecy rack,
But suddenly sits still in cloudless heavens,
She slumbers fearless in his steadfast gaze,
Peerless and unforbidding. O, to him
She is no more your bride! A statue fairer
Than ever rose enchanted from the stone,
Lies in that dim-lit chapel, clad like life.
Are you too slow to take my meaning yet?
He cannot loose the silken boddice *there!*
He cannot, *there,* upon the marble breast
Shower the dark locks from the golden comb!

TORTESA.

Hold!

ZIPPA.

Are you mov'd?   Has he no *end* to compass
In stealing her away from holy ground?
Will you not lock your bride up from his touch?

TORTESA.

No more! no more! I thought not of all this!
Perchance it is not true.   But twilight falls,
And I will home to doff this bridal gear,
And, after, set a guard upon the corse.
We'll walk together.   Come!

ZIPPA [*aside*].

(He shall not see her!)
[*Exeunt.*

SCENE III.

*A street in front of the Falcone Palace.   Night.   Enter
ISABELLA in her white bridal dress.   She falters to her
father's door, and drops exhausted.*

ISABELLA.

My brain swims round! I'll rest a little here!
The night's cold, chilly cold.   Would I could reach
The house of Angelo!   Alas! I thought
He would have kept *one* night of vigil near me,
Thinking me dead.   Bear up, good heart!   Alas!
I faint! Where am I? [*Looks around.*]
'Tis my father's door.
My undirected feet have brought me home—
And I must in, or die! [*Knocks with a painful effort.*]
So ends my dream!

FALCONE [*from above*].

Who's that would enter to a mourning house?

ISABELLA.

Your daughter!

FALCONE.

Ha! what voice is that I hear?

ISABELLA.

Poor Isabella's.

FALCONE.

Art thou come to tell me,
That with unnatural heart I killed my daughter?
Just heaven! thy retribution follows fast!
But oh, if holy and unnumbered masses
Can give thee rest, perturb'd and restless spirit!
Haunt thou a weeping penitent no more!
Depart! I'll in, and pass the night in prayer!
So shalt thou rest! Depart!

[*He closes the window, and* ISABELLA *drops with her forehead to the marble stair.*]

Enter TOMASO, *with a bottle in his hand.*

TOMASO.

It's like the day after the deluge. Few stirring and nobody
dry. I've been since twilight looking for somebody that
would drink. Not a beggar athirst in all Florence! I
thought that, with a bottle in my hand, I should be scented
like a wild boar. I expected drunkards would have come up
out of the ground—like worms in a shower. When was *I*
ever so difficult to find by a moist friend? Two hundred
ducats in good wine, and no companion! I'll look me up a
dry dog. I'll teach him to tipple, and give up the fellowship
of mankind.

ISABELLA [*faintly*].

Signor!

TOMASO.

Hey! What!

ISABELLA.

Help, Signor!

TOMASO.

A woman! Ehem! [*Approaching her.*] Would you take something to drink by any chance? [*Offers her the bottle.*] No? Perhaps you don't like to drink out of the bottle.

ISABELLA.

I perish of cold!

TOMASO.

Stay! Here's a cloak! My master's out for the night, and you shall home with me. Come! Perhaps when you get warmer, you'd like to drink a little. The wine's good! [*Assists her in rising.*] By St. Genevieve, a soft hand! Come! I'll bring you where there's fire and a clean flagon.

ISABELLA.

To any shelter, Signor!

TOMASO.

Shelter! nay, a good house, and two hundred ducats in ripe wine. Steady now! (This shall pass for a good action! If my master smell a rat, I'll face him out the woman's honest!) This way, now! Softly! that's well stepp'd! Come!

[*Goes out, assisting her to walk.*]

END OF THE FOURTH ACT.

ACT V.

SCENE I.

ANGELO's *Studio. A full-length picture, in a large frame, stands on the floor against an easel, placed nearly in the centre of the room. Two curtains, so arranged as to cover the picture when drawn together.* ANGELO *stands in an imploring attitude near the picture, his pencil and palette in his hands, appealing to* ISABELLA, *who is partly turned from him in an attitude of refusal. The back wall of the room such as to form a natural ground for a picture.*

ANGELO.

Hear me, sweet!

ISABELLA.

No, we'll keep a holiday,
And waste the hours in love and idleness.
You shall not paint to-day, dear Angelo!

ANGELO.

But listen!

ISABELLA.

Nay, I'm jealous of my picture;
For all you give to that is stol'n from me.
I like not half a look that turns away
Without an answer from the eyes it met!
I care not you should see my lips' bright color
Yet wait not for the breath that floats between!

ANGELO.

Wilt listen?

ISABELLA.

Listen? Yes! a thousand years!
But there's a pencil in those restless fingers,
Which you've a trick of touching to your lips—
And while you talk, my hand would do as well!
And if it's the same tale you told before

Of *certain vigils* you forgot to keep,
Look deep into my eyes till it is done—
For, like the children's Lady-in-the-well,
I only hark because you're looking in!
Will you talk thus to me?

ANGELO.

Come night I will!
But close upon thy voice, sweet Isabella!
A boding whisper sinks into mine ear
Which tells of sudden parting! If 'tis false,—
We shall have still a lifetime for our love,
But if 'tis true, oh think that, in my picture,
Will lie the footprint of an angel gone!
Let me but make it clearer!

ISABELLA.

Now, by heaven!
I think thou lov'st the picture, and not me!
So different am I, that, did I think
To lose thee presently, by death or parting,
For thy least word, or look, or slightest motion—
Nay, for so little breath as makes a sigh,
I would not take, to have it pass untreasured,
The empire of a star!

While she is uttering this reproach, ANGELO *has looked
at her with delight, and touched his portrait with a few
rapid strokes.*

ANGELO.

My picture's done!

[*Throws his pencil to the ground.*]

Break, oh enchanted pencil! thou wilt never
On earth, again, do miracle so fair!
Oh Isabella! as the dusky ore
Waits for the lightning's flash to turn to gold—
As the dull vapor waits for Hesperus,
Then falls in dew-drops, and reflects a star—

So waited I that fire upon thy lips,
To make my master-piece complete in beauty!

ISABELLA.

This is ambition where I look'd for love,
The fancy flattering where the heart should murmur.
I think you have no heart!

ANGELO.

        Your feet are on it!
The heart is ever lowly with the fortunes,
Tho' proud mind sits level with a kind!
I gave you long ago both heart and soul,
But only one has dared to speak to you!
Yet, if astonishment will cure the dumb,
Give it a kiss—

ISABELLA [*smiling*].

        Lo! Where it speaks at last!

[*A loud knock is heard.*]

Hark, Angelo!

He flies to the window, and looks out

ANGELO.

        Tortesa with a guard!
Alas! that warning voice! They've traced thee hither!
Lost! Lost!

ISABELLA [*hastily drawing the curtain and disappearing
behind it*].

        No! no! defend thy picture only,
And all is well yet!

ANGELO.

        Thee and it with life!

[*Draws his sword, and stands before the curtain in an attitude of defiance. Enter* TORTESA *with* OFFICERS *and*
GUARD.]

What is your errand?

TORTESA.

        I'm afraid, a sad one!
For, by your drawn sword and defying air,
Your conscious thought foretells it.

ANGELO.

        Why,—a blow—
(You took one, Signor, when you last were here—
If you've forgot it, well!)—but, commonly,
The giver of a blow needs have his sword
Promptly in hand. You'll pardon me!

TORTESA.

        I do!
For, if my fears are just, good Signor painter!
You've not a life to spare upon a quarrel!
In brief, the corse of a most noble lady
Was stol'n last night from holy sanctuary.
I have a warrant here to search your house;
And, should the body not be found therein,
I'm bid to see the picture of the lady—
Whereon, (pray mark me!) if I find a trace
Of charms fresh copied, more than may beseem
The modest beauty of a living maid,
I may arrest you on such evidence
For instant trial!

ANGELO.

        Search my house and welcome!
But, for my picture, tho' a moment's glance
Upon its pure and hallowed loveliness
Would give the lie to your foul thought of me,
It is the unseen virgin of my brain!
And as th' inviolate person of a maid
Is sacred ev'n in presence of the law,
My picture is my own—to bare or cover!
Look on it at your peril!

TORTESA [*to the* GUARD].

Take his sword.

The GUARDS *attack and disarm him.*

ANGELO.

Coward and villain!

TORTESA *parts the curtains with his sword, and* ANGELO *starts amazed to see* ISABELLA, *with her hands crossed on her breast, and her eyes fixed on the ground, standing motionless in the frame which had contained his picture. The tableau deceives* TORTESA, *who steps back to contemplate what he supposes to be the portrait of his bride.*

TORTESA.

Admirable work!
'Tis Isabella's self! Why, this is wondrous!
The brow, the lip, the countenance—how true!
I would have sworn that gloss upon the hair,
That shadow from the lash, were nature's own—
Impossible to copy! [*Looks at it a moment in silence.*]
                                        Yet methinks
The color on the cheek is something faint!

ANGELO [*hurriedly*].

                    Step this way farther

TORTESA [*changing his position*].

                            Ay—'tis better here!
The hand is not as white as Isabella's—
But painted to the life! If there's a feature
That I would touch again, the lip, to me,
Seems wanting in a certain scornfulness
Native to *her!* It scarcely marr'd her beauty.
Perhaps 'tis well slurr'd over in a picture!
Yet stay! I see it, now I look again!
How excellently well!

[GUARDS *return from searching the house.*]
What! found you nothing?

SOLDIER [*holding up* ISABELLA'S *veil*].
This bridal veil—no more.

ANGELO [*despairingly*].
Oh! luckless star!

TORTESA.

Signor! you'll trust me when I say I'm sorry
With all my soul! This veil, I know it well—
Was o'er the face of that unhappy lady
When laid in sanctuary. You are silent!
Perhaps you scorn to satisfy me here!
I trust you can—in your extremity!
But I must bring you to the Duke! Lead on!

ANGELO.

An instant!
TORTESA [*courteously*].
At your pleasure!

ANGELO [*to* ISABELLA, *as he passes close to her*].
I conjure you,
By all our love, stir not!

ISABELLA [*still motionless*].
Farewell!

TORTESA *motions for* ANGELO *to precede him with the* GUARD, *looks once more at the picture, and, with a gesture express- ive of admiration, follows. As the door closes,* ISABELLA *steps from the frame.*

ISABELLA.
I'll follow
Close on thy steps, beloved Angelo!

And find a way to bring thee home again!
My heart is light, and hope speaks cheerily!
And lo! bright augury!—a friar's hood
For my disguise! Was ever omen fairer!
Thanks! my propitious star!

[*Envelops herself in the hood, and goes out hastily.*]

SCENE II.

A Street. Enter TOMASO, *with his hat crushed and pulled sulkily over his eyes, his clothes dirty on one side, and other marks of having slept in the street. Enter* ZIPPA *from the other side, meeting him.*

ZIPPA.

Tomaso! Is't thou? Where's Angelo?

TOMASO.

It is I, and I don't know!

ZIPPA.

Did he come home last night?

TOMASO.

"*Did* he come home!" Look *there!* .[*Pulls off his hat, and shows his dirty side.*]

ZIPPA.

Then thou hast slept in the street!

TOMASO.

Ay!

ZIPPA.

And what has that to do with the coming home of Angelo?

TOMASO.

What had thy father to do with thy having such a nose as his?

[ZIPPA *holds up a ducat to him.*]

What! gave thy mother a ducat?—cheap as dirt!

ZIPPA.

Blockhead, no! I'll give thee the ducat if thou wilt tell me, straight on, what thou know'st of Angelo!

TOMASO.

I will—and thou shalt see how charity is rewarded.

ZIPPA.

Begin!—begin!

TOMASO.

Last night, having pray'd later than usual at vespers—

ZIPPA.

Ehem!

TOMASO.

I was coming home in a pious frame of mind—

ZIPPA.

—And a bottle in thy pocket.

TOMASO.

No!—in my hand. What should I stumble over—

ZIPPA.

—But a stone.

TOMASO.

A woman!

ZIPPA.

Fie! what's this you're going to tell me?

TOMASO.

She was dying with cold. Full of Christian charity.

ZIPPA.

—And new wine.

TOMASO.

Old wine, Zippa. The wine was old!

ZIPPA.

Well!

TOMASO.

I took her home.

ZIPPA.

Shame!—at thy years?

TOMASO.

And Angelo being out for the night—

ZIPPA.

There! there! you may skip the particulars.

TOMASO.

I say my own bed being in the garret—

ZIPPA.

Well, well!

TOMASO.

I put her into Angelo's.

ZIPPA.

Oh, unspeakable impudence! Didst thou do that?

TOMASO.

I had just left her to make a wine posset (for she was well nigh dead), when in popped my master,—finds her there —asks no questions,—kicks me into the street, and locks the door! *There's* the reward of virtue!

ZIPPA.

Did he not turn out the woman, too?

TOMASO.

Not as I remember.

ZIPPA.

Oh worse and worse! And thou hast not seen him since?

TOMASO.

I found me a soft stone, said my prayers, and went to sleep.

ZIPPA.

And hast thou not seen him to-day?

TOMASO.

Partly, I have!

ZIPPA.

Where? Tell me quickly!

TOMASO.

Give me the ducat.

ZIPPA [gives it him].

Quick! say on!

TOMASO.

I have a loose recollection, that, lying on that stone, Angelo called me by name. Looking up, I saw two Angelos, and two Tortesas, and soldiers with two spears each. [He figures in the air with his finger as if trying to remember.]

ZIPPA [aside].

(Ha! he is apprehended for the murder of Isabella! Say that my evidence might save his life! Not unless he love me!) Which way went he, Tomaso?

[TOMASO *points.*]

This way? (Then has he gone to be tried before the Duke.) Come with me, Tomaso! Come.

TOMASO.

Where?

ZIPPA.

To the Duke's palace! Come! [*Takes his arm.*]

TOMASO.

To the Duke's palace? There'll be kicking of heels in the ante-chamber!—Dry work! I'll spend thy ducat as we go along. Shall it be old wine, or new? [*Exeunt.*

SCENE III.

Hall of Judgment in the Ducal Palace. The DUKE *upon a raised throne on the left.* FALCONE *near his chair, and* ANGELO *on the opposite side of the stage with a guard.* ISABELLA *behind the* GUARD, *disguised as a monk.* TORTESA *stands near the centre of the stage, and* ZIPPA *and* TOMASO *in the left corner, listening eagerly.* COUNSELLORS *at a table, and crowd of spectators at the sides and rear.*

DUKE.

Are there more witnesses?

COUNSELLOR.

No more, my liege!

DUKE.

None for the prisoner?

COUNSELLOR.

He makes no defence
Beyond a firm denial.

FALCONE.

Is there wanting
Another proof, my liege, that he is guilty?

DUKE.

I fear he stands in deadly peril, Count.
[*To the* COUNSELLOR.]   Sum up the evidence.

[*He reads.*]

COUNSELLOR.

'Tis proved, my liege,
That for no honest or sufficient end,
The pris'ner practised on your noble Grace
And Count Falcone a contriv'd deceit,
Whereby he gained admittance to the lady.

TOMASO *exhibits signs of alarm.*

DUKE.

Most true!

COUNSELLOR.

That, till the eve before her death,
He had continual access to the palace;
And, having grown enamoured of the bride,
Essay'd by plots that never were matured,
And quarrels often forced on her betrothed,
To stay the bridal. That, against the will
Of her most noble father and the Duke,
The bride was resolute to keep her troth;
And so, preparing for the ceremony,
Upon her bridal morning was found dead.
'Tis proved again—that, while she lay in state,
The guard, at several periods of the night,
Did force the pris'ner from the chapel door;
And when the corse was stol'n from sanctuary
All search was vain, till, in the pris'ner's hands
Was found the veil that shrouded her. To these

And lighter proofs of sacrilege and murder
The prisoner has opposed his firm denial—
No more!

DUKE.

Does no one speak in his behalf?

TORTESA.

My liege! so far as turns the evidence
Upon the prisoner's quarrels with myself,
I'm free to say that they had such occasion
As any day may rise 'twixt men of honor.
As one of those aggriev'd by his offences,
You'll wonder I'm a suitor for his pardon—
But so I am! Besides that there is room
To hope him innocent, your Grace's realm
Holds not so wondrous and so rare a painter!
If he has kill'd the lady Isabella,
'Tis some amends that in his glorious picture
She's made immortal! If he stole her corse,
He can return, for that disfigured dust,
An Isabella fresh in changeless beauty!
Were it not well to pardon him, my lord?

ISABELLA [aside].

Oh brave Tortesa!

DUKE.

You have pleaded kindly

And eloquently, Signor! but the law
Can recognize no gift as plea for pardon.
For his rare picture he will have his fame;
But if the Isabella he has painted
Find not a voice to tell his innocence,
He dies at sunset!

ISABELLA [despairingly].

He is dead to me!

Yet he shall live!

[*She drops the cowl from her shoulders, and with her arms
folded, walks slowly to the feet of the* DUKE.]

FALCONE [*rushing forward*].

My daughter!

ANGELO [*with a gesture of agony*].

Lost!

TORTESA.

Alive!

ZIPPA [*energetically*].

Tortesa'll have her!

ISABELLA *retires to the back of the stage with her father,
and kneels to him, imploring in dumb show; the* DUKE *and
others watching*

TORTESA [*aside*].

So! all's right again?
Now for my lands, or Isabella?—Stay!
'Tis a brave girl, by heaven!

[*Reflects a moment.*]

A sleeping draught,
And so to Angelo. Her love for *me*
A counterfeit to take suspicion off!
It was well done! I feel my heart warm to her!

[*Reflects again.*]

Where could he hide her from our search to-day?

[*Looks round at* ISABELLA.

No? Yet the dress is like! It *was* the picture!
Herself—and *not* a picture! Now, by heaven,
A girl like that should be the wife of Cæsar!

[*Presses his hand upon his heart.*]

I've a new feeling here!

FALCONE comes forward, followed by ISABELLA *with gestures of supplication.*

FALCONE.

I will not hear you!
My liege, I pray you keep the prisoner
In durance till my daughter's fairly wed.
He has contriv'd against our peace and honor,
And howsoe'er this marvel be made clear,
She stands betroth'd, if he is in the mind,
To the brave Signor, yonder!

DUKE.

This were well—
What says Tortesa?

TORTESA.

If my liege permit,
I will address my answer to this lady.

[*Turns to* ISABELLA.]

For reasons which I need not give you now,
Fair Isabella! I became your suitor.
My motives were unworthy you and me—
Yet I was true—I never said I lov'd you!
Your father sold you me for lands and money—
(Pardon me, Duke! And you, fair Isabella!
You will—ere I am done!) I push'd my suit!
The bridal day came on, and clos'd in mourning;
For the fair bride it dawn'd upon was dead,
I had my shame and losses to remember—
But in my heart sat sorrow uppermost,
And pity—for I thought your heart was broken.

[ISABELLA *begins to discover interest in his story, and*
ANGELO *watches her with jealous eagerness.*]

I see you here again! You are my bride!
Your father holds me to my bargain for you!
The lights are burning on the nuptial altar—

The bridal chamber and the feast, all ready!
What stays the marriage now?—*my new-born love!*
That nuptial feast were fruit from Paradise—
I cannot touch it till *you* bid me welcome!
That nuptial chamber were the lap of heaven—
I cannot enter till *you* call me in!

[*Takes a ring from his bosom.*]

Here is the golden ring you should have worn.
Tell me to give it to my rival there—
I'll break my heart to do so! [*Holds it towards* ANGELO.]

ISABELLA [*looking at her father*].

Would I might!

TORTESA.

You shall if't please you!

FALCONE.

I command thee, never!
My liege, permit me to take home my daughter!
And, Signor, you—if you would keep your troth—
To-morrow come, and end this halting bridal!
Home! Isabella! [*Takes his daughter's hand.*]

TORTESA [*taking it from him*].

Stay, she is not yours!

[*Turns to the* DUKE.]

My gracious liege, there is a law in Florence,
That if a father, for no guilt or shame,
Disown, and shut his door upon his daughter,
She is the child of him who succors her;
Who, by the shelter of a single night,
Becomes endowed with the authority
Lost by the other. Is't not so?

DUKE.

So runs

The law of Florence, and I see your drift—
For, look, my lord! [*to* FALCONE] if that dread apparition
You saw last night, was this your living daughter,
You stand within the peril of that law.

FALCONE.

My liege!

ISABELLA [*looking admiringly at* TORTESA].

Oh, noble Signor!

TORTESA [*to* ISABELLA].

Was't well done?
Shall I give Angelo the ring?

As she is about to take it from him, TOMASO *steps in behind,
and pulls* ISABELLA *by the sleeve.*

TOMASO.

Stay there!
What wilt thou do for dowry? I'm thy father?
But—save some flasks of wine—

ISABELLA [*sorrowfully*].

Would I were richer
For thy sake, Angelo!

TORTESA *looks at her an instant, and then steps to the table
and writes.*

ANGELO [*coming forward with an effort*].

Look, Isabella!
I stand between thee and a life of sunshine.
Thou wert both rich and honor'd, *but for me!*
That thou *couldst* wed mē, beggar as I am,

Is bliss to think on—but see how I rob thee!
I have a loving heart—but am a beggar!
There is a loving heart—

[Points to TORTESA.]

—With wealth and honor!

TORTESA *steps between them, and hands a paper to* ANGELO.

TORTESA [to ISABELLA].

Say thou wilt wed the poorer.

ISABELLA [offers her hand to ANGELO].

So I will!

TORTESA.

Then am I blest, for he's as rich as I—
Yet, in his genius, has one jewel more!

ISABELLA.

What sayst thou?

ANGELO reads earnestly

TORTESA.

In a mortal quarrel, lady!

'Tis thought ill-luck to have the better sword;
For the good angels, who look sorrowing on,
In heavenly pity take the weaker side!

ISABELLA.

What is it, Angelo?

ANGELO.

A deed to *me*

Of the Falcone palaces and lands,
And all the moneys forfeit by your father!—
By heaven, I'll not be mocked!

TORTESA.

The deed is yours—
What mockery in that?

ISABELLA [*tenderly to* TORTESA].

It is not kind
To make refusal of your love a pain!

TORTESA.

I would 'twould *kill* you to refuse me, lady!
So should the blood plead for me at your heart!
Shall I give up the ring? [*Offers it.*]

ISABELLA [*hesitatingly*].

Let me look on it!

TORTESA [*withdrawing it*].

A moment yet! You'll give it ere you think!
Oh, is it fair that Angelo had *days*,
To tell his love, and I have not *one hour?*
How know you that I cannot love as well?

ISABELLA.

'Tis possible!

TORTESA.

Ah! Thanks!

ISABELLA.

But I have given
My heart to him!

TORTESA.

You gave your *troth* to me!
If, of these two gifts you must take back one,
Rob not the poorer! Shall I keep the ring?

ISABELLA *looks down.*

ANGELO.

She hesitates! I've waited here too long!

[*Tears the deed in two.*]

Perish your gift, and farewell Isabella!

ISABELLA [*advancing a step with clasp'd hands*].

You'll kill me, Angelo! Come back!

TORTESA [*seizing him by the hand as he hesitates and flinging
him back with a strong effort*].

He shall!

ANGELO.

Stand from my path! Or, if you care to try
Some other weapon than a glozing tongue,
Follow me forth where we may find the room!

TORTESA.

You shall not go.

ANGELO [*draws*].

Have at thee then!

[*Attacks* TORTESA, *who disarms him, and holds his sword-
point to his breast.* DUKE *and others come forward.*]

TORTESA.

The bar
'Twixt me and heaven, boy! is the life I hold
Now at my mercy! Take it, Isabella!
And with it the poor gift he threw away!
I'll write a new deed ere you've time to marry.
So take your troth back with your bridal ring,
And thus I join you!

[*Takes* ISABELLA's *hand, but* ANGELO *refuses his.*]

ANGELO [*proudly*].

                     Never! But for me,
The hand you hold were joyfully your own!
Shall I receive a life and fortune from you,
Yet stand 'twixt you and *that?*

ISABELLA [*turning from* ANGELO].

                  Thou dost not love me!

TORTESA.

Believe it not! He does! An instant more
I'll brush this new-spun cobweb from his eyes.

[*Approaches* ZIPPA.]

Fair Zippa! in this cross'd and tangled world
Few wed the one they could have lov'd the best,
And fewer still wed well for happiness!
We each have lost to-day what best we love.
But as the drops, that mingled in the sky,
Are torn apart in the tempestuous sea,
Yet with a new drop tremble into one,
We two, if you're content, may swim together!
What say you?

               ZIPPA [*giving her hand*].

                I have thought on it before,
When I believed you cold and treacherous,
'Tis easy when I know you kind and noble.

TORTESA.

To-morrow then we'll wed; and now, fair Signor,

[*To* ANGELO.]

Take you her hand, nor fear to rob Tortesa!

[*Turns to the* DUKE.]

Shall it be so, my liege?

DUKE.

You please me well.
And if you'll join your marriage feasts together
I'll play my part, and give the brides away!

TORTESA.

Not so, my liege! I could not see her *wed him*.
To *give her to him* has been all I could;
For I have sought her with the dearest pulses
That quicken in my heart, my *love and scorn*.
She's taught me that the high-born may be true.
I thank her for it—but, too close on that
Follow'd the love, whose lightning flash of honor
Brightens, but straight is dark again! My liege,
The poor who leap up to the stars for duty
Must drop to earth again! and here, if't please you,
I take my feet forever from your palace,
And, match'd as best beseems me, say farewell.

[*Takes* ZIPPA'S *hand, and the curtain drops.*]

THE END.

THE PEOPLE'S LAWYER

By Joseph S. Jones

DR. JOSEPH STEVENS JONES

(1809–1877.)

A book might well be written on the development of the Yankee type in the history of the American Drama. Such a consideration would involve something more than the fact that Royall Tyler, in "The Contrast", was the first American dramatist to sketch his outlines. It suggests the evaluation of a special kind of acting which gripped the country for many years, and resulted in rivalry among a number of actors, whose power of mimicry and appreciation of eccentricity were strongly developed.

The form of entertainment, which encouraged such Yankee delineation as James H. Hackett was accustomed to give— in which he varied the evening with passage from New England drawl to Irish wit, and then to French vivacity— was probably suggested by the success of Charles Mathews, the English actor, in this country. But the character of the Yankee was indigenous to the soil.

A long list of plays, accounted as being of distinction, exploited the Yankee type. Such a list includes L. Beach's "Jonathan Postfree; or, The Honest Yankee" (1807), A. B. Lindsley's "Love and Friendship; or, Yankee Notions" (1809), Micah Hawkins' "The Saw-Mill; or, a Yankee Trick" (1824), Samuel Woodworth's pastoral opera, "The Forest Rose; or, American Farmers" (1825), Mrs. Margaret Botsford's "The Reign of Reform; or, Yankee Doodle Court", David Humphrey's "The Yankee in England" (1815), and a long roll of plays written by dramatists who, like Dr. Jones, catered to the demands of one or more of the special Yankee actors.

Of these special actors, three in particular attract our attention: James H. Hackett, George Handel Hill (1809– 1848) and Dan Marble (1810–1849). There were others, of course, like Silsbee, but these magic three held the field. In

381

fact one of them gained so great a reputation that any communication, simply addressed to "Yankee" Hill, would have reached him with little delay.

None of these actors had any far-fetched notions that they were helping to develop a phase of American Drama. They dropped into the eccentric acting through their adaptability. In fact it is said that Dan Marble discovered his genius for New England dialect by imitating his landlady's daughter so inimitably that she, herself, called him down into the best parlor one evening to entertain her guests by "mocking" her.

And though we would not have the criticism apply generally, still we are of the belief that much of the Yankee acting of that day must have been akin to horseplay, to buffoonery, except where a genius heightened the characterization, and made it human. The rôle of *Solon Shingle,* for example, is scarcely discernible in all its Yankee attractiveness, on reading the text. But under the spell of Owens, it took on deeper and more colorful significance.

The different stage directions for the Yankee costume would indicate that the American dramatist, more than likely, had in mind the conventional *Yankee Doodle,* or else the noisy farmer, honest and common, as in Tom Taylor's "Our American Cousin". He was dressed either in a tall hat, with striped trousers, and swallow-tail-coat, wearing the conventional chin beard and red wig, or else a linen duster graced his person, capped by the broad-brimmed hat. The very character of his name shows the mixture of atmospheric truthfulness and cartoon humor in his make-up: *Deuteronomy Dutiful, Solon Shingle,* and *Sam Slick.* It was not a high-typed drama, but it was distinctly native.

Hackett held the field, *par excellence,* for the Yankee type, until the advent of "Yankee" Hill. In his "Recollections of Twenty-six Years as an Actor", Wemyss writes:

> Mr. Hackett created a new dramatic character, in the person of a Down East Yankee, which will place his name in a conspicious station in the future history of the American stage; although critics will exclaim against the alteration and mutilation of Colman's play of "Who Wants a Guinea?" and the Englishmen will hold up their hands in horror at the idea of *Soloman Grundy,* the

French cockney, being metamorphosed into *Jonathan,* a genuine Yankee; yet Hackett deserves, and will obtain the credit, for placing upon the stage a character which will supply the place to an American author of the Yorkshire clown of English comedy, so well handled by Morton.

Hackett was very tenacious of his position, and it was not long before he realized that it was being jeopardized by the increasing fame of Hill. The critics of the time throw their favor in the balance of the latter. For example, Ludlow, in his "Dramatic Life As I Found It", attributing Hackett's attitude to one of jealousy, writes of Hill in the following terms:

His delineations of the peculiarities of the genuine Down-Easter—the pure, unadulterated "Yankee" of the lower class—were, in my estimation, far ahead of those of any who have attempted that peculiar line, not even excepting Dan Marble, who certainly ranked next to him. It is said Mr. Hill first got the idea of introducing Yankee character on the stage from seeing Aleck Simpson, an excellent comedian, enact the character of *Jonathan Ploughboy.*

But though Hackett was to abandon his specialty, and to be known to the future as "Falstaff" Hackett, he did not relinquish his honours without an attempted fight. Ludlow, showing no sympathy for this attitude, quotes a letter from Hackett, which suggests his mood:

Philadelphia, 5th November, 1833.
My dear Wemyss:—
During my absence in England, *Mr. Hill* has had the *impudence,* as well as *injustice,* to perform, without my permission, my best Yankee character, *Solomon Swop,* (well-known as unpublished, and of my own originating) at the Park (some dozen times and elsewhere). I have, of course, a remedy *at law* against *him* and the *managers* who permit it, but a resort to it would be looked upon, perhaps, by the public, (who don't understand these

matters,) as a kind of *ill nature* on my part, and beneath me; and therefore to prevent my property being thus further hackneyed after being taken down from my mouth, or otherwise surreptitiously obtained, I have notified managers generally of the fact, and shall consider their *permitting* such an infringement of the most unalienable of literary rights, (the spinning of one's own brains) an act of open hostility to me, and proceed accordingly. Mr. Hill has character enough of his own, without carrying on that species of *Yankeeism,* and if I cannot protect myself from having my characters made stale by such depredations, I will resort to rigorous measures against both him and the manager, wherever the infringement transpires. Of course I do not fear *your* permitting or countenancing such *dishonesty,* but I thought I would drop you a line, as you might be ignorant of the *fact* of *Solomon Swop being,* in every respect, my own *exclusive property.* I have stopped him in *Boston, New-York,* and *here,* but understand he has been trying it in *Albany;* and though he will not attempt it *again there,* if I can catch him in *New-York,* where I am returning to-morrow, I must clap the "Grace upon him, for example's sake" . . .

This close competition, therefore, must have finally reduced itself to real merit in acting. For, speaking of Hill's performances, his biographer says:

It was this faculty, to use a hackneyed phrase, of throwing himself body and spirit, into a part, which gave to his Yankee a richness and truthfulness not approached by any actor before or since his time. He did not merely put on a flaxen wig, a long-tailed coat, a short vest, a bell-crowned hat, and straps to his pantaloons long enough for suspenders, nor thus attired did he content himself by imitating the peculiar drawl and queer expressions of the Yankee, for the veriest bungler on earth can do all this, but the spirit of Yankeedom pervaded every action of his body, peeped from his expressive eyes with such sly meaning, that it was difficult for the time being, not to believe it was a mistake in the bills, when they announced Mr. Hill as *Mr. Wheeler,* instead of announcing the veritable *Major Wheeler* himself.

It was because of these pronounced excellences, and because of the fact that, when he began his specialty there was not a great variety of Yankee parts, that, no sooner had Hill established himself in Woodworth's "Forest Rose", than he offered a prize of four hundred dollars for a play to fit his eccentricities. The judges, among them Verplanck and Washington Irving, failed to reach an agreement; so they awarded the money rather than the prize to Woodworth for his "The Foundling of the Sea". In 1834, Hill went to the New York Park Theatre, in John Augustus Stone's "Knight of the Golden Fleece", the originality of which has often been disputed. It was Hill's lack of education, according to Wemyss, that prevented him from reaching greater distinction in his work. Yet when he went to England he met with favor everywhere.

These men had repertories that grew by what they fed on. They increased from year to year, and the Yankee play became a specialty with certain dramatists. Dr. Jones was one of these specialists. The type did not bring much profit to the writers, who looked at them more as "skits" for entertainment than as sources of perpetual revenue. The consequence is, whatever money they received in return for their labor was as a reward rather than as their due. We shall find that to be the case with Dr. Jones's "The People's Lawyer", and we are told, in the record of Dan Marble's busy life, that it was the same with him. Speaking of Logan's "Yankee Land", the narrative says:

> The piece proved very successful, but lost the actor nothing, the author making the actor a present of that play, and soon after gave him another and excellent one —"The Wool-dealer"—and this was followed by a third, from the same author, same price—nothing.

This paragraph assists in establishing the authorship of a piece which Wegelin credits to no one, because the title-page of the published play, in the French edition, is without name.

I mean "The Vermont Wool-dealer", here referred to as "The Wool-dealer". Further references to the piece may be had by consulting the London papers the morning after Marble presented it, on September 30, 1844. There are others, also, who credit it to Cornelius Logan, a Cincinnati theatre-manager, and an ardent supporter of the stage against the onslaughts of the pulpit. He was the father of Olive Logan, the actress. Besides doing these plays for Dan Marble, he essayed a drama, "The Wag of Maine", for Hackett.

It is thus clear how the Yankee type received an impetus, and it was not long before the repertories increased rapidly. Marble, as *Zekiel Longshaw,* a cute Yankee in "Nighthawk", as *Sam Patch* in E. H. Thompson's play of that name, and in dramas by Jones, Bernard, Woodworth and Logan, was a striking example. Quick to recognize the foundation for other dramas, there was no etiquette as to the author who first conceived a part. It might be Thompson's *Sam Patch* which had caught fire; if Thompson had nothing further to contribute on the subject, it was passed on to another writer, in this particular case, J. P. Addams, a Boston comedian, who invented the adventures of "Sam Patch in France".

The very names of the pieces, in a way, suggest their scope and color. On Marble's list I find N. H. Bannister's "Bush Whacker", J. S. Robb's "People's Candidate", and other pieces of slight variety by H. J. Conway, Lawrence Labree, O. E. Durivage and Thomas R. Whitney. In the minds of the Yankee exploiter, the Yankee became the centre of the universe.

Dr. Jones rises from the level of his several hundred pieces on the wings of John E. Owens's excellence in the character of *Solon Shingle.* Born in 1809, he was an actor in his early life, and at various times was proprietor and manager of the Old National and the Tremont Theatres, in Boston. It was in 1843 that he graduated from the Harvard Medical School, and then he practised in Boston for several years. His career at the Tremont Theatre was partly aided by the fact that, for a time, he had John Gilbert as stage-manager. But the régime was not noteworthy, if the actor, George Vandenhoff, is to be believed in his "An Actor's Note-Book",

He went to the Tremont for an engagement, in November, 1842.

> Dr. Jones, a fair and easy-going, good-natured but not very enterprising man [he writes] was the manager; and, I think, with the exception of that excellent, solid, sterling actor, John Gilbert, and his wife, the company was about as poor a one, as a whole, as was ever assembled in the walls of a respectable theatre.

In his capacity as manager, Jones met Hill and Marble, and in this way was importuned to write for them. In fact, "The People's Lawyer" was first played at the Boston National, with "Yankee" Hill as *Solon Shingle*.

As a writer, Dr. Jones was ever active. To his credit, a staggering but incomplete list of plays might be assembled. From various sources we are able to gather such titles as "The Liberty Tree", "The Fire Warrior", "The Siege of Boston", "Moll Pitcher", "Stephen Burrough", "The Carpenter of Rouen", and its sequel, "The Surgeon of Paris; or, The Mask of the Huguenots", "Job and Jacob Gray", "The Last Dollar", "The Sons of the Cape", "Zofara", "Captain Lascar", and "Paul Revere," his last piece, produced at the Boston Museum during the season of 1875–76.

To his account may also be credited "The Usurper; or, Americans in Tripoli", "Captain Kidd; or, The Wizard of the Sea", "The Wheelwright", "The Green Mountain Boy", "The Last Days of Pompey", "Plymouth Rock", and he came very near writing for Marble, "Family Ties", about which an amusing conversation is recorded in Marble's "Reminiscences". The ease with which Dr. Jones turned forth these plays is seen from the preface to his "Moll Pitcher; or, The Fortune Teller of Lynn" (1855), wherein he writes:

> I have had objections to publishing my plays; one, that they were written to be acted to the people, and not to be read by them; another, that by the publication I lost my ownership, copyright giving no protection against representation upon the stage.
> . . . acquaint the critic that the construction of "Moll

Pitcher" occupied but two or three days; that it is a stage
drama. . . .

An examination of the titles of his plays will reveal the
fact that Dr. Jones was a good son of New England. Certainly, he was an honored citizen of Boston, for many years
occupying the position of City Physician. Rees claims that,
in addition, so well versed was he in his profession, he
lectured often on Physiology and Materia Medica. His death,
brought about partly by the news of the sudden death of a
daughter, occurred in Boston, on December 29, 1877. He
left four children, one of whom, Nathaniel D. Jones, was an
actor.

"The People's Lawyer" was first given by Hill in 1839.
At the Arch Street Theatre, in Philadelphia, it was produced
with Charles Burke, Jefferson's half-brother, in the rôle of
Solon Shingle. It was revived in Boston, at the Howard
Athenæum, with an excellent comedy cast. When Owens
stepped in and produced the play, he found *Solon* only an
incidental part. The reader will realize how true this is in
the printed text. But ever in accord with his method, Owens
enriched the meagre lines by that process of humanizing
which made his *John Unit* such a distinct creation. His voice,
according to his wife, seemed "to ruralize", and, if accounts
are to be believed, he must have been the medium of transformation, in the delineation of the stage Yankee, between
the broad work of Marble and Hill and the more realistic
work of Denman Thompson in "The Old Homestead".

The transformation made in Jones's manuscript was done
without consultation with him. The play was cut to farce
length, new business was introduced, and a copyright was
applied for a play under the title of "Solon Shingle". It
soon came to be used as an excellent "after-piece" in Owens's
repertory. He regarded it as of his own creation, and, when
he went to Boston, it was his desire to hunt out the author
of the original, and to thank him for furnishing the skeleton
to what turned out to be such a profitable venture.

The fact is, Owens realized more than two hundred and
fifty thousand dollars out of the rôle. Naturally, therefore,
his conscience prompted him to be gracious to the originator
of the part. And so, he sent the author a check in apprecia-

tion. To which Dr. Jones wrote the following acknowledgment:

Boston, September 23rd, 1871.

John E. Owens, Esq.

My dear Sir,—Your favour enclosing a check drawn by you and payable to my order, for "Five Hundred Dollars," was duly received. "The Souvenir," so gracefully tendered, I accept with peculiar gratification in consequence of its relation to one of my earliest efforts as a dramatist, "The People's Lawyer", written nearly two-score years ago.

You, sir, have made *Solon Shingle* famous, prolonged his stage existence, and preserved to this time this relic of the dramatic past.

My inclination would lead me to thank you, in the presence of the public, for your novel recognition of my claim to the authorship of the drama in which *Mr. Shingle* was first introduced. I have not considered it proper, without your approval, to reply to your note through the press.

I wish, however, that your gratuitous manifestation should be known to all who have interest in the success of plays and players.

Let me again repeat my appreciation of the gift, and the generous motive that suggested it.

Very truly yours,

Jos. S. Jones.

But whether through natural modesty, or through a strong desire not to overcloud his own creative work by the intrusion of another claim to authorship, Owens hastened to inform Jones that he did not care for any publicity.

The pleasure you express at the reception of the souvenir [he wrote] is not one-tenth of that which I experience in knowing that I have rendered to your gratification. Let that content us.

The Yankee type in literature became more subtle as the years advanced, and similar types for other localities began to arise. Lowell's "Bigelow Papers", Judge Baldwin's "Flushtimes in Alabama", Bret Harte's creations, are more refined cousins of the earlier attempts at the delineation of American character. Herne's "Shore Acres" excelled them all by the depth and truth of its realism. "David Harum", "Mrs. Wiggs of the Cabbage Patch", "The County Chairman", all have behind them the same incentive—to pick up the eccentricities of character and locality, and place them on the stage for themselves alone. The one great difference between the type play of to-day and yesterday is the fact that the type actor, who did as much creative work to a part as the dramatist, if not more, has gone out of fashion, and it is difficult to revive the species.

SOLON SHINGLE

Dramatis Personæ and Cast.

National Theatre, Boston, 1839.

Robert Howard, the People's Lawyer. Mr. Hudson Kirby.
Hugh Winslow, a Merchant..........Mr. W. Marshall.
Solon Shingle, a Country Teamster...Mr. G. H. Hill.
Charles Otis, a Clerk...............Mr. W. M. Leman.
John Ellsley, a Clerk...............Mr. C. H. Saunders.
Tripper, an Attorney-at-Law........Mr. G. H. Wyatt.
Judge of the Court.................Mr. Haynes.
Sheriff of the Court...............Mr. Robinson.
Clerk of the Court.................Mr. Beals.
Thompson, } Police Officers........ { Mr. Samuels.
Quirk,   }   { Mr. Thomas.
John, a Porter.....................Mr. Simonds.
Foreman of the Jury...............Mr. Sampson.
Timid, a Lawyer...................Mr. Clapp.
Eleven Jurymen.
Mrs. Otis..........................Mrs. Pelby.
Grace Otis........................Mrs. Anderson.

In the French "Acting Edition", *Solon Shingle's* costume is thus indicated: "Dark drab old-fashioned surtout with capes, sheep's grey trowsers, lead-coloured striped vest, old style black stock, cow-hide boots, broad-brimmed, low-crowned hat, bald-headed flaxen wig." Owens in the part may be judged by his picture in Winter's "The Wallet of Time", and by pictures in his "Memories".

BIBLIOGRAPHICAL NOTE

As an example of the mine of unused material waiting for the student of the American Theatre to systematize, I give here some references to Jones, sent me, on request, by the Librarian of the Boston Public Library.

The following material, relating to the Tremont Theatre under the management of J. S. Jones, may be consulted in the Brown Dramatic Collection:

The Tremont Theatre. Blotter. 1839–41. Journal. 1839–41. 101 pages. MS. Ledger, A. 1839–41. 104 pages.

The Tremont Theatre. Letters, financial statements, reports, applications for positions, etc. Scrap-book. Boston, 1842–43. The letters are addressed to J. S. Jones, the manager of the Tremont Theatre.

The Tremont Theatre. Playbills. Feb. 16, 1829—Dec. 31, 1839; Jan. 2, 1840—June 14, 1841. Two volumes.

"Return Book", being a statement in detail of every night's receipts, . . . the plays performed, the names of the stars, etc., for the entire season of 1839–40, 1840–41, 1842–45. When it was under the management of Jones. MS. Three volumes in one.

Tremont Theatre. Scrap-book of various manuscripts relating to. MSS. 1827–1843.

Thirty-four play-bills, dating from Feb. 3, 1829, to Jan. 14, 1841. Broadsides.

A History of the Tremont Theatre under J. S. Jones is in "A Record of the Boston Stage", by William W. Clapp, Jr. Boston: J. Munroe Co. 1853. Chap. xxv. pp. 362–375.

The Harvard Medical School. By Thomas F. Harrington, vol. 3, 1905, says that "Joseph Stevens Jones" was "born September 28, 1809, at Boston; died December 29, 1877, at Boston, where he practised."

THE PEOPLE'S LAWYER

ACT I.

SCENE I.—*A counting-room, opening into a loft, in which are seen barrels, cases, &c.; a desk on right; desk on left; table and chairs on left; a dry goods case near the desk; an iron safe. Door center.*

CHARLES OTIS *discovered at desk writing; enter* MR. TRIPPER.

TRIPPER. Mr. Winslow has not yet returned, Mr. Otis?

CHARLES. I have not seen him, sir. He has not been in the counting-room since my return.

TRIPPER. Is Mr. Ellsley in the store?

CHARLES. No sir, but he soon will be in, sir—

[*Continuing writing.*

TRIPPER. Smart young man is that Ellsley. He will one day be a rich man; I think, however, you are the favourite with Mr. Winslow.

CHARLES. I am happy to enjoy the confidence of my employer, and it shall be my constant effort to deserve it.

TRIPPER. Say to Mr. Winslow that I called, and if he wishes to see me, I shall remain an hour at my lodgings.

CHARLES. I will, sir—[TRIPPER *exits, passing* JOHN ELLSLEY, *who enters at the same time.*

JOHN. Charley, where's the old man?

CHARLES. I don't know.

JOHN. Do you know who that man was that just went out?

CHARLES. Mr. Winslow's attorney. He has been' complimenting you.

JOHN. Has he? I'm glad of it—I wish I could raise the wind somewhere; or Lawyer Tripper, or some other lawyer, will be jogging my memory, I'm afraid. I must take the benefit of the act, Charley—how much do you think I spent last week?

393

CHARLES. I cannot guess; I heard you say that you had been extravagant.

JOHN. A cool hundred—sleighrides, balls, etc., hot suppers do melt up the cash. But you know nothing about it; you won't go in for a bit of fun.

CHARLES. I cannot afford it,—you know it.

JOHN. Didn't I offer to stand the blunt? It would not have cost you a red cent.

CHARLES. Pleasures that I cannot afford to pay for, I cannot indulge in at the expense of others. John, there is one thing I cannot understand. Tell me, how can clerks with small salaries spend so much money in imitating the habits of men of fortune? You may indulge—your father is rich.

JOHN. Why, Charley, my boy, it is not the salary the clerk depends upon, so much as his perquisites. They tell the story.

CHARLES. Perquisites!

JOHN., Yes, the self-given privilege of investing the cash balances—helping themselves when they find themselves short, and their employers with something over.

CHARLES. Stealing?

JOHN. Stealing! that's the name of the science of abstraction; even if a fellow is so unlucky as to be found out, men who spend for their own purposes funds entrusted to their care, are not called thieves, but defaulters—not stealing, Charley, but financiering. Well, how much longer are you going to stay, working here by candle light? I shall close my books.

CHARLES. Mr. Winslow requested me to stay till he returned; as I must be here, I prefer work to idleness.

JOHN. You are a favourite of the old man's—I think the old man is in love with your pretty sister; if he should marry her, and take you in as a partner, how you would flourish.

CHARLES. Don't interrupt me now.

JOHN. There's a great ball to-night, and that pretty Miss Blazon is to be there; I am going, and the way I'll take the shine out of some of the boys will be high. I sha'n't go till nine. Charley, if Mr. Winslow wants me—I wish you'd go; I'll get you a ticket.

CHARLES. I cannot go; I have no wish to go.

JOHN. You need not tell the old man that I am going to a ball. He's too religious to believe in dancing. We clerks know a thing or two; and sometimes hear our master's voice through thin partitions, in places that they don't carry their wives. I mean to publish a book—call it the "Clerk's Guide," to show young men from the country how to forget ploughing, planting, sowing, hoeing, mowing. Well, Charley, if you won't go, I will; I shall go out the back way. Leave a key for me; I may want to come into the store after the ball is over. I'll have a night of it; good-bye, Charley. [*Exit.*

CHARLES. [*Comes forward.*] A night of it. He knows not of my poverty, or he would not have asked me to go to a ball, or wonder at my refusal. Daily, sums of gold and silver pass through my hands, sufficient to purchase splendour and independence,—yet not mine. Nightly do I go to a home where poverty is ever present, and distress may suddenly come with a temptation to use what is another's. The evil one shall not overcome me; I can bear my privations. I will be honest. [*Goes again to desk.*

MR. WINSLOW *enters.*

WINSLOW. Are you still here, Charles? Where is Mr. Ellsley?

CHARLES. He has just left the store, sir.

WINSLOW. I will not detain you long. I wish to speak to you on a subject of some importance. Has my attorney called?

CHARLES. He has, sir.

WINSLOW. Charles, you recollect, I dare say, that some time since, Colonel Spencer gave me a check on the Bank of Mobile?

CHARLES. I recollect seeing him sign a check, but I thought it was on a bank in the city.

WINSLOW. No, 'twas the Bank of Mobile; you remember he spoke of his extensive interest in it.

CHARLES. He did speak of a bank, but I still have an impression that the check related to a bank here.

WINSLOW. No doubt you think so; you are wrong—what are you doing now?

CHARLES. There's a trifling error in Mr. Ellsley's cash here, I'm trying to trace.

WINSLOW. Never mind that now. This check is of considerable consequence to me; and I assure you it will be greatly to your advantage to remember rightly; for should the matter be made the subject of a legal controversy, I must depend on your knowledge to evidence the facts in the case. Colonel Spencer is dead—I am apprehensive of trouble with his executors—just think again.

CHARLES. I am thinking, sir, but——

WINSLOW. The thing is undoubtedly coming to your mind as I represent it.

CHARLES. My memory is somewhat confused on the subject; but reflection seems only to confirm my first impression.

WINSLOW. 'Tis strange. By the way, Charles, your work is hard; I will raise your salary another hundred dollars. To-morrow, I believe, ends the quarter—take the advance.

CHARLES. Sir, I thank you; I will deserve your bounty.

WINSLOW. But about the check; you will have no objection to tell the good jury of the court, should we have a trial, that you saw Colonel Spencer give me a Mobile check, signed by him; remembering all the time that, in performing this little act of friendship, or I might say duty, you are materially benefiting yourself.

CHARLES. I will most cheerfully tell them all I know about it, for I should be glad to convince you of my devotion to your interests. But not for worlds would I testify to a circumstance, of the truth of which I'm not positive.

WINSLOW. Of course not—in this case you testify upon my word; should you make a small mistake, the blame be mine. The day may come, Charles, that will see you a partner in my establishment, as a reward for your devotion to my interests. There are profit and honour in connection with the name of Winslow, the merchant; think of it, Charles.

CHARLES. I cannot, for my life, sir, speak aught but the truth.

WINSLOW. The truth should not be spoken at all times; my lawyer shall instruct you what to say. He will lead you to the proper answers.

CHARLES. You have mistaken my character, sir; a lie is a lie, disguise it as you may. I am young, sir, but have not forgotten the precepts of my father, or the example of my mother.

WINSLOW. Your conscience, young man, is of too tender a

kind to aid you in the acquirement of wealth; you are poor—
this over-honesty will keep you so.

CHARLES. I own, I do feel the pangs of poverty; I have
left this place of toil for a home, where no meal was ready to
appease the cravings of hunger; a fireless hearth, a mother
with her children in tears, were my only welcome home. It
was home, the home of honesty; and sooner shall this body
be consumed by hunger, sooner shall my tongue be torn out
by the roots, than I infringe one little hair's breadth upon the
law which says, "Thou shalt not bear false witness against
thy neighbour."

Enter ROBERT HOWARD, *in a plain working-dress; he stops
center.*

WINSLOW. Then may my curses fall on thee, thou base son
of a baser father; and they shall, if my influence over thy
destiny is moved by hate. Hence; presume not again to set
your foot within my door; the character I will give you shall
shut you from all hopes of another situation. You have
goaded the lion, and may test his strength.

[CHARLES *closes his books and prepares to leave.*

HOWARD. [*Aside.*] The Lion, no, the Viper, is disturbed,
and he may feel his fangs.

CHARLES. Mr. Winslow, I have ever done my duty—good
night, sir—poor mother—poor sisters. [*Aside, and exit.*

WINSLOW. Fool! [*Seeing* HOWARD, *who comes down.*]
You have listened to my conversation, sir?

HOWARD. Unwillingly, sir, to your harsh reproof to your
clerk. I come, sir, on business. Will you give me immediate
answer to that proposition? [*Holding a paper.*] I called
this morning—you were out.

WINSLOW. [*Reads.*] "From the widow of Mr. Worthy."
I have but one answer—all that the law compels me to pay
is ready. I know my ground. She has no money; I have.
The time that must elapse before a judgment can be given
against me, with the expenses contingent upon the continuance of the suit, will force her to abandon her claim; you
have my answer.

HOWARD. And this is your answer. Do not deceive yourself, Mr. Winslow; the battle is not always for the strong.
I am instructed to inform you that the widow's claim will be

defended by competent counsel, who will, if necessary, furnish the requisite funds. I speak upon the authority of one who never pleads except where he sees oppression preying upon poverty and innocence.

WINSLOW. I know who you mean; a demagogue, seeking political advancement, basing his ambitious views upon affected generosity and patriotism. The man they style the "People's Lawyer," the people's friend. His services may be bought by my gold. I will retain him myself.

HOWARD. His services cannot be bought, sir. I have performed my duty, and will return your reply; as an humble citizen I may speak my thoughts. Hugh Winslow, do right; though you pile heaps of gold as stumbling blocks in the path of Justice, still will the righteous judgment overtake the evil doer.

WINSLOW. Go, sir; no longer insult me in my own house. I am determined.

HOWARD. To do wrong.

WINSLOW. Fellow, leave the place this instant, or I will throw you from a window to the street.

HOWARD. I have little to fear from your threat; I will spare you the attempt; I shun an affray, sir, but will defend myself from any assault. You *shall some day know who I am, and be sorry for this injustice.* [*Exit.*

WINSLOW. So much for the education of the poor. Here is a common mechanic, bullying a gentleman in college style. I thought Charles Otis had been more pliant to my will; if I cannot have his testimony, I must make sure he's not used against me. His good name is his pride, his honesty his great defense; I must find means to blast this airy fabric; Ellsley has a rich father—he is profligate. I'll try him, and at once. [*Sits at table.*

SOLON SHINGLE *enters.*

SOLON. Squire Winslow, how do you do? I most broke my shanks on your stairs.

WINSLOW. [*Interrupted—aside.*] Quite well, sir.

SOLON. I kinder conjured that your shop would be shut up, but I see'd a light through the winder, so I thought I'd come in.

WINSLOW. When did you come to town? [*Writing.*

SOLON. I come this morning, bright and early. Well, how do matters and things stand with you, considerin'?

[*Takes chair.*

WINSLOW. Much as usual, sir. [*Still writing and betraying much embarrassment.* SOLON *goes to table and looks over writing.*] This is a private affair, Mr. Shingle.

SOLON. Jest so; well, then, you don't keer about my reading on it. If I pester you any, jest say so; I'll take the hint without the kick.

WINSLOW. I'm happy to see you, but I wish you had come a little earlier; if you can, call to-morrow.

SOLON. Call to-morrow—I shall be dreadful busy to-morrow. I'll wait till you get through your pucker. I've got a case in court about a brindle cow, and Squire Dingle asked me how I was going tu sware, and I told him I should sware like lightning agin him; these are revolutionary times —my father fit in the Revolution, that is, he druv a baggage-wagon.

WINSLOW. [*Aside.*] What the devil sent him here now?

SOLON. Mr. Winslow, you are the head horse in the temperance team, and as I——

WINSLOW. You have some business with me?

SOLON. Jest so, Mr. Winslow—what's good to cure the mumps?

WINSLOW. Mr. Shingle, I am engaged this evening, on very particular business; I am now going out and shall not return.

SOLON. Jest so; well, my cattle are outside there—there's no danger on 'em, is there?

WINSLOW. I presume not. What have you got to say?

SOLON. I've got a little account agin your society, and I want to know who foots it?

WINSLOW. Some other time I'll see about it—John, you may close the store; Mr. Otis has gone home. Mr. Shingle, urgent business compels me to leave you—come to-morrow.

[WINSLOW *exits.*

SOLON. Jest so—[*Goes up to desk, takes ledger, sits down, puts on spectacles, and with candle in one hand is reading.*]— Jest so. [*Reading.*] Cash Dr.—Dr. Cash, for Rhubarb $2000 —what a dose. Dr. Cash. He is a great doctor; he cures every disease.

JOHN, *the porter, enters—replaces books—blows out candles.*
Having finished, he comes to SHINGLE.

SOLON. John, how du you du?

JOHN. Very well, sir—When you have done with that book, sir, I should like to put it in the case.

SOLON. Jest so. Pretty writing, ain't it, now?—whose is it?

JOHN. Mr. Ellsley's, sir.

SOLON. The dogs it is! Old Zack Ellsley's boy, John? His father and I were old cronies, and between you and I, John Ellsley come pretty near being my son instead of Zack's.

JOHN. Indeed, sir, how so?

JOHN *brings chair and sits next to him.—*SOLON *rests his leg
on* JOHN's *lap.*

SOLON. How so? Why, Zack and I courted the same gal, Patty Bigelow; and she had Zack instead of me—if she hadn't gin me the bag, John Ellsley might have been John Shingle; however, my gal, Nabby, and John are going to get married.

JOHN. I want to shut up the store and go home.

SOLON. Jest so; well, take the light and see if my team has started.

JOHN. I can't spare the time, Mr. Shingle.

Enter ELLSLEY.

ELLSLEY. Where's Mr. Otis?

SOLON. Gone home, sir. Mr. Winslow wants to see you at his house immediately.

ELLSLEY. The devil he does! I shall be too late for the ball, and I have no money. Ah, daddy Shingle, I'm glad to see you—[*Aside.*] What the devil sent him here?

SOLON. How de do? where's Nabby?

ELLSLEY. Nabby, yes,—she's well. John, go and tell Mr. Winslow that I will come to him directly. I will shut up the store and bring you the key.

JOHN. Yes, sir——   [*Gives him keys and exits.*

ELLSLEY. What does Winslow want with me to-night? Has he discovered the error in my account? Charles has made a memorandum; I will destroy that. [*Goes up to desk, finds paper left by* OTIS, *and tears it up; puts the pieces in his pocket.* SHINGLE *has followed him about.*] Mr. Shingle, have you got any money?

SOLON. No great amount in value.

ELLSLEY. I want fifty dollars. The key of the safe is not here. I'll give an order on my father for it.

SOLON. You shall have it, as you are going tu marry my darter. [*Takes out a very large bladder, inside of which is the bag with bank notes.*] Here's the money.

ELLSLEY. [*Has written the order at table.*] Thank ye, sir. [*Hands* SHINGLE *the paper, and takes the bills.*] This must replace the sum I spent last night. Mr. Shingle, just be kind enough to go into the loft, and bring me a small case you will find there. 'Tis a present for Nabby. A very small case.

SOLON. [*Having read the order, etc., lights a candle.*] A very small case, John.   [*Exit.*

ELLSLEY. What the devil sent that fool here this time of night? I wish he would fall through the scuttle—now for it. [*Opens the safe and deposits the money.*] All safe for this time; now to know what Mr. Winslow wants. [*Crash heard.*

SOLON. [*Without.*] Hollo, Mr. Ellsley! the light's gone out. [*Enter.*] I can't find no very small case there.
                    [*He is all over lampblack and flour.*

ELLSLEY. What have you been about?

SOLON. I went tu reach upon a shelf, the light went out, my foot slipped, and——

ELLSLEY. Lampblack and whiting fell upon you.

SOLON. Jest so, but I didn't find the case.

ELLSLEY. That's not strange, as there is none there. [*Aside.*] I advise you to take a warm bath. This way—I'll show you the way.   [*Exit.*

SOLON. Don't be so pesky quick. [SOLON *goes up to desk, examines it, and finds a revolver; takes it out—looks at it.*] What on earth is this, etc., etc. [*Re-enter* ELLSLEY, *slaps him on the shoulder—the pistol goes off. Scene closes quickly.*

Scene II.—*A street. Night.*

Robert Howard *enters in a blue cloak, followed by a man.*

Howard. Be sure that Thompson follows the directions I have given; remember that I do not wish it known that I am in the city. [Man *exits.*] She is indeed a charming girl; I blushed for the unfeeling, senseless blocks that treated her thus rudely; however, good may come out of it; in my disguise I shall try her affections, though I cannot doubt the purity of her heart in any situation or under any trial. My friends may deride my low-born bride—but she may decline my offer when 'tis made. If I do get a wife, I am determined it shall be my personal attractions, however slight their value, that shall win her. I'll make the trial. [Solon *outside.*

Solon. Whoa, there, Buck! go along! whoa, darn your skins, run, will you? I'll make you step out. [*Enter* Solon.

Howard. What's the matter, friend?

Solon. Them cattle of mine are acting like fried snakes; they ain't used to staying out late nights.

Howard. Why, Mr. Shingle, is this you?

Solon. Jest so, Mr. Howard. Can you tell me a good tavern tu go tu, and put up the darned critters. I went tu Mr. Winslow, just now, on business, and I left my cattle afore the door, and while I was gone somebody's gal, over the way, begun tu play on the pianner, and that got Satan into my team tu look in and see what made the music; and when I come out, I found the cattle all over the sidewalk, trying tu get into the winder.

Howard. I am sorry for your trouble; I will show you a good place to put up for the night.

Solon. I knew you would. I'm always unlucky when I come to the city—I'm on law business, too.

Howard. Indeed!

Solon. Yes; I wonder who is the best lawyer tu go tu, on a cow case? Squire Dingle offered to leave it out, if I'd gin him ten dollars—there's my cattle dancing agin—they don't know city fashions! Whoa! darn ye, Buck.

Howard. Come, sir, shall I show you a house for your accommodation? It is late.

SOLON. Jest so; I'm goin' into a bath, head and heels; then I'll see you. Whoa! there! etc., etc. [*Exit.*

SCENE III.—*A plain apartment, table with ornaments, two chairs on right, two chairs on left; table on right with drawings and books on it. A harp.*

GRACE *enters. Takes off her bonnet and shawl, placing them on a chair. Enter* MRS. OTIS.

MRS. OTIS. Grace, what detained you so long? I was alarmed; you are weeping!

GRACE. Am I?

MRS. OTIS. What has happened, Grace?

GRACE. Have the rich no feelings, or do they suppose the poor have no hearts? Mother, my blood hath run as molten lead through my veins.

MRS. OTIS. Did you not see the lady that advertised for the drawings?

GRACE. I did see the lady. I was shown into a room where were assembled a large party of the lady's friends. My threadbare dress was the mark for their ridicule, and their glasses were leveled at it. I blushed for the things, wearing the forms of men, that could thus cruelly insult a female for her poverty. I shall hate the rich.

MRS. OTIS. They are not all alike, my child.

GRACE. I conquered my feelings, and calmly walked to the table to display my drawings. As they passed from hand to hand, the lady asked her daughter what she thought of them. In most contemptuous terms she replied—"They look like my first attempt." My heart was bursting with suppressed emotion, when a voice, in manly tones, replied to her: "Then your first attempts were very beautiful, and I advise your mother to collect them immediately." But for this kind relief, I should have fallen on the floor. Mrs. Germain will send what she thinks the pictures worth.

MRS. OTIS. Don't weep, Grace. Ought we longer to keep that harp? Our best friends have hinted that so valuable a piece of furniture looks like extravagance in our humble dwelling.

GRACE. Don't ask me to part with that—the only present

from my dear father. I wish I knew who the gentleman was that spoke for me at Mrs. Germain's; I owe him double thanks.

MRS. OTIS. Did you not see him?

GRACE. I did not—

CHARLES OTIS *enters, pale and dejected.*

MRS. OTIS. Are you ill, Charles?

CHARLES. No, mother, I am well. I have been strangely tempted to be dishonest and rich.

MRS. OTIS. And you resisted?

CHARLES. I did, mother—I did resist—but heaven knows it may be the ruin of us all. Mr. Winslow has discharged me from his service.

MRS. OTIS. Discharged you? for what?

CHARLES. Because I would not lie.

MRS. OTIS. You have done well.

CHARLES. Mother, was my father an honest man?

MRS. OTIS. Who doubts it?

CHARLES. Mr. Winslow, in his rage at my refusal to do his wicked will, called me the base son of a baser father. 'Twas in my mind to kill him for the word, but I forbore.

MRS. OTIS. He uttered a falsehood, Charles. Your father's inflexible honesty was a bar to his specious plans for wealth.

GRACE. [*Who has been at the harp, comes down right.*] Mother, we must sell the harp.

MRS. OTIS. Grace, Charles has had no supper. Be composed; the storm of adversity is gathering over our heads, 'tis true, but there is a Power above that can dispel the clouds, and make all sunshine and brightness. [*Both exit.*

CHARLES. [*A knock heard at door.*] Come in. [*Enter* ELLSLEY.] John, is that you?

ELLSLEY. Yes; I have just heard that we are to lose you. I was going to the ball, but as soon as I heard of your quarrel with Winslow, I hastened to see you.

CHARLES. Quarrel—we have had no quarrel.

ELLSLEY. 'Tis the same thing. I'm sorry to lose your society. Mr. Winslow will be sorry, too, before long—and that reminds me of a secret I want you to help me keep.

CHARLES. I don't like secrets; they are apt to make mischief.

ELLSLEY. Not if they are well kept; this will hurt nobody. Now promise not to reveal what I am going to tell you.

CHARLES. I do.

ELLSLEY. Then here, [*taking out watch and chain*] here is the eye-tooth of our hard-hearted master.

CHARLES. Why, John, it cannot be possible that you have really practiced——

ELLSLEY. Hocus-pocus, you mean? agrimento, presto, cockolorum, change, as the jugglers say; nothing truer—master by this time has missed his time-keeper. He will suspect me, and I want you to keep it, till the first fuss is over; then you shall have half its worth.

CHARLES. Not for the world! Take it back, John, to Mr. Winslow—confess your fault. He will forgive you. I will not receive it.

ELLSLEY. Do you think that I am an idiot? take this back and ask forgiveness of a man whose creed is revenge? No. If you refuse, I must take my chance. He has wronged you, and if you had any spirit, you would set fire to his store, or in some way make him feel your revenge.

CHARLES. If you ever mention such things to me again, we cease to be friends.

ELLSLEY. I did this thing for you; at any rate, you will not betray me.

CHARLES. I have given my word, and you must return the property.

ELLSLEY. I will. What way shall I return it and save myself a mortifying acknowledgment?

CHARLES. Write a confession. I would.

ELLSLEY. Do it for me, Charles, will you?

CHARLES. I will, with pleasure—[*Sits down at the table and writes;* ELLSLEY, *looking over him, slips the watch and chain into* CHARLES' *pocket.*]

ELLSLEY. This will make all right, Charles; I am sorry I entered into the business; but as I have begun I must finish.

CHARLES. There, John, that is enough.

ELLSLEY. Nothing could be better; keep it for me until the morning. I am going to the ball; in the dance I might drop it. Mind, Charles, you let no person see it.

CHARLES. It shall be sacred—[*Takes the paper, folds it, and puts it into his pocket.*]

ELLSLEY. Thank you, Charles; good-night; I am sorry you can't come to the ball.

CHARLES. Good-night, John.   [*Exit* ELLSLEY.

GRACE *enters.*

GRACE. Charles, your supper is ready; 'tis not an inviting meal.

MRS. OTIS *enters.*

MRS. OTIS. Charles, what did John Ellsley want with you? I never liked that young man.

CHARLES. A friendly injunction of secrecy is imposed upon me. Grace, I have no appetite for food. [*A knock at the door.*] Come in.

HOWARD *enters, as a workman.*

HOWARD. Mrs. Otis, I have a note from Mrs. Germain to your daughter.

MRS. OTIS. [*Taking it.*] Grace, read it.

GRACE. [*Opens and reads;* HOWARD *observing* CHARLES *at table.*] "Mrs. Germain begs Miss Otis to accept the enclosed bank-note; upon a second examination of her drawings, she is pleased to say she discovered their beauties, and will feel obliged if Miss Otis will permit her to select from her collection still undisposed of."

MRS. OTIS. Well, Grace, that is kind, after all.

GRACE. Will you say to Mrs. Germain, I am gratified for her notice and kind enclosure?

HOWARD. I will do so, Miss Otis, in your own words.

GRACE. That voice—'tis he that saved me, mother—can it be? Sir, accept my thanks for your timely assistance this evening. I should have acknowledged the obligation at the door, but my escape, and the circumstances, embarrassed me.

HOWARD. I am repaid, Miss Otis, and regret the cause that needed a manly arm to protect, in the street of a city, a helpless woman from insult. I am most proud that from me the succor came.

CHARLES. What insult was this?

HOWARD. A drunken brawler that annoyed your sister on her return from Mrs. Germain's. 'Twas my fortune to be near, and it required a blow to convince him that he was a brute.

CHARLES. Sir, I thank you for my sister; though we are strangers, I trust I may know you better.

GRACE. 'Tis the voice of the gentleman—sir—do you know—I mean—seen—Mrs. Germain!

MRS. OTIS. But for your appearance, my daughter had thought she met you at Mrs. Germain's.

HOWARD. Appearance! I am what I appear,—a mechanic! I have learned my trade. I have, in this capacity, served Mrs. Germain, and shall be glad to work for your family. Still, I lose not, I trust, my right to the title of a gentleman, because my hands are hardened by labour.

MRS. OTIS. She is in error—you speak not like a mechanic—one bred to toil; but have more the manner of one that has studied in the halls of science.

HOWARD. What should hinder the son of toil, when genius stimulates, from acquiring the highest fund of knowledge that science gives. Our country is a free one, and education flows from the public fountain for all who thirst for its refreshing streams. Good-night. [*Is going—a loud knock.*] Shall I open the door?—

MRS. OTIS. If you please.   [HOWARD *opens the door.*]

THOMPSON *and* QUIRK *enter.*

THOMPSON. Which is Charles Otis?

CHARLES. I am the person.

THOMPSON. Then, sir, you are my prisoner.

CHARLES. Prisoner?

THOMPSON. Yes, sir, to execute your duty, we must search your person.

CHARLES. Stand off; would you treat me as a thief?

THOMPSON. A charge of theft is alleged against you.

HOWARD. Young man, offer no resistance to the officers in the discharge of their duty.

CHARLES. I have a paper entrusted to my care, which they must not see.

HOWARD. Give it to me.

GRACE *and* MRS. OTIS. Charles, what does this mean?

QUIRK *takes the watch from the pocket of* CHARLES.

THOMPSON. The property described in the warrant is here.
[*Shows watch.*

CHARLES. I am innocent.

GRACE. How comes the watch in your possession?

CHARLES. I know not what this means.

THOMPSON. Sir, I demand to see that paper.

HOWARD. Is that your brother's writing?

GRACE. It is. Charles, explain this.

HOWARD *after reading, hands paper to* THOMPSON.

MRS. OTIS. Charles Otis, am I the mother of a thief? Have I endured the stings of want, to rear a felon! speak— if you are guilty, may you fall dead at my feet!

CHARLES. Mother, I am not guilty.

MRS. OTIS. I believe you.

HOWARD. So do I.

WINSLOW *enters.*

WINSLOW. I do not. [THOMPSON *hands paper to* WINSLOW.] Why is not that thief in prison? Madam, he is like his father. By death he escaped my vengeance; so shall not the son.

CHARLES. Speak of me as you will; assail not the good name of my father. I am innocent.

WINSLOW. A jury's verdict will satisfy me better than your words—away with him.

HOWARD. Go not too far, Mr. Winslow.

WINSLOW. What I do here is no concern of yours.

HOWARD. I may choose to make it so.

WINSLOW. To prison with him. A virtuous family is here.

CHARLES. Slanderous villain! [GRACE *and* MRS. OTIS *holding him.*] Hold me not—

CHARLES *seizes a chair and is in the act of striking* WINSLOW, *when* HOWARD *interferes.*

TABLEAU.

QUICK DROP.

ACT II.

Scene I.—*Same as last scene of Act I, except there is no harp.* Grace *discovered—in her hands an open letter which she is reading.*

Mrs. Otis *enters.*

Grace. So soon returned, mother?

Mrs. Otis. Yes, child. I have seen Charles. The lawyer gives me but little hope, circumstances are so strong against him, and Mr. Winslow urges the trial.

Grace. Who purchased the harp?

Mrs. Otis. A stranger. I saw Robert. He assures me that Charles will be acquitted.

Grace. Then there is hope. Should Robert call in my absence, I will soon return—

[*As* Grace *is going, enter* Winslow.

Winslow. Do not leave the room, Miss Otis. I have something to say, which I wish you to hear.

Grace. Excuse me, sir.

Winslow. I may be of service to you. [Grace *turning away.*] Madam, in my zeal to bring the guilty to punishment, I may have gone too far. If you wish your son's release, it may be well to listen.

Mrs. Otis. Well, sir, be seated, we may listen,

[*All seated,* Winslow *in centre.*

Winslow. It is needless for me to allude to the peril which Charles is now in, or for me to mention your praiseworthy efforts in his defense. I have heard that you have disposed of part of your furniture to enable you to retain the services of a lawyer.

Grace. Sir, you will spare our feelings by confining your conversation to that which we do not know so well. My mother has reproved you; she is unable to bear calmly our mortifying and painful situation.

Winslow. I came in friendship; I wish not to wound your feelings. You deem me, I know not why, your enemy— why is this so?

Grace. Go to my brother's cell; ask that innocent boy,

torn from home, confined with thieves, ruffians, and murderers, hardened in crime, and amid the clank of chains—listen to his answer.

WINSLOW. I can save him from the verdict which will for years doom him to the horrors of a prison. I alone can save him; there is a way. I can point that way.

MRS. OTIS. Save my child, and buried be all former wrongs, forgotten present feelings.

GRACE. Save my brother, and heaven will reward you.

WINSLOW. I look for the reward here.

GRACE. The means of his deliverance, sir! Do not deceive us,—the means!

WINSLOW. I am the prosecutor—with my concurrence there are many ways a principal witness may be absent; I will not appear against him.

MRS. OTIS. This is evading justice, and may fail.

WINSLOW. Let him be convicted and appeal to another tribunal; I will assert my belief that he is not guilty, and be myself his bail; then send him in one of my vessels on a foreign voyage, to convince the world I believe him honest, and shield him from punishment.

GRACE. I am ignorant of the forms of law, but the principles of justice are deeply rooted here. I do not approve of your proposed means. Flight implies guilt. His good name is tarnished, mother; his country's verdict can alone wash clean the stain.

WINSLOW. So shall it be; your scruples are those of virtue, and they please me. I know he is innocent. I would have it appear so.

MRS. OTIS. With the feelings of a mother strong within me, I would welcome any means that gives Charles his liberty.

GRACE. I must go to him, and comfort him in his affliction.

WINSLOW. Stay, Miss Otis; if we both construe alike our thoughts, I may share your distresses and relieve them; again I tender you my hand, which, if you take, you take my wealth, and your brother's safety.

GRACE. I must decline the hand; I could not accept, if my life depended upon the act; there are reasons which render it impossible.

WINSLOW. Reasons! Madam, advise your daughter; you know her; you know me; much depends upon her answer.

MRS. OTIS. Her acts are free. I cannot bias her in such a choice.

GRACE. Mr. Winslow, I once before answered such a question. I am now betrothed to——

WINSLOW. Do I understand that you now reject me?

MRS. OTIS. Not so harshly, sir. Grace.

WINSLOW. The form of words affects not me; if you do reject me, your brother is a convicted thief ere the sun sets. Will your new lover marry the sister of a sentenced felon?—who is he? answer me.

HOWARD *enters*.

HOWARD. He is here, sir, and will answer for himself.

WINSLOW. Indeed! a powerful rival! A poor mechanic dares to thwart the wishes of a merchant! Have a care, sir, or I will prove you an accomplice in crime, with the one whose cause you espouse!

HOWARD. Sir, I know you—the difference of our positions in society gives me no cause of fear.

WINSLOW. Miss Otis, I congratulate you on your proposed alliance with this vagabond—

HOWARD. Vagabond, sir—[*Smiling.*]

WINSLOW. Vagabond, yes, I repeat the word—who are you? Marry him, Lady Otis. He is your brother's friend— the champion of a thief; himself no better.

MRS. OTIS. You are a brave man, sir, thus to inflict abuse upon two helpless women. I envy you not the delicacy of feeling you possess.

WINSLOW. There is the defender of the virtue of the name of Otis; let him redress your grievances. Why does he not answer for himself and you?

HOWARD. I make no hasty answers to angry men's words of passion; my answer will come, and like the thunder of heaven, it shall silence your voice of impotence—my tongue in this presence shall not speak your proper name.

WINSLOW. Beware how you glance at my character; speak, if you dare, aught against me.

GRACE. For heaven's sake, Robert, let him not anger you.

WINSLOW. Spiritless hind! even the weapon of speech he dare no longer use. How dare you, sir, hint aught against me!

HOWARD. Go on, sir.

WINSLOW. Retreat, sir, or with a blow I'll chastise you.

HOWARD. Vent your rage in words, and I will hear it; raise your arm to strike, and in mine own defense I stand; beware the consequences; no child's strength is here.

GRACE. Robert—Mr. Howard!

WINSLOW. A word with you. Here are the weapons gentlemen use, even in encounters with those beneath them. [*Produces pistols.*] To chastise you, I will raise you to my level. I talk not of vulgar blows.

MRS. OTIS. This is my house. Commit no murder here.

WINSLOW. If the ladies will withdraw, I will settle with the coward.

HOWARD. Coward! Do not hold my hand, madam! Stand from before him! I have listened to his insulting language; but for your presence, I had shown him that he was but man, and I his equal; leave us; he dare not die in any cause. I promise that no blood shall be spilled.

GRACE. You promise that?

HOWARD. I do.

MRS. OTIS. Robert, be not rash.

GRACE. He has promised, mother; come.

[*Exeunt* GRACE *and* MRS. OTIS.

HOWARD. We are alone, sir. The right of choice, by the barbarous code which governs men in their misnamed honourable meetings, is mine. If in this act I engage, I break my country's law and heaven's. You say I have wronged you; I will give you satisfaction; give me a weapon. [WINSLOW *gives him a pistol.*] Now, sir, prove your manly spirit; give me your hand; we are strangers; now, breast to breast, I fight you, thus: fire, if you dare; I give you my word—fire!

WINSLOW. Hold; this is murder.

HOWARD. Indeed! Give me your weapon, and talk of courage and honour elsewhere. I ask from you no degrading apology; you must respect me. I ask no more from friend or foe.

WINSLOW. I will take early opportunity to convince you, sir, what I dare do. I will have revenge for this.

[*Aside, and exit.*

HOWARD. 'Tis well. I know the limits of his power.

MRS. OTIS *and* GRACE *re-enter.*

GRACE. I am glad he is gone.

MRS. OTIS. I hope you have made no rash promise to meet this man.

HOWARD. Fear not; he will no more offend you by his presence here.

GRACE. Mr. Howard, we thank you.

HOWARD. Grace, dearest Grace, call me Robert; still, you have not known me long, 'tis true; I trust his offer has not made mine, humble as it is, of less value.

GRACE. Robert, your prospects in life may be blasted by a union with the sister of a felon.

HOWARD. Dearest Grace, let our marriage depend upon Charles' acquittal, and the measures I have taken will not be in vain.

GRACE. Prove my brother's innocence, and I am yours.

HOWARD. I will do so. You will pardon me for inquiring too closely into your affairs. Charles has told me his story; it shall be used to his advantage. This must be your home no longer. Take this letter, Grace, to the house with the Grecian portico—that which pleased you so well in our walk last Sunday—wait till the owner arrives; he will serve you and Charles. He has heard of your misfortunes, and would see you. When the trial is over I will bring you tidings of the result. Let no anxiety tempt you into the Court House; the forms of a criminal trial are too harsh for a sensitive mind—much less a mother's or a sister's, when a brother is arraigned.

GRACE. I hope all will go well. But for your persuasion I would have found the People's Lawyer, and begged him to act in Charles' cause; you know Mr. Winslow has threatened that he shall be against him at the trial.

HOWARD. I am sure he will not. Fear not. Our laws are just, our judges honest men, our jurors are our equals. The right will prevail. 'Tis near the hour; in our next meeting, Grace, I shall claim you for my wife. Mother, let me call you so, be of good heart. [*Exeunt* MRS. OTIS *and* GRACE.] Now, Hugh Winslow, beware! The snare your subtle thought set for the innocent shall close upon the guilty one.

[*Exit.*

SCENE II.—*A street, with signs of Attorneys, etc., repre-*
sented as Court Street, in Boston. SOLON SHINGLE *enters.*
with an old plaid cloak and umbrella. *Citizens, male and*
female, cross stage and exit.

SOLON. I wish I could catch the plaguy critter that stole
my apple-sarse. Where'bouts am I? [*Reading signs.*] I'm
among the law shops—jest the right place to find rogues. I
wonder where the Court House is. By Jove, I'll let folks
know I fout in the revolution. [*Goes up stage and talks to a*
man that is passing.

Enter WINSLOW.

WINSLOW. Just as I expected. The forgery is detected—
the draft returned, and it will be traced to me, and from the
obstinacy of this boy I may be ruined; I must hasten his
conviction. [*The man leaves* SOLON *laughing, and exits.*
SOLON. Jest so. [*Laughs.* Sees WINSLOW.] Ah, Mr.
Winslow, how de do? By Cain, I got lost this morning, or
I should have been in to see you.
WINSLOW. [*Aside.*] I wish, with all my heart, you had
never been found.
SOLON. That ain't all; I've lost my apple-sarse out of the
tail end of my waggin; it is sich a prime lot, tu; as good as
that I sold tu the chap from the Southard, and in your store.
WINSLOW. Man from the Southard—I remember—do you
know who we were talking about that day, Mr. Shingle?
SOLON. Yes, about the revolution; how the fellers had to
eat off the head of a barrel, without knives or forks. Mr.
Winslow, are you a judge of clothes? I bought this coat at
a vandue and this umbrella—what is it worth, cash down?
WINSLOW. I don't know, indeed; do you think you could
tell the story in court, if I wished it, about the check
Colonel Spencer gave me that day?
SOLON. The day I sold him the apple-sarse?—guess I
could; your clerk was there—he could tell better than me.
I was figuring out how much caliker it would take tu make
my Nabby a fashionable gown. But, I say, they du tell me
that your clerk was a rogue.
WINSLOW. To-day his trial comes on; after 'tis over, come

and see me. I should like to talk the matter over with you, about Colonel Spencer.

SOLON. How he laughed when I told him about the battle of Bunker Hill. [*Bell rings.*

WINSLOW. You had better come into court. I'll be there.
[*Exit* WINSLOW.

SOLON. Jest so, thank you; tell the judge I'll be there. Whenever I hear that bell, I always consate there is trouble brewing. Whenever I du go tu court, I'm sure tu make some alfired mistake or other; once I drove right straight intu the prisoner's stall; they told me tu stand up, and I did; they asked me if I had anything tu say; says I, no; and while they were trying me, the real rogue got off. But if this Otis boy stole the watch he might have stole my apple-sarse. I'll go in, and if there's any barin on the case, I'll speak. I don't like tu make a speech among these law chaps. They work a feller up so he don't know his head from his heels; I shall have law enough, I s'pose; for that John Ellsley won't marry my Nabby. I considered her as good as married, and now her markit's spoiled; my darter and the apple-sarse may work for the lawyers yet—jest so. [*Exit.*

SCENE III.—*Court House. The* JUDGE *discovered on the bench; before him the clerk, jury sitting. Lawyers.* CHARLES OTIS *in Prisoner's Box, Sheriff in his place;* ELLSLEY, THOMPSON, QUIRK *on seat near witness-stand.* WINSLOW *enters and sits near* ELLSLEY *as scene changes. The clerk is standing reading the indictment; the prisoner is also standing.*

CLERK. [*Finishing indictment.*] What say, you, Charles Otis—guilty or not guilty.

CHARLES. Not guilty.

TRIPPER. [*Rises.*] May it please your honor, gentlemen of the jury, in this case, Commonwealth *versus* Charles Otis, for stealing a watch and chain, the property of Hugh Winslow, we shall occupy but little of your time. The evidence offered will be found so conclusive that I shall probably not find it necessary to detain you with any argument. I shall proceed at once to the examination of the witnesses. The witnesses in this case will please come forward.

CLERK. Hugh Winslow, Peter Thompson, John Quirk, John Ellsley. [*Enter* SOLON SHINGLE. *He goes to table quietly, and shoves them all aside, lays down hat and whip, and offers to lay down umbrella; is prevented by officers.*

SOLON. I've got in, by Cain.

CLERK. Are you concerned in this case?

SOLON. Well, I s'pose it's likely I am, or I ought to be.

CLERK. Your name, sir?

SOLON. Solon Shingle.

CLERK. Solon Shingle?

SOLON. Jest so. [*Business.*

CLERK. Hold up your right hands. [*They do.*] You solemnly swear, etc. [*All are sworn.*

TRIPPER. Mr. Winslow, will you take the stand, sir? [*He does so.*] You have had your watch stolen?

WINSLOW. I have, sir.

TRIPPER. Is the watch in court. [*An officer hands the watch to him.*] Is that your watch?

WINSLOW. It is, sir.

TRIPPER. That is all, for the present, Mr. Winslow. Mr. Thompson, take the stand, if you please. [*He does so.*] You arrested the prisoner.

THOMPSON. I did.

TRIPPER. State to the Court, if you please, what you know.

THOMPSON. I had a warrant for the arrest of the prisoner; I found him at his house. When I made known my business, he was agitated, and denied the charge. I proposed to search him; he resisted.

SOLON *by this time has fallen asleep, and snores occasionally.*

TRIPPER. He resisted—well?

THOMPSON. We searched him, and upon his **person** found the lost property.

TRIPPER. This is the watch you found in the pocket of the prisoner?

THOMPSON. It is, sir. [SOLON *snores.*

TRIPPER. Very well. Mr. Quirk, take the stand.

QUIRK. [*Takes the stand.*] I went with Mr. Thompson. We found the watch and a paper, which he first gave to a young man, who was there.

TRIPPER. Did he refuse to give you that paper?

QUIRK. He did, sir.

TRIPPER. Very well, sir, stand down.

TIMID. I should like to ask the witness the nature of that paper, and, that is if——

TRIPPER. In time, sir; I will produce it soon enough for your client's good.

TIMID. The paper having been mentioned, I should like to know what it has to do with the case.

TRIPPER. I will not produce it now; I know my duty, and shall perform it; next witness.

WINSLOW *and* TRIPPER *are in conversation;* SHINGLE *being next in order, an officer awakens him, and he goes to the stand.*

SOLON. Jest so.

TRIPPER. Ah, Mr. Shingle, what· do you know of this affair?

SOLON. Well, sir, I can't say; you know there's no telling who's Governor till arter 'lection. So I guess.

TRIPPER. Mr. Shingle, I think I had the pleasure of examining you once before in a case.

SOLON. Yes, and you didn't get much ahead on me, did you?

TRIPPER. This time you may tell what you know in your own way.

SOLON. Jest so. But I don't tell all I know, for nothing—as I said in the last war, for my father fit in the Revolution.

TRIPPER. Never mind that, sir—an article has been stolen, as you are aware; now confine yourself to this fact.

SOLON. Jest so. I was in Mr. Winslow's the other night; I left my team in the street—two yoke o' cattle and a horse.

TRIPPER. Why tell us of that? let your team go.

SOLON. That's what I'm coming to—my team did go, for I couldn't bring 'em up into the shop; so I was talking to Mr. Ellsley there, about matters and things—my Nabby's getting married and so on, and how things worked; Squire, I wish you'd hand me a pen there tu pick my tooth. I eat three cents' worth of clams afore I came into court, and really believe there's a clam atween my eye tooth and tother one next tu it.

JUDGE. Mr. Shingle, this has nothing to do with the case.

SOLON. Well, I didn't say it had, Squire.

TRIPPER. Just confine yourself to the facts in the premises, if you please, Mr. Shingle.

SOLON. Well,—I don't exactly understand what you mean by premises.

TRIPPER. Why, sir, I thought every fool knew as much as that.

SOLON. Jest so; well, as I come out of the store, I knew that my cattle would natrally look tu me, and I took off the chain.

JUDGE. The watch chain, Mr. Shingle?

SOLON. No, Squire, the back chain.

TRIPPER. The back chain,—what's that?

SOLON. Why, I thought every fool knew what a back chain was. I had him there, Squire, by Cain.

JUDGE. Mr. Shingle, the loss of the article is proved without your evidence. 'Twas found in the prisoner's pocket—as you doubtless heard.

SOLON. In his pocket?

JUDGE. So said the witness.

SOLON. Then his pocket must have been as big as a hog-pen, to hold my barrel of apple-sarse.

JUDGE. 'Tis a watch that has been stolen.

SOLON. A watch—Then I must have been asleep while you have been goin' on. I knew nothing about any watch.

JUDGE. Then you know nothing about this case, it appears —there is some mistake, Mr. Tripper.

TRIPPER. So it appears. Mr. Shingle, how came you here?

SOLON. Well, I come to see about my apple-sarse; but either the clams that I eat, or a little rum toddy that I took arterwards, made me sleepy.

JUDGE. You may stand down, Mr. Shingle, for the present.

SOLON. Jest so; you've swar'd me then for nothing; however, I'm ready for the next time. [*Stands down.*

TRIPPER. John Ellsley. Mr. Ellsley, please to take the stand; you have been sworn, sir?

ELLSLEY. I have, sir.

TRIPPER. You are a clerk in the employment of Mr. Winslow?

ELLSLEY. I am, sir.

TRIPPER. You have been intimate with the prisoner?

ELLSLEY. Prisoner. I—you mean—yes, sir.

TRIPPER. Give us, if you please, a history of your knowledge of this affair.

CHARLES. John Ellsley—tell the truth.

JUDGE. Silence, prisoner—go on, Mr. Ellsley.

ELLSLEY. On the morning that Charles was discharged, I called on him at his house. He said he had a secret he wished me to keep. I declined—he then offered me a watch and chain, which I knew to be the property of our master. He told me he had taken it, and offered to give me half, if I would keep it for him, which I refused.

TRIPPER. Did you not advise him to return it?

ELLSLEY. I did. He promised to do so, and wrote a confession.

TRIPPER. Which I will now read—[*Reads.*] "To my wronged master.—Tempted by circumstances, which I will hereafter explain, I took from you your watch and chain. Conscience will not let me keep the ill-gotten bauble, and penitently I implore you to receive it, and forgive the commission of the crime."

TIMID. Let me see the paper,—it is not signed, or proved to have been written by my client.

TRIPPER. 'Twas found in his possession—we will soon settle that. Mr. Ellsley, is that the handwriting of the prisoner?

ELLSLEY. It is, sir—I saw him write it.

CHARLES. I did write the confession. I do not deny it.

TIMID. Do not speak, sir—admit nothing.

TRIPPER. Mr. Ellsley, you may stand down. I shall rest the case here, without remark. Mr. Timid, any question you may wish to propose, I am ready to hear.

TIMID. May it please the Court—the case appears circumstantially to be this. I mean to say that if evidence of good character can prevail, I can fill this court-room with such testimony. [HOWARD *enters and comes forward; speaks to* CHARLES *and shakes his hand—then comes to* TIMID *and whispers.*] I am not exactly prepared, but I do not doubt that if a little delay——

TRIPPER. Certainly, sir,—by all means.

HOWARD. I thank you, sir.—May it please your Honour, I

have listened to some of the evidence in this case, as well as the remarks of the learned gentlemen for the Government. I am here to speak in defence of that innocent young man.

TRIPPER. This is unfair, sir. I appeal to the Court, if this interference is not improper.

HOWARD. I shall be pleased to meet any fair argument against my appearance here, as counsel for that young man, the victim, in my opinion, of a base conspiracy—which I think I shall be able to prove, unless my right to practice in this court be denied me.

JUDGE. Go on, Mr. Howard, there can be no good excuse for objection.

SOLON. Why, that's the People's Lawyer—things will turn, I reckon. Mr. Howard, I've lost a barrel of apple-sarse.

SHERIFF. Silence in the court.

SOLON. Jest so. [*Sits down.*]

HOWARD. John Ellsley, take the stand again. [*He does so with evident unwillingness.*] Though the law may sometimes shield a villain with its broad hand of power, in honest hands 'tis an engine the evil-doer dreads. John Ellsley, you are under oath, a solemn oath, and upon the words spoken by you —under the penalty of broken oaths rests the fate of one who was your companion—your friend. I charge you, sir, with uttering what is untrue, and advise you to recall the dark deed which you have here committed.

TRIPPER. Is this brow-beating a witness—this sermonizing to be allowed, sir?

HOWARD. Speak not, sir; by courtesy—by right—the witness is mine. I will use him till he speaks the truth. Look at me, sir; knowest thou not that the eye of the eternal Judge is on you, that he has this day, with his pen of fire, written perjury against thy soul.

WINSLOW *and* TRIPPER *are in anxious conversation.* ELLSLEY *attempts to do as* WINSLOW *directs.*

HOWARD. Look not there. If you dare not meet my eye, look at your victim. Tell me how you will feel to see his youthful form wasting away in the walls of a state prison, his friends weeping over him as one dead, worse than dead— disgraced—and by thy false words. John Ellsley, ere it be too late, confess.

ELLSLEY. I will confess the truth. All I have uttered is false. I placed the watch in his pocket—for me he wrote the confession. I would have ruined my friend for paltry money. Mr. Winslow knew it all.

WINSLOW. 'Tis false. I knew nothing of it.

HOWARD. Hugh Winslow, silence. A day of judgment will come for you. I claim a verdict of acquittal for Charles Otis.

JUDGE. If Mr. Ellsley retract his evidence, the action cannot be sustained. Gentlemen of the jury, the case is for your decision.

The JURY *consult.* WINSLOW *is about leaving the court.*

HOWARD. Mr. Winslow, remain; I have procured an indictment against you for forgery.

WINSLOW. Sir, do you mean to insult me?

JUDGE. Silence.

FOREMAN OF THE JURY. We have agreed.

CLERK. What say you?

FOREMAN. Not guilty. [CHARLES *comes from box.*

HOWARD. [*Takes his hand.*] Officer, your duty.

[WINSLOW *is arrested.*

SOLON. Right side up; jest so.

MR. WINSLOW *in custody of two officers; animated tableau.*

SCENE IV.—*A street. A crowd of people pass over the stage as from a trial; with them* SOLON SHINGLE. *When all are off,* SOLON *speaks.*

SOLON. Well, now, who would have once thought of sich a thing. It's jest the way some fellows' mouths are jinted; they will strain 'em out of jint not to swaller a mouse or a grasshopper, and slide down an ox waggin, or a breaking-up plow, so tu speak. Well, my gal's lucky that she didn't marry that John, arter all; and as for myself, if ever anybody catches me inside of a court house agin, I'll agree to be proved non pompus—and that means a tarnal fool, according to law books. Yes, jest so.

HOWARD. [*Enters.*] Ah, my friend, you will find your

daughter at my house. I thank you for your assistance. I am now in haste; the widow Worthy shall have her rights.

[*Exit.*

SOLON. Well, Squire, that's first rate for the widder; but look here; off again; odd critter, that lawyer; so was his father; jest as odd as three oxen; he fit in the Revolution, tu. Well, it's no use my travelin' round all day. These city folks will skin me out of my old plaid cloak, that I bought ten years ago; hat, boots, and trowsers, tu, far as I know. I've been here long enough. I'll follow arter the Squire, find my Nabby, buy a load of groceries, and get home as quick as my team will go it. When I'm in this 'ere Boston, I get so bewildered I don't know a string of sausages from a cord of wood. Jest so.   [*Exit.*

SCENE V.—*A splendid drawing-room; pictures; the harp discovered.* MRS. OTIS *enters with* GRACE.

MRS. OTIS. 'Tis, indeed, a splendid mansion. Its beauties are dimmed by the thoughts of the news we may hear.

HOWARD. [*Enters.*] Have I kept you waiting, Grace? Charles has returned, has he not? He left the Court House with me.

MRS. OTIS. He has.

HOWARD. Mrs. Otis, request your son's attendance here.

MRS. OTIS. I will seek him.   [*Exit.*

GRACE. Robert, this place is a perfect paradise; what does it mean? How may one in your situation be intimate with the owner of such a mansion—and there, too, is my harp— what does this mean?

HOWARD. It means, my dearest Grace, that you are to be henceforth the mistress of this place, that you think a paradise. I purchased the harp for you, knowing how you valued it. Grace, a clergyman is in attendance with a few friends; that harp be the first present from your husband—this place is mine—I am rich,

CHARLES *and* MRS. OTIS *enter.*

CHARLES. Mother, there stands my deliverer—Robert Howard, the People's Lawyer.

GRACE. Is this so, Robert?

HOWARD. It is. I first saw you at Mrs. Germain's; your appearance interested me; your character, upon inquiry, pleased me—I determined that my riches should have no weight in the lady's choice selected to be my wife—hence my disguise.

GRACE. Then you are not a mechanic?

HOWARD. I am. My father, though wealthy, was governed by caprice, and insisted upon my learning a mechanical trade, besides educating me for his own profession, that of the bar, which I have practiced with success. In my character of a working man I became acquainted with the misdoings of Charles' master, which enabled me, as his attorney, to prove your brother's innocence.

CHARLES. For which, sir, accept my gratitude.

HOWARD. Let it be considered a family matter, now. I shall aid you in your future plans.   [SOLON *enters.*

SOLON. Mr. Howard, that plaster you put on to my friend Winslow, is likely to stick, and now he's gone to jail.

HOWARD. He will meet his just reward—his ill-gotten gains will scarcely shield him from the punishment due to fraud—he is accused of forgery.

SOLON. Jest so.—Mr. Howard, is this the gal you are going to marry?

HOWARD. Yes, sir—a friend of my father's.

GRACE. Your friends must be mine.—I'm glad to see you.

SOLON. My name's Shingle—I know'd your father, Miss Otis. Otis is a good name—but you change it for a good one tew. My darter, Nabby,—well, I guess I will not talk about her. I'll stay to the wedding, and take a bit of cake home to my old woman, and drink a glass of wine with you—and wish you good luck, and a dozen boys, if you want 'em.—Mrs. Otis, you mus'n't mind my talking; you might as well try to back a heavy load up a hill, as stop my thoughts coming right out in homely words.

MRS. OTIS. We doubt not your meaning is good.

HOWARD. Grace, this is your home; do with all as you please—and I trust more delicately than I can—you will explain my good intentions to your friends.

GRACE. Few words will suffice—for one who has for others

plead so well, I plead—I am interested in the result—for my sake—if not for his own—I trust that in the court you will admit to full practice—THE PEOPLE'S LAWYER.

THE END.

JACK CADE

By Robert T. Conrad

ROBERT T. CONRAD.

(1810–1858)

A large part of the history of the American Drama is a large part of the history of the Philadelphia stage. The pre-Revolutionary group of playwrights, Thomas Godfrey, Jr., Francis Hopkinson, John Leacock, hailed from the city of Philadelphia. At no period was that locality more prolific in its contribution of dramatists than when Edwin Forrest, the actor, was eagerly seeking, because of his dominant Americanism, for native material to suit his peculiar genius. Someone has said that Edwin Forrest should be considered one of the generous parents of American Drama. Had it not been for him, it is certain that at least nine, if not more, plays of variable merit would never have seen the light,— plays which were brought to notoriety through the power of acting distinctive of the period. These were Stone's "The Ancient Briton", but more important still, his "Metamora; or, The Last of the Wampanoags"; Bird's "Pelopidas", "Oralloosa", and "The Gladiator", together with his "The Broker of Bogata"; Richard Penn Smith's "Caius Marius"; George H. Miles's "Mahommed"; and finally Robert T. Conrad's "Jack Cade".

Of all these, there were only four that proved successful: "Metamora", "The Gladiator", "The Broker of Bogata", and "Jack Cade". There was another prominent person in the Philadelphia group of playwrights, who was not connected with Forrest's career,—George Henry Boker, and his play, "Francesca da Rimini", is contained in the third volume of this series.

A word of explanation is necessary regarding my choice of "Jack Cade" as representative of the Forrest régime. For many years the present editor has tried to locate the manu-script of "Metamora", but correspondence has not, as yet, brought to light any trace of it. Here and there stray

427

speeches are to be picked up, as representative of Forrest's triumphant delivery, and Alger gives a full synopsis of the play, so that with no difficulty the reader may patch together an impression of the drama as a whole. The prologue and the epilogue have also been preserved. At the Forrest Home, the repository of many Forrest relics, there are a few isolated parts to be picked up. But the play as a whole is as yet not to be had. At the present writing, I am assured by the former librarian of "The Players" that he is on the trail of "Metamora"; that an old actor of his acquaintance avers that in an ancient strong-box of his he has a complete manuscript. If it is to be had, the present editor has been promised its use. But in this second volume of "Representative Plays by American Dramatists", its omission is due to its still being unlocated. Forrest's magnificence in the rôle of the Indian Chieftain receives unending eulogy, wherever we meet with comment in theatrical reminiscences. Vandenhoff, in his "Leaves From An Actor's Note-Book", writes:

He acted with his accustomed vigor; and I freely acknowledge that, for power of destructive energy, I never heard anything on the stage so tremendous in its sustained *crescendo* swell, and crashing force of utterance, as his defiance of the Council, in that play. His voice surged and roared like the angry sea, lashed into fury by a storm; till, as it reached its boiling, seething climax, in which the serpent hiss of hate was heard, at intervals, amidst its louder, deeper, hoarser tones, it was like the falls of Niagara, in its tremendous downsweeping cadence: it was a whirlwind, a tornado, a cataract of illimitable rage.

The stage history of "Metamora", while it could be easily gathered, so as to leave an impression of its power and stateliness, is therefore passed over here until such time as fortune shall bring the play itself to light.

Regarding Dr. Robert Montgomery Bird, for whom Forrest had such a personal liking, it is necessary to state here that the only reason why an example of his dramaturgy is not given in the present volume is that the manuscripts were donated to the University of Pennsylvania by Dr. Bird's son,

and a prior claim to their use belongs to a member of the
English Department of that institution, Mr. Clement Foust,
through whose indefatigable researches, an entire collection
of Dr. Bird's manuscripts have been brought together. With
valuable data at his disposal, we are glad to think that the
student of American Drama is now able to read "The
Gladiator", which Mr. Foust has carefully collated from the
author's own manuscript corrections. And in his volume a
complete life of the dramatist is included, with extracts from
Bird's correspondence which throw direct light on his relations with Forrest.

There was left me, therefore, from the nine Forrest plays,
the one which may be regarded as an excellent example of
the character of work done by the Philadelphia group of
writers. Its history likewise is interesting, as showing how
a stage piece is sometimes evolved, and finally reaches the
interpreter for whom it is best suited. Conrad's *Jack Cade*
is not the *Jack Cade* of Shakespeare (2 Hen. VI.); the long
historical consideration of the character will show that Conrad's desire, as Alger states, was to breathe into the part
"the exaltation of popular liberty and equality." And then,
after the fashion of most writers who have tried to estimate
Forrest, Alger adds:

> The *Lear* of Forrest was the storm, and his *Broker
> of Bogata* the rainbow of his passion. *Othello* was his
> tornado, which, pursuing a level line of desolation, had
> on either side an atmosphere of light and love that
> illumined its dark wings. *Macbeth* was his supernatural
> dream, and entrancement of spasmodic action. *Hamlet*
> was his philosophic reverie and rambling in a charmed
> circle of the intellect. But *Jack Cade* was his incarnate
> tribuneship of the people, the blazing harangue of a
> later *Rienzi* inflamed by more frightful personal wrongs
> and inspired with a more desperate love of liberty.

These plays created by the Philadelphia group for Forrest
were produced within a definite period of that actor's career.
The dates of their first performances will show how closely
the dramatists followed each other; in fact, between 1829,
when "Metamora" was first put upon the boards, and 1835,

when Conrad wrote the first draft of what was afterwards to be called "Jack Cade", most of the other prize plays, in Forrest's repertory, had been performed. And there is no doubt that Conrad had seen them all, as each was given.

Forrest was able conscientiously to say that he had a deep interest in the future of American dramatic literature; but he was the type of personality to stamp his own requirements on any work, without which a play would be of no use to him. Forrest's genius was erratic, and so was his Americanism, which was mixed up with a certain amount of jealousy. He was constantly alert for any slight, real or imaginary, given to his own position as a leading American actor. It was this spirit in him which brought on the Astor Place riots, in New York, when he fought with Macready; it was this spirit which made him snap his fingers in the face of the genial comedian, John Gilbert; and it was the same temper, aroused because of personal grievance, which made him horsewhip the dramatist and *litterateur,* Nathaniel P. Willis, as the latter was walking down Fifth Avenue, in New York. He was, nevertheless, seriously interested in the American Drama, and his faith in what he accepted often led him into extravagant, not to say violent, praise. In a letter to Bird, now in the possession of the University of Pennsylvania, speaking of "The Broker of Bogota", he said, "It will live when our vile trunks are rotten."

One must expect, therefore, in the group of plays that was fostered under his care, a great predominance of his own personality. Very often the subjects were selected by him and handed over to the dramatists, after he had definitely conceived their proportions from the standpoint of his acting. Lawrence Barrett, in his brochure on Forrest, claims that his association with an Indian, *Push-ma-ta-ha,* while filling an engagement in New Orleans, suggested the character of *Metamora* to him. In this way the dramatist fades beneath the brightness of his own accomplishment. The fact of the matter is that Forrest was tenacious of his own rights, and he used the dramatists for his own purpose. And, in saying this, I do not in the least wish to detract from what the American Drama owes to him. But his prizes, which he offered from time to time, were not commensurate with what he might have easily offered. He held on with jealous hand

to his property. We shall see what he did with "Jack Cade".
And we are told that even such a personal friendship as
existed between himself and Dr. Bird, did not prevent the
latter from becoming discouraged with the rewards of the
stage, when he began to contemplate what unsatisfactory
returns he was receiving for such a play, for example, as
"The Gladiator", which made Forrest, as well as other actors,
a fortune. Yet, penurious though Forrest may have been
toward his dramatists, he was nonetheless erratically generous. When Stone, in a fit of despondency, committed
suicide, by throwing himself into the Schuylkill River, it was
Forrest who erected a monument above him, inscribed with
the "legend" that he was the creator of "Metamora".

Forrest's personality, when it was not roused in anger,
must have been attractive. Everyone spoke of him in glowing terms. We would think that they did so often in fear
of the consequences if they did not, were we not sure that
the force of Forrest's intellect was invigorating. Dr. Bird
travelled with him to South America for other reasons than
to gain Spanish atmosphere for his plays, "The Broker of
Bogata" and "Oralloosa". On all occasions we find his
dramatists loyal to him because of their admiration for him.
When he was given a dinner at the Merchants' Hotel in
Philadelphia (December 15, 1837), on his return from
Europe, he not only received encomium from Dunlap, but
was praised in speeches by Conrad and Richard Penn Smith.
Yet so impressed are we with the fact that Forrest was the
one American actor to place his trust in the American Drama,
that we are prone to forget others who did almost as much.
There is recalled to me, especially, E. L. Davenport. He was
to cross swords with Forrest regarding his sole rights to the
drama, "Jack Cade", and was to act in it as late as 1875.
History records likewise his appearance in Boker's "Calaynos", and in George H. Miles's "De Soto, the Hero of the
Mississippi".

Robert T. Conrad was a son of one of the members of the
publishing house that issued the works of Charles Brockden
Brown and Joel Barlow. Born in 1810, by the time he was
twenty-two he was writing plays, his first, entitled "Conrad
of Naples," having been produced at the Arch Street Theatre,
Philadelphia, on January 17, 1832. He was educated for the

bar, and early began to interest himself in local politics. He had read law with his uncle, but instead of immediately going into practise, he gave satisfaction to his interest in journalism, by publishing the *Daily Commercial Intelligencer,* later known as the *Philadelphia Gazette.* Here he must have exercised a political pen which was later to win him distinction. But his health could not stand the ardors of journalism, so he turned to the practise of law. Soon after, he was appointed Recorder of the City, and, holding office for a fortnight, he was elevated to the position of Judge of the Court of Criminal Sessions. In turn he was given a position on the bench in the Court of General Sessions. In June, 1854, the city and county of Philadelphia, being consolidated, he became the Mayoralty candidate for the American party, and was elected by an overwhelming majority.

This activity did not prevent him from devoting much of his spare time to the exercise of the poetic Muse. Rees refers to some lines of his on a blind boy soliciting charity by playing the flute, as comparable to anything by Wordsworth. To continue with that wrtier's estimate:

Mr. Conrad is better known as a political writer than for his labours in the flowery paths of literature. He writes with a pen of steel dipped in *aquafortis*—a dangerous talent, and one which, when freely exercised, seldom garners any other than a harvest of tares. We look upon this gentleman as possessing a talent of no ordinary calibre. He thinks deeply, sees clearly, and is not disposed to imbibe received notions, because endorsed by weighty names, without first casting them in the alembic of his own mind.

In fact, the "Judge", as he was called by those who knew him, was a man of varied talents and accomplishments, and one has to detach his dramatic activities from his journalistic interests. In 1841, we find him editing Graham's *American Monthly Magazine of Literature, Art, and Fashion;* and for many years he conducted the *North American.* His name is also attached, in an editorial capacity, to such reference works as Sanderson's "Biography of the Signers of the Declaration of Independence", which he revised for the 1846 edition; and to Joseph Reese Fry's "Life of Gen. Zachary Taylor", in which authentic incidents of his early years were added from material collected by Conrad. The literary interest was something that law, however exacting, could not stop.

In 1856, Governor Pollock appointed Conrad Judge of Quarter Sessions. Two years thereafter, on June 27, he died in his forty-eighth year.

Our interest is here concerned with the evolution of "Jack Cade". It was a slow development, and in the process it masqueraded under several names: "The Noble Yeoman", "Aylmere; or, The Bondman of Kent", and finally "Jack Cade". The story is told fully by Wemyss, and it is upon data furnished in his book that I rely for fact. It would seem that, soon after Conrad had met with success, when his "Conrad of Naples" was produced at the Philadelphia Arch Street Theatre, he was approached with a proposition to write a drama for A. A. Addams. And an agreement was reached to the effect that if the drama was approved by Addams, Wemyss should purchase it "at such a price as should be fixed upon by two gentlemen of literary taste." While Conrad decided upon "The Noble Yeoman" as the title of the new piece, it was Wemyss who finally changed it to "Jack Cade", it being more suggestive of the type of hero to be presented. It would appear that Addams was pleased with the rôle. So L. A. Godey and Morton McMichael, as judges, agreed that Wemyss should pay the dramatist the munificent sum of three hundred dollars, and the proceeds of the third night of the engagement were, in a way, to be regarded as a Conrad "benefit", after deducting two hundred dollars for expenses. On that occasion Wemyss and Conrad were to share and share alike. Such were the financial arrangements made in those days with a dramatic author.

On October 25, 1835, Addams went to Philadelphia for an engagement, and it was planned to give "Jack Cade" its first production then. But, when Wemyss joined him, he found that for some reason or other the actor was avoiding the ordeal, and was playing "Damon and Pythias" instead. The fact of the matter was that the entire scenery for the Conrad play was ready, but Addams was not. On December 2, the actor and his manager had a talk, and Addams agreed to begin rehearsals at once, inasmuch as he was "letter perfect" in his part. Night and day preparations went on, but not to the satisfaction of Conrad, who wrote to Wemyss, on December 4:

> I venture to say that no man in town is more rejoiced at your return than I am. I have had more trouble with the piece since it left my hands than in writing it. Immediately after you signified a desire to have it noticed, the *press* opened full-mouthed, but the piece thus announced *didn't come,* and I was forced to signify to my friends the necessity of silence, until we knew when it was coming out; or whether at all; for from the delay in the principal part I began to be apprehensive it would not be played. I was sedulous in visiting and urging Mr. Addams up to the day of my illness. To have had the piece blowing away all this time would have been awful. It is bad enough to undergo the puff, puff, puff, for a week, but night and day for a month, it would have made the piece and its author, the theatre and its manager, objects of universal merriment; so those of my friends who had their hands on the bellows stopped, until they were certain the iron was in the fire. Since they are assured of that, they will doubtless get to work to the tune of "Blow your trumpets, blow". If the piece fails, it won't be for the want of puffing. I am glad to learn that *you say* that Addams is up in the part—if he is, he will play it splendidly.
>
> Will you do me the favour to superintend such alterations as may be necessary. I don't care about the piece being cut, but should like some moderation being observed in leaving out or transposing scenes. If such is contemplated, will you see to it? Any change *you* approve will meet my full assent.
>
> Will you be so kind as to send by my brother my MS of the piece? I want to have several extracts made for the papers on Saturday.
>
> Yours truly,
R. T. Conrad.

The progress of the preparations received a halt when Addams suddenly absented himself from rehearsals. Questioned as to the reason for this vagary, he said that it was the better to concentrate on his rôle. Announcements had been sent forth that on Monday night would be the opening. On Monday morning, Miss Mary Duff notified the management that she was too ill to play *Mariamne,* so Miss Ann Waring was suddenly thrust into the part. But another blow was to be dealt. Addams was in trouble. Writes Wemyss: "I found him seated in an armchair, just recovering from an attack of *mania-à-potu!!!*" However much Addams might assure everybody that by evening he would be fit to go on, his doctors knew better. Distracted, Wemyss resorted to every expedient. "I offered (Mr. David Ingersoll) one hundred dollars to read the part, and play it for three nights." But that actor refused, declaring that by Wednesday night he would play it in the regular way. Wemyss was at sea. He had an eight hundred dollar audience on his hands, and he was obliged to refund half the money when he announced for that evening a substitute play, "Ambrose Gwinette."

The fact that Ingersoll was making ready for the chief rôle in "Jack Cade" drew from Conrad the following letter:

Philadelphia, Tenth day, 1835.
Dear Sir:

I perceive that Mr. Ingersoll is underlined for *Jack Cade,* on Thursday. I am sorry that it has been thought advisable to produce the piece at present, with Mr. Ingersoll, as I think that, reserved for Mr. Addams, who is now nearly well, and perfect in the part, we will be enabled to get up some excitement in its favour, and give it a *run* which will remunerate Wemyss for the expenses already incurred. Having been announced as written for Addams, he will certainly draw in it better than any one else. If Mr. Ingersoll plays it, Addams probably *will not,* and we lose all chance of making much of the piece. I mean no disrespect to Mr. Ingersoll. However well he may play the character, the circumstances of the case, I think, make it advisable to reserve it for Addams, with whom I think we can yet make the piece profitable, and without whom I am confident it will not draw *now.* I have no personal feeling in the matter, but am entirely anxious to see Mr. Wemyss repaid for the money laid out on the play.

R. T. CONRAD.

P. Warren (Present).

This point was made an issue, and one of the original judges, Mr. McMichael, questioned whether Wemyss had a right to force Ingersoll into the part without the consent of Conrad. Notwithstanding objections on all sides, however, at the Walnut Street Theatre, on the evening of December 9, 1835, "Jack Cade" was given, with the following cast:

Lord Say ....Mr. Connor.
Clifford ....Mr. Porter.
Walter Worthy ....Mr. Clarke.
Henry Mowbray ....Mr. Watson.
Vassal ....Mr. Mestayer.
Herald ....Mr. Smith.
Heneger ....Buttenham.
Sir Edward Lacy.....................Mr. Porter.
Courtnay ....Mr. Muzzy.
Faintheart ....Mr. Hadaway.
Pembroke ....Mr. Collinbourn.
Cade ....Mr. Ingersoll.
Helen Mortimer.....................Miss Ann Waring
Margaret ....Miss Charnock

The profits for the first three nights, as recorded by Wemyss, were as follows: 1st night—$339.25; 2nd night—$243.00; 3rd night (author's benefit)—$288.75. If the author's contract was observed, therefore, he received for that evening the munificent sum of $44.37. Certain it is that Addams was forced into finally giving the play; otherwise his contract would not have been renewed. This performance took place on February 1, 1836, and Wemyss claims that in no way could he be compared in force or power with Ingersoll. He gave it two times, also, in Pittsburgh, after which he dropped it altogether.

In 1839, Forrest was scheduled for an engagement at the Philadelphia Walnut Street Theatre, and Wemyss asked Conrad to re-write his play for that actor. This proposal drew from Forrest a curious opposition, although the correspondence which Wemyss gives between himself and the actor shows that from August, 1839, through March, 1840, great preparations were being made for the production. While these were in progress, C. Thorne, manager of the New York Chatham Theatre, offered Wemyss any amount of money just for a bare skeleton plan of "Jack Cade", for it seemed that Addams was anxious to do it in New York the same evening Forrest appeared in it in Philadelphia. In Wemyss's heart there must have been sore temptation to get an extra penny out of a play which already had cost him much in time and money. But, finally, he refused the offer, and thereafter prided himself on his resisting temptation. In fact, he hastened to let Forrest know about it in a characteristic letter:

Dear Forrest—

I have this day refused a tempting offer to do an action which might have affected the literary credit of my friend, Judge Conrad. I have been offered $200 for a copy of my *old play* of "Jack Cade". You are aware I paid the judge, some years ago, $300, and a portion of the receipts of the third night of the performance, announced as the Author's Benefit; you are also aware I first broached the subject of rewriting this part of *Jack Cade* for you, and was to have the advantage of the performance by you in your last engagement with me at the Walnut Street Theatre. I need hardly say that $200 to me, at this time, would have been a small fortune. However, I regret not what has been done; and should your play succeed, shall leave it hereafter to be decided by Conrad and yourself whether I deserve any consideration at your hands.

Yours sincerely,

F. C. W.

Forrest treated this letter in his individual way; he let it remain unanswered, however much Wemyss considered he should have been rewarded for his honesty. Were Forrest's correspondence in the matter at hand, it would doubtless be seen that he had questioned Wemyss's right to any claim on the old play of "Jack Cade", now that a new one was being presented by him. The fact is, in his usual manner, Forrest tried to lay claim to the entire rights, a procedure questioned by E. L. Davenport, at the time he decided to do "Jack Cade" himself. The play was first given by Forrest at the New York Park Theatre on May 24, 1841.

The long historical introduction which accompanies the printed play is measure of the seriousness which marks Judge Conrad's writing of the drama. When he re-wrote the manuscript, we can imagine his heightening the republican sentiment for the sake of Forrest's interest. In editing the text, I have omitted most of the technical stage directions, leaving only those which suggest certain obsolete physical features indicative of the state of the theatre of the time. The style of the dialogue is declamatory; that was in accord with the acting. But the movement of the play, its passion, and its healthy glow are felt, even without the acting, and that is a mark of its vitality. For stage directions, the reader is referred to the Samuel French Acting Edition. In after years, John McCullough, who added to his repertory many of Forrest's plays, appeared in "Jack Cade".

INTRODUCTION.

Mr. Malone has satisfactorily demonstrated that the caricature of the leader in the English insurrection of 1450, introduced in Shakspeare's second part of Henry VI., was borrowed from an old play, which, but for his touch of fire, would long since have sunk into oblivion. But it is the attribute of transcendent genius to impart immortality even to the grossest absurdity; and the idea of Jack Cade is now associated, in the popular mind, with all that is vulgar, brutal and barbarous. So general, indeed, is this impression, that the attempt, even in fiction, to render such a character an object of interest, is regarded as a poetical license so presumptuous as to demand apology. The author does not regret a necessity that enables him to correct an historical wrong, which, originating in the subserviency of contemporaneous chroniclers, has, either from a culpable carelessness, or from a characteristic disposition to derogate from every popular movement for the assertion of the equal rights of man, been repeated and sanctioned by more modern historians.

The insurrection of 1381, the first general rising of the English Commons, seems to date the dawn of popular liberty in that country. The period was pregnant with important revolutions. "The internal or constitutional history of the European nations," says Mackintosh, "threatened, in almost every continental country, the fatal establishment of absolute monarchy. . . . Parliaments and diets, states-general and cortes, were gradually disappearing from view, or reduced from august assemblies to insignificant formalities; and Europe seemed on the eve of exhibiting to the disgusted eye nothing but the dead uniformity of imbecile despotism, dissolute courts, and cruelly oppressed nations." Yet, even under these adverse auspices, the mind of man was winning momentous triumphs; and popular power was silently extended with popular knowledge. The discovery of the mariner's compass led the way to new worlds, and imparted energy and activity to intellect and enterprise; and the invention of the art of printing opened the cloistered knowledge of the age to the masses. Chaucer had already lashed with the scourge of satire the abuses of the Church; and under the bold attacks of Wickliffe, errors, long tolerated without question, became the subject of doubt and discussion. The revolt of the serfs, La Jacquerie, in France, the triumph of the burghers in the Netherlands, and the freedom of the peasants of the Alps, indicated that the popular mind was awakening from its long torpor; and that the movement had been commenced, which, after various delays, resulted in the abolition of villenage throughout the larger part of Europe. Nowhere was the manifestation of this spirit more remarkable for the wrongs which aroused, and the moderation which restrained it, than in England. It is an error to trace to the charters which the barons extorted from their monarchs, the liberties of England: the triumphs of the nobles were theirs alone, and enured almost exclusively to their own advantage. The mass of the people were villeins or serfs, and they were left, by those boasted charters, in their chains. The condition of the bondmen differed in degrees of degradation and cruelty (for the mere slaves—servi—were known by the names of theow, esne, and thrall, and distinguished from the villeins), but, even where most favourable, it was a dark and inhuman oppression. The villeins were incapable of property, destitute of legal redress, and bound to services ignoble in their nature and indeterminate in their degree; they were sold separately from the land, could not marry without consent, and were, in nowise, elevated above the beasts of burthen with which they drudged in their unrequited and hopeless labour. At length, their sufferings drove them into resistance; and that resistance, provoked and sanctified by unmeasured wrongs, has been, by almost every successive historian, made the subject of misrepresentation and obloquy. The old chroniclers, without exception, vie with each other in their zeal to blacken the champions of the people; and, as those patriots fell, without an arm to shield or a voice to vindicate them, their calumniators have hitherto triumphed. Yet, from materials thus corrupt and malignant, will we undertake to glean evidence, accidentally or unavoidably admitted, sufficient to justify their cause and vindicate their memory.

The insurrection generally known as Wat Tyler's, is ascribed by Holinshed to "the lewd demenor of some vndiscreete officers." The following extract from that author will afford an insight not only into the causes of the rebellion, but the spirit of hatred and detraction with which it is recorded. "The commons of the realme sore repining, not onely for the pole grotes that were demanded of them, by reason of the grant made in parlement (as yee have heard) but also (as some write) for that they were sore oppressed (as they tooke the matter) by their landlords, that demanded of them their ancient customes and services, set on by some diuelish instinct and persuasion of their owne beastlie intentions, as men not content with the state wherevnto they were called, rose in diuerse parts of this realme, and assembled togither in companies, purposing to inforce the prince to make them free and to release them of all seruitude, whereby they stood as bondmen to their lords and superiours."

Among the first and most fearless of the advocates of the abolition of villenage, was a mendicant friar, whose name is given as John Ball. The inferior clergy promoted manumission; but the Commons were opposed to the more elevated dignitaries of the church, except, as was stated by one of their leaders, "onelie friar mendicants that might suffice for the ministration of the sacraments." How far the clergy of the court deserved this condemnation may be judged by the following description of them from Holinshed. "Moreover such were preferred to bishoprikes, and other ecclesiasticall liuings, as neither could teach nor preach, nor knew anything of the scripture of God, but onelie to call for their tithes and duties: so that they were most unworthy the name of bishops, being lewd and most vaine persons disguised in bishops apparell. Furthermore, there reigned abundantlie the filthie sinne of leachery and fornication, with abominable adulterie, specialle in the king, but most cheeflie in the prelacie, whereby the whole realme by such their euill example, was so infected that the wrath of God was dailie provoked to vengeance for the sins of the prince and his people." John Ball presents, in strong contrast to this revolting picture, a character of singular simplicity, purity and devotedness. He is called by Froissart, "a foolish priest of Kent," and the doctrines he so boldly and perseveringly taught, and sealed at last with his blood, were then considered as iniquitous, as they were novel and startling. The most satisfactory account of him and of his dangerous mission is found in Holinshed. "This man had been a preacher the space of twentie years, and bicause his doctrine was not according to the religion then by the bishops mainteined, he was first prohibited to preach in anie church or chappell; and when he ceased not for all that, but set foorth his doctrine in the streets and fields where he might haue an audience, at length he was committed to prison, out of which he prophecied he should be deliuered with the force of twentie thousand men, and even so it came to passe in time of the rebellion of the Commons. When all the prisons were broken vp, and the prisoners set at libertie, he being therefore so deliuered, followed them, and at Blackheath when the greatest multitude was got togither (as some write) he made a sermon, taking this saieng or common prouerbe for his theame, whereupon to intreat:

> 'When Adam delued and Eve span;
> Who was then a gentleman?'

and so continuing his sermon, went about to proue by the words of that prouerbe, that from the beginning, all men by Nature were created alike, and that bondage or seruitude came in by uniust oppression of naughtie men. For if God would have had anie bondmen from the beginning, he would haue appointed who should be bond and who free. And therefore he exhorted them to consider, that now the time was come appointed to them by God, in which they might (if they would) cast off the yoke of bondage and recouer libertie. He counselled them therefore to remember themselues, and to take good hearts unto them, &c., &c. Manie other things are reported by writers of this John Ball, as the letter, which vnder a kinde of darke riddle he wrote to the captaine of the Essex rebels, the copie whereof was found in one of their purses that was executed at London."

"The tenour of the said seditious priest's letter."

"Ion Scheepe S. Marie, preest of York and now of Colchester, greeteth well Ion Nameless, and Iohn the Millea, and Iohn Carter, and biddeth them that they beware of guile in Bourrough, and stand togither in God's name, and biddeth Piers ploughman go to his worke, and chastise well Hob the robber, and Iohn Trewman and all his fellows, and no mo. Iohn the Miller Y ground small, small, small, the King's sonne of heaven shall paie for all. Be ware or ye be wo, know your friend from your foe, haue enough and saie ho, and doo well and better, flee sin and seeke peace, and hold you therein, and so biddeth Iohn Trewman and all his fellowes."

The doctrines of John Ball, urged with the enthusiasm of conscious right, and enforced by the sanction of religion, could not fail, in combination with the cruelty of the barons, the exactions of the court, the reckless depravity of the nobility, and the misery and degradation of the people, to excite deep and dangerous discontents. The overcharged feelings of the people were at length, by an outrage calculated in the highest degree to excite the passions of the multitude, let loose, and swept the land like a torrent. One of the insolent and rapacious officers for the collection of an oppressive poll-tax entered, during the absence of its proprietor, the cottage of a tiler—a man who seems to have been worthily esteemed by the populace. This tax was leviable upon females only when over fifteen years of age; and the licentious officer, alleging that the beautiful daughter of the Tiler was beyond that age, "therewith," (we quote again from Holinshed,) "began to misuse the maid, and search further than honestie would have permitted. The mother straightwaie made an outcrie, so that hir husband being in the towne at worke, and hearing of this adoo at his house, came running home with his lathing staffe in his hand, and began to question with the officer, asking him who made him so bold to keepe such a rule in his house: the officer being somewhat presumptuous, and high-minded, would forthwith have flowne upon the Tiler: but the Tiler, avoiding the officer's blow, caught him such a rap on the pate, that his braines flue out, and so presentlie he died. Great noise rose about this matter in the streets, and the poor folks being glad, everie man arraied himself to support John Tiler, and thus the Commons drew togither and went to Maidestone, and from thence to Blackheath, where their numbers so increased, that they were reckoned to be thirtie thousand. And the said John Tiler tooke vpon him to be their cheefe captaine, &c."

It would be difficult to imagine holier motives to justify resistance to oppression than those unwittingly and unwillingly disclosed by the chroniclers, who represent the Commons as the guiltiest malefactors. Their wrongs and sufferings were as dark and deadly as any which ever crushed a people. They had no hope of redress from courts or codes; their only reliance was in their own union or hardihood; and the invocation to resistance proclaimed in the outrage upon the helplessness of the Tiler's daughter, was as sacred and moving as that by which Brutus or Virginius aroused Rome. Nor does the purity and elevation of the cause suffer reproach from the conduct of its champions. Wat Tyler soon found himself at the head of one hundred thousand men, "the villeins and poor men" of Kent, Norfolk, Suffolk, Essex, Sussex, and other eastern counties. Illiterate, unused to freedom, infuriated by wrongs and desperate from misery, it might be supposed that so vast and disorganized a multitude would have rushed into boundless excesses. So far from it, it seems that, from the first, they not only disclaimed treasonable designs, but administered to all an oath that "they should be faithful to King Richard and the Commons." They soon obtained possession of London, and the Chancellor and the Primate suffered the death they merited, "as evil counsellors of the crown and cruel oppressors of the people." The approbation and confidence of the citizens afford evidence that neither their designs nor conduct inspired mistrust. The Mayor durst not, says Holinshed, shut the gates against them, "for fear of the Commons of the citie, who seemed to favour the cause of the rebels so apparentlie, that they threatened to kill the Lord Maior, and all other that would take vpon them to shut the gates against the Commons. The Londoners liked better of the Commons for that they protested that the cause of their assembling togither, was not but to seeke out the traitors of the realm, and when they had found them forth, and punished them according to what they had deserved, they ment to be quiet. And to give more credit to their saiengs, they suffered none of their companie to rob or spoile, but caused them to paie for that they tooke." That a certain amount of disorder and riot attended the presence of such a multitude cannot be doubted, and it could not have been otherwise. We learn that they destroyed the Savoy, the palace of the obnoxious Duke of Lancaster; and the angry chronicler informs us that· "the shamefull spoile which they made was wonderful, and yet the zeal of iustice, truth, and upright dealing which they would seeme to shew was as nice and strange on the other part in such kind of misgouerned people. One of them hauing thrust a faire silver piece into his bosome, meaning to conueie it awaie, was espied of his fellowes, who tooke him, and cast both him and the piece into the fire; saieng they might not suffer anie such thing, sith they professed themselves to be zealous of truth and iustice, and not thieves and robbers."

The conduct of this vast multitude, provoked by a thousand wrongs, and with the power to secure an ample vengeance, and glut to the uttermost their rapacity on the spoil of their unsparing oppressors, presents a singular contrast with the dishonourable perfidy and sanguinary cruelty exhibited by their lords. Mackintosh, the only historian who does them even stinted justice, says: "At this moment of victory, the demands of the serfs were moderate, and, except in one instance, just. They required the abolition of bondage, the liberty of buying and selling in fairs and markets, a general pardon, and the reduction of the rent of land to an equal rate. The last of these conditions was indeed unjust and absurd; but the first of them, though incapable of being carried into immediate execution without probably producing much misery to themselves, was yet of such indisputable justice on general grounds, as to make it most excusable in the sufferers to accept nothing less from their oppressors." But this usually accurate historian fails to inform us that the court, after a mature consideration of the demands of the Commons, regularly and formally conceded all that was required. Doubts being entertained, as the result proved not without reason, of the sincerity of the king and court, charters were demanded and granted, securing the abolition of bondage, the redress of grievances, and a full pardon to all engaged in the insurrection. The annals of royalty, clouded as they are with every crime of which human nature is capable, present few instances of such deliberate and atrocious perfidy, of craft so cowardly and base, consummated by cruelty so guilty and unsparing. The following is a copy of the charter literally transcribed from Holinshed, who informs us that: "the like there was granted to them of other counties, as well as these of Hertfordshire in ye same forme, the names of the counties being changed."

THE FORME OF THE KING'S CHARTER OF MANUMISSION.

RICHARDUS Dei gratia rex Angliæ & Franciæ & dominus Hiberniæ: omnibus balliuis & fidelibus suis, ad quos præsentes litteræ peruenerint, salutem. Sciatis quod de gratia nostra speciali manumisimus vniuersos ligeos & singulos subditos nostros et alios comitatus Hertfordiæ, & ipsos & eorum quemlibet ab omni bondagio exuimus, & quietos facimus per præsentes, ac etiam perdonamus eisdem ligeis ac subditis nostris omnimodas felonias, proditiones, transgressiones, & extortiones, per ipsos vel aliquem eorum qualitercunque factas siue perpetratas, ac etiam vtlagariam & vtlagarias si qua vel quæ in ipsos, vel aliquem ipsorum fuerit vel fuerint hijs occasionibus promulgata vel promulgatæ, & summam pacem nostram eis & eorum cuilibet inde concedimus. In cuius rei testimonium, has litteras nostras fieri fecimus patentes. Teste meipso apud London 15 die Junij. Anno regni nostri quarto.

"The Commons having received this charter departed home." The Essex men first left London, and those from other counties shortly followed. The leader of the Kentishmen, the unfortunate Wat Tyler, distrusted the fair dealing of the court, and in an interview with the king at Smithfield, met a melancholy realization of his fears. Mackintosh, in relating the facts, remarks: "It must not be forgotten that the partizans of Tyler had no historians." But a careful review of the servile chroniclers of the court will satisfy the reader that Tyler was, in the presence of the king, and under his guaranty of safety, basely, and without adequate, if any, provocation, assassinated.

This murder was but the first of thousands. The finale may

be readily imagined. The solemn and sacred pardon of the king was disregarded; the charter, with its sanction of covenants and oaths, was revoked. After the dispersion of the Commons, the men of Essex, says Holinshed, "sent to the king to know of him if his pleasure was, that they should inioy their promised liberties." The king, "in a great chafe," answered that "bondmen they were and bondmen they should be, and that in more vile manner than before." An army was sent against them, and all who did not escape into the woods were slain. Mackintosh admits that "the revolt was extinguished with the cruelty and bloodshed by which the masters of slaves seem generally anxious to prove that they are not of a race superior in any noble quality to the meanest of their bondmen. More than fifteen hundred perished by the hands of the hangman." But Henry Kniston states that: "Then the king, of his accustomed clemencie, being pricked with pitie, would not that the wretches should die, but spared them, being a rash and foolish multitude, and commanded them everie man to get him home to his owne house; howbeit manie of them at the king's going awaie suffered the danger of death. In this miserable taking were reckoned to the number of twentie thousand."

An impartial scrutiny of the evidence afforded by those who chronicled these events, overloaded as their statements are with unsustained accusations and bitter abuse, satisfactorily establishes that the origin and objects of the rising were just and rightful; that it was conducted with courage, with wisdom, and, in the main, with moderation; that its leaders were intelligent, temperate, and patriotic; and that, had not their triumph been baffled by a courtly breach of faith, their reforms would have anticipated, by centuries, the establishment of the liberties of England. On the other hand, their tyrants, uniting the principles of Machiavel with the perfidy of his pupil, Borgia, seem to have crowded into their policy every crime of which power can be guilty; and their servile scribes have carried the cruelty of their masters beyond the tomb, and burthened the memory of the unfortunate victims with the most unmerited obloquy.

Several of the acts and actors in these scenes have been, by the author of Jack Cade, interwoven with the insurrection which ensued in 1450. This liberty is induced and justified by the similarity of the two movements. They were provoked by the same wrongs, and were commenced in the same county; they both were contests between an imbecile monarch and his outraged subjects; in both, the Commons bore themselves with the same patriotic moderation, the court with the same feebleness and falsehood;—the people triumphed by valour, to be defeated by fraud, and spared their tyrants to be sacrificed, without mercy, themselves. The actors, in each, found fortune and history, their own generation and posterity, equally unjust and cruel.

The period which had, meanwhile, elapsed, had reduced England in 1450 to nearly the same condition as under the reign of Richard II. Again the degenerate son of a heroic father occupied the throne, from which he was doomed to be borne to a prison and a grave. Henry, indeed, was irresponsible to censure, for his weakness amounted to absolute and helpless idiocy. His foreign wife, wholly under foreign and criminal influences, was universally execrated for her tyranny and licentiousness. France, so gloriously won by the fifth Harry, was lost by weakness and treachery; and "the good Duke of Gloucester" had been basely murdered at the instigation of Suffolk, a counsellor of the realm, and, as Hall calls him, "the darling of the Queen." Villenage, with all its sufferings and debasement, continued, and the Commons were ground to the dust by the exactions of the court, and the unbridled oppression of the barons. Thus, with disgrace abroad and agony at home, the contrast with the glory of the recent reign was insupportable; and the popular discontent was manifested in risings, which, after the manner of the time, took the name of Blue Beard. So intense was the excitement against Say and Suffolk, that the latter, notwithstanding the efforts of the Queen to screen "her darling," met the fate which he so justly merited. Shortly after this execution, a body of the peasantry of Kent met in arms, at Blackheath, under the leader whose brief and eventful career has been made the subject of such unmeasured misrepresentation.

Even his name has, by the chroniclers, been left in doubt. "Stowe," says Mackintosh, "alone represents this leader's name to have really been Cade. In a contemporary record he is called Mr. John Aylmere, Physician." (Ellis's Letters, I., second series, 112.) This account seems to be fully en-

titled to credit: it accords with the language and deportment
of the chief of the Commons; and we doubt not that such
were his name and profession. It was, however, usual in
such commotions to give, to prominent actors, probably for
purposes of concealment and security, fictitious and popular
names. Thus we have seen that Wat Tyler assumed the
name of Jack Straw; and Fabyan says of William Mande-
ville that "for to draw the people unto him, he called himself
Jack Sharpe." All the popular leaders appear thus to have
borne names for the war. But Aylmere was not only called
Jack Cade: Polychronicon says that he was "of some named
John Mendall." The chronicles furnish no proof that he
ever acknowledged the name of Cade. In his communications
with the government, he used merely the title of "Captain of
the Commons." Mackintosh characterizes him as "a leader
of disputed descent, who had been transmitted to posterity
with the nickname of John Cade. On him they bestowed the
honourable name of John Mortimer, with manifest allusion
to the claims of the house of Mortimer to the succession;
which were, however, now indisputably vested in Richard,
Duke of York." It seems that the friends of the Duke of
York favoured the insurrection, a fact of itself sufficient to
attach dignity and importance to the movement. Hall and
Holinshed agree in this statement. "Those that fauoured
the Duke of Yorke, and wished the crowne upon his head,
for that (as they judged) he had more right thereto than
he that ware it, procured a commotion in Kent in this manner. A certeine young man of a goodlie stature and right
pregnaunt of wit, was intised to take upon him the name of
John Mortimer, coosine to the Duke of York, and not for a
small policie, thinking by that surname, that those which
fauored the house of the Earle of Marche would be assistant
to him. And so indeed it came to passe." If Aylmere permitted this title to be given him, he certainly did not use it
in his addresses to the King and Parliament, nor in his letters
which have been preserved. It is also certain that the name
of Mortimer could not, in any event, have promoted any personal design; and that he never claimed power, rank, or
reward for himself, his simple title being The Captain, and
his sole efforts confined to the amelioration of the condition
of the people. So far from seeking revolution, he most em-

phatically proclaimed his loyalty: and all his acts were in the name of the king. The title of Mortimer may have been given him as a demonstration of respect, for Fabyan says that "the multitude named him Mortimer, and this kept the people wondrously togither"—and not from a belief that he was connected with the popular line of John of Gaunt; or if the delusion actually existed, he may have forborne to correct it, from a desire to secure the sway over his people necessary to control them and repress disorder.

The leader who assumed this bold attitude of calm resistance must have been, if a physician at that period, superior to most of his opponents in the limited learning of the age. We have seen him described by the chroniclers as "a young man of goodly stature and right pregnant of wit." His letters, his addresses to the King and Parliament, his interview with the commissioners of the court, and the general tenor of his proceedings, prove the possession of an intellect of no ordinary cultivation and force; and his military skill and success indicate experience and sagacity as a soldier. His first measure, after assuming a position on Blackheath, was to proclaim distinctly the object of "the assembly of the Commons." We learn from Hall and Holinshed, that "this capteine assembling a great companie of tall personages, assured them that the enterprize which he tooke in hand was both honorable to God and the king, and profitable to the whole realme. For if either by force or policie they might get the king and queene into their hands, he would cause them to be honorablie used, and such order for the punishing and reforming of the misdemeanours of their bad counsellors, that neither fifteens should hereafter be demanded, nor once anie impositions or taxes be spoken of. The Kentish people, moved at these persuasions and other faire promises of reformation, in good order of battell (but not in greate number) came with their capteine vnto Blackheath, and there kept the field more than a month." During this period, "he made such ordinances among them that he brought a great number of people unto the Blackheath." (Fabyan.) He maintained also a correspondence with London, and his letters of safeguard to citizens passing to and from the camp and city are formally and well drawn, and prove that even then he received supplies of money and arms from the capital.

While thus organizing and disciplining his host, with a calmness and deliberation which manifest anything but the madness ascribed to him, "he devised,"—says Fabyan—"a bill of petitions to the king and his council, and shewed therein what injuries and oppressions the poor Commons suffered by such as were about the king." This proceeding is thus characterized by Holinshed: "And to the intent the cause of this glorious captain's coming thither, might be shadowed vnder a cloke of good meaning (though his intent nothing so) he sent vnto the king an humble supplication, affirming that his coming was not against his grace, but against such of his councellors, as were louers of themselues and oppressors of the poor commonaltie; flatterers of the king and enimies of his honour; suckers of his purse, and robbers of his subiects; parciall to their friends, and extreame to their enimies; through bribes corrupted, and for indifferencie dooing nothing." The Parliament was then in session; and this bill of complaint, together with the requests of the Commons, was sent to that body as well as to the King. The "Complaint of the Commons of Kent, and the causes of their assemblie on the Blackheathe" comprises fifteen items, set forth with great clearness and force, and manifesting as high an order of learning and ability as any state paper of the times. We extract the Bill of Complaints from Holinshed, as affording conclusive evidence that Aylmere, instead of being the ignorant, ferocious, and vulgar ruffian generally supposed, was a patriot eminently enlightened and discreet.

"The Request by the Capteine of the great assemblie in Kent.

"The Requests by the Capteine of the great assemblie in Kent.

"Imprimis, desireth the capteine of the Commons, the welfare of our souereigne lord the king, and all true lords spirituall and temporall, desiring of our said souereigne lord, and of all the true lords of his councell, he to take in all his demaines, that he maie reigne like a king roiall, according as he is borne our true and Christian king anointed; and who so will saie the contrarie, we all will liue and die in the quarrell as his true liege men.

"Item, desireth the said capteine, that he will avoide all the false progenie and affinitie of the Duke of Suffolke, the which been openlie knowne, and they to be punished after the custome and law of this land, and to take about his noble person the true lords of his roiall blood of this his realme, that is to saie, the high and mightie prince the Duke of York, late exiled from our said souereigne lord's presence (by the motion and stirring of the traitorous and false disposed the Duke of Suffolke and his affinitie), and the mightie princes and dukes of Exeter, Buckingham and Norffolke, and all the earles and barons of this land: and then shall he be the richest king Christian.

"Item, desireth the said capteine and Commons punishment vnto the false traitors, the which contriued and imagined the death of the high and mightfull and excellent prince the Duke of Gloucester, the which is too much to rehearse; the which duke was proclaimed as a traitor. Vpon the which quarrel, we purpose all to liue and die vpon that it is false.

"Item, the Duke of Exeter, our holie father the cardinall, the noble prince the Duke of Warwicke, and also the realme of France, the duchie of Normandie, Gascoigne, and Guion, Aniou and Maine, were deliuered and lost by means of the said traitors; and our true lords, knights and esquires and manie a good yeoman lost and sold yer they went, the which is a great pitie to hear, of the great and greevous losse to our souereigne and his realme.

"Item, desireth the said capteine and Commons, that all extortions vsed dailie among the common people might be laid down, that is to saie, the greene wax: the which is falselie vsed to the perpetuall destruction of the king's true Commons of Kent. Also the King's Bench, the which is too greefefull to the shire of Kent, without provision of our souereign lord and his true councell. And also in taking of wheate and other graines, beefe, mutton and all other vittles, the which is importable to the said Commons, without the breefe prouision of our said souereigne and his true councell, they may no longer beare it. And also vnto the statute of labourers and the great extortioners, the which is to saie the false traitors, Sleg, Cromer, Isle, and Robert Est."

These "requests" the council whom they accused, "disallowed and condemned"; and constrained the royal puppet in their keeping to march against the rebels. But so general and decided was the confidence in the rectitude of the motives and measures of the Commons and their leader, that not only the mass of the people, but many of the followers of the king and court, embraced their cause. Holinshed says that "the king removed from Westminster vnto Greenwich, from whence he would haue sent certaine lords with a power to haue distressed the Kentishmen, but the men said to their lords that they would not fight against them that laboured to amend the common weale: wherefore the lords were driuen to leaue their purpose. And bicause the Kentishmen cried out against the lord Saie the king's chamberleine, he was by the king committed to the Tower of London." The same course had been pursued in relation to Suffolk; and Say, against whom the nation was deeply and justly incensed, would also have been released by the court on the first opportunity, had not its action been anticipated by the Commons.

Some days after, the king marched against the force under Aylmere; but that leader seems to have been averse to the commencement of actual hostilities, especially against the king in person; and he retired before him, taking post at Seven-Oak, when the king returned to London. The withdrawal of Aylmere is considered, by the chroniclers, who can imagine no good of the people's chief, a mere feint to entice the royal army into a more unfavourable position. The queen, "that bare rule," shortly after sent Sir Humphrey Stafford, with an army, to disperse the rebels. The captain still desired to avoid the effusion of blood; and we are told by Fabyan that, "when Sir Humphrey with his company drew near to Seven-Oak, he was warned of the captain." But this generous caution and unusual moderation, doubtless ascribed to pusillanimity, did not avail; and Aylmere met the inevitable issue with the skill and courage of a tried soldier. "When," says the same author, "Sir Humphrey had counselled with the other gentlemen, he, like a manfull knight, set upon the rebels, and fought them long. But in the end the captain slew him and his brother, with many other, and caused the rest to give back. All which season the king's host lay still upon Blackheath, being among them sundry opinions; so that some and many favoured the captain. But finally when word came of the overthrow of the Staffords, they said plainly, boldly, that except the Lord Say and other rehearsed were committed to ward, they would take the captain's party." It was then that Say was sent to the Tower. The feeling must have been strong indeed, and well founded, that induced such a source, and that in a voice so potential and imperative as to enforce immediate acquiescence.

After this important victory, the leader of the Commons, says Mackintosh, "assumed the attire, ornaments and style of a knight; and, under the title of captain, he professed to preserve the country by enforcing the rigid observance of discipline among his followers." Having refreshed his people, he resumed his position on Blackheath, "where he strongly encamped himself, diverse idle and vagrant persons," says Holinshed, "out of Sussex, Surrie, and other places, still increasing his number." The king and his council were now fully aroused to a sense of their danger; and they determined to have recourse to the policy of negotiation, promises and perfidy, found so effective in the previous insurrection. They accordingly sent to the leader, whose humble "requests" they had received with such disdain, the Archbishop of Canterbury and the Duke of Buckingham, to treat of an accommodation. The report of this interview, derived, as it is from writers prompt to blacken Aylmere, and reluctant to admit the slightest point in his favour, establishes, beyond doubt, the elevation of his character and deportment. Fabyan says that the royal commissioners "had with him long communication, and found him right discrete in his answers. Howbeit, they could not cause him to lay down his people, and submit him (unconditionally) to the king's grace." Holinshed's account after Hall, is more full and expressive. "These lords found him sober in talke, wise in reasoning, arrogant in hart, and stiffe in opinion; as who that by no means would grant to dissolue his armie, except the king in person would come to him, and assent to the things he would require." The captain, it seems, remembered the ill faith practiced towards Wat Tyler, and was unwilling to place it in the power of the court to re-enact that tragedy. Subsequent events proved how just were his suspicions.

The king was alarmed by the firm attitude of Aylmere, and still more by the disaffection evident among his followers; and according to Holinshed, "upon the presumptuous answers and requests of this villainous rebell, beginning as much to doubt his owne meniall seruants as his vnknowen subiects (which spared not to speake, that the cauteine's cause was profitable to the commonwealth), departed in all hast to the castell of Killingworth, in Warwikeshire, leauing onlie behind him the Lord Scales to keepe the Tower of London." The captain, notwithstanding his recent victory, his great force, and the natural impatience of his host, had forborne to advance against the king; but his retreat rendered some decisive action now necessary. Nothing was to be expected from the court. Time was pressing; for delay multiplied his dangers, and increased the difficulty of holding together and restraining so vast and undiscipled a multitude. His only course was to take possession of the capital and redress, through such legal authorities as he found in existence, or upon the warrant of the nation's expressed will, the grievances under which the realm was groaning. This step was, however, attended with great difficulty and peril, arising from his own aversion to the assumption of permanent authority, and the absence of the Duke of York, who might then have taken upon him, as he did afterwards, the supreme control of affairs; and from the character of his force and the absence of regular resources for its maintenance. To prevent the excesses so much to be apprehended, he rigidly enforced the laws; or, as Fabyan has it, "to the end to blind the more people, and to bring him in fame that he kept good justice, he beheaded there a petty captain of his, named Parrys, for so much as he had offended against such ordinance as he had established in his host. And hearing that the king and his lords had thus departed, drew him near unto the city, so that upon the first day of July he entered the burgh of Southwark." Anxious to proceed with the strictest regard to the peace and the privileges of the city, Aylmere, next day, caused the authorities of London to be convened. "The Mayor called the Common Council at the Guildhall, for to purvey the understanding of these rebels, and other matters, in which assembly were divers opinions, so that some thought good that the said rebels should be received into the city, and some otherwise." (Fabyan.) He was, however, admitted. This submission to authority by a rebel at the head of a victorious army, is, the age and circumstances considered, a remarkable feature of the insurrection. "The same afternoon, about five of the clock, the captain with his people,

entered by the Bridge: and when he came upon the Draw-
bridge, he hew the ropes that drew the bridge in sunder with
his sword, and so passed into the city, and made in sundry
places thereof proclamations in the king's name, that no man,
upon pain of death, should rob or take anything perforce
without paying therefor. By reason whereof he won many
hearts of the Commons of the city; but," continues the charitable Fabyan, "all was done to beguile the people, as after
shall evidently appear. He rode through divers streets of the
city, and as he came by London stone, he strake it with his
sword, and said, 'Now is Mortimer lord of this city!' And
when he had thus showed himself in divers places in the city,
and showed his mind to the Mayor for the ordering of his
people, he returned into Southwark, and there he abode as he
had before done, his people coming and going at lawful hours
when they would." Thus, it seems that he acted in full concert with the authorities; that he did everything in his power
to prevent and punish disorder; and that so anxious was he
to avoid popular tumult, that he withdrew his force from the
city, and did not permit his people to enter it, except "at lawful times." The history of the times exhibits no instance of
such consideration for the welfare of the people, on the part
of monarchs or their barons, as is here manifested by "the
villainous rebel."

It was necessary that Lord Say should be brought to trial.
As he was in the custody of Lord Scales, this must have
taken place with the sanction and actual aid of the court.
"On the third day of July," says Fabyan, "the said captain
entered again the city, and caused the Lord Say to be fetched
from the Tower, and led into Guildhall, where he was arraigned before the mayor and other of the king's justices."
Of his guilt there seems to have been neither doubt nor
denial. Holinshed tells us that "being before the king's
justices put to answer, he desired to be tried by his peeres,
for the longer delaie of his life. The capteine perceiving his
dilatorie plea, by force tooke him from the officers, and
brought him to the standard in Cheape;" where he suffered
military execution, a result which, in the excited state of
public sentiment, probably could not have been averted, and
which the heavy catalogue of his crimes, and the certainty
that the queen, had time been afforded, would have shielded

him, perhaps justified. William Croumer, his brother-in-law and instrument, and one of those charged before Parliament, suffered at the same time. These executions are bitterly denounced by the chroniclers; but, according to their own accounts, Aylmere punished more of his own men for violations of the law, than he did of those whose crimes and cruelty had provoked the insurrection; and it may be doubted whether history affords an instance of greater moderation and lenity, under circumstances so peculiar, than were exhibited by him, with the oppressors of his country in his power, and a maddened people calling for justice.

The leader of the Commons continued, from a regard for the public safety, to occupy his position in Southwark until the sixth of July. During this period it is alleged that, in two instances, he made requisitions upon wealthy citizens of London; and, indeed, it was only by such means that so large a host could have been sustained. This appears to have alarmed the mayor and aldermen; and it is also probable that the utmost vigilance and rigour did not wholly repress occasional outrages of a character to excite the fears of the more wealthy citizens. The aid of Lord Scallys and Sir Matthew Gough, "then having the Tower in guiding," was, under these apprehensions, solicited to prevent the re-entrance of Aylmere into London. This induced a collision, "and a battle or bloody scuffle was continued during the night on London Bridge, in which success seemed to incline to the insurgents." (Mackintosh.) In the morning a truce for certain hours was effected, during which a negotiation took place between the Archbishop of Canterbury, representing the king, and the captain of the Commons. On the part of the former, everything would naturally be promised, for it was designed that no promise should be observed; and a covenant for all that was demanded was as readily violated as one for a part. The leader of the Commons must have been conscious that his force could only be maintained by a forcible and necessarily unpopular levy of contributions; and that even if maintained, their impatience of discipline and anxiety to return to their homes rendered them unfit for the protracted struggle that seemed impending. To continue in the field threatened the worst horrors of civil war, a war in which he could have but little hope of long restraining his followers. Every consideration of humanity and patriotism seemed therefore to dictate an acceptance of the proffered concessions of the court. The compact was therefore concluded; and the Commons thus won a seeming triumph. What was covenanted on the part of the court does not appear; for the chroniclers are silent on that head, and the people "had no historians." Fabyan, however, informs us that "the Archbishop of Canterbury, then Chancellor of England, sent a general pardon to the captain for himself, and another for his people; by reason whereof he and his company departed the same night out of Southwark, and so returned every man to his home."

The sequel is briefly told; it is the old tale of perfidy and blood. The pardon was immediately revoked. "Proclamations were made in divers places of Kent, of Southsex, and Sowthery, that who might take the aforesaid Jack Cade, either alive or dead, should have a thousand marks for his travayle." He was pursued and slain; "and so being dead was brought into Southwark. And upon the morrow, the dead corpse was drawn through the high streets of the city unto Newgate, and there headed and quartered, whose head was then sent to London Bridge, and his four quarters were sent to four sundry towns of Kent." (Fabyan.)

The following spirited extract, from the works of the late Mr. Leggett, is, perhaps, the only attempt hitherto made to do justice to the chivalrous and enlightened but unfortunate and much-maligned chieftain of the Commons. It was unknown to the author until after the production of the tragedy.

"It is heart-sickening to see men, citizens of this free republic and partakers of its equal blessings, assume without examination, and use without scruple, as terms of reproach, the epithets with which lying historians and panders to royalty have branded those, whose only crime was their opposing, with noble ardour and courage, the usurpations of tyranny, and setting themselves up as assertors of the natural and inalienable rights of their oppressed fellow-men.

"Have the editors who use the name of Cade as a word of scorn looked into the history of that heroic man? Have they sifted out, from the mass of prejudice, bigotry and servility, which load the pages of the old chroniclers, the facts in relation to his extraordinary career? Have they acquainted themselves with the oppressions of the times; the lawless violence of the nobles; the folly and rapacity of the monarch; the extortion and cruelty of his ministers; and the general contempt which was manifested for the plainest and dearest rights of humanity? Have they consulted the pages of Stow, and Hall, and Holinshed, who, parasites of royalty as they were, and careful to exclude from their chronicles whatever might grate harshly on the delicate ears of the privileged orders, have not yet been able to conceal the justice of the cause for which Cade contended, the moderation of his demands, or the extraordinary forbearance of his conduct? Have they looked into those matters for themselves, and divested the statements of the gloss of prejudice and servility, judged of the man by a simple reference to the facts of his conduct, and the nature and strength of his motives? Or have they been content to learn his character from the scenes of a play, or the pages of that king-worshipper, that pimp and pander to aristocracy, the tory Hume, who was ever ready to lick absurd pomp, and give a name of infamy to any valiant spirit that had the courage and true nobleness to stand forward in defence of the rights of his fellow-men?

"Let those who use the name of Cade as a term of reproach remember that the obloquy which blackens his memory flowed from the same slanderous pens that denounced as rebels and traitors, and with terms of equal bitterness, though not of equal contumely, the Hampdens and Sydneys of England— glorious apostles and martyrs in the cause of civil liberty! Let them remember, too, that, as the philosophic Mackintosh observes, all we know of Cade is through his enemies—a fact which of itself would impress a just and inquiring mind with the necessity of examination for itself, before adopting the current slang of the aristocracy of Great Britain.

"The very name of Jack Cade, if we take the pains to look into contemporary historians, is but a nickname conferred upon the leader of the Kentish insurrection, in order to increase the obloquy with which it was the policy of Henry IV. and his licentious nobles to load the memory of that heroic and treacherously murdered man. But whatever was his name or origin, and whatever might have been his private motives and character if we judge of him by the authentic facts of history alone, we shall find nothing that does not entitle him to the admiration of men who set a true value on liberty, and revere those who peril their lives, their fortunes, and their sacred honour, to achieve it from the grasp of tyrants, or defend it against their encroachments. Nothing can exceed the grossness of the oppressions under which the people laboured when Cade took up arms. Nothing can exceed the arbitrary violence with which their property was wrested from their hands, or the ignominious punishments which were causelessly inflicted on their persons. The kingdom was out of joint. An imbecile and rapacious monarch on the throne; a band of licentious and factious nobles around him—a Parliament ready to impose any exactions on the Commons—and all the minor offices of Government filled with a species of freebooters, who deemed the possessions of the people their lawful prey; in such a state of things, the burdens under which the great mass of Englishmen laboured must have been severe in the extreme.

"If Cade was the wretched fanatic which it has pleased the greatest dramatic genius of the world (borrowing his idea of that noble rebel from old Holinshed) to represent him, how did it happen that twenty thousand men flocked to his standard the moment it was unfurled? How did it happen that his statement of grievances was so true, and his demands for redress so moderate, that, even according to Hume himself, 'the council observing that nobody was willing to fight against men so reasonable in their pretensions, carried the king for safety to Kenilworth?' How did it happen, as related by Fabyan, that the Duke of Buckingham and the Archbishop of Canterbury being sent to negotiate with him were obliged to acknowledge that they found him 'right discrete in his answers'; howbeit they could not cause him to lay down his people, and to submit him (unconditionally) unto the king's grace." But we need not depend upon the opinions of historians for the reasonableness of his demands. Holinshed has recorded his list of grievances and stipulations of redress; and let those who think the term 'Jack Cade' synonymous with an ignorant and ferocious rebel and traitor, examine it; let them compare it with the grievances which led our fathers to take up arms against their mother-country, nor lay them down until they achieved a total separation; let them look at it in reference to what would be their own feelings under a tithe part of the wrongs; and, our life on it, they will pause before they again use the word in such a sense. Nay, more: let them follow Cade through his whole career; let them behold him in the midst of insurrection, checking the natural fierceness of his followers, restraining their passions, and compelling them by the severest orders to respect private property; see him withdrawing his forces each night from London, when he had taken possession of that city, that its inhabitants might sleep without fear or molestation; mark him continually endeavouring to fix the attention of the people solely on those great ends of public right and justice for which alone he had placed himself in arms against the king; let them look at Cade in these points of view, and we think their unfounded prejudices will speedily give way to very different sentiments.

"Follow him to the close of his career; see him deserted by his followers, under a general but deceitful promise of pardon from the government; trace him afterwards a fugitive· through the country with a reward set upon his head, in violation of the edict which but a few days before had absolved him of the crime of rebellion on condition of laying down his arms; behold him at last entrapped by a wretch and basely murdered; weigh his whole character as exhibited by all the prominent traits of his life and fortune, remembering,· too, that all you know of him is from those who dipped their pens in ink only to blacken his name, and you will at last be forced to acknowledge that instead of the scorn of mankind, he deserves to be ranked among those glorious martyrs who have sacrificed their lives in defence of the rights of man. The derision and contumely which have been heaped on Cade, would have been heaped upon those who achieved the liberty of this country, had they been equally unsuccessful in their struggle. It then ill becomes republicans, enjoying the freedom which they achieved, admiring the intrepidity of their conduct, and revering their memory, to use the name of one who sacrificed his life in an ill-starred effort in defence of the same glorious and universal principles of equal liberty, as a byword and term of mockery and reproach.

"Cade was defeated, and his very name lies buried underneath the rubbish of nations. But his example did not die. Those who are curious in historical research may easily trace the influence of the principles which Cade battled to establish, through succeeding reigns. If they follow the stream of history from the sixth Henry downwards, they will find that the same sentiments of freedom were continually breaking away from the restraint of tyranny, and that the same grievances complained of by the leader of the Kentish insurrection, were the main cause of all the risings of the Commons till at last the cup of oppression, filled to overflowing, was dashed to the earth by an outraged people, the power of the throne was shaken to its centre, and the evils under which men long had groaned were remedied by a revolution."

There has been no attempt in the following work to adhere strictly to the facts of history; though the author has endeavoured generally to portray the condition of the people and the causes and character of the insurrection. It is imagined, in the play, that the leader of the Commons was originally a villein by the name of Cade; afterwards a fugitive known as Aylmere; then, after an absence abroad, returning to England, he excites an insurrection, for the double purpose of avenging his own wrongs and of abolishing the institution, villeinage, which made him a bondman. After his triumph, he resumes his original name.—The tragedy, as originally written, comprises much that was not designed for, and is not adapted to the stage. To the judgment and taste of Mr. Forrest he is indebted for the suggestions which prepared "Aylmere" for the stage; and to the eminent genius of that unrivalled tragedian and liberal patron of dramatic literature, its flattering success at home and abroad may he justly ascribed.

JACK CADE.

New York Park Theatre, May 24, 1841.

Jack Cade .... Edwin Forrest.
Clifford .... Jas. Murdoch.
Kate .... Miss McCride.
Lord Say............................ W. Wheatley.
Buckingham .... A. Andrews.
Wat Worthy........................ ——— Chippendale.
Courtnay .... W. A. Chapman.
Dick Pembroke...................... ——— Fisher.
Mariamne.......................... Mrs. Geo. W. Jones.
Friar Lacy .... ——— Nickenson.
Mowbray .... C. W. Clarke.
Jack Straw .... ——— Bellamy.
Widow Cade........................ Mrs. Wheatley.

From the Lacy Acting Edition of "Jack Cade," we quote the following:

COSTUMES—PERIOD 1430-50—HENRY VI

AYLMERE.—*1st dress:* Dark turban cap, plain brown shirt with full sleeves and scollopped round the edges, black waist-belt with pouch and dagger, brown tights and buff ankle boots with pointed toes. *2nd dress:* Rich suit of plate armour of the time.

FRIAR LACY.—A grey robe, fleshings and sandals, rope round waist and rosary and cross.

WORTHY.—*1st dress:* Rather long leathern shirt, fleshings and ankle shoes. *2nd dress:* Armour.

STRAW AND THE OTHERS.—*1st dress:* Various coloured shirts with short sleeves, caps, and ankle shoes. *2nd dress:* Rudely armed.

SAY.—*1st dress:* Velvet shirt embroidered with hanging sleeves and scollopped edges, tights and ankle boots, belt with dagger, purse, and sword, gold neck chain. *2nd dress:* Complete suit of plate armour.

REST OF THE NOBLES.—The same as Say, of different colours.

The description of the costumes of Henry VI. written by the Editor for Cumberland's edition of that play, will be found to be perfectly suited for this drama. No beard or moustache should be worn. A representation of a suit of the armour of the time may be seen in Plate 1 of "Lacy's Female Costumes"—Joan of Arc.

MARIAMNE.—*1st dress:* Dark double dress with hanging sleeves. *2nd dress:* White, with dishevelled hair.

KATE.—Grey moreno double dress.

CHILD.—Plain tunic, &c.

JACK CADE.

ACT I.

SCENE FIRST.—*Sunrise landscape, with the hovels of the bond painted on flat.* JACK STRAW, *with long knife,* DICK PEMBROKE, *with pick-axe,* ROGER SUTTON, *with spade—bondmen dressed coarsely, with implements of labour, as if going to their work.*

STRAW. Of corn three stinted measures!
  And that doled
With scourge and curse! Rough fare, even for a bondman.
  PEMBROKE. Yet must he feed, from this, his wife and
    children;
They'll starve, of course. Courtnay cares not for that.
  STRAW. I'd cheerly toil, were Courtnay yoked this day
Unto my plough.
  PEMBROKE.   He seizes on the havings,
The little way found comforts of the bond,
Nor vouchsafes e'en a "Wi' your leave, good man."
  SUTTON. Man, matron, maid—alas, that it is so!
All are their victims.
  PEMBROKE.   Would we were not men,
But brutes—they are used kindlier!
  STRAW.   Men we are not.
Brutes only would bear this. Bond have there been
Who brooked it not.
  PEMBROKE. Who were they?
  STRAW.   Old Cade, one;
Who struck down the Lord Say;—not this base knave,
Courtnay, but e'en Lord Say, because he spurned him,
  PEMBROKE. He died for it.

STRAW.   But what of that? 'Tis better
To die than thus to live. His stripling son—
Young Cade—remember you Jack Cade?

PEMBROKE.   Not I.
Our Sutton must.

SUTTON.   He who, some ten years gone,
Fled from the barony?

STRAW.   The same. Well, he
A bondman and a boy, stood by, when Say
Wronged the pale widow Cade, by a base jest
Upon the husband he had scourged to death.
What think you did the boy?

PEMBROKE.   Rebuked his lordship?

STRAW. He struck him down, and 'scaped the barony.
He hath ne'er since been heard of. So he won
Both liberty and vengeance.

SUTTON.   A brave boy!
'Twas Friar Lacy taught him this: and he
Says that all men are in God's image made,
And all are equal.

PEMBROKE.   He hath preached through Kent,
Till bond and yeomen weary with their lot.
The down-trodden yet may, some day, turn and sting
The foot that tramples them.

STRAW.   I'm ready for it.
The yeomen are all with us. Master Mowbray,
A bold, hot spirit, and Wat Worthy too,
The old and doughty blacksmith, yeomen good,
Wealthy and well-approved, encourage Lacy
In his bold preaching of the poor man's right.

SUTTON. Mowbray is 'trothed to Master Worthy's daugh-
        ter;
And Courtnay, it is said, doth woo the girl.

STRAW. An' Mowbray want a stout heart and rough hand,
Jack Straw will thank him for a loving chance
Of braining the pet whelp.

PEMBROKE.   Work you to-day?

STRAW. My wife is sick to death: I must watch by her.
Yet little hope or comfort is there for her
In my poor hovel. Ha! the steward comes—
The crawling Courtnay.

Enter COURTNAY, *with staff, five feet long, gilt ball at top, bead and spike at bottom.*

COURTNAY. Sunrise and ye loiter!
Slaves, drudges, to your toil! or I'll scourge you!

SUTTON. We go, your worship. [*Crosses to right, bowing to* COURTNAY. *Exit* SUTTON.

COURTNAY. Get thee gone. And thou—
Why dost thou stand?

PEMBROKE. My children have no food;
Give me to feed them, ere I go afield.

COURTNAY. Dost murmur, rogue! This hath your beggar priest,
The shaveling who talks treason, taught you. Off!

PEMBROKE. Give me an hour to labour for a crust.
They pine, to perishing, for food!

COURTNAY. A trick—
A stale device!

PEMBROKE. No, by this light, it is not.

COURTNAY. What care I for your brats? Away to work!

PEMBROKE. Nay, gentle master Steward—

COURTNAY. Knave, dost argue?
I'll have thee instant i' the stocks.

PEMBROKE. [*Bowing very low to* COURTNAY.] I go, sir.
Alas, my children! [*Exit* PEMBROKE, *slowly.*

COURTNAY. And thou, what dost thou here? Art silent, patch?
Wilt not to work?

STRAW. No.

COURTNAY. Saucy carle, dar'st beard me?

STRAW. My wife is sick—sick unto death: I will not,
To pleasure any he that lives, leave her
To die alone.

COURTNAY. Thou lying knave! Dost think——

STRAW. I lie *not,* sir. O'ercome with toil, she fainted
I' the field: four days and nights I have watched o'er her,
And cannot toil—and would not, if I could.

COURTNAY. [*Raising his staff.*] Villain!

STRAW. [*Drawing his knife from his girdle.*] Strike, an' thou durst!

COURTNAY. [*Backing, and slowly letting his staff sink.*]
I'll have thee flayed
And hung for this.   [*Exit* COURTNAY.
STRAW.   I care not, I!
Why should I wish to live? Would I and mine
Were on the hillside lain, where bond and free
Are equal!   [*Exit* STRAW.

SCENE SECOND. *The cot of* WIDOW CADE. *Rustic interior.
Set door, table and two chairs, white table-cloth, and a
trencher.* WIDOW CADE *discovered at left of table.*

WIDOW. A heavy lot, and hopeless! Friendless, poor.
Stricken with years and sorrow, and bowed down
Beneath the fierce frown of offended power!
Would that widowhood and life could sink together
Into my husband's grave!
                    [*Knock at door;* WIDOW *opens it.*]
                    Good morrow, father!

Enter FRIAR LACY.

LACY. 'Tis strange! No aid yet from the castle, dame?
WIDOW. The castle? No, sir, no; they aid me not.
I am worn out with years, and toil, and sorrow;
And 'tis our steward's wont the useless bond
To turn adrift.
We only know our masters by our miseries.
LACY. The poor have no friends but the poor; the rich—
Heaven's stewards upon earth—rob us of that
They hold in trust for us, and leave us starvelings.
But good dame, to end
This idle railing, got you that, this morn
I sent you?
WIDOW.   Thanks! It stood 'twixt me and famine;
My boy, when he returns, will bless you for 't.
LACY. Still hoping, dame, thy boy's return? How brave
Is a mother's love! Why, ten long years have past,
And not a token from him.

WIDOW.   Oh, good father,
Do not divorce me from that hope! 'Tis fed
Upon my heart.

LACY.   A dream!

WIDOW.   An' if it be,
I would not give it for earth's brightest substance.
But 'tis no dream. I'm sure my dear son lives;
For when he fled, with his last kiss, poor boy!
He promised to be thoughtful of his weal,
Ev'n for my sake.

LACY.   He went with a high heart!
For I had taught him to look up to God
As his sole rightful lord. He sought a land
Where the poor peasant's heart may dare to throb
Without a master's leave: and "There," he said,
"There where the human soul has slipped its jesses,
I'll win my way, for I can do it."

WIDOW. My noble boy! "Though years may pass away,"
He said when he last clasped me, "ne'er despair;
I'll come again, and come in honour, mother."
And so he will! [*A knocking at the door.*]
                    A knocking at my door!
'Tis seldom poverty hath visitants,
Save want and terror. [*Goes up and opens door.*]

[*Enter* AYLMERE, MARIAMNE, *and* CHILD.]

                    Enter, enter, sir.
[*To* LACY.] Come they from the castle?

LACY.   They are strangers, dame.

AYLMERE. A wanderer, dame,
Houseless and heavy-hearted, craves a place
For these, his wife and child, beside your hearth.

WIDOW. Alack! I am but bond, fair sir; and want
And widowhood must be my only inmates.

AYLMERE. Nay, I have golden intercessors, dame;
Thou shalt not want.

WIDOW.   The home of a poor peasant
Doth not beseem your worship. At the castle
You will find fitting entertainment, sir.

AYLMERE. No, we are stricken fleers from the hunt,
Who seek a covert from the wild halloo,
Where the world's heartless rout may reach us not;
We would not flaunt our sorrows in the eyes
Of mocking greatness. Let us 'bide with thee;
And we will be as children to thee, dame,
And thou shalt be our mother.
    LACY. [*Interposing to* WIDOW CADE.] Let me speak
Good dame, a welcome for thee.
    WIDOW. [*To* LACY.] If you will it. [*Goes up stage.*
    LACY. [*Crosses to* AYLMERE.] Fair sir, if home so lowly
        be desired—
And 'tis not lowly, for 'tis virtue's home—
You will be welcome in it. [*They go up centre.*]
    WIDOW. [*Crosses to* MARIAMNE, *who meets her.*] Lady,
        if welcome and a willing service
Can make my poor cot rich, it is a palace.
Hast travelled far? [*To* MARIAMNE.]
    MARIAMNE. Even from Italy.
    WIDOW. His refuge!
        [WIDOW CADE, MARIAMNE, *and* CHILD *retire and con-*
        verse near table, the WIDOW *raising the* CHILD.]
    AYLMERE. [*To* LACY.—*He advances right,* AYLMERE
        left.] Hath our dame no child?
    LACY. No; she is alone.
    AYLMERE. Hath she been ever childless?
    LACY. She had a son, a noble boy,
So brave, so early wise! "Here's one," I said,
"That may be made the land's deliverer."
I took him to my cell, and in his soul
Poured all mine own. By day and night, for years,
I sought to foster in his breast a love
For all men, bond or noble, all that heaven
Hath quickened with its breath, and made to rank
Above earth's gilt nobility, with angels.
But thou'rt a stranger; haply I speak that
Which thou deem'st treason.
    AYLMERE.   Nay, say on, good father.
I come from Italy, free Italy, whose altars,
Unwarmed a thousand years, are now lit up

With the rekindled fires of freeborn Rome.
Thy pupil, proved he apt?
LACY. In sooth, he did.
In the hushed cloister's solitude, I taught him
That bond and baron had one sire, and all
Were brethren, equal all, all noble, save
Those whom their vice debased; and that the law
Of our blest faith is violate by the force
That makes the feeble bond. He caught the light
That flinty, high philosophy I taught him,
Which makes cold, hunger, suffering in the cause
Of a crushed people, luxuries sweeter far
Than ease and honour on their silken couch,
Tended by wan-eyed homage.
AYLMERE. Well, you made
His spirit free?
LACY. Aye, free and fearless too.
Nor life, nor death, had for his soul a terror.
AYLMERE. But thy wonder—
Did he, in all this budding promise, die?
WIDOW. [*Coming a little forward.*] That tone! Have
I not heard that voice before?
It must have been in dreams. [*Turns to* MARIAMNE.] For-
give me, lady. [*They resume their conversation.*]
LACY. His father, though a bondman, was a rough
And heady carle when wronged. He, on a day,
Was struck down by his lord, the Baron Say.
He was a man, albeit a slave, and rising,
He shouted: "Blow for blow, by Heaven!" and struck him.
For which offence, as a born serf, he was
Condemned and scourged to death.
AYLMERE. A most foul murder!
LACY. His father's fate,
Rooted, like nightshade, in the stripling's heart,
And angered o'er his brow with sterner thoughts
Than early life should know.
AYLMERE. You're wrong, you're wrong!
Wormlike and worthy spurning had he been,
Had not the memory of that wrong been food,
And drink and sleep, and life to him, until
It was avenged!

LACY. It made an exile of him. Thus it fell:
The proud Say, when a-hunting, happed to enter
The cot of her whom he had made a widow;
And spoke as tyrant power to weakness speaks,
In scorn and wrong. Young Cade, for he was bond,
The bondman, too, of Say, flung the foul scorn back.

AYLMERE. [*Quickly.*] He did, he did.

LACY. The proud lord would have spurned him, but young
Cade——

AYLMERE. I struck him to my feet! [*Laughs.*] I've not
forgot it!
How kissed his scarlet doublet the mean earth,
Beneath a bondsman's blow, and he a lord!
That memory hath made my exile green!

[WIDOW CADE *gives a scream of recognition.* AYLMERE
embraces her.]

Look up, my mother!
Could you read all my exile's history,
You would not blush for it. And now I've come
To shield and comfort thee.

WIDOW. [*Embraces* AYLMERE.] I knew thou would'st!
That I should know thee not, my gentle boy!

AYLMERE. [*Presenting* MARIAMNE *to* WIDOW.] A blessing for thy daughter!

WIDOW. [*To* MARIAMNE—*kisses her.*] Bless thee! Bless
thee.

AYLMERE. The star that shone upon my fate, when all
But that was clouded. [*To* LACY.] Bear with me, my
father,
My mind's father!

LACY.   Now has o'erwearied heaven
Granted its servant's prayer, and I am happy!
Thou hast outstripped thy promise. When thou fled'st,
A midnight fugitive, from the bondman's death,
I little hoped to meet thee thus. But, in.
Worn with long travel, you need food and rest.

AYLMERE. Come, mother, come.

[AYLMERE *conducts* WIDOW *out, followed by* LACY, *with*
MARIAMNE *and* BOY.]

SCENE THIRD. *Before* WORTHY's *cottage. A wedding festival. Male and female* PEASANTS *discovered—pastoral music, dance by* PEASANTS. *After dance, enter* WORTHY, MOWBRAY, *and* KATE.

WORTHY.   Now, may my anvil never ring again
To the merry sledge, an' I be not this day,
Happy as ere a man in Kent.
    MOWBRAY.   And I!
Think'st thou not, sweetheart, while I gaze on thee
Till my eyes fill, and I would play the child
And weep for very rapture, thus to know
Thou art mine own at last—think'st not I'm happier
Than the best peer in England?
    KATE.   Thine, Will, thine!
I am not thine! I'll yet say *nay,* when Father
Lacy asks the question.
    MOWBRAY.   Rebel! He comes.

Enter FRIAR LACY.

WORTHY. Welcome, father! Is not my Kate a brave one?
And yet that haggard Courtnay dared to think o' her!
No, Kate shall wed none but a jolly yeoman.

PEASANTS *form for a dance.*

LACY. They'd dance, good master; better we retire.
Age hath left little dancing in thy limbs,
Old yeoman.
    WORTHY. Right. My heart doth all my dancing
For this good day.

Enter COURTNAY.

MOWBRAY. The minion Courtnay!
    KATE.   Heed him not, dear Will!
MOWBRAY. [*Looking scornfully at* COURTNAY.] The leering slave!
    COURTNAY. [*To* MOWBRAY.] Nay, good Master Mowbray.
Look not so proudly fond. She's not thine yet.
Why should I falter thus? I'll speak. [*Aside.*] Fair
    mistress—

KATE. I know·thee not.

COURTNAY. Anon thou'lt know me better. **As for thee—**

MOWBRAY. Mongrel, what mean'st thou?

    [*Crosses to* COURTNAY.]

COURTNAY.   Nay, my master, **chafe not;**
I've done thee service—spoken to the lord,
And he will ban the bridal. Master Mowbray,
Art thou not grateful?

MOWBRAY.   So grateful, if 'tis true,
I'll wed my knife to thy dog's heart. Come, Kate.

    [*Takes* KATE *with him.*]

COURTNAY. Now comes my turn. Room, varlets, for Lord
    Say! [*Flourish—*PEASANTS *cross.*]

Enter ATTENDANTS *with cross-bows,* SAY, CLIFFORD, *and*
BUCKINGHAM.

SAY. How now? Art thou, carle, he who'd wed this
    maid?
Sirrah, when gave I leave thou should'st so wed?

KATE. [*Clinging to* MOWBRAY.] Answer him softly, Will!
    For my sake, Will!

MOWBRAY. I am a yeoman free, and free to wed
E'en when and where it pleasures me.

SAY.   Ho! ho!
Free, art thou, knave! We'll see anon—we'll see!
And thou, [*to* WORTHY] whom age should have taught
    duty, what
Hath set thee on to wed thy daughter where
I will she should not wed.

KATE. [*Leaving* MOWBRAY, *and clinging to* WORTHY.] Oh!
    be not rash! Anger him not, my father!

WORTHY. She's the free branch of a free stock; and I
May graft her where I list, and ask no leave
Of liege or lord. So speaks our law and charter.

SAY. [*To* LACY.] Accursed shaveling! Thou it is hast
    taught
This upstart spirit!

LACY. [*Meekly.*] I have taught the truth.

SAY. Vile monk, darest thou avow it to my face?

LACY. I dare speak truth to them, to thee, and any—
It is my mission.

SAY.   Priest! But for thy cowl,
Thy mission should be to the nearest tree,
With cord instead of cassock. As for thee, [*to* MOWBRAY]
And thee [*to* WORTHY] who prate of right; 'tis well you
    know
My will is charter and my rule is law.
The sun that sees you wed, shall, ere its setting,
Beam through your dungeon gates. Now get you gone.
    [*Goes and converses with* CLIFFORD. MOWBRAY *and* WOR-
        THY *whisper angrily together—*KATE *interposes.*]
    KATE. Nay, Will, be calm! I will be thine. Ne'er fear!
Father, speak not, but go: speak him no further.
    COURTNAY. [*Advances to right of* MOWBRAY.] What says
        thy bride? Who is the mongrel now?
    MOWBRAY. [*In a low voice.*] Thou! Slave and wretch,
        here is the only bride,
Thy heart shall clasp! [*His knife.*] Remember! *I'll* for-
        get not! [*Crosses to left of* KATE—WORTHY *is making
        a threatening action, but is urged off by* LACY;—*exeunt*
        MOWBRAY *and* KATE, PEASANTS, COURTNAY.]
    SAY. These are the mire-gendered knaves you praise!
Clifford, I swear 'tis strange, that thou, a noble,
Shouldst love these kern.
    CLIFFORD.   Nay, I but love their daughters.
But to be grave—[SAY *smiles*]—you smile—I *can* be grave—
They're men, as good in soul and sinew, ay,
Even in birth, as is the best of us.
    SAY. In birth! Why now thou'rt wild.
    CLIFFORD.   I said, in birth.
This crazy priest, his crazy couplet's right.

    "When Adam delved and Eve span,
        Who was then the gentleman?"

A potent question! Answer it, if you may.
    SAY. Why Heaven ne'er made the universe a level.
Some trees are loftier than the rest; some mountains
O'erspeak their fellows; and thus,
Some men are nobler than the mass, and should,
By nature's order, shine above their brethren.
    CLIFFORD. 'Tis true, the *noble* should: but who is noble?
Heaven and not heraldry makes noble men.

BUCKINGHAM. Art dead to all the burning thoughts that speak
A glorious past transmitted through long ages?

CLIFFORD. All this is well, or would be if 'twere true.
Men cannot put their virtues in their wills.
'Tis well to prate of lilies, lions, eagles, but
Your only heraldry, its true birth traced,
Is the plough, loom, or hammer! Without them, pray tell me
What were your nobles worth? Not much, I trow!

BUCKINGHAM. Thou speak'st as fame were nothing.

CLIFFORD.   Pish! for fame!

SAY. Yet, Clifford, hast thou fought, ay, hacked and hewed,
By the long day, in sweat and blood, for Fame.

CLIFFORD. Nor have, nor will. I'll fight for Love or Hate,
Or for divertisement; but not for Fame.
What! die for glory! Leap a precipice
To catch a shadow! What is it, this Fame?
Why, 'tis a brave estate to have and hold—
When? From and after death! Die t'enjoy fame!
'Tis as to close our eyes before the mirror
To know our sleeping aspects. No, by'r Lady!
I'll never be a miser of fair words,
And hoard up honour for posterity.
Die for glory! ha! ha! [Crosses to left.

SAY. Nay, an' thou die not, in a midnight brawl,
Fought for some black-eyed wench, thou'lt perish, coz,
Of thine own spleen. But let us leave word-tilting.
Did'st mark the sullen mood of yonder yeomen?

BUCKINGHAM. There's menace in their bearing; how is this?
What do they murmur at?

SAY.   At everything.
They prate of rights and wrongs; and talk in whispers
Of the people's power.

CLIFFORD.   Ha! they've found it out!
Believe me, Say, it is a frowning danger,
When a crushed people
Know they have power to right themselves.

SAY. What would you
That I should do?

CLIFFORD. Nay, I care not,—not I;
A game of buffets, if you please; but were I
Lord Say and Suffolk, Counsellors of the King,
I'd do the people right,—redress their wrongs—
And trust their gratitude.

SAY. Trust to the people!
The people! Whelps that lick the hand which beats
And chains them.

CLIFFORD. I care not for 'em;—but by my halidame,
I think they wrong not those that wrong not them.

SAY. The mob ne'er had a friend they did not murder.

CLIFFORD. Tell me,
Whose cot is that down by yon clump of trees?
Such casket ill beseems the gem that shines
Within. [*Points.*]

SAY. The Widow Cade's. Why, how now! grown
So musty in your taste—twoscore and ten!

CLIFFORD. Nay, not the widow, Say. The flower I'd cull
Is fresh and fair and coy—dewy with youth,
And bright with beauty. At the cot I saw her,
And would have known more of her, but your summons
Called me away. I'll mark the house, and seek
An hour to woo my rustic. [*All exeunt.*

SCENE FOURTH.—[*Same as Act I, Sc. 2.*]

Enter AYLMERE *and* FRIAR LACY.

AYLMERE. For thy blest charities to my poor mother,
My life is thine—all that I have and am.

LACY. Thy worth will do me justice.
Enough that thou, the bondman's station spurned,
Despised, oppressed, art where and what I'd have thee.

AYLMERE. Alas! not *all* that thou wouldst have me,
Father!
Ten years of freedom have not made me free.
I've grappled Fortune till she yielded up
Her brightest favours; I have wooed Ambition,

Wooed with a fiery soul and dripping **sword**,
And *would not* be denied;
Until my spirit walked with those who now
Are hailed, as brethren, by archangels:—yet,
Have I come home a slave,—a thing for chains
And scourges—ay, a dog,
Crouching, and spurned, and spat upon!

LACY.   Not so;
England hath yet brave hearts that will protect thee.
But Say will know thee not.
What name hast brought from exile? Thine own, **Cade,**
Would give thee up—so runs our feudal code—
As bondman unto Say.

AYLMERE.   When I left Kent,
A pallid fugitive, I took the name
Of Aylmere. After years heard that name shouted
A war-cry unto thousands!
But when I left the trade of blood, and sought
The gentle fruits of science, I was graced
With the mind's title of nobility,
And known as Doctor Aylmere.

LACY.   But thy title here
Must be plain Master Aylmere; thou must doff
The sage's sables, and in russet masque,
To 'scape the vigilant hate of Say. But thine,
My son, has been a life of marvel.

AYLMERE.   Italy became
My country, when *my* country cast me forth.
I joined the arms of those who struck for freedom,
And won,—for Fortune's soldier seldom fails,—
More than my hopes had spanned.

LACY.   You married.

AYLMERE.   In my stormiest hour, **Mariamne**
Left wealth and wooers nobler far, to share
My wayward lot.

LACY.   You were a dweller in a happy clime.

AYLMERE.   In that blest land the tiller is a prince.
No ruffian lord breaks Spring's fair promises,
And Summer's toils—for Freedom watches o'er them—
Are safe and happy;

There are no poor where freedom is;
For Nature's wealth is affluence for all.

LACY. Yet was this Italy a land enslaved.

AYLMERE. Once too, 'twas nobly free. That memory
Has, from the ashes of a glorious past,
Flashed its rekindled blaze into the gloom.
She has now
Sons that ne'er knew a fear, nor felt a shackle.

LACY. Of course, you were
Most happy there?

AYLMERE. Alas! 'twas not *my* country!—I thought
Of my pale mother; and of thee, my Father;
And of my brethren's wrongs, the herded bond.

LACY. Now Heaven be praised, thy heart was true.

AYLMERE. One night,
Racked by these memories, methought a voice
Summoned me from my couch. I rose—went forth.
The sky seemed a dark gulf, where fiery spirits
Sported; for o'er the concave the quick lightning
Quivered, but spoke not. In the breathless gloom
I sought the Coliseum, for I felt
The spirits of a manlier age were forth;
And there against the mossy wall I leaned,
And thought upon my country. Why was I
Idle, and she in chains? The storm now answered.
It broke as heaven's high masonry were crumbling.
And the wide vault, in one unpausing peal,
Throbbed with the angry pulse of Deity! [*Crosses left.*

LACY. Shrunk you not, 'mid these terrors?

AYLMERE. I felt I could amid the hurly laugh,
The heavens did speak like brothers to my soul,
And not a peal that leapt along the vault
But had an echo in my heart. Nor spoke
The clouds alone; for o'er the tempest's din,
I heard the genius of my country shriek
Amid the ruins, calling on her son—
On me! I answered her in shouts, and knelt—
Ev'n there in darkness, 'mid the falling ruins,
Beneath the echoing thunder peal—and swore,
(The while my father's pale form, stain'd with

The death-prints of the scourge, stood by and smiled,)
Then the air seemed thick with vengeance, clouded with
    blood,
I swore to make the bondman free!   [*Crosses right*

  LACY.   And here,
I link my soul to thine, and dedicate
The remnant of the days that Heaven hath spared,
"To make the bondman free!"   [AYLMERE *takes his hand.*

  AYLMERE. I sailed for England.

  LACY. Unhappy England! You beheld her lords
Rolling in reckless revel, while her people
Laboured beneath the lash, and mixed their blood
With the grudged crust that fed them. They may sow,
And Heaven give increase; but 'tis not for them!
The earth is curs'd to them, until it opens
To take their life-worn bodies in.

  AYLMERE.   Alas!
Alas! for England!
Her merry yeomen, and her sturdy serfs,
That made red Agincourt immortal, now
Are trod like worms into the earth.
Too much of this, the past and lost! The future
Be our care now; and for the iron wrongs
That pierce the gasping heart of our poor country,
Father, be sure they can and shall be righted.
Still in mine ear doth ring that mother's shrieks,
If I avenge her not—but we will in
And counsel on the means.

  LACY. I wait upon thee.

  AYLMERE. We'll do't, and quickly. Freedom ne'er came
    too soon
For wrongs like ours.   [*Exeunt.*

END OF ACT FIRST.

ACT II.

SCENE FIRST.—WIDOW CADE'S *cottage*.

Enter AYLMERE *and* MARIAMNE, *dressed as rustics*.

AYLMERE. Tired of thy truantry? What dost think now
Of our green merry England?
    MARIAMNE. The loveliest grove I found,—trellised with
    flowers,
And 'neath its trembling shade, the brightest stream,
I thought I was again in Italy.
Mind'st thou the day, when, by the Tiber's side,
In the cool shade of a mossed ruin, we
Sat, and thou told'st me of thy native land?
And how I won thee from thy heavy theme?
And how—go to! to thee these are but trifles.
    AYLMERE. Not trifles, Mariamne. No!
Life's better joys spring up thus by the wayside;
And the world calls them trifles. 'Tis not so.
Heaven is not prodigal, nor pours its joys
In unregarded torrents upon man;
They fall, as fall the riches of the clouds
Upon the parched earth, gently, drop by drop.
Nothing is trifling that love consecrates.
    MARIAMNE. But thou wert happier in those happy days,
And gentler too, my Aylmere.
    AYLMERE.   Gentler, wife!
Gentler! But it may be—Oppression's cloud
Hath shadowed thus my brow, and sharp-heeled wrong
So scotched my spirit, that I can no more
Forbear its writhing.
    MARIAMNE.   Mine own!
    AYLMERE.   Thine, girl! thine!
No! I am Say's—his bond! Oh, for the time
When I may doff this skulking masquerade,
And be mine own and thine!
    MARIAMNE. Nay, good my husband,

Fly with me from this place and these wild projects!
We'll follow Freedom wheresoe'er she bide,
And make her refuge ours!

AYLMERE.   This is my home,
And shall ere long be Freedom's.
Listen, wife.   I cannot be
The meek and gentle thing that thou wouldst have me.
The wren is happy on its humble spray,
But the fierce eagle revels in the storm.
Terror and tempest darken in his path;
He gambols 'mid the thunder; mocks the bolt
That flashes by his red, unshrinking eye,
And, sternly-joyful, screams amid the din:
Then shakes the torrent from his vigorous wing,
And soars above the storm, and looks and laughs
Down on its struggling terrors.   Safety still
Reward ignoble ease:—be mine the storm.

MARIAMNE.   The saints protect thee!   'Twere delight to
share
A peaceful lot with thee; but if Fate wills
The storm should gather o'er thee,—be it so,
By thy dear side I'll think it sunshine, Aylmere!

AYLMERE.   Like to thine own bright self!   And thou'lt be
cheerful?
Can'st thou be happy, love, so humbly lodged?

MARIAMNE.   Happy, an' I were safe from insult.

AYLMERE.   Insult!
Wife, insult!

MARIAMNE.   Scarce you left us, ere a lord
Approached, and spoke that your wife should not hear;
Deeming no doubt 'twas honour to a rustic.
I fled; when, Heaven be praised, the baron's summons
Called him away, or he had followed me!

AYLMERE.   More wrong! more wrong! was not the measure full!
Villain! but—but—his garb? his plume? his crest?

MARIAMNE.   I marked not that, but heard them call him
Clifford.

AYLMERE.   Down in my heart, that name, down, down,
Until I wash it in his blood!   [*Crosses.*

MARIAMNE.   Nay, Aylmere,
Be not thus moved; forget it, love!

[LACY *passes behind window.*

AYLMERE. Forget it!
Oh, I'll forget it! But no more; I see
The Father Lacy comes! speak not of this,
But fear not! I'll be near to watch o'er thee.
Now, gentlest, there! [*Embrace.*] Away!

[*Leads her to door, at which she exits.*

Enter LACY. AYLMERE *is turned from him.*

LACY. A goodly day toward, Aylmere! All goes cheerly.
Each heart is ripe to bursting with its wrongs.
Our young cause wears a brow of promise.
AYLMERE. [*Turning to* LACY.]   Know you
One Clifford—a hound in the pack of Say?
LACY. Why, what of him?
AYLMERE.   A villain! But ne'er mind—
Who is he? And what doth he i' the barony,
Beating about for game?
LACY.   He is a courtier,
But late from London, in the train of Say.
But what is Clifford unto thee?
AYLMERE.   Nought—nought.
You say the bond are ripe; how stand the yeomen?
LACY.   Full
Of moody discontents, resolved, and ready
To flash forth at a spark.
AYLMERE. Doth Mowbray brook
The ban upon his bridal?
LACY.   He is high
In wrath,—alas that we should suffer thus!
AYLMERE. 'Tis better, being slaves, that we should suffer.
Men must be thus, by chains and scourges, roused—
When the red hand of force is at their throats,
They know what freedom is.
LACY. All Kent is boiling over
With its o'ermeasured wrongs; and all demand
Thee as their leader.

AYLMERE.   They know me not
As Cade? [LACY *shakes his head dissentingly.*] The time
    will come when I,
The bond, the fugitive, will claim my name,
And wed it unto Honour. But, good Father,
Let none, not even the staunchest, know me now
As aught but Aylmere—as the stranger yeoman—
The champion of the bond.
    LACY.   Fear not; ten years
In a far clime have worked such change in thee,
Nor bond, nor yeomen see the stripling Cade
In the grave Aylmere.
    AYLMERE. 'Tis well, let us from cot to cot,
And pour the fury of each single heart
Into the general torrent—we cannot fail!
The right is with us, Heav'n is with the right
And victory with Heav'n!   [*Exeunt.*

A slight pause. Enter MARIAMNE.

MARIAMNE.   Where is Aylmere?
                                [*Looking about.*]
Would he were here! I grow of late sick-hearted,
And tremble with a wild and shadowy fear
Of—what I know not—when he is not by.

[*Enter* CLIFFORD.]

Lord Clifford here! Alas! what shall I do!
    CLIFFORD. [*Adjusting his dress.*] Good morrow to your
        beauty!
Well met! But why, my little lapwing, fled you
When last I saw you?
    MARIAMNE. [*With a rustic air.*] Saving your presence,
        sir,
(Pray Heaven my language not betray my husband!)
Wi' your leave. [*Going.*]
    CLIFFORD. [*Intercepting her.*] Nay, you leave me not,
        my Daphne.
There's not i' the manor maid so fair as thou—
I've seen 'em all—and, by this light, I love thee.
                                [*She is silent.*]

What! art not proud of a lord's love! no word?
Why, wench, art sullen? Is thy flax entangled?
What hap has ruffled thee? Sweet girl, art dumb?

    MARIAMNE. Let me away, sir.

    CLIFFORD. This is rare, I trow!
By your leave, girl, this is a fair, soft hand.
Nay, be not froward. Be your lips as soft?

    [Attempting to kiss her—he seizes her; she breaks
    from him, and crosses to left.

    MARIAMNE. Back, base lord! Get thee gone! Pass on
    thy way!
This humble door is marked, as were the cots
Of God's crushed people; and the curse of lust
Hath here no power.

    CLIFFORD. Cry you mercy, lady!
An' if thy garb belied thee 'tis no fault
Of mine; I chose it not. Forgive my rudeness;
But in all humbleness, whom speak I to?

    MARIAMNE. A woman! By that name entitled to
Each true man's courtesy. Thy mother bore it,
And scorning it, thou dost a wrong to her.

    CLIFFORD. If in thy cloud I thought thee bright, forgive
    me,
That now, thou shin'st undimmed—I worship thee.

    Enter AYLMERE, *unseen.—He draws his knife.*

Now, by this fair hand. *[Seizing it.]* Why dost struggle,
    love?

    MARIAMNE. Monster! thou durst not: off! mine eyes
    alone
Will with their lightnings blast thee, if thou lay'st
An impious hand upon me. Aylmere!   *[Struggling.*

    CLIFFORD.   Why,
Thine eyes, I own, are bright; but I am not
Frighted by lightning. Come, what hast to fear?

    *[*CLIFFORD *struggling with* MARIAMNE, *who shrieks.*
    AYLMERE *rushes forward—*MARIAMNE *gets to right*
    of AYLMERE.

    AYLMERE. Unmannered lord! hold off thy hand!

        *[*CLIFFORD *starts back.*

[*To* CLIFFORD *fiercely, and laughs.*] Ha! ha! ha!
This is a noble death! The bold Lord Clifford,
Stabbed by a peasant, for no braver feat
Than toying with his wife!
    CLIFFORD. Thou wilt not slay me, fellow?
    AYLMERE. Ay, marry will I! And why should I not?
                                [*Seizes him.*
    CLIFFORD. Thou durst not, carle.
    AYLMERE. [*Seizing him.*] Durst not!
    MARIAMNE. [*Clutches hold of his arm.*] Nay, Aylmere,
      strike not!
Lay not the weight of blood upon my memory,
Shed for mine honour!
AYLMERE.   Wife! Has he not flung
A shame on thee and me? And shall he live?
    CLIFFORD. Strike, if it be your will. I did the wrong,
And may, when tempted, do as much again.
    AYLMERE. [*Raises his knife.*] Dost mock me!
    MARIAMNE. [*Seizes his arm.*] Aylmere, an' thou lov'st
      me, hold!
    AYLMERE. I will not crush you, reptile, now: but mark
      me!
Steel knows no heraldry, and stoutly urged,
Visits the heart of a peer with no more grace
Than it would pierce a peasant's.
Get thee gone!   [*Hurls him from him to corner.*
    CLIFFORD. [*Going up to door.*] Sirrah, we're equal now—
    shame against shame.
When we next meet, a new compt we will open.
        [*Exit* CLIFFORD. AYLMERE *turns aside and presses
        his head.*
    MARIAMNE. Nay, do not press thy brow upon thy hand.
Heed not the reveller. Now that I am with thee,
I care not for this wrong: and such as he
Can bring to innocence no shame.
    AYLMERE.   No shame!
Now will this boaster go, and, o'er his cups, will tell
How fair the dame he clasped—And yet I slew him not!
    MARIAMNE.   Why should'st thou stain thee
With his licentious blood. It would but bring
New wrongs on thee and me.

AYLMERE. 'Tis well—very well! But get thee in.
                                        [*Crosses.*

MARIAMNE. [*Going, lingers, returns.*] Thou'rt not in
  anger with me?

AYLMERE. With thee, love!
Why was I ever? [*Embrace.*] Nay, girl, get thee in.
                      [*Leads her to door—exit* MARIAMNE.
[*Solus.*] And yet I slew him not! But, but, 'twill come!
It heaps my shame to heighten my revenge;
And I will feast it fully. Would 'twere here,
Here now! Oh, my arm aches, and every pulse
Frets like a war-horse on the curb, to strike
These bold man-haters down. 'Twill come, 'twill come!
And I will quench this fire in a revenge
Deep as our sufferings, sweeping as their wrongs! [*Exit.*

SCENE SECOND.—*Castle Interior.*

Enter SAY, *followed by* COURTNAY.

SAY. Sirrah, no more. Did I not say that thou
Shouldst have the wench? And yet methinks, it is
But splenetic envy of this fire-brained Mowbray:
Thou lovest her not.

COURTNAY. My lord, I love not Mowbray;
He follows the crazed priest whom they call prophet—
The mendicant Friar Lacy; and is leagued
With the faction o' the Commons—those who speak
So scurvily of your lordship.

SAY.   Have your wish.
I'd force this blacksmith knave give up his daughter,
If but to teach him that he is my thrall,
Even yeoman though he be. But how is this?
The barony holds another sturdy grumbller—
They must be weeded out—the stranger, dwelling
At th' house of Widow Cade. What call they him?

COURTNAY. Aylmere, so please you. 'Tis a bold,.strange
  man;
And in his breeding loftier than a peasant,
He hath great sway with the people,

SAY.   Well, sir, pray,
Are there no serving-men to seize such rogues?
No vaults in our keep to hold them?

Enter CLIFFORD.

                                 Good den, cousin!
[*To* COURTNAY.] Without! [*Exit* COURTNAY.] Ay, get
    thee gone, thou truest hound,
That power at weakness ere let slip. [*To* CLIFFORD.] How
    now?
Feather-witted coz, a wrinkle! What's befallen?
    CLIFFORD. A truce, my lord!
I'd have you know there is a devil unchained
In this your barony; and there is brewing
That which will raise such hurly round your **ears**
As England ne'er yet knew.
    SAY. Speakst thou of Aylmere?
What knowest thou of him?
    CLIFFORD.   Know! the knave, but now
Had his knife at my throat, and would have slain me
But for his wife. He has that in him, Say,
Will breed you griefs. The flash of such an eye,
Broke never from a bondman's heart. Be sure
He is not what he seems. And when I left him
He hurled a scornful menace after me
That spoke of trouble.
    SAY.   Yet, you'd have me pet
And palter with these ruffians. We must crush **them.**
A moody spirit doth possess the rout,
And every wind is murmur laden.
    CLIFFORD.   True,
And there is danger in it. Should not Aylmere
Be first looked to?
    SAY.   O' the instant. Ho! who waits!

Enter COURTNAY.

Have Aylmere, ere an hour, within the castle.
Take a sufficient force.
    COURTNAY.   It shall be done.

SAY. And, look ye, steward, that mangy hag, Cade's
  widow,
Expel her from the cot, and burn it, burn it!
Let her beg, starve, or leave the barony!
For years my plague! The wife of one sour slave,
Who struck me and died for 't, and the mother
Of a rough boy, who left a second shame
Upon my person, and escaped the barony
Ere my wrath reached him. Courtnay, leave it ashes!
  COURTNAY. It is a task I have good stomach for.
                                            [*Exit* COURTNAY.
  SAY. Thus will I crush the mad and moody slaves!
They'd better bow, and line their chains with down,
Than vainly struggling, dye them in their blood.
  CLIFFORD. Seize thou the husband—I will take the wife;
My yeoman stout—our new account is opened!
                      [*Exit* SAY, *right;* CLIFFORD, *left.*

SCENE THIRD.—*Rustic Interior. Door; bolt on door. Table
and two chairs, stool.* KATE, *seated;* MOMBRAY *seated
near* KATE; WORTHY, *seated on stool.*

  KATE. Nay, Will, content thee. I will never wed
The cringing steward. Women love no slaves
Except their own.
  MOWBRAY.   Our tyrant, Say, hath sworn
That if you wed not with his creature Courtnay,
He'll—
  KATE. Tush! I care not for him. Why should I?
These lords are no lords of a woman's will.
My father, thou, and Aylmere, with the Commons,
Can shield me.
  MOWBRAY. Right, brave Kate! why, let them come;
We'll entertain 'em in the good old style,
With the best edge of a stout yeoman's sword.
  WORTHY. Threescore tall men have I, whom Courtnay's
    knaves
Must hammer till they're cold as is my anvil,
Ere he shall touch her.   [*Three knocks.*
          Ha! it is the signal.

KATE. [*Crosses to right.*] Will, here is work that needs
　no woman's presence;
Stand to it, Will; strike for the bond and me! [*Exit.*
MOWBRAY. Will I not, my Kate?
WORTHY. [*At door.*] Ho! whom hold you with?
STRAW. [*From without.*] With Kent and the true Com-
　mons.
WORTHY. [*Opens the door.*] Enter, friends.

Enter STRAW, LACY, PEMBROKE, SUTTON, *and others.*

LACY. Blessings, my children, on your cause and you!
Pembroke, how fare your children?
PEMBROKE. 　　　　　　　　　　　As the lamp
That dies for want of feeding; they still flicker,
But I can only say they live.
LACY. [*To* STRAW.] How is it with your wife? But ill,
　I fear me.
From the cloud upon thy brow.
　　STRAW. 　　　　　　　　No, well, Father.
　　LACY. Your wife is then—
　　STRAW. 　　　　　　Beyond the whip and chain!
She's in her grave.
WORTHY. Dead! dead!
LACY. Heaven rest her soul! [*They all uncover and bow.*
WORTHY. And crush the lords who curse and cumber
　England!
LACY. Heaven, son, hath sent a champion and deliverer
Unto the poor.
WORTHY. 　　　Whom mean you?
LACY. 　　　　　　　　　　Master Aylmere.
STRAW. Know you Lord Say hath ordered he be taken
And thrown i' the castle dungeon?
LACY. 　　　　　　　　　　Men of Kent,
Shall this thing be; and he whom Heaven hath sent
To strike your chains off, be torn from you thus?
WORTHY. Where is Aylmere?

Enter ALYMERE *through door; he bolts it after him, then
　　comes down between* LACY *and* PEMBROKE.

AYLMERE. Here, Master Worthy. A brave morning,
　masters.

The sun hath not yet learned to frown upon
The poor. Friend Wat, hast yet given up thy daughter,
At thy lord's bidding, to his lacquey?

WORTHY.   Have not,
And will not. I will grind this steward's pate
Between my sledge and anvil, ere I yield
My free child up, a slave and a slave's wanton.

AYLMERE. [*Crosses to* MOWBRAY.] Good morrow, Mow-
    bray.
Now what sayest thou? Wilt give
Thy young bride humbly up to my lord's minion?

MOWBRAY. I'll dig his title—were it signed by Say—
A thousand Says—out of his rotten heart,
Ere he shall look upon her. [AYLMERE *smiles.*] But thou
    mock'st me.

AYLMERE. [*Crosses to* SUTTON.] Sutton, has the kind
    lord forgiven the wrong
Thou didst his lordship's hound? What, spurn the hound
Of thy liege lord! Irreverent man! Why, if
Such crimes should go unwhipped, it will anon
Be thought a poor man's child is nigh as noble
As a rich man's cur. Heaven shield his lordship's hound!

SUTTON. He threats me with the stocks.

AYLMERE.   The stocks, old man!
Thy hair's grown white, and thy limbs shrivelled, fighting
And toiling for this man! The stocks! Well, well;
'Tis vain to chafe. How bravely will this frame,
Honoured by time, adorn the felon's seat!
What sayest thou, good man? [*Crosses to* STRAW.] I could
    weep for thee,
And thy wife murdered, save that tears kill not.

STRAW. [*Lays his hand upon his knife.*] The tears shed
    for her shall be red and heart-drawn!

AYLMERE. Why, go to! thou know'st there's shame
On every honest brow, and grief in every honest heart
In Kent. We toil to feed their lusts; we bleed
To back their quarrels; coin our sweat and blood
To feed their wassail, and maintain their pomp!
And they in payment
Plunder our dwellings, spurn us as their dogs,
Stain those we love, and mock at our affliction!

Mowbray.   Are we men who brook it?

Aylmere.   Why should ye brook it?   Heav'n ne'er made
    a bondman,
Ne'er made one man to be his fellow's victim;
Ne'er curst the earth that its fair breast should yield
Unto the proud lord milk, but, to the peasant,
Nothing but poison.

Lacy.   Heaven, not Aylmere, speaks!

Worthy.   What should we do?
Mowbray.   Tell us what we shall do. } [*Eagerly.*]

Aylmere.   "Do!"   Listen,   Heaven!—"Do!"—wear a
    loyal smile,
And bow your heads, and bare you to the scourge;
And, on your supple knees, down, down, and pray,
For those who smite you!   Do!—Bear they a charter
From the highest,—
To make His earth a hell for us to howl in?
Or are these proud and pampered minions gods,
And we but dogs, and made to fawn and suffer?
Are your arms sinewless, or your hearts craven?
"What should ye do!"   What would ye, twine a serpent's
Slimy volumes round you?   Stoop?   Caress?
And stand to think and tremble?   No, you'd dash
The reptile to the earth, and trample on,
And crush it!   [*Crosses to right.   Pause.*

Worthy.   But if we rise, what should be our demands?

Aylmere.   All that just Nature gave and they have taken:
Freedom for the bond! and justice in the sharing
Of the soil given by Heaven to all.

Worthy.   They will not grant this.

Aylmere.   They shall,
If we are true unto ourselves!   But if
We rend a single link, we are rewarded.
Freedom's a good the smallest share of which
Is worth a life to win.   [*Knock at door.*

Worthy.   Are we surprised?   [*Louder knocking.*

Aylmere.   Open the door: if it be unto death,
Why let death enter: the crushed bondman knows
No better friend!   [Worthy *unbolts the door.*

Mariamne.   [*Without.*]   If you be Christians, shelter for
    my child!

AYLMERE. Just Heaven! it cannot be!

WORTHY *has opened the door*—MARIAMNE *staggers in, pale and dishevelled, carrying her child—she totters into the arms of* AYLMERE, *followed by* KATE—KATE *takes the child.*

MARIAMNE. My Aylmere, save us! save thy child! Oh Heaven!

AYLMERE. Thou art not hurt? Thou'rt well?
Our boy—no harm hath reached him? Look up, love!
Thou art with friends; it is thy Aylmere holds thee!
Heaven, what new horror's here?

MARIAMNE. [*Looks about wildly.*] Where am I?
Where is my child? [KATE *brings child down to her—she sees and clasps him.*] My husband? [*Looks wildly.*

AYLMERE. Mariamne!

MARIAMNE. Oh, Heaven! I thank thee! Clasp me closer, Aylmere!
I fear 'tis but a dream!

AYLMERE. Why flee the cot? Speak, for my heart is gasping
With a strange terror.

MARIAMNE. I know not.—How's this?—
My brain is 'wildered. Let me think. Yes, now,
It rushes on me! [*Shudders.*]

AYLMERE. Speak!

MARIAMNE. I cannot!

AYLMERE. Speak!
Speak, or I shall go mad.

MARIAMNE. Scarce had you left us,
Ere Say sent men to take you to the castle.
Not finding you, they went; but soon returned,
Led on by Say, drunken with pride and choler.
I, with our boy, fled to a near concealment,
And from my covert saw it, heard it all.

AYLMERE. What saw you?

MARIAMNE. In his rage, he fired the house. [*All start.*]
Dame Cade, affrighted, knelt to Say for mercy.
He thundered, "Where is Aylmere?" But she knew not.
"Thou lying hag! speak out, or I will slay thee,
And leave thy withered form to feed the flames."

AYLMERE. Oh, monster!

MARIAMNE.   She cried, "Mercy! All are gone—
Husband and son—add not another victim!
Spare me!"—In darker wrath, the savage raised
His arm, and, even as the Widow knelt,
He struck her down! [*All start.*]

AYLMERE.   Struck her down.
May every curse that hell's black confines know
Cling to and fester in him!

MARIAMNE.   The eddying smoke
Now drove them forth. A moment—and the flame
Flashed like an angry spirit through the cot.
The hot blast smote her; she arose and raised
Her hands to Heaven; she reeled—she shrieked—she fell!
>   [*Sinks back; they place her in a chair, which* KATE
>   *has brought down*—KATE *assists* MARIAMNE, *who
>   has fainted*—*All the Kentishmen are weeping.*]

AYLMERE. [*Pause.*] When he would sleep, that shriek be
    in his ears!
When he would drink, her blood be in his cup!
This is too much—too much—but I'll not weep.
>   [*Kneels.*] Witness, Heaven!
The orphan, whose sole heritage hath been
Blood, bonds, and shame, here swears to be avenged!
To follow Say as shades pursue the night,
Steady as conscience on his bloody track,
Certain as death!
The mountains shall not shield, the cavern hide,
The grave itself protect him! From his shroud
I'll drag him reeking forth, tear out his heart,
His false, foul heart, and trample—trample on it!
>   [*Staggers and falls into the arms of* LACY *and* WORTHY.

END OF ACT II.

ACT III.

SCENE FIRST.—*Blacksmith's forge, opening centre, backed
by landscape.*

WORTHY *discovered at forge.*

Enter LACY, MOWBRAY, PEMBROKE, STRAW, SUTTON.

WORTHY.   Good morrow, masters.
STRAW. Still at work, man! What's here?
WORTHY.   A work of love.
They're spear-heads for the hearts of our oppressors.
LACY. Have care your toil betray us not. [*All advance
down stage.*] My brethren,
I come from Essex.
WORTHY.   How stands Essex?
LACY.   Ready,
With twoscore thousand men, well mettled for
The cause.—What have ye?
WORTHY.   I, five hundred.
MOWBRAY.   I,
Nine; by the mass, true men as e'er gave buffets!
STRAW. I count two hundred, but they're men whom
wrong
Hath made in love with death.
LACY.   And Pembroke, thou?
PEMBROKE. Three hundred.
LACY. Good. How stand our other musters?
WORTHY. All now are full. Kent is prepared to rise.
MOWBRAY. But Aylmere hath not, since the Widow Cade
Was murdered, been amongst us.
WORTHY.   How his heart
Swells for the wretched! That pale widow's death—
A stranger to him—save he made her cot
A time his home—hath moved him nigh to madness.
MOWBRAY. A noble heart! Where is our leader, Father?

LACY. Upon the heels of that affliction, came
Outlawry; and his head is now the wolf's,
Which any serf may take.
MOWBRAY.   Where has he fled?
LACY. I took him, with his pale wife and his child,
That sickened by the way, unto a cave
Far hid i' the forest. There, alas! I left them.
Heaven wot how fare they.
WORTHY.   Bore they with them food?
LACY. We fled hot foot, and not a morsel with us.
WORTHY. Then will they perish, and the Commons lose
Their leader; for Say's creatures guard the forest
On this side; and the neighboring barony
Is churlish and will render no relief.
Pray Heaven they starve not!
LACY.   He may reach the town.
WORTHY. But find no aid. These citizens own no God
But Mammon. No aid from them!
LACY. Heaven be with Aylmere then. My heart bleeds
    for him.
MOWBRAY. Father, strange sayings stir the barony.
'Tis whispered that the gracious Mortimer,
Poor England's rightful king, not only lives,
But is the Commons' friend: and, to be plain,
That our loved Aylmere is none other than
Lord Mortimer.
LACY.   Is it so spoken, son?
MOWBRAY. And is at large believed.
LACY.   I'll think of this.
WORTHY. If he be Mortimer, all England will
Proclaim him King o' the Commons.   [A shriek without.

Enter KATE.

KATE. Mowbray! father!
            [Rushes to MOWBRAY, then turns to her father.
WORTHY. Who hath thus frightened thee?
KATE. Courtnay—
MOWBRAY.   The hound! where is he?
KATE.   Flushed with drink.
He hath—he's here! Protect me!
                    [Crosses to right of MOWBRAY.

Enter COURTNAY.

COURTNAY. Stay, girl—ho!
I've fallen among the plotters! Spear-heads too!
[*Kicks them about.*]
Well, well! But, Kate, think not I heed these knaves.
I love thee, by this light! I'll not be foiled!
I'll have my sport!
WORTHY. Just Heaven! must we bear this!
MOWBRAY. [*To* WORTHY.] Give way! I'll slay him!
LACY. Be not rash.
WORTHY. Back, Mowbray!
I yet am her protector!
COURTNAY. Here's a coil!
I have Say's leave, and care not. [*About to cross to her.*
WORTHY. Touch her not!
Or, spite of every lord in Kent, I'll brain thee!
[WORTHY *goes to anvil and seizes hammer.*
Back! I say!
COURTNAY. [*Coming towards* KATE.] I am the steward.
I care not for carles.
I love thee, and will clasp thee!
[*Attempts to embrace her; she breaks from him and
runs off; he follows.* WORTHY *rushes after them.*
MOWBRAY *has crossed to the friar, who is inter-
posing.*]
COURTNAY. [*Without.*] Slave! dog! [*A struggling.*]
WORTHY. [*Without.*] Die, villain, die! [KATE *shrieks.*]

WORTHY *re-enters, bearing his hammer, which is bloody,
followed by* MOWBRAY. KATE *clings to him in terror.*

LACY. What hast thou done?
WORTHY. What I would do again!
MOWBRAY. And I!
STRAW. And I! } [*Energetically,*]
PEMBROKE. And I!
WORTHY. By Heaven,
Were he our king I'd slay him; ay and love
The weapon that smote him! [*Throws hammer up stage.*
LACY. Thou hast burst our plot,

The veil is rent; and you must now throw by
All save your swords.

    MOWBRAY.   Our swords are ready, Father!

    PEMBROKE. We must away, or Say will be upon us.

    WORTHY. To Seven-Oaks then, at dawn!

    LACY.   So be it! Let
The word be passed at once. And, Mowbray, thou
And Straw, with a true band, seek Aylmere's refuge,
And guard him to our meeting. Bear food with you.

    STRAW. We'll instant to our errand.

                        [All going up stage.

    LACY.   At dawn, remember!
Then with the sun, will liberty arise
From the long night of wrong; and the crushed spirit
Will soar, as does the lark, to meet its light!
Away! There's much before us.

    OMNES. Away! away!   *[Exeunt.*

SCENE SECOND.—*A room in the castle.*

Enter SAY, CLIFFORD, BUCKINGHAM, *and* OFFICER.

    SAY. See they are watched; and if the villains murmur,
They shall—or priest or peasant—hang like dogs.

                        [Exit OFFICER.

    CLIFFORD. Know you, Say, 'tis whispered
Their leader, Aylmere, is Lord Mortimer?
Start not!—all Kent believes it.

    SAY.   What!
Lord Mortimer! It is believed he lives;
If it be he, why, woe to our King Henry!

    BUCKING. Aylmere is of his aspect. And why comes he
Thus darkly into Kent? And why, though gentle,
Herds he but with the bond?

    CLIFFORD.   For 'tis his humour.
Tush! Turn ye pale at this—at dreams and guesses?

    SAY. There's danger in it.

    CLIFFORD.   Where there is no fear,
There is no peril.

    SAY.   Would
That we had seized and sent him bound to London!

He's fled to the forest; we will yet secure him.
There he must famish or surrender to us.
As to these plotting serfs—why, let 'em plot!
The people's anger!—Tell it to the waves,
Which, like the mob, beneath the tempest's lash,
Will writhe and rage awhile, but meet the calm
With meek and mirrored smile.

   CLIFFORD.   Hunt you to-day?

   SAY. [*Crosses to the left.*]   Ay, and we will to horse.—
    If other game
We start not, we will beat the forest through,
For this same masquer, Mortimer.   [*Exeunt.*

SCENE THIRD.—*A Cave in the forest. Opening. Bank.*
  Lights down in front of cave, and up behind the opening.
  MARIAMNE *left of bank. The child asleep on a rude*
  pallet.

   MARIAMNE. Sleep hath fallen on him; yet
His limbs still toss, and his wan brow is wrung with agony.
Heaven be with thee, my babe! Would I might feed thee,
Famished one, on my heart!
Strange, Aylmere comes not. Images of gloom
Throng o'er my soul, like birds of evil omen
Waked by the night's low voice! He may be taken,—
Dragged to the castle! Hist'! the branches rustle,
And the dry twigs are crushed as by a foot.
Am I discovered? Heaven protect me!—Yet
It may be Aylmere—now 'tis nearer!—nearer!
Ha! my husband!

       Enter AYLMERE. *They embrace.*

Hist! our poor boy is sleeping!
   AYLMERE. Alas! thy cheek's e'en paler than it was!
   MARIAMNE. And thou art faint and worn, and on thy
    brow
How the chill dew has gathered!
   AYLMERE.   I've been far,
And have suffered much.
   MARIAMNE.   Thou hast brought us food?

AYLMERE.   My path has been beset by Say's retainers.
Each cot is guarded.

MARIAMNE.   Sought you not the town?

AYLMERE.   And reached it.

MARIAMNE.   And they gave thee food?

AYLMERE.   Alas!

MARIAMNE.   Our boy is starving.

AYLMERE.   I begged, till my brow
Blackened with blushes, and my thick tongue faltered.
None would relieve!   The pitying poor dare not
From dread of Say; the rocky-hearted rich
List to my plaint of agony with sneers.

MARIAMNE.   Be calmed, my Aylmere; thou'lt awake our
    boy,
And he but wakes to wail.

AYLMERE.   My Mariamne,
Alas, thine eye is dim, and thy hand trembles.

MARIAMNE.   I faint for food.   Our store, 'twas but a
    crust,
I gave unto our boy; and yet he sinks!
Since you departed, years of agony
Have crowded into hours.   Our child slept on
My knee; and as I watched his troubled slumber,
Sudden his face grew dark, his eyelids raised,
And his eye glared with a strange horror on me!
I thought 'twas death, and shrieked—oh! that hour!

AYLMERE.   Now Heaven be with us, for our griefs are
    many!

MARIAMNE.   Since then, his wail is feebler; and his eye,
Which when you went was fever-lit, is now
Heavy and lustreless.   He asked for thee,
But knew me not; alas! why knew he not
His mother?   Then he sunk into a stupor.
    [AYLMERE *goes to the pallet silently, and lifts the cover
        —starts;* MARIAMNE *stands near him, on his left.*

AYLMERE.   Is this my boy!—The lid is raised,
But the eye sees not!   Hist! how faint and low
His breathing!   Oh, my boy!   His brow is damp
With a chill dew!   [*Kneels and kisses his son.*

MARIAMNE.   [*Left of him, clinging to him and looking
    terrified in his face.*]   Aylmere!

AYLMERE.   My boy! my boy!
MARIAMNE. That he should die for lack of food!
AYLMERE. [*Starts up.*] He shall not!—shall not!
Madness and death! They've filched my share
Of Nature's equal boon; and by my wrongs,
Though death stand by, I'll wrench it back again!
       [*Going up centre;* MARIAMNE *stands to the right.*
MARIAMNE. Leave us not, Aylmere!
AYLMERE.   I'll be here anon.
                      [*She goes up to bank.*
Oh, oppression! 'Tis not thine own crimes only,
Fell as they are, will frown on thee at compt;
But every desperate deed, in frenzy done
By maddened innocence, will claim thee sire,
And thunder-toned, pronounce thee guilty! guilty!
       [AYLMERE *rushes out.* MARIAMNE *goes to bank, and*
       weeps over her child.

SCENE FOURTH.—*The Forest.*

Enter SAY.

SAY. Where loiters Clifford! Now, beshrew the lag-
    gards!
They shame the sport. If in this sombre wood,
Where Nature's king, where the poor slave's a man
And I no more,—should I these plotters meet,
'Twere a grave peril. Would I'd vexed 'em not!
But there's no pausing-place in wrong.—'Tis done.
No time for thoughts or fears. The venturous hind,
Who clambers up the steepy precipice,
When the rock crumbles 'neath his wary foot,
And falls, far echoing, in the flood below,
Stays not to tremble, turns him not to gaze;
But upward looks and onward works his way.
Thanks for the lesson! Tho' my foothold be
As frail as love, yet, yet will I not falter.
Ha! who is he approaches?

Enter AYLMERE.

AYLMERE. Well met, sir.
SAY. Why, how now, knave!

AYLMERE. Knave! Be it so—I'm poor
And thou art wealthy. I would have some gold.
    SAY. Thou darest not rob me!
    AYLMERE.   What will misery dare not?
I dare!
    SAY. Sirrah! I am a peer!
    AYLMERE.   And so
Am I—thy peer, and any man's—ten times
Thy peer, and thou'rt not honest.
    SAY.   Insolent!
My fathers were made noble by a king!
    AYLMERE. And mine by Heaven! The people are God's
        own
Nobility; and wear their stars not *on*
Their breasts, but *in* them!
    SAY.   Dost not fear justice?
    AYLMERE. The justice o' the court?
Nursled on blood! A petted falcon which
You fly at weakness! I do know your justice!
Crouching and meek to proud and purpled Wrong;
But tiger-toothed and ravenous o'er pale Right.
I do nor love nor fear it.
    SAY.   What art thou
That speakest thus rashly?
    AYLMERE. What thou see'st—a man—
Poor and in need of gold—desperate—wild!
Yield thee; or—[*Threatens.*]
    SAY.   Slave! I will not yield.
    AYLMERE.   By Heaven!
But I would do no crime! My lord, I am
The wretched father of a boy whom now
I left, hard by, to perish, and for bread.
Give me a piece! but one! and I will bless thee! [*Kneels
        to him and clings to his dress.*]
    SAY.   Out of my way!
    AYLMERE. My lord, let him not perish!
Oh, save my child!
    SAY. [*Throws* CADE *off, who starts up revengefully.*]
        Off, carle! or thus I spurn thee!
    AYLMERE. Ha! then have at thee! Thy gold or thy base
        life! [*Draws his knife.*]

SAY. Hold, slave! Thou art mad!
I am the treasurer of the realm. Lord Say!

AYLMERE. [*Bursts into a fierce laugh of exultation.*] Ha,
ha, ha!

SAY. Doth he laugh at me!

AYLMERE. Heaven hath sent him to me
For sacrifice! The years have yielded up
That hour so long and bitterly awaited!

SAY. Give way! [*Crosses to left;* AYLMERE *stops him.*

AYLMERE. Stir not;
I am thy executioner.

SAY. What mean you!

AYLMERE. That thou must die!

SAY. Thou wouldst not slay me, fellow!

AYLMERE. Slay thee! Ay, by this light, as thou wouldst
slay
A wolf! Bethink thee; hast not used thy place
To tread the weak and poor to dust; to plant
Shame on each cheek, and sorrow in each heart?
Hast thou not plundered, tortured, hunted down
Thy fellow-men like brutes? Why now, what devil is it
That palters with thee, to believe that thou
Canst do such deeds and live!

SAY. I am unarmed;

AYLMERE. Ha, ha, ha! [*Laughs scornfully.*] Well said,
well said! Hence, toy. [*Throws away the dagger.*]
We're equal now; and I would have no arms
But those the tiger hath against thee! Now
For vengeance, justice for the bond!

[*Throws himself upon* SAY. *Enter* CLIFFORD, BUCK-
INGHAM, *and train—four* GUARDS *and two* OFFICERS,
right, two OFFICERS *left. They interpose.*]

CLIFFORD. Hold! ruffian!
Strike him down! So, secure him.

[OFFICERS *advance left to seize* AYLMERE, *who throws
them off; two* OFFICERS *from right seize him as he
is in the act of going towards* SAY. GUARDS *present
spears.*]

AYLMERE. [*Struggling with* OFFICERS.] Back, slaves!
Baffled!
Oh, for one moment,—one—to grind the viper

Into the earth he poisons!

CLIFFORD. [*Aside to* SAY.]   By Heaven!
'Tis Aylmere! Mark you, Say, his form, his carriage,
All over Mortimer!

SAY.   'Tis Mortimer!
Let him not see we know him.
Now, sirrah.

AYLMERE. [*Sullenly.*] Well, sir.

SAY. Who art thou?

AYLMERE. Thy foe inexorable.

SAY.   Know you
Your crime's need? 'Tis——

AYLMERE.   I care not what——

SAY.   'Tis death.

AYLMERE. So be it!
Death! the bondman's last, best friend!
In the grave there is no echo for the tyrant's lash;
He who has learned to die, forgets to serve
Or suffer!

Enter MARIAMNE; *when she enters,* SAY *and others go
up stage.*

MARIAMNE.   My Aylmere!
It is my husband, and be his doom mine. [*Rushes to his
arms.*]
Think not [*to* AYLMERE] to part our fates. We'll die
together!

AYLMERE.   Why, alas!
Didst draw this ruin on thee, Mariamne?

MARIAMNE. Wrong me not, Aylmere, so to think I'd bear
An unshared safety.

AYLMERE. How fares our boy, my Mariamne? [*She
averts her face.*]
He is——he is——[*She turns, bursts into an agony of tears,
and throws herself on his bosom.*]

MARIAMNE. Happy, Aylmere!

AYLMERE. Desolate! desolate! my heart is desolate! [*He
falls on the shoulder of* MARIAMNE *and weeps.*]

SAY. [*Advancing.*] Part them. [OFFICERS *advance.*]

AYLMERE. Hold! I pray you, hold!

SAY. What wouldst thou?

AYLMERE. Not many paces hence, we have a child,
A poor, a sinless child, whom thou hast driven
To famine and to death. Let us once more look on his
Lifeless form, and kiss his cold cheek?

SAY. Away!

AYLMERE. Oh, execrable wretch! A day will come
When thy polluted heart shall writhe for this!
When the unbaffled fiend, Remorse, shall show the blood
Of white-haired Cade, dark stained on thy brow.
Then every wind shall stir in billow clouds
Her ashes 'gainst thee whom, but yesterday,
Thou gavest to the flames.

SAY. Away!

END OF ACT III.

ACT IV.

SCENE FIRST.—*A room in the castle; door. A table and
two chairs; lights on table.*

MARIAMNE. To London sent! And to be tried! Alas,
Tried! He's condemned even now! Child, husband, lost!
I have no friend! Yes, one is left me—this! [*A dagger.*]
Beyond thy point no shame can pass;
For when thou can'st not guard this feeble citadel,
Still thou wilt ope a door to let the hunted spirit out!
'Twere well to die now. Oh, my Aylmere, why,
Why left we Italy? [*Weeps.*]

Enter CLIFFORD.

CLIFFORD. [*Approches* MARIAMNE.] Nay, gracious lady,
  weep not. Thou
Wilt find me no ungentle warder o'er thee.
Look up! These torrent tears have swept the roses
From thy fair cheek.

MARIAMNE. It is not well to mock
The friendless.

CLIFFORD. Nay, thou art not friendless here.

My bosom aches o'er all thy sufferings. Trust me—
I am thy friend.

MARIAMNE. Enough—thou art Lord Clifford—
Friend of Say. Woe and weakness
Will make the simplest wise. I trust thee not.

CLIFFORD. Thou dost me wrong, fair casuist; and, in me
Wrong'st one awakened from a dream of evil,
To be the friend of virtue.

MARIAMNE. Give me, then,
My husband!

CLIFFORD. If I could, lady, and I think I can——

MARIAMNE. Oh, all good men would bless thee!
And Heaven, that loves just deeds, would hear my prayer,
And on thy gracious head shower rich blessings. [*Kneels.*

CLIFFORD. Nay, rise, fair lady, 'tis for me to kneel.
Thy husband shall be saved; if thou wilt——

MARIAMNE. What?
I will do anything; toil till I faint,
And be lashed back to life to toil again!
I'll live with midnight darkness in thy dungeons.

CLIFFORD. I ask not this; thy heaviest task is pleasure.
Thou shalt be mine, sweet lady.

MARIAMNE. Said I not
I knew thee? Wretch! [*Crosses to left.*

CLIFFORD. Stay, lady, and bethink thee;
Thy husband's freedom.

MARIAMNE. Purchased with dishonour!
'Twere well to buy his freedom with his curse.
Unlink his chains and turn him forth to draw
The thick and tainted air of infamy—
Be pointed at by every honest hand,
There goes the wanton's husband!—this thy blessing!

CLIFFORD. Smile upon me.
I'll give thee riches.

MARIAMNE. I spurn thy bounty. Can the clink of gold
Shut out the hiss of shame?

CLIFFORD. The loftiest rank,
Observance, title, are thine own, if thou
Art mine. Thou shalt be honoured——

MARIAMNE. By wretches like thyself! Away, thou'rt
loathly!

CLIFFORD. Aylmere and thou are parted, and for ever.
[*She starts; he makes a slight pause.*]
I feigned a power I have not when I said
He could be saved.
MARIAMNE. Thou'dst tell me—thou hast lied,
Thou honourable lord!
CLIFFORD.   Still hear me, lady.
Aylmere must die; smile on me, and I'll wed thee;
And raise thee 'mid the loftiest of the land!
MARIAMNE. Never! now do I scorn thee more! Wed
thee!
I'd rather clasp a pestilence! Go to
The charnel-house and wed the dead, than wed
With thee!
CLIFFORD. Insolent minion, have a care!
MARIAMNE. I'd rather be a living death,
And perish thus by piecemeal, than thy bride!
CLIFFORD. I am no more thy suitor, but thy fate!
And what I will—I will! [*Seizes her.*]
MARIAMNE. Off! tyrant, monster!
[*Struggles with* CLIFFORD—*taking the dagger from her
bosom.*]
CLIFFORD. Nay, 'tis too late, no struggling! [*Struggles
with her.*]
MARIAMNE. This for Aylmere! [*Stabs him—he falls.*]
CLIFFORD. Hold, lady.
MARIAMNE. What have I done!
CLIFFORD. I have deserved this death:
But happier is it, than will be thy life,
Gloomed by the memory of this murder. [*Dies.*]
MARIAMNE.   Murder!
Dead! Why, how now? My brain reels. 'Tis too much!
[*Sinks down shudderingly.*]

Enter SAY, BUCKINGHAM, *and* OFFICERS.

SAY. What means this noise?
BUCKING. Horror! 'Tis Clifford, dead.
SAY. What bloody act is here? Is she, too, dead? [*She
is partly raised up, looks wildly round, laughs.*]
MARIAMNE. [*In a whisper.*] Where am I?

Aylmere, didst speak?—   [*Still bewildered.*
I did it for thine honour.

> [*She stands up, sees the red dagger, which she still
> holds; looks down and sees the body of* CLIFFORD;
> *shrieks and falls.*

SCENE SECOND.—*The Forest. Distant alarums.*

Enter STRAW *and* WORTHY.

STRAW. How quick their leasy legions shrunk! 'Fore
    Heaven,
I like not such lame sport. But, good master,
Have we freed Mortimer?
    WORTHY.   No, by my troth;
He freed himself; for when we burst upon them,
He snatched a sword, and in a moment spread
A solitude around him. Now beshrew me,
I know my hammer not, as he the sword.

Enter LACY, PEMBROKE, MOWBRAY, *and six* KENTISHMEN.

WORTHY. Where's Mortimer?
    LACY.   Foremost in the pursuit.
    MOWBRAY. He rages like a wounded lion. Who
Would from so calm a cloud, expect a bolt
So fierce and blasting? Is this man our Aylmere?
    LACY. Some fearful spirit seems to swell his frame,
When, like a slaughter-god, he scatters death,
And shouts and laughs in killing. It appalled me.
    WORTHY. Behold! He comes! he comes!

Enter AYLMERE, *with drawn sword.*

LACY. [*Takes* AYLMERE *by the hand.*] Thank Heaven!
    thou'rt free!
    AYLMERE. [*Laughs.*] Ay, once more free! within my
    grasp a sword,
And round me freemen! Free! as is the storm
About your hills; the surge upon your shore!
Free as the sunbeams on the chainless air;
Or as the stream that leaps the precipice,

And in eternal thunder, shouts to Heaven,
That it is free, and will be free for ever!

STRAW.   Now for revenge! Full long we've fed on wrong:
Give us revenge!

AYLMERE.   For you and for myself!
England from all her hills, cries out for vengeance!
The angry waves
Repeat the sound in thunder; and the heavens,
From their blue vaults, roll back a people's cry
For liberty and vengeance!   [*Crosses to right.*

MOWBRAY.   The Lord Say
Knows of the Commons' rising, and hath sent
For force from London; all the Kentish lords
Are arming, and Lord Buckingham is up.

AYLMERE.   Up, up! why so are we! Here [*His sword*]
    be our answer!
Now by yon Heaven, it glads me! I would have
Some stirring work to wake my soul withal;
I pant to try my wing so long unfluttered;
And here's a sky to soar in! Mowbray, where
Meet our musters?

MOWBRAY.   At Seven-Oak.

AYLMERE.   Thither, then!
        [MOWBRAY *crosses to right front; all others on left.*
But only with hot hearts that will hug danger.
Let falterers—pale-lipped slaves who would be men
But dare not—back to whip and chain!
Remembering that they could be free, but would not!

WORTHY.   Fear not; the sons of Kent are better mettled.

AYLMERE.   For Seven-Oak, ho!

MOWBRAY
    and   }Ay, on! for Mortimer!
KENTISHMEN.

        [*Exeunt all but* AYLMERE *and* LACY.

AYLMERE.   For Mortimer! What means this? When
    they rushed
Upon my guard, the cry was "Mortimer
Unto the rescue!" Why this iteration
Of a name now the tomb's?

LACY.   It is believed
He lives; even Say thinks thou art none but he;—

The Rightful King of England!

AYLMERE.　　　　　　　　　　Ha! 'twas oft
Said that my favour semblanced his.

LACY.　　　　　　　　　　　　The people
Have caught the thought, and ne'er will deem thee other.
Mortimer is a name to conjure up
Thousands of daring spirits for the cause.

AYLMERE. It is?

LACY.　　　　　That spell hath called this host together:
Unspeak it, and they scatter with the wind.

AYLMERE. Thou wouldst not have me bear a noble name
Not mine?

LACY.　　　Thou now bear'st name not thine,
Aylmere;—why not a prince's name as well?
Our host is glued together with the name
Of Mortimer:—disclaim it—all is o'er,
And England may crawl back into her chains!　　[A pause.

AYLMERE. I will be Mortimer unto the world;—but only
Until our chains are molten in the glow
Of kindled spirits; for I seek not power,
I know no glory,—save the godlike joy of making
The bondman free. When we *are* free, Jack Cade
Will back unto his hills, and proudly smile
Down on the spangled meanness of the court,
Claiming a title higher than their highest,—
An honest man—a freeman!

LACY.　　　　　　　　　I am cheered
To see thy spirit mounting thus. I feared
Thy Mariamne's danger—

AYLMERE.　　　　　　Alas! alas!

LACY. I thought not to have moved thee thus. Forgive
me!

AYLMERE. Have I then lost her?

LACY.　　　　　　　　　Nay—doubt not, she is safe.

AYLMERE. Oh! she was lovely as the smile of hope,
And gentle as the dewy star of eve!

　　　　　　　　　　　　　　　[A distant march.

LACY. Say's force is in motion.

AYLMERE. By Heaven, I do forget myself, this while!
War, iron war's my only bride this day,
And by the people's wrongs, I'll woo her bravely.

How are our men? Do their souls bear an edge
Keen and well-tempered for the morrow's fight?

LACY. They will not shame old Kent, unconquered Kent!

AYLMERE. I'd have their veins flow to the coming fight,
Like the fierce torrent to the cataract!
Come, Father, unto our host! Bid each man strike,
In God's name, for God's gifts.
We'll meet no more, or meet as freemen, Father!

[*Exeunt.*

SCENE THIRD.—*London. Old London stone, centre.*

Enter SAY, BUCKINGHAM, OFFICERS, *and* SOLDIERS. *March
till* SAY *is on.* GUARDS *form across stage.*

BUCKING. They dream not such a force as yours can fall
In peril;—nor foresee that Kent and Essex
Should thus unkennel all their bloodhounds on us.
Meanwhile
Let the worst swell the worst—thou'lt yield not?

SAY.   Yield!
By Heaven, it shall be death to speak of it!
Yield to the insolent kern!

BUCKING.   Ne'er heed the mob.
What though the rout,
The compost of the realm, is smoking now
With its vile heat? Show them the whip, they'll flee
Like beaten whelps.

SAY.   The name of Mortimer
Gathers the bond like bees. His valour, too,
In his late rescue glitters in their eyes.

BUCKING. Mad but the mettled fool, he'll rush on ruin,
As eagles pounce upon a baited spear.

SAY. I have his wife. He knows not she is maniac:
And with this gripe upon his heart, I'll yet
Bow him to terms.   [*Shouts and drum.*

Enter OFFICER, *in haste.*

OFFICER.   My lord, the bond have fallen
In thousands on our camp. They are led on
By our late prisoner.

SAY. These bondmen fight like fiends.

BUCKING.   'Tis Mortimer
That makes them heroes. [*Distant shout.*] Hark! they
    follow hard
Upon us.
[*Distant shout.*] Again!
Let us unto the Tower: there we are safe.

    SAY. Not long, I fear; [*shout*] they are upon us.
     Hence!   [*Exeunt.*
        [*A cry of "Mortimer! Mortimer!"*

Enter WORTHY, MOWBRAY, LACY, PEMBROKE, *and others of
the party of Commons, and* AYLMERE, *to the left, dressed
as a knight.*

    AYLMERE. Now Mortimer is lord o' the city. Thus,
                       [*Striking London stone.*
Thus upon London do I lay my sword!
As she is to the bond—so I to her!
[*To his sword.*] Thou friend of those who have no friend
    beside,
Be with me, till the name of slave is known not!
Then rest and rust for ever. [*Sheathing it.*] *Master
    Mowbray,*
What of the King?

    MOWBRAY.   He's fled to Kenilworth.

    AYLMERE. And Say and Buckingham?

    MOWBRAY.   Have doubtless taken
Refuge in the Tower.

    AYLMERE. [*To* MOWBRAY.] Let it be invested;
And on thy life have care that Say escape not.
                          [*Exit* MOWBRAY.
Escape! As well the night escape the dawn!
Earth hath no shelter for him.

    WORTHY.   Good my lord,
The jarring nobles in the north have leagued
Against thee.

    AYLMERE. I care not. They'll fall asunder.
Pembroke, be it proclaimed throughout our host,
The Commons rise for right—a holy right—
And not for lawless license. Whoso robs

Or doth a wrong unto the citizens,
Shall, in the king's name, suffer death. Proclaim it.
[Exit PEMBROKE.

And lest the night should breed excess, at sunset
Lead our force from out the city, Master Worthy,
Unto your posts. Keep a wary eye upon
Your followers. Power even in the cause of freedom
Not always studies right.

Enter STRAW and PEMBROKE with a PRISONER.

STRAW. Good my lord, we found this knave
Rifling the house of one whom he had slain.
PRISONER. I am of Kent, and hold with Mortimer.
AYLMERE. The men of Kent are true men, and not
robbers.
Your duty.—Take him hence.
PRISONER.   Oh, spare me! Mercy!
AYLMERE. Mercy to thee, would whet the tooth of rapine,
And urge it on to murder.
[Waves them off—exeunt STRAW and KENTISHMEN.
He fears death!
Why, I would totter to its gentle arms,
As a tired infant to its mother's bosom!
He who knows life yet fears to die, is mad,
Mad as the dungeon slave who dreads his freedom.
Father, hast been among our host?
LACY.   Ay! And find them
Drunken with triumph. They think toil and care
Are over now, and deem that, when they're free,
Life will be but a lawless long-drawn revel.
AYLMERE. Liberty gives nor light nor heat itself;
It but permits us to be good and happy.
It is to man, what space is to the orbs,
The medium where he may revolve and shine,
Or, darkened by his vices, fall for ever!
LACY. Already they are struggling for their rank.
All would be great, all captains, leaders, lords.
AYLMERE. Life's story still! all would o'ertop their fel-
lows;
And every rank—the lowest—hath its height

To which hearts flutter, with as large a hope
As princes feel for empire! But in each,
Ambition struggles with a sea of hate.
He who toils up the ridgy grades of life,
Finds, in each station, icy scorn above,
Below him hooting envy.

Enter WORTHY, SUFFOLK, *and four* LORDS, *prisoners.*

WORTHY.　My lord, the prisoners.
AYLMERE.　　　　　　　　　How hushed and meek
Are now those thunderers! Why call ye not
The thong, the rack, the axe, for us, your slaves?
Oh, ye are men now, only men;—methought
Ye were the gods of the crushed earth! How say ye?
SUFFOLK.　You will not dare to hold us?
AYLMERE.　　　　　　　　　Heaven forfend!
Hold a lord captive! Awful sacrilege!
What! hold a lord!
SUFFOLK.　　　　　He mocks us.
AYLMERE.　Pembroke, take hence, and strip these popin-
jays,
Garb their trim forms and perfumed limbs in russet,
And drive them to the field! We'll teach you, sirs,
To till the glebe you've nurtured with our blood.
SUFFOLK.　Thou wilt not use us thus?
AYLMERE.　　　　　　　　　And wherefore not?
SUFFOLK.　Heaven gave us rank, and freed that rank from
labour.
AYLMERE.　Go to! thou speak'st not truth!
Heaven were not Heaven were such as ye its chosen.

Re-enter STRAW.

STRAW.　　　　　　The king's council,
Who audience crave with Mortimer.
AYLMERE.　　　　　　　　Admit them.
　　[*Exit* STRAW, *and re-enter with* BUCKINGHAM *and two*
　　　OFFICERS *of* SAY, *who stand to the right.*
BUCKING.　In the King's name, Lord Mortimer, we come,
To ask why thus you fright his peaceful realm
With wild rebellion?

AYLMERE. Why!—You mock us!
Are ye so deaf that England's shrieks ye hear not?
So blind, ye see not her wan brow sweat blood?

BUCKING. My lord, if you seek power in this, remember
The greatness which is born in anarchy,
And thrown aloft in tumult, cannot last.

AYLMERE. [*Rises and comes forward.*] Sagely said!
Go back unto the court, and preach it, where
Fraud laughs at faith, and force at right, and where
Success is sainted if it come from hell!
And seek the right—the right!

BUCKING. Disband your force;
We promise mercy.

AYLMERE. Now 'fore Heaven, you're kind,
You've scourged, and chained, and mocked us; made God's
earth
A dungeon, and a living grave; and now,
When we are free,—our swords in our right hands,
Our tyrants shivering at our feet—ye prate
Of promised mercy. Hark ye! if you yield not,
The wolf shall howl in your spoiled palaces!
Better were England made a wild, than be
The home of bondmen!

BUCKING. What do you demand?
We would have peace, if not too dearly bought.

AYLMERE. We're deaf. Say lives! 'Till he be rendered
up,
We know no word like peace!

BUCKING. He is in ward,
And, to appease the Commons, shall be tried.

AYLMERE. Pah! He is tried and sentenced by a nation!
Give him, or—we will take him!—We can do it;
And, gentle sirs, ye know it!

BUCKING. Be it so;
[*To* OFFICER.] Bring from the Tower Lord Say!
[*Exit* OFFICER.

AYLMERE. [*Aside.*] It is no dream—no dream!
The hour has come!

BUCKING. We'll yield thee Say:—what further?

AYLMERE. That the king grant this charter to his people.
[*Exhibiting the scroll, which he unrolls.*

BUCKING. What doth it covenant?

AYLMERE.   Freedom for the bond!

BUCKING. For all?

AYLMERE.   For all; all who breathe England's air
Henceforward shall be free!

[BUCKINGHAM *and* SUFFOLK *confer.*

BUCKING.   This too, we grant—
Conditioned you withdraw your host.

AYLMERE. [*Places chart on London stone—*LACY *gives
pen.*] A pen, a pen!
Now I can die in peace. I will, my lord—I will.
Your name, my Lord of Suffolk.

[SUFFOLK *signs, and goes back to place.*
                                      Yours, my lord.

BUCKING. [*Signs.*] Art now content?

AYLMERE.   Not till the realm's broad seal
Makes the deed sacred. [*Brings charter forward with him.*

BUCKING.   Nay—

AYLMERE. [*Impatiently.*]   The seal—the seal!

BUCKING. [*Takes charter.*] As you will. [*To* OFFICER.]
    Bear this to the Tower, and bid
My secretary stamp this charter with
The great seal of the realm.

AYLMERE. [*To* MOWBRAY.] And, Mowbray, go
With him and haste! And when
'Tis done, shout the glad tidings to our host;
And bid their hearts and voices tell the heavens
That they are slaves no more!

[*Exeunt* MOWBRAY *and* OFFICER, *with charter.*

Enter PEMBROKE, *with* SAY.

                              Ha! ha! ha! ha!
Now do I almost love thee, for this hour!
Why, bridegroom ne'er met bride with such a joy
As I meet thee!

SAY. Thou fierce and savage man!

AYLMERE.   Fierce! I am gentle;
                    [*Goes to him and eyes him savagely.*
Gentle and joyous. Fierce! You see I laugh!
[*Sternly.*] Thou hadst a bondman once—his name was Cade,
A white-haired man.

SAY.   I had.

AYLMERE.   And for some toy
That harmless man was scourged; and thou stood'st by
And saw the red whip pierce his quivering flesh.

SAY. The villain was my bond.

AYLMERE.   Your bond! His child,
A pale boy, struck you down, and spurned you—spurned you.
                    [*Very strong and sarcastic.*
And he, too, was your bond!

SAY.   The carle escaped.

AYLMERE. Ay, but forgot you not, though years and
     troubles
Passed darkly o'er him! But thy victim's widow—
Ha! doth her name appal thee? Thine the arm—
Coward! that smote her! Thou it was that gave
Her wasted form to the fierce flames! thou! thou!
Thought'st thou not of her boy? The poor Jack Cade
Is now the avenger! Mortimer no more—
Behold me—Cade the bondman!
                    [*All start with surprise, except* LACY.

SAY.   Thou! Heaven shield me!

AYLMERE. Even I! Ha! ha! The grace of noble birth!
Poor Cade, the bondman, worshipped as a prince!
Poor Cade, the bondman, giving laws to princes!
But no! Cade is no bondman! England's sun
Sees not a slave; and her glad breeze floats by,
And bears no groans save those of her oppressors.
Now for thy doom. Quick, let me set it down. The scourge
     that slew my father
Shall, from thy shrinking flesh lap up the blood,
Till ragged from the lash. Then to the stake!
My father's torture and my mother's death!

SAY. [*Aside.*] No, never by the torture will I die—
Nor die alone! I have a weapon still.
[*Tauntingly.*] How fareth Mariamne?

AYLMERE. [*Half aside.*]   Wretch!

SAY. Clifford was a rough wooer.

AYLMERE. And wooed his death.

SAY.   The murd'ress sank a maniac;
And dainty warders had she in the castle.
Her mingled shrieks and laughter liked me not.

I sent her to the dungeon. And, as she raved,
To the damp wall, unlit and cold, we bound her.
On you she called, in mingled shrieks and prayers.
  AYLMERE.   God of Heaven!
  SAY. 'Tis said the scourge will tame the wildest maniac.
And—
  AYLMERE. And what?
  SAY.   I bade the steward bring
The hangman's whip.
  AYLMERE.   The whip! I'll hear no more!
Die, dog, and rot!

    [AYLMERE *stabs* SAY. *They grapple.* SAY *strikes*
    AYLMERE *with his dagger.* ATTENDANTS *interpose.*
    SAY *falls into* OFFICER'S *arms;* LACY *and* WORTHY
    come forward to AYLMERE.

  AYLMERE. Take down to hell my curse, thou blackest
  fiend
That e'er its gates let forth! Hence with him—
Gibbet and flames shall be thy portion—hence with him.
  LACY. [*To* AYLMERE.] You bleed!
  SAY.   He bleeds? Why then I triumph still!
My steel was venomed and its point is fate.
            [SAY *is dragged off.*

Enter MARIAMNE; *he rushes to her and embraces her; she*
  shrieks and breaks from him shudderingly.

  MARIAMNE. [*Crossing* AYLMERE *to centre.*] Off! I scorn,
  I loathe thee!
  AYLMERE. She knows me not! Her brain is wandering!
  This
With the rest, oh Heaven!
  MARIAMNE.   Wed thee, monster? never!
Or ere upon thy breast I'd lay my head,
I'd hide me in a charnel-house, and sport
With the red worm among the carrion dead.
  AYLMERE. Knowest me, Mariamne?
  MARIAMNE. I know thee! thou art—no, thou art not
  Clifford.
Thou'lt wrong me not! Hist! [*whispers*] they've hid

My sweet boy in the earth—the cold—cold earth;
And I would dig my gentle darling out.
And thou wilt aid me? But what is this?—A corpse!
'Tis Clifford's! and 'twas I that did it—I! I!

> [*She sinks down, covering her face.*

AYLMERE. Anything but this!
I could have seen her die, and kissed her lips,
And caught her last low sigh. I could have lain
Her gentle form in earth, and never murmured!
I think—I think—I could! But thus to see her!
Thus!

MARIAMNE. [*Rises.*] Have I been dreaming? or have I
been mad?
The smoke that palled my brain
Flies from life's deadening embers now away,
And leaves me but the ashes. Ha! my Aylmere!

> [*She totters to his arms.*

AYLMERE. Thou knowest me? Dost thou not? Now
blessings on thee!

MARIAMNE. Nearer, my Aylmere, nearer! I do lose thee!
Is not this death? Our boy, they tore me from him:
Buried they him?

AYLMERE. Alas, I know not. [*She faints.*] Faint
not!
'Tis I—'tis Aylmere holds thee, Mariamne!

> [*Getting down on his knees with her.*

MARIAMNE. I see thee not, nor hear thee.—Bless thee!
Bless thee. [*Dies.*

AYLMERE. Look up, love! Wife! My Mariamne! cold!
Dead! dead!

> [*Weeps—he rises—sinks again—is caught and supported
> by* LACY *and* WORTHY.

Say struck home!
The charter—is it come?

LACY. Not yet.

AYLMERE. All slain!
Say hath slain all! I come, my Mariamne!

> [*He sinks upon her body. A distant shout. Another
> and nearer.* AYLMERE *partly rises.*

That shout?

LACY.　　　　Mowbray proclaims the charter.

AYLMERE.　　　　　　　　　　　　　　Doth he?

　　　　　　　　　　　　　　[*Another shout, louder.*

Again!　　　[*A cry without,* "The charter! the charter!"

MOWBRAY *rushes in, bearing the charter unrolled, and exhibiting the seal.*

MOWBRAY.　The charter! seal and all!

　　　　[AYLMERE *starts up with a wild burst of exultation, rushes to him, catches the charter, kisses it, and clasps it to his bosom.*

AYLMERE.　　　　　　　　　　　　　　Free! free!

The bondman is avenged, my country free!

　　　　　　　　　　[*Totters towards* MARIAMNE *and sinks.*

THE END.

FASHION

By Mrs. Anna Cora Mowatt

MRS. ANNA CORA (OGDEN) MOWATT RITCHIE

(1819–1870)

The study of social manners is one of the most interesting phases of the drama. However unliterary some of the early American plays may be, they nonetheless reflect the social life of the time, and one can trace, with the advance of the theatres up Broadway in New York, from the Battery to Union Square, the advance in social standards and the changes in social usage. It was around the Battery that the young ladies in Royall Tyler's "The Contrast" used to parade on Sundays, thence to the Astor House, on Vesey Street, opposite the old Park Theatre; at Union Square, grand opera was given at the Academy of Music, and is talked about in Augustin Daly's "Under the Gas Light"; then New York's dramatic centre advanced to the Madison Square Theatre, where David Belasco's "milk and water" drama first introduced to the stage the realistic or quiet acting. If we do not take "The Contrast" as the first attempt at depicting New York manners—(that play has all the credit it deserves in the fact that the first stage Yankee came out of it)—then Mrs. Mowatt's "Fashion" marks a distinct epoch in American society drama. Those who are interested in manners will find it a profitable study, as I have before intimated, to take Mrs. Mowatt's "Fashion" and contrast it with Mrs. Bateman's "Self" of later date, with Bronson Howard's "Saratoga", and with Langdon Mitchell's "The New York Idea", which is the American "School for Scandal", both in its acid test and in its native wit.[1]

[1] Laurence Hutton, in his "Curiosities of the American Stage", has an interesting chapter on "The Local New York Drama", in which he differentiates the distinctly local from such plays as Mead, ——, "Wall Street; or, Ten Minutes Before Three" (1819); McCracken, J. L. H., "Earning a Living" (1849); Smith, Mrs. E. Oakes, "Old New York; or, Democracy in 1689" (1853); Boucicault, Dion, "The Poor o New York" (1857), and such additional dramas as John Brougham's "The Lottery of Life" and "Life in New York", B. A. Baker's "A Glance at New York", and G. P. Wilkinson's "Young New York".

Mrs. Mowatt's "Fashion" was an accident. The fact of the matter is, Mrs. Mowatt, as an actress, was herself almost an accident, pushed on the stage by the vagaries of ill-fortune. So excellently well has she outlined the perturbations of mind which prompted her to write this piece, and so graphically has she described the troubles of rehearsals, that no one writing about Mrs. Mowatt can afford to ignore that part of her "Autobiography of an Actress; or, Eight Years on the Stage", which follows "Fashion's" production.

Mrs. Mowatt was one of the striking New York literary figures in the time when Edgar Allan Poe—"one of my sternest critics", she characterizes him—was doing dramatic criticism and book reviewing for one of the local papers,— *The Broadway Journal.* She was born abroad [1] and acquired some of the French vivacity which surrounded her in her early years. Brought up as a member of a large family, she, being the tenth child, early acquired a taste for private theatricals, which did not abate in the least when her father, Samuel Ogden, moved his family to New York. At the age of fifteen, Anna married a lawyer, James Mowatt, the courtship taking place very largely during the girl's journeys to and from school. The consequence is, when she was married under the romantic conditions of an elopement, the husband continued with her the education thus suddenly interrupted.

According to the traditions of the time, there was little outlet for any show of native powers in a woman, the only channel open to her being the art of letters. Thus, we find Mrs. Mowatt posing, not only as a poetess, but as a novelist, writing under the romantic pseudonyms of "Isabel" and "Helen Berkley". She received recognition from most of the literary critics of the day, and entered the portals of Rufus Griswold's monumental book, "Female Poets of America." [2]

It is not our province here to discuss Mrs. Mowatt's poems

---

[1] In Bordeaux, France, in 1819. She died at Twickenham on the Thames, July 28, 1870, having lived mostly abroad during the latter years of her life. Mowatt died in 1851, and. in 1854, after her farewell tour through the United States, Mrs. Mowatt married William F. Ritchie, a journalist, of Richmond, Va.

[2] In 1840, she wrote a play, "Gulzara; or, The Persian Slave", for which she bought scenes and dresses in Paris, and which was given a production at her home on her return to New York. Her long story, "The Fortune Hunter, A Novel by Helen Berkley", was issued in 1842.

of numerous cantos, her quick-witted replies to some of her
critics, her novels, cast in the tedious and sometimes quaint
mould of the period of 1845, or her other literary activities.
She lived in that part of New York now known as Mott
Haven, and probably would have continued in her quiet
social way, writing pleasant poems and two-volumed novels,
had it not been that Mr. Mowatt met with financial reverses,
due to speculation in Wall Street, and this turned his wife's
attention to immediate means of a livelihood. She decided
that a series of dramatic readings, bringing into account
her native elocutionary powers, would probably reap her a
reward which, if it were not quite as much as that reaped by
Fanny Kemble, and by the elder Vandenhoff, would at least
bring her an income, and help Mr. Mowatt over a difficult
time. One who reads her "Autobiography" will sense some
of that stress of mind which she had when she made her
first public appearance as a reader in Boston, and then
turned to New York—all the time being subject to the
decided disapproval of her intimate friends. It is just here
that the narrative of "Fashion" begins in her "Autobiography".

Most of the "female" poets of the time, if their own
friends are to be believed, were thrust into publication
through the admiring persuasion of their friends. So, Mrs.
Mowatt was confronted by one "E. S." (most probably
Epes Sargent), with the proposal that she write a play and
submit it to the managers of the Park Theatre. She records
the conversation between them thus:

"'Why do you not write plays?' said E. S., to me one
morning. 'You have more decided talent for the stage
than for any thing else. If we can get it accepted by
the Park Theatre, and if it should succeed, you have a
new and wide field of exertion opened to you—one in
which success is very rare, but for which your turn of
mind has particularly fitted you.'

"'What shall I attempt, comedy or tragedy?'

"'Comedy, decidedly; because you can only write
what you feel, and you are "nothing if not critical"—
besides, you will have a fresh channel for the sarcastic
ebullitions with which you so constantly indulge us.'"

The very fact that Mrs. Mowatt asked whether it should be comedy or tragedy shows well enough that she had not thought of the theatre as a vehicle for artistic expression, nor had she weighed her ability, nor fathomed her vivacity. "E. S.", however, was wiser than she. Mrs. Mowatt confesses that this was true,—that in conversation as well as in writing, her sharpness of tongue sometimes got the better of her. And so her mind instantly turned to American *parvenuism*, a treatment of which inevitably brought down upon her the accusation that, in "Fashion", she was holding some of her acquaintances up to ridicule. This she flatly denied, even though she acknowledged that *Adam Trueman* was a portrait from life.

There were no attempts in "Fashion" at fine writing, she declares, and we agree with her. "I designed the play wholly as an *acting* comedy [and it acts well even to-day]. A dramatic, not a literary success, was what I desired to achieve. Caution suggested my not aiming at both at once."

In due time the finished manuscript was offered to Manager Simpson, of the Park Theatre, and it was not long before the play was accepted, with the assurance that it would be produced with suitable magnificence. According to her own account, the contract called for a benefit to be given to Mrs. Mowatt on the third evening, and for a certain percentage of the nightly receipts of the theatre for every performance of the play after it had run a stipulated number of times. Mrs. Mowatt was naïve in the contemplation of her initial step as a dramatist. Of Simpson's acceptance, she makes the following confession:

I very quietly asked myself whether I was awake. It took some time, and needed some practical experiments upon my own sensibilities, before I could feel assured that I was not enjoying a pleasant dream. I was almost too much surprised to be elated.

Evidently, it was not the theatrical custom of the Park Theatre, Mr. Barry, the stage-manager, being a wise man, to conduct open rehearsal. The fact is, Mrs. Mowatt did not attend rehearsals of "Fashion" until the day before the opening performance. Then it was that she became anxious. "It is an author's privilege to attend the rehearsal of his own productions", she said, "his acknowledged seat being at the Manager's table upon the stage."

She and Mr. Mowatt were introduced by Mr. Blake, the "box-keeper" of the Park Theatre, and thereupon, in her autobiographical account, follows Mrs. Mowatt's first impressions of a stage rehearsal beneath the glare of stage lights. If this was the day before the opening performance, the actors must have been slow indeed in the learning of their lines, for Mrs. Mowatt says, "Every actor held his part to which he referred constantly."

"Fashion" was first presented at the New York Park Theatre, on March 24, 1845, and it was with some misgivings that Mrs. Mowatt took a seat in the box, her "anxious heart" being overtaxed by the fact of the "gloomy rehearsal on the day previous."

The prologue was written by Epes Sargent (in whose play, "Velasco", both Mrs. Mowatt and E. L. Davenport appeared), and, in its spirit, it excellently well displayed the prejudice theatre audiences of the day held against the native drama, which made them accept anything of a London stamp as being perfect. The fact is, American actors, going abroad at this period, always wrote back home that they were being discriminated against because of their Yankee crudeness. Forrest's fight with Macready was on that score. There was tremendous ill-feeling existent between the American and English actor. When Davenport joined forces with Mrs. Mowatt, and went to London with her play, he was continually flaunting his native characteristics in the face of the English, his pride being repeatedly ruffled by the slurs put upon him because he was an American actor. The consequence is, when Epes Sargent said in his prologue,

"Bah! home-made calicoes are well enough,
But home-made dramas *must* be stupid stuff,
Had it the *London* stamp, 'twould do—but then,
For plays, we lack the manners and the men!"

he was reflecting some of the spirit of the moment, some of the international strain which resulted in Dickens's "American Notes" and Lowell's essay, "On a Certain Condescension in Foreigners."

There was another point brought out by Epes Sargent, to

which we have already referred, and which may here be quoted without comment:

"*Fashion!* what's here? (*Reads.*) It never can succeed!
What! from a woman's pen? It takes a man
To write a comedy—no woman can."

With all the modesty of the novitiate, Mrs. Mowatt claims that it ("Fashion") could not have succeeded had it not been for the wonderful acting of Chippendale as *Adam Trueman,* the bluff old farmer; or of Skerrett as *Zeke,* and so on throughout the entire cast.

The next morning, rehearsal was called for "cutting". Attended by Mr. Mowatt, the author of "Fashion" for the first time in her life went upon the stage, the dress rehearsal having been witnessed from the auditorium. In a most unaffected way, Mrs. Mowatt relates that "Mr. Barry arranged the 'cuts', requesting my approval in a manner which left me very little alternative."

It was soon after the opening that Poe, with the carefulness which always marked him as a reviewer, wrote to Mrs. Mowatt, asking her the loan of the script of "Fashion", and received from her the following note:

Thursday Evening (1845)

Edgar A. Poe, Esqr.,—(I regret that) I have not a more legible manuscript of the Comedy to submit to your perusal, or even one containing all the corrections made at the suggestion of critical advisers. The only fair copy is in the hands of the managers, and that I could not procure. Your criticisms will be prized—I am sorry that they could not have been made before preparations for the performance of the Comedy had progressed so far.

Will you have the goodness to return the manuscript at your earliest convenience, addressed James Mowatt, care Messrs. Judd & Taylor, No. 2 Astor House?

Respectfully yrs, &c.

(Signature missing)

4th Avenue 5 doors above
Twentieth Street.
   Anna Cora Mowatt.
      (Endorse.)

Regarding the third evening of "Fashion", the benefit called for in the contract or agreement, Mrs. Mowatt writes the following:

On the occasion, the house was literally crammed from pit to dome. Owing to the judicious cutting, the performance was more rapid than on the first night, and went off with even greater spirit. At the falling of the curtain, there was a call for the author. This I had anticipated, and, instead of bowing from a private box, according to the established usage, I sent Mr. Barry a few lines expressive of my thanks, and desired him to deliver them before the curtain. "Mr. Barry then came forward" (said one of the newspapers the next morning), "and spoke as follows:

"LADIES AND GENTLEMEN: I am commissioned by Mrs. Mowatt to offer you her sincere and most grateful acknowledgments for the favour with which you have received this comedy. She desires me to express the hope that you will take it rather as an earnest of what she may hereafter do than as a fair specimen of what American dramatic literature ought to be. (*Loud applause*.) With your permission, ladies and gentlemen, I will announce the comedy of 'Fashion' every night until further notice.' (*Loud and continued applause*.)"

Then "Fashion" began its successful career, so successful, indeed, that, during its run in New York, it was likewise given a production in Philadelphia, under the excellent stage-management of W. Rufus Blake, at the Walnut Street Theatre, where Mr. Blake, himself famed for his old men, enacted the part of *Adam Trueman*. With her accustomed generosity, Mrs. Mowatt praised each one of the cast in her "Autobiography".

It was on this first night that Mrs. Mowatt, in her box, was given a white satin play bill, printed in gold letters, after the style of the day, whenever a Jubilee occasion occurred; and it was here that, for the first time, she was obliged to rise and curtsey to an enthusiastic house. She confesses, "I little thought that in less than two months I should curtsey to an audience from the stage of that very theatre."

There is no need to go into the small details of the stage history of "Fashion". These may be found, not only in Mrs. Mowatt's confessions, but in the records connected with the life of E. L. Davenport. We know, however, that though it was received with *éclat,* and though Edgar Allan Poe, writing for the *Broadway Journal,* as dramatic critic, went repeatedly to see the play in order not to miss any of its good points, he was finally obliged to write in a derogatory manner, on March 29, 1845, condemning it for its lack of originality and invention, and disliking its theatricalism, which to him took the place of real dramatic quality. Of the play he also wrote:

> We are really ashamed to record our deliberate opinion that if "Fashion" succeed at all (and we think, upon the whole, that it will) it will owe the greater portion of its success to the very carpets, the very ottomans, the very chandeliers, and the very conservatories that gained so decided a popularity for that most inane and utterly despicable of all modern comedies,— the "London Assurance" of Boucicault.

And once more he comments:

> We presume that not even the author of a plot such as this would be disposed to claim for it anything on the score of originality or invention. Had it, indeed, been designed as a burlesque upon the arrant conventionality of stage incidents in general, we should have regarded it as a palpable hit. . . . It will no longer do to copy, even with absolute accuracy, the whole tone of even so ingenious and really spirited a thing as the "School for Scandal". It was comparatively good in its day, but it would be positively bad at the present day, and imitations of it are inadmissable at any day.

On April 5th, 1845, Poe, considering "Fashion" again, began his analysis in this manner:

> So deeply have we felt interested in the question of "Fashion's" success or failure, that we have been to see it every night since its first production; making careful

note of its merits and defects as they were more and more distinctly developed in the gradually perfected representation of the play.

We mention this, not so much for the sake of discovering any great shifting of opinion, as for the purpose of illustrating the conscientiousness of Poe, the dramatic critic—a conscientiousness which has certainly died out of the profession since that day!

Whether or not the success of "Fashion" brought to Mrs. Mowatt many offers from the theatre managers is not of great import. Certain it is, however, that her attention was more and more being drawn to the stage, and that pressure was being brought to bear upon her, since she had won for herself unstinted praise as a reader, to try her own hand at acting. There is a general impression that Mrs. Mowatt herself played in "Fashion" during these initial days. But there was no part in this drama that attracted her sufficiently to undertake it, except on one or two rare occasions, after she had determined to go upon the stage: for instance, in Philadelphia, for the benefit of Mr. Blake, and at the New York Park Theatre, on May 15, 1846.

Her health at the time was not of the best, and this in a way limited her public engagements. However, her attitude toward the theatre,—an attitude, which the society of the time had taken, about the social inequality of actors,—was changing considerably, probably because of her personal association with members of her companies at the Park Theatre and at the Walnut Street Theatre.

Nevertheless, Mrs. Mowatt had much to consider and to sacrifice in becoming an actress, because of the fact that she was so closely connected with society life. This did not deter her, however, once she had squared things with her own conscience, and she was abetted by Mr. Mowatt, whose interest in the theatre was very pronounced. The consequence is, after careful weighing of the matter, she made her first appearance on the stage, June, 1845, as *Pauline,* in "The Lady of Lyons". Poe went to see her in the play, and gives this description of her:

Her figure is slight—even fragile—but eminently graceful. Her face is a remarkably fine one, and of that precise character best adapted to the stage. The forehead is the least prepossessing feature, although it is by no means an unintellectual one. The eyes are grey, brilliant, and expressive, without being full. The nose is well formed, with the Roman curve, and strongly indicative of energy; this quality is also shown in the prominence of the chin. The mouth is somewhat large, with brilliant and even teeth, and flexible lips, capable of the most effective variations of expression. A more radiantly beautiful smile we never remember having seen. Mrs. Mowatt has also the personal advantage of a profusion of rich auburn hair.

In 1847, she appeared in a new play of hers, entitled "Armand; or, The Peer and the Peasant", the Park Theatre (September 27, 1847), and during the year she went to England, where, as I have said, she was ably supported by that estimable American actor, E. L. Davenport. Together, in 1846, they had played *Romeo* and *Juliet, Benedick* and *Beatrice, Fazio* and *Bianca,* touring the South and acting as far as Mobile, Alabama, and New Orleans. It was during their European trip that Mrs. Mowatt's acting came under the observation of Macready, and one may obtain from his diaries and reminiscences comments on her work. It was likewise on this trip that she produced "Armand", January 18, 1849, and "Fashion", January 9, 1850.

This, therefore, is the stage history of "Fashion", which Mrs. Mowatt, as well as Poe, confessed is not marked by any undue literary quality, but which certainly has reflected, in its dialogue, the quaint manners of the period of the forties. The first act was revived in New York, in the spring of 1917, by the New York Centre of the Drama League of America, and was quite the most successful part of a long program—successful because the actors tried to reproduce the artificial stage manners of the times. This artificiality was largely due to the "asides" which were delivered across the foot-lights in confidence to the audience, in the burlesque qualities exploited in the character of *Zeke,* a negro with dialect as impossible as the negro dialect then in vogue among American writers. Examples of it are to be found in "Uncle Tom's Cabin".

In its entirety "Fashion" was given at the Provincetown Playhouse, Macdougal Street, New York, during the season of 1923–24, and met with general commendation. It was arranged after the manner of "The Beggar's Opera", and the contemporary music, together with the accentuated humor of the "asides" and the glaring "unreality" of the scenery, at once were measure of its weakness and its vitality.

The contrasts in "Fashion" are accentuated beyond reasonable proportions, with the result that *Adam Trueman,* bluff in manner and homely in speech, is a cartoon of American character, lacking in any subtlety, a character fashioned after the model of the time, used by both Tom Taylor and Dion Boucicault in England. It was a long while before the American Theatre could escape the stage American. In like manner, it took the Irish renaissance, led by Yeats, Synge and Lady Gregory, a long while to obliterate the stage Irishman, perpetuated by Lever and Boucicault.

In giving an impression of Mrs. Mowatt, we must not lose sight of her intellectual worth. She was a woman of rare abilities, one who never allowed the artistic to escape her notice or commendation, one who was fair in all her estimates of art conditions. She was a traveller of true worth, as is seen by her accounts of Italian life and legends (1870); her "Autobiography of an Actress" (1854) is filled with reflections of her professional associations, as is also her "Mimic Life, or, Before and Behind the Curtain", published in 1855. One could write an entire thesis about "Fashion", which would bring into play all the manners of the epoch, and would draw for inspiration from much of the literary life of New York during 1845.

The text of the play is based on the first London edition.

PROLOGUE TO FASHION

Written by Epes Sargent.

(Enter a Gentleman—Mr. Crisp—reading a newspaper.)

" '*Fashion, A Comedy.*' I'll go; but stay—
Now I read farther, 'tis a *native* play!
Bah! home-made calicoes are well enough,
But home-made dramas must be stupid stuff.
Had it the *London* stamp, 'twould do—but then,
For plays, we lack the manners and the men!"

Thus speaks *one* critic.   Hear *another's* creed:—
" '*Fashion!*'—What's here? (*Reads.*) It never can succeed!
What! from a *woman's* pen? It takes a *man*
To write a comedy—no woman can."

Well, sir, and what say *you?* And why that frown?
His eyes uprolled, he lays the paper down:—
"Here! take," he says, "the unclean thing away!
'Tis tainted with a notice of a *play!*"

But, sir!—but, gentlemen!—you, sir, who think
No comedy can flow from *native* ink,—
Are we such *perfect* monsters, or such *dull,*
That wit no traits for ridicule can cull?
Have we no follies here to be redressed?
No vices gibetted? no crimes confessed?

"But then, a female hand can't lay the lash on!"
"How know you *that*, sir, when the theme is 'Fashion'?"

And now, come forth, thou man of sanctity!
How shall I venture a reply to thee?
The *Stage*—what is it, though beneath *thy* ban,

But a *Daguerreotype* of life and man?
Arraign poor human nature, if you will,
But let the *Drama* have her mission still!
Let her, with honest purpose, still reflect
The faults which keen-eyed Satire may detect.
For there *be* men, who fear not an hereafter,
Yet tremble at the Hell of public laughter!

Friends, from these scoffers we appeal to you!
Condemn the *false,* but O! applaud the *true.*
Grant that *some* wit may grow on native soil,
And Art's fair fabric rise from *woman's* toil—
While we exhibit but to reprehend
The social vices, 'tis for *you* to mend!

FASHION

Dramatis Personæ

Adam Trueman, a Farmer from Catteraugus.
Count Jolimaitre, a fashionable European Importation.
Colonel Howard, an Officer in the U. S. Army.
Mr. Tiffany, a New York Merchant.
T. Tennyson Twinkle, a Modern Poet.
Augustus Fogg, a Drawing-Room Appendage.
Snobson, a rare species of Confidential Clerk.
Zeke, a coloured Servant.

Mrs. Tiffany, a Lady who imagines herself fashionable.
Prudence, a Maiden Lady of a certain age.
Millinette, a French Lady's Maid.
Gertrude, a Governess.
Seraphina Tiffany, a Belle.
        Ladies and Gentlemen of the Ball-Room.

Cast of Characters

As produced at the Royal Olympic Theatre,
January 9, 1850, under the direction of
Mr. George Ellis, Stage Manager.

Adam Trueman...... Mr. Davenport. (Mr. Chippendale)
Count Jolimaitre..... Mr. A. Wigan. (Mr. Crisp)
Colonel Howard ..... Mr. Belton. (Mr. Dyott)
Mr. Tiffany .... Mr. J. Johnstone. (Mr. Barry)
Twinkle .... Mr. Kinloch. (Mr. DeWalden)
Fogg .... Mr. J. Howard. (Mr. J. Howard)
Snobson .... Mr. H. Scharf. (Mr. Fisher)
Zeke .... Mr. J. Herbert. (Mr. Skerrett)
Mrs. Tiffany........ Mrs. H. Marston. (Mrs. Barry)
Prudence .... Mrs. Parker. (Mrs. Knight)
Millinette .... Mrs. A. Wigan. (Mrs. Dyott)
Gertrude .... Miss F. Vining. (Miss Ellis)
Seraphina .... Miss Gougenheim. (Miss Horn)

The names in parenthesis constitute the cast of "Fashion",
as given at the New York Theatre, March 24, 1845.

PREFACE.

The Comedy of *Fashion* was intended as a good-natured satire upon some of the follies incident to a new country, where foreign dross sometimes passes for gold, while native gold is cast aside as dross; where the vanities rather than the virtues of other lands are too often imitated, and where the stamp of *Fashion* gives currency even to the coinage of vice.

The reception with which the Comedy was favoured proves that the picture represented was not a highly exaggerated one.

It was first produced at the Park Theatre, New York, in March, 1845.

The splendid manner in which the play was put upon the stage, and the combined efforts of an extremely talented company, ensured it a long continued success. It was afterwards received with the same indulgence in all the principal cities of the United States, for which the authoress is doubtless indebted to the proverbial gallantry of Americans to a countrywoman.   A. C. M.

LONDON,
January, 1850.

COSTUMES.

ADAM TRUEMAN.—First dress: A farmer's rough overcoat, coarse blue trousers, heavy boots, broad-brimmed hat, dark coloured neckerchief, stout walking-stick, large bandanna tied loosely around his neck.—Second dress: Dark grey old-fashioned coat, black and yellow waistcoat, trousers as before.—Third dress: Black old-fashioned dress coat, black trousers, white vest, white cravat.

COUNT JOLIMAITRE.—First dress: Dark frock coat, light blue trousers, patent leather boots, gay coloured vest and scarf, profusion of jewellery, light overcoat.—Second dress: Full evening dress; last scene, travelling cap and cloak.

MR. TIFFANY.—First dress: Dark coat, vest, and trousers.—Second dress: Full evening dress.

MR. TWINKLE.—First dress: Green frock coat, white vest and trousers, green and white scarf.—Second dress: Full evening dress.

MR. FOGG.—First dress: Entire black suit.—Second dress: Full evening dress, same colour.

SNOBSON.—First dress: Blue Albert coat with brass buttons, yellow vest, red and black cravat, broad plaid trousers.—Second dress: Evening dress.

COL. HOWARD.—First dress: Blue undress frock coat and cap, white trousers.—Second dress: Full military uniform.

ZEKE.—Red and blue livery, cocked hat, &c.

MRS. TIFFANY.—First dress: Extravagant modern dress.—Second dress: Hat, feathers, and mantle, with the above.—Third dress: Morning dress.—Fourth dress: Rich ball dress.

SERAPHINA.—First dress: Rich modern dress, lady's tarpaulin on one side of head.—Second dress: Morning dress.—Third dress: Handsome ball dress, profusion of ornaments and flowers.—Fourth dress: Bonnet and mantle.

GERTRUDE.—First dress: White muslin.—Second dress: Ball dress, very simple.

MILLINETTE.—Lady's Maid's dress, very gay.

PRUDENCE.—Black satin, very narrow in the skirt, tight sleeves, white muslin apron, neckerchief of the same, folded over bosom, old-fashioned cap, high top and broad frill, and red ribbands.

FASHION

ACT I.

Scene I.

A splendid Drawing-Room in the House of Mrs. Tiffany. *Open folding doors centre, discovering a Conservatory. On either side glass windows down to the ground. Doors on right and left. Mirror, couches, ottomans, a table with albums, &c., beside it an arm-chair.* Millinette *dusting furniture, &c.* Zeke *in a dashing livery, scarlet coat, &c.*

Zeke. Dere's a coat to take de eyes ob all Broadway! Ah! Missy, it am de fixins dat make de natural *born* gemman. A libery for ever! Dere's a pair ob insuppressibles to 'stonish de colored population.

Millinette. Oh, *oui,* Monsieur Zeke. [*Very politely.*] I not *comprend* one word he say! [*Aside.*]

Zeke. I tell 'ee what, Missy, I'm 'stordinary glad to find dis a bery 'spectabul like situation! Now as you've made de acquaintance ob dis here family, and dere you've had a supernumerary advantage ob me—seeing dat I only receibed my appointment dis morning. What I wants to know is your publicated opinion, privately expressed, ob de domestic circle.

Millinette. You mean vat *espèce,* vat kind of personnes are Monsieur and Madame Tiffany? Ah! Monsieur is not de same ting as Madame,—not at all.

Zeke. Well, I s'pose he ain't altogether.

Millinette. Monsieur is man of business,—Madame is lady of fashion. Monsieur make the money,—Madame spend it. Monsieur nobody at all,—Madame everybody altogether. Ah! Monsieur Zeke, de money is all dat is *necessaire* in dis country to make one lady of fashion. Oh! it is quite anoder ting in *la belle France!*

539

ZEKE. A bery lucifer explanation. Well, now we've disposed ob de heads of de family, who come next?

MILLINETTE. First, dere is Mademoiselle Seraphina Tiffany. Mademoiselle is not at all one proper *personne.* Mademoiselle Seraphina is one coquette. Dat is not de mode in *la belle France;* de ladies, dere, never learn *la coquetrie* until dey do get one husband.

ZEKE. I tell 'ee what, Missy, I disreprobate dat proceeding altogeder!

MILLINETTE. Vait! I have not tell you all *la famille* yet. Dere is Ma'mselle Prudence—Madame's sister, one very *bizarre* personne. Den dere is Ma'mselle Gertrude, but she not anybody at all; she only teach Mademoiselle Seraphina *la musique.*

ZEKE. Well now, Missy, what's your own special defunctions?

MILLINETTE. I not understand, Monsieur Zeke.

ZEKE. Den I'll amplify. What's de nature ob your exclusive services?

MILLINETTE. *Ah, oui! je comprend.* I am Madame's *femme de chambre*—her lady's maid, Monsieur Zeke. I teach Madame *les modes de Paris,* and Madame set de fashion for all New York. You see, Monsieur Zeke, dat it is me, *moi-même,* dat do lead de fashion for all de American *beau monde!*

ZEKE. Yah! yah! yah! I hab de idea by de heel. Well now, p'raps you can 'lustrify my officials?

MILLINETTE. Vat you will have to do? Oh! much tings, much tings. You vait on de table,—you tend de door,—you clean de boots,—you run de errands,—you drive de carriage, —you rub de horses,—you take care of de flowers,—you carry de water,—you help cook de dinner,—you wash de dishes,—and den you always remember to do everyting I tell you to!

ZEKE. Wheugh, am dat *all?*

MILLINETTE. All I can tink of now. To-day is Madame's day of reception, and all her grand friends do make her one *petite* visit. You mind run fast ven de bell do ring.

ZEKE. Run? If it wasn't for dese superfluminous trimmings, I tell 'ee what, Missy, I'd run—

MRS. TIFFANY. [*Outside.*] Millinette!

MILLINETTE. Here comes Madame! You better go, Monsieur Zeke.

ZEKE. Look ahea, Massa Zeke, doesn't dis open rich! [*Aside.*] [*Exit* ZEKE.

Enter MRS. TIFFANY *right, dressed in the most extravagant height of fashion.*

MRS. TIFFANY. Is everything in order, Millinette? Ah! very elegant, very elegant indeed! There is a *jenny-says-quoi* look about this furniture,—an air of fashion and gentility perfectly bewitching. Is there not, Millinette?

MILLINETTE. Oh, *oui,* Madame!

MRS. TIFFANY. But where is Miss Seraphina? It is twelve o'clock; our visitors will be pouring in, and she has not made her appearance. But I hear that nothing is more fashionable than to keep people waiting.—None but vulgar persons pay any attention to punctuality. Is it not so, Millinette?

MILLINETTE. Quite *comme il faut.*—Great personnes always do make little personnes wait, Madame.

MRS. TIFFANY. This mode of receiving visitors only upon one specified day of the week is a most convenient custom! It saves the trouble of keeping the house continually in order and of being always dressed. I flatter myself that *I* was the first to introduce it amongst the New York *ee-light.* You are quite sure that it is strictly a Parisian mode, Millinette?

MILLINETTE. Oh, *oui,* Madame; entirely *mode de Paris.*

MRS. TIFFANY. This girl is worth her weight in gold. [*Aside.*] Millinette, how do you say *arm-chair* in French?

MILLINETTE. *Fauteuil,* Madame.

MRS. TIFFANY. *Fo-tool!* That has a foreign—an out-of-the-wayish sound that is perfectly charming—and so genteel! There is something about our American words decidedly vulgar. *Fowtool!* how refined. *Fowtool! Arm-chair!* what a difference!

MILLINETTE. Madame have one charmante pronunciation. *Fowtool!* [*Mimicking aside.*] Charmante, Madame!

MRS. TIFFANY. Do you think so, Millinette? Well, I

believe I have. But a woman of refinement and of fashion can always accommodate herself to everything foreign! And a week's study of that invaluable work—"*French without a Master*," has made me quite at home in the court language of Europe! But where is the new valet? I'm rather sorry that he is black, but to obtain a white American for a domestic is almost impossible; and they call this a free country! What did you say was the name of this new servant, Millinette?

MILLINETTE. He do say his name is Monsieur Zeke.

MRS. TIFFANY. Ezekiel, I suppose. Zeke! Dear me, such a vulgar name will compromise the dignity of the whole family. Can you not suggest something more aristocratic, Millinette? Something *French!*

MILLINETTE. *Oh, oui,* Madame; *Adolph* is one very fine name.

MRS. TIFFANY. A-dolph! Charming! Ring the bell, Millinette! [MILLINETTE *rings the bell.*] I will change his name immediately, besides giving him a few directions. [*Enter* ZEKE, *left.* MRS. TIFFANY *addresses him with great dignity.*] Your name, I hear, is *Ezekiel.*—I consider it too plebeian an appellation to be uttered in my presence. In future you are called A-dolph. Don't reply,—never interrupt me when I am speaking. A-dolph, as my guests arrive, I desire that you will inquire the name of every person, and then announce it in a loud, clear tone. *That* is the fashion in Paris.

[MILLINETTE *retires up the stage.*

ZEKE. Consider de office discharged, Missus.

[*Speaking very loudly.*

MRS. TIFFANY. Silence! Your business is to obey and not to talk.

ZEKE. I'm dumb, Missus!

MRS. TIFFANY. [*Pointing up stage.*] A-dolph, place that *fow-tool* behind me.

ZEKE. [*Looking about him.*] I habn't got dat far in de dictionary yet. No matter, a genus gets his learning by nature. [*Takes up the table and places it behind* MRS. TIFFANY, *then expresses in dumb show great satisfaction.* MRS. TIFFANY, *as she goes to sit, discovers the mistake.*

MRS. TIFFANY. You dolt! Where have you lived not to

know that *fow-tool* is the French for *arm-chair?* What ignorance! Leave the room this instant.

[MRS. TIFFANY *draws forward an arm-chair and sits.* MILLINETTE *comes forward suppressing her merriment at* ZEKE'S *mistake and removes the table.*

ZEKE. Dem's de defects ob not having a libery education.
[*Exit left.*

PRUDENCE *peeps in, right.*

PRUDENCE. I wonder if any of the fine folks have come yet. Not a soul,—I knew they hadn't. There's Betsy all alone. [*Walks in.*] Sister Betsy!

MRS. TIFFANY. Prudence! how many times have I desired you to call me *Elizabeth?* *Betsy* is the height of vulgarity.

PRUDENCE. Oh! I forgot. Dear me, how spruce we do look here, to be sure,—everything in first rate style now, Betsy. [MRS. TIFFANY *looks at her angrily.*] *Elizabeth* I mean. Who would have thought, when you and I were sitting behind that little mahogany-coloured counter, in Canal Street, making up flashy hats and caps—

MRS. TIFFANY. Prudence, what *do* you mean? Millinette, leave the room.

MILLINETTE. *Oui,* Madame.

[MILLINETTE *pretends to arrange the books upon a side table, but lingers to listen.*

PRUDENCE. But I always predicted it,—I always told you so, Betsy,—I always said you were destined to rise above your station!

MRS. TIFFANY. Prudence! Prudence! have I not told you that—

PRUDENCE. No, Betsy, it was *I* that told *you,* when we used to buy our silks and ribbons of Mr. Antony Tiffany— *"talking Tony"* you know we used to call him, and when you always put on the finest bonnet in our shop to go to his,— and when you staid so long smiling and chattering with him, I always told you that *something* would grow out of it—and didn't it?

MRS. TIFFANY. Millinette, send Seraphina here instantly. Leave the room.

MILLINETTE. *Oui,* Madame. So dis Americaine ladi of fashion vas one *milliner?* Oh, vat a fine country for *les*

merchandes des modes! I shall send for all my relation by
de next packet! [*Aside.*]   [*Exit* MILLINETTE.

MRS. TIFFANY. Prudence! never let me hear you mention
this subject again. Forget what we *have* been, it is enough
to remember that we *are* of the *upper ten thousand!*

[PRUDENCE *goes left and sits down.*]

Enter SERAPHINA, *very extravagantly dressed.*

MRS. TIFFANY. How bewitchingly you look, my dear!
Does Millinette say that that head-dress is strictly Parisian?

SERAPHINA. Oh yes, Mamma, all the rage! They call it
a *lady's tarpaulin,* and it is the exact pattern of one worn
by the Princess Clementina at the last court ball.

MRS. TIFFANY. Now, Seraphina my dear, don't be too
particular in your attentions to gentlemen not eligible.
There is Count Jolimaitre, decidedly the most fashionable
foreigner in town,—and so refined,—so much accustomed to
associate with the first nobility in his own country that he
can hardly tolerate the vulgarity of Americans in general.
You may devote yourself to him. Mrs. Proudacre is dying
to become acquainted with him. By the by, if she or her
daughters should happen to drop in, be sure you don't introduce them to the Count. It is not the fashion in Paris to
introduce—Millinette told me so.

Enter ZEKE.

ZEKE. [*In a very loud voice.*] Mister T. Tennyson
Twinkle!

MRS. TIFFANY. Show him up.   [*Exit* ZEKE.

PRUDENCE. I must be running away.   [*Going.*

MRS. TIFFANY. Mr. T. Tennyson Twinkle—a very literary
young man and a sweet poet! It is all the rage to patronize
poets! Quick, Seraphina, hand me that magazine.—Mr.
Twinkle writes for it.

[SERAPHIA *hands the magazine;* MRS. TIFFANY *seats
herself in an arm-chair and opens the book.*

PRUDENCE. [*Returning.*] There's Betsy trying to make
out that reading without her spectacles. [*Takes a pair of
spectacles out of her pocket and hands them to* MRS. TIF-
FANY.] There, Betsy, I knew you were going to ask for them.
Ah! they're a blessing when one is growing old!

MRS. TIFFANY. What do you mean, Prudence? A woman of fashion *never* grows old! Age is always out of fashion.

PRUDENCE. Oh, dear! what a delightful thing it is to be fashionable. [*Exit* PRUDENCE. MRS. TIFFANY *resumes her seat.*

Enter TWINKLE. *He salutes* SERAPHINA.

TWINKLE. Fair Seraphina! the sun itself grows dim,
       Unless you aid his light and shine on him!

SERAPHINA. Ah! Mr. Twinkle, there is no such thing as answering you.

TWINKLE. [*Looks around and perceives* MRS. TIFFANY.] The "New Monthly Vernal Galaxy." Reading my verses, by all that's charming! Sensible woman! I won't interrupt her. [*Aside.*]

MRS. TIFFANY. [*Rising and coming forward.*] Ah! Mr. Twinkle, is that you? I was perfectly *abimé* at the perusal of your very *distingué* verses.

TWINKLE. I am overwhelmed, Madam. Permit me. [*Taking the magazine.*] Yes, they do read tolerably. And you must take into consideration, ladies, the rapidity with which they were written. Four minutes and a half by the stop watch! The true test of a poet is the *velocity* with which he composes. Really, they do look very prettily, and they read tolerably—*quite* tolerably—*very* tolerably,—especially the first verse. [*Reads.*] "To Seraphina T————."

SERAPHINA. Oh! Mr. Twinkle!

TWINKLE. [*Reads.*] "Around my heart"—

MRS. TIFFANY. How touching! Really, Mr. Twinkle, quite tender!

TWINKLE. [*Recommencing.*] "Around my heart"—

MRS. TIFFANY. Oh, I must tell you, Mr. Twinkle! I heard the other day that poets were the aristocrats of literature. That's one reason I like them, for I do dote on all aristocracy!

TWINKLE. Oh, Madam, how flattering! Now pray lend me your ears! [*Reads.*]
       "Around my heart thou weavest"—

SERAPHINA. That is such a *sweet* commencement, Mr. Twinkle!

TWINKLE. [*Aside.*] I wish she wouldn't interrupt me!
[*Reads.*] "Around my heart thou weavest a spell"—

MRS. TIFFANY. Beautiful! But excuse me one moment,
while I say a word to Seraphina! Don't be too affable, my
dear! Poets are very ornamental appendages to the drawing
room, but they are always as poor as their own verses.
They don't make eligible husbands! [*Aside to* SERAPHINA.]

TWINKLE. [*Aside.*] Confound their interruptions! My
dear Madam, unless you pay the utmost attention you cannot
catch the ideas. Are you ready? Well, now you shall hear
it to the end! [*Reads.*]—

"Around my heart thou weavest a spell
"Whose"—

Enter ZEKE.

ZEKE. Mister Augustus Fogg! A bery misty lookin'
young gemman? [*Aside.*]

MRS. TIFFANY. Show him up, A-dolph! [*Exit* ZEKE.

TWINKLE. This is too much!

SERAPHINA. Exquisite verses, Mr. Twinkle,—exquisite!

TWINKLE. Ah, lovely Seraphina! your smile of approval
transports me to the summit of Olympus.

SERAPHINA. Then I must frown, for I would not send
you so far away.

TWINKLE. Enchantress! It's all over with her. [*Aside.*]
[*Retire up right and converse.*

MRS. TIFFANY. Mr. Fogg belongs to one of our oldest
families,—to be sure he is the most difficult person in the
world to entertain, for he never takes the trouble to talk, and
never notices anything or anybody,—but then I hear that
nothing is considered so vulgar as to betray any emotion,
or to attempt to render oneself agreeable!

Enter MR. FOGG, *fashionably attired but in very dark clothes.*

FOGG. [*Bowing stiffly.*] Mrs. Tiffany, your most obedient.
Miss Seraphina, yours. How d'ye do, Twinkle?

MRS. TIFFANY. Mr. Fogg, how do you do? Fine weather,
—delightful, isn't it?

FOGG. I am indifferent to weather, Madam.

MRS. TIFFANY. Been to the opera, Mr. Fogg? I hear that
the *bow monde* make their *debutt* there every evening.

Fogg. I consider operas a bore, Madam.

Seraphina. [*Advancing.*] You must hear Mr. Twinkle's verses, Mr. Fogg!

Fogg. I am indifferent to verses, Miss Seraphina.

Seraphina. But Mr. Twinkle's verses are addressed to me!

Twinkle. Now pay attention, Fogg! [*Reads.*]—
"Around my heart thou weavest a spell
"Whose magic I"—

Enter Zeke.

Zeke. Mister—No, he say he ain't no Mister—

Twinkle. "Around my heart thou weavest a spell
"Whose magic I can never tell!"

Mrs. Tiffany. Speak in a loud, clear tone, A-dolph!

Twinkle. This is terrible!

Zeke. Mister Count Jolly-made-her!

Mrs. Tiffany. Count Jolimaitre! Good gracious! Zeke, Zeke—A-dolph, I mean.—Dear me, what a mistake! [*Aside.*] Set that chair out of the way,—put that table back. Seraphina, my dear, are you all in order? Dear me! dear me! Your dress is so tumbled! [*Arranges her dress.*] What are you grinning at? [*To* Zeke.] Beg the Count to *honour* us by walking up! [*Exit* Zeke.] Seraphina, my dear [*aside to her*], remember now what I told you about the Count. He is a man of the highest,—good gracious! I am so flurried; and nothing is so ungenteel as agitation! what will the Count think! Mr. Twinkle, pray stand out of the way! Seraphina, my dear, place yourself on my right! Mr. Fogg, the conservatory—beautiful flowers,—pray amuse yourself in the conservatory.

Fogg. I am indifferent to flowers, Madam.

Mrs. Tiffany. Dear me! the man stands right in the way,—just where the Count must make his *entray!* [*Aside.*] Mr. Fogg,—pray—

Enter Count Jolimaitre, *very dashingly dressed; he wears a moustache.*

Mrs. Tiffany. Oh, Count, this unexpected honour—

Seraphina. Count, this inexpressible pleasure—

COUNT. Beg you won't mention it, Madam! Miss Seraphina, your most devoted!

MRS. TIFFANY. What condescension! [*Aside.*] Count, may I take the liberty to introduce—Good gracious! I forgot. [*Aside.*] Count, I was about to remark that we never introduce in America. All our fashions are foreign, Count.

[TWINKLE, *who has stepped forward to be introduced, shows great indignation.*

COUNT. Excuse me, Madam, our fashions have grown antediluvian before you Americans discover their existence. You are lamentably behind the age—lamentably! 'Pon my honour, a foreigner of refinement finds great difficulty in existing in this provincial atmosphere.

MRS. TIFFANY. How dreadful, Count! I am very much concerned. If there is anything which I can do, Count—

SERAPHINA. Or I, Count, to render your situation less deplorable—

COUNT. Ah! I find but one redeeming charm in America —the superlative loveliness of the feminine portion of creation,—and the wealth of their obliging papas. [*Aside.*]

MRS. TIFFANY. How flattering! Ah! Count, I am afraid you will turn the head of my simple girl here. She is a perfect child of nature, Count.

COUNT. Very possibly, for though you American women are quite charming, yet, demme, there's a deal of native rust to rub off!

MRS. TIFFANY. *Rust?* Good gracious, Count! where do you find any rust?   [*Looking about the room.*

COUNT. How very unsophisticated!

MRS. TIFFANY. Count, I am so much ashamed,—pray excuse me! Although a lady of large fortune, and one, Count, who can boast of the highest connections, I blush to confess that I have never travelled,—while you, Count, I presume are at home in all the courts of Europe.

COUNT. *Courts?* Eh? Oh, yes, Madam, very true. I believe I am pretty well known in some of the courts of Europe— [*aside*] police courts. In a word, Madam, I had seen enough of civilized life—wanted to refresh myself by a sight of barbarous countries and customs—had my choice between the Sandwich Islands and New York—chose New York!

MRS. TIFFANY. How complimentary to our country! And, Count, I have no doubt you speak every conceivable language? You talk English like a native.

COUNT. Eh, what? Like a native? Oh, ah, demme, yes, I am something of an Englishman. Passed one year and eight months with the Duke of Wellington, six months with Lord Brougham, two and a half with Count d'Orsay—knew them all more intimately than their best friends—no heroes to me—hadn't a secret from me, I assure you,—*especially of the toilet.* [*Aside.*]

MRS. TIFFANY. Think of that, my dear! Lord Wellington and Duke Broom! [*Aside to* SERAPHINA.]

SERAPHINA. And only think of Count d'Orsay, Mamma! [*Aside to* MRS. TIFFANY.] I am so wild to see Count d'Orsay!

COUNT. Oh! a mere man milliner. Very little refinement out of Paris! Why, at the very last dinner given at Lord— Lord Knowswho, would you believe it, Madam, there was an individual present who wore a *black* cravat and took *soup twice!*

MRS. TIFFANY. How shocking! the sight of him would have spoilt my appetite! Think what a great man he must be, my dear, to despise lords and counts in that way. [*Aside to* SERAPHINA.] I must leave them together. [*Aside.*] Mr. Twinkle, your arm. I have some really very *foreign exotics* to show you.

TWINKLE. I fly at your command. I wish all her exotics were blooming in their native soil!

[*Aside, and glancing at the* COUNT.

MRS. TIFFANY. Mr. Fogg, will you accompany us? My conservatory is well worthy a visit. It cost an immense sum of money.

FOGG. I am indifferent to conservatories, Madam; flowers are such a bore!

MRS. TIFFANY. I shall take no refusal. Conservatories are all the rage,—I could not exist without mine! Let me show you,—let me show you.

[*Places her arm through* MR. FOGG'S, *without his consent. Exeunt* MRS. TIFFANY, FOGG, *and* TWINKLE *into the conservatory, where they are seen walking about.*

SERAPHINA. America, then, has no charms for you, Count?

COUNT. Excuse me,—some exceptions. I find you, for instance, particularly charming! Can't say I admire your country. Ah! if you had ever breathed the exhilarating air of Paris, ate creams at Tortoni's, dined at the Café Royale, or if you had lived in London—felt at home at St. James's, and every afternoon driven a couple of Lords and a Duchess through Hyde Park, you would find America—where you have no kings, queens, lords, nor ladies—insupportable!

SERAPHINA. Not while there was a Count in it!

Enter ZEKE, *very indignant.*

ZEKE. Where's de Missus?

Enter MRS. TIFFANY, FOGG, *and* TWINKLE, *from the conservatory.*

MRS. TIFFANY. Whom do you come to announce, A-dolph?

ZEKE. He said he wouldn't trust me—no, not eben wid so much as his name; so I wouldn't trust him up stairs; den he ups wid *his stick* and I *cuts mine.*

MRS. TIFFANY. Some of Mr. Tiffany's vulgar acquaintances. I shall die with shame. [*Aside.*] A-dolph, inform him that I am *not at home.* [*Exit* ZEKE.] My nerves are so shattered, I am ready to sink. Mr. Twinkle, that *fow-tool,* if you please!

TWINKLE. What? What do you wish, Madam?

MRS. TIFFANY. The ignorance of these Americans! [*Aside.*] Count, may I trouble you? That *fow-tool,* if you please!

COUNT. She's not talking English, nor French, but I suppose it's American. [*Aside.*]

TRUEMAN. [*Outside.*] Not at home!

ZEKE. No, Sar—Missus say she's not at home.

TRUEMAN. Out of the way, you grinning nigger!

Enter ADAM TRUEMAN, *dressed as a farmer, a stout cane in his hand, his boots covered with dust.* ZEKE *jumps out of his way as he enters. Exit* ZEKE.

TRUEMAN. Where's this woman that's not *at home* in her own house? May I be shot! if I wonder at it! I shouldn't think she'd ever feel *at home* in such a show-box as this!

[*Looking round.*]

MRS. TIFFANY. What a plebeian looking old farmer! I wonder who he is? [*Aside.*] Sir—[*Advancing very agitatedly.*] What do you mean, sir, by this *ow*dacious conduct? How dare you intrude yourself into my parlor? Do you know who I am, sir? [*With great dignity.*] You are in the presence of Mrs. Tiffany, sir!

TRUEMAN. Antony's wife, eh? Well now, I might have guessed that—ha! ha! ha! for I see you make it a point to carry half your husband's shop upon your back! No matter; that's being a good helpmate—for he carried the whole of it once in a pack on his own shoulders—now you bear a share.

MRS. TIFFANY. How dare you, you impertinent, *ow*dacious, ignorant old man! It's all an invention. You're talking of somebody else. What will the Count think! [*Aside.*]

TRUEMAN. Why, I thought folks had better manners in the city! This is a civil welcome for your husband's old friend, and after my coming all the way from Catteraugus to see you and yours! First a grinning nigger tricked out in scarlet regimentals—

MRS. TIFFANY. Let me tell, you, sir, that liveries are all the fashion!

TRUEMAN. The fashion, are they? To make men wear the *badge of servitude* in a free land,—that's the fashion, is it? Hurrah for republican simplicity! I will venture to say now, that you have your coat-of-arms too!

MRS. TIFFANY. Certainly, sir; you can see it on the panels of my *voyture.*

TRUEMAN. Oh! no need of that. I know what your escutcheon must be! A bandbox *rampant,* with a bonnet *couchant,* and a pedlar's pack *passant!* Ha, ha, ha! that shows both houses united!

MRS. TIFFANY. Sir! you are most profoundly ignorant,—what do you mean by this insolence, sir? How shall I get rid of him? [*Aside.*]

TRUEMAN. [*Looking at* SERAPHINA.] I hope that is not Gertrude! [*Aside.*]

MRS. TIFFANY. Sir, I'd have you know that—Seraphina, my child, walk with the gentlemen into the conservatory. [*Exeunt* SERAPHINA, TWINKLE, FOGG *into conservatory.*] Count Jolimaitre, pray make due allowances for the errors of this rustic! I do assure you, Count— [*Whispers to him.*]

TRUEMAN. Count! She calls that critter with a shoe-brush over his mouth, Count! To look at him, I should have thought he was a tailor's walking advertisement!

[*Aside.*]

COUNT. [*Addressing* TRUEMAN, *whom he has been inspecting through his eye-glass.*] Where did you say you belonged, my friend? Dug out of the ruins of Pompeii, eh?

TRUEMAN. I belong to a land in which I rejoice to find that you are a foreigner.

COUNT. What a barbarian! He doesn't see the honor I'm doing his country! Pray, Madam, is it one of the aboriginal inhabitants of the soil? To what tribe of Indians does he belong—the Pawnee or Choctaw? Does he carry a tomahawk?

TRUEMAN. Something quite as useful,—do you see that?

[*Shaking his stick.* COUNT *runs to right, behind* MRS. TIFFANY.

MRS. TIFFANY. Oh, dear! I shall faint! Millinette! [*Approaching right.*] Millinette!

Enter MILLINETTE, *without advancing into the room.*

MILLINETTE. *Oui*, Madame.

MRS. TIFFANY. A glass of water! [*Exit* MILLINETTE.] Sir, [*crossing to* TRUEMAN] I am shocked at your plebeian conduct! This is a gentleman of the highest standing, sir! He is a *Count,* sir!

Enter MILLINETTE, *bearing a salver with a glass of water. In advancing towards* MRS. TIFFANY, *she passes in front of the* COUNT, *starts and screams. The* COUNT, *after a start of surprise, regains his composure, plays with his eye-glass, and looks perfectly unconcerned.*

MRS. TIFFANY. What is the matter? What is the matter?

MILLINETTE. Noting, noting,—only—[*looks at* COUNT *and turns away her eyes again*] only—noting at all!

TRUEMAN. Don't be afraid, girl! Why, did you never see a live Count before? He's tame,—I dare say your mistress there leads him about by the ears.

MRS. TIFFANY. This is too much! Millinette, send for Mr. Tiffany instantly!

[*Crosses to* MILLINETTE, *who is going.*

MILLINETTE. He just come in, Madame!

TRUEMAN. My old friend! Where is he? Take me to him,—I long to have one more hearty shake of the hand!

MRS. TIFFANY. Shake of the fist, you mean. [*Crosses to him.*] If I don't make him shake his in your face, you low, *ow*-dacious—no matter, we'll see. Count, honor me by joining my daughter in the conservatory, I will return immediately.

[COUNT *bows and walks towards conservatory,* MRS. TIFFANY *following part of the way and then returning to* TRUEMAN.

TRUEMAN. What a Jezebel! These women always play the very devil with a man, and yet I don't believe such a damaged bale of goods as *that* [*looking at* MRS. TIFFANY] has smothered the heart of little Antony!

MRS. TIFFANY. This way, sir, sal vous plait.

[*Exit, with great dignity.*

TRUEMAN. *Sal vous plait.* Ha, ha, ha! We'll see what Fashion has done for him.

[*Exit.*

END OF ACT I.

ACT II.

SCENE I.

Inner apartment of MR. TIFFANY'S *Counting-House.* MR. TIFFANY *seated at a desk looking over papers.* MR. SNOBSON *on a high stool at another desk, with a pen behind his ear.*

SNOBSON. [*Rising, advances to the front of the stage, regards* TIFFANY *and shrugs his shoulders.*] How the old boy frets and fumes over those papers, to be sure! He's working himself into a perfect fever—ex-actly,—therefore *bleeding's* the prescription! So here goes! [*Aside.*] Mr. Tiffany, a word with you, if you please, sir?

TIFFANY. [*Sitting still.*] Speak on, Mr. Snobson. I attend.

SNOBSON. What I have to say, sir, is a matter of the first importance to the credit of the concern—the *credit* of the concern, Mr. Tiffany!

TIFFANY. Proceed, Mr. Snobson.

SNOBSON. Sir, you've a handsome house—fine carriage—nigger in livery—feed on the fat of the land—everything first rate—

TIFFANY. Well, sir?

SNOBSON. My salary, Mr. Tiffany!

TIFFANY. It has been raised three times within the last year.

SNOBSON. Still it is insufficient for the necessities of an honest man,—mark me, an *honest* man, Mr. Tiffany.

TIFFANY. [*Crossing.*] What a weapon he has made of that word! [*Aside.*] Enough—another hundred shall be added. Does that content you?

SNOBSON. There is one other subject which I have before mentioned, Mr. Tiffany,—your daughter,—what's the reason you can't let the folks at home know at once that I'm to be *the man?*

TIFFANY. Villain! And must the only seal upon this scoundrel's lips be placed there by the hand of my daughter? [*Aside.*] Well, sir, it shall be as you desire.

SNOBSON. And Mrs. Tiffany shall be informed of your resolution?

TIFFANY. Yes.

SNOBSON. Enough said! That's the ticket! The CREDIT *of the concern's safe,* sir! [*Returns to his seat.*

TIFFANY. How low have I bowed to this insolent rascal! To rise himself, he mounts upon my shoulders, and unless I can shake him off he must crush me! [*Aside.*]

Enter TRUEMAN.

TRUEMAN. Here I am, Antony, man! I told you I'd pay you a visit in your money-making quarters. [*Looks around.*] But it looks as dismal here as a cell in the State's prison!

TIFFANY. [*Forcing a laugh.*] Ha, ha, ha! State's prison! You are so facetious! Ha, ha, ha!

TRUEMAN. Well, for the life of me I can't see anything so amusing in that! I should think the State's prison plaguy uncomfortable lodgings. And you laugh, man, as though you fancied yourself there already.

TIFFANY. Ha, ha, ha!

TRUEMAN. [*Imitating him.*] Ha, ha, ha! What on earth do you mean by that ill-sounding laugh, that has nothing of a laugh about it! This *fashion*-worship has made heathens and hypocrites of you all! *Deception* is your household god! A man laughs as if he were crying, and cries as if he were laughing in his sleeve. Everything is something else from what it seems to be. I have lived in your house only three days, and I've heard more lies than were ever invented during a Presidential election! First your fine lady of a wife sends me word that she's not at home— I walk up-stairs, and she takes good care that *I* shall not be *at home*—wants to turn me out of doors. Then *you* come in—take your old friend by the hand—whisper, the deuce knows what, in your wife's ear, and the tables are turned in a tangent! Madam curtsies—says she's enchanted to see me—and orders her grinning nigger to show me a room.

TIFFANY. We were exceedingly happy to welcome you as our guest!

TRUEMAN. Happy? *You* happy? Ah! Antony! Antony! that hatchet face of yours, and those criss-cross furrows tell quite another story! It's many a long day since you were *happy* at anything! You look as if you'd melted down your flesh into dollars, and mortgaged your soul in the bargain! Your warm heart has grown cold over your ledger—your light spirits heavy with calculation! You have traded away your youth—your hopes—your tastes for wealth! and now you *have* the wealth you coveted, what does it profit you? Pleasure it cannot buy; for you have lost your *capacity* for enjoyment. Ease it will not bring; for the love of gain is never satisfied! It has made your counting-house a penitentiary, and your home a fashionable *museum* where there is no niche for you! You have spent so much time *ciphering* in the one, that you find yourself at last a very *cipher* in the other! See me, man! seventy-two last August!—strong as a hickory and every whit as sound!

TIFFANY. I take the greatest pleasure in remarking your superiority, sir.

TRUEMAN. Bah! no man takes pleasure in remarking the superiority of another! Why the deuce can't you speak the truth, man? But it's not the *fashion,* I suppose! I have not seen one frank, open face since—no, no, I can't say that either, though lying *is* catching! There's that girl, Gertrude, who is trying to teach your daughter music —but Gertrude was bred in the country!

TIFFANY. A good girl; my wife and daughter find her very useful.

TRUEMAN. Useful? Well, I must say you have queer notions of *use!*—But come, cheer up, man! I'd rather see one of your old smiles, than know you'd realized another thousand! I hear you are making money on the true, American, high-pressure system—better go slow and sure —the more steam, the greater danger of the boiler's bursting! All sound, I hope? Nothing rotten at the core?

TIFFANY. Oh, sound—quite sound!

TRUEMAN. Well that's pleasant—though I must say you don't look very pleasant about it!

TIFFANY. My good friend, although I am solvent, I may say, perfectly solvent—yet you—the fact is, you can be of some assistance to me!

TRUEMAN. That's the *fact,* is it? I'm glad we've hit upon one *fact* at last! Well—

[SNOBSON, *who during this conversation has been employed in writing, but stops occasionally to listen, now gives vent to a dry chuckling laugh.*

TRUEMAN. Hey? What's that? Another of those deuced ill-sounding, city laughs! [*Sees* SNOBSON.] Who's that perched up on the stool of repentance—eh, Antony?

SNOBSON. The old boy has missed his text there—*that's* the stool of repentance!

[*Aside, and looking at* TIFFANY'S *seat.*

TIFFANY. One of my clerks—my confidential clerk!

TRUEMAN. Confidential? Why, he looks for all the world like a spy—the most inquisitorial, hang-dog face—ugh! the sight of it makes my blood run cold! Come, [*crosses right*] let us talk over matters where this critter can't give us the benefit of his opinion! Antony, the next time you choose a confidential clerk, take one that carries his credentials in his face—those in his pocket are not worth much without!

[*Exeunt* TRUEMAN *and* TIFFANY.

SNOBSON. [*Jumping from his stool and advancing to the centre.*] The old prig has got the tin, or Tiff would never be so civil! All right—Tiff will work every shiner into the concern—all the better for me! Now I'll go and make love to Seraphina. The old woman needn't try to knock me down with any of her French lingo! Six months from to-day, if I ain't driving my two footmen tandem down Broadway— and as fashionable as Mrs. Tiffany herself, then I ain't the trump I thought I was! that's all. [*Looks at his watch.*] Bless me! eleven o'clock, and I haven't had my julep yet? Snobson, I'm ashamed of you! [*Exit.*

SCENE II.

The interior of a beautiful conservatory; walk through the centre; stands of flower-pots in bloom; a couple of rustic seats. GERTRUDE, *attired in white, with a white rose in her hair, watering the flowers.* COLONEL HOWARD *regarding her.*

HOWARD. I am afraid you lead a sad life here, Miss Gertrude?

GERTRUDE. [*Turning round gaily.*] What! amongst the flowers? [*Continues her occupation.*

HOWARD. No, amongst the thistles, with which Mrs. Tiffany surrounds you; the tempests, which her temper raises!

GERTRUDE. They never harm me. Flowers and herbs are excellent tutors. I learn prudence from the reed, and bend until the storm has swept over me!

HOWARD. Admirable philosophy! But still this frigid atmosphere of fashion must be uncongenial to you? Accustomed to the pleasant companionship of your kind friends in Geneva, surely you must regret this cold exchange?

GERTRUDE. Do you think so? Can you suppose that I

could possibly prefer a ramble in the woods to a promenade in Broadway? A wreath of scented wild flowers to a bouquet of these sickly exotics? The odour of new-mown hay to the heated air of this crowded conservatory? Or can you imagine that I could enjoy the quiet conversation of my Geneva friends, more than the edifying chit-chat of a fashionable drawing-room? But I see you think me totally destitute of taste?

HOWARD. You have a merry spirit to jest thus at your grievances!

GERTRUDE. I have my *mania,*—as some wise person declares that all men have,—and mine is a love of independence! In Geneva, my wants were supplied by two kind old maiden ladies, upon whom I know not that I have any claim. I had abilities, and desired to use them. I came here at my own request; for here I am no longer *dependent! Voilà tout,* as Mrs. Tiffany would say.

HOWARD. Believe me, I appreciate the confidence you repose in me!

GERTRUDE. Confidence! Truly, Colonel Howard, the *confidence* is entirely on your part, in supposing that I confide that which I have no reason to conceal! I think I informed you that Mrs. Tiffany only received visitors on her reception day—she is therefore not prepared to see you. Zeke—Oh! I beg his pardon—Adolph made some mistake in admitting you.

HOWARD. Nay, Gertrude, it was not Mrs. Tiffany, nor Miss Tiffany, whom I came to see; it—it was—

GERTRUDE. The conservatory perhaps? I will leave you to examine the flowers at leisure!   [*Crosses left.*

HOWARD. Gertrude—listen to me. If I only dared to give utterance to what is hovering upon my lips! [*Aside.*] Gertrude!

GERTRUDE. Colonel Howard!

HOWARD. Gertrude, I must—must—

GERTRUDE. Yes, indeed you *must,* must leave me! I think I hear somebody coming—Mrs. Tiffany would not be well pleased to find you here—pray, pray leave me—that door will lead you into the street.

[*Hurries him out through door, takes up her watering-pot, and commences watering flowers, tying up branches, &c.*

What a strange being is man! Why should he hesitate to say—nay, why should I prevent his saying, what I would most delight to hear? Truly, man *is* strange—but woman is quite as incomprehensible!

[*Walks about gathering flowers.*

Enter COUNT JOLIMAITRE.

COUNT. There she is—the bewitching little creature! Mrs. Tiffany and her daughter are out of ear-shot. I caught a glimpse of their feathers floating down Broadway, not ten minutes ago. Just the opportunity I have been looking for! Now for an engagement with this captivating little piece of prudery! 'Pon my honour, I am almost afraid she will not resist a *Count* long enough to give value to the conquest. [*Approaches her.*] *Ma belle petite,* were you gathering roses for me?

GERTRUDE. [*Starts on first perceiving him, but instantly regains her self-possession.*] The roses here, sir, are carefully guarded with thorns—if you have the right to gather, pluck for yourself!

COUNT. Sharp as ever, little Gertrude! But now that we are alone, throw off this frigidity, and be at your ease.

GERTRUDE. Permit me to *be alone,* sir, that I *may be at* my ease!

COUNT. Very good, *ma belle,* well said! [*Applauding her with his hands.*] Never yield too soon, even to a *title!* But, as the old girl may find her way back before long, we may as well come to particulars at once. I love you; but that you know already. [*Rubbing his eye-glass unconcernedly with his handkerchief.*] Before long I shall make Mademoiselle Seraphina my wife, and, of course, you shall remain in the family!

GERTRUDE. [*Indignantly.*] Sir—

COUNT. 'Pon my honour you shall! In France we arrange these little matters without difficulty!

GERTRUDE. But I am an *American!* Your conduct proves that you are not one! [*Going, crosses right.*

COUNT. [*Preventing her.*] Don't run away, my immaculate *petite Americaine!* Demme, you've quite overlooked my condescension—the difference of our stations—you a species of upper servant—an orphan—no friends.

Enter TRUEMAN *unperceived*.

GERTRUDE. And therefore more entitled to the respect and protection of every *true gentleman!* Had you been one, you would not have insulted me!

COUNT. My charming little orator, patriotism and declamation become you particularly! [*Approaches her.*] I feel quite tempted to taste—

TRUEMAN. [*Thrusting him aside.*] An American hickory switch! [*Strikes him.*] Well, how do you like it?

COUNT. Old matter-of-fact! [*Aside.*] Sir, how dare you?

TRUEMAN. My stick has answered that question!

GERTRUDE. Oh! now I am quite safe!

TRUEMAN. Safe! not a bit safer than before! All women would be safe, if they knew how virtue became them! As for you, Mr. Count, what have you to say for yourself? Come, speak out!

COUNT. Sir,—aw—aw—you don't understand these matters!

TRUEMAN. That's a fact! Not having had *your* experience, I don't believe I *do* understand them!

COUNT. A piece of pleasantry—a mere joke—

TRUEMAN. A joke, was it? I'll show you a joke worth two of that! I'll teach you the way we natives joke with a puppy who don't respect an honest woman! [*Seizing him.*

COUNT. Oh! oh! demme—you old ruffian! let me go. What do you mean?

TRUEMAN. Oh! a piece of pleasantry—a mere joke—very pleasant, isn't it?

[*Attempts to strike him again;* COUNT *struggles with him. Enter* MRS. TIFFANY *hastily, in her bonnet and shawl.*

MRS. TIFFANY. What is the matter? I am perfectly *abimé* with terror. Mr. Trueman, what has happened?

TRUEMAN. Oh! we have been *joking!*

MRS. TIFFANY. [*To* COUNT, *who is re-arranging his dress.*] My *dear* Count, I did not expect to find you here— how kind of you!

TRUEMAN. Your *dear* Count has been showing his *kindness* in a very *foreign* mànner. Too *foreign*, I think, he found it to be relished by an *unfashionable native!* What do you think of a puppy, who insults an innocent girl all in the way of *kindness?* This Count of yours—this importation of—

COUNT. My dear Madam, demme, permit me to explain. It would be unbecoming—demme—particularly unbecoming of you—aw—aw—to pay any attention to this ignorant person. [*Crosses to* TRUEMAN.] Anything that he says concerning a man of my standing—aw—the truth is, Madam—

TRUEMAN. Let us have the truth, by all means,—if it is only for the novelty's sake!

COUNT. [*Turning his back to* TRUEMAN.] You see, Madam, hoping to obtain a few moments' private conversation with Miss Seraphina—with *Miss Seraphina*, I say—and—aw —and knowing her passion for flowers, I found my way to your very tasteful and *recherché* conservatory. [*Looks about him approvingly.*] *Very* beautifully arranged—does you great credit, Madam! Here I encountered this young person. She was inclined to be talkative; and I indulged her with—with a—aw—demme—a few *commonplaces!* What passed between us was mere *harmless badinage*—on *my* part. You, Madam, you—so conversant with our European manners—you are aware that when a man of fashion—that is, when a woman—a man is bound—amongst noblemen, you know—

MRS. TIFFANY. I comprehend you perfectly—*parfittement*, my dear Count.

COUNT. 'Pon my honour, that's very obliging of her.
[*Aside.*]

MRS. TIFFANY. I am shocked at the plebeian forwardness of this conceited girl!

TRUEMAN. [*Walking up to* COUNT.] Did you ever keep a reckoning of the lies you tell in an hour?

MRS. TIFFANY. Mr. Trueman, I blush for you!
[*Crosses to* TRUEMAN.

TRUEMAN. Don't do that—you have no blushes to spare!

MRS. TIFFANY. It is a man of rank whom you are addressing, sir!

TRUEMAN. A rank villain, Mrs. Antony Tiffany! A *rich* one he would be, had he as much *gold* as *brass!*

MRS. TIFFANY. Pray pardon him, Count; he knows nothing of *how ton!*

COUNT. Demme, he's beneath my notice. I tell you what, old fellow—[TRUEMAN *raises his stick as* COUNT *approaches; the latter starts back*] the sight of him discomposes me— aw—I feel quite uncomfortable—aw—let us join your charming daughter? I can't do you the honour to shoot you, sir, —[*to* TRUEMAN] you are beneath me—a nobleman can't fight a commoner! Good-bye, old Truepenny! I—aw—I'm insensible to your insolence!

[*Exeunt* COUNT *and* MRS. TIFFANY.

TRUEMAN. You won't be insensible to a cow-hide in spite of your nobility! The next time he practises any of his foreign fashions on you, Gertrude, you'll see how I'll wake up his sensibilities!

GERTRUDE. I do not know what I should have done without you, sir.

TRUEMAN. Yes, you do—you know that you would have done well enough! Never tell a lie, girl! not even for the sake of pleasing an old man! When you open your lips, let your heart speak. Never tell a lie! Let your face be the looking-glass of your soul—your heart its clock—while your tongue rings the hours! But the glass must be clear, the clock true, and then there's no fear but the tongue will do its duty in a woman's head!

GERTRUDE. You are very good, sir!

TRUEMAN. That's as it may be!—How my heart warms towards her! [*Aside.*] Gertrude, I hear that you have no mother?

GERTRUDE. Ah! no, sir; I wish I had.

TRUEMAN. So do I! Heaven knows, so do I! [*Aside, and with emotion.*] And you have no father, Gertrude?

GERTRUDE. No, sir—I often wish I had!

TRUEMAN. [*Hurriedly.*] Don't do that, girl! don't do that! Wish you had a mother—but never wish that you had a father again! Perhaps the one you had did not deserve such a child!

Enter PRUDENCE.

PRUDENCE. Seraphina is looking for you, Gertrude.

GERTRUDE. I will go to her. [*Crosses.*] Mr. Trueman, you will not permit me to thank you, but you cannot prevent my gratitude! [*Exit,*

TRUEMAN. [*Looking after her.*] If falsehood harbours there, I'll give up searching after truth!

[*Retires up the stage musingly, and commences examining the flowers.*

PRUDENCE. What a nice old man he is, to be sure! I wish he would say something! [*Aside. Walks after him, turning when he turns—after a pause.*] Don't mind *me*, Mr. Trueman!

TRUEMAN. Mind you? Oh! no, don't be afraid [*Crosses.*] —I wasn't minding you. Nobody seems to mind you much!

[*Continues walking and examining the flowers.*—PRU-DENCE *follows.*

PRUDENCE. Very pretty flowers, ain't they? Gertrude takes care of them.

TRUEMAN. Gertrude? So I hear—[*Advancing.*] I suppose you can tell me now who this Gertrude—

PRUDENCE. Who she's in love with? I *knew* you were going to say that! I'll tell you all about it! Gertrude, she's in love with—Mr. Twinkle! and he's in love with her. And Seraphina, she's in love with Count Jolly—what-d'ye-call-it: but Count Jolly don't take to her at all—but Colonel Howard —he's the man—he's desperate about her!

TRUEMAN. Why, you feminine newspaper! Howard in love with that quintessence of affectation! Howard—the only frank, straightforward fellow that I've met since—I'll tell him my mind on the subject! And Gertrude hunting for happiness in a rhyming dictionary! The girl's a greater fool than I took her for?   [*Crosses right.*

PRUDENCE. So she is—you see I know all about them!

TRUEMAN. I see you do! You've a wonderful knowledge —wonderful—of *other people's concerns!* It may do here, but take my word for it, in the county of Catteraugus you'd get the name of a great *busy-body*. But perhaps you know that, too?

PRUDENCE. Oh! I always know what's coming. I feel it beforehand all over me. I knew something was going to happen the day you came here—and what's more I can always tell a married man from a single—I felt right off that you were a bachelor?

TRUEMAN. Felt right off I was a bachelor, did you? you were sure of it—sure?—quite sure? [PRUDENCE *assents de-*

lightedly.] Then you felt wrong!—a bachelor and a widower are not the same thing!

PRUDENCE. Oh! but it all comes to the same thing—a widower's as good as a bachelor any day! And besides, I knew that you were a farmer *right off*.

TRUEMAN. On the spot, eh? I suppose you saw cabbages and green peas growing out of my hat?

PRUDENCE.. No, I didn't—but I knew all about you. And I knew—[*looking down and fidgetting with her apron*] I knew you were for getting married soon! For last night I dreamt I saw your funeral going along the streets, and the mourners all dressed in white. And a funeral is a sure sign of a wedding, you know! [*Nudging him with her elbow.*]

TRUEMAN. [*Imitating her voice.*] Well, I can't say that I *know* any such thing! you know! [*Nudging her back.*]

PRUDENCE. Oh! it does, and there's no getting over it! For my part, I like farmers—and I know all about setting hens and turkeys, and feeding chickens, and laying eggs, and all that sort of thing!

TRUEMAN. May I be shot! if mistress newspaper is not putting in an advertisement for herself! This is your city mode of courting, I suppose, ha, ha, ha! [*Aside.*]

PRUDENCE. I've been west, a little; but I never was in the county of Catteraugus, myself.

TRUEMAN. Oh! you were not? And you have taken a particular fancy to go there, eh?

PRUDENCE. Perhaps I shouldn't object—

TRUEMAN. Oh!—ah!—so I suppose. Now pay attention to what I am going to say, for it is a matter of great importance to yourself.

PRUDENCE. Now it's coming—I know what he's going to say! [*Aside.*]

TRUEMAN. The next time you want to tie a man for life to your apron-strings, pick out one that don't come from the county of Catteraugus—for green-horns are scarce in those parts, and modest women plenty! [*Exit.*

PRUDENCE. Now, who'd have thought he was going to say that! But I won't give him up yet—I won't give him up. [*Exit.*

END OF ACT II.

ACT III.

SCENE I.

Mrs. Tiffany's *Parlor. Enter* Mrs. Tiffany, *followed by* Mr. Tiffany.

Tiffany. Your extravagance will ruin me, Mrs. Tiffany!

Mrs. Tiffany. And your stinginess will ruin me, Mr. Tiffany! It is totally and *toot a fate* impossible to convince you of the necessity of *keeping up appearances*. There is a certain display which every woman of fashion is forced to make!

Tiffany. And pray who made *you* a woman of fashion?

Mrs. Tiffany. What a vulgar question! All women of fashion, Mr. Tiffany—

Tiffany. In this land are *self-constituted,* like you, Madam—and *fashion* is the cloak for more sins than charity ever covered! It was for *fashion's* sake that you insisted upon my purchasing this expensive house—it was for *fashion's* sake that you ran me in debt at every exorbitant upholsterer's and extravagant furniture warehouse in the city—it was for *fashion's* sake that you built that ruinous conservatory—hired more servants than they have persons to wait upon—and dressed your footman like a harlequin!

Mrs. Tiffany. Mr. Tiffany, you are thoroughly plebeian, and insufferably *American,* in your grovelling ideas! And, pray, what was the occasion of these very *mal-appro-pos* remarks? Merely because I requested a paltry fifty dollars to purchase a new style of head-dress—a *bijou* of an article just introduced in France.

Tiffany. Time was, Mrs. Tiffany, when you manufactured your own French head-dresses—took off their first gloss at the public balls, and then sold them to your shortest-sighted customers. And all you knew about France, or French either, was what you spelt out at the bottom of your fashion-plates—but now you have grown so fashionable, forsooth, that you have forgotten how to speak your mother tongue!

MRS. TIFFANY. Mr. Tiffany, Mr. Tiffany! Nothing is more positively vulgarian—more *unaristocratic* than any allusion to the past!

TIFFANY. Why, I thought, my dear, that *aristocrats* lived principally upon the past—and traded in the market of fashion with the bones of their ancestors for capital?

MRS. TIFFANY. Mr. Tiffany, such vulgar remarks are only suitable to the counting-house; in my drawing-room you should—

TIFFANY. Vary my sentiments with my locality, as you change your *manners* with your *dress!*

MRS. TIFFANY. Mr. Tiffany, I desire that you will purchase Count d'Orsay's "Science of Etiquette," and learn how to conduct yourself—especially before you appear at the grand ball, which I shall give on Friday!

TIFFANY. Confound your balls, Madam; they make *footballs* of my money, while you dance away all that I am worth! A pretty time to give a ball when you know that I am on the very brink of bankruptcy!

MRS. TIFFANY. So much the greater reason that nobody should suspect your circumstances, or you would lose your credit at once. Just at this crisis a ball is absolutely *necessary* to save your reputation! There is Mrs. Adolphus Dashaway—she gave the most splendid fête of the season—and I hear on very good authority that her husband has not paid his baker's bill in three months. Then there was Mrs. Honeywood—

TIFFANY. Gave a ball the night before her husband shot himself—perhaps you wish to drive me to follow his example?   [*Crosses right.*

MRS. TIFFANY. Good gracious! Mr. Tiffany, how you talk! I beg you won't mention anything of the kind. I consider black the most unbecoming color. I'm sure I've done all that I could to gratify you. There is that vulgar old torment, Trueman, who gives one the lie fifty times a day—haven't I been very civil to him?

TIFFANY. Civil to his *wealth*, Mrs. Tiffany! I told you that he was a rich old farmer—the early friend of my father—my own benefactor—and that I had reason to think he might assist me in my present embarrassments. Your civility was *bought*—and like most of your *own* purchases has yet to be *paid* for.   [*Crosses to right.*

MRS. TIFFANY. And will be, no doubt! The condescension of a woman of fashion should command any price. Mr. Trueman is insupportably indecorous—he has insulted Count Jolimaitre in the most outrageous manner. If the Count was not so deeply interested—so *abimé* with Seraphina, I am sure he would never honor us by his visits again!

TIFFANY. So much the better—he shall never marry my daughter!—I am resolved on that. Why, Madam, I am told there is in Paris a regular matrimonial stock company, who fit out indigent dandies for this market. How do I know but this fellow is one of its creatures, and that he has come here to increase its dividends by marrying a fortune?

MRS. TIFFANY. Nonsense, Mr. Tiffany. The Count, the most fashionable young man in all New York—the intimate friend of all the dukes and lords in Europe—not marry my daughter? Not permit Seraphina to become a Countess? Mr. Tiffany, you are out of your senses!

TIFFANY. That would not be very wonderful, considering how many years I have been united to you, my dear. Modern physicians pronounce lunacy infectious!

MRS. TIFFANY. Mr. Tiffany, he is a man of fashion—

TIFFANY. Fashion makes fools, but cannot *feed* them. By the bye, I have a request,—since you are bent upon ruining me by this ball, and there is no help for it,—I desire that you will send an invitation to my confidential clerk, Mr. Snobson.

MRS. TIFFANY. Mr. Snobson! Was there ever such an *you-nick* demand! Mr. Snobson would cut a pretty figure amongst my fashionable friends! I shall do no such thing, Mr. Tiffany.

TIFFANY. Then, Madam, the ball shall not take place. Have I not told you that I am in the power of this man? That there are circumstances which it is happy for you that you do not know—which you cannot comprehend,—but which render it essential that you should be civil to Mr. Snobson? Not you merely, but Seraphina also? He is a more appropriate match for her than your foreign favorite.

MRS. TIFFANY. A match for Seraphina, indeed!

[*Crosses.*] Mr. Tiffany, you are determined to make a *fow pas.*

TIFFANY. Mr. Snobson intends calling this morning.

[*Crosses to left.*

MRS. TIFFANY. But, Mr. Tiffany, this is not reception day—my drawing-rooms are in the most terrible disorder—

TIFFANY. Mr. Snobson is not particular—he must be admitted.

Enter ZEKE.

ZEKE. Mr. Snobson.

Enter SNOBSON; *exit* ZEKE.

SNOBSON. How d'ye do, Marm? [*Crosses to centre.*] How are you? Mr. Tiffany, your most!—

MRS. TIFFANY. [*Formally.*] *Bung jure. Comment vow portè vow, Monsur Snobson?*

SNOBSON. Oh, to be sure—very good of you—fine day.

MRS. TIFFANY. [*Pointing to a chair with great dignity.*] *Sassoyez vow, Monsur Snobson.*

SNOBSON. I wonder what she's driving at? I ain't up to the fashionable lingo yet! [*Aside.*] Eh? what? Speak a little louder, Marm?

MRS. TIFFANY. What ignorance! [*Aside.*]

TIFFANY. I presume Mrs. Tiffany means that you are to take a seat.

SNOBSON. Ex-actly—very obliging of her—so I will. [*Sits.*] No ceremony amongst friends, you know—and likely to be nearer—you understand? *O. K.,* all correct. How *is* Seraphina?

MRS. TIFFANY. Miss Tiffany is not visible this morning.

[*Retires up.*

SNOBSON. Not visible? [*Jumping up, crosses.*] I suppose that's the English for can't see her? Mr. Tiffany, sir—[*walking up to him*] what am I to understand by this *de-fal-ca-tion,* sir? I expected your word to be as good as your bond—beg pardon, sir—I mean *better*—considerably better —no humbug about it, sir.

TIFFANY. Have patience, Mr. Snobson. [*Rings bell.*]

Enter ZEKE.

ZEKE, desire my daughter to come here.

MRS. TIFFANY. [*Coming down centre.*] A-dolph—I say, A-dolph— [ZEKE *straightens himself and assumes foppish airs, as he turns to* MRS. TIFFANY.

TIFFANY. Zeke.

ZEKE. Don't know any such nigga, Boss.

TIFFANY. Do as I bid you instantly, or off with your livery and quit the house!

ZEKE. Wheugh! I'se all dismission. [*Exit.*

MRS. TIFFANY. A-dolph, A-dolph! [*Calling after him.*

SNOBSON. I brought the old boy to his bearings, didn't I though! Pull that string, and he is sure to work right. [*Aside.*] Don't make any stranger of me, Marm—I'm quite at home. If you've got any odd jobs about the house to do up, I sha'n't miss you. I'll amuse myself with Seraphina when she comes—we'll get along very cosily by ourselves.

MRS. TIFFANY. Permit me to inform you, Mr. Snobson, that a French mother never leaves her daughter alone with a young man—she knows your sex too well for that!

SNOBSON. Very *dis*-obliging of her—but as we're none French—

MRS. TIFFANY. You have yet to learn, Mr. Snobson, that the American *ee-light*—the aristocracy—the *how-ton*—as a matter of conscience, scrupulously follow the foreign fashions.

SNOBSON. Not when they are foreign to their interests, Marm—for instance—[*Enter* SERAPHINA.] There you are at last, eh, Miss? How d'ye do? Ma said you weren't visible. Managed to get a peep at her, eh, Mr. Tiffany?

SERAPHINA. I heard you were here, Mr. Snobson, and came without even arranging my toilette; you will excuse my negligence?

SNOBSON. Of everything but *me*, Miss.

SERAPHINA. I shall never have to ask your pardon for *that*, Mr. Snobson.

MRS. TIFFANY. Seraphina—child—really—

[*As she is approaching* SERAPHINA, MR. TIFFANY *plants himself in front of his wife.*

TIFFANY. Walk this way, Madam, if you please. To see

that she fancies the surly fellow takes a weight from my heart. [*Aside.*]

MRS. TIFFANY. Mr. Tiffany, it is highly improper and not at all *distingué* to leave a young girl—

Enter ZEKE.

ZEKE. Mr. Count Jolly-made-her!

MRS. TIFFANY. Good gracious! The Count—Oh, dear!—Seraphina, run and change your dress,—no, there's not time! A-dolph, admit him. [*Exit* ZEKE.] Mr. Snobson, get out of the way, will you? Mr. Tiffany, what are you doing at home at this hour?

Enter COUNT JOLIMAITRE, *ushered by* ZEKE.

ZEKE. Dat's de genuine article ob a gemman. [*Aside.*]
[*Exit.*

MRS. TIFFANY. My dear Count, I am overjoyed at the very sight of you.

COUNT. Flattered myself you'd be glad to see me, Madam —knew it was not your *jour de reception.*

MRS. TIFFANY. But for you, Count, all days—

COUNT. I thought so. Ah, Miss Tiffany, on my honour, you're looking beautiful. [*Crosses right.*

SERAPHINA. Count, flattery from you—

SNOBSON. What? Eh? What's that you say?

SERAPHINA. Nothing but what etiquette requires.
[*Aside to him.*

COUNT. [*Regarding* MR. TIFFANY *through his eye-glass.*] Your worthy Papa, I believe? Sir, your most obedient.
[MR. TIFFANY *bows coldly;* COUNT *regards* SNOBSON *through his glass, shrugs his shoulders and turns away.*

SNOBSON. [*To* MRS. TIFFANY.] Introduce me, will you? I never knew a Count in all my life—what a strange looking animal!

MRS. TIFFANY. Mr. Snobson, it is not the fashion to introduce in France!

SNOBSON. But, Marm, we're in America. [MRS. TIFFANY *crosses to* COUNT.] The woman thinks she's somewhere else than where she is—she wants to make an *alibi?* [*Aside.*]

MRS. TIFFANY. I hope that we shall have the pleasure of seeing you on Friday evening, Count?

COUNT. Really, Madam, my invitations—my engagements —so numerous—I can hardly answer for myself: and you Americans take offence so easily—

MRS. TIFFANY. But, Count, everybody expects you at our ball—you are the principal attraction—

SERAPHINA. Count, you *must* come!

COUNT. Since you insist—aw—aw—there's no resisting you, Miss Tiffany.

MRS. TIFFANY. I am so thankful. How can I repay your condescension. [COUNT *and* SERAPHINA *converse.*] Mr. Snobson, will you walk this way?—I have *such* a cactus in full bloom—remarkable flower! Mr. Tiffany, pray come here—I have something particular to say.

TIFFANY. Then speak out, my dear—I thought it was highly improper just now to leave a girl with a young man?
[*Aside to her.*

MRS. TIFFANY. Oh, but the Count—that is different!

TIFFANY. I suppose you mean to say there's nothing of *the man* about him?

Enter MILLINETTE *with a scarf in her hand.*

MILLINETTE. A-dolph tell me he vas here. [*Aside.*] Pardon, Madame, I bring dis scarf for Mademoiselle.

MRS. TIFFANY. Very well, Millinette; you know best what is proper for her to wear.

[MR. *and* MRS. TIFFANY *and* SNOBSON *retire up; she engages the attention of both gentlemen.*

[MILLINETTE *crosses towards* SERAPHINA, *gives the* COUNT *a threatening look, and commences arranging the scarf over* SERAPHINA'S *shoulders.*

MILLINETTE. Mademoiselle, *permettez-moi.* Perfide! [*Aside to* COUNT.] If Mademoiselle vil stand *tranquille* one *petit moment.* [*Turns* SERAPHINA'S *back to the* COUNT, *and pretends to arrange the scarf.*] I must speak vid you to-day, or I tell all—you find me at de foot of de stair ven you go. *Prend garde!* [*Aside to* COUNT.]

SERAPHINA. What is that you say, Millinette?

MILLINETTE. Dis scarf make you so very beautiful, Mademoiselle—*Je vous salue, mes dames.* [*Curtsies.*] [*Exit.*

COUNT. Not a moment to lose! [*Aside.*] Miss Tiffany, I have an unpleasant—a particularly unpleasant piece of intelligence—you see, I have just received a letter from my friend—the—aw—the Earl of Airshire; the truth is, the Earl's daughter—beg you won't mention it—has distinguished me by a tender *penchant.*

SERAPHINA. I understand—and they wish you to return and marry the young lady; but surely you will not leave us, Count?

COUNT. If *you* bid me stay—I shouldn't have the conscience—I couldn't *afford* to tear myself away. I'm sure that's honest. [*Aside.*]

SERAPHINA. Oh, Count!

COUNT. Say but one word—say that you shouldn't mind being made a Countess—and I'll break with the Earl tomorrow.

SERAPHINA. Count, this surprise—but don't think of leaving the country, Count—we could not pass the time without you! I—yes—yes, Count—I do consent!

COUNT. I thought she would! [*Aside, while he embraces her.*] Enchanted, rapture, bliss, ecstasy, and all that sort of thing—words can't express it, but you understand. But it must be kept a secret—positively it *must!* If the rumour of our engagement were whispered abroad—the Earl's daughter —the delicacy of my situation, aw—you comprehend? It is even possible that our nuptials, my charming Miss Tiffany, *our nuptials* must take place in private!

SERAPHINA. Oh, that is quite impossible!

COUNT. It's the latest fashion abroad—the very latest! Ah, I knew that would determine you. Can I depend on your secrecy?

SERAPHINA. Oh, yes! Believe me.

SNOBSON. [*Coming forward in spite of* MRS. TIFFANY's *efforts to detain him.*] Why, Seraphina, haven't you a word to throw to a dog?

TIFFANY. I shouldn't think she had after wasting so many upon a puppy. [*Aside.*]

Enter ZEKE, *wearing a three-cornered hat.*

ZEKE. Missus, de bran new carriage am below.

MRS. TIFFANY. Show it up,—I mean,—very well, A-dolph.

[*Exit* ZEKE.

Count, my daughter and I are about to take an airing in our new *voyture,*—will you honour us with your company?

COUNT. Madam, I—I have a most *pressing* engagement. A letter to write to the *Earl of Airshire*—who is at present residing in the *Isle of Skye.* I must bid you good-morning.

MRS. TIFFANY. Good-morning, Count. [*Exit* COUNT.

SNOBSON. I'm quite at leisure, [*crosses to* MRS. TIFFANY] Marm. Books balanced—ledger closed—nothing to do all the afternoon,—I'm for you.

MRS. TIFFANY. [*Without noticing him.*] Come, Seraphina, come! [*As they are going,* SNOBSON *follows them.*

SNOBSON. But, Marm—I was saying, Marm, I am quite at leisure—not a thing to do; have I, Mr. Tiffany?

MRS. TIFFANY. Seraphina, child—your red shawl—remember—Mr. Snobson, *bon swear!*

[*Exit, leading* SERAPHINA.

SNOBSON. Swear! Mr. Tiffany, sir, am I to be fobbed off with a *bon swear?* D—n it, I will swear!

TIFFANY. Have patience, Mr. Snobson, if you will accompany me to the counting-house—

SNOBSON. Don't count too much on me, sir. I'll make up no more accounts until these are settled! I'll run down and jump into the carriage in spite of her *bon swear.* [*Exit.*

TIFFANY. You'll jump into a hornet's nest, if you do! Mr. Snobson, Mr. Snobson! [*Exit after him.*

SCENE II.

Housekeeper's Room. Enter MILLINETTE.

MILLINETTE. I have set dat bête, Adolph, to vatch for him. He say he would come back as soon as Madame's voiture drive from de door. If he not come—but he vill—he vill—he *bien étourdi,* but he have *bon cœur.*

Enter COUNT.

COUNT. Ah! Millinette, my dear, you see what a good-natured dog I am to fly at your bidding—

MILLINETTE. Fly? Ah! *trompeur!* Vat for you fly from

Paris? Vat for you leave me—and I love you so much? Ven you sick—you almost die—did I not stay by you—take care of you—and you have no else friend? Vat for you leave Paris?

COUNT. Never allude to disagreeable subjects, *mon enfant!* I was forced by uncontrollable circumstances to fly to the land of liberty—

MILLINETTE. Vat you do vid all de money I give you? The last sou I had—did I not give you?

COUNT. I dare say you did, ma petite—wish you'd been better supplied! [*Aside.*] Don't ask any questions here—can't explain now—the next time we meet—

MILLINETTE. But, ah! ven shall ve meet—ven? You not deceive me, not any more.

COUNT. Deceive you! I'd rather deceive myself—I wish I could! I'd persuade myself you were once more washing linen in the Seine! [*Aside.*]

MILLINETTE. I vil tell you ven ve shall meet—On Friday night Madame give one grand ball—you come *sans doute*—den ven de supper is served—de Americans tink of noting else ven de supper come—den you steal out of de room, and you find me here—and you give me one grand *explanation!*

Enter GERTRUDE, *unperceived.*

COUNT. Friday night—while supper is serving—*parole d'honneur* I will be here—I will explain everything—my sudden departure from Paris—my—demme, my countship—every thing! Now let me go—if any of the family should discover us—

GERTRUDE. [*Who during the last speech has gradually advanced.*] They might discover more than you think it advisable for them to know!

COUNT. The devil!

MILLINETTE. *Mon Dieu!* Mademoiselle Gertrude!

COUNT. [*Recovering himself.*] My dear Miss Gertrude, let me explain—aw—aw—nothing is more natural than the situation in which you find me—

GERTRUDE. I am inclined to believe that, sir.

COUNT. Now—'pon my honour, that's not fair. Here is Millinette will bear witness to what I am about to say—

GERTRUDE. Oh, I have not the slightest doubt of that, sir,

COUNT. You see, Millinette happened to be lady's-maid in the family of—of—the Duchess Chateau D'Espagne—and I chanced to be a particular friend of the Duchess—*very particular* I assure you! Of course I saw Millinette, and she, demme, she saw me! Didn't you, Millinette?

MILLINETTE. Oh! *oui*—Mademoiselle, I knew him ver vell.

COUNT. Well, it is a remarkable fact that—being in correspondence with this very Duchess—at this very time—

GERTRUDE. That is sufficient, sir—I am already so well acquainted with your extraordinary talents for improvisation, that I will not further tax your invention—

MILLINETTE. Ah! Mademoiselle Gertrude, do not betray us—have pity!

COUNT. [*Assuming an air of dignity.*] Silence, Millinette! My word has been doubted—the word of a nobleman! I will inform my friend, Mrs. Tiffany, of this young person's audacity. [*Going.*]

GERTRUDE. His own weapons alone can foil this villain! [*Aside.*] Sir—sir—Count! [*At the last word the* COUNT *turns.*] Perhaps, sir, the least said about this matter the better!

COUNT. [*Delightedly.*] The least said? We won't say anything at all. She's coming round—couldn't resist me! [*Aside.*] Charming Gertrude—

MILLINETTE. Quoi? Vat that you say?

COUNT. My sweet, adorable Millinette, hold your tongue, will you? [*Aside to her.*]

MILLINETTE. [*Aloud.*] No, I vill not! If you do look so from out your eyes at her again, I vill tell all!

COUNT. Oh, I never could manage two women at once, —jealousy makes the dear creatures so spiteful. The only valour is in flight [*Aside.*] Miss Gertrude, I wish you good-morning. Millinette, *mon enfant,* adieu. [*Exit.*

MILLINETTE. But I have one word more to say. Stop! Stop! [*Exit after him.*

GERTRUDE. [*Musingly.*] Friday night, while supper is serving, he is to meet Millinette here and explain—what? This man is an impostor! His insulting me—his familiarity with Millinette—his whole conduct—prove it. If I tell Mrs. Tiffany this, she will disbelieve me, and one word may place this so-called Count on his guard. To convince Seraphina would be equally difficult, and her rashness and infatuation may render her miserable for life. No—she shall be saved! I must devise some plan for opening their eyes. Truly, if I *cannot* invent one, I shall be the first woman who was ever at a loss for a stratagem—especially to punish a villain or to shield a friend. [*Exit.*

END OF ACT III.

ACT IV.

SCENE I.

Ball-room splendidly illuminated. A curtain hung at the further end. MR. *and* MRS. TIFFANY, SERAPHINA, GERTRUDE, FOGG, TWINKLE, COUNT, SNOBSON, COLONEL HOWARD, *a number of guests—some seated, some standing. As the curtain rises, a cotillion is danced;* GERTRUDE *dancing with* HOWARD, SERAPHINA *with* COUNT.

COUNT. [*Advancing with* SERAPHINA *to the front of the stage.*] To-morrow then—to-morrow—I may salute you as my bride—demme, my Countess!

Enter ZEKE *with refreshments.*

SERAPHINA. Yes, to-morrow.
　　[*As the* COUNT *is about to reply,* SNOBSON *thrusts himself in front of* SERAPHINA.
SNOBSON. You said you'd dance with me, Miss—now take my fin, and we'll walk about and see what's going on.
　　[COUNT *raises his eye-glass, regards* SNOBSON, *and leads* SERAPHINA *away;* SNOBSON *follows, endeavouring to attract her attention, but encounters* ZEKE, *bearing a waiter of refreshments; stops, helps himself, and puts some in his pockets.*
Here's the treat! get my to-morrow's luncheon out of Tiff.

Enter TRUEMAN, *yawning and rubbing his eyes.*

TRUEMAN. What a nap I've had, to be sure! [*Looks at his watch.*] Eleven o'clock, as I'm alive! Just the time when country folks are comfortably *turned in*, and here your grand *turn-out* has hardly begun yet!

[*To* TIFFANY, *who approaches.*

GERTRUDE. [*Advancing.*] I was just coming to look for you, Mr. Trueman. I began to fancy that you were paying a visit to dream-land.

TRUEMAN. So I was child—so I was—and I saw a face—like yours—but brighter!—even brighter. [*To* TIFFANY.] There's a smile for you, man! It makes one feel that the world has something worth living for in it yet! Do you remember a smile like that, Antony? Ah! I see you don't—but I do—I do! [*Much moved.*]

HOWARD. [*Advancing.*] Good evening, Mr. Trueman.

[*Offers his hand.*

TRUEMAN. That's right, man; give me your whole hand! When a man offers me the tips of his fingers, I know at once there's nothing in him worth seeking beyond his fingers' ends.

[TRUEMAN *and* HOWARD, GERTRUDE *and* TIFFANY *converse.*

MRS. TIFFANY. [*Advancing centre.*] I'm in such a fidget lest that vulgar old fellow should disgrace us by some of his plebeian remarks! What it is to give a ball, when one is forced to invite vulgar people!

[MRS. TIFFANY *advances towards* TRUEMAN; SERAPHINA *stands conversing flippantly with the gentlemen who surround her; amongst them is* TWINKLE, *who, having taken a magazine from his pocket, is reading to her, much to the undisguised annoyance of* SNOBSON.

Dear me, Mr. Trueman, you are very late—quite in the fashion, I declare!

TRUEMAN. Fashion! And pray what is *fashion*, Madam? An agreement between certain persons to live without using their souls! to substitute etiquette for virtue—decorum for purity—manners for morals! to affect a shame for the works of their Creator! and expend all their rapture upon the works of their tailors and dressmakers!

MRS. TIFFANY. You have the most *ow-tray* ideas, Mr. Trueman—quite rustic, and deplorably *American!* But pray walk this way. [MRS. TIFFANY *and* TRUEMAN *go up stage.*

COUNT. [*Advancing to* GERTRUDE, *who stands centre,* HOWARD *a short distance behind her.*] Miss Gertrude—no opportunity of speaking to you before—in demand, you know!

GERTRUDE. I have no choice, I must be civil to him. [*Aside.*] What were you remarking, sir?

COUNT. Miss Gertrude—charming Ger—aw—aw—I never found it so difficult to speak to a woman before. [*Aside.*]

GERTRUDE. Yes, a very charming ball—many beautiful faces here.

COUNT. Only one!—aw—aw—one—the fact is—
[*Talks to her in dumb show.*

HOWARD. What could old Trueman have meant by saying she fancied that puppy of a Count—that paste-jewel thrust upon the little finger of society.

COUNT. Miss Gertrude—aw—'pon my honour—you don't understand—really—aw—aw—will you dance the polka with me?

[GERTRUDE *bows and gives him her hand; he leads her to the set forming;* HOWARD *remains looking after them.*

HOWARD. Going to dance with him, too! A few days ago she would hardly bow to him civilly—could old Trueman have had reasons for what he said? [*Retires.*

[*Dance, the polka;* SERAPHINA, *after having distributed her bouquet, vinaigrette and fan amongst the gentlemen, dances with* SNOBSON.

PRUDENCE. [*Peeping in, as dance concludes.*] I don't like dancing on Friday; something strange is always sure to happen! I'll be on the look out.

[*Remains peeping and concealing herself when any of the company approach.*

GERTRUDE. [*Advancing hastily to centre.*] They are preparing the supper—now, if I can only dispose of Millinette while I unmask this insolent pretender! [*Exit.*

PRUDENCE. [*Peeping.*] What's that she said? It's coming!

Re-enter GERTRUDE, *bearing a small basket filled with bouquets; approaches* MRS. TIFFANY; *they walk to the front of the stage.*

GERTRUDE. Excuse me, Madam—I believe this is just the hour at which you ordered supper?

MRS. TIFFANY. Well, what's that to you! So, you've been dancing with the Count—how dare you dance with a nobleman—*you?*

GERTRUDE. I will answer that question half an hour hence. At present I have something to propose, which I think will gratify you and please your guests. I have heard that at the most elegant balls in Paris, it is customary—

MRS. TIFFANY. What? what?

GERTRUDE. To station a servant at the door with a basket of flowers. A bouquet is then presented to every lady as she passes in—I prepared this basket a short time ago. As the company walk in to supper, might not the flowers be distributed to advantage?

MRS. TIFFANY. How *distingué!* You are a good creature, Gertrude—there, run and hand the *bokettes* to them yourself! You shall have the whole credit of the thing.

GERTRUDE. Caught in my own net! [*Aside.*] But, Madam, *I* know so little of fashions—Millinette, being French, herself will do it with so much more grace. I am sure Millinette—

MRS. TIFFANY. So am I. She will do it a thousand times better than you—there, go call her.

GERTRUDE. [*Giving basket.*] But, Madam, pray order Millinette not to leave her station till supper is ended—as the company pass out of the supper room she may find that some of the ladies have been overlooked.

MRS. TIFFANY. That is true—very thoughtful of you, Gertrude. [*Exit* GERTRUDE.] What a *recherché idea!*

Enter MILLINETTE.

Here, Millinette, take this basket. Place yourself there, [*centre*] and distribute these *bokettes* as the company pass in to supper; but remember not to stir from the spot until supper is over. It is a French fashion, you know, Milli-

nette. I am so delighted to be the first to introduce it—it
will be all the rage in the *bow-monde!*

MILLINETTE. Mon Dieu! dis vill ruin all! [*Aside.*]
Madame, Madame, let me tell you, Madame, dat in France, in
Paris, it is de custom to present *les* bouquets ven everybody
first come—long before de supper. Dis vould be *outré!
barbare!* not at all *la mode!* Ven dey do come in, dat is de
fashion in Paris!

MRS. TIFFANY. Dear me! Millinette, what is the difference? besides I'd have you to know that Americans always
improve upon French fashions! here, take the basket, and
let me see that you do it in the most *you-nick* and genteel
manner.

[MILLINETTE *poutingly takes the basket and retires up
stage. A march. Curtain hung at the further end
of the room is drawn back, and discloses a room, in
the centre of which stands a supper-table, beautifully decorated and illuminated; the company
promenade two by two into the supper room;*
MILLINETTE *presents bouquets as they pass;* COUNT
leads MRS. TIFFANY.

TRUEMAN. [*Encountering* FOGG, *who is hurrying alone to
the supper room.*] Mr. Fogg, never mind the supper, man!
Ha, ha, ha! Of course you are indifferent to suppers!

FOGG. Indifferent! suppers—oh, ah—no, sir—suppers?
no—no—I'm not indifferent to suppers!

[*Hurries away towards table.*

TRUEMAN. Ha, ha, ha! Here's a new discovery I've
made in the fashionable world! Fashion don't permit the
critters to have *heads* or *hearts,* but it allows them stomachs!
[*To* TIFFANY, *who advances.*] So, it's not fashionable to
feel, but it's fashionable to *feed,* eh, Antony? ha, ha, ha!

[TRUEMAN *and* TIFFANY *retire towards supper room.*

Enter GERTRUDE, *followed by* ZEKE.

GERTRUDE. Zeke, go to the supper room instantly,— whisper to Count Jolimaitre that all is ready, and that he must
keep his appointment without delay,—then watch him, and as
he passes out of the room, place yourself in front of Millinette in such a manner, that the Count cannot see her nor

she him. Be sure that they do not see each other—everything depends upon that. [*Crosses to right.*

ZEKE. Missy, consider dat business brought to a scientific conclusion. [*Exit into supper room. Exit* GERTRUDE.

PRUDENCE. [*Who has been listening.*] What can she want of the Count? I always suspected that Gertrude, because she is so merry and busy! Mr. Trueman thinks so much of her, too—I'll tell him this! There's something wrong—but it all comes of giving a ball on a Friday! How astonished the dear old man will be when he finds out how much I know! [*Advances timidly towards the supper room.*

SCENE II.

Housekeeper's room; dark stage; table, two chairs. Enter GERTRUDE, *with a lighted candle in her hand.*

GERTRUDE. So far the scheme prospers! and yet this imprudence—if I fail? Fail! to lack courage in a difficulty, or ingenuity in a dilemma, are not woman's failings!

Enter ZEKE, *with a napkin over his arm, and a bottle of champagne in his hand.*

Well, Zeke—Adolph!

ZEKE. Dat's right, Missy; I feels just now as if dat was my legitimate title; dis here's de stuff to make a nigger feel like a gemman!

GERTRUDE. But is he coming?

ZEKE. He's coming! [*Sound of a champagne cork heard.*] Do you hear dat, Missy? Don't it put you all in a froth, and make you feel as light as a cork? Dere's nothing like the *union brand,* to wake up de harmonies ob de heart. [*Drinks from bottle.*

GERTRUDE. Remember to keep watch upon the outside—do not stir from the spot; when I call you, come in quickly with a light—now, will you be gone!

ZEKE. I'm off, Missy, like a champagne cork wid de strings cut. [*Exit.*

GERTRUDE. I think I hear the Count's step. [*Crosses left;*

stage dark; she blows out candle.] Now, if I can but disguise my voice, and make the best of my French.

Enter COUNT.

COUNT. Millinette, where are you? How am I to see you in the dark?

GERTRUDE. [*Imitating* MILLINETTE'S *voice in a whisper.*] Hush! *parle bas.*

COUNT. Come here and give me a kiss.

GERTRUDE. Non—non—[*retreating, alarmed;* COUNT *follows*] make haste, I must know all.

COUNT. You did not use to be so deuced particular.

ZEKE. [*Without.*] No admission, gemman! Box-office closed, tickets stopped!

TRUEMAN. [*Without.*] Out of my way; do you want me to try if your head is as hard as my stick?

GERTRUDE. What shall I do? Ruined, ruined!

[*She stands with her hands clasped in speechless despair.*

COUNT. Halloa! they are coming here, Millinette! Millinette, why don't you speak? Where can I hide myself? [*Running about stage, feeling for a door.*] Where are all your closets? If I could only get out—or get in somewhere; may I be smothered in a clothes' basket, if you ever catch me in such a scrape again! [*His hand accidentally touches the knob of a door opening into a closet.*] Fortune's favorite yet! I'm safe!

[*Gets into closet, and closes door. Enter* PRUDENCE, TRUEMAN, MRS. TIFFANY, *and* COLONEL HOWARD, *followed by* ZEKE, *bearing a light.*

PRUDENCE. Here they are, the Count and Gertrude! I told you so! [*Stops in surprise on seeing only* GERTRUDE.

TRUEMAN. And you see what a lie you told!

MRS. TIFFANY. Prudence, how dare you create this disturbance in my house? To suspect the Count, too—a nobleman!

HOWARD. My sweet Gertrude, this foolish old woman would—

PRUDENCE. Oh! you needn't talk—I heard her make the appointment—I know he's here—or he's been here. I wonder if she hasn't hid him away!

[*Runs peeping about the room.*

TRUEMAN. [*Following her angrily.*] You're what I call a confounded—troublesome—meddling—old—prying—(*As he says the last word,* PRUDENCE *opens closet where the* COUNT *is concealed.*) Thunder and lightning!

PRUDENCE. I told you so!

[*They all stand aghast;* MRS. TIFFANY, *with her hands lifted in surprise and anger;* TRUEMAN, *clutching his stick;* HOWARD, *looking with an expression of bewildered horror from the* COUNT *to* GERTRUDE.

MRS. TIFFANY. [*Shaking her fist at* GERTRUDE.] You depraved little minx! this is the meaning of your dancing with the Count!

COUNT. [*Stepping from the closet and advancing.*] I don't know what to make of it! Millinette not here! Miss Gertrude—oh! I see—a disguise—the girl's desperate about me—the way with them all. [*Aside.*]

TRUEMAN. I'm choking—I can't speak—Gertrude—no—no—it is some horrid mistake! [*Partly aside, changes his tone suddenly.*] The villain! I'll hunt the truth out of him, if there's any in—[*Approaches* COUNT *threateningly.*] Do you see this stick? You made its first acquaintance a few days ago; it is time you were better known to each other.

[*As* TRUEMAN *attempts to seize him,* COUNT *escapes, and shields himself behind* MRS. TIFFANY, TRUEMAN *following.*

COUNT. You ruffian! would you strike a woman?—Madam—my dear Madam—keep off that barbarous old man, and I will explain! Madam, with—aw—your natural *bon gout*—aw—your fashionable refinement—aw—your—aw—your knowledge of *foreign customs*—

MRS. TIFFANY. Oh! Count, I hope it ain't a *foreign custom* for the nobility to shut themselves up in the dark with young women? We think such things *dreadful* in *America*.

COUNT. Demme—aw—hear what I have to say, Madam—I'll satisfy all sides—I am perfectly innocent in this affair—'pon my honor I am! That young lady shall inform you that I am so herself!—can't help it, sorry for her. Old matter-of-fact won't be convinced any other way,—that club of his is so particularly unpleasant! [*Aside.*] Madam, I was summoned here *malgré moi*, and not knowing whom I was to meet—Miss Gertrude, favor this company by saying whether or not you directed—that—aw—aw—that coloured individual to conduct me here?

GERTRUDE. Sir, you well know—

COUNT. A simple yes or no will suffice.

MRS. TIFFANY. Answer the Count's question instantly, Miss.

GERTRUDE. I did—but—

COUNT. You hear, Madam—

TRUEMAN. I won't believe it—I can't! Here, you nigger, stop rolling up your eyes, and let us know whether she told you to bring that critter here?

ZEKE. I'se refuse to gib ebidence; dat's de device ob de skilfullest counsels ob de day! Can't answer, Boss—neber git a word out ob dis child—Yah! yah!   [Exit.

GERTRUDE. Mrs. Tiffany,—Mr. Trueman, if you will but have patience—

TRUEMAN. Patience! Oh, Gertrude, you've taken from an old man something better and dearer than his patience—the one bright hope of nineteen years of self-denial—of nineteen years of—

[Throws himself upon a chair, his head leaning on table.

MRS. TIFFANY. Get out of my house, you owdacious—you ruined—you abimé young woman! You will corrupt all my family. Good gracious! don't touch me,—don't come near me. Never let me see your face after to-morrow. Pack.

[Goes up stage.

HOWARD. Gertrude, I have striven to find some excuse for you—to doubt—to disbelieve—but this is beyond all endurance!   [Exit.

Enter MILLINETTE *in haste.*

MILLINETTE. I could not come before— [Stops in surprise at seeing the persons assembled.] Mon Dieu! vat does dis mean?

COUNT. Hold your tongue, fool! You will ruin everything. I will explain to-morrow. [Aside to her.] Mrs. Tiffany—Madam—my dear Madam, let me conduct you back to the ball-room. [She takes his arm.] You see I am quite innocent in this matter; a man of my standing, you know,—aw, aw—you comprehend the whole affair.

[Exit COUNT leading MRS. TIFFANY.

MILLINETTE. I vill say to him von vord, I vill! [*Exit.*

GERTRUDE. Mr. Trueman, I beseech you—I insist upon being heard,—I claim it as a right!

TRUEMAN. Right? How dare you have the face, girl, to talk of rights? [*Comes down stage.*] You had more rights than you thought for, but you have forfeited them all! All right to love, respect, protection, and to not a little else that you don't dream of. Go, go! I'll start for Catteraugus to-morrow,—I've seen enough of what fashion can do!

[*Exit.*

PRUDENCE. [*Wiping her eyes.*] Dear old man, how he takes on! I'll go and console him! [*Exit.*

GERTRUDE. This is too much! How heavy a penalty has my imprudence cost me!—his esteem, and that of one dearer —my home—my— [*Burst of lively music from ball-room.*] They are dancing, and I—I should be weeping, if pride had not sealed up my tears.

[*She sinks into a chair. Band plays the polka behind till Curtain falls.*

END OF ACT IV.

ACT V.

SCENE I.

MRS. TIFFANY'S *Drawing-room—same scene as Act I.* GERTRUDE *seated at a table, with her head leaning on her hand; in the other hand she holds a pen. A sheet of paper and an inkstand before her.*

GERTRUDE. How shall I write to them? What shall I say? Prevaricate I cannot—[*rises and comes forward*] and yet if I write the truth—simple souls! how can they comprehend the motives for my conduct? Nay—the truly pure see no imaginary evil in others! It is only vice, that reflecting its own image, suspects even the innocent. I have no time to lose—I must prepare them for my return. [*Re-*

sumes her seat and writes.] What a true pleasure there is in daring to be frank! [*After writing a few lines more, pauses.*] Not so frank either,—there is one name that I cannot mention. Ah! that he should suspect—should despise me. [*Writes.*]

Enter TRUEMAN.

TRUEMAN. There she is! If this girl's soul had only been as fair as her face,—yet she dared to speak the truth,—I'll not forget that! A woman who refuses to tell a lie has one spark of heaven in her still. [*Approaches her.*] Gertrude, [GERTRUDE *starts and looks up*] what are you writing there? Plotting more mischief, eh, girl?

GERTRUDE. I was writing a few lines to some friends in Geneva.

TRUEMAN. The Wilsons, eh?

GERTRUDE. [*Surprised, rising.*] Are you acquainted with them, sir?

TRUEMAN. I shouldn't wonder if I was. I suppose you have taken good care not to mention the dark room—that foreign puppy in the closet—the pleasant surprise—and all that sort of thing, eh?

GERTRUDE. I have no reason for concealment, sir! for I have done nothing of which I am ashamed!

TRUEMAN. Then I can't say much for your modesty.

GERTRUDE. I should not wish you to say more than I deserve.

TRUEMAN. There's a bold minx! [*Aside.*]

GERTRUDE. Since my affairs seem to have excited your interest—I will not say *curiosity*,—perhaps you even feel a desire to inspect my correspondence? There, [*handing the letter*] I pride myself upon my good nature,—you may like to take advantage of it?

TRUEMAN. With what an air she carries it off! [*Aside.*] Take advantage of it? So I will [*Reads.*] What's this? "French chambermaid—Count—impostor—infatuation—Seraphina—Millinette—disguised myself—expose him." Thunder and lightning! I see it all! Come and kiss me, girl! [GERTRUDE *evinces surprise.*] No, no—I forgot—it won't do to come to that yet! She's a rare girl! I'm out of my senses with joy! I don't know what to do with myself! Tol, de rol, de rol, de ra!   [*Capers and sings.*

GERTRUDE. What a remarkable old man! [*Aside.*] Then you do me justice, Mr. Trueman?

TRUEMAN. I say I don't! Justice? You're above all dependence upon justice! Hurrah! I've found one true woman at last! *True?* [*Pauses thoughtfully.*] Humph! I didn't think of that flaw! Plotting and manœuvering—not much truth in that? An honest girl should be above stratagems!

GERTRUDE. But my *motive,* sir, was good.

TRUEMAN. That's not enough—your *actions* must be *good* as well as your *motives!* Why could you not tell the silly girl that the man was an impostor?

GERTRUDE. I did inform her of my suspicions—she ridiculed them; the plan I chose was an imprudent one, but I could not devise—

TRUEMAN. I hate devising! Give me a woman with the *firmness* to be *frank!* But no matter—I had no right to look for an angel out of Paradise; and I am as happy—as happy as a lord! that is, ten times happier than any lord ever was! Tol, de rol, de rol! Oh! you—you—I'll thrash every fellow that says a word against you!

GERTRUDE. You will have plenty of employment then, sir, for I do not know of one just now who would speak in my favor!

TRUEMAN. Not *one,* eh? Why, where's your dear Mr. Twinkle? I know all about it—can't say that I admire your choice of a husband! But there's no accounting for a girl's taste.

GERTRUDE. Mr. Twinkle! Indeed you are quite mistaken!

TRUEMAN. No—really? Then you're not taken with him, eh?

GERTRUDE. Not even with his rhymes.

TRUEMAN. Hang that old mother meddle-much! What a fool she has made of me. And so you're quite free, and I may choose a husband for you myself? Heart-whole, eh?

GERTRUDE. I—I—I trust there is nothing *unsound* about my heart.

TRUEMAN. There it is again. Don't prevaricate, girl! I

tell you an *evasion* is a *lie in contemplation,* and I hate lying!
Out with the truth! Is your heart *free* or not?

GERTRUDE.   Nay, sir, since you *demand* an answer, permit
me to demand by what right you ask the question?

Enter HOWARD.

Colonel Howard here!

TRUEMAN.   I'm out again! What's the Colonel to her?
[*Retires up stage.*

HOWARD.   [*Crosses to her.*]   I have come, Gertrude, to
bid you farewell.   To-morrow I resign my commission and
leave this city, perhaps for ever.   You, Gertrude, it is you
who have exiled me!   After last evening—

TRUEMAN.   [*Coming forward to* HOWARD.]   What the
plague have you got to say about last evening?

HOWARD.   Mr. Trueman!

TRUEMAN.   What have you got to say about last evening?
and what have you to say to that little girl at all?   It's
Tiffany's precious daughter you're in love with.

HOWARD.   Miss Tiffany?   Never!   I never had the slightest pretension—

TRUEMAN.   That lying old woman!   But I'm glad of it!
Oh! Ah! Um!   [*Looking significantly at* GERTRUDE *and then
at* HOWARD.]   I see how it is.   So you don't choose to marry
Seraphina, eh?   Well now, whom do you choose to marry?
[*Glancing at* GERTRUDE.

HOWARD.   I shall not marry at all!

TRUEMAN.   You won't?   [*Looking at them both again.*]
Why, you don't mean to say that you don't like—
[*Points with his thumb to* GERTRUDE.

GERTRUDE.   Mr. Trueman, I may have been wrong to boast
of my good nature, but do not presume too far upon it.

HOWARD.   You like frankness, Mr. Trueman, therefore I
will speak plainly.   I have long cherished a dream from
which I was last night rudely awakened.

TRUEMAN.   And that's what you call speaking plainly?
Well, I differ with you!   But I can guess what you mean.
Last night you suspected Gertrude there of—[*angrily*] of
what no man shall ever suspect her again while I'm above
ground!   You did her injustice,—it was a mistake!   There,

now that matter's settled. Go, and ask her to forgive you, —she's woman enough to do it! Go, go!

HOWARD. Mr. Trueman, you have forgotten to whom you dictate.

TRUEMAN. Then you won't do it? you won't ask her pardon?

HOWARD. Most undoubtedly I will not—not at any man's bidding. I must first know—

TRUEMAN. You won't do it? Then, if I don't give you a lesson in politeness—

HOWARD. It will be because you find me your *tutor* in the same science. I am not a man to brook an insult, Mr. Trueman! but we'll not quarrel in the presence of the lady.

TRUEMAN. Won't we? I don't know that— [*Crosses.*

GERTRUDE. Pray, Mr. Trueman—Colonel Howard, [*crosses to centre*] pray desist, Mr. Trueman, for my sake! [*Taking hold of his arm to hold him back.*] Colonel Howard, if you will read this letter it will explain everything.

[*Hands letter to* HOWARD, *who reads.*

TRUEMAN. He don't deserve an explanation! Didn't I tell him that it was a mistake? Refuse to beg your pardon! I'll teach him, I'll teach him!

HOWARD. [*After reading.*] Gertrude, how I have wronged you!

TRUEMAN. Oh! you'll beg her pardon now?

[*Between them.*

HOWARD. Hers, sir, and yours! Gertrude, I fear—

TRUEMAN. You needn't,—she'll forgive you. You don't know these women as well as I do,—they're always ready to pardon; it's their nature, and they can't help it. Come along, I left Antony and his wife in the dining-room; we'll go and find them. I've a story of my own to tell! As for you, Colonel, you may follow. Come along, come along!

[*Leads out* GERTRUDE, *followed by* HOWARD.

Enter MR. *and* MRS. TIFFANY. MR. TIFFANY *with a bundle of bills in his hand.*

MRS. TIFFANY. I beg you won't mention the subject again, Mr. Tiffany. Nothing is more plebeian than a discussion upon economy—nothing more *ungenteel* than looking over and fretting over one's bills!

TIFFANY. Then I suppose, my dear, it is quite as ungenteel to *pay* one's bills?

MRS. TIFFANY. Certainly! I hear the *ee*-light never condescend to do anything of the kind. The honor of their invaluable patronage is sufficient for the persons they employ!

TIFFANY. *Patronage* then is a newly invented food upon which the working-classes fatten? What convenient appetites poor people must have! Now listen to what I am going to say. As soon as my daughter marries Mr. Snobson—

Enter PRUDENCE, *a three-cornered note in her hand.*

PRUDENCE. Oh, dear! oh, dear! what shall we do! Such a misfortune! Such a disaster! Oh, dear! oh, dear!

MRS. TIFFANY. Prudence, you are the most tiresome creature! What *is* the matter?

PRUDENCE. [*Pacing up and down the stage.*] Such a disgrace to the whole family! But I always expected it. Oh, dear! oh, dear!

MRS. TIFFANY. [*Following her up and down the stage.*] What are you talking about, Prudence? Will you tell me what has happened?

PRUDENCE. [*Still pacing,* MRS. TIFFANY *following.*] Oh! I can't, I can't! You'll feel so dreadfully! How could she do such a thing! But I expected nothing else! I never did, I never did!

MRS. TIFFANY. [*Still following.*] Good gracious! what do you mean, Prudence? Tell me, will you tell me? I shall get into such a passion! What *is* the matter?

PRUDENCE. [*Still pacing.*] Oh, Betsy, Betsy! That your daughter should have come to that! Dear me, dear me!

TIFFANY. Seraphina? Did you say Seraphina? What has happened to her? what has she done?

[*Following* PRUDENCE *up and down the stage on the opposite side from* MRS. TIFFANY.

MRS. TIFFANY. [*Still following.*] What *has* she done? What *has* she done?

PRUDENCE. Oh! something dreadful—dreadful—shocking!

TIFFANY. [*Still following.*] Speak quickly and plainly—you torture me by this delay,—Prudence, be calm, and speak! What is it?

PRUDENCE. [*Stopping.*] Zeke just told me—he carried her travelling trunk himself—she gave him a whole dollar! Oh, my!

TIFFANY. Her trunk? where? where?

PRUDENCE. Round the corner!

MRS. TIFFANY. What did she want with her trunk? You are the most vexatious creature, Prudence! There is no bearing your ridiculous conduct!

PRUDENCE. Oh, you will have worse to bear—worse! Seraphina's gone!

TIFFANY. Gone! where?

PRUDENCE. Off!—eloped—eloped with the Count! Dear me, dear me! I always told you she would!

TIFFANY. Then I am ruined!

[*Stands with his face buried in his hands.*

MRS. TIFFANY. Oh, what a ridiculous girl! And she might have had such a splendid wedding! What could have possessed her?

TIFFANY. The devil himself possessed her, for she has ruined me past all redemption! Gone, Prudence, did you say gone? Are you *sure* they are gone?

PRUDENCE. Didn't I tell you so! Just look at this note—one might know by the very fold of it—

TIFFANY. [*Snatching the note.*] Let me see it! [*Opens the note and reads.*] "My dear Ma,—When you receive this I shall be a *countess!* Isn't it a sweet title? The Count and I were forced to be married privately, for reasons which I will explain in my next. You must pacify Pa, and put him in a good humour before I come back, though now I'm to be a countess I suppose I shouldn't care!" Undutiful huzzy! "We are going to make a little excursion and will be back in a week. Your dutiful daughter—Seraphina." A man's curse is sure to spring up at his own hearth,—here is mine! The sole curb upon that villain gone, I am wholly in his power! Oh! the first downward step from honour—he who takes it cannot pause in his mad descent and is sure to be hurried on to ruin!

MRS. TIFFANY. Why, Mr. Tiffany, how you do take on! And I dare say to elope was the most fashionable way after all!

Enter TRUEMAN, *leading* GERTRUDE, *and followed by* HOWARD.

TRUEMAN. Where are all the folks? Here, Antony, you are the man I want. We've been hunting for you all over the house. Why—what's the matter? There's a face for a thriving city merchant! Ah! Antony, you never wore such a hang-dog look as that when you trotted about the country with your pack upon your back! Your shoulders are no broader now—but they've a heavier load to carry—that's plain!

MRS. TIFFANY. Mr. Trueman, such allusions are highly improper! What would my daughter, *the Countess,* say!

GERTRUDE. The Countess? Oh! Madam!

MRS. TIFFANY. Yes, the Countess! My daughter Seraphina, the Countess *dee* Jolimaitre! What have you to say to that? No wonder you are surprised after your *recherché, abimé* conduct! I have told you already, Miss Gertrude, that you were not a proper person to enjoy the inestimable advantages of my patronage. You are dismissed—do you understand? Discharged!

TRUEMAN. Have you done? Very well, it's my turn now. Antony, perhaps what I have to say don't concern you as much as some others—but I want you to listen to me. You remember, Antony, [*his tone becomes serious*] a blue-eyed, smiling girl—

TIFFANY. Your daughter, sir? I remember her well.

TRUEMAN. None ever saw her to forget her! Give me your hand, man. There—that will do! Now let me go on. I never coveted wealth—yet twenty years ago I found myself the richest farmer in Catteraugus. This cursed money made my girl an object of speculation. Every idle fellow that wanted to feather his nest was sure to come courting Ruth. There was one—my heart misgave me the instant I laid eyes upon him—for he was a city chap, and not over-fond of the truth. But Ruth—ah! she was too pure herself to look for guile! His fine words and his fair looks—the old story—she was taken with him—I said, "no"—but the girl liked her own way better than her old father's—girls always do! and one morning—the rascal robbed me—not of my money,—he would have been welcome to that—but of the only treasure I cherished—my daughter!

TIFFANY. But you forgave her!

TRUEMAN. I did! I knew she would never forgive herself—that was punishment enough! The scoundrel thought he was marrying my gold with my daughter—he was mistaken! I took care that they should never want; but that was all. She loved him—what will not woman love? The villain broke her heart—mine was tougher, or it wouldn't have stood what it did. A year after they were married, he forsook her! She came back to her old home—her old father! It couldn't last long—she pined—and pined—and —then—she died! Don't think me an old fool—though I am one—for grieving won't bring her back. [*Bursts into tears.*]

TIFFANY. It was a heavy loss!

TRUEMAN. So heavy that I should not have cared how soon I followed her, but for the child she left! As I pressed that child in my arms, I swore that my unlucky wealth should never curse it, as it had cursed its mother! It was all I had to love—but I sent it away—and the neighbors thought it was dead. The girl was brought up tenderly but humbly by my wife's relatives in Geneva. I had her taught true independence—she had hands—capacities—and should use them! Money should never buy her a husband! For I resolved not to claim her until she had made her choice, and found the man who was willing to take her for herself alone. She turned out a rare girl! and it's time her old grandfather claimed her. Here he is to do it! And there stands Ruth's child! Old Adam's heiress! Gertrude, Gertrude!—my child! [GERTRUDE *rushes into his arms.*

PRUDENCE. [*After a pause.*] Do tell; I want to know! But I knew it! I always said Gertrude would turn out somebody, after all!

MRS. TIFFANY. Dear me! Gertrude an heiress! My dear Gertrude, I always thought you a very charming girl— quite YOU-NICK—an heiress! I must give her a ball! I'll introduce her into society myself—of course an heiress must make a sensation! [*Aside.*]

HOWARD. I am too bewildered even to wish her joy. Ah!

there will be plenty to do that now—but the gulf between us is wider than ever. [*Aside.*]

TRUEMAN. Step forward, young man, and let us know what you are muttering about. I said I would never claim her until she had found the man who loved her for herself. I *have* claimed her—yet I never break my word—I think I *have* found that man! and here he is. [*Strikes* HOWARD *on the shoulder.*] Gertrude 's yours! There—never say a word, man—don't bore me with your thanks—you can cancel all obligations by making that child happy! There—take her!—Well, girl, and what do you say?

GERTRUDE. That I rejoice too much at having found a parent for my first act to be one of disobedience!

[*Gives her hand to* HOWARD.

TRUEMAN. How very dutiful! and how disinterested!

[TIFFANY *retires—and paces the stage, exhibiting great agitation.*

PRUDENCE. [*To* TRUEMAN.] All the *single folks* are getting married!

TRUEMAN. No they are not. You and I are single folks, and we're not likely to get married.

MRS. TIFFANY. My dear Mr. Trueman—my sweet Gertrude, when my daughter, the Countess, returns, she will be delighted to hear of this *deenooment!* I assure you that the Countess will be quite charmed!

GERTRUDE. The Countess? Pray, Madam, where *is* Seraphina?

MRS. TIFFANY. The Countess *dee* Jolimaitre, my dear, is at this moment on her way to—to Washington! Where, after visiting all the fashionable curiosities of the day—including the President—she will return to grace her native city!

GERTRUDE. I hope you are only jesting, Madam? Seraphina is not married?

MRS. TIFFANY. Excuse me, my dear, my daughter had this morning the honor of being united to the Count *dee* Jolimaitre!

GERTRUDE. Madam! He is an impostor!

MRS. TIFFANY. Good gracious! Gertrude, how can you

talk in that disrespectful way of a man of rank? **An heiress, my dear, should have better manners! The Count—**

Enter MILLINETTE, *crying.*

MILLINETTE. Oh! Madame! I will tell everyting—oh! dat monstre! He break my heart!

MRS. TIFFANY. Millinette, what is the matter?

MILLINETTE. Oh! he promise to marry me—I love him much—and now Zeke say he run away vid Mademoiselle Seraphina!

MRS. TIFFANY. What insolence! The girl is mad! Count Jolimaitre marry my *femmy de chamber!*

MILLINETTE. Oh! Madame, he is not one Count, not at all! Dat is only de title he go by in dis country. De foreigners always take de large title ven dey do come here. His name *à Paris* vas Gustave Tread-mill. But he not one Frenchman at all, but he do live one long time *à Paris.* First he live vid Monsieur Vermicelle—dere he vas de head cook! Den he live vid Monsieur Tire-nez, de barber! After dat he live wid Monsieur le Comte Frippon-fin—and dere he vas le Comte's valet! Dere, now I tell everyting, I feel one great deal better!

MRS. TIFFANY. Oh! good gracious! I shall faint! Not a Count! What will everybody say? It's no such thing! I say he *is* a Count! One can see the foreign *jenny says quoi* in his face! Don't you think I can tell a Count when I see one? I say he *is* a Count!

Enter SNOBSON, *his hat on—his hands thrust in his pocket— evidently a little intoxicated.*

SNOBSON. I won't stand it! I say I won't!

TIFFANY. [*Rushing up to him.*] Mr. Snobson, for heaven's sake—[*Aside.*]

SNOBSON. Keep off. I'm a hard customer to get the better of! You'll see if I don't come out strong!

TRUEMAN. [*Quietly knocking off* SNOBSON's *hat with his stick.*] Where are your manners, man?

SNOBSON. My business ain't with you, Catteraugus; you've waked up the wrong passenger!—Now the way I'll put it into Tiff will be a caution. I'll make him wince! That extra mint julep has put the true pluck in me. Now for it! [*Aside.*] Mr. Tiffany, sir—you needn't think to come over me, sir—you'll have to get up a little earlier in the morning before you do *that,* sir! I'd like to know, sir, how you came to assist your daughter in running away with that foreign loafer? It was a downright swindle, sir. After the conversation I and you had on that subject she wasn't your property, sir.

TRUEMAN. What, Antony, is that the way your city clerk bullies his boss?

SNOBSON. You're drunk, Catteraugus—don't expose yourself—you're drunk! Taken a little too much toddy, my old boy! Be quiet! I'll look after you, and they won't find it out. If you want to be busy, you may take care of my *hat*—I feel so deuced weak in the chest, I don't think I *could* pick it up myself.—Now to put the screws to Tiff. [*Aside.*] Mr. Tiffany, sir—you have broken your word, as no virtuous individual—no honorable member—of—the—com—mu—ni—ty—

TIFFANY. Have some pity, Mr. Snobson, I beseech you! I had nothing to do with my daughter's elopement! I will agree to anything you desire—your salary shall be doubled—trebled—   [*Aside to him.*

SNOBSON. [*Aloud.*] No you don't. No bribery and corruption.

TIFFANY. I implore you to be silent. You shall become partner of the concern, if you please—only do not speak. You are not yourself at this moment.   [*Aside to him.*

SNOBSON. Ain't I though. I feel *twice* myself. I feel like two Snobsons rolled into one, and I'm chock full of the spunk of a dozen! Now Mr. Tiffany, sir—

TIFFANY. I shall go distracted! Mr. Snobson, if you have one spark of manly feeling—   [*Aside to him.*

TRUEMAN. Antony, why do you stand disputing with that drunken jackass? Where's your nigger? Let him kick the critter out, and be of use for once in his life.

SNOBSON. Better be quiet, Catteraugus. This ain't your hash, so keep your spoon out of the dish. Don't expose yourself, old boy.

TRUEMAN. Turn him out, Antony!

SNOBSON. He daren't do it! Ain't I up to him? Ain't he in my power? Can't I knock him into a cocked hat with a word? And now he's got my steam up—I *will* do it!

TIFFANY. [*Beseechingly.*] Mr. Snobson—my friend—

SNOBSON. It's no go—steam's up—and I don't stand at anything!

TRUEMAN. You won't *stand* here long unless you mend your manners—you're not the first man I've *upset* because he didn't know his place.

SNOBSON. I know where Tiff's place is, and that's in the *States' Prison!* It's bespoke already. He would have it! He wouldn't take pattern of me, and behave like a gentleman! He's a *forger,* sir!

[TIFFANY *throws himself into a chair in an attitude of despair; the others stand transfixed with astonishment.*

He's been forging Dick Anderson's endorsements of his notes these ten months. He's got a couple in the bank that will send him to the wall anyhow—if he can't make a raise. I took them there myself! Now you know what he's worth. I said I'd expose him, and I have done it!

MRS. TIFFANY. Get out of the house! You ugly, little, drunken brute, get out! It's not true. Mr. Trueman, put him out; you have got a stick—put him out!

Enter SERAPHINA, *in her bonnet and shawl—a parasol in her hand.*

SERAPHINA. I hope Zeke hasn't delivered my note.
[*Stops in surprise at seeing the persons assembled.*

MRS. TIFFANY. Oh, here is the Countess!
[*Advances to embrace her.*

TIFFANY. [*Starting from his seat, and seizing* SERAPHINA *violently by the arm.*] Are—you—married?

SERAPHINA. Goodness, Pa, how you frighten me! No, I'm not married, *quite.*

TIFFANY. Thank heaven.

MRS. TIFFANY. [*Drawing* SERAPHINA *aside.*] What's the matter? Why did you come back?

SERAPHINA. The clergyman wasn't at home—I came back

for my jewels—the Count said nobility couldn't get on without them.

TIFFANY. I may be saved yet! Seraphina, my child, you will not see me disgraced—ruined! I have been a kind father to you—at least I have tried to be one—although your mother's extravagance made a *madman* of me! The Count is an impostor—you seemed to like him—[*Pointing to* SNOBSON.] Heaven forgive me! [*Aside.*] Marry *him* and save *me*. You, Mr. Trueman, you will be my friend in this hour of extreme need—you will advance the sum which I require —I pledge myself to return it. My wife—my child—who will support them were I—the thought makes me frantic! You will aid me? You had a child yourself.

TRUEMAN. But I did not *sell* her—it was her own doings. Shame on you, Antony! Put a price on your own flesh and blood! Shame on such foul traffic!

TIFFANY. Save me—I conjure you—for my father's sake.

TRUEMAN. For your *father's* SON's sake I will *not* aid you in becoming a greater villain than you are!

GERTRUDE. Mr. Trueman—Father, I should say—save him —do not embitter our happiness by permitting this calamity to fall upon another—

TRUEMAN. Enough—I did not need your voice, child. I am going to settle this matter my own way.

[*Goes up to* SNOBSON—*who has seated himself and fallen asleep—tilts him out of the chair.*

SNOBSON. [*Waking up.*] Eh? Where's the fire? Oh! it's you, Catteraugus.

TRUEMAN. If I comprehend aright, you have been for some time aware of your principal's forgeries?

[*As he says this, he beckons to* HOWARD, *who advances as witness.*

SNOBSON. You've hit the nail, Catteraugus! Old chap saw that I was up to him six months ago; left off throwing dust into my eyes—

TRUEMAN. Oh, he did!

SNOBSON. Made no bones of forging Anderson's name at my elbow.

TRUEMAN. Forged at your elbow? You saw him do it?

SNOBSON. I did.

TRUEMAN. Repeatedly?

SNOBSON. Re—pea—ted—ly.

TRUEMAN. Then you, Rattlesnake, if he goes to the States' Prison, you'll take up your quarters there too. You are an accomplice, an *accessory!*

> [TRUEMAN *walks away and seats himself.* HOWARD *rejoins* GERTRUDE. SNOBSON *stands for some time bewildered.*

SNOBSON. The deuce, so I am! I never thought of that! I must make myself scarce. I'll be off. Tiff, I say Tiff! [*going up to him and speaking confidentially*] that drunken old rip has got us in his power. Let's give him the slip and be off. They want men of genius at the West,—we're sure to get on! You—you can set up for a writing-master, and teach copying *signatures;* and I—I'll give lectures on *temperance!* You won't come, eh? Then I'm off without you. Good-bye, Catteraugus! Which is the way to California?
> [*Steals off.*

TRUEMAN. There's one debt your city owes me. And now let us see what other nuisances we can abate. Antony, I'm not given to preaching, therefore I shall not say much about what you have done. Your face speaks for itself,— the crime has brought its punishment along with it.

TIFFANY. Indeed it has, sir! In *one year* I have lived a *century* of misery.

TRUEMAN. I believe you, and upon one condition I will assist you—

TIFFANY. My friend—my first, ever kind friend,—only name it!

TRUEMAN. You must sell your house and all these gewgaws, and bundle your wife and daughter off to the country. There let them learn economy, true independence, and home virtues, instead of foreign follies. As for yourself, continue your business—but let moderation, in future, be your counsellor, and let *honesty* be your confidential clerk.

TIFFANY. Mr. Trueman, you have made existence once more precious to me! My wife and daughter shall quit the city to-morrow, and—

PRUDENCE. It's all coming right! It's all coming right! We'll go to the county of Catteraugus.
> [*Walking up to* TRUEMAN.

TRUEMAN. No you won't,—I make that a stipulation, Antony; keep clear of Catteraugus. None of your fashionable examples there!

JOLIMAITRE *appears in the Conservatory and peeps into the room unperceived.*

COUNT. What can detain Seraphina? We ought to be off!

MILLINETTE. [*Turns round, perceives him, runs and forces him into the room.*] Here he is! Ah, Gustave, mon cher Gustave! I have you now and we never part no more. Don't frown, Gustave, don't frown—

TRUEMAN. Come forward, Mr. Count! and for the edification of fashionable society confess that you're an impostor.

COUNT. An impostor? Why, you abominable old—

TRUEMAN. Oh, your feminine friend has told us all about it, the cook—the valet—barber, and all that sort of thing. Come, confess, and something may be done for you.

COUNT. Well then, I do confess I am no count; but really, ladies and gentlemen, I may recommend myself as the most capital cook.

MRS. TIFFANY. Oh, Seraphina!

SERAPHINA. Oh, Ma!   [*They embrace and retire.*

TRUEMAN. Promise me to call upon the whole circle of your fashionable acquaintances with your own advertisements and in your cook's attire, and I will set you up in business to-morrow. Better turn stomachs than turn heads!

MILLINETTE. But you will marry me?

COUNT. Give us your hand, Millinette! Sir, command me for the most delicate *paté*—the daintiest *croquette à la royale*—the most transcendent *omelette soufflé* that ever issued from a French pastry-cook's oven. I hope you will pardon my conduct, but I heard that in America, where you pay homage to titles while you profess to scorn them—where *Fashion* makes the basest coin current—where you have no kings, no princes, no *nobility*—

TRUEMAN. Stop there! I object to your use of that word. When justice is found only among lawyers—health among physicians—and patriotism among politicians, *then* may you say that there is no *nobility* where there are no titles! But we *have* kings, princes, and nobles in abundance—of

Nature's stamp, if not of *Fashion's,*—we have honest men, warm-hearted and brave, and we have women—gentle, fair, and true, to whom no *title* could add *nobility.*

EPILOGUE.

PRUDENCE.   I told you so!   And now you hear and see.
I told you *Fashion* would the fashion be!
TRUEMAN.   Then both its point and moral I distrust.
COUNT.   Sir, is that liberal?
HOWARD.   Or is it just?
TRUEMAN.   The guilty have escaped!
TIFFANY.   Is, therefore, sin
Made charming?   Ah! there's punishment within'
Guilt ever carries his own scourge along.
GERTRUDE.   Virtue her own reward!
TRUEMAN.   You're right, I'm wrong.
MRS. TIFFANY.   How we have been deceived!
PRUDENCE.   I told you so.
SERAPHINA.   To lose at once a title and a beau!
COUNT.   A count no more, I'm no more of *account.*
TRUEMAN.   But to a nobler title you may mount,
And be in time—who knows?—an honest man!
COUNT.   Eh, Millinette?
MILLINETTE.   Oh, *oui,* I know you can!
GERTRUDE.   [*To audience.*]   But, ere we close the scene, a
       word with you,—
We charge you answer,—Is this picture true?
Some little mercy to our efforts show,
Then let the world your honest verdict know.
Here let it see portrayed its ruling passion,
And learn to prize at its just value—*Fashion.*

THE END.

UNCLE TOM'S CABIN

By GEORGE L. AIKEN

GEORGE L. AIKEN'S DRAMATIZATION

OF

UNCLE TOM'S CABIN

There are many instances of a drama becoming so popular through several generations that the playwright is totally eclipsed, and finds himself not identified with its success. In the present collection, two such plays have been selected,— plays whose evolution embraces much fascinating history: I mean "Uncle Tom's Cabin" and "Rip Van Winkle".

It is easy to answer the question, Who wrote "Uncle Tom's Cabin"? It is not so easy to say who dramatized the story. There are records before me of twelve different stage versions, and there is no telling how many more are extant. There was a mushroom growth of these plays, made all the more easy of accretion because of the fact that, when Mrs. Harriet Beecher Stowe published her slave novel, she failed to reserve to herself the dramatic rights. The consequence is that, though "Uncle Tom's Cabin" has probably been given some three hundred thousand performances in America and abroad, according to the computations of Mrs. Stowe's son, neither Mrs. Stowe nor her estate profited by one cent from the popularity of the story on the stage. The fault was one of established prejudice against the stage, for, as we shall see, Mrs. Stowe had her attention called many times to the potency of the theatre, and to the influence of the dramatization of her novel on the popular mind.

It is common knowledge how quickly the story of "Uncle Tom's Cabin" caught fire, after its publication on March 20, 1852. By August of the same year, according to Mrs. Stowe's neighbor, at Hartford, Connecticut, Charles Dudley Warner, it had been dramatized. It would seem that the book suggested a stage version almost immediately to Asa Hutchinson, for he wrote Mrs. Stowe, asking for the rights.

The reply to his letter brought out the typical New England spirit of the time. She wrote:

> I have considered your application and asked advice of my different friends, and the general sentiment of those whom I have consulted so far agrees with my own, that it would not be advisable to make that use of the work which you propose. It is thought, with the present state of theatrical performances in this country, that any attempt on the part of Christians to identify themselves with them will be productive of danger to the individual character, and to the general cause. If the barrier which now keeps young people of Christian families from theatrical entertainments is once broken down by the introduction of respectable and moral plays, they will then be open to all the temptations of those who are not such, as there will be, as the world now is, five bad plays to one good. However specious may be the idea of reforming dramatic entertainments, I fear it is wholly impracticable, and as a friend to you should hope that you would not run the risk of so dangerous an experiment. The world is not good enough yet for it to succeed. I preserve a very pleasant recollection of your family, and of the gratification I have derived from the exercise of your talents, and it gives me pleasure to number you among my friends.

This attitude was, however, no deterrent to others, who immediately seized the opportunity of catering to popular appeal. There was no social fervor in their point of view, but theatrical expediency; and, in the particular case of Aiken, the book was selected because of the immediate fitness of the character of *Little Eva*. Everywhere, hands began tinkering with the incidents of the story, and a comparative study of the versions, a casual and fruitless task, would show how easily manipulated were the many novelties introduced. Like *Topsy*, the stage versions just grew by what they fed on, and we are told that one of the first, that by Charles Taylor, who was connected with the Albany Museum, and later with Purdy's New York National, in Chatham Street, ignored both *Eva* and *Topsy* in the cast.

Yet, in this unfinished state, it was seen in New York, on August 24, 1852.

Other dramatizations will be mentioned, simply as a matter of record, but the evolution of the version that came into being at the Troy Museum, under the hand of George L. Aiken, is our chief concern. Be it stated that during the period of its growth, the fame of "Uncle Tom's Cabin" had spread abroad, and it was advertised as being played in two London theatres, during the fall of 1852,—the Royal Victoria and the Great National Standard. So states Mrs. Stowe's son. I also have a record of a dramatization made by Mark Lemon and Tom Taylor, entitled "Slave Life", and presented at the London Adelphi Theatre, in November, 1852.

But these dates were after Aiken's version had been given its trial at the Troy Museum. George L. Aiken, the dramatist, was a typical man of the theatre, both in his tastes and in his connections. Born, according to Wemyss, in Boston, on December 19, 1830, his first appearance as an actor was in Providence, R. I., in "Six Degrees of Crime", June, 1848. During May, 1852, he was filling an engagement at the Boston National Theatre.

Aiken was a cousin of George C. Howard, who, during this year of 1852, was manager of the Troy Museum, and whose daughter, Cordelia, was winning reputation as an infant prodigy. In fact, according to Phelps, she was only four years old when she was taken on the stage in a dramatization of "Oliver Twist", and made a decided emotional impression in the rôle of *Little Dick*. With the approbation of the crowd so easily won, the proud father looked about for other rôles to conquer.

It is not recorded who first suggested the part of *Little Eva* for the precocious child. But the fact remains that, once it was decided, Howard's cousin, George, was called into service, and, in less than a week, a dramatization of "Uncle Tom's Cabin" was ready for rehearsals. This was a family affair, and it remained so for some while, inasmuch as the first *Uncle Tom,* one of the famous Fox brothers, could claim Mrs. Howard as his sister.

That Aiken was equal to the melodramatic task set before him is readily discernible by his taste, shown in his other literary work. Phelps designates him as a dramatist who catered to the fashion of the day by writing "sensation dramas". He dramatized many of the New York *Ledger* stories, like "The Gun-maker of Moscow", "The Mystic Bride", and "Orion, the Gold Beater", all of them recorded as having been produced in Albany. He also turned his hand to the creation of many ten-cent novellettes, which brought the George Munroe publishing house into fame, and the Library of Congress credits him with such fictions as "Chevalier, the French Jack Sheppard" (1868) and "A New York Boy Among the Indians" (1872). It is small wonder, therefore, that he should discover in "Uncle Tom's Cabin" those broad strokes of sensation which his pen so quickly utilized, in preference to what admirers of the book designate as its "lowly" side.

Through the painstaking researches of Edgar W. Ames, we are given some idea of the manner in which the play was advertised for its first production, which occurred on the evening of September 27, 1852. The Troy papers announced that "The doors open at seven—to commence at eight. Admission 25 cents, children half-price. Boys to the gallery, 12½ cents. Box seats, 12½ cents extra. Orchestra spring seats and cushioned armchairs, 25 cents extra." On the first program the author's name was not given.

Evidently Aiken at first was embarrassed by the riches of the book, or else he was so deeply concerned with the necessity of catering to *Little Eva* that he could not utilize the whole story, for he immediately prepared a new drama, entitled "The Death of Uncle Tom; or, The Religion of the Lowly". This further dramatization was immediately produced, but must have impressed the management with its lack of coherency, detached from the first part of the story. For the notice in the Troy papers of November 15, 1852, according to Mr. Ames, reveals that Aiken finally welded the two plays into one. The advertisement read: "Grand combination of the two dramas on the same evening. . . . Little Cordelia Howard as *Eva.*" Comment on the performance may be easily traced in the Troy *Northern Budget* and the Troy *Daily Times.* Mr. Ames infers that the Troy *Daily Whig* was too much engrossed with the coming presidential

election, with Pierce as the candidate, to send a reporter to
the theatre.

It is the Aiken version I have selected for the present
collection. Although, so elastic are all the dramatizations
of "Uncle Tom's Cabin", that we conjecture even this must
be considerably different from Aiken's original manuscript.
The play ran for one hundred nights in Troy, Aiken himself
playing *George Shelby*, and then it was brought to the New
York Chatham Street Theatre, where, on July 18, 1853, it
began a run which lasted for three hundred and twenty-five
nights. The original version was in six acts, eight tableaux,
and thirty scenes.

For the time, it was a massive production, requiring ingenuity of stage set, and, when one recalls that realism was
just coming into vogue, that Mrs. John Drew was considered remarkable for her introduction of a carpet in one of
the scenes of "London Assurance", that Dion Boucicault
was creating a stir by the use of real water in his "Colleen
Bawn", the measure of the scenic demands of "Uncle Tom's
Cabin" is easily estimated. But the production was an inno-
vation in another direction, if Howard is to be believed.
He is quoted as having said:

I was the first, I may say, to introduce one-play
entertainments. That is, till the advent of "Uncle Tom"
in New York, no evening at the theatre was thought
complete, without an afterpiece, or a little ballet-
dancing. When I told the manager "Uncle Tom" must
constitute the entire performance, he flouted the idea;
said he would have to shut up in a week. But I carried
my point, and we didn't shut up, either. People came to
the theatre by hundreds, who were never inside its doors
before; we raised our prices, which no other theatre in
New York could do, and we played "Uncle Tom" over
three hundred times during that engagement.

Tradition has it that the *Little Eva* of Cordelia Howard
was so poignantly played it drew tears from Edwin Forrest
and the poet, Bryant, when they witnessed it. We are fortunate in having preserved for us an account of Mrs. Stowe's
impressions of Aiken's version of her novel, and of those

who visualized the characters. It is from the pen of the
Hon. Francis H. Underwood, in 1889 United States Consul
to Glasgow, and originally one of the projectors and the
managing editor of the *Atlantic Monthly*. He writes:

In the winter of 1852 or 1853 a dramatization of
"Uncle Tom's Cabin" was performed at the National
Theatre, Boston,—a fine, large theatre, in the wrong
place—that is to say, in one of the worst districts of
Boston. It was burned a few years later, and never
rebuilt. The dramatization was not very artistic, and
the scenes introduced were generally the most ghastly
ones of the painful story. Of the lightness and gayety
of the book there was no sign. The actors were fairly
good, but none of them remarkable, except the child who
personated *Eva,* and the woman (Mrs. Howard) who
played *Topsy.* Mrs. Howard was beyond comparison
the best representative of the dark race I ever saw. She
was a genius whose method no one could describe. In
every look, gesture, and tone there was an intuitive
revelation of the strange, capricious, and fascinating
creature which Mrs. Stowe had conceived.

I asked Mrs. Stowe to go with me to see the play.
She had some natural reluctance, considering the position her father had taken against the theatre, and considering the position of her husband as a preacher; but
she also had some curiosity as a woman and as an
author to see in flesh and blood the creations of her
imagination. I think she told me she had never been
in a theatre in her life. I procured the manager's box,
and we entered privately, she being well muffled. She
sat in the shade of the curtains of our box, and watched
the play attentively. I never saw such delight upon a
human face as she displayed when she first compre-
hended the full power of Mrs. Howard's *Topsy.* She
scarcely spoke during the evening; but her expression
was eloquent,—smiles and tears succeeding each other
through the whole.

It must have been for her a thrilling experience to
see her thoughts bodied upon the stage, at a time when
any dramatic representation must have been to her so

vivid. Drawn along by the threads of her own romance, and inexperienced in the deceptions of the theatre, she could not have been keenly sensible of the faults of the piece or the shortcomings of the actors.

I remember that in one scene *Topsy* came quite close to our box, with her speaking eyes full upon Mrs. Stowe. Mrs. Stowe's face showed all her vivid and changing emotions, and the actress must surely have divined them. The glances when they met and crossed reminded me of the supreme look of Rachel when she repeated that indescribable *Hélas!* There was but one slight wooden barrier between the novelist and the actress—but it was enough! I think it a matter of regret that they never met.

The *Eliza* of the evening was a reasonably good actress, and skipped over the floating ice of the Ohio River with frantic agility.

The *Uncle Tom* was rather stolid—such a man as I have seen preaching among the negroes, when I lived in Kentucky.

Having thus established what may be truly regarded as the stage version of "Uncle Tom's Cabin", the record of other dramatizations needs must follow. The list is gathered from Allston Brown and others. Clifton W. Tayleure's play was given in Detroit, Michigan, on October 2, 1852; C. W. Taylor's version, as already noted, was presented at the New York Chatham Theatre, on August 23, 1853; H. J. Conway's drama was seen at the Boston Museum, on November 15, 1852, with William Warren and a fine cast, and was later taken to Barnum's Museum (New York). Under the stage management of F. C. Wemyss, and at the New York Bowery Theatre, on January 16, 1854, there was produced a version by Henry E. Stevens. Other dramatizations are Robert Johnson's (October 20, 1879), Clay Greene's (August 18, 1888), and Harkin and Barbour's (1897). An English dramatization was made by T. H. Lacey, and was produced at the Manchester Theatre Royal, on February 1, 1853. There are extant many versions in Spanish, Italian, Portuguese, and German. Among the French adaptations are recorded Dennery's "La Case de l'Oncle Tom", in eight acts and fifty-five scenes, presented at the Théâtre de l'Ambigu-Comique, on January 18, 1853, which was rehashed for Rio Janiero, in the Spanish of Dumanoiu ("A Cabana de pai Thomaz", 1881); Beauplan's "Elisa; ou, un chapître de l'Oncle Tom" (1853), and finally Texier and Wailly's version, produced at the Théâtre de la Gaieté, in Paris, on January 23, 1853.

Everywhere, it was regarded as a typical negro play, and students became interested in the question of the negro as a stage character. They went back to Mrs. Aphra Behn's "The Widdow Ranter; or, The History of Bacon in Virginia", and they discussed Thomas Southerne's "Oroonoko" in comparison with Mrs. Behn's "Oroonoko; or, The Royal Slave". They had not seriously considered the development of the Ethiopian drama in America, which had begun years before the advent of "Uncle Tom", nor had they realized that long before Joseph Jefferson appeared in this play, he had, as a little fellow, blackened up and made his stage début with "Jim Crow" Rice in dance and song. But popularly, "Uncle Tom's Cabin" is regarded as one of our very early negro plays.

It would be impossible to attempt to record the famous casts that have made up the different performances of "Uncle Tom's Cabin". Nearly every well-known American actor has, at one time or another, served his apprenticeship in it. The original cast, as given at the Troy theatre, is recorded in its proper place. At the Chestnut Street Theatre, in Philadelphia, we note that John Gilbert was playing *Uncle Tom,* Joseph Jefferson was scheduled as *Gumption Cute,* and John Sleeper Clark assumed the rôle of *Marks.* In Detroit, whither Aiken went to play the part of *George Harris,* James H. Hackett was the *St. Clare* of the occasion. In 1858, when "Uncle Tom" reached McVicker's Theatre, in Chicago, Mary McVicker, who was afterwards the first Mrs. Edwin Booth, played *Little Eva.*

There came a time when the play was so well established in the affections of the people that no theatre, however high its reputation, thought it out of place to revive "Uncle Tom" with ideal casts. Such a performance is recorded as taking place at Booth's Theatre, on December 20, 1880. Around the play there grew a tradition; each manager tried to out-do every other manager in the multifariousness of new detail, in the number of people, in the introduction of new songs and dances. I find John E. Owens boasting that his production of "Uncle Tom" was the first to go below the Mason and Dixon line, a rather bold venture, considering the reputation of the book among Southerners. A fascinating adventure, partly realized by Frank P. Stockbridge, in the *Green Book,* for January, 1913, would be to trace the advertisements and "printings" for the many productions of "Uncle Tom's Cabin", illustrating the "circus" quality of the entertainment. The stage directions to the printed play give much latitude to the producer, who might halt the action at any auspicious moment, to introduce solos or quartettes or breakdowns for the purpose of atmosphere.

It is an easy matter to determine how faithful Aiken was to Mrs. Stowe's book. Deprived of its spirit of special pleading, visualized for its different situations, it is small wonder that Mrs. Stowe found its subtler qualities gone from the stage. Yet, a reading of the play will show that Aiken has retained the stilted manner of the time, has but slightly heightened the villainy of slavery as seen through the eyes of Mrs. Stowe, has retained all the pious sentimentality of *Little Eva* and the religious fervor of *Uncle Tom.* The colors are all there. Even in the reading one can get a certain note of sincerity which prompted Aiken in the dramatization. He was himself undoubtedly impressed with the potency of Mrs. Stowe's work. We have seen that he at first wrote two plays covering the story. It has been likewise conclusively proven that he tried his hand at another dramatization—Mrs. Stowe's "Dred, a Tale of the Great Dismal Swamp", besides making ready for the stage a "Key to Uncle Tom's Cabin."

Granting, therefore, that, however lacking his work may be in its literary value, at least it held for many seasons on the stage, "Uncle Tom's Cabin", as dramatized by Aiken, must be considered one of the mile-posts in any estimate of what the tastes of audiences must have been during the early days in the National Period of the American Theatre.

UNCLE TOM'S CABIN

DRAMATIS PERSONÆ AND CAST FOR THE PRODUCTION

Troy Museum, September 27, 1852.

Uncle Tom	Mr. G. C. Germon.
George Harris	} Mr. G. L. Aiken.
George Shelby	
St. Clare	Mr. G. C. Howard.
Phineas Fletcher	} Mr. C. Fox.
Gumption Cute	
Mr. Wilson	} Mr. LeMoyne.
Deacon Perry	
Shelby	Mr. Allen.
Haley	} Mr. Davis.
Legree	
Tom Loker	Mr. Cushman.
Marks	Mr. F. Aiken.
Sambo	————
Quimbo	Mr. Salter.
Doctor	————
Waiter	————
Harry, a Child	Master Groat.
Eva	Cordelia Howard.
Eliza	} Mrs. G. C. Germon.
Cassy	
Marie	Miss Emmons.
Ophelia	Mrs. E. Fox.
Chloe	} Mrs. G. C. Howard.
Topsy	

UNCLE TOM'S CABIN

ACT I.

Scene I.—*Plain Chamber.*

Enter Eliza, *meeting* George.

Eliza. Ah! George, is it you? Well, I am so glad you've come! [George *regards her mournfully.*] Why don't you smile, and ask after Harry?

George. [*Bitterly.*] I wish he'd never been born!—I wish I'd never been born myself!

Eliza. [*Sinking her head upon his breast and weeping.*] Oh, George!

George. There, now, Eliza; it's too bad for me to make you feel so. Oh! how I wish you had never seen me—you might have been happy!

Eliza. George! George! how can you talk so? What dreadful thing has happened, or is going to happen? I'm sure we've been very happy till lately.

George. So we have, dear. But oh! I wish I'd never seen you, nor you me.

Eliza. Oh, George! how can you?

George. Yes, Eliza, it's all misery! misery! The very life is burning out of me! I'm a poor, miserable, forlorn drudge! I shall only drag you down with me, that's all! What's the use of our trying to do anything—trying to know anything—trying to be anything? I wish I was dead!

Eliza. Oh! now, dear George, that is really wicked. I know how you feel about losing your place in the factory, and you have a hard master; but pray be patient—

George. Patient! Haven't I been patient? Did I say a word when he came and took me away—for no earthly reason—from the place where everybody was kind to me?

I'd paid him truly every cent of my earnings, and they all say I worked well.

ELIZA. Well, it *is* dreadful; but, after all, he is your master, you know.

GEORGE. My master! And who made him my master? That's what I think of! What right has he to me? I'm as much a man as he is! What right has he to make a dray-horse of me?—to take me from things I can do better than he can, and put me to work that any horse can do? He tries to do it; he says he'll bring me down and humble me, and he puts me to just the hardest, meanest and dirtiest work, on purpose.

ELIZA. Oh, George! George! you frighten me. Why, I never heard you talk so. I'm afraid you'll do something dreadful. I don't wonder at your feelings at all; but oh! do be careful—for my sake, for Harry's.

GEORGE. I have been careful, and I have been patient, but it's growing worse and worse—flesh and blood can't bear it any longer. Every chance he can get to insult and torment me he takes. He says that though I don't say anything, he sees that I've got the devil in me, and he means to bring it out; and one of these days it will come out, in a way that he won't like, or I'm mistaken.

ELIZA. Well, I always thought that I must obey my master and mistress, or I couldn't be a Christian.

GEORGE. There is some sense in it in your case. They have brought you up like a child—fed you, clothed you and taught you, so that you have a good education—that is some reason why they should claim you. But I have been kicked and cuffed and sworn at, and what do I owe? I've paid for all my keeping a hundred times over. I won't bear it!—no, I *won't!* Master will find out that I'm one whipping won't tame. My day will come yet, if he don't look out!

ELIZA. What are you going to do? Oh! George, don't do anything wicked; if you only trust in heaven and try to do right, it will deliver you.

GEORGE. Eliza, my heart's full of bitterness. I can't trust in heaven. Why does it let things be so?

ELIZA. Oh, George! we must all have faith. Mistress says that when all things go wrong to us, we must believe that heaven is doing the very best.

GEORGE. That's easy for people to say who are sitting on their sofas and riding in their carriages; but let them be where I am—I guess it would come some harder. I wish I could be good; but my heart burns and can't be reconciled. You couldn't, in my place, you can't now, if I tell you all I've got to say; you don't know the whole yet.

ELIZA. What do you mean?

GEORGE. Well, lately my master has been saying that he was a fool to let me marry off the place—that he hates Mr. Shelby and all his tribe—and he says he won't let me come here any more, and that I shall take a wife and settle down on his place.

ELIZA. But you were married to *me* by the minister, as much as if you had been a white man.

GEORGE. Don't you know I can't hold you for my wife if he chooses to part us? That is why I wish I'd never seen you—it would have been better for us both—it would have been better for our poor child if he had never been born.

ELIZA. Oh! but my master is so kind.

GEORGE. Yes, but who knows?—he may die, and then Harry may be sold to nobody knows who. What pleasure is it that he is handsome and smart and bright? I tell you, Eliza, that a sword will pierce through your soul for every good and pleasant thing your child is or has. It will make him worth too much for you to keep.

ELIZA. Heaven forbid!

GEORGE. So, Eliza, my girl, bear up now, and good-by, for I'm going.

ELIZA. Going, George! Going where?

GEORGE. To Canada; and when I'm there I'll buy you— that's all the hope that's left us. You have a kind master, that won't refuse to sell you. I'll buy you and the boy— heaven helping me, I will!

ELIZA. Oh, dreadful! If you should be taken?

GEORGE. I won't be taken, Eliza—I'll *die* first! I'll be free, or I'll die!

ELIZA. You will not kill yourself?

GEORGE. No need of that; they will kill me, fast enough. I will never go down the river alive.

ELIZA. Oh, George! for my sake, do be careful. Don't lay hands on yourself, or anybody else. You are tempted too much, but don't. Go, if you must, but go carefully, prudently, and pray heaven to help you!

GEORGE. Well, then, Eliza, hear my plan. I'm going home quite resigned, you understand, as if all was over. I've got some preparations made, and there are those that will help me; and in the course of a few days I shall be among the missing. Well, now, good-by.

ELIZA. A moment—our boy.

GEORGE. [*Choked with emotion.*] True, I had forgotten him; one last look, and then farewell!

ELIZA. And heaven grant it be not forever!   [*Exeunt.*

SCENE II.—*A dining-room.—Table and chairs.—Dessert, wine, &c., on table.*—SHELBY *and* HALEY *discovered at table.*

SHELBY. That is the way I should arrange the matter.

HALEY. I can't make trade that way—I positively can't, Mr. Shelby.   [*Drinks.*

SHELBY. Why, the fact is, Haley, Tom is an uncommon fellow! He is certainly worth that sum anywhere—steady, honest, capable, manages my whole farm like a clock!

HALEY. You mean honest, as niggers go.   [*Fills glass.*

SHELBY. No; I mean, really, Tom is a good, steady, sensible, pious fellow. He got religion at a camp-meeting, four years ago, and I believe he really *did* get it. I've trusted him since then, with everything I have—money, house, horses, and let him come and go round the country, and I always found him true and square in everything!

HALEY. Some folks don't believe there is pious niggers, Shelby, but *I do*. I had a fellow, now, in this yer last lot I took to Orleans—'twas as good as a meetin' now, really, to hear that critter pray; and he was quite gentle and quiet like. He fetched me a good sum, too, for I bought him cheap of a man that was 'bliged to sell out, so I realized six hundred on him. Yes, I consider religion a valeyable thing in a nigger, when it's the genuine article and no mistake.

SHELBY. Well, Tom's got the real article, if ever a fellow had. Why, last fall I let him go to Cincinnati alone, to do business for me and bring home five hundred dollars.

"Tom," says I to him, "I trust you, because I think you are a Christian—I know you wouldn't cheat." Tom comes back sure enough; I knew he would. Some low fellows, they say, said to him—"Tom, why don't you make tracks for Canada?" "Ah, master trusted me, and I couldn't," was his answer. They told me all about it. I am sorry to part with Tom, I must say. You ought to let him cover the whole balance of the debt, and you would, Haley, if you had any conscience.

HALEY. Well, I've got just as much conscience as any man in business can afford to keep, just a little, you know, to swear by, as 'twere; and then I'm ready to do anything in reason to 'blige friends, but this yer, you see, is a leetle too hard on a fellow—a leetle too hard!   [*Fills glass again.*

SHELBY. Well, then, Haley, how will you trade?

HALEY. Well, haven't you a boy or a girl that you could throw in with Tom?

SHELBY. Hum! none that I could well spare; to tell the truth, it's only hard necessity makes me willing to sell at all. I don't like parting with any of my hands, that's a fact.

HARRY *runs in.*

Hulloa! Jim Crow! [*Throws a bunch of raisins towards him.*] Pick that up now.   [HARRY *does so.*

HALEY. Bravo, little 'un! [*Throws an orange, which* HARRY *catches. He sings and dances around the stage.*] Hurrah! Bravo! What a young 'un! That chap's a case, I'll promise. Tell you what, Shelby, fling in that chap, and I'll settle the business. Come, now, if that ain't doing the thing up about the rightest!

ELIZA *enters.—Starts on beholding* HALEY, *and gazes fearfully at* HARRY, *who runs and clings to her dress, showing the orange, &c.*

SHELBY. Well, Eliza?

ELIZA. I was looking for Harry, please, sir.

SHELBY. Well, take him away, then.

ELIZA *grasps the child eagerly in her arms, and casting another glance of apprehension at* HALEY, *exits hastily.*

HALEY. By Jupiter! there's an article, now. You might make your fortune on that ar gal in Orleans any day. I've seen over a thousand in my day, paid down for gals not a bit handsomer.

SHELBY. I don't want to make my fortune on her. Another glass of wine. [Fills the glasses.

HALEY. [Drinks and smacks his lips.] Capital wine—first chop! Come, how will you trade about the gal? What shall I say for her? What'll you take?

SHELBY. Mr. Haley, she is not to be sold. My wife wouldn't part with her for her weight in gold.

HALEY. Ay, ay! women always say such things, 'cause they hain't no sort of calculation. Just show 'em how many watches, feathers and trinkets one's weight in gold would buy, and that alters the case, I reckon.

SHELBY. I tell you, Haley, this must not be spoken of—I say no, and I mean no.

HALEY. Well, you'll let me have the boy tho'; you must own that I have come down pretty handsomely for him.

SHELBY. What on earth can you want with the child?

HALEY. Why, I've got a friend that's going into this yer branch of the business—wants to buy up handsome boys to raise for the market. Well, what do you say?

SHELBY. I'll think the matter over and talk with my wife.

HALEY. Oh, certainly, by all means; but I'm in a devil of a hurry, and shall want to know as soon as possible, what I may depend on. [Rises and puts on his overcoat, which hangs on a chair.—Takes hat and whip.]

SHELBY. Well, call up this evening, between six and seven, and you shall have my answer.

HALEY. All right. Take care of yourself, old boy! [Exit.

SHELBY. If anybody had ever told me that I should sell Tom to those rascally traders, I should never have believed it. Now it must come for aught I see, and Eliza's child too. So much for being in debt, heigho! The fellow sees his advantage and means to push it. [Exit.

SCENE III.—Snowy landscape.—UNCLE TOM'S Cabin.—Snow on roof.—Practicable door and window.—Dark Stage.—Music.

Enter ELIZA hastily, with HARRY in her arms.

ELIZA. My poor boy; they have sold you, but your mother will save you yet!

*[Goes to Cabin and taps on window.—*Aunt Chloe *appears at window with a large white night-cap on.*

Chloe. Good Lord! what's that? My sakes alive if it ain't Lizy! Get on your clothes, old man, quick! I'm gwine to open the door.

The door opens and Chloe *enters, followed by* Uncle Tom, *in his shirt sleeves, holding a tallow candle.*

Tom. [*Holding the light towards* Eliza.] Lord bless you! I'm skeered to look at ye, Lizy! Are ye tuck sick, or what's come over ye?

Eliza. I'm running away, Uncle Tom and Aunt Chloe, carrying off my child! Master sold him!

Tom and Chloe. Sold him!

Eliza. Yes, sold him! I crept into the closet by mistress' door to-night, and heard master tell mistress that he had sold my Harry, and you, Uncle Tom, both, to a trader, and that the man was to take possession to-morrow.

Chloe. The good Lord have pity on us! Oh! it don't seem as if it was true. What has he done that master should sell *him?*

Eliza. He hasn't done anything—it isn't for that. Master don't want to sell, and mistress—she's always good. I heard her plead and beg for us, but he told her 'twas no use—that he was in this man's debt, and he had got the power over him, and that if he did not pay him off clear, it would end in his having to sell the place and all the people and move off.

Chloe. Well, old man, why don't you run away, too? Will you wait to be toted down the river, where they kill niggers with hard work and starving? I'd a heap rather die than go there, any day! There's time for ye; be off with Lizy—you've got a pass to come and go any time. Come, bustle up, and I'll get your things together.

Tom. No, no—I ain't going. Let Eliza go—it's her right. I wouldn't be the one to say no—'tain't in natur for her to stay; but you heard what she said? If I must be sold, or all the people on the place, and everything go to rack, why, let me be sold. I s'pose I can bar it as well as any one. Mas'r always found me on the spot—he always will. I never have broken trust, nor used my pass no ways contrary to my word, and I never will. It's better for me to go alone, than to break up the place and sell all. Mas'r ain't to blame, and he'll take care of you and the poor little 'uns! [*Overcome.*

CHLOE. Now, old man, what is you gwine to cry for? Does you want to break this old woman's heart? [*Crying.*

ELIZA. I saw my husband only this afternoon, and I little knew then what was to come. He told me he was going to run away. Do try, if you can, to get word to him. Tell him how I went and why I went, and tell him I'm going to try and find Canada. You must give my love to him, and tell him if I never see him again on earth, I trust we shall meet in heaven!

TOM. Dat is right, Lizy, trust in the Lord—He is our best friend—our only comforter.

ELIZA. You won't go with me, Uncle Tom?

TOM. No; time was when I would, but the Lord's given me a work among these yer poor souls, and I'll stay with 'em and bear my cross with 'em till the end. It's different with you—it's more'n you could stand, and you'd better go if you can.

ELIZA. Uncle Tom, I'll try it!

TOM. Amen! The Lord help ye!

[*Exit* ELIZA *and* HARRY.

CHLOE. What is you gwine to do, old man? What's to become of you?

TOM. [*Solemnly.*] Him that saved Daniel in the den of lions—that saved the children in the fiery furnace—Him that walked on the sea and bade the winds be still—He's alive yet! and I've faith to believe He can deliver me!

CHLOE. You is right, old man.

TOM. The Lord is good unto all that trust Him, Chloe.

[*Exeunt into Cabin.*

SCENE IV.—*Room in Tavern by the river side.—A large window, through which the river is seen, filled with floating ice.—Moonlight.—Table and chairs brought on.*

Enter PHINEAS.

PHINEAS. Chaw me up into tobaccy ends! how in the name of all that's onpossible am I to get across that yer pesky river? It's a reg'lar blockade of ice! I promised Ruth to meet her to-night, and she'll be into my har if I don't come. [*Goes to window.*] Thar's a conglomerated prospect for a loveyer! What in creation's to be done? That thar river looks like a permiscuous ice-cream shop come to an awful state of friz. If I war on the adjacent bank, I wouldn't care a teetotal atom. Rile up, you old varmint, and shake the ice off your back!

Enter ELIZA *and* HARRY.

ELIZA. Courage, my boy—we have reached the river. Let it but roll between us and our pursuers, and we are safe! [*Goes to window.*] Gracious powers! the river is choked with cakes of ice!

PHINEAS. Holloa, gal!—what's the matter? You look kind of streaked.

ELIZA. Is there any ferry or boat that takes people over now?

PHINEAS. Well, I guess not; the boats have stopped running.

ELIZA. [*In dismay.*] Stopped running?

PHINEAS. Maybe you're wanting to get over—anybody sick? Ye seem mighty anxious.

ELIZA. I—I—I've got a child that's very dangerous. I never heard of it till last night, and I've walked quite a distance to-day, in hopes to get to the ferry.

PHINEAS. Well, now, that's onlucky; I'm re'lly consarned for ye. Thar's a man, a piece down here, that's going over with some truck this evening, if he duss to; he'll be in here to supper to-night, so you'd better set down and wait. That's a smart little chap. Say, young 'un, have a chaw tobaccy?

[*Takes out a large plug and a bowie-knife.*

ELIZA. No, no! not any for him.

PHINEAS. Oh! he don't use it, eh? Hain't come to it yet? Well, I have. [*Cuts off a large piece, and returns the plug and knife to pocket.*] What's the matter with the young 'un? He looks kind of white in the gills!

ELIZA. Poor fellow! he is not used to walking, and I've hurried him on so.

PHINEAS. Tuckered, eh? Well, there's a little room there,

with a fire in it. Take the babby in there, make yourself comfortable till that thar ferryman shows his countenance— I'll stand the damage.

ELIZA. How shall I thank you for such kindness to a stranger?

PHINEAS. Well, if you don't know how, why, don't try; that's the teetotal. Come, vamoose! [*Exit* ELIZA *and* HARRY.] Chaw me into sassage meat, if that ain't a perpendicular fine gal! she's a reg'lar A No. 1, sort of female! How'n thunder am I to get across this refrigerated stream of water? I can't wait for that ferryman. [*Enter* MARKS.] Halloa! what sort of a critter's this? [*Advances.*] Say, stranger, will you have something to drink?

MARKS. You are excessively kind: I don't care if I do.

PHINEAS. Ah! he's a human. Halloa, thar! bring us a jug of whisky instantaneously, or expect to be teetotally chawed up! Squat yourself, stranger, and go in for enjoyment. [*They sit at table.*] Who are you, and what's ycur name?

MARKS. I am a lawyer, and my name is Marks.

PHINEAS. A land shark, eh? Well, I don't think no worse on you for that. The law is a kind of necessary evil; and it breeds lawyers just as an old stump does fungus. Ah! here's the whisky.

Enter WAITER, *with jug and tumblers. Places them on table.*

Here, you—take that shin-plaster. [*Gives bill.*] I don't want any change—thar's a gal stopping in that room—the balance will pay for her—d'ye hear?—vamoose! [*Exit* WAITER.—*Fills glass.*] Take hold, neighbour Marks—don't shirk the critter. Here's hoping your path of true love may never have an ice-choked river to cross! [*They drink.*

MARKS. Want to cross the river, eh?

PHINEAS. Well, I do, stranger. Fact is, I'm in love with the teetotalist pretty girl, over on the Ohio side, that ever wore a Quaker bonnet. Take another swig, neighbour.

[*Fills glasses, and they drink.*

MARKS. A Quaker, eh?

PHINEAS. Yes—kind of strange, ain't it? The way of it was this:—I used to own a grist of niggers—had 'em to work on my plantation, just below here. Well, stranger, do you know I fell in with that gal—of course I was considerably smashed—knocked into a pretty conglomerated heap—and I told her so. She said she wouldn't hear a word from me so long as I owned a nigger!

MARKS. You sold them, I suppose?

PHINEAS. You're teetotally wrong, neighbour. I gave them all their freedom, and told 'em to vamoose!

MARKS. Ah! yes—very noble, I dare say, but rather expensive. This act won you your lady-love, eh?

PHINEAS. You're off the track again, neighbour. She felt kind of pleased about it, and smiled, and all that; but she said she could never be mine unless I turned Quaker! Thunder and earth! what do you think of that? You're a lawyer—come, now, what's your opinion? Don't you call it a knotty point?

MARKS. Most decidedly. Of course you refused.

PHINEAS. Teetotally; but she told me to think better of it, and come to-night and give her my final conclusion. Chaw me into mincemeat, if I haven't made up my mind to do it!

MARKS. You astonish me!

PHINEAS. Well, you see, I can't get along without that gal;—she's sort of fixed my flint, and I'm sure to hang fire without her. I know I shall make a queer sort of Quaker, because you see, neighbour, I ain't precisely the kind of material to make a Quaker out of.

MARKS. No, not exactly.

PHINEAS. Well, I can't stop no longer. I must try to get across that candaverous river some way. It's getting late—take care of yourself, neighbour lawyer. I'm a teetotal victim to a pair of black eyes. Chaw me up to feed hogs if I'm not in a ruinatious state! [*Exit.*

MARKS. Queer genius, that, very!

Enter TOM LOKER.

So you've come at last.

LOKER. Yes. [*Looks into jug.*] Empty! Waiter! more whisky!

WAITER *enters with jug, and removes the empty one.—*
Enter HALEY.

HALEY. By the land! if this yer ain't the nearest, now, to

what I've heard .people call Providence! Why, Loker, how are ye?

LOKER. The devil! What brought you here, Haley?

HALEY. [*Sitting at table.*] I say, Tom, this yer's the luckiest thing in the world. I'm in a devil of a hobble, and you must help me out!

LOKER. Ugh! aw! like enough. A body may be pretty sure of that when you're glad to see 'em, or can make something off of 'em. What's the blow now?

HALEY. You've got a friend here—partner, perhaps?

LOKER. Yes, I have. Here, Marks—here's that ar fellow that I was with in Natchez.

MARKS. [*Grasping* HALEY'S *hand.*] Shall be pleased with his acquaintance. Mr. Haley, I believe?

HALEY. The same, sir. The fact is, gentlemen, this morning I bought a young 'un of Shelby up above here. His mother got wind of it, and what does she do but cut her lucky with him; and I'm afraid by this time that she has crossed the river, for I tracked her to this very place.

MARKS. So, then, ye're fairly sewed up, ain't ye? He! he! he! It's neatly done, too.

HALEY. This young 'un business makes lots of trouble in the trade.

MARKS. Now, Mr. Haley, what is it? Do you want us to undertake to catch this gal?

HALEY. The gal's no matter of mine—she's Shelby's—it's only the boy. I was a fool for buying the monkey.

LOKER. You're generally a fool!

MARKS. Come now, Loker, none of your huffs; you see, Mr. Haley's a-puttin' us in a way of a good job, I reckon; just hold still—these yer arrangements are my forte. This yer gal, Mr. Haley—how is she?—what is she?

[ELIZA *appears, with* HARRY, *listening.*

HALEY. Well, white and handsome—well brought up. I'd have given Shelby eight hundred or a thousand, and then made well on her.

MARKS. White and handsome—well brought up! Look here, now, Loker, a beautiful opening. We'll do a business here on our own account. We does the catchin'; the boy, of course, goes to Mr. Haley—we takes the gal to Orleans to speculate on. Ain't it beautiful? [*They confer together,*

ELIZA. Powers of mercy, protect me! How shall I escape these human bloodhounds? Ah! the window—the river of ice! That dark stream lies between me and liberty! Surely the ice will bear my trifling weight. It is my only chance of escape—better sink beneath the cold waters, with my child locked in my arms, than have him torn from me and sold into bondage. He sleeps upon my breast—Heaven, I put my trust in thee! *[Gets out of window.*

MARKS. Well, Tom Loker, what do you say?

LOKER. It'll do!

[Strikes his hand violently on the table.—ELIZA screams.— They all start to their feet.—ELIZA disappears.

HALEY. By the land, there she is now!
[They all rush to the window.

MARKS. She's making for the river!

LOKER. Let's after her!
[They all leap through the window.—Change.

SCENE V.—*Snowy Landscape.*

Enter ELIZA, with HARRY, hurriedly.

ELIZA. They press upon my footsteps—the river is my only hope! Heaven grant me strength to reach it, ere they overtake me! Courage, my child!—we will be free—or perish! *[Rushes off.*

Enter LOKER, HALEY and MARKS.

HALEY. We'll catch her yet; the river will stop her!

MARKS. No, it won't, for look! she has jumped upon the ice! She's a brave gal, anyhow!

LOKER. She'll be drowned!

HALEY. Curse that young 'un! I shall lose him, after all.

LOKER. Come on, Marks, to the ferry!

HALEY. Aye, to the ferry!—a hundred dollars for a boat!
[They rush off.

SCENE VI.—*The entire depth of stage, representing the Ohio River filled with Floating Ice. Bank on right hand.*

ELIZA *appears, with* HARRY, *on a cake of ice, and floats slowly across.—*HALEY, LOKER *and* MARKS, *on bank, right hand, observing.—*PHINEAS *on opposite shore.*

END OF ACT I.

ACT II.

SCENE I.—*A Handsome Parlour.*

MARIE *discovered reclining on a sofa.*

MARIE. [*Looking at a note.*] What can possibly detain St. Clare? According to this note, he should have been here a fortnight ago. [*Noise of carriage without.*] I do believe he has come at last.

EVA *runs in.*

EVA. Mamma!
[*Throws her arms around* MARIE'S *neck, and kisses her.*
MARIE. That will do—take care, child—don't you make my head ache!   [*Kisses her languidly.*

Enter ST. CLARE, OPHELIA, *and* TOM, *nicely dressed.*

ST. CLARE. Well, my dear Marie, here we are at last. The wanderers have arrived, you see. Allow me to present my cousin, Miss Ophelia, who is about to undertake the office of our housekeeper.

MARIE. [*Rising to a sitting posture.*] I am delighted to see you. How do you like the appearance of our city?

EVA. [*Running to* OPHELIA.] Oh! is it not beautiful? My own darling home!—is it not beautiful?

OPHELIA. Yes, it is a pretty place, though it looks rather old and heathenish to me.

ST. CLARE. Tom, my boy, this seems to suit you?

TOM. Yes, mas'r, it looks about the right thing.

ST. CLARE. See here, Marie, I've brought you a coachman, at last, to order. I tell you, he's a regular hearse for blackness and sobriety, and will drive you like a funeral, if you wish. Open your eyes, now, and look at him. Now, don't say I never think about you when I'm gone.

MARIE. I know he'll get drunk.

ST. CLARE. Oh! no he won't. He's warranted a pious and sober article.

MARIE. Well, I hope he may turn out well; it's more than I expect, though.

St. Clare. Have you no curiosity to learn how and where I picked up Tom?

Eva. *Uncle* Tom, papa; that's his name.

St. Clare. Right, my little sunbeam!

Tom. Please, mas'r, that ain't no 'casion to say nothing 'bout me.

St. Clare. You are too modest, my modern Hannibal. Do you know, Marie, that our little Eva took a fancy to Uncle Tom—whom we met on board the steamboat—and persuaded me to buy him?

Marie. Ah! she is so odd!

St. Clare. As we approached the landing, a sudden rush of the passengers precipitated Eva into the water—

Marie. Gracious heavens!

St. Clare. A man leaped into the river, and, as she rose to the surface of the water, grasped her in his arms, and held her up until she could be drawn on the boat again. Who was that man, Eva?

Eva. Uncle Tom!

[*Runs to him.—He lifts her in his arms.—She kisses him.*

Tom. The dear soul!

Ophelia. [*Astonished.*] How shiftless!

St. Clare. [*Overhearing her.*] What's the matter now, pray?

Ophelia. Well, I want to be kind to everybody, and I wouldn't have anything hurt, but as to kissing—

St. Clare. Niggers! that you're not up to, hey?

Ophelia. Yes, that's it—how can she?

St. Clare. Oh! bless you, it's nothing when you are used to it!

Ophelia. I could never be so shiftless!

Eva. Come with me, Uncle Tom, and I will show you about the house. [*Crosses with* Tom.

Tom. Can I go, mas'r?

St. Clare. Yes, Tom; she is your little mistress—your only duty will be to attend to her! [Tom *bows and exits.*

Marie. Eva, my dear!

Eva. Well, mamma?

Marie. Do not exert yourself too much!

Eva. No, mamma! [*Runs out.*

Ophelia. [*Lifting up her hands.*] How shiftless!

S<small>T</small>. C<small>LARE</small> *sits next to* M<small>ARIE</small> *on sofa.*—O<small>PHELIA</small> *next to* S<small>T</small>. C<small>LARE</small>.

S<small>T</small>. C<small>LARE</small>. Well, what do you think of Uncle Tom, Marie?

M<small>ARIE</small>. He is a perfect behemoth!

S<small>T</small>. C<small>LARE</small>. Come, now, Marie, be gracious, and say something pretty to a fellow!

M<small>ARIE</small>. You've been gone a fortnight beyond the time!

S<small>T</small>. C<small>LARE</small>. Well, you know I wrote you the reason.

M<small>ARIE</small>. Such a short, cold letter!

S<small>T</small>. C<small>LARE</small>. Dear me! the mail was just going, and it had to be that or nothing.

M<small>ARIE</small>. That's just the way; always something to make your journeys long and letters short!

S<small>T</small>. C<small>LARE</small>. Look at this. [*Takes an elegant velvet case from his pocket.*] Here's a present I got for you in New York—a daguerreotype of Eva and myself.

M<small>ARIE</small>. [*Looks at it with a dissatisfied air.*] What made you sit in such an awkward position?

S<small>T</small>. C<small>LARE</small>. Well, the position may be a matter of opinion, but what do you think of the likeness?

M<small>ARIE</small>. [*Closing the case snappishly.*] If you don't think anything of my opinion in one case, I suppose you wouldn't in another.

O<small>PHELIA</small>. [*Sententiously, aside.*] How shiftless!

S<small>T</small>. C<small>LARE</small>. Hang the woman! Come, Marie, what do you think of the likeness? Don't be nonsensical now.

M<small>ARIE</small>. It's very inconsiderate of you, St. Clare, to insist on my talking and looking at things. You know I've been lying all day with the sick headache, and there's been such a tumult made ever since you came, I'm half dead!

O<small>PHELIA</small>. You're subject to the sick headache, ma'am?

M<small>ARIE</small>. Yes, I'm a perfect martyr to it!

O<small>PHELIA</small>. Juniper-berry tea is good for sick headache; at least, Molly, Deacon Abraham Perry's wife, used to say so; and she was a great nurse.

S<small>T</small>. C<small>LARE</small>. I'll have the first juniper-berries that get ripe in our garden by the lake brought in for that especial purpose. Come, cousin, let us take a stroll in the garden. Will you join us, Marie?

M<small>ARIE</small>. I wonder how you can ask such a question, when you know how fragile I am. I shall retire to my chamber, and repose till dinner time. [*Exit.*

OPHELIA. [*Looking after her.*] How shiftless!

ST. CLARE. Come, cousin! [*As he goes out.*] Look out for the babies! If I step upon anybody, let them mention it.

OPHELIA. Babies under foot! How shiftless! [*Exeunt.*

SCENE II.—*A Garden.*

TOM *discovered, seated on a bank, with* EVA *on his knee—his button-holes are filled with flowers, and* EVA *is hanging a wreath around his neck. Enter* ST. CLARE *and* OPHELIA, *observing.*

EVA. Oh, Tom; you look so funny.

TOM. [*Sees* ST. CLARE, *and puts* EVA *down.*] I begs pardon, mas'r, but the young missis would do it. Look yer, I'm like the ox, mentioned in the Good Book, dressed for the sacrifice.

ST. CLAIRE. I say, what do you think, Pussy? Which do you like the best—to live as they do at your uncle's, up in Vermont, or to have a house full of servants, as we do?

EVA. Oh! of course our way is the pleasantest.

ST. CLARE. [*Patting her head*] Why so?

EVA. Because it makes so many more round you to love, you know.

OPHELIA. Now, that's just like Eva—just one of her odd speeches.

EVA. Is it an odd speech, papa?

ST. CLARE. Rather, as this world goes, Pussy. But where has my little Eva been?

EVA. Oh! I've been up in Tom's room, hearing him sing.

ST. CLARE. Hearing Tom sing, hey?

EVA. Oh, yes! he sings such beautiful things about the new Jerusalem, and bright angels, and the land of Canaan.

ST. CLARE. I dare say; it's better than the opera, isn't it?

EVA. Yes; and he's going to teach them to me.

ST. CLARE. Singing lessons, hey? You are coming on.

EVA. Yes, he sings for me, and I read to him in my Bible, and he explains what it means. Come, Tom.

[*She takes his hand and they exit.*

St. Clare. [*Aside.*] Oh, Evangeline! Rightly named; hath not heaven made thee an evangel to me?

Ophelia. How shiftless! How can you let her?

St. Clare. Why not?

Ophelia. Why, I don't know; it seems so dreadful.

St. Clare. You would think no harm in a child's caressing a large dog, even if he was black; but a creature that can think, reason and feel, and is immortal, you shudder at. Confess it, cousin. I know the feeling among some of you Northerners well enough. Not that there is a particle of virtue in our not having it, but custom with us does what Christianity ought to do: obliterates the feeling of personal prejudice. You loathe them as you would a snake or a toad, yet you are indignant at their wrongs. You would not have them abused, but you don't want to have anything to do with them yourselves. Isn't that it?

Ophelia. Well, cousin, there may be some truth in this.

St. Clare. What would the poor and lowly do without children? Your little child is your only true democrat. Tom, now, is a hero to Eva; his stories are wonders in her eyes; his songs and Methodist hymns are better than an opera, and the traps and little bits of trash in his pockets a mine of jewels, and he the most wonderful Tom that ever wore a black skin. This is one of the roses of Eden that the Lord has dropped down expressly for the poor and lowly, who get few enough of any other kind.

Ophelia. It's strange, cousin; one might almost think you was a *professor,* to hear you talk.

St. Clare. A professor?

Ophelia. Yes, a professor of religion.

St. Clare. Not at all; not a professor as you town folks have it, and, what is worse, I'm afraid, not a *practicer,* either.

Ophelia. What makes you talk so, then?

St. Clare. Nothing is easier than talking. My forte lies in talking, and yours, cousin, lies in doing. And speaking of that puts me in mind that I have made a purchase for your department. There's the article now. Here, Topsy!

[*Whistles.*

TOPSY *runs on.*

OPHELIA. Good gracious! what a heathenish, shiftless looking object! St. Clare, what in the world have you brought that thing here for?

ST. CLARE. For you to educate, to be sure, and train in the way she should go. I thought she was rather a funny specimen in the Jim Crow line. Here, Topsy, give us a song, and show us some of your dancing.

[TOPSY *sings a verse and dances a breakdown.*

OPHELIA. [*Paralyzed.*] Well, of all things! If I ever saw the like!

ST. CLARE. [*Smothering a laugh.*] Topsy, this is your new mistress—I'm going to give you up to her. See now that you behave yourself.

TOPSY. Yes, mas'r.

ST. CLARE. You're going to be good, Topsy, you understand?

TOPSY. Oh, yes, mas'r.

OPHELIA. Now, St. Clare, what upon earth is this for? Your house is so full of these plagues now, that a body can't set down their foot without treading on 'em. I get up in the morning and find one asleep behind the door, and see one black head poking out from under the table—one lying on the door mat, and they are moping and mowing and grinning between all the railings, and tumbling over the kitchen floor! What on earth did you want to bring this one for?

ST. CLARE. For you to educate—didn't I tell you? You're always preaching about educating; I thought I would make you a present of a fresh caught specimen, and let you try your hand on her and bring her up in the way she should go.

OPHELIA. I don't want her, I am sure; I have more to do with 'em now than I want to.

ST. CLARE. That's you Christians, all over. You'll get up a society, and get some poor missionary to spend all his days among just such heathens; but let me see one of you that would take one into your house with you, and take the labour of their conversion upon yourselves.

OPHELIA. Well, I didn't think of it in that light. It might be a real missionary work. Well, I'll do what I can. [*Advances to* TOPSY.] She's dreadful dirty and shiftless! How old are you, Topsy?

TOPSY. Dunno, missis.

OPHELIA. How shiftless! Don't know how old you are? Didn't anybody ever tell you? Who was your mother?

TOPSY. [*Grinning.*] Never had none.

OPHELIA. Never had any mother? What do you mean? Where was you born?

TOPSY. Never was born.

OPHELIA. You mustn't answer me in that way. I'm not playing with you. Tell me where you was born, and who your father and mother were?

TOPSY. Never was born, tell you; never had no father, nor mother, nor nothin'. I war raised by a speculator, with lots of others. Old Aunt Sue used to take care on us.

ST. CLARE. She speaks the truth, cousin. Speculators buy them up cheap, when they are little, and get them raised for the market.

OPHELIA. How long have you lived with your master and mistress?

TOPSY. Dunno, missis.

OPHELIA. How shiftless! Is it a year, or more, or less?

TOPSY. Dunno, missis.

ST. CLARE. She does not know what a year is; she don't even know her own age.

OPHELIA. Have you ever heard anything about heaven, Topsy? [TOPSY *looks bewildered and grins.*] Do you know who made you?

TOPSY. Nobody, as I knows on, he, he, he! I 'spect I growed. Don't think nobody never made me.

OPHELIA. The shiftless heathen! What can you do? What did you do for your master and mistress?

TOPSY. Fetch water—and wash dishes—and rub knives—and wait on folks—and dance breakdowns.

OPHELIA. I shall break down, I'm afraid, in trying to make anything of you, you shiftless mortal!

ST. CLARE. You find virgin soil there, cousin; put in your own ideas—you won't find many to pull up. [*Exit laughing.*

OPHELIA. [*Takes out her handkerchief.—A pair of gloves falls.—*TOPSY *picks them up slyly and puts them in her sleeve.*] Follow me, you benighted innocent!

TOPSY. Yes, missis.

As OPHELIA *turns her back to her, she seizes the end of the ribbon she wears around her waist, and twitches it off.—* OPHELIA *turns and sees her as she is putting it in her other sleeve.—*OPHELIA *takes ribbon from her.*

OPHELIA. What's this? You naughty, wicked girl, you've been stealing this?

TOPSY. Laws! why, that ar's missis' ribbon, ain't it? How could it got caught in my sleeve?

OPHELIA. Topsy, you naughty girl, don't you tell me a lie —you stole that ribbon!

TOPSY. Missis, I declare for't, I didn't—never seed it till dis yer blessed minnit.

OPHELIA. Topsy, don't you know it's wicked to tell lies?

TOPSY. I never tells no lies, missis; it's just de truth I've been telling now, and nothing else.

OPHELIA. Topsy, I shall have to whip you, if you tell lies so.

TOPSY. Laws, missis, if you's to whip all day, couldn't say no other way. I never seed dat ar—it must a got caught in my sleeve. [*Blubbers.*

OPHELIA. [*Seizes her by the shoulders.*] Don't you tell me that again, you barefaced fibber! [*Shakes her.—The gloves fall on stage.*] There you, my gloves too—you outrageous young heathen! [*Picks them up.*] Will you tell me, now, you didn't steal the ribbon?

TOPSY. No, missis; stole de gloves, but didn't steal de ribbon. It was permiskus.

OPHELIA. Why, you young reprobate!

TOPSY. Yes—I's knows I's wicked!

OPHELIA. Then you know you ought to be punished. [*Boxes her ears.*] What do you think of that?

TOPSY. He, he, he! De Lord, missus; dat wouldn't kill a 'skeeter! [*Runs off laughing.—*OPHELIA *follows indignantly.*

SCENE III.—*The Tavern by the River.—Table and chairs.— Jug and glasses on table.—On flat is a printed placard, headed:—*"Four Hundred Dollars Reward—Runaway— George Harris!"

PHINEAS *is discovered, seated at table.*

PHINEAS. So yer I am; and a pretty business I've under-took to do. Find the husband of the gal that crossed the river on the ice two or three days ago. Ruth said I must do it, and I'll be teetotally chawed up if I don't do it. I see they've offered a reward for him, dead or alive. How in creation am I to find the varmint? He isn't likely to go round looking natural, with a full description of his hide and figure staring him in the face.

Enter MR. WILSON.

I say, stranger, how are ye?   [*Rises and comes forward.*

WILSON. Well, I reckon.

PHINEAS. Any news?   [*Takes out plug and knife.*

WILSON. Not that I know of.

PHINEAS. [*Cutting a piece of tobacco and offering it.*] Chaw?

WILSON. No, thank ye—it don't agree with me.

PHINEAS. Don't, eh? [*Putting it in his own mouth.*] I never felt any the worse for it.

WILSON. [*Sees placard.*] What's that?

PHINEAS. Nigger advertised. [*Advances towards it and spits on it.*] There's my mind upon that.

WILSON. Why, now stranger, what's that for?

PHINEAS. I'd do it all the same to the writer of that ar paper, if he was here. Any man that owns a boy like that, and can't find any better way of treating him than branding him on the hand with the letter H, as that paper states, *deserves* to lose him. Such papers as this ar' a shame to old Kaintuck! that's my mind right out, if anybody wants to know.

WILSON. Well, now, that's a fact.

PHINEAS. I used to have a gang of boys, sir—that was before I fell in love—and I just told 'em:—"Boys," says I, "run now! Dig! put! jest when you want to. I never shall come to look after you!" That's the way I kept mine. Let 'em know they are free to run any time, and it jest stops their wanting to. It stands to reason it should. Treat 'em like men, and you'll have men's work.

WILSON. I think you are altogether right, friend, and this man described here is a fine fellow—no mistake about that. He worked for me some half dozen years in my bagging factory, and he was my best hand, sir. He is an ingenious fellow, too; he invented a machine for the cleaning of hemp—

a really valuable affair; it's gone into use in several factories. His master holds the patent of it.

PHINEAS. I'll warrant ye; holds it, and makes money out of it, and then turns round and brands the boy in his right hand! If I had a fair chance, I'd mark him, I reckon, so that he'd carry it *one* while!

Enter GEORGE HARRIS, *disguised.*

GEORGE. [*Speaking as he enters.*] Jim, see to the trunks. [*Sees* WILSON.] Ah! Mr. Wilson here?

WILSON. Bless my soul, can it be?

GEORGE. [*Advances and grasps his hand.*] Mr. Wilson, I see you remember me, Mr. Butler, of Oaklands, Shelby county.

WILSON. Ye—yes—yes—sir.

PHINEAS. Halloa! there's a screw loose here somewhere. That old gentleman seems to be struck into a pretty considerable heap of astonishment. May I be teetotally chawed up! if I don't believe that's the identical man I'm arter. [*Crosses to* GEORGE.] How are ye, George Harris?

GEORGE. [*Starting back and thrusting his hands into his breast.*] You know me?

PHINEAS. Ha, ha, ha! I rather conclude I do; but don't get riled, I ain't a bloodhound in disguise.

GEORGE. How did you discover me?

PHINEAS. By a teetotal smart guess. You're the very man I want to see. Do you know I was sent after you?

GEORGE. Ah! by my master?

PHINEAS. No; by your wife.

GEORGE. My wife! Where is she?

PHINEAS. She's stopping with a Quaker family over on the Ohio side.

GEORGE. Then she is safe?

PHINEAS. Teetotally!

GEORGE. Conduct me to her.

PHINEAS. Just wait a brace of shakes and I'll do it. I've got to go and get the boat ready. 'Twon't take me but a minute—make yourself comfortable till I get back. Chaw me up! but this is what I call doing things in short order.

[*Exit.*

WILSON. George!

GEORGE. Yes, George!

WILSON. I couldn't have thought it!

GEORGE. I am pretty well disguised, I fancy; you see I don't answer to the advertisement at all.

WILSON. George, this is a dangerous game you are playing; I could not have advised you to it.

GEORGE. I can do it on my own responsibility.

WILSON. Well, George, I suppose you're running away—leaving your lawful master, George (I don't wonder at it), at the same time, I'm sorry, George, yes, decidedly. I think I must say that it's my duty to tell you so.

GEORGE. Why are you sorry, sir?

WILSON. Why, to see you, as it were, setting yourself in opposition to the laws of your country.

GEORGE. *My* country! What country have *I*, but the grave? And I would to heaven that I was laid there!

WILSON. George, you've got a hard master, in fact he is—well, he conducts himself reprehensibly—I can't pretend to defend him. I'm sorry for you, now; it's a bad case—very bad; but we must all submit to the indications of Providence, George, don't you see?

GEORGE. I wonder, Mr. Wilson, if the Indians should come and take you a prisoner away from your wife and children, and want to keep you all your life hoeing corn for them, if you'd think it your duty to abide in the condition in which you were called? I rather imagine that you'd think the first stray horse you could find an indication of Providence, shouldn't you?

WILSON. Really, George, putting the case in that somewhat peculiar light—I don't know—under those circumstances—but what I might. But it seems to me you are running an awful risk. You can't hope to carry it out. If you're taken it will be worse with you than ever; they'll only abuse you, and half kill you, and sell you down river.

GEORGE. Mr. Wilson, I know all this. I *do* run a risk, but—[*Throws open coat and shows pistols and knife in his belt.*] There! I'm ready for them. Down South I never *will* go! no, if it comes to that, I can earn myself at least six feet of free soil—the first and last I shall ever own in Kentucky!

WILSON. Why, George, this state of mind is awful—it's

getting really desperate. I'm concerned. Going to break the laws of your country?

GEORGE. My country again! Sir, I haven't any country any more than I have any father. I don't want anything of *your* country, except to be left alone—to go peaceably out of it; but if any man tries to stop me, let him take care, for I am desperate. I'll fight for my liberty, to the last breath I breathe! You say your fathers did it; if it was right for them, it is right for me!

WILSON. [*Walking up and down, and fanning his face with a large yellow silk handkerchief.*] Blast 'em all! Haven't I always said so—the infernal old cusses! Bless me! I hope I ain't swearing now! Well, go ahead, George, go ahead. But be careful, my boy; don't shoot anybody, unless—well, you'd *better* not shoot—at least I wouldn't *hit* anybody, you know.

GEORGE. Only in self-defense.

WILSON. Well, well. [*Fumbling in his pocket.*] I suppose, perhaps, I ain't following my judgment—hang it, I won't follow my judgment. So here, George.

[*Takes out a pocket-book and offers* GEORGE *a roll of bills.*

GEORGE. No, my kind, good sir, you've done a great deal for me, and this might get you into trouble. I have money enough, I hope, to take me as far as I need it.

WILSON. No; but you must, George. Money is a great help everywhere; can't have too much, if you get it honestly. Take it, do take it, *now* do, my boy!

GEORGE. [*Taking the money.*] On condition, sir, that I may repay it at some future time, I will.

WILSON. And now, George, how long are you going to travel in this way? Not long or far, I hope? It's well carried on, but too bold.

GEORGE. Mr. Wilson, it is *so bold,* and this tavern is so near, that they will never think of it; they will look for me on ahead, and you yourself wouldn't know me.

WILSON. But the mark on your hand?

GEORGE. [*Draws off his glove and shows scar.*] That is a parting mark of Mr. Harris' regard. Looks interesting, doesn't it? [*Puts on glove again.*

WILSON. I declare, my very blood runs cold when I think of it—your condition and your risks!

GEORGE. Mine has run cold a good many years; at present, it's about up to the boiling point.

WILSON. George, something has brought you out wonderfully. You hold up your head, and move and speak like another man.

GEORGE. [*Proudly.*] Because I'm a *freeman!* Yes, sir; I've said "master" for the last time to any man. *I'm free!*

WILSON. Take care! You are not sure; you may be taken.

GEORGE. All men are free and equal *in the grave*, if it comes to that, Mr. Wilson.

Enter PHINEAS.

PHINEAS. Them's my sentiment, to a teetotal atom, and I don't care who knows it! Neighbour, the boat is ready, and the sooner we make tracks the better. I've seen some mysterious strangers lurking about these diggings, so we'd better put.

GEORGE. Farewell, Mr. Wilson, and heaven reward you for the many kindnesses you have shown the poor fugitive!

WILSON. [*Grasping his hand.*] You're a brave fellow, George. I wish in my heart you were safe through, though—that's what I do.

PHINEAS. And ain't I the man of all creation to put him through, stranger? Chaw me up if I don't take him to his dear little wife, in the smallest possible quantity of time. Come, neighbour, let's vamoose.

GEORGE. Farewell, Mr. Wilson.

WILSON. My best wishes go with you, George. [*Exit.*

PHINEAS. You're a trump, old Slow-and-Easy.

GEORGE. [*Looking off.*] Look! look!

PHINEAS. Consarn their picters, here they come! We can't get out of the house without their seeing us. We're teetotally treed!

GEORGE. Let us fight our way through them!

PHINEAS. No, that won't do; there are too many of them for a fair fight—we should be chawed up in no time. [*Looks round and sees trap door.*] Holloa! here's a cellar door. Just you step down here a few minutes, while I parley with them. [*Lifts trap.*

GEORGE. I am resolved to perish sooner than surrender!
[*Goes down trap.*

PHINEAS. That's your sort! [*Closes trap and stands on it.*] Here they are!

Enter HALEY, MARKS, LOKER *and three* MEN.

HALEY. Say, stranger, you haven't seen a runaway darkey about these parts, eh?

PHINEAS. What kind of a darkey?

HALEY. A mulatto chap, almost as light-complexioned as a white man.

PHINEAS. Was he a pretty good-looking chap?

HALEY. Yes.

PHINEAS. Kind of tall?

HALEY. Yes.

PHINEAS. With brown hair?

HALEY. Yes.

PHINEAS. And dark eyes?

HALEY. Yes.

PHINEAS. Pretty well dressed?

HALEY. Yes.

PHINEAS. Scar on his right hand?

HALEY. Yes, yes.

PHINEAS. Well, I ain't seen him.

HALEY. Oh, bother! Come, boys, let's search the house.
[*Exeunt.*

PHINEAS. [*Raises trap.*] Now, then, neighbour George.

GEORGE *enters, up trap.*

Now's the time to cut your lucky.

GEORGE. Follow me, Phineas. [*Exit.*

PHINEAS. In a brace of shakes. [*Is closing trap as*

HALEY, MARKS, LOKER, *&c., re-enter.*

HALEY. Ah! he's down in the cellar. Follow me, boys! [*Thrusts* PHINEAS *aside, and rushes down trap, followed by the others.* PHINEAS *closes trap and stands on it.*

PHINEAS. Chaw me up! but I've got 'em all in a trap. [*Knocking below.*] Be quiet, you pesky varmints! [*Knock-*

ing.] They're getting mighty oneasy. [*Knocking.*] Will you be quiet, you savagerous critters! [*The trap is forced open.* HALEY *and* MARKS *appear.* PHINEAS *seizes a chair and stands over trap.*] Down with you or I'll smash you into apple-fritters!   [*Tableau.*

SCENE IV.—*A Plain Chamber.*

TOPSY. [*Without.*] You go 'long. No more nigger dan you be! [*Enters—shouts and laughter without—looks off.*] You seem to think yourself white folks. You ain't nerry one —black *nor* white. I'd like to be one or turrer. Law! you niggers, does you know you's all sinners? Well, you is— everybody is. White folks is sinners too—Miss Feely says so—but I 'spects niggers is the biggest ones. But Lor'! ye ain't any on ye up to me. I's so awful wicked there can't nobody do nothin' with me. I used to keep old missis a-swarin' at me half de time. I 'spects I's de wickedest critter in de world.

[*Song and dance introduced.*

Enter EVA.

EVA. Oh, Topsy! Topsy! you have been very wrong again.

TOPSY. Well, I 'spects I have.

EVA. What makes you do so?

TOPSY. I dunno; I 'spects it's cause I's so wicked.

EVA. Why did you spoil Jane's earrings?

TOPSY. 'Cause she's so proud. She called me a little black imp, and turned up her pretty nose at me 'cause she is whiter than I am. I was gwine by her room, and I seed her coral earrings lying on de table, so I threw dem on de floor, and put my foot on 'em, and scrunched 'em all to little bits— he! he! he! I's so wicked.

EVA. Don't you know that was very wrong?

TOPSY. I don't car' I despises dem what sets up for fine ladies, when dey ain't nothin' but cream-coloured niggers! Dere's Miss Rosa—she gives me lots of 'pertinent remarks. T'other night she was gwine to ball. She put on a beau'ful dress that missis give her—wid her har curled, all nice and pretty. She hab to go down de back stairs—dey am dark—and I puts a pail of hot water on dem, and she put her foot into it, and den she go tumblin' to de bottom of de stairs, and de water go all ober her, and spile her dress, and scald her dreadful bad! He! he! he! I's so wicked!

Eva. Oh! how could you!

Topsy. Don't dey despise me 'cause I don't know nothin'? Don't dey laugh at me 'cause I'm brack, and dey ain't?

Eva. But you shouldn't mind them.

Topsy. Well, I don't mind dem; but when dey are passing under my winder, I trows dirty water on 'em, and dat spiles der complexions.

Eva. What does make you so bad, Topsy? Why won't you try and be good? Don't you love anybody, Topsy?

Topsy. Can't recommember.

Eva. But you love your father and mother?

Topsy. Never had none; ye know, I telled ye that, Miss Eva.

Eva. Oh! I know; but hadn't you any brother, or sister, or aunt, or——

Topsy. No, none on 'em—never had nothin' nor nobody. I's brack—no one loves me!

Eva. Oh! Topsy, I love you! [*Laying her hand on* Topsy's *shoulder.*] I love you because you haven't had any father, or mother, or friends. I love you, and I want you to be good. I wish you would try to be good for my sake. [Topsy *looks astonished for a moment, and then bursts into tears.*] Only think of it, Topsy—*you* can be one of those spirits bright Uncle Tom sings about!

Topsy. Oh! dear Miss Eva—dear Miss Eva! I will try— I will try! I never did care nothin' about it before.

Eva. If you try, you will succeed. Come with me.

[*Takes* Topsy's *hand.*

Topsy. I will try; but den, I's so wicked!

[*Exit* Eva, *followed by* Topsy, *crying.*

Scene V.—*Chamber.*

Enter George, Eliza *and* Harry.

George. At length, Eliza, after many wanderings, we are again united.

Eliza. Thanks to these generous Quakers, who have so kindly sheltered us.

GEORGE.   Not forgetting our friend Phineas.

ELIZA.   I do indeed owe him much. 'Twas he I met upon the icy river's bank, after that fearful but successful attempt, when I fled from the slave-trader with my child in my arms.

GEORGE.   It seems almost incredible that you could have crossed the river on the ice.

ELIZA.   Yes, I did.   Heaven helping me, I crossed on the ice, for they were behind me—right behind—and there was no other way.

GEORGE.   But the ice was all in broken-up blocks, swinging and heaving up and down in the water.

ELIZA.   I know it was—I know it; I did not think I should get over, but I did not care—I could but die if I did not! I leaped on the ice, but how I got across I don't know; the first I remember, a man was helping me up the bank—that man was Phineas.

GEORGE.   My brave girl! you deserve your freedom—you have richly earned it!

ELIZA.   And when we get to Canada I can help you to work, and between us we can find something to live on.

GEORGE.   Yes, Eliza, so long as we have each other, and our boy.   Oh, Eliza, if these people only knew what a blessing it is for a man to feel that his wife and child belong to *him!*   I've often wondered to see men that could call their wives and children *their own,* fretting and worrying about anything else.   Why, I feel rich and strong, though we have nothing but our bare hands.   If they will only let me alone now, I will be satisfied—thankful!

ELIZA.   But we are not quite out of danger; we are not yet in Canada.

GEORGE.   True; but it seems as if I smelt the free air, and it makes me strong!

Enter PHINEAS, *dressed as a Quaker.*

PHINEAS.   [*With a snuffle.*]   Verily, friends, how is it with thee?—hum!

GEORGE.   Why, Phineas, what means this metamorphosis?

PHINEAS.   I've become a Quaker! that's the meaning on't.

GEORGE.   What—you?

PHINEAS. Teetotally! I was driven to it by a strong argument, composed of a pair of sparkling eyes, rosy cheeks, and pouting lips. Them lips would persuade a man to assassinate his grandmother! [*Assumes the Quaker tone again.*] Verily, George, I have discovered something of importance to the interests of thee and thy party, and it were well for thee to hear it.

GEORGE. Keep us not in suspense!

PHINEAS. Well, after I left you on the road, I stopped at a little, lone tavern, just below here. Well, I was tired with hard driving, and, after my supper, I stretched myself down on a pile of bags in the corner, and pulled a buffalo hide over me—and what does I do but get fast asleep.

GEORGE. With one ear open, Phineas?

PHINEAS. No, I slept ears and all for an hour or two, for I was pretty well tired; but when I came to myself a little, I found that there were some men in the room, sitting round a table, drinking and talking; and I thought, before I made much muster, I'd just see what they were up to, especially as I heard them say something about the Quakers. Then I listened with both ears and found they were talking about you. So I kept quiet, and heard them lay off all their plans. They've got a right notion of the track we are going to-night, and they'll be down after us, six or eight strong. So, now, what's to be done?

ELIZA. What *shall* we do, George?

GEORGE. I know what I shall do! [*Takes out pistols.*]

PHINEAS. Ay—ay, thou seest, Eliza, how it will work—pistols—phitz—poppers!

ELIZA. I see; but I pray it come not to that!

GEORGE. I don't want to involve any one with or for me. If you will lend me your vehicle, and direct me, I will drive alone to the next stand.

PHINEAS. Ah! well, friend, but thee'll need a driver for all that. Thee's quite welcome to do all the fighting thee knows; but I know a thing or two about the road that thee doesn't.

GEORGE. But I don't want to involve you.

PHINEAS. Involve me! Why, chaw me—that is to say—when thee does involve me, please to let me know.

ELIZA. Phineas is a wise and skillful man. You will do

well, George, to abide by his judgment. And, oh! George, be not hasty with these—young blood is hot!

[*Laying her hand on pistols.*

GEORGE. I will attack no man. All I ask of this country is to be left alone, and I will go out peaceably. But I'll fight to the last breath before they shall take from me my wife and son! Can you blame me?

PHINEAS. Mortal man cannot blame thee, neighbour George! Flesh and blood could not do otherwise. Woe unto the world because of offenses, but woe unto them through whom the offense cometh! That's gospel, teetotally!

GEORGE. Would not even you, sir, do the same, in my place?

PHINEAS. I pray that I be not tried; the flesh is weak— but I think my flesh would be pretty tolerably strong in such a case; I ain't sure, friend George, that I shouldn't hold a fellow for thee, if thee had any accounts to settle with him.

ELIZA. Heaven grant we be not tempted.

PHINEAS. But if we are tempted too much, why, consarn 'em! let them look out, that's all.

GEORGE. It's quite plain you was not born for a Quaker. The old nature has its way in you pretty strong yet.

PHINEAS. Well, I reckon you are pretty teetotally right.

GEORGE. Had we not better hasten our flight?

PHINEAS. Well, I rather conclude we had; we're full two hours ahead of them, if they start at the time they planned; so let's vamoose. [*Exeunt.*

SCENE VI.—*A Rocky Pass in the Hills.—Large set rock and platform.*

PHINEAS. [*Without.*] Out with you in a twinkling, every one, and up into these rocks with me! run *now*, if you *ever* did run!

PHINEAS *enters, with* HARRY *in his arms.*—GEORGE *supporting* ELIZA.

Come up here; this is one of our old hunting dens. Come up. [*They ascend the rock.*] Well, here we are. Let 'em get us if they can. Whoever comes here has to walk single file between those two rocks, in fair range of your pistols—d'ye see?

GEORGE. I do sec. And now, as this affair is mine, let me take all the risk, and do all the fighting.

PHINEAS. Thee's quite welcome to do the fighting, George; but I may have the fun of looking on, I suppose. But see, these fellows are kind of debating down there, and looking up, like hens when they are going to fly up onto the roost. Hadn't thee better give 'em a word of advice, before they come up, jest to tell 'em handsomely they'll be shot if they do.

LOKER, MARKS, *and three* MEN *enter.*

MARKS. Well, Tom, your coons are fairly treed.

LOKER. Yes, I see 'em go up right here; and here's a path—I'm for going right up. They can't jump down in a hurry, and it won't take long to ferret 'em out.

MARKS. But, Tom, they might fire at us from behind the rocks. That would be ugly, you know.

LOKER. Ugh! always for saving your skin, Marks. No danger; niggers are too plaguy scared!

MARKS. I don't know why I shouldn't save my skin; it's the best I've got; and niggers do fight like the devil sometimes.

GEORGE. [*Rising on the rock.*] Gentlemen, who are you down there, and what do you want?

LOKER. We want a party of runaway niggers. One George and Eliza Harris, and their son. We've got the officers here, and a warrant to take 'em too. D'ye hear? Ain't you George Harris, that belonged to Mr. Harris, of Shelby county, Kentucky?

GEORGE. I am George Harris. A Mr. Harris, of Kentucky, did call me his property. But now I'm a freeman, standing on Heaven's free soil! My wife and child I claim as mine. We have arms to defend ourselves, and we mean to do it. You can come up if you like, but the first one that comes within range of our bullets is a dead man.

MARKS. Oh, come—come, young man, this ain't no kind of talk at all for you. You see we're officers of justice. We've got the law on our side, and the power and so forth; so you'd better give up peaceably, you see—for you'll certainly have to give up at last.

GEORGE. I know very well that you've got the law on your side, and the power; but you haven't got us. We are standing here as free as you are, and by the great power that made us, we'll fight for our liberty till we die!

During this, MARKS *draws a pistol, and when he concludes fires at him.—*ELIZA *screams.*

GEORGE. It's nothing, Eliza; I am unhurt.

PHINEAS. [*Drawing* GEORGE *down.*] Thee'd better keep out of sight with thy speechifying; they're teetotal mean scamps.

LOKER. What did you do that for, Marks?

MARKS. You see, you get jist as much for him dead as alive in Kentucky.

GEORGE. Now, Phineas, the first man that advances I fire at; you take the second, and so on. It won't do to waste two shots on one.

PHINEAS. But what if you don't hit?

GEORGE. I'll try my best.

PHINEAS. Creation! chaw me up if there ain't stuff in you!

MARKS. I think I must have hit some on 'em. I heard a squeal.

LOKER. I'm going right up for one. I never was afraid of niggers, and I ain't a going to be now. Who goes after me?

LOKER *dashes up the rock.—*GEORGE *fires.—He staggers for a moment, then springs to the top.—*PHINEAS *seizes him.— A struggle.*

PHINEAS. Friend, thee is not wanted here!

[*Throws* LOKER *over the rock.*

MARKS. [*Retreating.*] Lord help us—they're perfect devils!

MARKS *and* PARTY *run off.* GEORGE *and* ELIZA *kneel in an attitude of thanksgiving, with the* CHILD *between them.—* PHINEAS *stands over them exulting.*

END OF ACT II.

ACT III.

SCENE I.—*Chamber.*

Enter ST. CLARE, *followed by* TOM.

ST. CLARE. [*Giving money and papers to* TOM.] There, Tom, are the bills, and the money to liquidate them.

TOM. Yes, mas'r.

ST. CLARE. Well, Tom, what are you waiting for? Isn't all right there?

TOM. I'm 'fraid not, mas'r.

ST. CLARE. Why, Tom, what's the matter? You look as solemn as a coffin.

TOM. I feel very bad, mas'r. I allays have thought that mas'r would be good to everybody.

ST. CLARE. Well, Tom, haven't I been? Come, now, what do you want? There's something you haven't got, I suppose, and this is the preface.

TOM. Mas'r allays been good to me. I haven't nothing to complain of on that head; but there is one that mas'r isn't good to.

ST. CLARE. Why, Tom, what's got into you? Speak out— what do you mean?

TOM. Last night, between one and two, I thought so. I studied upon the matter then—mas'r isn't good to *himself.*

ST. CLARE. Ah! now I understand; you allude to the state in which I came home last night. Well, to tell the truth, I *was* slightly elevated—a little more champagne on board than I could comfortably carry. That's all, isn't it?

TOM. [*Deeply affected—clasping his hands and weeping.*] All! Oh! my dear young mas'r, I'm 'fraid it will be *loss of all—all,* body and soul. The Good Book says, "It biteth like a serpent and stingeth like an adder," my dear mas'r.

ST. CLARE. You poor, silly fool! I'm not worth crying over.

TOM. Oh, mas'r! I implore you to think of it before it gets too late.

ST. CLARE. Well, I won't go to any more of their cursed nonsense, Tom—on my honour, I won't. I don't know why

I haven't stopped long ago; I've always despised *it,* and myself for it. So now, Tom, wipe up your eyes and go about your errands.

Tom. Bless you, mas'r. I feel much better now. You have taken a load from poor Tom's heart. Bless you!

St. Clare. Come, come, no blessings! I'm not so wonderfully good, now. There, I'll pledge my honour to you, Tom, you don't see me so again. [*Exit* Tom.] I'll keep my faith with him, too.

Ophelia. [*Without.*] Come along, you shiftless mortal!

St. Clare. What new witchcraft has Topsy been brewing? That commotion is of her raising, I'll be bound.

Enter Ophelia, *dragging in* Topsy.

Ophelia. Come here now; I will tell your master.

St. Clare. What's the matter now·?

Ophelia. The matter is that I cannot be plagued with this girl any longer. It's past all bearing; flesh and blood cannot endure it. Here I locked her up and gave her a hymn to study; and what does she do but spy out where I put my key, and has gone to my bureau, and got a bonnet-trimming and cut it all to pieces to make dolls' jackets! I never saw anything like it in my life!

St. Clare. What have you done to her?

Ophelia. What have I done? What haven't I done? Your wife says I ought to have her whipped till she couldn't stand.

St. Clare. I don't doubt it. Tell me of the lovely rule of woman. I never saw above a dozen women that wouldn't half kill a horse, or a servant, either, if they had their own way with them—let alone a man.

Ophelia. I am sure, St. Clare, I don't know what to do. I've taught and taught—I've talked till I'm tired; I've whipped her, I've punished her in every way I could think of, and still she's just what she was at first.

St. Clare. Come here, Tops, you monkey! [Topsy *crosses to* St. Clare, *grinning.*] What makes you behave so?

Topsy. 'Spects it's my wicked heart—Miss Feely says so.

St. Clare. Don't you see how much Miss Ophelia has

done for you? She says she has done everything she can think of.

Topsy. Lor', yes, mas'r! old missis used to say so, too. She whipped me a heap harder, and used to pull my ha'r, and knock my head agin the door; but it didn't do me no good. I 'spects if they's to pull every spear of ha'r out o' my head, it wouldn't do no good neither—I's so wicked! Laws! I's nothin' but a nigger, no ways! [*Goes up.*

Ophelia. Well, I shall have to give her up; I can't have that trouble any longer.

St. Clare. I'd like to ask you one question.

Ophelia. What is it?

St. Clare. Why, if your doctrine is not strong enough to save one heathen child, that you can have at home here, all to yourself, what's the use of sending one or two poor missionaries off with it among thousands of just such? I suppose this girl is a fair sample of what thousands of your heathen are.

Ophelia. I'm sure I don't know; I never saw such a girl as this.

St. Clare. What makes you so bad, Tops? Why won't you try and be good? Don't you love any one, Topsy?

Topsy. Dunno nothing 'bout love; I loves candy and sich, that's all.

Ophelia. But, Topsy, if you'd only try to be good, you might.

Topsy. Couldn't never be nothing but a nigger, if I was ever so good. If I could be skinned and come white, I'd try then.

St. Clare. People can love you, if you are black, Topsy. Miss Ophelia would love you, if you were good. [Topsy *laughs.*] Don't you think so?

Topsy. No, she can't b'ar me, 'cause I'm a nigger—she'd's soon have a toad touch her. There can't nobody love niggers, and niggers can't do nothin'! I don't car'! [*Whistles.*

St. Clare. Silence, you incorrigible imp, and begone!

Topsy. He! he! he! didn't get much out of dis chile!

[*Exit.*

Ophelia. I've always had a prejudice against negroes, and it's a fact—I never could bear to have that child touch me, but I didn't think she knew it.

St. Clare. Trust any child to find that out; there's no keeping it from them. But I believe all the trying in the world to benefit a child, and all the substantial favours you can do them, will never excite one emotion of gratitude, while that feeling of repugnance remains in the heart. It's a queer kind of fact, but so it is.

Ophelia. I don't know how I can help it—they are disagreeable to me, this girl in particular. How can I help feeling so?

St. Clare. Eva does, it seems.

Ophelia. Well, she's so loving. I wish I was like her. She might teach me a lesson.

St. Clare. It would not be the first time a little child had been used to instruct an old disciple, if it were so. Come, let us seek Eva, in her favourite bower by the lake.

Ophelia. Why, the dew is falling; she mustn't be out there. She is unwell, I know.

St. Clare. Don't be croaking, cousin—I hate it.

Ophelia. But she has that cough.

St. Clare. Oh, nonsense, of that cough—it is not anything. She has taken a little cold, perhaps.

Ophelia. Well, that was just the way Eliza Jane was taken—and Ellen—

St. Clare. Oh, stop these hobgoblin, nurse legends. You old hands get so wise, that a child cannot cough or sneeze, but you see desperation and ruin at hand. Only take care of the child, keep her from the night air, and don't let her play too hard, and she'll do well enough.   [*Exeunt.*

Scene II.—*The flat represents the lake.—The rays of the setting sun tinge the waters with gold.—A large tree.— Beneath this a grassy bank, on which* Eva *and* Tom *are seated side by side.—*Eva *has a Bible open on her lap.*

Tom. Read dat passage again, please, Miss Eva?

Eva. [*Reading.*] "And I saw a sea of glass, mingled with fire." [*Stopping suddenly and pointing to lake.*] Tom, there it is!

Tom. What, Miss Eva?

Eva. Don't you see there? There's a "sea of glass, mingled with fire."

Tom. True enough, Miss Eva. [*Sings.*]
    Oh, had I the wings of the morning,
    I'd fly away to Canaan's shore;
    Bright angels should convey me home,
    To the New Jerusalem.

Eva. Where do you suppose New Jerusalem is, Uncle Tom?

Tom. Oh, up in the clouds, Miss Eva.

Eva. Then I think I see it. Look in those clouds; they look like great gates of pearl; and you can see beyond them—far, far off—it's all gold! Tom, sing about 'spirits bright.'

Tom. [*Sings.*]
    I see a band of spirits bright,
    That taste the glories there;
    They are all robed in spotless white,
    And conquering palms they bear.

Eva. Uncle Tom, I've seen *them*.

Tom. To be sure you have; you are one of them yourself. You are the brightest spirit I ever saw.

Eva. They come to me sometimes in my sleep—those spirits bright—
    They are all robed in spotless white,
    And conquering palms they bear.
Uncle Tom, I'm going there.

Tom. Where, Miss Eva?

Eva. [*Pointing to the sky.*] I'm going *there,* to the spirits bright, Tom; I'm going before long.

Tom. It's jest no use tryin' to keep Miss Eva here; I've allays said so. She's got the Lord's mark in her forehead. She wasn't never like a child that's to live—there was always something deep in her eyes.
[*Rises and comes forward.—*Eva *also comes forward, leaving Bible on bank.*]

Enter St. Clare.

St. Clare. Ah! my little pussy, you look as blooming as a rose! You are better now-a-days, are you not?

Eva. Papa, I've had things I wanted to say to you a great while. I want to say them now, before I get weaker.

 St. Clare. Nay, this is an idle fear, Eva; you know you grow stronger every day.

Eva. It's all no use, papa, to keep it to myself any longer. The time is coming that I am going to leave you; I am going, and never to come back.

St. Clare. Oh, now, my dear little Eva! you've got nervous and low-spirited; you mustn't indulge such gloomy thoughts.

Eva. No, papa, don't deceive yourself, I am *not* any better; I know it perfectly well, and I am going before long. I am not nervous—I am not low-spirited. If it were not for you, papa, and my friends, I should be perfectly happy. I want to go—I long to go!

St. Clare. Why, dear child, what has made your poor little heart so sad? You have everything to make you happy that could be given you.

Eva. I had rather be in heaven! There are a great many things here that make me sad—that seem dreadful to me; I had rather be there; but I don't want to leave you—it almost breaks my heart!

St. Clare. What makes you sad, and what seems dreadful, Eva?

Eva. I feel sad for our poor people; they love me dearly, and they are all good and kind to me. I wish, papa, they were all *free!*

St. Clare. Why, Eva, child, don't you think they are well enough off, now?

Eva. [*Not heeding the question.*] Papa, isn't there a way to have slaves made free? When I am dead, papa, then you will think of me, and do it for my sake?

St. Clare. When you are dead, Eva? Oh, child, don't talk to me so! You are all I have on earth!

Eva. Papa, these poor creatures love their children as much as you do me. Tom loves his children. Oh, do something for them!

St. Clare. There, there darling; only don't distress yourself, and don't talk of dying, and I will do anything you wish.

Eva. And promise me, dear father, that Tom shall have his freedom as soon as—[*hesitating*]—I am gone!

St. Clare. Yes, dear, I will do anything in the world—

anything you could ask me to. There, Tom, take her to her chamber; this evening air is too chill for her. [*Kisses her.*
[Tom *takes* Eva *in his arms, and exit.*

St. Clare. [*Gazing mournfully after* Eva.] Has there ever been a child like Eva? Yes, there has been; but their names are always on grave-stones, and their sweet smiles, their heavenly eyes, their singular words and ways, are among the buried treasures of yearning hearts. It is as if heaven had an especial band of angels, whose office it is to sojourn for a season here, and endear to them the wayward human heart, that they might bear it upward with them in their homeward flight. When you see that deep, spiritual light in the eye, when the little soul reveals itself in words sweeter and wiser than the ordinary words of children, hope not to retain that child; for the seal of heaven is on it, and the light of immortality looks out from its eyes! [*Exit.*

Scene III.—*A corridor.*

Enter Tom; *he listens at door and then lies down.*

Enter Ophelia, *with candle.*

Ophelia. Uncle Tom, what alive have you taken to sleeping anywhere and everywhere, like a dog, for? I thought you were one of the orderly sort, that liked to lie in bed in a Christian way.

Tom. [*Rises.—Mysteriously.*] I do, Miss Feely, I do, but now—

Ophelia. Well, what now?

Tom. We mustn't speak loud; Mas'r St. Clare won't hear on't; but Miss Feely, you know there must be somebody watchin' for the bridegroom.

Ophelia. What do you mean, Tom?

Tom. You know it says in Scripture, "At midnight there was a great cry made, behold the bridegroom cometh!" That's what I'm 'spectin' now, every night, Miss Feely, and I couldn't sleep out of hearing, noways.

Ophelia. Why, Uncle Tom, what makes you think so?

Tom. Miss Eva, she talks to me. The Lord, he sends his messenger in the soul. I must be thar, Miss Feely; for when that ar blessed child goes into the kingdom, they'll open the door so wide, we'll all get a look in at the glory!

OPHELIA. Uncle Tom, did Miss Eva say she felt more unwell than usual to-night?

TOM. No; but she told me she was coming nearer—thar's them that tells it to the child, Miss Feely. It's the angels—it's the trumpet sound afore the break o' day!

OPHELIA. Heaven grant your fears be vain! Come in, Tom. [*Exeunt.*

SCENE IV.—EVA's *Chamber.*

EVA *discovered on a couch.—A table stands near the couch, with a lamp on it. The light shines upon* EVA's *face, which is very pale.—Scene half dark.—*UNCLE TOM *is kneeling near the foot of the couch.—*OPHELIA *stands at the head.—*ST. CLARE *at back.—Scene opens to plaintive music.—Enter* MARIE, *hastily.*

MARIE. St. Clare! Cousin! Oh! what is the matter now?

ST. CLARE. [*Hoarsely.*] Hush! she is dying!

MARIE. [*Sinking on her knees, beside* TOM.] Dying!

ST. CLARE. Oh! if she would only wake and speak once more. [*Bending over* EVA.] Eva, darling!

EVA. [*Uncloses her eyes, smiles, raises her head and tries to speak.*]

ST. CLARE. Do you know me, Eva?

EVA. [*Throwing her arms feebly about his neck.*] Dear papa! [*Her arms drop and she sinks back.*

ST. CLARE. Oh, heaven! this is dreadful! Oh! Tom, my boy, it is killing me!

TOM. Look at her, mas'r. [*Points to* EVA.

ST. CLARE. Eva! [*A pause.*] She does not hear. Oh, Eva! tell us what you see. What is it?

EVA. [*Feebly smiling.*] Oh! love! joy! peace! [*Dies.*

TOM. Oh! bless the Lord! it's over, dear mas'r, it's over.

ST. CLARE. [*Sinking on his knees.*] Farewell, beloved child! the bright eternal doors have closed after thee. We shall see thy sweet face no more. Oh! wo for them who watched thy entrance into heaven, when they shall wake and find only the cold, gray sky of daily life, and thou gone forever. [*Solemn music, slow curtain.*

END OF ACT III.

ACT IV.

SCENE I.—*A street in New Orleans.*

Enter GUMPTION CUTE, *meeting* MARKS.

CUTE. How do ye dew?

MARKS. How are you?

CUTE. Well, now, squire, it's a fact that I am dead broke and busted up.

MARKS. You have been speculating, I suppose?

CUTE. That's just it and nothing shorter.

MARKS. You have had poor success, you say?

CUTE. Tarnation bad, now I tell you. You see I came to this part of the country to make my fortune.

MARKS. And you did not do it?

CUTE. Scarcely. The first thing I tried my hand at was keeping school. I opened an academy for the instruction of youth in the various branches of orthography, geography, and other graphies.

MARKS. Did you succeed in getting any pupils?

CUTE. Oh, lots on 'em! and a pretty set of dunces they were, too. After the first quarter, I called on the respectable parents of the juveniles, and requested them to fork over. To which they politely answered—don't you wish you may get it?

MARKS. What did you do then?

CUTE. Well, I kind of pulled up stakes and left those diggin's. Well, then I went into Spiritual Rappings for a living. That paid pretty well for a short time, till I met with an accident.

MARKS. An accident?

CUTE. Yes; a tall Yahoo called on me one day, and wanted me to summon the spirit of his mother—which, of course, I did. He asked me about a dozen questions which I answered to his satisfaction. At last he wanted to know what she died of—I said, Cholera. You never did see a critter so riled as he was. "Look yere, stranger," said he, "it's my opinion that you're a pesky humbug! for my mother was blown up in a *Steamboat!*" With that he left the premises. The next day the people furnished me with a conveyance, and I rode out of town.

MARKS. Rode out of town?

CUTE. Yes; on a rail!

MARKS. I suppose you gave up the spirits, after that?

CUTE. Well, I reckon I did; it had such an effect on my spirits.

MARKS. It's a wonder they didn't tar and feather you.

CUTE. There was some mention made of that, but when they said *feathers,* I felt as if I had wings, and flew away.

MARKS. You cut and run?

CUTE. Yes; I didn't like their company and I cut it. Well, after that I let myself out as an overseer on a cotton plantation. I made a pretty good thing of that, though it was dreadful trying to my feelings to flog the darkies; but I got used to it after a while, and then I used to lather 'em like Jehu. Well, the proprietor got the fever and ague and shook himself out of town. The place and all the fixings were sold at auction, and I found myself adrift once more.

MARKS. What are you doing at present?

CUTE. I'm in search of a rich relation of mine.

MARKS. A rich relation?

CUTE. Yes, a Miss Ophelia St. Clare. You see, a niece of hers married one of my second cousins—that's how I came to be a relation of hers. She came on here from Vermont to be housekeeper to a cousin of hers, of the same name.

MARKS. I know him well.

CUTE. The deuce you do!—well, that's lucky.

MARKS. Yes, he lives in this city.

CUTE. Say, you just point out the locality, and I'll give him a call.

MARKS. Stop a bit. Suppose you shouldn't be able to raise the wind in that quarter, what have you thought of doing?

CUTE. Well, nothing particular.

MARKS. How should you like to enter into a nice, profitable business—one that pays well?

CUTE. That's just about my measure—it would suit me to a hair. What is it?

MARKS. Nigger catching.

CUTE. Catching niggers! What on airth do you mean?

MARKS. Why, when there's a large reward offered for a runaway darkey, we goes after him, catches him, and gets the reward.

CUTE. Yes, that's all right so far—but s'pose there ain't no reward offered?

MARKS. Why, then we catches the darkey on our own account, sells him, and pockets the proceeds.

CUTE. By chowder, that ain't a bad speculation!

MARKS. What do you say? I want a partner. You see, I lost my partner last year, up in Ohio—he was a powerful fellow.

CUTE. Lost him! How did you lose him?

MARKS. Well, you see, Tom and I—his name was Tom Loker—Tom and I were after a mulatto chap, called George Harris, that run away from Kentucky. We traced him through the greater part of Ohio, and came up with him near the Pennsylvania line. He took refuge among some rocks, and showed fight.

CUTE. Oh! then runaway darkies show fight, do they?

MARKS. Sometimes. Well, Tom—like a headstrong fool as he was—rushed up the rocks, and a Quaker chap, who was helping this George Harris, threw him over the cliff.

CUTE. Was he killed?

MARKS. Well, I didn't stop to find out. Seeing that the darkies were stronger than I thought, I made tracks for a safe place.

CUTE. And what became of this George Harris?

MARKS. Oh! he and his wife and child got away safe into Canada. You see, they will get away sometimes, though it isn't very often. Now what do you say? You are just the figure for a fighting partner. Is it a bargain?

CUTE. Well, I rather calculate our teams won't hitch, no how. By chowder, I hain't no idea of setting myself up, as a target for darkies to fire at—that's a speculation that don't suit my constitution.

MARKS. You're afraid, then?

CUTE. No, I ain't; it's against my principles.

MARKS. Your principles—how so?

CUTE. Because my principles are to keep a sharp lookout

for No. 1. I shouldn't feel wholesome if a darkey was to throw me over that cliff to look after Tom Loker.

[*Exeunt, arm-in-arm.*

SCENE II.—*Gothic Chamber.*

ST. CLARE *discovered, seated on sofa.* TOM *to the left.*

ST. CLARE. Oh! Tom, my boy, the whole world is as empty as an egg-shell.

TOM. I know it, mas'r, I know it. But oh! if mas'r could look up—up where our dear Miss Eva is—

ST. CLARE. Ah, Tom! I do look up; but the trouble is, I don't see anything when I do. I wish I could. It seems to be given to children and poor, honest fellows like you, to see what we cannot. How comes it?

TOM. "Thou hast hid from the wise and prudent, and revealed unto babes; even so, Father, for so it seemed good in thy sight."

ST. CLARE. Tom, I don't believe—I've got the habit of doubting—I want to believe and I cannot.

TOM. Dear mas'r, pray to the good Lord: "Lord, I believe; help thou my unbelief."

ST. CLARE. Who knows anything about anything? Was all that beautiful love and faith only one of the ever-shifting phases of human feeling, having nothing real to rest on, passing away with the little breath? And is there no more Eva—nothing?

TOM. Oh! dear mas'r, there is. I know it; I'm sure of it. Do, do, dear mas'r, believe it!

ST. CLARE. How do you know there is, Tom? You never saw the Lord.

TOM. Felt Him in my soul, mas'r—feel Him now! Oh, mas'r, when I was sold away from my old woman and the children, I was jest a'most broken up—I felt as if there warn't nothing left—and then the Lord stood by me, and He says, "Fear not, Tom," and He brings light and joy into a poor fellow's soul—makes all peace; and I's so happy, and loves everybody, and feels willin' to be jest where the Lord wants to put me. I know it couldn't come from me, 'cause I's a poor, complaining creature—it comes from above, and I know He's willin' to do for mas'r.

ST. CLARE. [*Grasping* TOM'S *hand.*] Tom, you love me!

TOM. I's willin' to lay down my life this blessed day for you.

ST. CLARE. [*Sadly.*] Poor, foolish fellow! I'm not worth the love of one good, honest heart like yours.

TOM. Oh, mas'r! there's more than me loves you—the blessed Saviour loves you.

ST. CLARE. How do you know that, Tom?

TOM. The love of the Saviour passeth knowledge.

ST. CLARE. [*Turns away.*] Singular! that the story of a man who lived and died eighteen hundred years ago, can affect people so yet. But He was no man. [*Rises.*] No man ever had such long and living power. Oh! that I could believe what my mother taught me, and pray as I did when I was a boy! But, Tom, all this time I have forgotten why I sent for you. I'm going to make a freeman of you; so have your trunk packed, and get ready to set out for Kentuck.

TOM. [*Joyfully.*] Bless the Lord!

ST. CLARE. [*Dryly.*] You haven't had such very bad times here, that you need be in such a rapture, Tom.

TOM. No, no, mas'r, 'tain't that; it's being a *freeman*—that's what I'm joyin' for.

ST. CLARE. Why, Tom, don't you think, for your own part, you've been better off than to be free?

TOM. No, *indeed,* Mas'r St. Clare—no, indeed!

ST. CLARE. Why, Tom, you couldn't possibly have earned, by your work, such clothes and such living as I have given you.

TOM. I know all that, Mas'r St. Clare—mas'r's been too good; but I'd rather have poor clothes, poor house, poor everything, and have 'em *mine,* than have the best, if they belonged to somebody else. I had *so,* mas'r; I think it's natur', mas'r.

ST. CLARE. I suppose so, Tom; and you'll be going off and leaving me in a month or so—though why you shouldn't no mortal knows.

TOM. Not while mas'r is in trouble. I'll stay with mas'r as long as he wants me, so as I can be any use.

ST. CLARE. [*Sadly.*] Not while I'm in trouble, Tom? And when will my trouble be over?

Toм. When you are a believer.

Sт. Clare. And you really mean to stay by me till that day comes? [*Smiling and laying his hand on* Toм's *shoulder.*] Ah, Tom! I won't keep you till that day. Go home to your wife and children, and give my love to all.

Toм. I's faith to think that day will come—the Lord has a work for mas'r.

Sт. Clare. A work, hey? Well, now, Tom, give me your views on what sort of a work it is—let's hear.

Toм. Why, even a poor fellow like me has a work; and Mas'r St. Clare, that has larnin', and riches, and friends, how much he might do for the Lord.

Sт. Clare. Tom, you seem to think the Lord needs a great deal done for him.

Toм. We does for him when we does for his creatures.

Sт. Clare. Good theology, Tom. Thank you, my boy; I like to hear you talk. But go now, Tom, and leave me alone. [*Exit* Toм.] That faithful fellow's words have excited a train of thoughts that almost bear me, on the strong tide of faith and feeling, to the gates of that heaven I so vividly conceive. They seem to bring me nearer to Eva.

Ophelia. [*Outside.*] What are you doing there, you limb of Satan? You've been stealing something, I'll be bound.

Ophelia *drags in* Topsy.

Topsy. You go 'long, Miss Feely, 'tain't none o' your business.

Sт. Clare. Heyday! what is all this commotion?

Ophelia. She's been stealing.

Topsy. [*Sobbing.*] I hain't neither.

Ophelia. What have you got in your bosom?

Topsy. I've got my hand dar.

Ophelia. But what have you got in your hand?

Topsy. Nuffin'.

Ophelia. That's a fib, Topsy.

Topsy. Well, I 'spects it is.

Ophelia. Give it to me, whatever it is.

Topsy. It's mine—I hope I may die this bressed minute, if it don't b'long to me.

Ophelia. Topsy, I order you to give me that article;

don't let me have to ask you again. [Topsy *reluctantly takes the foot of an old stocking from her bosom and hands it to* Ophelia.] Sakes alive! what is all this? [*Takes from it a lock of hair, and a small book, with a bit of crape twisted around it.*

Topsy. Dat's a lock of ha'r dat Miss Eva give me—she cut it from her own beau'ful head herself.

St. Clare. [*Takes book.*] Why did you wrap *this* [*pointing to crape*] around the book?

Topsy. 'Cause—'cause—'cause 'twas Miss Eva's. Oh! don't take 'em away, please! [*Sits down on stage, and, putting her apron over her head, begins to sob vehemently.*

Ophelia. Come, come, don't cry; you shall have them.

Topsy. [*Jumps up joyfully and takes them.*] I wants to keep 'em, 'cause dey makes me good; I ain't half so wicked as I used to was. [*Runs off.*

St. Clare. I really think you can make something of that girl. Any mind that is capable of a *real sorrow* is capable of good. You must try and do something with her.

Ophelia. The child has improved very much; I have great hopes of her.

St. Clare. I believe I'll go down the street, a few moments, and hear the news.

Ophelia. Shall I call Tom to attend you?

St. Clare. No, I shall be back in an hour. [*Exit.*

Ophelia. He's got an excellent heart, but then he's so dreadful shiftless! [*Exit.*

[In a prompt copy of this play, owned by the New York Public Library, a scene is here inserted (in manuscript), laid in a bar-room, between Marks, Cute, and Legree. St. Clare also. It suggests the brutality of Legree. This scene likewise explains the cause of St. Clare's death in Scene IV. Also it explains Act VI, Sc. IV. It is as follows:]

Scene.—*A bar-room. Tables and chairs. Newspapers on table.* Marks *and* Cute *discovered.*

Cute. Any news, Squire?

Marks. . . . 'scaped to death!

Cute. Squire, it's lucky that the staves of that barrel wasn't made of yellow pine.

Marks. Why so, Cute?

Cute. Because she might have got a pine-knot hole in both her eyes, and been blind for life.

Marks. . . . from him immediately.

CUTE. Don't want to enter into any such speculation. Hello, Squire, who is this feller coming up street?

MARKS. Can't say, Cute, never having seen the individual before.

CUTE. Rather an odd-looking fish, ain't he, Judge?

MARKS. . . . Mr. Simon Legree.

CUTE. Do you think him and I will agree?

MARKS. . . . pretty rough.

CUTE. Trot him out, Squire, I'm tough!

LEGREE *enters*.

LEGREE. How are you, Marks? What are you doing down here?

MARKS. . . . Cute, Legree; Legree, Cute.

[LEGREE *squeezes* CUTE's *hand*.

CUTE. I'll trouble for that when you get through with it. Darn his picture! My hand's like a duck's foot.

[ST. CLARE *enters, and seats himself at table.*

CUTE. I cal'ate you're some on your muscle, Squire?

LEGREE. Just so, stranger.

CUTE. Say, I cal'ate you'd handle a fellar pretty rough.

LEGREE. Just so, stranger.

CUTE. Well, say, do you want to hire an overseer to boss your darkies?

LEGREE. Why so?

CUTE. 'Cause I'd like to hire myself out for a few months to oversee.

LEGREE. I can oversee my own niggers, I reckon.

CUTE. You look as if you could, by thunder!

LEGREE. 'Umph! Do you see that 'ere right hand? There's a fist that's grown hard a smacking down niggers! Just feel the weight on't, stranger!

CUTE. Land of hope and blessed promise! Now, I shouldn't wonder if your heart was just about as hard as your hand.

LERGEE. Just so, stranger.

CUTE. Nevertheless, you've one soft spot about you.

LEGREE. 'Umph, indeed, whereabouts?

CUTE. Your head, you darned cuss!

LEGREE. What! [*Rushes at him with bowie-knife.* ST. CLARE *attempts to separate them. Business and scene closes.*

Scene III.—*Front Chamber.*

Enter Topsy.

Topsy. Dar's somethin' de matter wid me—I isn't a bit like myself. I haven't done anything wrong since poor Miss Eva went up in de skies and left us. When I's gwine to do anything wicked, I tinks of her, and somehow I can't do it. I's getting to be good, dat's a fact. I 'spects when I's dead I shall be turned into a little brack angel.

Enter Ophelia.

Ophelia. Topsy, I've been looking for you; I've got something very particular to say to you.

Topsy. Does you want me to say the catechism?

Ophelia. No, not now.

Topsy. [*Aside.*] Golly! dat's one comfort.

Ophelia. Now, Topsy, I want you to try and understand what I am going to say to you.

Topsy. Yes, missis, I'll open my ears drefful wide.

Ophelia. Mr. St. Clare has given you to me, Topsy.

Topsy. Den I b'longs to you, don't I? Golly! I thought I always belonged to you.

Ophelia. Not till to-day have I received any authority to call you my property.

Topsy. I's your property, am I? Well, if you say so, I 'spects I am.

Ophelia. Topsy, I can give you your liberty.

Topsy. My liberty?

Ophelia. Yes, Topsy.

Topsy. Has you got 'um with you?

Ophelia. I have, Topsy.

Topsy. Is it clothes or wittles?

Ophelia. How shiftless! Don't you know what your liberty is, Topsy?

Topsy. How should I know when I never seed 'um?

Ophelia. Topsy, I am going to leave this place; I am going many miles away—to my own home in Vermont.

Topsy. Den what's to become of dis chile?

Ophelia. If you wish to go, I will take you with me.

TOPSY. Miss Feely, I doesn't want to leave you no how, I loves you, I does.

OPHELIA. Then you shall share my home for the rest of your days. Come, Topsy.

TOPSY. Stop, Miss Feely; does dey hab any oberseers in Varmount?

OPHELIA. No, Topsy.

TOPSY. Nor cotton plantations, nor sugar factories, nor darkies, nor whipping, nor nothing?

OPHELIA. No, Topsy.

TOPSY. By golly! de quicker you is gwine de better den.

Enter TOM, *hastily.*

TOM. Oh, Miss Feely! Miss Feely!

OPHELIA. Gracious me, Tom! what's the matter?

TOM. Oh, Mas'r St. Clare! Mas'r St. Clare!

OPHELIA. Well, Tom, well?

TOM. They've just brought him home and I do believe he's killed.

OPHELIA. Killed?

TOPSY. Oh, dear! what's to become of de poor darkies now?

TOM. He's dreadful weak. It's just as much as he can do to speak. He wanted me to call you.

OPHELIA. My poor cousin! Who would have thought of it? Don't say a word to his wife, Tom; the danger may not be so great as you think; it would only distress her. Come with me; you may be able to afford some assistance.

[*Exeunt.*

SCENE IV.—*Handsome Chamber.*

ST. CLARE *discovered seated on sofa.* OPHELIA, TOM *and* TOPSY *are clustered around him.* DOCTOR *back of sofa, feeling his pulse.*

ST. CLARE. [*Raising himself feebly.*] Tom—poor fellow!

TOM. Well, mas'r?

ST. CLARE. I have received my death wound.

TOM. Oh, no, no, mas'r!

ST. CLARE. I feel that I am dying—Tom, pray!

TOM. [*Sinking on his knees.*] I do pray, mas'r! I do pray!

ST. CLARE. [*After a pause.*] Tom, one thing preys upon my mind.—I have forgotten to sign your freedom papers. What will become of you when I am gone?

TOM. Don't think of that, mas'r.

ST. CLARE. I was wrong, Tom, very wrong, to neglect it. I may be the cause of much suffering to you hereafter. Marie, my wife—she—oh!—

OPHELIA. His mind is wandering.

ST. CLARE. [*Energetically.*] No! it is coming *home* at last! [*Sinks back.*] at last! at last! Eva, I come! [*Dies.*

END OF ACT IV.

ACT V.

SCENE I.—*An Auction Mart.*

UNCLE TOM *and* EMMELINE *at back*—ADOLF, SKEGGS, MARKS, MANN, *and various spectators discovered.* MARKS *and* MANN *come forward.*

MARKS. Hulloa, Alf! what brings you here?

MANN. Well, I was wanting a valet, and I heard that St. Clare's lot was going; I thought I'd just look at them.

MARKS. Catch me ever buying any of St. Clare's people. Spoilt niggers, every one—impudent as the devil.

MANN. Never fear that; if I get 'em, I'll soon have their airs out of them—they'll soon find that they've another kind of master to deal with than St. Clare. 'Pon my word, I'll buy that fellow—I like the shape of him.

[*Pointing to* ADOLF.

MARKS. You'll find it'll take all you've got to keep him— he's deucedly extravagant.

MANN. Yes, but my lord will find that he *can't* be extravagant with *me*. Just let him be sent to the calaboose a few times, and thoroughly dressed down, I'll tell you if it don't bring him to a sense of his ways. Oh! I'll reform him, up hill and down, you'll see. I'll buy him, that's flat.

Enter LEGREE; *he goes up and looks at* ADOLF, *whose boots are nicely blacked.*

LEGREE. A nigger with his boots blacked—bah! [*Spits on them.*] Holloa, you! [*To* TOM.] Let's see your teeth. [*Seizes* TOM *by the jaw and opens his mouth.*] Strip up your sleeve and show your muscle. [TOM *does so.*] Where was you raised?

TOM. In Kentuck, mas'r.

LEGREE. What have you done?

TOM. Had care of mas'r's farm.

LEGREE. That's a likely story. [*Turns to* EMMELINE.] You're a nice looking girl enough. How old are you?

[*Grasps her arm.*

EMMELINE. [*Shrieking.*] Ah! you hurt me.

SKEGGS. Stop that, you minx! No whimpering here. The sale is going to begin. [*Mounts the rostrum.*] Gentlemen, the next article I shall offer you to-day is Adolf, late valet to Mr. St. Clare. How much am I offered? [*Various bids are made.* ADOLF *is knocked down to* MANN *for eight hundred dollars.*] Gentlemen, I now offer a prime article— the quadroon girl, Emmeline, only fifteen years of age, warranted in every respect. [*Business as before.* EMMELINE *is sold to* LEGREE *for one thousand dollars.*] Now, I shall close to-day's sale by offering you the valuable article known as Uncle Tom, the most useful nigger ever raised. Gentlemen in want of an overseer, now is the time to bid.

Business as before. TOM *is sold to* LEGREE *for twelve hundred dollars.*

LEGREE. Now look here, you two belong to me.

[TOM *and* EMMELINE *sink on their knees.*

TOM. Heaven help us, then!

[*Music*—LEGREE *stands over them exulting. Picture.*

SCENE II.—*The Garden of* MISS OPHELIA'S *House in Vermont.*

Enter OPHELIA *and* DEACON PERRY.

DEACON. Miss Ophelia, allow me to offer you my congratulations upon your safe arrival in your native place. I hope it is your intention to pass the remainder of your days with us?

OPHELIA. Well, Deacon, I have come here with that express purpose.

DEACON. I presume you were not over pleased with the South?

OPHELIA. Well, to tell the truth, Deacon, I wasn't; I liked the country very well, but the people there are so dreadful shiftless.

DEACON. The result, I presume, of living in a warm climate.

OPHELIA. Well, Deacon, what is the news among you all here?

DEACON. Well, we live on in the same even jog-trot pace. Nothing of any consequence has happened.—Oh! I forgot. [*Takes out his handkerchief.*] I've lost my wife; my Molly has left me. [*Wipes his eyes.*

OPHELIA. Poor soul! I pity you, Deacon.

DEACON. Thank you. You perceive I bear my loss with resignation.

OPHELIA. How you must miss her tongue!

DEACON. Molly certainly was fond of talking. She always would have the last word—heigho!

OPHELIA. What was her complaint, Deacon?

DEACON. A very mild and soothing one, Miss Ophelia; she had a severe attack of the lockjaw.

OPHELIA. Dreadful!

DEACON. Wasn't it? When she found she couldn't use her tongue, she took it so much to heart that it struck to her stomach and killed her. Poor dear! Excuse my handkerchief; she's been dead only eighteen months.

OPHELIA. Why, Deacon, by this time you ought to be setting your cap for another wife.

DEACON. Do you think so, Miss Ophelia?

OPHELIA. I don't see why you shouldn't—you are still a good-looking man, Deacon.

DEACON. Ah! well, I think I do wear well—in fact, I may say remarkably well. It has been observed to me before.

OPHELIA. And you are not much over fifty?

DEACON. Just turned of forty, I assure you.

OPHELIA. Hale and hearty?

DEACON. Health excellent—look at my eye! Strong as a lion—look at my arm! A No. 1 constitution—look at my leg!!!

OPHELIA. Have you no thoughts of choosing another partner?

DEACON. Well, to tell you the truth, I have.

OPHELIA. Who is she?

DEACON. She is not far distant. [*Looks at* OPHELIA *in a languishing manner.*] I have her in my eye at this present moment.

OPHELIA. [*Aside.*] Really, I believe he's going to pop. Why, surely, Deacon, you don't mean to—

DEACON. Yes, Miss Ophelia, I do mean; and believe me, when I say—[*Looking off.*] The Lord be good to us, but I believe there is the devil coming!

TOPSY *runs on with bouquet. She is now dressed very neatly.*

TOPSY. Miss Feely, here is some flowers dat I hab been gathering for you.　　　　　　　　　[*Gives bouquet.*

OPHELIA. That's a good child.

DEACON. Miss Ophelia, who is this young person?

OPHELIA. She is my daughter.

DEACON. [*Aside.*] Her daughter! Then she must have married a colored man off South. I was not aware that you had been married, Miss Ophelia?

OPHELIA. Married? Sakes alive! what made you think I had been married?

DEACON. Good gracious! I'm getting confused. Didn't I understand you to say that this—somewhat tanned—young lady was your daughter?

OPHELIA. Only by adoption. She is my adopted daughter.

DEACON. O—oh! [*Aside.*] I breathe again.

TOPSY. [*Aside.*] By golly! dat old man's eyes stick out of 'um head dre'ful. Guess he never seed anything like me afore.

OPHELIA. Deacon, won't you step into the house and refresh yourself after your walk?

DEACON. I accept your polite invitation. [*Offers his arm.*] Allow me.

OPHELIA. As gallant as ever, Deacon. I declare, you grow younger every day.

DEACON. You can never grow old, madam.

OPHELIA. Ah, you flatterer! [*Exeunt.*

TOPSY. Dar dey go, like an old goose and gander. Guess dat ole gemblemun feels kind of confectionary—rather sweet on my old missis. By golly! she's been dre'ful kind to me ever since I come away from de South; and I loves her, I does, 'cause she takes such car' on me and gives me dese fine clothes. I tries to be good, too, and I's getting 'long 'mazin' fast. I'se not so wicked as I used to was. [*Looks out.*] Hulloa! dar's some one comin' here. I wonder what he wants now. [*Retires, observing.*

Enter GUMPTION CUTE, *very shabby—a small bundle, on a stick, over his shoulder.*

CUTE. By chowder, here I am again. Phew! it's a pretty considerable tall piece of walking between here and New Orleans, not to mention the wear of shoe-leather. I guess I'm about done up. If this streak of bad luck lasts much longer, I'll borrow sixpence to buy a rope, and hang myself right straight up! When I went to call on Miss Ophelia, I swow if I didn't find out that she had left for Vermont; so I kind of concluded to make tracks in that direction myself, and as I didn't have any money left, why I had to foot it, and here I am in old Varmount once more. They told me Miss Ophelia lived up here. I wonder if she will remember the relationship. [*Sees* TOPSY.] By chowder, there's a darkey. Look here, Charcoal!

TOPSY. [*Comes forward.*] My name isn't Charcoal—it's Topsy.

CUTE. Oh! your name is Topsy, is it, you juvenile specimen of Day & Martin?

TOPSY. Tell you I don't know nothin' 'bout Day & Martin. I's Topsy and I belong to Miss Feely St. Clare.

CUTE. I'm much obleeged to you, you small extract of Japan, for your information. So Miss Ophelia lives up there in the white house, does she?

TOPSY. Well, she don't do nothin' else.

CUTE. Well, then, just locomote your pins.

TOPSY. What—what's dat?

CUTE. Walk your chalks!

TOPSY. By golly! dere ain't no chalk 'bout me.

CUTE. Move your trotters.

TOPSY. How you does spoke! What you mean by trotters?

CUTE. Why, your feet, Stove Polish.

TOPSY. What does you want me to move my feet for?

CUTE. To tell your mistress, you ebony angel, that a gentleman wishes to see her.

TOPSY. Does you call yourself a gentleman? By golly! you look more like a scar'-crow.

CUTE. Now look here, you Charcoal, don't you be sassy. I'm a gentleman in distress; a done-up speculator; one that has seen better days—long time ago—and better clothes too, by chowder! My creditors are like my boots—they've no soles. I'm a victim to circumstances. I've been through much and survived it. I've taken walking exercise for the benefit of my health; but as I was trying to live on air at the same time, it was a losing speculation, 'cause it gave me such a dreadful appetite.

TOPSY. Golly! you look as if you could eat an ox, horns and all.

CUTE. Well, I calculate I could, if he was roasted—it's a speculation I should like to engage in. I have returned like the fellow that run away in Scripture; and if anybody's got a fatted calf they want to kill, all they got to do is to fetch him along. Do you know, Charcoal, that your mistress is a relation of mine?

TOPSY. Is she your uncle?

CUTE. No, no, not quite so near as that. My second cousin married her niece.

TOPSY. And does you want to see Miss Feely?

CUTE. I do. I have come to seek a home beneath her roof, and take care of all the spare change she don't want to use.

TOPSY. Den just yo' follow me, mas'r.

CUTE. Stop! By chowder, I've got a great idee. Say, you Day & Martin, how should you like to enter into a speculation?

TOPSY. Golly! I doesn't know what a spec—spec—cu— what-do-you-call-'um am.

CUTE. Well, now, I calculate I've hit upon about the right thing. Why should I degrade the manly dignity of the Cutes by becoming a beggar—expose myself to the chance of receiving the cold shoulder as a poor relation? By chowder, my blood biles as I think of it! Topsy, you can make my fortune, and your own, too. I've an idee in my head that is worth a million of dollars.

Topsy. Golly! is your head worth dat? Guess you wouldn't bring dat out South for de whole of you.

Cute. Don't you be too severe, now, Charcoal; I'm a man of genius. Did you ever hear of Barnum?

Topsy. Barnum! Barnum! Does he live out South?

Cute. No, he lives in New York. Do you know how he made his fortin?

Topsy. What is him fortin, hey? Is it something he wears?

Cute. Chowder, how green you are!

Topsy. [*Indignantly.*] Sar, I hab you to know I's not green; I's brack.

Cute. To be sure you are, Day & Martin. I calculate, when a person says another has a fortune, he means he's got plenty of money, Charcoal.

Topsy. And did he make the money?

Cute. Sartin sure, and no mistake.

Topsy. Golly! now I thought money always growed.

Cute. Oh, git out! You are too cute—you are cuter than I am; and I'm Cute by name and cute by nature. Well, as I was saying, Barnum made his money by exhibiting a *woolly* horse; now wouldn't it be an all-fired speculation to show you as the woolly gal?

Topsy. You want to make a sight of me?

Cute. I'll give you half the receipts, by chowder!

Topsy. Should I have to leave Miss Feely?

Cute. To be sure you would.

Topsy. Den you hab to get a woolly gal somewhere else, Mas'r Cute.   [*Runs off.*

Cute. There's another speculation gone to smash, by chowder!   [*Exit.*

SCENE III.—*A Rude Chamber.*

TOM *is discovered, in old clothes, seated on a stool; he holds in his hand a paper containing a curl of* EVA's *hair. The scene opens to the symphony of* "Old Folks at Home."

TOM. I have come to de dark places; I's going through de vale of shadows. My heart sinks at times and feels just like a big lump of lead. Den it gits up in my throat and chokes me till de tears roll out of my eyes; den I take out dis curl of little Miss Eva's hair, and the sight of it brings calm to my mind and I feels strong again. [*Kisses the curl and puts it in his breast—takes out a silver dollar, which is suspended around his neck by a string.*] Dere's de bright silver dollar dat Mas'r George Shelby gave me the day I was sold away from old Kentuck, and I've kept it ever since. Mas'r George must have grown to be a man by this time. I wonder if I shall ever see him again.

SONG.—*"Old Folks at Home."*

Enter LEGREE, EMMELINE, SAMBO *and* QUIMBO.

LEGREE. Shut up, you black cuss! Did you think I wanted any of your infernal howling? [*Turns to* EMMELINE.] We're home. [EMMELINE *shrinks from him. He takes hold of her ear.*] You didn't ever wear earrings?

EMMELINE. [*Trembling.*] No, master.

LEGREE. Well, I'll give you a pair, if you're a good girl. You needn't be so frightened; I don't mean to make you work very hard. You'll have fine times with me and live like a lady; only be a good girl.

EMMELINE. My soul sickens as his eyes gaze upon me. His touch makes my very flesh creep.

LEGREE. [*Turns to* TOM, *and points to* SAMBO *and* QUIMBO.] Ye see what ye'd get if ye'd try to run off. These yer boys have been raised to track niggers, and they'd just as soon chaw one on ye up as eat their suppers; so mind yourself. [*To* EMMELINE.] Come, mistress, you go in here with me.

[*Taking* EMMELINE's *hand, and leading her away.*

EMMELINE. [*Withdrawing her hand, and shrinking back.*] No, no! let me work in the fields; I don't want to be a lady.

LEGREE. Oh! you're going to be contrary, are you? I'll soon take all that out of you.

EMMELINE. Kill me, if you will.

LEGREE. Oh! you want to be killed, do you? Now, come here, you Tom—you see I told you I didn't buy you jest for the common work; I mean to promote you and make a driver of you, and to-night ye may jest as well begin to get yer hand in. Now, ye jest take this yer gal, and flog her; ye've seen enough on't to know how.

TOM. I beg mas'r's pardon—hopes mas'r won't set me at that. It's what I ain't used to—never did, and can't do—no way possible.

LEGREE. Ye'll larn a pretty smart chance of things ye never did know before I've done with ye. [*Strikes* TOM *with whip, three blows.—Music chord each blow*.] There! now will ye tell me ye can't do it?

TOM. Yes, mas'r! I'm willing to work night and day, and work while there's life and breath in me; but this yer thing I can't feel it right to do, and, mas'r, I *never* shall do it, *never!*

LEGREE. What! ye black beast! tell *me* ye don't think it right to do what I tell ye! What have any of you cussed cattle to do with thinking what's right? I'll put a stop to it. Why, what do ye think ye are? Maybe ye think yer a gentleman, master Tom, to be telling your master what's right and what ain't! So you pretend it's wrong to flog the gal?

TOM. I think so, mas'r; 'twould be downright cruel, and it's what I never will do, mas'r. If you mean to kill me, kill me; but as to raising my hand agin any one here, I never shall—I'll die first!

LEGREE. Well, here's a pious dog at last, let down among us sinners—powerful holy critter he must be. Here, you rascal! you make believe to be so pious, didn't you never read out of your Bible, "Servants, obey your masters?" Ain't I your master? Didn't I pay twelve hundred dollars, cash, for all there is inside your cussed old black shell? Ain't you mine, body and soul?

TOM. No, no! My soul ain't yours, mas'r; you haven't bought it—ye can't buy it; it's been bought and paid for by one that is able to keep it, and you can't harm it!

LEGREE. I can't? we'll see, we'll see! Here, Sambo! Quimbo! give this dog such a breaking in as he won't get over this month!

EMMELINE. Oh, no! you will not be so cruel—have some mercy! [*Clings to* TOM.

LEGREE. Mercy? you won't find any in this shop! Away with the black cuss! Flog him within an inch of his life!

SAMBO *and* QUIMBO *seize* TOM *and drag him up stage.* LEGREE *seizes* EMMELINE, *and throws her.—She falls on her knees, with her hands lifted in supplication.—*LEGREE *raises his whip, as if to strike* TOM.—*Picture.*

SCENE IV.—*Plain Chamber.*

Enter OPHELIA, *followed by* TOPSY.

OPHELIA. A person inquiring for me, did you say, Topsy? TOPSY. Yes, missis.

OPHELIA. What kind of a looking man is he?

TOPSY. By golly! he's very queer looking man, anyway; and den he talks so dre'ful funny. What does you think?— yah! yah! he wanted to 'xibite me as de woolly gal! yah! yah!

OPHELIA. Oh! I understand. Some cute Yankee, who wants to purchase you, to make a show of—the heartless wretch!

TOPSY. Dat's just him, missis; dat's just his name. He tole me dat it was Cute—Mr. Cute Speculashum—dat's him.

OPHELIA. What did you say to him, Topsy?

TOPSY. Well, I didn't say much; it was brief and to the point—I tole him I wouldn't leave you, Miss Feely, no how.

OPHELIA. That's right, Topsy; you know you are very comfortable here—you wouldn't fare quite so well if you went away among strangers.

TOPSY. By golly! I know dat; you takes care on me, and makes me good. I don't steal any now, and I don't swar, and I don't dance breakdowns. Oh! I isn't so wicked as I used to was.

OPHELIA. That's right, Topsy; now show the gentleman, or whatever he is, up.

TOPSY. By golly! I guess he won't make much out of Miss Feely. [*Exit.*]

OPHELIA. I wonder who this person can be? Perhaps it is some old acquaintance, who has heard of my arrival, and who comes on a social visit.

Enter CUTE.

CUTE. Aunt, how do ye do? Well, I swan, the sight of you is good for weak eyes. [*Offers his hand.*

OPHELIA. [*Coldly drawing back.*] Really, sir, I can't say that I ever had the pleasure of seeing you before.

CUTE. Well, it's a fact that you never did. You see I never happened to be in your neighborhood afore now. Of course you've heard of me? I'm one of the Cutes—Gumption Cute, the first and only son of Josiah and Maria Cute, of Onion-town, on the Onion river, in the north part of this ere State of Varmount.

OPHELIA. Can't say I ever heard the name before.

CUTE. Well then, I calculate your memory must be a little ricketty. I'm a relation of yours.

OPHELIA. A relation of mine! Why, I never heard of any Cutes in our family.

CUTE. Well, I shouldn't wonder if you never did. Don't you remember your niece, Mary?

OPHELIA. Of course I do. What a shiftless question!

CUTE. Well, you see, my second cousin, Abijah Blake, married her; so you see that makes me a relation of yours.

OPHELIA. Rather a distant one, I should say.

CUTE. By chowder! I'm *near* enough, just at present.

OPHELIA. Well, you certainly are a sort of connection of mine.

CUTE. Yes, kind of sort of.

OPHELIA. And of course you are welcome to my house, as long as you choose to make it your home.

CUTE. By chowder! I'm booked for the next six months —this isn't a bad speculation.

OPHELIA. I hope you left all your folks well at home?

CUTE. Well, yes, they're pretty comfortably disposed of. Father and mother's dead, and Uncle Josh has gone to California. I am the only representative of the Cutes left.

OPHELIA. There doesn't seem to be a great deal of *you* left. I declare, you are positively in rags.

CUTE. Well, you see, the fact is, I've been speculating—trying to get bank-notes—specie-rags, as they say—but I calculate I've turned out rags of another sort.

OPHELIA. I'm sorry for your ill luck, but I am afraid you have been shiftless.

CUTE. By chowder! I've done all that a fellow could do. You see, somehow, everything I take hold of kind of bursts up.

OPHELIA. Well, well, perhaps you'll do better for the future; make yourself at home. I have got to see to some household matters, so excuse me for a short time. [*Aside.*] Impudent and shiftless! [*Exit.*

CUTE. By chowder! I rather guess that this speculation will hitch. She's a good-natured old critter; I reckon I'll be a son to her while she lives, and take care of her valuables arter she's a defunct departed. I wonder if they keep the vittles in this ere room? Guess not. I've got extensive accommodations for all sorts of eatables. I'm a regular vacuum, throughout—pockets and all. I'm chuck full of emptiness. [*Looks out.*] Holloa! who's this elderly individual coming upstairs? He looks like a compound essence of starch and dignity. I wonder if he isn't another relation of mine. I should like a rich old fellow now for an uncle.

Enter DEACON PERRY.

DEACON. Ha! a stranger here!

CUTE. How d'ye do?

DEACON. You are a friend to Miss Ophelia, I presume?

CUTE. Well, I rather calculate that I am a leetle more than a friend.

DEACON. [*Aside.*] Bless me! what can he mean by those mysterious words? Can he be her——no, I don't think he can. She said she wasn't——well, at all events, it's very suspicious.

CUTE. The old fellow seems kind of stuck up.

DEACON. You are a particular friend to Miss Ophelia, you say?

CUTE. Well, I calculate I am.

DEACON. Bound to her by any tender tie?

CUTE. It's something more than a tie—it's a regular double-twisted knot.

DEACON. Ah! just as I suspected. [*Aside.*] Might I inquire the nature of that tie?

CUTE. Well, it's the natural tie of relationship.

DEACON. A relation—what relation!

CUTE. Why, you see, my second cousin, Abijah Blake, married her niece, Mary.

DEACON. Oh! is that all?

CUTE. By chowder, ain't that enough?

DEACON. Then you are not her husband?

CUTE. To be sure I ain't. What put that 'ere idee into your cranium?

DEACON. [*Shaking him vigorously by the hand.*] My dear sir, I'm delighted to see you.

CUTE. Holloa! you ain't going slightly insane, are you?

DEACON. No, no fear of that; I'm only happy, that's all.

CUTE. I wonder if he's been taking a nipper?

DEACON. As you are a relation of Miss Ophelia's, I think it proper that I should make you my confidant; in fact, let you into a little scheme that I have lately conceived.

CUTE. Is it a speculation?

DEACON. Well, it is, just at present; but I trust before many hours to make it a surety.

CUTE. By chowder! I hope it won't serve you the way my speculations have served me. But fire away, old boy, and give us the prospectus.

DEACON. Well, then, my young friend, I have been thinking, ever since Miss Ophelia returned to Vermont, that she was just the person to fill the place of my lamented Molly.

CUTE. Say, you couldn't tell us who your lamented Molly was, could you?

DEACON. Why, the late Mrs. Perry, to be sure.

CUTE. Oh! then the lamented Polly was your wife?

DEACON. She was.

CUTE. And now you wish to marry Miss Ophelia?

DEACON. Exactly.

CUTE. [*Aside.*] Consarn this old porpoise! if I let him do that he'll Jew me out of my living. By chowder! I'll put a spoke in his wheel,

DEACON. Well, what do you say? will you intercede for me with your aunt?

CUTE. No! bust me up if I do!

DEACON. No?

CUTE. No, I tell you. I forbid the bans. Now, ain't you a purty individual, to talk about getting married, you old superannuated Methuselah specimen of humanity! Why, you've got one foot in eternity already, and t'other ain't fit to stand on. Go home and go to bed! have your head shaved, and send for a lawyer to make your will; leave your property to your heirs—if you hain't got any, why leave it to me—I'll take care of it, and charge nothing for the trouble.

DEACON. Really, sir, this language, to one of my standing, is highly indecorous—it's more, sir, than I feel willing to endure, sir. I shall expect an explanation, sir.

CUTE. Now, you see, old gouty toes, you're losing your temper.

DEACON. Sir, I'm a deacon; I never lost my temper in all my life, sir.

CUTE. Now, you see, you're getting excited; you had better go; we can't have a disturbance here!

DEACON. No, sir! I shall not go, sir! I shall not go until I have seen Miss Ophelia. I wish to know if she will countenance this insult.

CUTE. Now keep cool, old stick-in-the-mud! Draw it mild, old timber-toes!

DEACON. Damn it all, sir, what—

CUTE. Oh! only think, now, what would people say to hear a deacon swearing like a trooper?

DEACON. Sir—I—you—this is too much, sir.

CUTE. Well, now, I calculate that's just about my opinion, so we'll have no more of it. Get out of this! start your boots, or by chowder! I'll pitch you from one end of the stairs to the other.

Enter OPHELIA.

OPHELIA. Hoity toity! What's the meaning of all these loud words.

CUTE.
DEACON. } [*Together.*] { Well, you see, Aunt—
                          Miss Ophelia, I beg—

CUTE. Now, look here, you just hush your yap! How can I fix up matters if you keep jabbering?

OPHELIA. Silence! for shame, Mr. Cute. Is that the way you speak to the deacon?

CUTE. Darn the deacon!

OPHELIA. Deacon Perry, what is all this?

DEACON. Madam, a few words will explain everything. Hearing from this person that he was your nephew, I ventured to tell him that I cherished hopes of making you my wife, whereupon he flew into a violent passion, and ordered me out of the house.

OPHELIA. Does this house belong to you or me, Mr. Cute?

CUTE. Well, to you, I reckon.

OPHELIA. Then how dare you give orders in it?

CUTE. Well, I calculated you wouldn't care about marrying old half-a-century there.

OPHELIA. That's enough; I will marry him; and as for you, [*points to the right*] get out.

CUTE. Get out?

OPHELIA. Yes; the sooner the better.

CUTE. Darned if I don't serve him out first though.

[CUTE *makes a dash at* DEACON, *who gets behind* OPHELIA. TOPSY *enters with a broom and beats* CUTE *around stage.—* OPHELIA *faints in* DEACON'S *arms.—*CUTE *falls, and* TOPSY *butts him, keeling over him.—Quick drop.*

END OF ACT V.

ACT VI.

SCENE I.—*Dark Landscape.—An old, roofless shed.*

TOM *is discovered in shed, lying on some old cotton bagging.* CASSY *kneels by his side, holding a cup to his lips.*

CASSY. Drink all ye want. I knew how it would be. It isn't the first time I've been out in the night, carrying water to such as you.

TOM. [*Returning cup.*] Thank you, missis.

CASSY. Don't call me missis. I'm a miserable slave like yourself—a lower one than you can ever be! It's no use,

my poor fellow, this you've been trying to do. You were a
brave fellow. You had the right on your side; but it's all
in vain for you to struggle. You are in the Devil's hands:
he is the strongest, and you must give up.

Tom. Oh! how can I give up?

Cassy. You see *you* don't know anything about it; I do.
Here you are, on a lone plantation, ten miles from any other,
in the swamps; not a white person here who could testify,
if you were burned alive. There's no law here that can do
you, or any of us, the least good; and this man! there's no
earthly thing that he is not bad enough to do. I could make
one's hair rise, and their teeth chatter, if I should only tell
what I've seen and been knowing to here; and it's no use
resisting! Did I *want* to live with him? Wasn't I a woman
delicately bred? and he!—Father in Heaven! what was he
and is he? And yet I've lived with him these five years, and
cursed every moment of my life, night and day.

Tom. Oh, heaven! have you quite forgot us poor critters?

Cassy. And what are these miserable low dogs you work
with, that you should suffer on their account? Every one
of them would turn against you the first time they get a
chance. They are all of them as low and cruel to each other
as they can be; there's no use in your suffering to keep from
hurting them!

Tom. What made 'em cruel? If I give out, I shall get
used to it and grow, little by little, just like 'em. No, no,
missis, I've lost everything, wife, and children, and home,
and a kind master, and he would have set me free if he'd
only lived a day longer—I've lost everything in *this* world,
and now I can't lose heaven, too; no, I can't get to be wicked
besides all.

Cassy. But it can't be that He will lay sin to our account;
he won't charge it to us when we are forced to it; he'll
charge it to them that drove us to it. Can I do anything
more for you? Shall I give you some more water?

Tom. Oh missis! I wish you'd go to Him who can give
you living waters!

Cassy. Go to Him! Where is He? Who is He?

Tom. Our Heavenly Father!

Cassy. I used to see the picture of Him, over the altar,
when I was a girl; but *he isn't here!* there's nothing here but

sin, and long, long despair! There, there, don't talk any more, my poor fellow. Try to sleep, if you can. I must hasten back, lest my absence be noted. Think of me when I am gone, Uncle Tom, and pray, pray for me.

[*Exit* Cassy.—Tom *sinks back to sleep.*

Scene II.—*Street in New Orleans.*

Enter George Shelby.

GEORGE. At length my mission of mercy is nearly finished; I have reached my journey's end. I have now but to find the house of Mr. St. Clare, re-purchase old Uncle Tom, and convey him back to his wife and children, in old Kentucky. Some one approaches; he may, perhaps, be able to give me the information I require. I will accost him.

Enter Marks.

Pray, sir, can you tell me where Mr. St. Clare dwells?

MARKS. Where I don't think you'll be in a hurry to seek him.

GEORGE. And where is that?

MARKS. In the grave!

GEORGE. Stay, sir! you may be able to give me some information concerning Mr. St. Clare.

MARKS. I beg pardon, sir, I am a lawyer; I can't afford to *give* anything.

GEORGE. But you would have no objections to selling it?

MARKS. Not the slightest.

GEORGE. What do you value it at?

MARKS. Well, say five dollars, that's reasonable.

GEORGE. There they are. [*Gives money.*] Now answer me to the best of your ability. Has the death of St. Clare caused his slaves to be sold?

MARKS. It has.

GEORGE. How were they sold?

MARKS. At auction—they went dirt cheap.

GEORGE. How were they bought—all in one lot?

MARKS. No, they went to different bidders.

GEORGE. Was you present at the sale?

MARKS. I was.

GEORGE. Do you remember seeing a negro among them called Tom.

MARKS. What, Uncle Tom?

GEORGE. The same—who bought him?

MARKS. A Mr. Legree.

GEORGE. Where is his plantation?

MARKS. Up in Louisiana, on the Red River; but a man never could find it unless he had been there before.

GEORGE. Who could I get to direct me there?

MARKS. Well, stranger, I don't know of any one just at present, 'cept myself, could find it for you; it's such an out-of-the-way sort of hole; and if you are a mind to come down handsomely, why, I'll do it.

GEORGE. The reward shall be ample.

MARKS. Enough said, stranger; let's take the steamboat at once. [*Exeunt.*

SCENE III.—*A Rough Chamber.*

Enter LEGREE.—*Sits.*

LEGREE. Plague on that Sambo, to kick up this yer row between me and the new hands.

CASSY *steals on, and stands behind him.*

The fellow won't be fit to work for a week now, right in the press of the season.

CASSY. Yes, just like you.

LEGREE. Hah! you she-devil! you've come back, have you? [*Rises.*

CASSY. Yes, I have; come to have my own way, too.

LEGREE. You lie, you jade! I'll be up to my word. Either behave yourself, or stay down in the quarters and fare and work with the rest.

CASSY. I'd rather, ten thousand times, live in the dirtiest hole in the quarters, than be under your hoof!

LEGREE. But you are under my hoof, for all that, that's one comfort; so sit down here and listen to reason. [*Grasps her wrist.*

CASSY. Simon Legree, take care! [LEGREE *lets go his hold.*] You're afraid of me, Simon, and you've reason to be; for I've got the Devil in me!

LEGREE. I believe to my soul you have. After all, Cassy, why can't you be friends with me, as you used to?

CASSIE. [*Bitterly.*] Used to!

LEGREE. I wish, Cassy, you'd behave yourself decently.

CASSY. *You* talk about behaving decently! and what have you been doing? You haven't even sense enough to keep from spoiling one of your best hands, right in the most pressing season, just for your devilish temper.

LEGREE. I was a fool, it's a fact, to let any such brangle come up; but when Tom set up his will he had to be broke in.

CASSY. You'll never break *him* in.

LEGREE. Won't I? I'd like to know if I won't! He'll be the first nigger that ever come it round me! I'll break every bone in his body but he shall give up.

Enter SAMBO, *with a paper in his hand; he stands bowing.*

LEGREE. What's that, you dog?

SAMBO. It's a witch thing, mas'r.

LEGREE. A what?

SAMBO. Something that niggers gits from witches. Keep 'em from feeling when they's flogged. He had it tied round his neck with a black string.

LEGREE *takes the paper and opens it.—A silver dollar drops on the stage, and a long curl of light hair twines around his finger.*

LEGREE. Damnation. [*Stamping and writhing, as if the hair burned him.*] Where did this come from? Take it off! burn it up! burn it up! [*Throws the curl away.*] What did you bring it to me for?

SAMBO. [*Trembling.*] I beg pardon, mas'r; I thought you would like to see 'um.

LEGREE. Don't you bring me any more of your devilish things. [*Shakes his fist at* SAMBO *who runs off.—*LEGREE *kicks the dollar after him.*] Blast it! where did he get that? If it didn't look just like—whoo! I thought I'd forgot that. Curse me if I think there's any such thing as forgetting anything, any how.

CASSY. What is the matter with you, Legree? What is there in a simple curl of fair hair to appal a man like you— you who are familiar with every form of cruelty.

LEGREE. Cassy, to-night the past has been recalled to me— the past that I have so long and vainly striven to forget.

CASSY.   Hast aught on this earth power to move a soul like thine?

LEGREE.   Yes, for hard and reprobate as I now seem, there has been a time when I have been rocked on the bosom of a mother, cradled with prayers and pious hymns, my now seared brow bedewed with the waters of holy baptism.

CASSIE.   [*Aside.*]   What sweet memories of childhood can thus soften down that heart of iron?

LEGREE.   In early childhood a fair-haired woman has led me, at the sound of Sabbath bells, to worship and to pray. Born of a hard-tempered sire, on whom that gentle woman had wasted a world of unvalued love, I followed in the steps of my father.   Boisterous, unruly and tyrannical, I despised all her counsel, and would have none of her reproof, and, at an early age, broke from her to seek my fortunes on the sea.   I never came home but once after that; and then my mother, with the yearning of a heart that must love something, and had nothing else to love, clung to me, and sought with passionate prayers and entreaties to win me from a life of sin.

CASSY.   That was your day of grace, Legree; then good angels called you, and mercy held you by the hand.

LEGREE.   My heart inly relented; there was a conflict, but sin got the victory, and I set all the force of my rough nature against the conviction of my conscience.   I drank and swore, was wilder and more brutal than ever.   And one night, when my mother, in the last agony of her despair, knelt at my feet, I spurned her from me, threw her senseless on the floor, and with brutal curses fled to my ship.

CASSY.   Then the fiend took thee for his own.

LEGREE.   The next I heard of my mother was one night while I was carousing among drunken companions.   A letter was put in my hands.   I opened it, and a lock of long, curling hair fell from it, and twined about my fingers, even as that lock twined but now.   The letter told me that my mother was dead, and that dying she blest and forgave me!

[*Buries his face in his hands.*

CASSY.   Why did you not even then renounce your evil ways?

LEGREE.   There is a dread, unhallowed necromancy of evil, that turns things sweetest and holiest to phantoms of horror and affright. That pale, loving mother,—her dying prayers, her forgiving love,—wrought in my demoniac heart of sin only as a damning sentence, bringing with it a fearful looking for of judgment and fiery indignation.

CASSY. And yet you would not strive to avert the doom that threatened you.

LEGREE. I burned the lock of hair and I burned the letter; and when I saw them hissing and crackling in the flame, inly shuddered as I thought of everlasting fires! I tried to drink and revel, and swear away the memory; but often in the deep night, whose solemn stillness arraigns the soul in forced communion with itself, I have seen that pale mother rising by my bed-side, and felt the soft twining of that hair around my fingers, 'till the cold sweat would roll down my face, and I would spring from my bed in horror—horror! [*Falls in chair.—After a pause.*] What the devil ails me? Large drops of sweat stand on my forehead, and my heart beats heavy and thick with fear. I thought I saw something white rising and glimmering in the gloom before me, and it seemed to bear my mother's face! I know one thing; I'll let that fellow Tom alone, after this. What did I want with his cussed paper? I believe I am bewitched sure enough! I've been shivering and sweating ever since! Where did he get that hair? It couldn't have been that! I *burn'd* that up, I know I did! It would be a joke if hair could rise from the dead! I'll have Sambo and Quimbo up here to sing and dance one of their dances, and keep off these horrid notions. Here, Sambo! Quimbo! [*Exit.*

CASSY. Yes, Legree, that golden tress was charmed; each hair had in it a spell of terror and remorse for thee, and was used by a mightier power to bind thy cruel hands from inflicting uttermost evil on the helpless! [*Exit.*

SCENE IV.—*Street.*

Enter MARKS, *meeting* CUTE, *who enters, dressed in an old faded uniform.*

MARKS. By the land, stranger, but it strikes me that I've seen you somewhere before.

CUTE. By chowder! do you know now, that's just what I was a going to say?

MARKS. Isn't your name Cute?

CUTE. You're right, I calculate. Yours is Marks, I reckon.

MARKS. Just so.

CUTE. Well, I swow, I'm glad to see you. [*They shake hands.*] How's your wholesome?

MARKS. Hearty as ever. Well, who would have thought of ever seeing you again. Why, I thought you was in Vermont?

CUTE. Well, so I was. You see I went there after that rich relation of mine—but the speculation didn't turn out well.

MARKS. How so?

CUTE. Why, you see, she took a shine to an old fellow—Deacon Abraham Perry—and married him.

MARKS. Oh, that rather put your nose out of joint in that quarter.

CUTE. Busted me right up, I tell you. The deacon did the handsome thing though; he said if I would leave the neighbourhood and go out South again, he'd stand the damage. I calculate I didn't give him much time to change his mind, and so, you see, here I am again.

MARKS. What are you doing in that soldier rig?

CUTE. Oh, this is my sign.

MARKS. Your sign?

CUTE. Yes; you see, I'm engaged just at present in an all-fired good speculation; I'm a Fillibusterow.

MARKS. A what?

CUTE. A Fillibusterow! Don't you know what that is? It's Spanish for Cuban Volunteer; and means a chap that goes the whole porker for glory and all that ere sort of thing.

MARKS. Oh! you've joined the order of the Lone Star!

CUTE. You've hit it. You see I bought this uniform at a second-hand clothing store; I puts it on and goes to a benevolent individual and I says to him,—appealing to his feelings,—I'm one of the fellows that went to Cuba and got massacred by the bloody Spaniards. I'm in a destitute condition—give me a trifle to pay my passage back, so I can whop the tyrannical cusses and avenge my brave fellow soger what got slewed there.

MARKS. How pathetic!

CUTE. I tell you it works up the feelings of benevolent individuals dreadfully. It draws tears from their eyes and money from their pockets. By chowder! one old chap gave me a hundred dollars to help on the cause.

MARKS. I admire a genius like yours.

CUTE. But I say, what are you up to?

MARKS. I am the travelling companion of a young gentleman by the name of Shelby, who is going to the plantation of a Mr. Legree, on the Red River, to buy an old darky who used to belong to his father.

CUTE. Legree—Legree? Well, now, I calculate I've heard that ere name afore.

MARKS. Do you remember that man who drew a bowie knife on you in New Orleans?

CUTE. By chowder! I remember the circumstance just as well as if it was yesterday; but I can't say that I recollect much about the man, for you see I was in something of a hurry about that time and didn't stop to take a good look at him.

MARKS. Well, that man was this same Mr. Legree.

CUTE. Do you know, now, I should like to pay that critter off?

MARKS. Then I'll give you an opportunity.

CUTE. Chowder! how will you do that?

MARKS. Do you remember the gentleman that interfered between you and Legree?

CUTE. Yes—well?

MARKS. He received the blow that was intended for you, and died from the effects of it. So, you see, Legree is a murderer, and we are the only witnesses of the deed. His life is in our hands.

CUTE. Let's have him right up and make him dance on nothing to the tune of Yankee Doodle!

MARKS. Stop a bit. Don't you see a chance for a profitable speculation?

CUTE. A speculation! Fire away, don't be bashful; I'm the man for a speculation.

MARKS. I have made a deposition to the Governor of the State of all the particulars of that affair at Orleans.

CUTE. What did you do that for?

MARKS. To get a warrant for his arrest.

CUTE. Oh! and have you got it?

MARKS. Yes; here it is. *[Takes out paper.*

CUTE. Well, now, I don't see how you are going to make anything by that bit of paper?

MARKS. But I do. I shall say to Legree, I have got a warrant against you for murder; my friend, Mr. Cute, and myself are the only witnesses who can appear against you. Give us a thousand dollars, and we will tear up the warrant and be silent.

CUTE. Then Mr. Legree forks over a thousand dollars, and your friend Cute pockets five hundred of it. Is that the calculation?

MARKS. If you will join me in the undertaking.

CUTE. I'll do it, by chowder!

MARKS. Your hand to bind the bargain.

CUTE. I'll stick by you thro' thick and thin.

MARKS. Enough said.

CUTE. Then shake. *[They shake hands.*

MARKS. But I say, Cute, he may be contrary and show fight.

CUTE. Never mind, we've got the law on our side, and we're bound to stir him up. If he don't come down handsomely, we'll present him with a neck-tie made of hemp!

MARKS. I declare you're getting spunky.

CUTE. Well, I reckon I am. Let's go and have something to drink. Tell you what, Marks, if we don't get *him,* we'll have his hide, by chowder! *[Exeunt, arm in arm.*

SCENE V.—*Rough Chamber.*

Enter LEGREE, *followed by* SAMBO.

LEGREE. Go and send Cassy to me.

SAMBO. Yes, mas'r. *[Exit.*

LEGREE. Curse the woman! she's got a temper worse than the devil! I shall do her an injury one of these days, if she isn't careful.

Re-enter SAMBO, *frightened.*

What's the matter with you, you black scoundrel?

SAMBO. S'help me, mas'r, she isn't dere.

LEGREE. I suppose she's about the house somewhere?

SAMBO. No, she isn't, mas'r; I's been all over de house and I can't find nothing of her nor Emmeline.

LEGREE. Bolted, by the Lord! Call out the dogs! saddle my horse! Stop! are you sure they really have gone?

SAMBO. Yes, mas'r; I's been in every room 'cept the haunted garret, and dey wouldn't go dere.

LEGREE. I have it! Now, Sambo, you jest go and walk that Tom up here, right away! [*Exit* SAMBO.] The old cuss is at the bottom of this yer whole matter; and I'll have it out of his infernal black hide, or I'll know the reason why! I *hate* him—I *hate* him! And isn't he *mine?* Can't I do what I like with him? Who's to hinder, I wonder?

TOM *is dragged on by* SAMBO *and* QUIMBO.

LEGREE. [*Grimly confronting* TOM.] Well, Tom, do you know I've made up my mind to *kill* you?

TOM. It's very likely, Mas'r.

LEGREE. *I—have—done—just—that—thing,* Tom, unless you tell me what do you know about these yer gals? [TOM *is silent.*] D'ye hear? Speak!

TOM. I hain't got anything to tell, mas'r.

LEGREE. Do you dare to tell me, you old black rascal, you don't know? Speak! Do you know anything?

TOM. I know, mas'r; but I can't tell anything. *I can die!*

LEGREE. Hark ye, Tom! ye think, 'cause I have let you off before, I don't mean what I say; but, this time, I have made *up my mind,* and counted the cost. You've always stood it out agin me; now, I'll *conquer ye or kill ye!* one or t'other. I'll count every drop of blood there is in you, and take 'em, one by one, 'till ye give up!

TOM. Mas'r, if you was sick, or in trouble, or dying, and I could save, I'd *give* you my heart's blood; and, if taking every drop of blood in this poor old body would save your precious soul, I'd give 'em freely. Do the worst you can, my troubles will be over soon; but if you don't repent, yours won't never end.

[LEGREE *strikes* TOM *down with the butt of his whip.*

LEGREE. How do you like that?

SAMBO. He's most gone, mas'r!

TOM. [*Rises feebly on his hands.*] There ain't no more you can do! I forgive you with all my soul.

[*Sinks back, and is carried off by* SAMBO *and* QUIMBO.

LEGREE. I believe he's done for finally. Well, his mouth is shut up at last—that's one comfort.

Enter GEORGE SHELBY, MARKS *and* CUTE.

Strangers! Well, what do you want?

GEORGE. I understand that you bought in New Orleans a negro named Tom?

LEGREE. Yes, I did buy such a fellow, and a devil of a bargain I had of it, too! I believe he's trying to die, but I don't know as he'll make it out.

GEORGE. Where is he? Let me see him!

SAMBO. Dere he is!   [*Points to* TOM.

LEGREE. How dare you speak?

[*Drives* SAMBO *and* QUIMBO *off.*—GEORGE *exits.*

CUTE. Now's the time to nab him.

MARKS. How are you, Mr. Legree?

LEGREE. What the devil brought you here?

MARKS. This little bit of paper. I arrest you for the murder of Mr. St. Clare. What do you say to that?

LEGREE. This is my answer! [*Makes a blow at* MARKS, *who dodges, and* CUTE *receives the blow—he cries out and runs off.* MARKS *fires at* LEGREE, *and follows* CUTE.] I am hit!—the game's up! [*Falls dead.* QUIMBO *and* SAMBO *return and carry him off laughing.*]

GEORGE SHELBY *enters, supporting* TOM.—*Music. They advance and* TOM *falls, centre.*

GEORGE. Oh! dear Uncle Tom! do wake—do speak once more! look up! Here's Master George—your own little Master George. Don't you know me?

TOM. [*Opening his eyes and speaking in a feeble tone.*] Mas'r George! Bless de Lord! it's all I wanted! They hav'n't forgot me! It warms my soul; it does my old heart good! Now I shall die content!

GEORGE. You sha'n't die! you mustn't die, nor think of it. I have come to buy you, and take you home.

TOM. Oh, Mas'r George, you're too late. The Lord has bought me, and is going to take me home.

GEORGE. Oh! don't die. It will kill me—it will break my heart to think what you have suffered, poor, poor fellow!

TOM. Don't call me poor fellow. I *have* been poor fellow; but that's all past and gone now. I'm right in the door, going into glory! Oh, Mas'r George! *Heaven has come!* I've got the victory! the Lord has given it to me! Glory be to His name!   [*Dies.*

[*Solemn music.*—GEORGE *covers* UNCLE TOM *with his cloak, and kneels over him. Clouds work on and conceal them, and then work off.*

SCENE VII.—*Gorgeous clouds, tinted with sunlight.* EVA, *robed in white, is discovered on the back of a milk-white dove, with expanded wings, as if just soaring upward. Her hands are extended in benediction over* ST. CLARE *and* UNCLE TOM, *who are kneeling and gazing up to her. Impressive music.—Slow curtain.*

THE END.

SELF

By Mrs. Sidney F. Bateman

MRS. SIDNEY F. BATEMAN

1823–1881

I have selected Mrs. Bateman's "Self" for inclusion in the present collection, not because it differs so materially from Mrs. Mowatt's "Fashion", as because of its resemblance to the latter play. The similarity almost reduces itself to a convention which can be sharply estimated by a comparison of the two dramas, and a further comparative process with Bronson Howard's "Saratoga". There is no doubt that Mrs. Bateman must have had "Fashion" in mind as to plot and characterization. Of the two, I should say that Mrs. Mowatt is more spontaneous in her style, and that "Fashion", for its fame, was less dependent on E. L. Davenport's success in the rôle of *Adam Trueman,* than was "Self" on the wonderfully creative acting of John E. Owens, in the rôle of *John Unit.*

"Self" is highly local, and constant references show it a typical play of the moment. The local allusions are plentiful. We find that "presidents may Schuylerize", that Broadway has Russ pavements, that Rushton's drug store is a thinly disguised place on the Avenue. Patent medicines are lampooned with some personal feeling or else some timely meaning; wildcat banks are mentioned with newspaper casualness; slavery is referred to as it could not help but be mentioned in the general conversation of the day; daguerreotypes are spoken of with the wonder of new inventions. Probably "Self's" claim to ultra-modernism could be based on its mention of women's rights. These are a few of its timely excrescences.

Mrs. Bateman brought to her task of writing a thorough knowledge of the theatre. Before her marriage, she was Sidney Frances Cowell, daughter of the English low comedian, who was so closely associated with the early history of the American Theatre, and whose "Reminiscences", now

697

scarce in the first edition, are filled with his ebullient wealth of anecdote. From her mother, she inherited some of the verve of the French. She was born in New York, on March 29, 1823. Theatrical dates are never to be relied on; contradictory statements are everywhere to be met with. The London *Times* claims that Mrs. Bateman was a native of Maryland; the London *Era Almanack* states that she died at the age of fifty-six, which would make her birth year 1825. This date is sustained in Davenport Adams's "Dictionary of the Drama". But the *Dictionary of National Biography*, which adheres to 1823, also states that Mrs. Bateman was the daughter of Cowell, by a second wife. Brought up on a farm in Ohio, Sidney received her education in Cincinnati. During this farm existence, she was not removed from artistic influence; it is recorded how she sat upon the knee of the elder Booth, with awe in her eyes, during a visit of the great actor to her father, and how she won her way into his eccentric heart.

Joe Cowell reveals himself fully in his "Thirty Years Passed Among the Players of England and America", but, in a letter written to the present editor by a granddaughter of the old actor, we are given a further glimpse. "I have a very fond recollection of my grandfather," she writes. "He seemed a very grand old man to me—very full 'of wise saws and modern instances.' Do you know that he was a naturalized citizen of America?—and that he adored his adopted country?"

Sidney was the only daughter, her brother Samuel being well-known as a comedian and comic singer in London during the 50's and 60's. Her histrionic talent manifested itself at an early age. She must have made her professional début around her fourteenth year, for there is record of her playing in New Orleans during the season of 1837–38. She married Hezekiah Linthicum Bateman, in St. Louis, on November 10, 1839, and their careers are indissolubly linked, for they both were actors and they both ended their days as managers of theatres in London. From his early career as a director, Bateman showed genius for coping with the impossible, and it is probable that his domineering character was developed in an atmosphere of getting, at this time, exactly what he wanted.

The one curb to his temper was his awful name, about which he was most sensitive. After John E. Owens had bought the entire rights to "Self", and engaged Bateman to accompany him on the road, many are the humorous encounters the two had because of the vagaries of the latter. "I really think, Bateman," declared Owens, one day, "if in the next world you are fortunate enough to be placed with the sheep, you will think it looks pleasanter among the goats." We learn from Owens's "Memories" that Bateman possessed indomitable energy, was a most indefatigable worker, as a director, and his keen wit was seen to excellent advantage as a raconteur. He requested everyone to address him as Henry L. Bateman. Thus he coped with his parental endowment. But Owens used "Hezekiah Linthicum" as a sure weapon of defence. At one time actor and manager had a heated debate, and correspondence passed between them, with such eloquence on the part of Bateman that Owens threatened, unless the letters stopped at once, to address his replies to the accursed Hezekiah. Bateman immediately stopped. "I have heard my father say", writes Miss Cowell, "that Mrs. Bateman in her youth was a delightful actress and a beautiful woman. She was very gentle and retiring, but of very fine judgment and executive ability. She was always the power behind the throne in all the elaborate productions credited to her husband and daughter."

Such strength of character was seen in every emergency which marked her busy life. Whatever she did was approached with energy and thoroughness, from the education of her famous daughters to the planning of those dramas which, in London, proved to be the commencement of Henry Irving's illustrious career. Her literary talent was early developed. For "Self" was written and produced in St. Louis, at the People's Theatre, on April 6, 1857. Mr. Bateman, so we are informed, was the first *John Unit,* although French's Acting Edition of the play gives Mark Smith. Her next piece, "Geraldine; or, The Master Passion", originally produced in Philadelphia, in 1859, was given at the London Adelphi, on June 12, 1865, with Bateman in the cast, and his daughter, Kate, assuming the title-rôle, originally played in America by Matilda Heron. In 1855, Bateman managed a theatre in St. Louis, and, in 1859, removed to New York. A fast growing family—for the Batemans had eight children—demanded much of Mrs. Bateman's time and care, and she retired from the stage while still a young woman. Whatever distinction later fell to the lot of her children, Kate, Ellen, Isabel, and Virginia, was largely due to the thorough training given them by their mother.

By the time Mr. and Mrs. Bateman had moved to London, they had completely forgotten their claim to the play "Self." In fact, no English biographer of the theatre credits Mrs. Bateman with its authorship, though they all do not fail to mention her other plays. It was brought to New York, and was played at Burton's Chambers Street Theatre, on October 27, 1856, with the excellent comedy cast of a noted stock company. The *dramatis personae* is given elsewhere in full. On the morning after the production, the dramatic writer for the New York *Times* showed discrimination and reasonable reticence. "Whether it will obtain a permanent place in the limited repertoire of the native drama," he wrote, "admits of some doubt." Scoring in detail, he added: "The costumes were rich enough, but the changes were not numerous, and the ball-dresses had to do service in the street or store as well as drawing-room. It is in matters of this kind that Mr. Burton is specially negligent."

Evidently Owens must have seen in the rôle of *John Unit* many possibilities; for he was not long in signing up with Bateman to star in "Self". There followed the building up of a part which no printed text could ever suggest; the fitting in of stage business to accord with the individual interpretation and feeling. It is another instance of a play dragged out of oblivion by creative acting. "Self" had practically failed, and yet Owens risked, even as Sothern risked when he was given twenty-three lines of *Dundreary* and was told by Miss Keene that he might enlarge it as he saw fit. We are told by the actor's wife and biographer that in the costuming of the part of *John Unit,* Owens modelled after the manner and dress of a prominent citizen of Cincinnati. From the very first, he was a complete success, and he hastened to buy from Bateman all the rights to the comedy. With the purchase must have gone a business arrangement with Bateman to manage the tour. During this association, a plan was discussed, to form an American Comedy Company for the purpose of travelling through England. But it never came to anything. It may be that Mrs. Bateman recalled this plan, when, as a manageress in London, on her own initiative, she brought over an entire American company in Joaquin Miller's "The Danites".

Owens's work in the rôle of *John Unit* was one of those complete portraitures in which American stage history is so rich. Mrs. Owens writes:

> His grasp of the character was perfect, and every light and shade stood forth intensely life-like. Prominent in perfection, the library scene may be considered the gem of the part. The soliloquy, after having made his will, was like the unfolding of the inner nature of the old banker, giving glimpses of its asperity and of its tenderness. The ingenuous retrospection of his life— realization that his methods had brought him to a lonely old age, recollections of boyhood and home, yearnings for family ties, were delineated with such depth of sentiment and rugged pathos as to invoke sympathetic response. During Owens's first visit to California, this scene had intense effect upon the rough, red-shirted miners in the galleries. . . .

Owens's *John Unit* pleased such a critic as Laurence Hutton more than his *Solon Shingle,* discussed in the introduction to "The People's Lawyer". In popularity it was accorded a place beside his delineation of *Caleb Plummer.*

It must have been either in 1869, or very early in the '70's, that the Batemans went to London. For we find record of Mrs. Bateman's third play mentioned,—"Fanchette, the Will o' the Wisp", an adaptation from "Die Grille," a German version of George Sand's "La Petite Fadette". It was given at the Theatre Royal, Edinburgh, with Isabel Bateman in the title part, and was later seen at the Lyceum Theatre, London, on September 11, 1871, with Henry Irving in the cast.

This establishes the date of Bateman's undertaking the management of the Lyceum, the lease of which theatre he held until his death, on March 22, 1875. The ups and downs

of fortune, which the two experienced were shared by the
then rising young actor, Irving, who awaited the stamp of
public recognition when, under the Batemans, he appeared in
"The Bells." This success not only established him, but
likewise refounded the fortunes of the Batemans, whose
treasury was none too full for the ambitions of their house.
This was in November, 1871. By the time Irving had gained
his position, the Bateman children were also well-established
in theatrical life, and we find two of the daughters, Kate
and Virginia, in the cast of Tennyson's "Queen Mary",
presented in Ap l, 1876. Kate's reputation was associated
with the play, "Leah, the Forsaken", adapted from Mosen-
thal's "Deborah" by Augustin Daly. When Miss Bateman
played *Juliet* in America, her *Romeo* was John Wilkes
Booth.

Toward the latter part of her career, and after Irving
assumed control of the Lyceum, Mrs. Bateman, never loath
to try new ventures, leased Sadler's Wells Theatre, and,
according to the London *Times,* her régime there made it
likely that the old playhouse would regain some of the prestige it held during the days of Samuel Phelps. It was here
that she brought "The Danites".

Mrs. Bateman died in London, on January 13, 1881, much
honored by the theatrical profession. In recording her
literary attainments, there has been no mention made of
"Self", as I have said, and there are several other plays
by her which have failed of record. Evidently her taste
for poetry was pronounced, for not only was "Geraldine"
written in blank verse, but she attempted a dramatization of
Longfellow's "Evangeline" for her daughter, Kate. I find
two other plays accredited to Mrs. Bateman: "The Golden
Calf", a comedy, published in 1857, by the St. Louis Republican Office, and "The Dead Secret", a drama adapted by
permission of Wilkie Collins, and printed in London, 1877.
There must have been other writings, for she was ever ready
with her pen; especially ready when she had to defend an
artistic policy. I have read an open letter written by her
to Dr. Furnivall, in defense of the Shakespearean productions given by Irving at the Lyceum, and it was written with
full knowledge and equal determination. Clement Scott
leaves a contemporary impression. "Bateman thought his

good wife was the best writer and judge of plays in existence," he says in his "The Drama of Yesterday and Today". And he adds: "She certainly was a very clever and charming woman". [1]

[1] The editor has been fortunate in being able to consult with Miss Sidney Cowell, one of the honored residents of the Forrest Home, regarding her family. She is the daughter of Samuel, mentioned above, and therefore is a niece of "Aunt Sidney". On inquiry as to a picture of Mrs. Bateman, Miss Cowell's reply throws further light on the family. She states: "I am writing to my niece, Miss Sydney Fairbrother, who is at present playing in 'Chin-Chu-Chow' (that's as near as I can get it), at His Majesty's Theatre, London. It is possible that she or her mother may have— or know of—a likeness. . . . Sydney is the last dramatic representative of the Cowell family, and a most worthy one—a great favorite in London. . . . I hope you will not consider me obtrusive, but I might also mention my sister, *née* Florence Cowell, Mrs. Florence Tapping, who is widely known and admired as a *grande dame* and character actress. She has been associated for some years with that wonderful producing company, Miss Horniman's Players of Manchester, England. My sister Florence and I were Sam Cowell's only daughters. She is five years my junior, and is still in the meridian of her talents and popularity."

Miss Cowell, herself, had a distinctive theatrical career, and as recorded in the "Memoirs" of David Belasco, was in her ascendency during the initial years of that manager's success in the West.

Of the Bateman daughters, much interesting data is to be had by consulting Pascoe's "The Dramatic List," and other theatrical records of the time. Isabel was associated with her mother in the management of Sadler's Wells Theatre, and Virginia married Edward Compton, a son of the famous comedian of that name. Kate, by far the most noteworthy actress of the sisters, died at the beginning of the year 1917. She and Ellen were probably most closely associated in the public mind as the Bateman Children.

SELF

DRAMATIS PERSONÆ AND CAST

As given at Burton's Chambers Street Theatre,
October 27, 1856.

Mr. John Unit......................	Mr Burton.
Mr. Apex, *a New York Merchant*.....	Mr. C. Fisher.
Charles Sanford, *his stepson*..........	Mr. Morton.
Cypher Cynosure, Esq., *a travelled nonentity*...........................	Mr. T. Placide.
Mr. Promptcash, *a Dry Goods Merchant*...........................	Mr. Setchell.
Mr. Ellwide, *his partner*..............	Mr. J. Moore.
Jones	Mr. Tree.
Brown } *Dry Goods Clerks*........... {	Mr. Lawson.
Smith } {	Mr. Everett.
Thompson...........................	Mr. Paul.
Servant to Apex.....................	Mr. C. Parsloe.
Servant to Unit.....................	Mr. Hurley.
Mrs. Apex, *a fashionable Lady*.........	Mrs. A. Parker.
Mary Apex, *her step-daughter*........	Mrs. E. Davenport.
Mrs. Radius	Mrs. C. Howard.
Mrs. Corderoy Codliver, *a wealthy Vulgarian*...........................	Miss P. Marshall.
Aunt Chloe, *an old colored Nurse*......	Mrs. Dunn.
Miss Sallie Simper..................	Miss Florence.
Miss Ida Indolence..................	Miss Tree.
Miss Dorothea Dumpling.............	Miss Morton.
Miss Fanny Fortuna	Miss Stella.
Servant at Boarding House..........	Mrs. Bell.

Locality, New York.
Time, Two Days.
Costume, modern (i.e., 1856).

SELF

ACT I.

SCENE I.—*A Fashionable Dry Goods Store, in Broadway.— Sign, "ELLWIDE & PROMPTCASH," over door. Counter and shelves; goods displayed; frames, with mantillas, carpets, shawls, &c., suspended from ceiling. Entrance to store. JONES, SMITH, CLARK, and THOMPSON discovered at counter, arranging and displaying dresses and goods.*

ELLWIDE *and* PROMPTCASH *discovered.*

ELLWIDE. Trade slow to-day—[*pulls out watch*]—past eleven! High time some of our customers got down town. Oh, by the way! that embroidered velvet must be sold at once, or shipped to California. We shall lose by that investment. It's growing vulgar to wear such high-priced goods, since the sporting gentry began buying them for their wives. So, unless we can get some of our fashionable folks by the ears about it, the seven hundred dollar velvet will go a-begging.

PROMPTCASH. That won't do. I paid twenty-five cents a line to Napless, for a first-rate notice. That won't do! Cost of importation and puffing—a heavy loss!

ELLWIDE. The truth is, every store hangs out placards of "Wet Goods" and "Immense Reduction," until nobody believes them. We must strike out a new dodge to catch the public. That Napless is a perfect case. He said that the velvet was made at Genoa, by an Italian Princess, who had learned the art of weaving, in consequence of her love of democracy, and because she had been robbed by the Austrians of all her estates and cash. Ha, ha, ha!

PROMPTCASH. [*Taking up newspaper.*] Pretty good! Barnum ought to get Napless to take him in hand. But this *imperial* dodge, in to-day's paper, is the best. The mysterious report he invented, that this dress was designed expressly for the Empress Eugénie; but that she refused it, because Miss Sneade had one just the same color. Ha, ha, ha!

ELLWIDE. That story will sell it for us—if we can only get Mrs. Apex to take a fancy to it.

PROMPTCASH. Oh, she would buy it fast enough, but her payments are rather slow. Do you know, Ellwide, it would not astonish me, from the talk on 'change, if Apex were to break.

ELLWIDE. Nonsense, man! He is at the very head of all mercantile affairs in New York. He break! Why, they say the sea is dotted with his ships!

PROMPTCASH. But they may sink.

ELLWIDE. His warehouses are said to be crammed with goods.

PROMPTCASH. But they may all burn down.

ELLWIDE. Report says, he owns shares in half the railroads in the country.

PROMPTCASH. But the presidents may Schuylerize.

ELLWIDE. Bah! Man, you believe in nothing!

PROMPTCASH. Yes I do. I believe that short credits make long friends—that a bird in the hand is worth two in the bush—that the way to keep your credit up——

ELLWIDE. Stop! stop! You are worse than a revised edition of "Poor Richard's Almanac."

PROMPTCASH. Better hear "Poor Richard" now, than poor Promptcash when our firm is ruined by bad debts.

ELLWIDE. Hark!—there is a carriage. Hush—hush! It is the very woman we were talking of—the fashionable and extravagant Mrs. Apex. Good morning, Mrs. Apex!

Enter MRS. APEX, *elegantly attired, in walking dress.* MR. ELLWIDE *goes up stage, and receives her with great ceremony.*

MRS. APEX. Good morning, Mr. Ellwide. I want to see if you have got anything really elegant to show me, in dress goods. I give a large party to-morrow evening, and don't like the dress I had prepared for the occasion. Now, have you something really magnificent?

ELLWIDE. We have just got a case from Paris, with the most superb embroidered velvet—but don't be startled at the price.

MRS. APEX. The price is not usually an object of paramount importance with me, Mr. Ellwide.

PROMPTCASH. [*At desk, aside.*] It seldom is with people who run up accounts!

MRS. APEX. I only fear you have nothing worth looking at. Since our European tour, I think American goods are so vulgar.

PROMPTCASH. [*Aside.*] So, I'm afraid, is paying for them!

ELLWIDE. [*Takes paper-box, unties ribbon, &c.*] But this dress, Mrs. Apex, is really a superb affair—embroidered expressly for the Empress Eugénie!

MRS. APEX. Ah, yes! That is the one I should like to see. I read something about it in this morning's paper.

PROMPTCASH. [*Aside.*] Mem! Secret of business success is advertising.

ELLWIDE. [*Opening box, and displaying dress.*] This color would become you exactly. Mrs. Radius, I know, is crazy to buy it, but I determined you should see it first. Now, did you ever see anything so truly rich and elegant?

MRS. APEX. Oh, that is certainly charming! What is the price?

ELLWIDE. Seven hundred dollars.

MRS. APEX. No doubt it is worth that, particularly as it was made for the Empress.

ELLWIDE. It cost us six hundred and fifty dollars to import.

PROMPTCASH. [*Aside.*] And fifty dollars to puff it.

MRS. APEX. You have nothing more expensive!

ELLWIDE. Nothing. But when Madame Tulle Rubon has trimmed and made it up in the style now worn, it will cost certainly half as much again.

PROMPTCASH. [*Aside.*] That's the first word of truth I've heard for some time!

MRS. APEX. Send the dress home; no—to Tulle Rubon's, and add the amount to my bill.

[*Going. Passing desk,* PROMPTCASH *steps out and intercepts her.*

PROMPTCASH. Excuse me, madam, but business is business. My partner attends upon the ladies, but I attend to the books. Now, your account has been sent in regularly, half-yearly, for two years, and I should prefer not adding so large an item to the $5,964.39 already due.

MRS. APEX. [*Aside.*] Impudent shopkeeper! Mr. Ellwide, you are a gentleman. [ELLWIDE *down.*] I will take the dress, and pay your account, in full, to-morrow morning, but I am sorry to say I must discontinue my patronage!

ELLWIDE. [*Aside to* PROMPTCASH.] I told you how it would be! [*To* MRS. APEX.] You must excuse Mr. Promptcash, madam—he has not that glacé—no, I mean, smooth style of addressing ladies which sarsnett—no, etiquette requires to a moiré antique—no, I mean a middle-aged—that is to say—I—[*Aside.*] Once out of the dry-goods line, and I'm out of my element!

MRS. APEX. I accept your apology for Mr. Promptcash—poor man—he is desperately ignorant of the forms of politeness; but we cannot expect much—they say he used to be a dirty boy, who swept out his employer's store.

[*Turns up stage to counter.*

ELLWIDE. Here is something very rich! Mr. Jones, open some of those new embroideries, and show them to Mrs. Apex.

PROMPTCASH. [*Returns to desk as* ELLWIDE *comes down.*] Shop-boy! I wonder if she never heard of her old grandfather? I remember his Irish phiz whenever I look in her face! Here comes another of her own sort. The mother kept a boarding-house, and the daughter had luck enough to catch a wealthy husband, whose dollars, I must admit, she distributes very liberally.

Enter MRS. RADIUS, ELLWIDE *receiving her. Comes down stage, not seeing* MRS. APEX, *who is still up at counter.*

MRS. RADIUS. Oh, Mr. Ellwide, I thought I should never be able to get here! I wish they would arrange some other street for the canaille, and not permit them to obstruct Broadway. Do you know, I had to wait three-quarters of an hour, because a dray-load of emigrants—(dirty, dreadful wretches!)—ran against a wagon full of barrels; the horses slipped on the Russ pavement; some of the people were thrown down and hurt; three of the animals were killed, and I was obliged patiently to wait until they removed the bodies —a most provoking circumstance, for I was dying to get here before Mrs. Apex, as I hear you have something very handsome, and I am resolved, at any rate, to have the refusal of it!

ELLWIDE. I am sorry, but she has been here beforehand. The seven hundred dollar velvet is gone.

MRS. RADIUS. Has the creature been here already? and has she made such a purchase, when her husband's probable insolvency and her son's dissipation have become the talk of the town? That woman's extravagance is——

[*Turns and sees* MRS. APEX. PROMPTCASH *chuckles over a prospective quarrel.* MRS. RADIUS *and* MRS. APEX *meet.*

MRS. RADIUS. Ah! my dear Clemanthe! how are you after last night's excitement?   [*Kisses her.*

PROMPTCASH. [*Aside at desk.*] I knew she would kiss her! What hypocrites these women are!

MRS. RADIUS. You look pale, dear! Ah! no wonder; you must be very anxious about your son, Charles. He was quite tipsy last night; it was the talk of the party, and very naturally grief is written upon your face to-day.

MRS. APEX. Not at all, love; Charles was with friends, whose position in society insures them respect, even in their excesses.

MRS. RADIUS. Perhaps so. Some of the recent failures must make Mr. Apex very anxious about his business relations, and, of course, so devoted a wife as yourself must sympathize deeply in his anxiety.

MRS. APEX. [*Yawning.*] Indeed, dear Harriet, you seem infinitely more interested in my affairs than I am. [*Aside.*] Deceitful monster!—but she is too fashionable to quarrel with!

MRS. RADIUS. [*Aside.*] Artificial creature! I am resolved to mortify her! [*Aloud.*] I came down to get some handsome satin, Mr. Ellwide, for a dress. [ELLWIDE *comes down.*] They say you have some embroidered goods, but pray don't show them to me—all ornament is voted vulgar by *really* fashionable people. It is only the lower class patronize the flaunty style of dress. Don't you think so, love?

MRS. APEX. Perhaps gaudy and valueless goods, may be; but what is really handsome, is always admired. Show Mrs. Radius the dress I just purchased, Mr. Ellwide.

[ELLWIDE *displays dress.* MRS. RADIUS *laughs.*

MRS. RADIUS. Now, that is too droll! It is an exact fac-simile of the one I wore last season, when that style was most fashionable! Yes, love, it was quite pretty when it was what was worn!

MRS. APEX. Imposible!—This is certainly new,—was woven expressly for Eugénie, and exhibited at the Great Industrial Fair, this season! How fortunate!—here comes Mr. Cynosure, who has just returned from Paris, and as he moved in the most aristocratic circles abroad, he has no doubt seen, and will remember this exquisite pattern.

Enter CHARLES SANDFORD *and* CYNOSURE, *both elegantly dressed in modern style;* MRS. RADIUS *and* MRS. APEX *curtsey to* CYNOSURE.

CHARLES. Oh! ladies, both, good morning! We saw your carriages at the door, and came in to make our morning salutations. You both look charming, to-day. [*Apart, to* CYNOSURE.] Hang it, Cy, say something!

CYNOSURE. [*Aside.*] Why—ah—eh—you said good morning, and I don't happen to think of anything to say—ya-as!

CHARLES. [*Aside.*] Tell them both how well they look! That's the way I always manage to please mother, and the other dragon is just as vain!

CYNOSURE. Never saw you looking so well! I hope Miss Mary is lovely as ever? Nothing out of Paris can compare with her for beauty and amiability! I really think so—ah—eh—ya-as!

MRS. APEX. She is quite well; and will be much flattered by your kind inquiries.

CYNOSURE. Of course, having just left Paris, I am quite able to decide what is, or what is not worthy of admiration, and this gives my opinion weight—oh—eh—ya-as!

CHARLES. Ah—the opinion would not weigh so heavily if your pockets were light, Cy, my boy!—don't forget that, old fellow!

CYNOSURE. You never let me forget it—you help me so often to lighten them—eh—ah—ya-as!

[CHARLES *goes, and talks to* ELLWIDE.

MRS. APEX. Your opinion is all important just now. Mrs. Radius and I have a little dispute, which you can settle by a word. Just look at this, and tell me if you ever saw it before.

[ELLWIDE *holds up box.*

CYNOSURE. Really, I have seen so much, I—eh—ah— ya-as!

MRS. APEX. Yes, but this you must remember: at the last fête, just before you left Paris—

CYNOSURE. Oh—yes—it was used for pavilion drapery— eh—ah—ya-as!   [MRS. APEX *turns up offended.*

MRS. RADIUS. Oh, you mischievous creature! Poor, dear Mrs. Apex thinks it is a new style of dress, lately worn by the Empress Eugénie.

CYNOSURE. [*Looking at dress again.*] Eh—ah—exactly —that is it. I could not remember—eh—ah—ya-as!

MRS. APEX. [*Comes down.*] There, Madame, I knew what he would say, when he was allowed time to consider.

MRS. RADIUS. [*Aside.*] We all know what reasons influence his change of opinion. I have no pretty daughter to keep out of the way of poor admirers, and dazzle rich boobies with! Ha! ha! ha! Adieu, love: I must leave you, to commence my purchases. I shall tell everywhere how droll you were to-day, Mr. Cynosure, to say the pavilion covers were like Mrs. Apex's gaudy dress! Ha! ha! ha! you wicked creature! Ha! ha! ha! such a satirical fellow! Ha! ha! ha!

[ELLWIDE *ushers her to centre door very politely.*—MRS.
   APEX *goes to counter, and looks at goods; comes to
   right of centre, during* CYNOSURE'S *speech.*

CYNOSURE. First impression I have made since I appeared in Broadway, in my landscape trowsers, with the last eruption of Vesuvius on one leg, and the fall of the Mamelon on the other! Excuse me—must meet Gourdtell at the club, at twelve. Good morning. Come Charles. Ya-as.

[*Exit, affectedly.*

MRS. APEX *comes down.*

CHARLES. Will join you in an instant. Mother, you look very handsome this morning! Did old Tulle Rubon manufacture that bonnet? It gives you the air of a girl of eighteen. I say, mother, let me have some money. The Governor grows stingier every day, and I can't keep up an appearance by the side of fellows like Cy, without two or three hundred dollars always at my disposal.

MRS. APEX. Dear Charles, you know I can't bear to deny you anything, but I gave you four hundred last week—you are really too bad!

CHARLES. Just as you please. It's all up, though, my being able to persuade Cy into marrying Mary, the only thing we require to make our family the richest in New York, for he is worth at least a million, and can talk familiarly about all the crowned heads in Europe. Of course I can't be his bosom friend, and all that, and be hampered for a few paltry dollars.

MRS. APEX. It is not my fault, Charles. Mr. Apex grows so penurious, I can scarcely get enough for current expenses. But here, Charles, are two hundred dollars. [*Opens port-monnaie.*] Now, pray be careful.

CHARLES. Oh, this will do for a week or two. Thank you, my handsome mamma! I am going to call you sister— it is too bad—a great awkward fellow like me should have such a beautiful mother! [*Aside.*] There, that's worth the full amount to the old lady. I knew I could talk her over. [*Aloud.*] Good-bye, *Sister,* I must catch Cy; he has not gone far, however. What a slow lot he would be, if he had no money. Did you see his walk? Look, mother! Ha, ha, ha!

[*Mimics* CYNOSURE, *and exits,* MRS. APEX *laughing and admiring.*

MRS. APEX. The dear fellow, he is a little extravagant, but he is so unselfish; his only desire is to secure a good match for his sister, and then, he is so very handsome, and so young, and so *fashionable!*—I am so proud of him. Ah! a mother's love is a truly unselfish feeling! There is that parvenue, Mrs. Codliver, at the door. I must get away at once. Good morning, Mr. Ellwide, don't forget to send the package at once, and the bill to-morrow morning. It shall be settled punctually, Mr. Promptcash.

ELLWIDE. The dress shall be sent at once. Good morning. Much obliged, ma'am.

PROMPTCASH. So shall the bill, ma'am.

[MRS. APEX *exits, casting haughty glances at* PROMPTCASH.

ELLWIDE. [*Coming down, rubbing his hands.*] That puff has been worth three hundred dollars to us this morning, net profit on the dress: but you must not talk so plainly, P., you will destroy our connexion.

PROMPTCASH. [*Comes down centre.*] Nonsense! with liberal advertising, handsome clerks, and good goods, we can laugh at the caprices of fashionable ladies. We must get the bill paid, for I tell you, Apex will fail, unless Unit, his old partner, assists him.

ELLWIDE. Unit assists nobody but Unit, not he! Apex and he once stood equally in money matters, when they dissolved partnership, but that Unit is a close, careful man of business, and he has more than trebled his former gains by a series of prudent speculations, and then he has neither chick nor child, and lives for himself, while Apex is the most liberal man in the world. The honours of New York are not given until Apex dines a distinguished stranger. Ah! here comes a cash customer, the fat widow Codliver! Sympathize with her imaginary afflictions, and we can persuade her into pretty extensive purchases. [*Goes up to meet her.*

Enter MRS. CODLIVER, *muffled, with fan, &c.*—ELLWIDE *courteously places a chair.*

MRS. CODLIVER. Good morning. I was under the compression that it was very cold, but the heat, on the contrary, is most concessive. This is the dreadfullest climacteric!

ELLWIDE. Dreadful, indeed, for a delicate invalid like yourself. We have some beautiful Welsh flannel I should like to show you; it is of the finest texture, just suited to the present season.

MRS. CODLIVER. Well, maybe,—but that 'ere I bought last, the context got quite shrunk, and I may say emashuated, after it was washed.

ELLWIDE. This I am sure you will be pleased with. Do you find your health improve under Homœpathic treatment?

MRS. CODLIVER. Oh, dear, no! Them twitterations and globes ain't of no use in medicine, if they are in 'jography!—I have just commenced a new course of Townsend's Sassyparilla,—not the young doctor, but the old doctor. He must be a smart man, for his picter is on the bottle, and he has got such a noble forehead!

ELLWIDE. Do you find yourself able to attend parties this season?

MRS. CODLIVER. Oh, my, yes—and I want to buy something real stylish, for Mr. Codliver has been dead eighteen months, and I'm sure it's high time I laid aside my sombrero accoutrements. But I am too much fatigued to look over your goods this morning,—besides, I have an engagement to lunch o' lobster salad and ice cream, at Mrs. Notable's, and she is such a good housekeeper, I wouldn't miss it for the world!

ELLWIDE. We will be happy to send the articles for your inspection. Allow me to escort you to your carriage.

MRS. CODLIVER. You are real polite, and I don't care if I do take your arm. I'm so weak—I never teched a bit of breakfast this morning, but a young chicken, seven eggs, and a few cups of chocolate, so I feel quite exasperated with the exertions I have made. Do remind me to tell the coachman to call at Rushton's, that I may get a dozen boxes of Abernethy's dinner pills.

ELLWIDE. Certainly.—This way, Mrs. Codliver—I will have the articles sent. Allow me.

[*Exeunt, very ceremoniously, with* MRS. CODLIVER.— PROMPTCASH *chuckling, &c., at desk.*

PROMPTCASH. Ha, ha, ha! Ellwide is a jewel of a partner! There he goes, ushering out more gluttony and ignorance, in the form of a grumbling old woman, than all New York contains beside, yet he shows her as much attention as if she was a Venus! A man, to succeed in our business, must be forgetful of everything but the main chance, and never fail to be smooth and polite to the ugliest old frumps in the city! Ah, here comes a fresh batch!—now all the goods in the store will be pulled down, and perhaps nothing bought.

Enter ELLWIDE *with a party of ladies,* MISS SALLY SIMPER, MISS DOLLY DIMPLE, MISS IDA INDOLENCE, &c.

ELLWIDE. [*As they come down.*] This way, ladies! What can I show you?

MISS SIMPER. Oh! I want to see some of the handsomest brocades you have got.

PROMPTCASH. [*Aside.*] Of course she does,—and will buy a paper of pins! Who would be a storekeeper!

MISS SIMPER. And I want you to take back the lawns I got last week, for they don't wash, and I want a quarter of a yard of blue silk, exactly this color, and an eighth of a yard of this green, but it must be matched precisely!

ELLWIDE. [*Aside.*] Now for everything to be pulled down, and thrown over the store! Oh, patience! patience! How much we poor shopkeepers need thee!

[*Ladies approach counter.* ELLWIDE *and* CLERKS *pull down goods.*

SCENE II.—*Parlour in the House of* MR. APEX.

Enter AUNT CHLOE.

AUNT CHLOE. Lord knows, things can't go on in this way much longer! There ain't a mornin' when I gits up, but I hears pussons a-knockin' at de do' for money! I does wish mass'r had staid on de plantation, and neber come here to dis hea' New York to set up merchant. 'Tain't all his fault do—it all comes of marrin' agin, and gittin' one of dese stuck-up Norf ladies, 'stead of a Virginny gal like Miss Mary war—not dis hea' Miss Mary, kase she's hez child. Eh! eh! ain't she de picter of her mammy! How mass'r George could marry agin wid de eyes of de done gone wife lookin' at him out of de chile's head, beats dis nigga's time! But dis wife, she's mighty peart and pretty—eh! eh! de night dey had de party down stairs—I see Mrs. Apex—(I don't call her my miss)—steppin' out on de flo', buzzin' round de buildin' like a blue-bottle fly dat's done got shut in dos in July! Here comes Mrs. Apex! She's mad, too! I see dat by de way she screws her mouf up!

Enter Mrs. Apex, *with bonnet and scarf.*

Mrs. Apex. Here, Chloe, take these things to my room, and give them to my maid, and say I shall be with her soon to dress for dinner. Has any one called since I went out this morning?

Chloe. Oh, yes, ma'am, dere's been a sight of company. De cards was lef in de drawing-room.

Mrs. Apex. Oh, yes—but any business callers?

Chloe. Yes, ma'am, dere's been a sight of dem, too. Dey—Diu—Diuf—

Mrs. Apex. Diurnal?

Chloe. Dat's de one! He says de French Madame say dat she mus' have de money for her work, or she'll keep de things you sent up dar to be made.

Mrs. Apex. And I have just sent her my new dress to make for the party to-morrow! Impertinent creature!—I will withdraw my patronage from her forever!

Chloe. And de 'fectioner say dat all his French sugar things is nigh 'spended, and he can't afford to trust no longer, and de things you ordered can't be sent 'cept de cash comes for dem.

Mrs. Apex. This is Mrs. Radius' work! She has warned them to refuse me credit out of malice, because my parties are far more select and magnificent than her own. But I'll be revenged upon her, and if it cost my peace of mind for-ever, I will give my party to-morrow evening!

Chloe. Den de flower-maker, and de furniture-store man, and de carpet man, and a heap of 'em, talk mighty sassy, and say mass'r Apex better pay for what he gits if he wants so much.

Mrs. Apex. Silence!—don't repeat their insolence to me! Perhaps you are like the rest and want your wages, that you may be off and leave your mistress without a servant. My maid grows daily more insolent, and you are all alike!

Chloe. Dat's de place whar you make a mistake. Dem maids you hire for money care nuffin for you but to git dere wages, but I love dat little white chile dat I raised, and to-morrow if she lost all her friends she would hab a home in de heart of her ole black mammy, if she was poor as dat ole Scripture turkey dat Job done got, and he was so poor dat he couldn't 'ford more dan one fedder in his tail! Keu! keu! keu! [*Exit.*

MRS. APEX. She speaks truly. She loves Mary, and would work for her without hire; but no one loves me—not even my husband, or my own child! I lead a false life among thousands as false as myself. With superficial accomplishments, I assume to be a patroness of the arts, and, though of low extraction, I affect in the position of leader of the *ton,* the pride and importance of a duchess. With a husband whose wealth is the envy of his fellow-merchants, I am kept so impoverished by his avarice that I am sneered at by trades-people and servants, whose just claims I am unable to satisfy! Oh, false—false life! Hollow and heartless as I have proved you, still I cling to the high position which I have bartered health, content, affection—all that is worth living for—to obtain. The lesson of to-day was most bitter, and still I feel it is but one of a series of agonizing and humiliating mortifications! But my party *shall* be given —*shall* be admired, let me get money how or where I can! What do I see!—Mr. Apex returned so soon! This is most unusual! Can there be any truth in the report about his probable failure, so industriously circulated by Mrs. Radius? No, no! it is impossible! His face looks haggard and careworn;—no matter, he shall hear the degradation his parsimony has exposed me to.

Enter APEX.

APEX. Good morning, Madam. I scarcely hoped to find you at home—a most unusual place to meet so fashionable a lady! A friend will dine with me—my former partner, Mr. Unit. He comes at my request, to assist me in projecting a mercantile scheme I have long thought of,—and I wish,—no —I *insist*—that the extravagance of your expenditure may be concealed before him. The last time he visited our house, he estimated the probable cost of your last party,—and startled me by the magnitude of the amount.

MRS. APEX. I am sorry I did not add a few figures to the real amount, and thus astonish you both still more. My dear Mr. Apex, your position, as the first merchant in New York, demands that your wife should preside with elegance and taste over a sumptuous establishment. I believe the voice of the fashionable world will acknowledge my ability to fulfil my part, at least, as well as any of my rivals. Your task, Mr. Apex, is to supply me a liberal allowance, and I will engage the mansion of the American merchant will be more sumptuous and elegant than the hereditary palaces of a foreign aristocracy.

APEX. There Madam,—that is the rock on which you split. Your European tour has unfitted you to live as becomes a plain American citizen.

MRS. APEX. [*Takes stage to left, laughing.*] Now that is too droll, coming from you—"an American citizen."—You are just the man would like to dress in linsey-woolsey, and cowhide brogans, while Mary and I, in check aprons and shilling calicoes, did our own chores! You are just the man to admire the primitive style! Ha! ha! ha!

[*Takes stage to right.*

APEX. You may laugh, Madam, but what you so sneer at may be our ultimate fate,—nor is it so very far beneath the condition *you were born to fill, Mrs. Apex.*

MRS. APEX. [*Crossing to him.*] But I left that condition, Mr. Apex, and do you think I will be dragged down to it? No—never! Do you suppose the young widow was only won by the fine person of the wealthy Southern planter? Had fame not whispered of the great estate with which the woman who came as mistress would be endowed, rest assured I should have sought a different destiny.

APEX. Your sneers pass by harmless! The world believes us to be a happy couple, and I will not permit the wilful insolence of a spoiled beauty to degrade the position of my family,—but remember this,—you must retrench your expenditure,—understand me, Madam,—*must!*

MRS. APEX. Threats! Oh, this is Southern chivalry, I suppose?

APEX. You will not find them empty threats. Your son, Charles, is a graceless profligate,—from gambling-house to drinking-saloon he passes the fresh days of his boyhood. You would tell me this is fashionable life,—it may be,—at least it is the life of a spendthrift!—He must amend at once, or not one dollar shall he henceforth receive from me! Yet more, that your expenditure may be restrained within the bounds of propriety, I shall allow you only a stated sum, amply sufficient for your position, but not for the dower of a duchess. You will thus be unable to supply his headlong extravagance, and will be taught to limit your own overweening desires.

MRS. APEX. Go on, sir,—this is so gentlemanly—to insult your wife—by reproaches aimed at her only child. [*Weeps.*

APEX. Madam, tears will not serve your purpose. Let us understand each other. I am involved—fearfully involved, and nothing but retrenchment can redeem my tottering credit! Will you assist me?—or must I regard as my most dangerous enemy, the woman who, did she realize the importance of her marriage obligation, would prove now my truest friend?

MRS. APEX. Sentiment will not serve *your purpose.—I* am involved—fearfully involved, and nothing but your immediate acquiescence in my request that you furnish me with ten thousand dollars, with which to discharge the debts I have incurred, can save me, and through me, yourself, from the indelible disgrace of a series of petty suits for sums of money you should blush to hear your wife asked for twice,— but your parsimony——

APEX. Parsimony! In the name of heaven, Madam, I stand upon the brink of failure!

MRS. APEX. This is all a pretext to avoid what you feel to be a just request. The money I require, I must and will have to-morrow! I have been brow-beaten in stores, taunted by servants, rudely questioned by collectors, until my heart is bursting with resentment! I will bear this no longer! I have issued cards for a party to-morrow night. If unable to discharge the petty debts that weigh me to the earth, the party is either given up or postponed. The thousand tongues of Rumor will soon proclaim the cause, and thus shall I lose my prestige in fashionable circles, and sink into insignificance—like that more domestic pattern, your *first wife!*

APEX. Hold, Madam! do not dare profane the name of one who fulfilled so gracefully the sweet domestic duties at which you sneer!

MRS. APEX. For the last time, Mr. Apex, I ask you, will you furnish me the money I require?

APEX. I cannot—and if I could, I *would not!* Your extravagance has become a proverb, and I shall best sustain my failing credit by disputing the payment of your overgrown accounts. I understand it all; your son is in arrears for some debts of *Honour,* and you would deceive me into furnishing the means of payment for him. Every account you have, I have furnished you the money, repeatedly, to discharge, but for the last time. And I here tell you, unless you reform, I shall be left without—

Enter SERVANT.

SERVANT. Mr. Unit, sir.

APEX. Show him in.

     [SERVANT *ushers in* MR. UNIT, *bows, and exits.* Come in, Unit, come in,—glad to see you.

UNIT. How dy'e do? how d'ye do, ma'am—both look as if you had been in a passion—bad plan, sir, never pays! No, sir,—lose your temper, lose your wit—yes, sir,—wit gone, lose your money, and that won't do—no, sir, it won't pay!

MRS. APEX. I in a passion? You deceive yourself, Mr. Unit, in spite of your great penetration. I never was in better spirits, and to prove that I am very good natured, I'll do the very thing you wish me,—I'll go away, and leave you to talk business together. I see you are looking at my dress, and no doubt you are adding up the probable price of the embroidery, and lace, and ribbon, and all the little trifles that combine to produce this charming negligé! But pray don't take so much pains to show me my faults, for I shall always be a sad, extravagant creature, so don't try to improve me— for it won't pay—ha, ha, ha! No, sir,—it won't pay! Ha, ha, ha!   [*Exit laughing.*

UNIT. Tears in her eyes, and laughing! pale cheeks, looking ghastly with passion underneath the rouge!—that's the way with your fashionable people. Like the meat pies they gave the boys at boarding-school,—all top-crust, and nothing inside! That can't pay, sir.

APEX. Hang it, Unit, to hear you talk, one would think you had been fed on the apples that grow on the borders of the Dead Sea, and that the taste of the bitter ashes had risen on your stomach ever since.

UNIT. So they would, if I had ever married. I should have been all sackcloth and ashes, like yourself and the rest of the married men are, sir. Women are an unprofitable lot, sir,—yes, sir,—the investment will not cover the taxation,— no, sir,—never pays to get married—no, sir.

APEX. I confess my wife runs up my domestic taxes pretty high, but she is a fine woman, and I am proud of her, with all her extravagance. When I see her drive down Broadway, with her elegant equipage, and her stately figure, and hear the passers-by exclaim: "Look at Mrs. Apex, the beautiful wife of the great merchant—is not that a fine carriage and horses—and is she not a splendid woman!"—I feel as proud, ay, prouder than you do, Unit, when stocks rise, and all the world knows that you have made a lucky speculation. Just now, when you came in, we were having a little disagreement; but did you not see how cleverly she disguised it all, and laughed it all off?

UNIT. Yes, sir,—yes. She is as artful as women generally are.—Never trust them,—if you do, sure to be taken in. Never trusted a woman in my life, but I repented it. Yes, sir, always found out too late that it didn't pay.

APEX. How did you become such a confirmed woman-hater?

UNIT. Got bit once myself.—Yes, sir.—widow, sir,— afraid ever since. Burnt child dreads fire, sir.

APEX. What, *you!* do let me hear the particulars. I never knew you to allow yourself to be entrapped by the fair enslavers! When were you victimized?

UNIT. Just come to the city—verdant—saw advertisement for a husband. Said she was thirty; twenty thousand dollars; no ready-made incumbrances. Answered the letter; had meeting; found an adventuress; pretty face; no money; less principle. People heard of it; got laughed at; cost me twelve hundred dollars to hush the matter up. Never forgot it, sir. Keep the women at a distance now, sir.—Yes, sir. Only way to get along. No other way will pay, sir.

APEX. Ha, ha, ha! I'm glad to find the women have been too much for you, also. But come, we have a great deal that is important to talk over to-day. I want your advice, and perhaps your assistance; and from our old intimacy, I know I can depend upon you.

Unit. For advice, yes,—but not for my money. Your way is not my way. Ten years ago, I told you how it would end. Your headlong career has run you into difficulty, just as I said,—yes, sir,—just exactly, sir!

Apex. Well, don't reproach me, Unit—I—

Enter Servant.

Servant. Dinner is served, sir.

Apex. In my study?

Servant. Yes, sir, covers laid for two, as you ordered, sir.   [*Exit* Servant.

Unit. Then we shall not see Mary—I am sorry for that —Mary is a good girl, sir—noble girl! The man that calls her his child, has something to be proud and grateful for. She is one out of a million, sir!

Apex. Mary is a good girl, but she is so selfishly pre-occupied in her private amusements, that she seldom joins the family circle. In fact, her plain dress and simple manners add nothing to the importance of the family.

Unit. Importance! Bah! She is worth fifty fashionable dawdles, like the wife you are so proud of. Poor girl! she feels neglected in her stepmother's house, and seeks in solitude, with her books and flowers, the happiness her father's kind smile should afford her. You'll repent this when it is too late, sir,—yes, sir,—too late!

Apex. Why, she is as avaricious as you, Unit! Saves and economises her little income, and last week, when she came of age, and I told her that the $15,000 her aunt left her was placed in bank, subject to her order, instead of rushing off to draw the amount, and spending half the day at a jeweller's, selecting a set of diamonds, she replied very quietly, "If you think the bank a solvent one, papa, it may as well remain there," and proceeded just as usual with her needlework.

Enter Servant.

Servant. Dinner will be quite cold, sir.   [*Exit.*

Apex. Hang the dinner, I forgot all about it.

Unit. Of course you did, because you are a hasty man, sir—proud and hasty—both bad qualities. Hasty about dinner, slow about digestion—never hurry over my meals, sir,—

take time enough to masticate, sir—can make a calculation at the same time. Bad digestion, sir—broken constitution,— ending in a metallic sarcophagus, bought at a high price by your executor—never could afford it in the world, sir! Take my word for it—it won't pay! [*Exeunt.*

SCENE III.—*A Boudoir neatly furnished. Birds, flowers, work-table, &c., all the appointments of a young lady's parlor.* MARY *discovered at a small work-table, sewing.—* CHLOE, *sitting on a stool near, with spectacles on, and a Child's Primer in her hand, saying her letters to* MARY, *who laughs as she attempts to repeat them. Two lighted candles.—Piano.*

CHLOE. A—B—C—D—[*Repeat.*] See, hea', 'tain't worth while spending your precious words on this hea' ole woman: kase I neber could learn, no how. Dey done tried to teach me when I was a little bit of a gal, but I never could get further than D, and dat am de berry place whar I sticks yit. I was a right cute little nigga, too, I was dat; but de readin' —dat got me, shure.

MARY. Never mind, mammy, you know I always read to you; so, it don't make much matter; and, by-and-bye, when you grow very old, I'll be as good as a pair of spectacles for you: you shall see out of my eyes, and hear with my ears; and when I am Mrs. Doctor Lever, we will have a nice, quiet, cosy little home, and you, dear mammy, shall order every-thing your own way.

CHLOE. Lord knows, honey child, I don't blame you to want to git shut of dis hea' home, for dey done plague you to deff! Mrs. Apex, she keeps telling your Pa heap of stories 'bout you, and makes him believe you ain't your own self at all, just kase she wants dat Charles Sandford to git your share of de property when Mass'r pegs out! Dat boy of her'n, he'll make her sup sorrow by de gourdfull, as Mass'r Solomon say in de good book!

MARY. Oh, you must not talk so, mammy, or you and I will quarrel. Although Charles is wild, and over-indulged, he loves me with all his heart.

CHLOE. Dat ain't nuffin! Who don't love you? But don't he let his ma pick your pockets to lend him money to put in his own? And don't your pa think you spend it for yourself, when all de time you lend it to Mrs. Apex?

MARY. Never mind, mammy, it will be all right some day, and if my little income helps to keep peace in a divided household, I am sure it is well bestowed. Hark! I hear some one at the door. It is mama!

Enter MRS. APEX *in evening dress.*

MRS. APEX. Mary, I have something to say to you. Send the old woman away. [*Goes up to piano.*

MARY. Yes, mamma! Leave the room a little while, mammy. I will call you directly.

CHLOE. I'll come back in de space of a short time, Miss Mary. [*Aside.*] Dat Mrs. Apex call me "old woman." I spec she knows my name. I don't suppose dere's such a mighty sight of difference of age between us two, if I had dat'ar' red and white paint on, dat she is!

[*Exit, muttering.*

MRS. APEX. [*Brings down chair.*] That old negro grows insufferably familiar. She evidently presumes upon her position in the family as your nurse, and considers herself in the light of an equal!

MARY. Don't mistake the innocent and affectionate familiarity of a faithful, tho' humble friend, for rudeness. Believe me, she would shed her heart's blood for her foster-child.

MRS. APEX. It is very evident that you have spoilt her. But no matter. I have snatched a few moments, before the carriage drives up, to take me to Mrs. Culminate's, to ask a favour of you.

MARY. A favor of me, mama? What can it be?

MRS. APEX. You know that for the last three years, since you returned from school, you have loaned me three hundred dollars a year out of your private income of four hundred dollars, settled on you by your mother's jointure. My reason for borrowing this sum was to assist in the education of your half-brother, my son Charles and, as your father has never known what disposal you have made of the money, I must again urge your silence on this point.

MARY. Indeed I have been scrupulously silent. [*Aside.*]

Although the good I desired to do has been misrepresented by the very person obliged.

Mrs. Apex. I now wish you to add to the obligation I feel I am under to you. Some accounts have been for some time standing: it is imperatively necessary they should be settled at once. They amount to more than twelve thousand dollars.

Mary. Can it be possible? This is truly alarming! Does my father——

Mrs. Apex. Your father positively refuses to advance the money, in order, he says, that I may be taught the perils of extravagance. But he shall learn another version of the results of his parsimony. Now, the legacy your aunt lately left you is deposited in the bank, and I wish you to give me a check for the full amount, $15,000, to be repaid, with the nine hundred I previously borrowed of you, either when you are married, or immediately that I can rally your father out of his present economical humor.

Mary. Mama, I should be happy to give you the money, if I thought I should thus increase my father's happiness. But you yourself say that he refuses to furnish you with the amount, in order that you may receive a lesson on the dangers and miseries of debt. For me to supply you with what he has purposely denied, would be acting in direct opposition to my father's expressed will, and, therefore, you must forgive me, but I ought, and do refuse.

Mrs. Apex. [*Looks a moment astonished.—Aside.*] Is it possible! This pliant child, whom I have been able at will to exile from her father's affections, and whose very thoughts I have constrained to serve my interests, has rebelled against me! [Mary *comes down left.*] Mary, I have requested this money—I now implore it of you! I cannot tell what may be the result of your refusal!

Mary. Indeed it gives me pain to deny your request, but my father's wish is paramount.

Mrs. Apex. Cold-hearted girl, this hypocrisy will not serve you. Your selfish heart bids you deny my request because you fear you may never again be repaid your paltry fortune! I leave you to the enjoyment of your generous reflections! [*Curtseys proudly, and exits.*

Mary. To a sensitive mind, what can prove a source of

deeper anguish than to be thus misjudged by those we love? And this has been through life my doom! Oh, with what yearning tenderness have I prayed for a child's sweet privilege, to steal unquestioned into a father's heart; but, alas! it has been denied me! Hark! another visitor?—I must dry my tears, lest the cause be suspected!

Enter APEX, *agitated.*

Why, it is dear father! He looks care-worn and so anxious; I would not for the world cause him another sorrow!

APEX. Do I disturb you, Mary?

MARY. Disturb me? Dear papa, you can't think how glad and happy I am to see you! Sit on this chair: this is the easiest one; and I worked the cushions myself. It was to have been your birthday gift; but I was afraid it was not handsome enough for the new furniture in your study.

APEX. Not handsome enough for a father, when his child was the manufacturer? Oh, you selfish little rogue, you wanted to keep it for yourself!

MARY. For myself? [*Aside.*] Oh, mama! how much you have to answer for!

APEX. How quiet and home-like this little room is? Do you know, it is the most comfortable place in the house? How glad I should be, when the parlors are thronged with gay company, to steal up here and rest my poor tired brain!

MARY. Why don't you, dear papa? It would make me so happy if you would! [*Brings chair to left of him.*

APEX. Why, your mama says you don't like to be disturbed, or I should often visit you.

MARY. Indeed, papa! that would be a joyful disturbance to one who loves you so well!

APEX. To tell the truth, I am myself a little selfish in coming up to-night; for I want you to grant me a favour.

MARY. A favour! Oh, dear, dear father! what can I do? How can I show you how dearly I love you? How proud and happy it will make me to aid you in anything!

APEX. By a succession of unexpected circumstances, I am straitened for ready money. A merchant, my child, should seem to possess inexhaustible coffers; for, in an emergency, a trivial sum may be necessary to maintain the idea of his firmly established position. I am placed in this strait: **there** are numbers of whom I could readily borrow, but I dare not let them understand that I require a loan. Unit, your old god-father, dined with me to-day; but as I approached the subject, my pride bade me be silent. Now, your little fortune would, at this moment, be of essential service, and, you know, such a sum is a mere trifle to me, which I can pay tenfold, when this period of embarrassment passes over.

Mary. Repay it! Oh, dear father! I am so glad, so proud, so happy that you will let me enjoy the great delight I feel in being useful to you! I don't believe you really want the money: you only say so to give me the pleasure of returning a tythe of the gratitude I owe you! What must I do? Write a cheque dated? Oh, I know all about business! I'll come to your counting-room to be your confidential clerk, if you will let me! [*Runs up to table, and writes eagerly.*

Apex. [*Aside.*] There has been some strange misrepresentation, here! God bless the child!—her eyes are sparkling with joy!—the flush of excitement and duteous affection lights up her face!

Mary. [*Comes down.*] There, papa! there is the cheque, and how I wish it was twenty times more!

Apex. [*Folds cheque, and places it in pocket-book.*] This will be as useful, Mary, as a great sum.

Mary. I am so proud to think I am the foolish little mouse that has gnawed the net, and set the lion free!

Apex. Dear child! another net has been broken, in which I have been artfully entangled; but it is over now, and we won't talk of that; but I shall never call you little selfish again!

Mary. Oh, I am so glad to hear you say so! And you will come and sit with me often, won't you, papa, when you see I am not disturbed?

Apex. That I will, my child! But if anything should occur, Mary, to prevent my repaying this, I am sure you will believe I did not intentionally deceive you, and this paltry sum will never breed distrust between father and child?

Mary. Can you think me so unworthy?

Apex. Ah, my child, you little know the power of this simple bit of paper, to alienate the heart's best and dearest affections. To an inordinate love of gain,—not for its own sake, but for the sake of the importance wealth would bestow upon me,—I may trace all my misfortunes! I trust this madness has forever left me, but, alas! who is the master of his own thoughts? A thousand passions, I scarcely know, exist, lie dormant in my breast, and only wait the kindling spark of an incentive, to burst forth into a volcano of impulsive action! And money, my child, is that all-powerful agent, that unites, that separates, that creates, that destroys, that wields a rod of mysterious power to sway the destinies of humanity! But it is too late for moralizing: you must retire, or the fresh roses will fade on those blooming cheeks. Good night, my darling! Sleep calmly in the thought that you have made your father's mind more tranquil than it has been for months, not by the loan of your little fortune, but by the sweet and dutiful affection which has prompted each word you have uttered, and has borne hope and gladness to his world-wearied heart! God bless you, my child! Good night!

[*Kisses her; goes up to door. She rushes up, and throws her arms around his neck. Embrace. Exit* APEX.

MARY. Oh, I am so happy! So happy that my heart would burst for joy, if it were not for these blessed tears! Oh! my dear mother!—the thought of whose all-pervading presence has proved a charm to chase away the many sorrows of my orphan childhood!—from you, from you, blessed spirit, has descended this great joy into my saddened breast! My father loves me—blesses me! I am his child once more! —his past harshness—the neglect, the coldness of bygone years, I here forget forever! Dear, dear father! I am again your child! [*Picture.*]

END OF ACT I.

ACT II.

SCENE I.—*Breakfast Room in* APEX'S *House. Table and chair, pen, ink, and paper.*

Enter MRS. APEX, *in morning costume; she walks uneasily about the stage.*

MRS. APEX. What a wretched night have I passed! It was four o'clock when I returned from that intolerable party, and I have tossed uneasily upon my sleepless couch, unable to close my eyes until now! The refusal of that girl, Mary, and Mr. Apex's determination or inability to assist me, are most perplexing. What is to be done? If through pecuniary embarrassment my party is postponed, what a triumph will my humiliation afford Mrs. Radius, my envious rival. If I had only discharged those terrible debts, when Mr. Apex gave me the amount long since to do so, all would now be well. Oh, the slavery of indebtedness! Who would groan under its humiliating chains, who remembered the blessings of freedom?

Enter CHARLES.—MRS. APEX *brings down chair.*

CHARLES. Alone, mother?—how fortunate! I have something to tell you of importance. Last night, at the Club, I had the misfortune to lose nearly five thousand dollars. Don't look so terrified! We can manage matters so that Papa Apex will never hear what has occurred.

MRS. APEX. Charles! Charles! this is beyond belief! It was but yesterday I emptied my purse for you, and you promised that you would not apply to me again for some time.

CHARLES. Well, hang it! I did not intend to do so, but I was with gentlemen, and I must appear like others of my set. Cynosure would not change a muscle if he lost twice the sum, and you have always told me to go in the best society, and never let others eclipse me.—Now, I suppose, you wish to upbraid me for obeying you?

MRS. APEX. This is unpardonable! I wished you to be fashionable—not extravagant.

CHARLES. Mother, you talk like my tailor! You told me, when I was expelled from college, to strive, above all things, to make a figure in the best society, that I might catch an heiress, or at least, attract rich and fashionable young men to your parties, and now you blame me, and grumble about a few paltry thousands! You married old Crœsus for his money, and would you deny me the advantage I ought to derive from it?

MRS. APEX. Dear Charles, don't reproach me.—I cannot bear it from you! I have sacrificed everything for your interest,—for your sake I married Mr. Apex, and have strained every nerve to place you in a high position.

CHARLES. High position! What useful thing have you taught me? What am I? What can I do? Look at my hands—what are they fit for, but to be encased in kid gloves, or to handle a billiard cue, or a pack of cards? I will not reproach you; your conscience will do that sufficiently here-after. But I tell, you, you have brought me up badly, and the result will be disgrace to us both.

MRS. APEX. Oh! the agony of these ungrateful words!

CHARLES. Mother, don't mistake me. I am deeply grateful for the kindness you intended, but I am aroused to a sense of the reality of my position. For what should I be grateful to you? For the fine clothes and dainty ruffles that decked my little limbs in childhood, and forbade free motion and joyous play? For the silly fondness that pampered me with unwholesome sweets, that winked at my neglect of useful study, that laughed at my deceptive arts, until low cunning was engrafted on my boy nature? For the false reasoning that taught me to believe industry and economy were low, and that enjoyment consisted only in a feeble attempt to ape the follies of a corrupt aristocracy, the very follies that are causing the tottering kingdoms of long centuries to tremble before the onward step of a republic created and sustained by the very labor you have taught me was degrading.

MRS. APEX. Go on. I can bear your reproaches. I did all for the best.

CHARLES. If you think so, mother, I forgive you, and forgive me, too, if I have spoken painful truths. I will get a situation as clerk, and will spend only what I can earn; and if my *fast* friends should cut me, why, I'll pull my hat over my eyes, and thank heaven that although they despise me, I am, in my own estimation, a more useful and respectable member of society than the idle butterflies whose favour I have lost.

MRS. APEX. You a clerk!—Oh! Charles, you will break your mother's heart.

CHARLES. Better be a working man than a thief, mother. The man who buys what he knows he has not means to pay for, is a thief, in that court of higher law, to which so many appeals are now taken.

MRS. APEX. Is the money for the payment of this debt essential to you?

CHARLES. [*Brings chair down.*] Essential! I will not live if I am forced to forfeit the respect of my companions. I can brave their ridicule or their scorn of my endeavours to earn an honest living, but I could not endure their just contempt for the presumptuous boy who thrust himself into the society of those whose wealth countenances their extravagance, and then shrunk, like a sneak, from the indebtedness his pride and folly had led him to incur.

MRS. APEX. My position is equally agonizing. I am overwhelmed with debts, which Mr. Apex refuses me one dollar to discharge.

CHARLES. Have you no friend of whom you could borrow the amount we both require?

MRS. APEX. Not one that would not give the sum twice told to see me humbled.

CHARLES. And I, among the intimates with whom I spend my days, have not a friend whose outstretched hand would strive to save me.

MRS. APEX. But when friends fail, and we are forced upon our own resources, the brain is quickened to create them. You must remember in childhood that Mary (although younger than yourself) so far surpassed you at her tasks, that once, when complaints had reached your father's ears of your remissness, she resolved to help you?

CHARLES. Like the dear girl she always is. She taught me to write, or I should never have gone beyond straight marks, I verily believe.

MRS. APEX. Your writing now resembles hers so closely that it is impossible to distinguish your letters from hers.

CHARLES. I cannot name a difference myself, except that what she writes is always pure and good, and I—but I will grow better, and more worthy of that dear sister.

MRS. APEX. But if you are disgraced by this fatal loss, if your name becomes a byword and a reproach?

CHARLES. Still, she will not despise, though she may grieve for me.

MRS. APEX. Listen to a plan that will preserve us both. Mary has $15,000 in the bank; subject to her order, the legacy just left her by her aunt.

CHARLES. She will lend it?

MRS. APEX. Not so—she has refused.

CHARLES. She will not refuse me.

MRS. APEX. Do not deceive yourself; she will—urged by an idea that she thus obeys your stepfather's desire that we should be taught prudence by necessity.

CHARLES. If Mary thinks it right to refuse, it is in vain to ask her.—The last hope is gone.

MRS. APEX. Not so. Suppose we were to obtain it without her knowledge, and immediately repay it?

CHARLES. A lucky thought; but how can this be accomplished?

MRS. APEX. Easily. Do you write a check in Mary's name for the money, and take it to be cashed. [CHARLES *looks astonished.*] Our debts can be cancelled, and, perhaps, in three days Mr. Apex will regret his harshness and give me back my accustomed control over his purse-strings. We can again deposit the money, and Mary, sitting in her quiet room, will never suspect how cleverly we managed to accomplish our purpose. Why do you look so terrified? we only want to borrow for a few days what Mary is not likely to require, and what we can replace at once. So what is there so alarming?

CHARLES. Oh, mother!—a forgery!!

MRS. APEX. Nonsense, Charles! do you suppose I think there is any sin in such an act as this? Would your mother counsel you to commit forgery? These over-nice scruples are ridiculous!

CHARLES. But, mother, I,—*is* there no other way?

MRS. APEX. Why seek for another, when this is so simple and apparent? Come, come, be a man and not a child, frightened at a spectre of your own creation! I wish to borrow some money of your sister, for a few days, and you call it *forgery!*—such baby-fears are only fit for the nursery.

[*Goes to table and prepares paper, &c.*

CHARLES. Hang it! it is nonsense to hesitate about writing Mary's name. It is not like writing father's, or a president, or a cashier of a bank, to swindle some one. Swindle! what an ugly word that is, and, somehow, others just like it come thronging into my mind, and I have inwardly repeated swindler, cheat, forger, impostor, and thief, ever since you proposed, and I agreed, to this sw—no,—borrowing transaction!

MRS. APEX. [*Having prepared check.*] Come, here are pens, ink and paper—not a moment is to be lost!

CHARLES. [*Right of table.*] See how my hand shakes! Does that look like the stroke of an honest pen? [*Writes on, reads.*] Pay to bearer—[*Writes, and then throws down pen.*] I can't and won't write it! [*Crossing down.*

MRS. APEX. Then your poor mother will, and she will lend you the money you require, if she is fortunate enough to obtain it,—if her feeble imitation of Mary's signature does not lead to exposure and disgrace.

CHARLES. [*Goes to right of table.*] No, no, no! I will write it myself—no one will discover, then, that it is a forgery, or, if they do, I am the fittest victim! Mother, this will make me a changed man. I am as much a convict in heart as if I were already the tenant of a prison!

MRS. APEX. Pshaw! these scruples——

CHARLES. Are ridiculous—I cannot help it! I know I am acting like a thief, if my intentions are honourable. [*Writes with agitation, stopping occasionally, and throwing down pen.*] There it is—done, and may God forgive you, mother, if this leads to any evil.

MRS. APEX. My dear boy, that is impossible; look at the bright side—all our anxieties will now be ended. Take the check at once, and get it cashed—discharge your debts, and send the remainder to me by a trusty messenger; the door's besieged by duns, and not a moment is to be lost.

CHARLES. I'll hasten to the bank, and bring the amount in half an hour. Don't let me meet Mary; I could not look in her honest eyes without feeling doubly degraded. Oh, what a cowardly wretch is the man whose own conscience judges and condemns him! [*Exit.*

MRS. APEX. [*Brings down chair, and sits, thinking.*] I did not look at this matter in so serious a light as Charles seems to do. If I thought it would really expose him to any danger—but that is impossible—and I will not torture myself with such a supposition! The money can be repaid at once, and this scheme of ours will never be suspected; but should Mr. Apex be really involved, and I unable to return the amount, then, indeed, I'll call him back—Charles, Charles— I——[*Runs nervously to door and calls anxiously.*]

Enter SERVANT.

SERVANT. Mr. Diurnal, the collector, madam. I told him you were engaged, but he says he must see you.

MRS. APEX. Say I am coming—show him to the study. [*Exit* SERVANT.] He is one of my most unsparing tormentors, but their day of triumph shall be short. This morning I will pay every debt I owe in the world, and I solemnly vow never to incur another! I will bid this man return in an hour to receive the money he so perseveringly demands, and then I shall be free from his rude cross-questioning. Who would exchange the calm and peaceful thoughts of those who have shunned the Demon, Debt, for all the gorgeous splendours that charm the eye, but rack the heart of the humiliated slave—a debtor? [*Exit.*

SCENE II.—*Drawing-Room in* APEX'S *House.*—*Sofa, tables, chairs, a hand-bell, books, and smelling-bottle.*

Enter MRS. RADIUS, *shown in by* SERVANT.—SERVANT *brings forward table and chair.*

SERVANT. I will take up your card, Madam. Be seated. [*Exit.*

MRS. RADIUS. Not down stairs yet,—I thought so! It is a serious undertaking, at her time of life, to conceal the ravages of a night of dissipation. I am determined to find out whether my labours have been successful, and whether her unfortunate creditors will not be able to break off this much-talked-of party.

Enter MARY, *followed by* SERVANT, *who passes off.*

MARY. Good morning, Mrs. Radius, mama is slightly indisposed, and requests me to receive you in her stead, but she will be here in a few moments. I hope you enjoyed yourself last evening?

MRS. RADIUS. Oh, yes, dear.—I always enjoy myself,—there is so much to criticize and to laugh at in this droll world of ours! Why did you not come with your mama? Oh, I suppose she would not permit you,—her pride in her youthful appearance makes her dread a dangerous rival in her beautiful step-daughter. Everybody says she keeps you shut up, lest you should be too much admired.

MARY. Then foolish people do mama great injustice. You, who are so familiar with the affairs of *others,* are doubtless aware that I am engaged, and as my engagement has been kept private, I prefer not going to large parties. Your inference, therefore, was unjust, Mrs. Radius.

MRS. RADIUS. Ah? you never forget to keep up the character of a sweet and amiable creature, as I dare say you are,—and don't say how much you are imposed upon, but everybody knows your step-mother has completely turned your father's heart against you.

MARY. There you are equally misinformed, for I assure you he never was so kind and affectionate as he has been quite lately.

MRS. RADIUS. It is of no use to attempt deceiving me. I am sure he must be uncommonly cross just now, for I know his business perplexities are driving him almost crazy. Fortunately, you have a little property of your own, and are engaged, so, even if your father does fail, it will not materially affect your prospects, unless Dr. Lever should do as many have done before,—look with different eyes upon the daughter of the wealthy merchant and the bankrupt.

MARY. You are conjuring up imaginary evils to combat, Madam. My father is not on the eve of failure,—but if he was, the affection existing between Edward and myself was not cemented by dollars, and could bear a greater shock than my father's bankruptcy.

MRS. RADIUS. Yes, you think so,—poor dear child, but I know the world a great deal better than you do, and know that men are not to be trusted, not even the best of them. As to Dr. Lever, I consider him to be a most unscrupulous young man——

Enter MRS. CODLIVER; *she has a large bottle, labelled and wrapped in paper, and large pill box, also labelled.*

MRS. CODLIVER. Good mornin' all! Have you got here a' ready? Mrs. Radius, I wish Dr. Lever was here! How very handy! If I should by any contrary temps be taken poorly, he could be at hand to proscribe, you know.

MARY. [*To* MRS. CODLIVER,—*crossing to her.*] Mama will be here directly, Mrs. Codliver. Pray be seated.

MRS. CODLIVER. That's right, for I have eaten nothin' but three plates of oysters and some blue monge since ten o'clock, and it's now nearly twelve, and I do feel more exasperated than I have been for a long time.

MARY. Permit me to order something.   [*Rings bell.*

Enter SERVANT.—*As* MARY *gives orders to him,* MRS. COD-LIVER *goes up and suggests something.*

MRS. RADIUS. That's right, my dear. She is always ready to feed.

MRS. CODLIVER. [*Coming down.*] Oh, I wish the doctor was here! I wanted to know his opinion of "Sprouts' Sovereign Specific."

MARY. I really fear he has no opinion of it at all.

MRS. CODLIVER. [*Seated at table.*] Ah, I know how it is! —them people with medical faculties and diplomacy, never says nothin' in favour of Swain, or Brandreth, or Moffit, or Perry,—Davis, or any of them savants that's just took up docterin' out of pity for the afflictions of uncomfortable human nater. [*Shows bottle, labelled with wood-cut.*] Jist read the kiver of this bottle! What a great cure it perfected on Mrs. R., who had childblains, scrufula, nervous headache, and rhumatiz in her elbow, and got cured of every one of them melodys after she had taken a bottle and three-quarters,—and here's a picter of her, in a balloon, bearing the glad tidings to a tormented world! [*All laugh.*] You may laugh, but if you suffered as I do——

Enter SERVANT, *with tray.*—MRS. CODLIVER *commences eating greedily.*

Ah! it looks very nice!

Enter CYNOSURE.

CYNOSURE. Good morning, ladies. Miss Mary—most devoted. Feel quite done up this morning—thought the sight of you would do me good—only girl worth seeing out of Paris—ah, really, y-a-a-s.

MARY. Here comes mama, Mr. Cynosure, and she can merit and receive your compliments, as gracefully as you can bestow them.

Enter MRS. APEX, *in splendid morning dress.—She has changed her dress during scene.—*MRS. CODLIVER *crosses to her.*

MRS. APEX. How do you all do? Delighted to find you here! Such a charming party last night,—enjoyed myself so much, but it has left me a shade fatigued to-day,—the reaction, you know. Why were you not there, Mr. Cynosure? I had promised myself the pleasure of dancing with you.

CYNOSURE. Much flattered, but American balls are so commonplace—nothing like the Tuilleries! Paris is the place where a gentleman can live. Americans only exist— really—eh—yes!

MRS. APEX. Oh, that's too true! but Mrs. Culminate is careful to invite no one to her reunions but the most distingué people in New York. [*Goes up to* MRS. CODLIVER.

CYNOSURE. But somehow, I think the more distingué our parties, the slower they are—eh—oh—yes——

MRS. RADIUS. [*Crosses to* CYNOSURE.] Very true, and do you know, I have heard people say that they thought your advantages had been greatly thrown away, and actually regretted that some painter or poet had not made the tour of Europe, instead of a well-dressed puppet who has nothing to say, like gilded Gourdtelle.

CYNOSURE. Me! quite likely to be true—never heard witty people talk until I went to Paris—afraid now to say anything, lest I should prove myself as foolish as the rest of you—eh—oh—yes——

Enter SERVANT, *who crosses to* MRS. APEX *and whispers to her. She expresses agitation. Exit* SERVANT.

MRS. APEX. Excuse me one moment. [*Exit hurriedly.*

MRS. RADIUS. [*As* MRS. CODLIVER *comes down.*] Poor dear soul!—a creditor, no doubt; the poor woman scarcely draws a quiet breath for them. I heard to-day,—but you will not mention it?

MRS. CODLIVER. Oh, my, no! I am as silent as a Hippopotamus.

CYNOSURE. And I never talk of anything but myself,—
and Paris—eh—oh—yes——

MRS. RADIUS. Well, then, they do say——

[*They draw together, and whisper significantly.*
And so, my dear, the whole affair will be exposed, and the
young man will become quite a wretch.

CYNOSURE. Don't believe such a story can be true, but if
so, he is a lucky fellow to create an American sensation.
In Paris, he would have made much shorter work of it,—
got a pan of charcoal, or blown his brains out—eh—yes——

MRS. CODLIVER. Charcoal? Oh, yes! that's the stuff that
penetrates the pores of your lungs and stupefies the action
of your skin. I read all about it, in the extracts of a physi-
ognomy, published by Doctor Ayer, in the almanac that tells
what day of the month to take his Cherry's Spectre, that
stuff that tastes like apple sass, and cures brown keeters.

MRS. RADIUS. Medicine, or sickness, or your appetite, or
something, has greatly changed you since the death of poor
dear Corderoy Codliver. You look as pale as a ghost; so
does our friend Mrs. Apex. [*Looking off*.] See! she is
quite ghastly. [MRS. CODLIVER *goes up to lunch*.

Enter MRS. APEX.

MRS. APEX. Pray excuse me. I was unexpectedly detained.

MRS. RADIUS. We were doing very well without you.

[*Goes up to* CYNOSURE.

MRS. APEX. [*Aside*.] That silly boy, Charles, was so
overcome with horror at what he had done, that he has
resolved to leave town for a few days, to avoid the sister
he imagines he has injured. Dear, foolish boy, I will not
believe he is in any danger.

Enter UNIT.

UNIT. Good morning—heard talking, so knew you were
at home—came to see Mary—went to her room, but it was
empty—did not send card; only extravagance for nothing—
waste a card to-day, want one to-morrow. That is my
motto, sir,—always pays, sir, always pays.

MRS. RADIUS. But you don't know what the world says
of your economy, Mr. Unit.

UNIT. Don't care, and that is more to the purpose, ma'am! I know all about the world's opinion—opinions are bought with dollars, ma'am—have *got* the dollars, ma'am,—could buy opinions with them, if it paid—but I don't believe it would pay.

CYNOSURE. It does in Paris. Public opinion makes a man an emperor, it does really—ya-as.

UNIT. Bah! wouldn't be an emperor if I could, sir. Empty honour, sir, without profit—spend income keeping up dignity—no chance to save money. Some day mad Frenchman cut your throat—dead loss of net profit of time employed in keeping up grandeur to date of murder—don't pay in the end—no, sir, a high position that is not founded upon merit never can be made to pay.

CYNOSURE. But just think of living *in* Paris—leader of the ton—Boulevards, Tuilleries, Versailles, eh, oh!

UNIT. Don't pay!

MRS. CODLIVER. Think of them French doctors, and the made-up dishes—the eatings them cooks can fix up—the *têtcs de veau,* with sassages, and the *Maître de Hotel* tripe.

UNIT. Don't pay!

MRS. APEX. And the importance of your position, with unlimited resources, and leader of every fashion.

UNIT. All these things don't pay. You are all the better off as you are. You are not as happy now, ma'am, as you were long before Codliver died, when you kept that low groggery, until the railroad bought your property at an immense over-valuation, and so made your fortune. No temperance movement then; cheap liquor, in tin cups, paid heavy profit,—yes, made you able to support a dozen quack doctors. You'd be better off than Louis Napoleon now, if you would try a little hard work, ma'am; to get rid of your dyspepsia, nothing like work,—at last it is a thing that may be said to always pay.

MRS. CODLIVER. What an impolite barbarossa he is! Dear me! I feel such a swimmin' in my head! I wish, whenever he begins to tell a body's Geology, he would bring a bottle of Watt's Nervous Anecdote!

[MRS. APEX *leads* MRS. CODLIVER *to a chair, then comes down.*

MRS. RADIUS. You must not be so severe on our friend,

MR. UNIT. Don't you see how fat and delicate she has got since she has eaten so much and worked so little? Poor thing!—she is a good-natured parvenue, and we overlook her ignorance and vulgarity for the sake of——

UNIT. I know you do—for the sake of her dollars. I don't—don't want her money, ma'am, and can afford to tell the truth. One of the great privileges of being a moneyed man is that you can tell the truth and have your joke—like a joke when it pays! Have a good memory, ma'am—know your early history, too,—have not forgotten your mother keeping a boarding-house on Greenwich-street, when you got little Radius entrapped into marrying you! Bad plan, ma'am—I would have stood a law-suit for breach of promise first!—law-suit not half so troublesome or expensive as an extravagant wife,—drag a man down if he was rich as John Jacob Astor! Yes, sir!—worse than a mill-stone around the neck,—sure to ruin him in the end—an extravagant woman never pays!

MRS. APEX. Ah! Mr. Unit, you know you mean that for me, and if you do, I shall have to scold you.

UNIT. Better not, ma'am; I may return it unpleasantly. Your pride and ostentation are no credit to the memory of your worthy old grandfather!

MRS. RADIUS. Had Mrs. Apex a worthy old grandfather? Then, of course, he was wealthy? Really, now, I should never have thought it, dear!

CYNOSURE. Had a grandfather?—quite uncommon in this country. Those Dukes, and that sort of thing—they always have them in Paris—eh—oh—ya-as!

UNIT. Yes, sir; yes, he was a worthy old man—kept his money hidden in a worsted mit, sewed in the corner of his bed—better place for a deposit than a *Wild Cat Bank!*

MRS. RADIUS. Dear old man, how eccentric! Just like you!

UNIT. Don't say I'm a dear old man!—I know you don't mean it, and it won't pay! Yes, her grandfather was a worthy old wood-sawyer. Many a time I have seen him with his buck and saw in his hand, and a pad tied on his knee, trying to get a job—and it paid in the end—he died a wealthy man—yes, sir! Industry always pays!

Mrs. Apex. [*Aside.*] If Mrs. Radius had only been away!—I shall choke with vexation!

Cynosure. Ladies, don't look so uncomfortable! I don't care who knows that my father was a successful tailor. It is quite fashionable at Paris to laugh at pedigree, and talk about merit, and not money, and all that sort of thing—eh—oh!—ya-as!

Unit. That is the first Parisian fashion I ever thought worth following. But that is too vulgar a theory for us Republicans. Upstarts here make money by cheating government in contracts, swindling Indians with glass beads and bad whiskey—lucky investments in old cabbage-gardens, —all ends in the same thing—children grow up, and are the "first people"—ride in carriages with livery servants—take daughters to big hotels—Saratoga and Newport, on exhibition, to be knocked down to the highest bidder! Sons are idle spendthrifts, and bring the family down again to poverty —just as Charles Sandford is doing—he is a fair sample of lot, and a damaged lot it is, sir—one that won't pay! No, sir—never can be made to pay!

[Cynosure, Mrs. Radius, *and* Mrs. Codliver *retire up*.

Mrs. Apex. My son, Mr. Unit, is——

Unit. Gambling every night—I know it—lost five thousand dollars last night!

Re-enter Mary.—*She crosses to right of* Unit.

Mary. [*Aside.*] Heavens! can this be what Edward referred to?

Mrs. Apex. [*Aside.*] If this reaches his father's ears, he is ruined!   [*Goes up to table.*

Mary. How do you do, Mr. Unit? I am afraid you are a little cross to-day. Don't pretend to be cross to me, for I know you a great deal better than you do yourself, and I'm sure you don't wish to give pain to any one.

Unit. Yes, I do, when they deserve it! But if they were all like you, I would not wish to hurt their feelings, for then it wouldn't pay.

Mary. Oh, it never pays to be unkind! Now, do me a favour. Don't mention this dreadful loss of brother Charles to papa, because it will, perhaps, cause him to discard him.

UNIT. All the better for you. Cut him off with a shilling—leave you his entire fortune, as he ought to do—it always pays to expose extravagance and folly. Tell the truth, Mary—best way—in the end it's sure to pay!

MARY. But, dear uncle Unit, you will not expose poor Charles this time, for my sake!

[*Puts her arm on his shoulder.*

UNIT. N-o—though I came on purpose! Must go now—no time to spare. Your father's affairs are in great confusion, Mary. Do you take care of the little sum you lately came in possession of—don't lend it—mind—never get it again—don't pay to lend—understand me, don't pay! Good morning, ladies. And you, Mr. Cynosure—know you are glad I am going—don't care if you are—know too much about you—all butterflies—don't pay in the end. Ruin the country with your extravagance—yes, sir—an idle population, consuming and not producing, can never be made to pay! [*Exit.—*MARY *goes to table.*

MRS. APEX. He is gone at last! Now, my dear friends, I pledge myself you shall never meet him here again. Mr. Apex is partial to him from old associations, and Mary imagines that elements of good are hid beneath his rough manners and address, but I believe he is as much a bear in heart as in behaviour.

CYNOSURE. For my own part, I quite like him—he is a character! Americans are all alike. He would be a favourite in Paris. I must go now. [*Crosses to* MRS. APEX.] Mrs. Apex, I kiss your hand. Adieu, Miss Mary. Ladies, most obedient. Eh! oh! [*Exit, affectedly.*

MRS. CODLIVER. I am very glad he has made an exclusion of his ruminiscences. I must go myself, for I am engaged to dine with Mrs. Slocum, and dinner is sure to be put on the table within the punctuation of a railroad conductor. Good mornin'. If that there is Sally Volatile, Miss Mary, do lend it to me, I have such a pain in my poor head—indeed, I may say, I have what the French call, a *melody in the tete!*

[*Exit, fanning herself. All laugh.*

MRS. RADIUS. I must away, too; I have made a long call, but I have enjoyed it so much, particularly Mr. Unit's comical reminiscences!

MRS. APEX. Let us keep each other's counsel. Dear Mrs.

Codliver is too stupid, and little Cynosure too preoccupied, to remember what they have heard, so let us preserve mutual silence on the subject.

MRS. RADIUS. [*Going—returns.*] The very thing I meant to propose. Adieu, love!—one kiss! That is sad news about dear Charles, but I hope it is not true; people are always manufacturing and circulating such ill-natured stories. Good-bye, dear! Good-bye, Mary—do call and see me soon. I shall come early, if nothing prevents your party from coming off to-morrow evening. Adieu. [*Exit.*

MRS. APEX. [*Brings down a chair.*] I feel strangely nervous! I almost wish Mrs. Radius had stayed. Why does the girl still linger here? It is very silly, but I scarcely dare look at her. [*Aside.*

MARY. [*Comes down to left of* MRS. APEX.] Mama, you look anxious. I don't believe this report about my brother can be true. Have you seen Charles this morning, mother?

MRS. APEX. No—yes—I—[*Aside.*] What weakness and folly have usurped my better reason! [*Aloud.*] I saw him for a few moments.

MARY. [*Aside.*] Her agitation reveals what her lips refuse to utter! The sad story is true, and my poor brother is ruined!

MRS. APEX. Silence, for heaven's sake! Here's your father! [*Goes up right.*

Enter APEX, *hurriedly.—*MRS. APEX *goes to entrance, but pauses irresolutely, and conceals herself behind chair.*

APEX. You caused me much anxiety this morning, Mary. Luckily, I shall not require the money you gave me a check for until to-morrow.

MRS. APEX. [*Aside.*] Great heavens! what do I hear!

APEX. But when I presented the check this morning, the teller handed me a duplicate which he had already paid.

MRS. APEX. [*Aside.*] Oh, horror, horror! Into what an abyss of agony have I dragged my child!

APEX. Of course you have drawn the money, thinking to give me pleasure by your alacrity, but, though very good and thoughtful of you, love, it was not business-like.
    [*Goes to table, takes out a large pocket-book, and selects papers, till the following dialogue is over.*

MARY. What fearful idea presents itself to my mind! But—no—no—no—it is impossible!

MRS. APEX. [*Comes down right.*] Say you have used the money! Say so! Your brother's life and mine hang on your answer!

MARY. Oh! I am faint—and sick at heart!

MRS. APEX. Do not betray us. Do not, I implore you!

MARY. I promise you—I will not!

MRS. APEX. Bless you! Bless you!

[MRS. APEX *retires up, quickly to right;* APEX *comes down with check in his hand.*

APEX. Here is the check—and now, my child, give me the money.

MARY. Father—I cannot.

APEX. What do I hear? Unit has cautioned you against trusting this money in my hands? Can it be possible that you have listened to him, after all you said last night?

MARY. No—no—father. I—do not despise me! I cannot give you the money—it is gone!

APEX. Did you not draw the money from the bank this morning? for your own purposes?

MRS. APEX. [*Aside.*] She is silent! Oh, my boy—my boy!

MARY. I—did!

APEX. Cold-hearted, selfish wretch! Henceforth this house is no home for you! Take all you have; and when, to-morrow, you hear of my bankruptcy, remember my worst foe was my own child!—who, with love in her eyes, and fair words on her lips, induced me to trust all to her generous proffers, and then repented of the risk she ran to save her father!

MRS. APEX. Oh! Suspend your decision, let me entreat you! Mary may not be to blame!

APEX. Silence, madam! The voice of Nature, in my breast, can offer no excuse for her unnatural conduct. Why, then, do *you* waste words on me? Go, heartless wretch! My daughter never more! I stand here in my misery—a childless, beggared man!

MARY. [*Kneeling at his feet.*] My heart will break! Father, only hear me. I cannot now explain my seeming guilt—but, believe me, I am innocent of any design.

APEX. You are all design! Your apparent readiness to aid me, all was art, cunning, and hypocrisy! Out of my sight, *viper* that you are!

Enter CHLOE.

CHLOE. De Lord! Is this hea' ole nigga awake—to hea' Mass'r George talk dat kind talk to my blessed Miss Mary!

APEX. [*Throws* MARY *off.*] Leave the house, I say, if you would not have me curse you!

MARY. Have I no friend? Is there no one to speak for me?

CHLOE. Yes, Miss Mary! You' poor old black mammy will speak for you, and *do* for you, too! You must be crazy, Mass'r George, to speak dat way to your own child!

APEX. Leave the house, you insolent old hag! Go together, and take care your generous young mistress does not sell you for your pains!

[*Sinks into chair, and buries his face in his hands. MRS. APEX is in corner. MARY approaches her father; he pushes her roughly away.—She falls into CHLOE's arms.*

MARY. [*Weeping.*] I have no father now.

CHLOE. Yes, you has, honey! The great Shepherd above is you' fadder, and you' old black mammy is your friend.

END OF ACT II.

ACT III.

SCENE I.—*A Room in a Boarding-house.—Plain Furniture.—* MARY *discovered.*

Enter CHLOE.

MARY. Did you have your tea, mammy?

CHLOE. I had some bilin' water, honey!—Eh—eh! dis hea' boarding-house eatin'! I often heard tell ob dese hea' places, whar dem people lives dat gits low wages, and wants to cut a big figger, but, sakes! Miss Ma'y, I never thought 'twas half as bad as dis!

MARY. Don't be discontented, mammy,—Edward and I parted unkindly this morning—father has cast me off, and heaven only knows how long I shall be able to pay for even these accommodations! No doubt our acquaintances would open their doors to receive me, but it would be rather to mortify my step-mother, whom they hate, than to show me kindness, and I would rather decline their heartless hospitality.

CHLOE. Dat's true, honey,—but, Miss Ma'y, you done starve to def in dis house! You didn't take no tea, but I did —so I peeped through de window, war de white folks war eatin', and sakes! Miss Mary!—it wasn't nothin' like old Virginny,—de tables was peppered all over wid a sight of little dishes, 'most like cup-plates, and each one had three crumbs of cake, and a quarter of a slice of bread, cut so thin, it looked like a piece of white stickin' plaster,—and a scrap of dried beef, so mity small, it wouldn't do to bait a fish-hook, and dey all sot around dem little scraps, and 'tendin' to eat, just like little gals a playin' tea-party! And de dressin' an' de primpin' took dis nigga rite off at de heels! Dem old maids, wid de wide ribbons, and de har all comb'd out 'bout a yard 'cross de face, a mumblin' dem remnants,— 'fraid to laugh, fear dey'd spill dey false teef, and sittin' so sober, just like dey was gittin' took in a doggerytype! It was killin'! I got so chuck full of laugh I was mighty pleased to git up sta'rs; fear dey'd call me a sassy nigga!

MARY. We must try and content ourselves, Chloe. I do not think my father's anger will continue.

CHLOE. Massy's sake! I hope, as de coloured preacher say,—de time of probashum will be short!

MARY. I must endeavour immediately to get some employment that will pay our expenses. Perhaps my former music teacher may be able to recommend me to some pupils.

CHLOE. Now, Miss Ma'y, don't talk dat way 'cept you want to break your old mammy's heart! You sit down to teach de pianner, and hear de little gals tum, tum, tum, till your head gits most busted? I'll never give my 'sent to you doin' no such thing! I'd rather sell myself to Georgia! Sakes! I'd rather sell myself to de debbil!

MARY. Hush, mammy, you must not talk so, and indeed, when I am busy, I shall feel happier than when I sit quietly and think.   [*Bursts into tears.*

CHLOE. Now, honey, sugar child, shut up **dem** tears!

When I was a little nigga, dey done told me, when I git a lickin' dat it was for my good. So, I suppose dese hea' crosses is for your good in de end, honey. So, don't git undone, but wait for de good time comin'. I kin be more help dan you s'pose. I ain't quite a broke down old nigga yet, and I will go and see some coloured ladies what does up clothes, and git work from dem. I tell you I don't turn my back upon no person to do up fine tings! Den I got a heap of money saved up, too! I never told no one so: kase I feared some one might come and chloroform me to git it; so I jus' kep it tied up in dis hea' old handkercher. I never had no use for money, and I'm rite glad to git shut of it; I only wish it was more, Miss Ma'y. But just you count it over, and see how much dey is. I never could count fur—time I gits all de fingers, and de toes counted, I begins to cave in!

MARY. Oh, mammy! I should be as base as father thinks me, if I could accept your little saving. Pray, don't ask me.

CHLOE. Den, if you's so mighty stuffy, I'll hunt up a nigga trader dis blessed night, and sell myself souf! What I gwine to do wid money, chile? I 'spect you is crazy, makin' such a fuss about dese dimes. You done give 'em to me, and if I can't do what I chooses wid 'em, it's time to leave! I see what's de matter: you 'spises my mite, kase I is coloured!

MARY. You, too, suspect me? [Weeps.

CHLOE. Bless de Lord! no, chile; I just 'tend so, to make you take de old nigga's money!

[A knock at door; CHLOE goes to it.

SERVANT. A card for Miss Apex. The gentleman is down stairs.

CHLOE. [Gives card to MARY.] Here, Miss Mary, Mr. What-you-call-um is down sta'rs.

MARY. It is Mr. Cynosure!—I cannot see him.

CHLOE. May be he brings some message from you' pa. You better see him, honey.

MARY. It is only one trial more! Desire him to walk up.

CHLOE. [Delivers message at door.] Now, honey, don't you be feerd to tell dis man de trufe, kase dey'll git a sight of lies up agin you, an' you just clar your own skeerts!

[A knock. CHLOE opens door, and then retires up.

Enter CYNOSURE.

MARY. I am much indebted for the friendly interest which has prompted your call, Mr. Cynosure.

CYNOSURE. It was not exactly friendship, Miss Mary; it was a rather warmer feeling. I—oh—eh!— have long admired—that is to say, I—I wish I knew how fellows propose in Paris. [*Aside.*

MARY. I'm sure you will excuse me, Mr. Cynosure, when I say that such language in my present situation is, to say the least of it, ill-timed.

CYNOSURE. 'Pon my soul I should never have mentioned the subject, although my sentiments are well known; but I understood there had been a change in your circumstances to-day, from some unknown cause, and I thought a trip to Europe might be acceptable—if so, I offer you my hand and heart, and Paris for a dwelling-place. I assure you nothing shall be left undone to secure your happiness,—that is, not only nothing I can do, but nothing that can be done in Paris! Don't answer hastily, but reflect upon what I say. I can make no sensation at all in Paris as a bachelor, but with you for a wife, I would be the envy of our set. By Jove! I would be the envy of all Paris—eh!—really, ya-as.

MARY. Permit me most positively to decline your proposal, and request you to terminate an interview so painful to my feelings.

CYNOSURE. No hope of changing your determination? Well, Miss Mary, I deeply regret it. It will make me a desperate man—perfectly desperate! I—I shall go home, and cut——

CHLOE. Not your troat, honey! Don't you do dat, kase it won't never grow agin!

CYNOSURE. No, not my throat, but the straps of my trowsers. I'll let my beard grow—no, I've done that. I'll shave— I'll buy a suit of clothes in Chatham Square, and a hat in Catharine Market. I'll have my boots made by an Englishman. I'll let my hair return to its natural colour. I'll forswear all society and lead the life of a misanthrope! Yes, I'll forswear Paris, and go to Coney Island, and dig clams for your sake. [*Rushes out.*

CHLOE. If dat Cynosure comes foolin' here agin, I'll give

him Bunker Hill! shu. Tell you what do, Miss Ma'y; go see Mass'r Unit, and see what he'll done told you. He kin fix you' pa all right, shu.

MARY. A happy thought! Come, dear, dear mammy; perhaps this may lead to a more fortunate result than even my rising hopes predict. [*Exit.*

CHLOE. Dat's jus' de way. Dey talk de fine talk, and go off widout a speck of bonnet! Dat's jus' de way wid gals in love! Miss Ma'y. Dem people in love is crazier dan a young nigger a shoutin' hallalujerin' at a camp-meetin'!
[*Exit* CHLOE.

SCENE II.—UNIT'S *Study.—Furniture of black walnut—desk, with pens, ink, and paper—tea table—a large chair—a stool—a lighted candle on desk—chairs and stool covered with black haircloth—a fireplace.*

UNIT *discovered writing Will; folds and places it in drawer of desk; locks and puts key in his pocket.*

UNIT. Made my will to-night—settled all my affairs—might die suddenly—object to long sickness—doctors' bills and nurses very expensive, and often help to kill you. In that case, don't pay! Hired nurses never *do* pay—want some one that really cares for you, when you are ill, when your eyes get dim, and you can't raise your hand to wait upon yourself, it pays then to have some one who really loves you, to do the pillow-smoothing business. Yes, sir, it pays then. Don't know, though—sometimes wife and children stand quarrelling for the spoil, before the breath is out of the old father's body—seen 'em do it often! Worse than lawyers are some children when a rich man dies; they make a grab-game of it—but it don't pay—litigation swallows up estate, and avarice kills affection. Have no heirs—left half my money to Mary—good girl, economical—left the rest to orphans,—no children of my own,—help to support other people's. Don't like colleges—education no use, except figures.—Arithmetic is the only study that pays! My birthday, to-day—no one knew it—no one left to care—used to have new clothes, when I was a little boy, kind faces looking love at me,—all gone now—have not seen such a look for forty years! World grows dreary—have outlived my generation—left home when I was twenty—cried like a baby—never saw my family again—scarcely thought of them—but, somehow remember them to-night—wish I could bring them back—household ties, familiar names, kind friendly words—I thought they didn't pay, but they do. Yes, yes, when you are old and lonely, you feel they can be made to pay. [*A knock at door.*] Who can that be?—never expect a visitor—nothing to be made by coming to see me, and they know it. [*Goes to door.*] Why, Mary!

Enter MARY *and* CHLOE.

What brought you here, child?—Come in—sit down! What's the matter? look pale—been crying—must not cry!—never pays!—Yes, it does—best investment a woman can make are tears—cost nothing, and are sure to conquer. Yes—tears can be made to pay.

MARY. I thought I should surprise you, Uncle Unit; but indeed you must forgive my intrusion. Go down stairs, mammy, and wait in the housekeeper's room until I call.

CHLOE. Yes, Miss Ma'y, I'se gwine! De Lor' send de blessed chile may melt dat ar' ole man's froze up heart! She kin do it, if anybody kin, but it's bin cold so long, it's got childblains all over it.   [*Exit, looking back.*

MARY. Now, I've come to ask you a great favour—the greatest favour I could ask of you, almost, and I am sure you won't refuse me, will you Uncle Unit? I won't call you that ugly name—I'll call you John—Uncle John—that is better, I am sure—is it not?

UNIT. Yes, yes, I like to hear my old name once more—have not been called John for forty years! This is my birthday, Mary; I am sixty years of age to-day, and in a few years more the old man will be off, and then you will find that your good feeling for him has paid!—Yes, Mary, respect and attention from the young to the old always pays!

MARY. Promise me you won't talk about anything paying again to-night—because I want to speak to you about something—something bad, and something foolish, and something that I know can't pay.

UNIT. Well, I'll not say it again; but this business—if it is about your family, I don't want to listen; they are all headstrong, and will find, ere long, that extravagance leads to ruin, and that pride and vanity can't——

Mary. [*Stopping him.*] Ah?

Unit. Prosper! [*Laughs.*] Mary, I only wish you were my daughter, instead of my godchild. I have not forgotten you, and you will find that I have not, some day.

Mary. But that, Uncle John, will be such a sad, sad day, —when I can no longer look in your face and thank you,— when I cannot clasp your hand and tell you I am grateful.— when all my pleasure at the gift will be embittered by a sorrowful remembrance of the giver. [*Weeps.*] But I have come to ask you a favour, and I am so anxious to hear you say that you will grant it, that I cannot wait another moment.

Unit. Yes, you must—you must wait till I get my tea. Always do business up to time—see, [*pulls out watch*] seven o'clock, and here comes tea.

Enter Servant, *with tray, teapot, &c.—He places them on table, and exits.*

Always comes in time—if it didn't, would discharge housekeeper! Punctuality always p—no—prospers.

Mary. Now I will pour out the tea for you,—[*they sit*] —and tell you my story at the same time. You must promise to hear me out, and not to be displeased with any one.

Unit. No,—can't promise that—always displeased with folly and pretension. Can't promise—don't——[*Checking himself.*]

Mary. Pray don't say so, until you have heard me out. Papa wished very much to borrow the legacy my aunt left me——

Unit. I knew it—I was sure of it! And you lent it?

Mary. I——

Unit. Did you refuse him?

Mary. Oh, no!

Unit. Glad to hear you say so. You will never get it again, but I don't like selfishness at your age. Time enough when you get old and soured, as I am. Want me to forgive you for not taking my advice? All right—like you the better —good girl—shall lose nothing by it—filial affection always p——

Mary. Prevails in the end. Ah! I only hope you will let

me say so, when you hear all! Now, after I had promised
papa the money, some very pressing debts came in, and my
step-mother and Charles were so anxious to save my father
any anxiety on their account, and never dreaming that he
wanted to borrow my little legacy,—they——

UNIT. Applied to you for it! You had not got it to lend,
—so came to get some money for their use, from me?—No—
no—no! Wouldn't let you have it on any account—despise
them both. Idleness and pride deserve humiliation—they
never can be made to p——

MARY. Pray let me give you some more tea? Shall I put
more sugar in your next cup?

UNIT. No use—can't sweeten the acid of my temper,
when I see extravagance and folly.

MARY. Let me warm this toast for you. [*Goes to fire-place.*] No, dear Uncle John, you did not guess quite cor-
rectly. In their great need of money—and feeling quite sure
they could replace it—they did borrow it of me.

UNIT. Did you not say you had lent it to your father?

MARY. No,—I gave him a check for it—but this morning——

UNIT. Eh!—don't stand by that fire—your face is burning!

MARY. The amount was already drawn!

UNIT. I knew it. That scamp, Charles Sandford, has
forged your signature! I'll have him arrested! [*Going.*]

MARY. Not for ten thousand times the sum! I don't
value the money—I am glad and happy it has been of use to
them, and I would not, for the world, have the artifice they
have practised, discovered. I have sworn to keep their
secret, but papa is in such distress for the money, which he
thinks I have withheld.—If you would only lend me the
amount until I can repay you, that I may give it to him,—I
will bless you, and love you,—oh, so gratefully! Only think!
Papa imagines I have drawn the money, and have kept it
for myself,—and he has sent me away. Oh, aid me in this
deep affliction! I have no hope but you!

UNIT. A bad piece of business!—very bad! Fifteen
thousand dollars! A large sum—no matter—you shall have
it, on condition that the whole affair is exposed. Rascality
should never be cloaked from the world's scorn. Show up

the rascals and honour honest men—true system—too much lenity will never pay,—it engenders vice.

MARY. But mercy often engenders reformation. Think of the poor boy—his character for ever blasted! Think of my step-mother—her proud heart broken with remorse at the ruin brought upon her darling! Think of my father— his lofty head bowed down by the disgrace of those he loves! Never—never! Better that I should remain a homeless wanderer, than such evil should befall those who are dearest to me.

UNIT. But you say that your father believes you have acted selfishly? Perhaps, in his anger and disappointment, he almost cursed you? You must clear yourself—very bad to be under sentence for faults never committed,—very bad!

MARY. No matter. If he cannot learn that I am innocent of all unkindness towards him, save by the sacrifice of my step-mother and her son, it will give him less pain to believe the child he never loved a heartless monster, than to know that his wife and son have incurred a penalty so disgrace- ful that its execution would bring him to the grave. It is hard to be misjudged, but there will come a day hereafter, when he will know the truth, and perhaps when he hears all he will love me better.

UNIT. Good girl!—good heart—sound head—quite right! Exposure would punish the innocent more than the guilty. Will compromise with you: you shall have the money to save your father's credit—twice the sum if he requires it. But he must be told the truth if the world must not. Charles Sandford must go to work; and your step-mother, she must join the church. No more feathers and furbelows, debts and diamonds, for her! All that must be given up, or your father is a ruined man.

MARY. They will do all you wish—I am sure they will; for the fearful lesson they have received cannot be in vain, and, oh! how grateful—how deeply grateful,—will all be to you—our benefactor—our saviour!

UNIT. Don't speak of gratitude; no necessity for any words about it—made my will to-day. Choose to let you have an instalment in advance—best investment I can make to let you have the money—expect to receive ten per cent. per annum, in attention, kindness and cheerful words.—Yes, sir—fine investment for an old fellow, with no one belonging to him, to secure the kind offices of a good, true-hearted woman, when you can find one.—Yes, sir—that will pay—the gratitude of a noble nature must pay!

MARY. I will let you say *that* pays, for indeed it does! But how much injustice you do yourself—how few would believe that so much generosity and kindness lay hidden beneath.

UNIT. My crusty exterior?—Yes, sir; yes—a human cocoa-nut—rough, coarse, fibrous outside covering—that's my clothes and my manner—hard shell beneath—that's my worldliness and prudence—yes, and my politics, too! But there is a little of the milk of human kindness in the old man's heart, and a large share of it belongs to you, Mary, for you are a good girl and deserve it!

MARY. Indeed, you praise me much more than I deserve.

UNIT. Not a bit!—you have good sense—common sense, it is called, but I find it uncommon—but it is the kind that always can be made to pay! If you had come here to-night and gone into hysterics, like the heroine of a novel or a melo-drama, I should have sent you away with a scolding; but you came like a girl of sense, poured out my tea, told a straight-forward story, and only showed, by emotion you could not repress, the deep interest you felt in getting my aid.

MARY. Don't praise me any more, but let me call up my dear old mammy, who has been my friend in all my trials, and let her share my joy as she has done my disgrace.

UNIT. Of course; call up the old coloured woman;—another specimen that outside covering is not to be depended upon. Good old woman—does her duty—respect her more than twenty fashionable dawdles if she was dyed in the wool!   [MARY *beckons to* CHLOE.

CHLOE. Sakes, Miss Mary! I done got thinkin' you would never git done talk! Good evening, mass'r—I feels myself 'tickler well, I thank you!

MARY. Now, Chloe and I will go home and tell papa—but—I am afraid he will not listen to me.

UNIT. No, no, we will all go together. A lesson must be taught them all they never can forget! Now that it is too late, I have discovered, Mary, a fatal mistake in my ledger of life.

MARY. You can soon correct it, Uncle John.

UNIT. No, Mary; there are but few more entries to be made before the balance-sheet is struck, and the accounts put into the hands of parties holding judgment against me! I have made a great mercantile error—I have given unlimited credit to self-interest, economy, system, and a host of business qualifications, and refused to trust affection, generosity, and kindness, and too late I have discovered that my favourite customers are bankrupts, and that in the down-hill path a man walks at sixty years of age, the assets that benevolent actions towards our fellow-beings leave in the shape of love, respect, and sympathy, are the only ones worth having—the only things that pay!   [*Exeunt.*

SCENE III.—*Splendid drawing-room in* APEX *house, brilliantly illuminated.—Mirrors, chandeliers, &c.,—chandeliers reflected on large mirror at back—sofa, &c.*

Enter MRS. APEX, *elegantly dressed.*

MRS. APEX. What a day of agony I have endured! The image of Mary, driven from her home, haunts me—her pale face is ever before me—the echo of her sobs rings in my ears! What can I do? If I reveal the truth, I sacrifice my poor boy, whom I have persuaded into an action fatal to his future character! Oh! the hollow worthlessness of worldly ambition! I am now on the eve of enjoying the triumph I so much wished for—all is prepared for the reception of my guests, and yet the hour of their arrival finds me almost mad! The glare of the chandeliers burns into my aching brain—the distant sound of music falls upon my ears like the expiring shriek of some lost soul! These flowers and garlands are fetters bound round a wretched convict, and he is ever before me in the person of my son! Again I hear my words urging him to commit the fatal act, while the false friends and envious rivals,—to gain a triumph over whom I have sacrificed all!—laugh exultingly, and point their scornful fingers to taunt the selfish mother who, for an empty triumph, broke down the barriers of conscience that heaven had placed around the young soul of her child!

Enter APEX, *in evening dress.*

APEX. All is prepared, I see, for your party. Well, let it proceed: to-morrow I shall be a bankrupt; and it will be droll to mark how different shall be the greetings we will receive from those who now are all courtesy to the host and hostess of this splendid mansion!

MRS. APEX. More confidence on your part towards me might have saved us both much sorrow! Had I even dreamed the true condition of your affairs, I would have retrenched, reformed!

APEX. It is too late now to speak of the past. We have both been grievously to blame; but I feel my own faults too keenly to think of yours with harshness. I could look forward to the morrow with calmness, almost content, if the remembrance of that selfish and cold-hearted girl did not perpetually haunt me!

MRS. APEX. [*Aside.*] Oh, what anguish his words cause me!

APEX. When long accumulating liabilities render a crash inevitable, the disgrace and mortification of failure, the dread of the world's sneers, and worse, its pity, are far more unendurable, when pictured by the merchant's fancy in the dim future, than when the avalanche falls and the poor victim lies stunned and helpless beneath the accumulated load! But that a child should refuse to aid her father in such a strait, that she should be able, and yet unwilling, to stretch out a hand to save him,—that thought breaks my heart!

MRS. APEX. [*Aside.*] I can bear no more!—I must, I will tell him! I will be the victim! He need never know that Charles was aware the check was forged! [*Aloud.*] Let that thought no longer grieve you! My extravagance, and mine alone, has brought——

Enter MRS. RADIUS.

[*Aside.*] Mrs. Radius!—that woman is my fate!

MRS. RADIUS. Ah, my dear friends!—so glad to see you! Enjoying a matrimonial tête-à-tête, no doubt,—sorry if I disturb you. [*Aside.*] She has tears in her eyes, and he looks white with anger! No doubt they had a dreadful quarrel! [*Goes up.*

Mrs. Apex. [*Aside.*] I could have told him all that moment; but now to be degraded, and before her!—I cannot!

Apex. [*Aside.*] Curses on this false life! Smiles on my lips, and groans in my heart! [*Aloud.*] Most happy you have come so early, Mrs. Radius!

Mrs. Radius. [*This speech spoken jestingly.*] Why, to tell you the truth, there are some terrible rumours abroad about you both, my dear friends, and I felt as if I would not be showing a proper regard for you if I did not endeavour to be the first guest in your drawing-room, so that if Mrs. Apex had taken strychnine, or you had shot yourself, I could have dismissed the company, directed the laying out, ordered the funeral, and told the whole story properly for you to-morrow! Ha! ha! ha!

Mrs. Apex. Ha, ha, ha! How very droll you are, my dear Mrs. Radius, to indulge in such laughable ideas! I was never in better health or spirits, I assure you; and I hope you think I look well, for I have on the Eugénie dress you tried so hard to purchase before me.

Mrs. Radius. No, dear; you mean the gaudy dress so like an old one of mine. [*Aside.*] It is very badly made, and is terribly unbecoming! [*Aloud.*] What a pity it is not worth the high price and the high words the world says it cost you, love!

Apex. The world says many things, Mrs. Radius, that a lady like yourself should be too wise either to listen to or repeat!

Mrs. Radius. So my friends tell me; but it is purely disinterested on my part. Of course, there can be no benefit to me in repeating the unpleasant things I hear said of my intimate acquaintances; but I think it so useful for them to know the reports ill-natured persons spread abroad, that they may guard against them.

Apex. There is no evil more to be dreaded, and harder to guard against, than the whispers of scandal-mongers!

Mrs. Radius. Oh, yes! I think profligate and ungrateful children are evils most to be dreaded. I am very glad I have none, lest they should turn out to be misers or rakes, like the daughters and sons of some of my acquaintance. Apropos, where is dear Charles?—I have not seen him since he lost that terrible sum at the Club.

APEX. [*Aside.*] Charles gambling again! Can it be possible that Mary lent him——

Enter MRS. CODLIVER. APEX *is seated.*

MRS. CODLIVER. Good evenin'! I heard some inklings that something might happen to break off the party to-night; leastways, Mrs. Radius told me so.

[MRS. RADIUS *expresses confusion, and signs* MRS. COD-
LIVER *to be silent.*

As I knows you always gets your suppers from Maillard's, and he is notorious for his pattys of four greyes, I thought I had better come early to pick a bit, and talk over your trouble in a friendly way. It would be the greatest of pities such a sight of good cookin' should go for nothin'; and as I hate friends that turn their backs upon people in conflictions, I shall eat just as hearty as if it was all paid for; and I've brought a bottle of Pepsin, and some Abernethy's Dinner Pills, to make late suppers not be injurious to my indelicate conjestion!

MRS. APEX. [*With forced composure.*] Very happy to see you! I cannot think what ill-natured person could put such unfounded reports into circulation.

MRS. CODLIVER. No more can I! But there always is some person a palpitating around with confounded reports in every communipaw, and why shouldn't we have 'em, too? I only hope the great chloroform movement will give woman so much demijohnism to attend to, that they won't have no time to spare for meddling with other people's concerns!

MRS. RADIUS. They will never give up scandal, my dear, rest assured! They may say what they please about medicine, law, or politics, but I am convinced that regulating the affairs of our neighbours is indisputably woman's peculiar mission.

Enter CYNOSURE.

CYNOSURE. Ladies, good evening! Mr. Apex, most obedient. Heard something was likely to take place, and, in great want of excitement to-night, feel disposed to do something desperate myself!! Intend to commence shaving to-morrow, or else shall take steamer and return at once to Paris!

Enter SERVANT.

SERVANT. A gentleman wishes to speak to Mr. Apex for a few moments. [*Exit.*

APEX. Pray, excuse me. [*Going.*

MRS. RADIUS. Oh, no, see your friend here: we will go down to the music-room. [*Aside.*] We can peep in presently, and see who it is, and it may not unlikely prove something very mysterious,—a sheriff's officer to arrest her, or something startling! Come, who's for the music-room?

[MRS. RADIUS *takes* CYNOSURE'S *arm, and exeunt.*

MRS. CODLIVER. Not me, for one! If anything is going to happen now, I am too exasperated to be of a bit of use; so, I'll go down to the supper-room, and get a few slices of boned turkey, and a few bowls of oyster soup, or some other little relish, and then I will join you; so, if any contrairy-temps does occur, it won't do me half the injury it would on an empty stomach. [*Exit.*

MRS. APEX. [*Aside.*] I must see this stranger! The dread of detection haunts me!

Enter CHARLES *hastily, his dress disordered, his face pale and agitated.*

CHARLES. Oh, sir!—what have I heard? Mary!—where is she? I could not believe the cruel story I heard, and hastened here to seek her. Her room is desolate! Her sweet face, that always welcomed the truant brother, was not there! Where is dear Mary?

APEX. Miss Apex is with such friends as her money will purchase her. She left her home last night, after refusing to aid me in a time of unexpected difficulties, and her cruel selfishness renders me indifferent whether I either see or hear from her again!

CHARLES. Oh, that the earth would open to receive me! Father, you are deceived, cruelly deceived! Mary is all that you would wish her! Recall your unhappy child, and let the just sentence of your wrath fall upon——

MRS. APEX. [*Comes hastily forward; apart to* CHARLES.] We are undone! Charles, why are you here, in this dress, and with such wild and haggard looks? Go to your room, child: your father's guests demand his care!

CHARLES. Oh, mother!—did you know of this? Did you know that Mary was driven from her home in disgrace? Tell me it was unknown to you, or I shall hate you!

APEX. The boy's warm heart is apology enough for all his faults! Charles, I wish your sister was more worthy of affection. Your generous nature should teach you to despise her selfish cupidity.

CHARLES. You are deceived——

MRS. APEX. Are you mad! Would you see your mother a corpse at your feet?

APEX. [Turns suddenly.] What mystery is this?

MRS. RADIUS. [Peeps in at door.] That's just what I say! I am listening carefully, but I can't catch a word!

[Spoken quickly.

CHARLES. [Takes his mother by the hand.] Mother, this is no place for you—leave us for a few moments. This must be explained!

MRS. RADIUS. [At door.] Provoking! I must keep out of the way, and am expiring with curiosity!

[Must be spoken very quickly.

MRS. APEX. No, no, I cannot go! Charles, you will break my heart!

APEX. What does this mean?

CHARLES. That I alone am answerable for Mary's conduct! The dear, generous girl, that has for years given mother her little income for my use, was deprived of her fortune by a forgery which I committed on the bank this morning. For which act I am here to surrender myself to the officers of justice!

MRS. APEX. [Crosses to APEX.] No, no, no! do not believe him!—you cannot believe him—he is so young—his soul is free from guilt! It was me alone—me—to gain an empty triumph—to gall my hated rivals!—I bartered my peace of mind forever—and now they laugh at me! Ha! ha! ha!

[Sinks into the arms of CHARLES, laughing hysterically.

CHARLES. You see, sir, she is mad! The knowledge of my guilt has overcome her! Send me away at once, before returning reason bids her feel the horrors of this moment!

APEX. Charles, do not deceive me! It is time the truth was told.

Enter UNIT.

UNIT. So I say, too—came here to tell it—[*looks towards door*]—not before witnesses. [*Slams door where* MRS. RADIUS *was peeping.—A slight scream heard.*] Smashed her fingers—good for her—mind her own business! [CHARLES *leads forward* MRS. APEX.] Now for the truth! Your wife, who is an unscrupulous woman, has led this boy to commit an act they both repent.

CHARLES. No, Mr. Unit; my mother knew nothing of this —it was me alone!

UNIT. Don't lie—lies never pay. She told you to do it— and you know it! Don't you, ma'am?

MRS. APEX. I did—I did! Let the punishment, the disgrace, fall only upon me—but save my unhappy son!

UNIT. The disgrace, I trust, we shall be able to avert, for everybody's sake—the punishment you shall share. Will you give up parties, balls, dress, and extravagance? Will you mean what you say when you pray to be delivered from envy, hatred, malice, and all uncharitableness?—that is, will you cut your fashionable connections, darn your husband's stockings, nurse your grand-children, when you have any, and live as a middle-aged woman should do?

MRS. APEX. I will, indeed—indeed, I will!—if my husband can only forgive me! [*Crosses to* APEX.] I will suit myself to his altered fortunes, and endeavour to prove the friend and helpmate I swore to be at the altar!

UNIT. Never mind; if your repentance is sincere, all right. You have had a hard lesson, but you wanted it—look ten years older since yesterday! [MRS. APEX *goes up to sofa.*] Don't go to the glass—a very good sign!—Apex, I will help you through this trouble, though you don't deserve it, for the sake of Mary!

APEX. Where is she?—the dear, wronged, patient child!

UNIT. Where might she not have been if she had not come to seek the aid of her old godfather? You owe everything to that child—yes, sir—she is a treasure! If I thought I would have a daughter like Mary, I'd marry to-morrow— yes, sir—to-morrow!—but I'm afraid it wouldn't pay! Come in, Mary! [*Going up.—*APEX *goes up to* MRS. APEX, *on sofa.*]

CHARLES. Let me go first—I cannot bear to meet her—in the prison I justly merit—

UNIT. No, no—would not pay to send you to prison. Go to prison an unscrupulous boy—come out an accomplished rascal! No, sir—prison education very seldom pays! No—set you to work, instead—know you hate work, and despise workers!

CHARLES. If you think I am worthy of a trial, you shall see that I look back with regret upon the useless folly of my past career, and it shall not be my fault——

UNIT. There, there, don't promise too much—large promises seldom pay. Like you better than I did, for coming to clear Mary—also for trying to save your mother—neither of you are so bad as I thought; but take care of a relapse—always more fatal than first attack! But Mary is waiting all this time. [*Goes to door.*] Come in, Mary—all explained!

Enter MARY.

Go ask your father to forgive you. No—tell him you forgive him—there—forgive each other all round!

[MARY *embraces* APEX, &c. *They, with* MRS. APEX *and* CHARLES, *retire up stage.*

UNIT. Now to admit the vultures; their last visit to this house for some time, I hope: so, let them see a happy family, —worst punishment I can inflict. Yes, to envy, a united household is, indeed, a baneful sight! [*Opens door.*

Enter MRS. RADIUS *and* CYNOSURE.

MRS. RADIUS. Dear me! what an interesting group! quite a tableau! How odd that Mary should have been sent away, and that Charles should look so altered! How I should have liked to hear the particulars of the reconciliation!

UNIT. I know you would: that is the reason I closed the door. How is your finger?

[MRS. RADIUS *retires up with* CYNOSURE.

Enter MRS. CODLIVER.

MRS. CODLIVER. If anything's the matter with it, try Dolly's Musical Pain Distractor! I'll tell you what has done me good to-night, though,—the sight of them there happy faces!

CYNOSURE. So it has me—quite unusual to see anybody look happy in America; but very common in Paris.

UNIT. Has it done you good?—then you are both better fellows than I took you for! Take my advice, old lady, eat three times a day, instead of twenty—throw your physic bottles out of the window—cut all your fashionable friends, and call into your big house all your poor, hard-working relations, and you'll be a healthy and a happy woman—two things that always pay, ma'am—that are sure to pay!

MRS. CODLIVER. I will so. I'll go and see Aunt Jemima to-morrow morning, if she did used to take in washing.

CYNOSURE. I'm in a desperate state of mind myself. I've a great mind to become an active partner in the old firm, and get a fine supply of clothing from Paris.

MRS. RADIUS. Do, and stand outside the store every morning in a different suit. It is just the occupation Nature intended for you.

UNIT. And the first you ever tried that will be sure to pay. Never be afraid of the friends or habits of your early years, if they are only honest ones.

MARY. There is one early friend I should like to see among our happy group,—my dear old mammy.

UNIT. That's right, Mary—same good girl always—never forget your old friends; that is a point in your character that must always pay! [*Goes to door.*] Come in, Queen Sheba, and see the happiness of your young mistress.

Enter CHLOE.

CHLOE. Jus' what I'se bound to see, Mass'r Unit, but I—sakes! I don't like to 'trude 'mong all dis hea' company—so I was gittin' a squint tro' de do'. Bless dat chile! her eyes is jus' a poppin' out of her head wid joy.

APEX. I owe you an apology, my good old Chloe.

CHLOE. Now, Mass'r, ain't you ashamed to talk dat talk to dis hea' nigga; if you say sich a word again, I'll go straight to de kitchen, and never 'trude among white folks agin.

MARY. Intrude? oh, no, mammy; the honest, faithful heart that beats within your breast should make you the welcome inmate of a royal palace.

APEX. True, Mary, she has shown her forgetfulness of the pervading sin of human nature—selfishness. To that engrossing passion may be traced all our sorrows, and in the absence of that degraded feeling, the old nurse may boast her supremacy over us all, save you, my darling child, and you, my good old friend.

UNIT. Not so sure of that—Mary, good girl—old darkey pays—but for me—no, no—just as bad as the rest of you.

MARY. Oh, no, dear Uncle John.

UNIT. Yes, I tell you, yes: tell the truth—it pays. I serve you by lending you money I don't want, to gain gratitude and affection, which I do. All the same in the end—all selfish—all human beings are selfish. [*To audience.*] Perhaps you think that our exertions to-night were induced by a desire to please you? No, sir, no—not a bit of it—all a mistake.

MARY. If so, Uncle John, it is because the deep delight we feel in their approval, gives us so much more pleasure than our exertions merit, that——

UNIT. Yes—just as I said—that, after all, our labours are prompted by that great motive power of human nature— *Self!*

CURTAIN.*

* In a prompt copy of this play, owned by the New York Public Library, there is a manuscript epilogue, written on paper headed New Orleans. The book was once the property of J. B. Wright, and contains copious "cuts."

HORSESHOE ROBINSON

By Clifton W. Tayleur

HORSESHOE ROBINSON

During the first fifty years of the national period, the American writers were greatly concerned about the creation of a native literature. They strove self-consciously to divest themselves of the British yoke. The full-blooded attitude was to be found in the correspondence of Cooper and Simms, of Irving and Brown, of Paulding and Kennedy. It was also to be found in the fiction they created. These men were only indirectly interested in the stage. Their famous creations were utilized in dramatizations. We have already seen how nearly Irving came to being a real dramatist in his associative work with Payne. We shall see later, in the third volume, how insistently his "Rip van Winkle" appealed to the dramatic instinct of playwrights. Even his "Knickerbocker History" attracted the attention of James H. Hackett, who had a play made from it, written around three of the famous Dutch Governors. A consideration of Simms will throw light on theatrical conditions in the South, and particularly in Charleston. And Cooper in dramatization has held the stage for many years past. Paulding and Kennedy, of this group, are the ones who had no deep-founded interest in the theatre. As the biographer of the former claimed, he had little "dramatic inclination." But Paulding did actually essay the dramatic form, whereas Kennedy only approached it through the labor of another.

The consequence is, Paulding's "American Comedies," published in 1847, is merely interesting from the stage standpoint, as it applies to the acting of Hackett. In 1830, this comedian offered a prize for an original comedy, "wherein an American should be the leading character." Bryant, Halleck, and Wetmore were the judges. Hackett went to Paulding and begged him to enter the competition, even suggesting to him a title. In some way it got bruited about that the prize play had been pre-determined, and that the character was to be Davy Crockett. This picturesque gentleman was, at that time, a member of the House of Representatives, and Paulding hastened to assure him that no dramatic liberties were being taken with his career. To which a most characteristic reply was received. The result of Paulding's work was the excellent picture of *Colonel Nimrod Wildfire,* a figure which Hackett made familiar to the playgoers of every large city in the United States.

The prize drama was "manipulated" by John Augustus Stone, so we are told, and, when Hackett went abroad in 1832–33, it was further "adapted" by Bayle Bernard. So that Paulding, as a dramatist, dwindles to the minus *n*th power. Even in the volume of "American Comedies," the majority of the plays—two out of the three—were written by William I. Paulding.

In the same indirect manner, John P. Kennedy, whose connection with the United States Navy was so similar to that of Paulding, became associated with the American theatre. He wrote a book which is an excellent example of the early historical romance of the Revolution. "Horseshoe Robinson: A Tale of the Tory Ascendency" was published in 1835, and twenty years afterwards it was put upon the stage by Clifton W. Tayleure. Kennedy must have been a theatregoer, for, in his "memoir," we have a glimpse of the drama in Baltimore during his youth. But, in his correspondence with Irving and Simms, on the subject of his novel, he in no way ever suggested that it might be made into a play, and certainly gave no hint of his familiarity with the fact that Hackett was already playing it. In other words, his interest in the stage was nil. The fact is, when he actually saw "Horseshoe Robinson" on the stage, he was inclined to be annoyed over the skeleton impression he received of the novel. In his diary, under date of Baltimore, May 5, 1856, he writes:

To see the new drama of "Horseshoe Robinson," fabricated by Mr. T—— of the Holliday Street Theatre, out of my novel. It was the first performance of it. A great crowd was there and greeted it with vehement applause. It is amazingly noisy, and full of battles, and amuses the gallery hugely. Mr. Ford was very kind in giving me a private box to witness it. It has had a most successful run since that night for a week.

It would appear from every evidence that another version of the play was in existence long before Kennedy saw it. And the very fact that Hackett is not mentioned in that portion of Kennedy's diary quoted by his biographer would lead us to believe he had never seen that actor in the rôle of *Galbraith Robinson*. Ireland refers to a version of the play which was presented the very year of the novel's publication, and he credits the same to Charles Dance, a prolific dramatist of the day. But though Ireland claims that it was played at the New York National, in 1836, he gives a wrong date, October 23 (it was November 23 instead), which fell on Sunday. Brown records the fact that the piece was presented at the New York Park Theatre, on March 19, 1841, and the New York *Herald* for the next morning has a review, but does not reveal the authorship. It only remarks, very much in the manner of Kennedy: "The first scenes are excellent, but it flags in interest, and ends in a battle of Bosworth's Field, quite too much *à la* Richard."

Granting this, the question next arises as to whether the version of "Horseshoe Robinson," which is here presented, is an entirely new dramatization, or whether it is the Hackett version, revamped by Clifton W. Tayleure, who must have served at the Holliday Street Theatre in Baltimore in the capacity of stock dramatist. Here it was given, April, 1856. There is very little history preserved in available shape concerning this famous theatre to throw any light on the subject. And the only reference I could find was in Colonel J. Thomas Scharf's "Chronicles of Baltimore", in which we learn that Tayleure took his farewell, as an actor, from the stage, on May 3, 1856, remaining, however, connected with the theatre until 1859. Then it was that he was admitted to the bar, and was associated with the press of Baltimore and Richmond. It was in the latter city, in 1857, that Mrs. Tayleure played the part of *Mary Musgrove*, in "Horseshoe Robinson". Whether or not she was his wife, is not conclusively proven by this statement, or some other Mrs. Tayleure, inasmuch as we are given to understand that, in 1856, Miss Mary Ann Graham, who had been connected as an actress with the Baltimore Museum, retired from the stage, and it was after this that she married Mr. Tayleure.

Tayleure served at one time as a reporter on the Baltimore *Clipper,* and John T. Ford, on August 15, 1857, entrusted to him the editorship of *Our Opinion.* According to all accounts, he remained thus employed until John E. Owens went to England, in 1865, when Tayleure accompanied him as his business manager.

This is sufficient to lay claim to the fact that Tayleure was a man of varied abilities. He made a version of "Uncle Tom's Cabin", dramatized "East Lynn", was the author of an original play, "Won Back", and had the reporter's instinct for theatrical incident. What connection his version of "Horseshoe Robinson" has with the version presented by Hackett, will remain unproven until Mr. James K. Hackett has unearthed his father's old manuscripts and made them available to the student.[1]

The present text is based on the acting edition issued by Samuel French. It reveals the conventional stagecraft of the day, and shows certain crude characteristics peculiar to the writing of the time. Compare, for example, the negro dialect here with the dialect in "Uncle Tom's Cabin" and in Poe's "The Gold Bug". The reader will be instantly struck by the ease with which Tayleure appropriates words and phrases from others for his dramatic necessity. For instance, *Butler* uses Hale's words about regretting he had but one life to sacrifice for his country, and I have been told by a bibliophile that probably Tayleure had been reading Isaac W. Stuart's biography of Hale, first issued at that time.

The play is included here because it is my conviction that it forms a link between the early period of pioneer story and the mid-period, represented by Murdock's "Davy Crockett." And without it, probably, if literary analogies have any significance, "The Great Divide" might have been other than it is. It has the attempted ruggedness of early backwoods American drama.

[1] A letter from Mr. Hackett states his intention of having a systematic search made among his father's effects for the original dramatization of "Horseshoe Robinson." His recollection is that Dance was the author.

Ireland gives the following cast of characters for the first performance of "Horseshoe Robinson", the New York National Theatre, November 23, 1836:

Galbraith	Mr. Hackett.
Philip Lindsay	Mr. Stevenson.
Arthur Butler	Mr. C. Thorne.
Hugh Habershaw	Mr. W. Johnson.
Dame Crosby	Mrs. Stevenson.
Mrs. Adair	Mrs. C. Thorne.
Mary Musgrove	Mrs. Flynn.
Mildred Lindsay	Miss C. Woodhull.

The cast for the New York Park Theatre, March 16, 1841, was as follows:

Galbraith Robinson	Mr. Hackett.
Philip Lindsay	Mr. Gann.
Henry Lindsay	Mr. C. W. Clarke.
Capt. St. Jermyn	Mr. A. Andrews.
Ensign St. Jermyn	Mrs. C. Pritchard.
Arthur Butler	Mr. Hield
Sergt. Curry	Mr. Nickinson.
Wat Adair	Mr. W. A. Chapman.
Hugh Habershaw	Mr. Chippendale.
Mike Lynch	Mr. Fisher.
Mildred Lindsay	Mrs. Chippendale.
Mary Musgrove	Miss McBride.
Dame Crosby	Mrs. Wheatley.
Mrs. Adair	Mrs. Barry Wheatley.

The cast as given at the Holiday Street Theatre, Baltimore, May, 1856, was as follows:

Horseshoe Robinson	Mr. Wm. Ellis.
Major Arthur Butler	Mr. G. C. Boniface.
Henry Lindsay	Mr. J. Albaugh.
Col. James Williams	Mr. W. H. Briggs.
Mr. Lindsay	Mr. J. H. Jack.

Allen Musgrove ....Mr. J. Drake.
Chris Shaw ....Mr. H. S. Chapman.
Steve Foster ....Mr. I. B. Phillips.
Wat Adair ....Mr. W. H. Bokee.
Hugh Habershaw...................Mr. Joseph Parker.
Col. St. Jermyn...................Mr. J. W. Wallace.
Edgar St. Jermyn..................Mr. A. F. Blake.
Captain Du Poistre................Mr. B. Clarke.
James Curry ....Mr. H. A. Langdon.

Mildred Lindsay ....Mrs. I. B. Phillips.
Mary Musgrove ....Miss V. Kemble.
Mrs. Adair ....Mrs. G. C. Boniface.
Mrs. Crosby ....Mrs. H. Muzzy.

Other interesting casts are given in the French Acting version.

COSTUMES.[1]

MAJOR BUTLER.—*First dress:* Gentleman's costume of that period—dark square-cut coat—waistcoat—buff knee-breeches—Hessian boots—round slouched hat, with white cockade—cloak. *Second dress:* Full continental costume.

ROBINSON.—Coarse gray coatee—dark linsey-woolsey trousers—shoes—broad-rimmed round slouched hat—red neckerchief, carelessly tied—deer-skin pouch, powder horn, and long rifle—brown wig, tied in long queue behind.

MR. LINDSAY.—Black square-cut suit of the period—powdered wig—shoes and buckles.

HENRY.—Green jacket and trousers—green cloth cap—laced shoes—black polished waist-belt.

CURRY.—English sergeant's uniform of the period.

TYRRELL.—English colonel's uniform—powdered wig.

ENSIGN ST. JERMYN.—English ensign's uniform—powdered wig.

ALLEN MUSGROVE.—Light square-cut suit—shoes and buckles.

---

[1] These costume descriptions are in the edition of "Horseshoe Robinson" published in *French's Standard Drama* (No. CCXIII).

CHRIS SHAW.—Light small clothes and slouched hat—miller's over-shirt.

ADAIR.—Coarse green hunting-shirt, open at collar—black leather waist-belt—moccasins—rude fur cap—long knife.

HABERSHAW.—Very stoutly padded, bald crown—meager red whiskers—greasy cocked hat, plentifully bedecked with feathers of all kinds—old square-cut brown coat—threadbare epaulets—buckskin waist-belt and brass buckle—long rusty sabre and knife—dark breeches—long black boots.

COL. WILLIAMS.—Hunting-shirt, with fringe—leggings—slouched hat, with buck-tail.

COL. CAMPBELL.—Ibid.

AMERICAN SOLDIERS.—The same, varying in color.

MILDRED LINDSAY.—Neat tuck-up. *Second dress:* Riding habit.

MARY MUSGROVE.—Plain tuck-up and flat.

MRS. ADAIR.—Coarse homespun dress.

MRS. CROSBY—Ibid.

HORSESHOE ROBINSON.

ACT I.

SCENE I.—*Picturesque Valley in Virginia, through which the Rock-fish River passes. Beyond the river, lofty verdure-covered hills.*

ROBINSON. [*Speaking outside.*] You devil, Capen Peter Lynch! what are you 'bout? You obstropolous beast!

Enter MAJOR BUTLER *and* ROBINSON.

BUTLER. Well, here we are at last, Horseshoe, and, to my thinking, the lower road would have been better, even with its increased chances of meeting a few rascally Tories.

ROBINSON. Whist! Major Butler; I'm an older, and, consequently, wiser man than you, The road which we have just come up swarms with Tories, whom I have outflanked by coming through the hills, and probably saved ourselves from tumbling into a hornet's nest. It's an observation I've made, Major, that the best way to get along through the world is, not to be quarrelsome.

BUTLER. There's an observation of my own, Sergeant, I'd like to mention—'tis one, too, upon which all philosophers agree—and that is: a man must rest when he is tired, and eat when he is hungry; now, as my appetite has been somewhat sharpened by my long journey, I'll make bold to inquire what provender your wallet contains?

ROBINSON. [*Kneeling and examining wallet.*] Here's the rear division of a roast pig, flanked by two *biled* chickens, a blood puddin', four johnny cakes, two slices of *briled* ham; besides these, I can throw in half-a-dozen apple-jacks, three corn cakes, and——

BUTLER. [*Interrupting.*] Mercy on us, Galbraith! your wallet appears as inexhaustible as a conjuror's bag.

ROBINSON. [*Producing flask.*] Here's an egg from the

same nest. A bottle of what Corporal Robson calls "exhilarating peach-brandy." [*Offers it.*] Try some, Major.

BUTLER. Not any, thank you, Sergeant.

ROBINSON. Well, excuse me, Major, whilst I wash down the gutter arter camp fashion. [*Wipes flask with cuff of coat, cleanses his mouth of tobacco, and drinks.*] Mayhap, Major, afore we proceed further, you'll tell me what game you're arter in this neighborhood?

[*Replaces articles in wallet, leaving it near.*

BUTLER. Suppose I say, Sergeant, there's a bird nestles in these woods I'm fond of hearing sing.

ROBINSON. [*Laughingly.*] Oh ho! Whether in peace or in war, these wimmen critters keep the upper hand of us. But come, Major, let's fall to and eat. [*Two reports of muskets fired in rapid succession, heard. Both start, seize arms, and place themselves in posture of defense. Looking off.*] Ah! thar's game afoot, and if that shot hasn't taken effect, it may be my turn next. Ah! yonder he goes—a monstrous fine buck. He's hit!

Enter HENRY LINDSAY *and* STEVE FOSTER, *armed with rifles.*

STEVE. It's no use talkin', Mass Harry—dat was my shot.

HENRY. I say 'twas *my* shot, Steve, that dropped him. [*Surprised, seeing* BUTLER.] Ah! strangers!

BUTLER. Henry Lindsay as I live! this is indeed fortunate.

HENRY. [*Eagerly advancing and grasping his hand.*] What!—Captain Arthur Butler——

ROBINSON. *Major* Butler, if it's all the same to you, young sir. The Captain's been promoted by the wiping out of a few friends at Fort Moultrie.

BUTLER. I need scarcely ask you, Harry—for that smiling face assures me all *is* well at the Dove Cote—but Mildred, my dear lad—is she well and happy?—Has she received my letter?

HENRY. Stay, Captain—Major I meant—one question at a time. Mildred is as well as any girl can be who has a bushel of crosses to keep her out of spirits. For your second question—she got your letter about a week ago, and has had me patrolling the ridges every day since, to keep a look-out for you. Your arrival will soon put her in good spirits.

BUTLER. I would to heaven we had all cause to be of

better cheer. But the gloom of disaster has fallen upon our cause, leaving us scarce a glimmer of hope.

HENRY. The clouds will soon disperse, Major. You know, I presume, that General Gates has passed South, and a great battle is expected shortly. They're all mustering in our neighborhood—we've already raised a corps of mounted riflemen, of which I am appointed deputy-corporal. Steve Foster here is my body-guard.

STEVE. [*Bowing.*] Just so, Mass Harry, I'm your body-black-guard! Ha! ha! ha!

BUTLER. I crave your pardon, brother officer—does so bitter a royalist as your father permit his son to ride in the ranks of the friends of liberty?

HENRY. Oh! sister Mildred persuaded him that, as I was a mere lad, there was no harm in my playing the soldier; but I'm tired of this boy-play. I go for the rebel cause heart and soul—give me sharp steel—throw me upon the world— and I'll be sworn to make my way better than many who have more years to boast of!

ROBINSON. Well spoken! 'Tis just so I love to hear an American lad talk!

BUTLER. This is a famous soldier, Harry—Horseshoe Robinson—he can tell you more of wars than you have ever read; and so accustomed is he to hard knocks, that I question whether a musket-ball could penetrate his tough hide.

STEVE. [*Aside.*] What a rhinocererhoss!

HENRY. I am really delighted to know you, Sergeant.

[ROBINSON *bows—goes up and beckons* STEVE—*presents him flask—they drink.*

BUTLER. When, and where, can I see Mildred?

HENRY. It will be best for me to get her out on pretense of a stroll, and you can hold your interview here.

BUTLER. I trust to your discretion, Harry; only delay as little as possible; my stay in this neighborhood must be short —I should even now be on my way South.

HENRY. I understand, my valiant Major, and will be with you in brief time. [*Blows signal on bugle.*] That's my signal to "prepare to receive commanding officer." Milly will know it refers to you. Come, Steve. [*They exeunt.*

BUTLER. Galbraith, I know your honesty, and would trust you with my life. In case of aught befalling me, 'tis neces-

sary you should know something of my plans and purposes—
you will keep my counsel?

ROBINSON. As I would the heart in my body, Major!

BUTLER. The letter you delivered me was from Colonel
Pinckney, apprising me of things in the upper country.
Clarke there meditates an attempt to regain Augusta and
Ninety-Six; and we have reason to believe that some levies
will be made by our confederates in Virginia and elsewhere.
My business is to co-operate in the undertaking. 'Tis essential, therefore, I should have the guidance of some true and
trusty man, acquainted with the country. These red coats,
you know, hold possession of all our strongholds, and Tories
swarm like the locusts of Egypt. The Colonel has selected
you—and a better man I am confident he could not have
picked out. Besides, Galbraith, old acquaintance has bred
an affection between us.

ROBINSON. I'm a man that can eat my allowance, Major,
and you're not likely to suffer, if a word or blow of mine
would do you any good.

BUTLER. So much for duty; and if you'll not deem it more
irksome to stand by a comrade in love than in war, you can
materially aid me!

ROBINSON. The war part of it, Major, comes naturally
enough to my hand; but for the love part—exceptin' so far
as carryin' a message, or in case of a runaway, keeping off
a gang of pestiferous intermeddlers—my sarvices won't be
of much account.

BUTLER. Mr. Lindsay's daughter is an especial friend to
me, and to our cause. There are reasons which forbid my
entering the house, and she will meet me here:—it concerns
me deeply that this meeting should be kept free from inter-
lopers and——

ROBINSON. I understand you, Major; and if anybody
should pop in while you're talking, I'll do my best to entertain 'em till you're disengaged. [*Bugle heard.*] Yonder
comes the young Corporal with her you were talkin' of.

Enter HENRY *and* MILDRED LINDSAY.—*She rushes into* BUT-
LER'S *embrace.*

ROBINSON. [*Beckoning* HENRY *up.*] Excuse me, Mister
—two is company.   [*Pulls him out.*

BUTLER. Dear Mildred! There is, in the unknown time to

come, no suffering I would not hold a cheap purchase, for one moment like this!

MILDRED. Ah! Arthur, what have I not suffered at the thought of the dangers which beset your path! I cannot say how joyfully I received the intelligence of your escape from the fatal siege of Charleston!

BUTLER. Many—alas! too many—of our country's bravest defenders fell there, to rise no more. I was sent, the bearer of dispatches to Congress, previous to the surrender, and so was spared the mortification of being a prisoner beneath England's yoke.

MILDRED. Oh! that peace would end this unhappy strife!

BUTLER. We have put our hands to the ploughshare, and will not now turn or look back till the cause of freedom and of right shall have gloriously triumphed!

MILDRED. Think not I seek to dissuade you from the path your duty and your conscience have adopted. No! I praised your first resolve to join the patriot army, loved you for it, and I would not, for the sake of my weak womanish fears, say one word to withhold your arm!

BUTLER. My loved enthusiast! you inspire my soul with fresh ardor and zeal.

MILDRED. Could this feeble arm avail, its strength should be bestowed upon that cause you have made mine, and which even now, I learn, trembles upon the verge of ruin, despite the exertions and sacrifices of Washington—that Washington who loves his country and her soldiers as a bride loves her husband, or a father his children!

BUTLER. The longest troubles have an end; there are bold hearts and stout arms yet to spare for this quarrel, and the present enterprise, in which I am engaged, may strip these invaders of their power.

Enter HENRY.—HORSESHOE *restraining him.*

HENRY. [*Coming forward.*] I can't help it, Sergeant: I must interrupt them. Major, you and Milly have been talking long enough to settle the plan of a campaign. Her absence may excite surmise and I shouldn't be surprised if Tyrrell, or his lurking spy, Curry, should come tracking us.

BUTLER. Who is Tyrrell? [2]

[2] It will be noted that the character of Tyrrell is not recorded in any of the Casts given. He is accounted for in the costume indications. The plot reveals that he is Col. St. Jermyn.

MILDRED. One whom I could almost wish had been in his grave ere he saw my father! He goes further than you would believe in his efforts to entrap my father into an active support of the royal cause.

BUTLER. Dear girl! and you must be left alone to battle against his pernicious wiles and art.

HENRY. Leave me to protect her, Major. I've *my* eye upon him, and when Milly gives the signal, down comes the game.

CURRY *appears.—Crosses behind.*

MILDRED. Since you needs must go, Arthur, may the God of right bless and protect you! You'll leave behind you an aching heart, that, morning, noon and night, will weary heaven with prayers for your safety.

BUTLER. Sergeant, will you prepare our horses? [ROBIN-SON *exits.*] Dear Mildred, I will accompany you a few steps upon the road; perhaps fortune may favour me with a glimpse of this Tyrrell or his myrmidon.

[*Exeunt* BUTLER, HENRY *and* MILDRED.

CURRY. [*Coming forward.*] Say you so, my rebel bird? This, then, is Major Arthur Butler. 'Twill be rare and de-lightful news for Colonel St. Jermyn; a short cut through the woods will enable me to reach the mansion in a few minutes, and apprise the Colonel of this bit of luck, sent him by the devil, no doubt. [*Is moving off.—Comes in collision with* ROBINSON, *who then enters.*] What do you mean, Mr. Bump-kin?

ROBINSON. [*Sternly eyeing him.*] Whar *mought* you be from?

CURRY. What *mought* be your right to know?

ROBINSON. It's the custom in my country—whatever else it mought be in yours—to despise all sorts of contwistifications and spyin' tricks.

CURRY. I don't understand your lingo, Mr. Clown—it's neither sense, English, nor grammar.

ROBINSON. You're a damned onmannerly scoundrel! do you understand *that?* That's sense, English and grammar—all three.

CURRY. [*Threateningly.*] Lubberly booby! know you to whom you are speaking?

ROBINSON. [*Significantly.*] Better than you think for.

CURRY. I'm a free born subject of King George, and may teach you that, because a portion of his people have turned *rebels,* I'll not be questioned by every inquisitive idler I may meet.

ROBINSON. Now, look-a-here, you cringing whelp of an Englisher! it doesn't suit such sixpenny-a-day fellers as you, who march right and left, at the bidding of your master, to rob a church, or to root up a peaceful man's hearth-stone, and without daring to have so much as a thought about the righteousness of the matter—it doesn't suit such slavish curs, I say, to be nicknaming them as fight for home, for church, and for liberty. So mend your speech, or I mought handle you rather more roughly than your mammy would! [*Crossing to right.*]

CURRY. Say you so, bully? Take that! [*He strikes at* ROBINSON, *who suddenly turns and grasps* CURRY *by the throat.*] Confound the fellow! He has a grip like a vice! Who the devil are you?

ROBINSON. Yes, that's it. My name's Brimstone. I'm fust cousin to Beelzebub. I know *you,* Jeems Curry—you're a double-faced, savage-hearted beast, that gnashes his teeth when he darsn't bite. [*Releasing him.*] Oh! don't scowl, man, or I'll alter your complexion in quicker time than you would bob your head at the sight of one of your royal masters.

CURRY. [*Going right.*] You shall pay dearly for your advantage.

ROBINSON. If I do, it will be in the same coin I've just given you. But I ain't afeerd on ye. I've made an observation, that foul-mouthed blood-thirsty boasters like you are always beastly cowards! [*Crosses to his wallet, and busies himself replacing articles in it.*

CURRY. [*Apart.*] Man or imp, he knows me, and shall pay dear for his knowledge. [*Drawing pistol, fires at* ROBINSON, *who darts upon* CURRY, *and dashes him to the earth, as he draws and levels a second pistol.*

ROBINSON. [*Putting his foot upon him.*] No, no! Jeems Curry, you twistin' prevaricationer! lie there, where every mother's son of ye English wolves ought to be—under an American freeman's foot! Lie there, you pestiferous piece of pestilence! and know, that if I don't blow your brains out, 'tis because I wouldn't accommodate the devil by throwing into his clutches such a lump of putrefaction!

[CURRY *rises*—ROBINSON *takes up* CURRY's *pistols—examines flints—and ostentatiously, though not to* CURRY, *pours contents of his flask over priming.*]

CURRY. [*Crosses right.*] With your heart's blood you shall wash out this indignity!

ROBINSON. Stop, Jeems Curry! take your shootin' irons— they're marked G. R., which, I hearn tell, are the initials of your master's name— and there's many an Englishman I know that would take anything marked G. R. with thanks, even if it were a cat-o'-nine-tails. [*Throws pistols to* CURRY, *who secures them.*] Take 'em, for, cuss me if I'd honour 'em with a place in an American pocket. [CURRY *exits.— Returns instantly.*—ROBINSON *bends over wallet, watching, from under his arm, with ready cocked rifle, the manœuvres of* CURRY—*the latter levels and snaps his pistol at* ROBINSON, *who immediately retorts with a rifle-shot.*] Ah! would you!

[CURRY *darts off with an exclamation*—BUTLER *rushes in with drawn sword*—ROBINSON *laughing—Picture— Scene closes.*

SCENE II.—*Chamber at* MR. LINDSAY's *Mansion—Enter* LINDSAY *and* TYRRELL—*the latter in plain clothes.*

LINDSAY. Nay, Mr. Tyrrell, Sir Henry Clinton overrates my influence amongst the gentry of this province.

TYRRELL. I could scarcely expect you to speak otherwise than you do, but I who have the opportunity to know, take it upon myself to say, that many gentlemen of note in this province look with anxiety to you. They repose faith in your discretion, and would implicitly follow your lead.

LINDSAY. 'Tis a thorny path you would have me tread. Am I not girded about by the hot champions of independence, and your mission here, were it but known, might cost us both our lives.

TYRRELL. And can you tamely bow to this oppression, when one act of yours may confer success on that cause with which the prosperity of this country is indissolubly united. One battle may decide, and any estate, belonging to the rebels, you may desire of Lord Cornwallis, shall be the guerdon of your sacrifice.

LINDSAY. [*Smiling.*] Cornwallis, remember, has yet to win the ground he occupies.

TYRRELL. And think you that the starved and ragged squads now creeping through the pines of Carolina, under command of that braggart Gates—or that the skulking cowards led by Marion, Sumter and Pickens—are the men to dispute with his majesty's forces the right to any inch of soil they may choose to occupy?

LINDSAY. By my honour! they *have* disputed, and successfully, too, the right you claim!

TYRRELL. 'Tis for you now to decide upon the single question, whether you will unite yourself actively with our cause, or desert your monarch in his need.

LINDSAY. You present the alternatives most harshly, sir. I have yet to learn how my single arm could ensure success to my monarch's now prospering cause; while I have many and powerful motives for keeping aloof from this struggle— my family—my daughter——

TYRRELL. Could you not remove her to Charleston?— there she would be safe among friends, and leave you free to act.

LINDSAY. You speak of Mildred as if her thought and will lay at my disposal—you do not know her; I have long striven in vain to subdue an attachment that has bound her to our worst enemy——

TYRRELL. The rebel Butler? Soon will I force him to yield his hopeless aim; measures are now being taken, at my instance, to confiscate his lands in Carolina, and transfer their possession to myself. He will then—and that soon—be penniless.

LINDSAY. 'Twill win you no favour with Mildred to tell her that.

TYRRELL. Have you broached to her the subject of my ardent passion for her?

LINDSAY. I have not; but from my knowledge of the love she bears this Butler, and which has grown to be her faith— her honour—her religion—I feel she will never be yours.

TYRRELL. [*Enraged.*] What an infatuation! by heaven! Prefer an outlawed and doomed rebel to one of my position!

proud and wayward girl! her traitorous lover shall swing within sight of her window, and she shall be taught to feel——

LINDSAY. [*Haughtily.*] Remember yourself, sir. This is neither the tone nor language to use in speaking of my daughter. [*Crossing right.*] When your strange and unnecessary excitement shall have subsided into a sense of proper respect, I may then, sir, listen further to you.

[*Bows haughtily and exits.*

TYRRELL. Stay, Mr. Lindsay—sir—fool that I was, thus to yield to an angry impulse. Yet, insolent girl! her contempt, so insolently expressed, might excite to madness colder blood than courses through my veins.

Enter CURRY.

How now, Curry—what has occurred?

CURRY. I have just seen Major Butler.

TYRRELL. Ah! Butler in this neighborhood—**where?**

CURRY. Not one mile from this spot, sir.

TYRRELL. [*Exultingly.*] It does appear as if the very Fates had leagued to defeat those rebels, in love as in war. He must be secured. Butler once in my power, I may dictate terms to my haughty beauty. Whither does he journey?

CURRY. To join Clarke at Ninety-Six.

TYRRELL. Ha! on his route to Ninety-Six! Then he must pass Wat Adair's cabin. [*Crosses.*] Follow me as rapidly as you can to Wat Adair's, and, hark ye, scoundrel! no loitering. [*Exit.*

CURRY. Peremptory scoundrel! Curses on the mischance which has placed me subject to the beck and nod of every epauletted fool!

Enter STEVE.

Well, Blacky, what do you want?

STEVE. Well, sir, I has several wants; my most urgent one, at dis present period of time, is my supper. Say, boss, is you near-sighted?

CURRY. Near-sighted! you black idiot, what do you mean?

STEVE. Nothin', sir—only dat massa told me to show you

de door, and less you are d'yam blind, you ought to be able to see um without my pinting um out.

Curry. [*Incensed.*] Insolent slave——

Steve. Look yer, soldier man, don't come yer to 'buse me; I'm a native American nigger; but it am suxceptible of de strongest kind of proof dat I ain't no more a slave than you chaps, wot's got to do just as your ossifers tell you. If I disobeys massa, he larrups me—if you disobey your ossifer— dat's *your* massa—he shoots you. I think I'se a d'yam sight de best off of de two.

Curry. Ha! ha! ha! Well, this impudence pleases me!

Steve. Ha! ha! ha! it pleases me, too.

Curry. There must be some rebel spirit in this house; you and your traitorous instructor shall be taught to know King George——

Steve. Know King George!—why, I does know him! Dat is, I has a sort of general acquaintance wid him: we boff patronize de same shop.

Curry. Indeed! And what shop is it so favoured with your patronage?

Steve. De perfume shop [*Produces a cologne bottle.*] Dar 'tis—my Cologne bottle—dar 'tis, printed in de plainest kind of print—"Toady Tufkins, Perfumer to his Majesty, George the Third." I mean to gib him special permission to add, "Perfumer also to Steve Foster, of Ole Wirginny."

Curry. [*Violently.*] Dog!

Steve. Don't you do it! Dar's de door—put yourself on toder side of it, or I'll call massa.

Curry. On my return, scoundrel, I'll see if a thrashing won't improve your bearing.   [*Exit.*

Steve. Ha! ha! ha! I'm afraid dat Englisher don't feel well.   [*Exit laughingly. Slow music at change.*

SCENE III.—*Interior of* WAT ADAIR'S *Log Cabin—furs hanging against wall—loaded gun leaning against flat near window.*

MARY MUSGROVE *discovered at spinning-wheel—*MRS. ADAIR *at wash-tub—*MRS. CROSBY *crouching before fireplace, smoking pipe, and swaying to and fro—*TYRRELL *and* ADAIR *seated at table.*

TYRRELL. [*As if continuing conversation.*] He must pass the ford; then remember my instructions.

[*They come forward.*

ADAIR. I'll not forget 'em. Mike is on the lookout now, and Curry has gone forward to warn Hugh. I'll take good keer they shall travel the path to the ford; and the devil help 'em once Hugh Habershaw's cut-throats lays paws on 'em.

TYRRELL. [*Giving purse to* WAT.] Take this gold for the present. [ADAIR *pockets it exultingly.*

MRS. CROSBY. Gold—gold—gold! It's a sweet sound, though they do say devils swim in melted gold. Ha! ha! ha!

ADAIR. Silence! you cursed old hag, or I'll squeeze your wizen for you!

MRS. CROSBY. [*Muttering.*] Gold—gold——

ADAIR. Do you want 'em killed?—or have you forgotten how a rebel looks when he's swinging, and wants a private exhibition of your own?

TYRRELL. A deeper feeling than any which curiosity prompts, now actuates me. The officer I must have alive— the other can be shot—I care not. [*Whistle heard.*

ADAIR. That's Mike. They're coming! follow me—I'll guide you to your horse. Wife, if I'm axed for, say I'll be back soon, and don't be too darned perlite, as you usually ain't. [*Exit with* TYRRELL.

MRS. ADAIR. Oh! git out, you old fool!

MARY. [*Coming forward.*] Oh! what a dreadful plot I've overheard! Whoever the victims are, once in the power of these dreadful men, their chance of life is weak, indeed. Who would have thought Uncle Adair such a cold-blooded and cruel man! [*Loud knocking at door.*

MRS. ADAIR. Who's that making such a racket at a peaceable house?

ROBINSON. [*Outside.*] We want a night's lodging, and must have it. We've capital appetites—could eat a nigger baby with the small-pox.

MRS. ADAIR. [*Opening window and levelling gun.*] Oh! you are hungry, are you? How would you like a bit of cold lead?

ROBINSON. [*Appearing at window.*] Well, I'm not over partial to it. But there's no necessity for your gun, Mrs.

Adair. We're friends of Wat, and he'll be right glad to see us.

MRS. ADAIR. [*Opening door.*] Oh, if you're friends of Watty, that alters the case; but people put on so many pretenses now-a-days, there's no telling who's who.

Enter ROBINSON *and* BUTLER, *closely enveloped in cloaks.*

BUTLER. Pardon our intrusion, Madam; we were recommended to Mr. Adair, as a friend to whom I could speak without suspicion.

MRS. ADAIR. Wat Adair's a fool, who's never satisfied unless he has other people thrusting their spoons into his mess.

ROBINSON. Wat Adair's a wiser man than his wife, and takes care no man thrusts a spoon into his mess without paying for it.

MRS. ADAIR. And who are you, to talk of Wat Adair? I warrant, you come on no honest business—you and your tramping friend. It is such as you, and your drinking, rioting, broadsword cronies that have given us all our troubles.

ROBINSON. Hello! not so fast; why, you're as spiteful as a hen with a fresh brood; if I was a thief, instead of Wat's friend, Horseshoe Robinson, you couldn't treat me worse.

[MRS. CROSBY *starts up and comes forward.*

MRS. CROSBY. Hey-day! hey-day! who's a-talking of Horseshoe Robinson? Is this Horseshoe? Come yer, my good man, and let me look at ye! come closer, 'cause my old eyes is weak and watery! 'Tis Horseshoe, as I'm a sinner! all the way from Waxhaws. Who'd o' thought to find you here, among Tories, such a racketing Whig as you!—hey-day!

ROBINSON. [*Playfully.*] Whist! Granny, don't call names!—it's onpolite. [*Leans his rifle against wall.*

MRS. CROSBY. We're all Tories here now, sence that han'-some English officer was here to see Watty, and count his gold out like pebblestones. Ha! ha! ha!

MRS. ADAIR. [*Crossing to right of* MRS. CROSBY.] Shut up, or I'll shake the breath out of you!

MRS. CROSBY. Well-a-day! I see how it is. That's the

way of the world. Old granny's a dried-up tree, and doesn't look well among the flowers of the family. The old granny's room is more wanted than her company. She ought to be nailed up in her coffin, and put under ground! [*Weeping.*

MRS. ADAIR. Well, what did you say Watty seed an English officer for?

MRS. CROSBY. Golden guineas Watty got—all gold—and a proud clinking they made in Watty's home-spun pockets. Watty's nose cocked up so high, too—like a proud gander!— ha! ha! ha!—both his pockets full, too. Here, Meg, come wipe my eyes.

MRS. ADAIR. [*Dragging her towards right.*] Here, come to bed!

MRS. CROSBY. Oh! I'm gettin' old now. Granny hasn't got both pockets filled with gold, as Watty has—ha! ha! ha! Here, Meg, fill my pipe. Gold—gold!—yes, yes! Granny ain't no han'some English officer!

[MRS. ADAIR *jerks her violently out.*

BUTLER. [*Apart to* ROBINSON.] I have a strange misgiving of Adair's honesty.

ROBINSON. Wat daresn't play us a trick; he knows I'd shake the life out of his carcase if he'd turn traitor. Still, there ain't no trustin' anything in this duberous country: so as Wat doesn't know you, we'll keep your name and business a secret. The old woman's talk 'bout the English officer smacked mightily of the truth. I think we'd better push straight forrad, and not trouble Wat to accommodate us to-night.   [MARY *advances.*

BUTLER. [*Accosting* MARY.] Are you a daughter of Wat Adair, my pretty lass?

MARY. [*Curtseying.*] Oh! no, sir. My name is Mary Musgrove;—I'm the daughter of Allen Musgrove, whose mill is on the Ennoree River, a few miles from here.

[ROBINSON *goes up stage.*

BUTLER. Then, you are the miller's pretty daughter, for that's what you are called, I'll wager.

MARY. The men sometimes call me so, sir; but the women call me plain Mary Musgrove.

BUTLER. Faith, my dear, the men come nearer the truth than the women.

MARY. They say not, sir—I've read in good books—at

least, they called 'em good—that you mustn't believe what the men say.

BUTLER. Indeed! And why not?

MARY. I don't know, sir. But I'm young yet, and may learn.

BUTLER. Nay, heaven forbid you should ever learn by experience.

MARY. I'm seventeen, sir; and though I have traveled backwards and forwards from here to Ennorree, and once to Camden, which, you know, sir, is a good deal of the world to see—I never knew anybody that thought hard of me: though I don't dispute there are men to be afraid of, and some that nobody could like, yet, I'm sure, sir, a good man could be told by his face.

BUTLER. Do you think so?

MARY. Yes, sir, father says so, too. My father would be glad to know you, sir.

BUTLER. Now, my pretty miller's daughter, why do you think so?

MARY. Because you are a gentleman, sir.

BUTLER. How know you that?

MARY. You talk differently from our people, and I saw just now a beautiful gold picture hanging to that ribbon around your neck.

BUTLER. [*Apart.*] Mildred's portrait! For heaven's sake, keep that to yourself, child!

MARY. [*Aside.*] These must be the people they are going to murder. Oh! if I could but warn him. [*To* BUTLER.] Father tells me, sir, to pray for General Washington and his soldiers, and—and—I'm sorry you've come here.

[ROBINSON *advances.*

BUTLER. Indeed, Mary; and why?

MARY. [*Whispering.*] Because I've just found out Uncle Wat Adair's a bad man—harm is meant you—leave here, and take the *left* hand road to the ford.

MRS. ADAIR *re-enters.*

MRS. ADAIR. Wat's a-comin'! [*Opens door.*

Enter WAT ADAIR.

WAT. [*Advancing and slapping* ROBINSON *familiarly on the shoulder.*] Why, Galbraith, my man, have you been running from the red coats, or hunting up Tories, eh? 'Twas only to-day I said I should mightily like to see Horseshoe Robinson—ho! ho! ho!

ROBINSON. You were ashamed of your own company, Wat, and wanted to see a decent man once more—ho! ho! ho!

BUTLER. Mr. Adair, I'm desirous of getting into Georgia by the nearest route, and that least frequented. We've been directed to you, and if you'll undertake our guidance, I will pay you liberally.

ADAIR. You ain't a-goin' on to-night!

ROBINSON. Well, we didn't intend to go at fust, but, putting our heads together, my friend here, and I, think 'tis best.

[WAT *whispers to his wife, who comes down.—She goes up, and is seen emptying priming from* ROBINSON'S *gun.*

WAT. [*To* MAJOR.] Why, do you see, Major Butler——
[ROBINSON *and* MAJOR *start.*

ROBINSON. [*Surprised.*] Eh?—what's that?—who said he was Major Butler?

ADAIR. [*Confused.*] Did I say Major?

ROBINSON. Most ondoubtedly you did.

ADAIR. I must have dreamed it—or didn't you speak about him yourself, Horseshoe?

ROBINSON. Most certainly not.

ADAIR. Then I dreamed it!—well, Horseshoe, the path is quite easy. Go straight forrad till you come to the fork; there take the *right-hand* road; about two miles further you'll come to another prong;—there strike the *right-hand* road, which leads you to the ford. [*Confidentially to* ROBINSON, *leaning familiarly on his shoulder.*] What are you arter in Georgy, Horseshoe?

ROBINSON. [*Imitating his manner.*] There are two kinds of men in this world, Wat—them as axes questions, and them as won't answer questions. I leave you to decide which class I b'long to. [*They go up stage, as if to depart.*

ADAIR. Well, good-bye—luck attend you.

MARY. [*Whispering to* BUTLER *as he passes.*] The *left-hand* road to the ford—remember!

ADAIR. [*Detecting her.*] Whispering, are you? Treacherous minx—I'll sarve you out! [*Rushes across and seizes* *her by right arm.—*Butler *casts aside cloak, and hurls* Adair *round.*]

Butler. Harm that girl, coward as you are, and traitor as I suspect you to be, and I'll put a bullet through your brain!

Adair. Oh! you will, eh?

[*Seizes rifle leaning against wall, and levels at* Butler—Mary *strikes up piece as it is discharged—*Major *levels his pistol, and* Robinson *his rifle, at* Adair—*They both miss fire—*Robinson *clubs rifle and fells* Adair—Mrs. Adair *interposing, shields her husband—*Mary *at door, as if in the act of making her egress—*Robinson *with upraised gun—Tableau.*

Scene IV.—*Front Wood.*

Enter Robinson *and* Butler.

Robinson. The cantankerous, double-faced scoundrel! he may thank his lucky star that my rifle so unaccountably missed fire, or by this time he'd be holding a confidential chat with his particular friend, "Old Nick."

Butler. My pretty miller's daughter fled in this direction. I fear she may, through fright, be lost in the woods.

Robinson. Oh, never fear for her. She'll find her way home as safe and snug as a cat. When next I meet with that Wat Adair, I'll argufy with him in a manner not pleasant to his feelings. Thar's danger about, Major.

Butler. If the worst comes to the worst, we can run or fight.

Robinson. [*Priming afresh.*] We can manage either nicely, for we've had a good deal of both to do lately. At present, a quick eye, nimble foot, and steady hand are our truest friends. [*Exeunt.*

Scene V.—*Grindall's Ford on Pacolet River—Cut wood in fourth groove—Large set tree, at foot of which a camp-fire burns—Rifles leaning against trees.*

Twelve Soldiers *discovered, in various outré costumes, reclining before camp-fires—*Hugh Habershaw *and* Curry *playing cards.*

HABERSHAW. [*Dashing cards in fire.*] Damn the luck! There's an end of Backbiter, the best horse betwixt the Pedee and the Savannah. You've luck enough to worry the nine lives out of a cat.

CURRY. [*Coming forward.*] The luck was against you, valiant Captain Hugh Habershaw.

HABERSHAW. [*Blustering.*] Harkee! You imp of Satan, you've the luck of winning, and I suspect you're a light-fingered Jack. Do you hear that, Master Peppercorn?

CURRY. How now, bully; are you turning boy in your old age, that you must fall to whining because you've lost a turn at play? Come, my noble Captain, there's no time for us to be quarrelling—we've other business cut out; and as to Back-biter—the rat-tailed, spavined bone-setter—curse me if I'd have him as a gift! He isn't worth the cards that won him— eh, boys? [*Men all laugh.*

HABERSHAW. Silence! you tailors' bastards. [*To* CURRY.] Would you breed a mutiny in the camp?—look around you; do you expect me to preserve discipline among these wild wood-scourers, with your loud haw-haws to my very teeth? You make too free, Peppercorn—you make too free.

CURRY. I crave your pardon, noble Captain; I mistook the extent of your good nature. Ha! ha! ha!

HABERSHAW. When I'm at the head of my men, you must preserve discipline. But I let it pass this time; and, harkee, as you underrate Backbiter, I'll hold you to your word as a gentleman, and take him back; now, there's an end of it, and let's have no more talking.

CURRY. Ha! ha! ha! right, my noble Captain! I'll uphold the discipline of valiant Captain Hugh Habershaw against all babblers the world over. By the god of war, I wonder you haven't had a commission from his Majesty!

HABERSHAW. [*Importantly.*] The time *will* come, Pepper-corn, when I'll teach 'em all the elements of military tactics.

CURRY. Hurrah for Captain Tiger of Habershaw—I mean Captain Habershaw of Tiger. [SOLDIERS *hurrah.*

HABERSHAW. Peace, you rapscallions! Stop your bellowing! Is this your discipline—when you should be as silent as cats in a kitchen?

CURRY. Oughtn't our friends to be near at hand?

HABERSHAW. I've sent Black Jack on the road; he'll bring

us news of their coming fast enough. But it's allers well to be in time, so, Master Orderly, call the roll.

CURRY. Ready—always ready when you command. Shall I call the ragamuffins by their nicknames, or will you have 'em handled like Christians?

HABERSHAW. On secret service allers stick to the nick-names.

CURRY. As when they go house-burning, throat-cutting, horse-stealing——

HABERSHAW. Order, sir—no ondecencies.

CURRY. Attention! you devils' babes—horse and gun, every mother's imp of you!

[*Men rise and range themselves in line.—As* CURRY *calls roll, each one answers "here," to his name.*
Pimple, Long Shanks, Black Jack——

HABERSHAW. On patrol.

CURRY. Platter-Breech, Marrow-Bone, Fire-Nose, Screech-Owl, Clapper-Claw, Bow-Legs, Red-Eye, Bullet-Head—they're all here, Captain—your entire valiant army—hello! I forgot one name!

HABERSHAW. Forgot a name, eh? who's that?

CURRY. [*Laughing.*] Why, Moon-face Bragger, captain of the squad.

HABERSHAW. [*Half drawing sword.*] Peppercorn, now may all the devils ride over me if I don't drive my sword through your heart, if you infringe on my discipline again.

Enter BLACK JACK, *hurriedly.*

BLACK JACK. [*To* HABERSHAW.] They're comin'!

HABERSHAW. Now scatter to your hiding-holes, you rascals, till I give the signal—then bang away. But look out for Horseshoe Robinson—he's a dog as bites without barking.

[*The entire party conceal themselves—*SOLDIERS *behind cut-wood.*

Enter ROBINSON *and* MAJOR.

BUTLER. We have lost the path.

ROBINSON. I thought I heard voices just now. Look to your pistols, Major, and prime afresh.

[HABERSHAW *darts forward and engages* BUTLER.

HABERSHAW. [*Through din.*] Cut down the rebels!
ROBINSON. Fight, Major. The Tories are upon us——
CURRY. [*Appearing.*] This from James Curry!

[*Fires at* ROBINSON, *who returns the fire ineffectually*—
MAJOR *disarms and cuts down* HABERSHAW—*About to
dispatch him, when he is seized by numbers of the
Tories.*

BUTLER. [*Through noise.*] We are outnumbered! Fly,
Horseshoe!—escape!

[*Simultaneously with* BUTLER'S *action,* ROBINSON
struggles briefly with CURRY, *and hurls him.* HABER-
SHAW *places himself, sword in hand, to intercept* ROB-
INSON'S *flight.*—*The latter, clubbing his rifle, fells him
to the earth, and escapes.*

HABERSHAW. [*In sitting posture.*] He escapes! Fire on
the rebel! [SOLDIERS *fire at* ROBINSON.

END OF ACT I.

ACT II.

SCENE I.—*Musgrove's Mill, on the Ennoree River, South
Carolina*—*Set house with upper window practicable*—*Set
tree above house, near enough to be reached from window
*—*Set mill and water-wheel*—*Set waters across stage*—
Soldiers' arms stacked. Stage half dark.

ENSIGN ST. JERMYN *and six English* SOLDIERS *discovered
bearing bags of meal from mill off*—ALLEN MUSGROVE *and
CHRIS SHAW *discontentedly watching proceedings.*

CHRIS. [*As if counting.*] Seven! [*To* ENSIGN.] Ain't
you got enough yet?
ENSIGN. [*To* MUSGROVE.] That is sufficient for our present purpose, Musgrove. These "orders on Lord Rawdon's
commissary," [*giving papers*] will secure your remuneration.
[*To* MEN.] See the wagon's quickly loaded; I perceive signs
of an approaching squall, and we have yet to stop at Ramsay's. Good-bye, Musgrove—your sacrifices in our cause
shall not be unremembered!

[Exit ENSIGN *and* SOLDIERS—CHRIS *follows them to "wing," threateningly.*

CHRIS. Oh! I would so like to give him a gentle crack under the chin; just here, where Adam's apple is. Nunkey, there's just so much labor and meal thrown away. You'll never git paid for it. The onhealthy, carnivorous beasts, with their everlastin' talk about "the cause." If Master Popinjay knew how little we cared about his unholy cause, mebbe, instead of hollow promises of reward, we wouldn't have a shelter for our heads to-night.

MUSGROVE. Heaven knows, Chris, I begrudge 'em the grain;—but there's no disputin' with these whiskered foot-pads, with bayonets in their hands.

CHRIS. Oh, ain't there, though? Do you see the mill-race there? Well, if I had my way, the first red-coat that came here to rob us of our labor, I'd sew him up in the strongest meal-bag I could find, and give him a dip that would deprive him of all appetite for meal forever afterwards.

[Stage three-quarters dark—Low thunder and lightning at intervals.

MUSGROVE. Bide your time, Chris, bide your time, lad. *[Distant thunder.]* But see, there's a storm gathering, and neither Mrs. Musgrove nor Mary are at home.

CHRIS. I wonder Mary can stay so long at that dirty old boar—Wat Adair's. The old Tory *pisens* everything he touches; even his cabbages stop growing when he looks at 'em. It's goin' to rain—Bull-frogs and sulphur! hadn't I better run over to Ramsay's, and escort aunty home?—mebbe some rascally red-coat, with a heart as sour as a barrel of vinegar, may insult her. I half wish they'd try it. I fairly hanker arter thrashing a red-coat or a Tory.

MUSGROVE. You speak truly, Chris. She may be insulted. Go for your aunt, and if Mary doesn't return by morning, you shall go and fetch her.

*Distant thunder—*MUSGROVE *exits into house—*CHRIS *goes off right—*ROBINSON, *travel-worn, enters, left.*

ROBINSON. Sakes alive! it's a smart run I've had, and many a narry escape from the ongodly Tories. But here I am, at last, whar I can once more see a friendly face. [*Knocks loudly at house.*] Allen Musgrove! Allen Musgrove! Come out, man!

MUSGROVE. [*Within.*] Who are you?—friend or foe?

ROBINSON. A very worthless friend to any man at the present speaking, and one not fit to be counted a foe, till he's had something to eat. If you're Allen Musgrove, come out, man. You'll find me as harmless as a barn-yard fowl.

MUSGROVE *re-enters*.

Allen Musgrove, give us your hand! I've hearn tell of you often;—you're obliged to keep fair weather with these Tories, but your heart is with the boys who fight for liberty! —mayhap you've hearn tell of one Horseshoe Robinson?

MUSGROVE. Frequently;—and as one worthy every true man's esteem!

ROBINSON. Well, I won't tell you he stands before you, lest you should git into hot water with the cursed Tories, for harbouring such a nev-to-do-well. But I will say, you see a man before you that's had a mighty tight race to git *yer*.

MUSGROVE. [*Grasping his hand.*] I understand, friend, and will aid and protect you at all hazards.

ROBINSON. An officer in the Continental army—Major Butler—and myself, were journeying to these parts, and have been ambuscaded by a half wild-cat, half bull-dog kind of chap called Hugh Habershaw!

MUSGROVE. Heaven have mercy on the man who falls into the power of Hugh Habershaw!

ROBINSON. Amen! for a surlier piece of flesh doesn't live in these woods, giving you the choice of *panter,* catamount, or rattlesnake. Well, Wat Adair was the chap as deluded us into this wild-cat's claws—though a tidy, spruce little pet, calling herself your daughter, gave us somehow or t'other a warning there was something wrong a-hatchin'. We followed her advice, but it didn't do.

MUSGROVE. Mercy on me! I trust my child has not been harmed!

ROBINSON. Well, I reckon not; but there's no tellin' sure, for when a kind of scrimmage, on her account, broke out atwixt Wat and ourselves, she scampered out inter the woods, and that's the last I've heard or seed of her. Mayhap, Allen, you kin give me some information of the doin's of these Englishers and Tories. How fur off is their nearest post?

MUSGROVE. Colonel St. Jermyn has a camp within two miles.

ROBINSON. Ha! ha! ha! That's a post Jim Williams, of South Car'liny, will soon be dipping his spoon inter.

MUSGROVE. You're now in a very dangerous position, friend; all the posts in this neighborhood are in the possession of the British, while the roads between are filled with Tories; a man must have his wits about him to get through.

ROBINSON. We Whigs, Musgrove, have a touch of the hobgoblin about us, and travel just where we please.

MARY *runs in.*

MARY. [*Embracing* ALLEN.] Oh! my dear father! how glad I am to have reached home. I am frightened nearly out of my wits—there has been such doings. [*Seeing* ROBINSON—*eagerly.*] Ah! Mr. Horseshoe—where's Major Butler?

ROBINSON. Blessings on you, for a wise and brave girl! We were ambuscaded, and the Major is still a prisoner. I thank you all the same, though. You're a stout-hearted American lass, and 'twould be happier for our country if more of her sons owned a share of your courage!

CHRIS *rushes in breathless, his nose bleeding and clothes dishevelled.*

MARY. Oh! Chris, what's the matter?—do speak!

CHRIS. I will—as soon as—as I get my second wind!— Oh!—sich a time with them dogs!

ROBINSON. Red-coats?

CHRIS. Yes—over at Ramsay's. There was Ensign St. Jermyn and his biled lobsters helpin' themselves most promiscuously to all the fowls, ducks and geeses they could lay hands on. It made my blood bile, I tell you, to see 'em cuttin' up, frightening all the women-folks into prayin' convulsions. Say, nunkey, is my nose swelled much?

MUSGROVE. No, no. Let's have it.

CHRIS. Yes, and I let them have it. One of the rascals chased a pet lamb, that ran and hid its head in little Julia Ramsay's lap, bleating just as if it knowed they were butchers, and ran there for protection and mercy. Say, nunkey, my nose feels mighty queer;—the rascals hit me on it with the butt of a musket.

MARY. Never mind your nose, Chris—go on.

CHRIS. Well, the hyena never heeded the lamb, or little Julia's prayers, but cut the lamb's throat while its little mistress's arms were clasping its neck. Dang it! I couldn't stand that, so I told him he was a bloody-minded villain. Consequently and accordingly, he pitched inter me. 'Twas rough and tumble—nip and tuck for a while, but I got the best of it. I was a-chawing his under lip off quite comfortably, when I got this smash over the nose from a musket, which drew my attention from him for awhile.   [*Slight thunder.*

ROBINSON. Did they leave then?

CHRIS. Yes, the Ensign—drat his skin!—said it looked squally, and he'd hurry off to camp afore it rained, 'cause he had to attend a court-plaster, or some sich thing, on a Corporal or Colonel Butler.

ROBINSON. [*Starting.*] Ha! That's the game, is it?

                                      [*Rain slightly.*

CHRIS. He said if it did rain, they could shelter in the old ruined meetin'-house, 'cross the fields, whar I *dessay* they now are, and whar I hope they'll all be struck by lightning!

ROBINSON. The old meetin'-house stands, if I don't disremember, about half way atwixt here and their camp, eh?

CHRIS. Exactly so, squire.

ROBINSON. This rain will soon come down heavily, and 'tis likely they've sheltered. An idee's took possession of my mind that's worth the trial. [*To* CHRIS.] How would you like a scrimmage with these chicken-thieves?

CHRIS. How would I like it?—better than peach-brandy!

ROBINSON. [*Crossing to* MUSGROVE.] Musgrove, what arms have you in the house?

MUSGROVE. We've a rifle only.

CHRIS. And my big horse-pistol—don't you remember that?

ROBINSON. Well, I'll take the liberty of borryin' your rifle, if you'll fetch it for me.

CHRIS. Nunkey, bring my horse-pistol while you're about it.   [MUSGROVE *exits into house.*

MARY. What are you going to do, Mr. Horseshoe? Pray

don't take Chris! He's such a desperate little fellow, he'll be sure to grow rash, and rush into danger.

ROBINSON. There's no danger, my lass. I'll only want him to bring home the prisoners I'll captur'.

MARY. Yes, but you can't take prisoners, Mr. Horseshoe, without fighting.

ROBINSON. As a general thing, you're right; but in this partick'lar instance, I'll adopt Pat's mode of warfare, and "surround the divils."

Re-enter MUSGROVE, *with rifle and pistol. Rain descends hard.*

Now, Corporal Chris, I'll lead the army—do you bring up the rear.

MARY. Well, Chris, if you're determined upon going, I hope you'll behave like a hero.

CHRIS. Won't I!—I begin to feel heroic already. Do you see any change in my countenance? Don't I look sublimely heroic?—I know I do! Come, Mister—I'm ready. Forrad—march!

> [*Music, "Yankee Doodle"*—CHRIS *locks step with* ROBINSON—*Exeunt,* MARY *and* MUSGROVE *watching their departure.*

SCENE II.—*Front Wood—Rain, heavily—Thunder and lightning.*

ROBINSON *and* CHRIS *enter in the order of the previous exit.*

ROBINSON. Keep the lock of your pistol down, and cover it with the flap of your jacket, to preserve it from the rain. By the smoke rising from the old cabin, I know they're snugly stored there. Cautiously, Chris.

CHRIS. [*In a whisper.*] All right, Mr. Horseshoe.

ROBINSON. Don't call me Mister, mind you, in the hearing of these rascals. Let it be Captain, Corporal, Major, or anything but Mister.   [*Thunder.*

CHRIS. All right, Mr. Major.

ROBINSON. I'll creep along the edge of the woods, and dash in among 'em unawares. They'll be mighty apt to think they're surrounded, and surrender.

CHRIS. I don't want 'em to surrender till arter I've licked 'em.

ROBINSON. The moment they surrender, dash in and secure the arms. If they show fight, make the best of your way off.

CHRIS. What! and desert you? No, I'll be dog-goned if I will. That ain't a Southern principle. I'll stick by you, Quartermaster, as long as I can see and smell. [*Rain, heavily.*

ROBINSON. Keep your primin' dry. Now, quietly!

[*Exeunt cautiously.*

SCENE III.—*Interior of a dilapidated Hut—Practicable door and window—Muskets stacked against wall—Rain, heavily—Thunder—Lightning.*

Camp-fire, around which five English SOLDIERS *are gathered, with* ENSIGN ST. JERMYN, *right.*

ENSIGN. Confound this climate! It's as variable as a coquette's humor. Unless the squall ceases soon, I shall be detained here beyond the hour fixed for the trial of the rebel, Butler.

CORPORAL. Ensign, you seem to have a grudge against this Butler?

ENSIGN. And with good cause. He is an implacable enemy of my brother.

ROBINSON *peeps on, at door.*

CORPORAL. Indeed! why, when I stood sentry over him last night, he asked who our commanding officer was. I told him Colonel St. Jermyn, and he said he did not know him.

ENSIGN. That may be. My brother met him in Virginia, where circumstances rendered a change of name necessary, and he is known to this rebel only as Tyrrell, an English officer. There can scarcely exist a doubt of his guilt; he'll surely be convicted—— [ROBINSON *has now entered and placed himself before the arms of the party*] and die the death of a dog.

ROBINSON. [*With levelled rifle.*] I reckon not! [*They all start, and rush forward to grasp their arms.*] Don't budge, or you're a dead man! [*Calling off.*] File off right and left!—surround the house, and some of you search the woods.

CHRIS. [*Outside.*] All right, Captain—I mean Corporal.

ROBINSON. Now, surrender, you pestiferous chicken-thieves! I'll blow out the brains of the first man who moves a foot! [*They appear determined to rush upon him.*] Ah! would you? Move, and I'll pull the trigger!

ENSIGN. Cowards! would you be intimidated by one man? Seize your arms, and annihilate the lurking rebels!

ROBINSON. Come on, you chicken thieves! but the fust that advances is a dead rooster!

CHRIS *appears at window, levelling pistol at* ENSIGN.

CHRIS. How are you, Insign? what's the price of flour now? Say, General, sha'n't I blaze away among 'em? [*Calling off.*] Here, boys—come in and take a hand.

ROBINSON. No! no!—Keep 'em outside!

CHRIS *enters through window.*

Ensign, my men are gitting impatient; I don't keer about harming you, so you'd better surrender to the Continental Congress: and this scrap of its army I command.

ENSIGN. [*To English party.*] We are, indeed, surrounded. Lower your rifle, sir. Taken by surprise and by a superior force, I shall offer no further resistance.

ROBINSON. I'll trouble you, Ensign, to lay down your pistol and sword, and whatever other ammunition of war you mought chance to have about you. [ENSIGN *casts his pistol and sword upon floor.*] Advance, Corporal, and receive them ere articles.

[CHRIS *creeps cautiously, and secures arms, presenting his pistol at every fancied move of the* ENSIGN.

CHRIS. [*During movement.*] Ah! I see you. I'll perforate your gizzard if you budge!

ROBINSON. Now we're safe, Chris. Two to six is desp'rit odds, but we've won the game!

ENSIGN. What! duped—tricked—by two clodpoles! On 'em, lads!—they are but two!

ROBINSON. [*With levelled rifle.*] Ay!—but two armed and determined men.

CHRIS. Me in partic'lar. I'm the most determinedest little chap you ever seed; so keep cool, or you'll have a chunk of lead on visiting terms with the vitalest part of your everlastin' gizzard.

ENSIGN. Feeling that no mercy is to be expected at the hands of savages, who war by cunning, I shall offer no further resistance.

ROBINSON. Savages, are we? No marcy from us! Did your butcher, Tarleton, show marcy to *us*, when, at the Waxhaws, he mercilessly butchered Colonel Buford's two hundred men *arter* they had surrendered? was marcy shown to brave Colonel Isaac Hayne, whom ye hung within sight of his family? *We* savages! I tell you, Ensign, the shrieks of women ravished by your comrades—the groans of parents murdered, and the sighs of wives, whose bodies you've ripped open for refusing to disclose the hiding-places of their sons and husbands—and the prayers of the hundreds of noble patriots daily martyred!—rise hourly to the throne of Eternal Justice, calling for divine vengeance upon men whose cruelty, in this war, finds no parallel in history!

CHRIS. Corporal—I mean Captain—let me shoot one!— just one. There's that little cross-eyed chap in the corner. He ain't no use to anybody!

ROBINSON. You prate of marcy—when scarcely a minute since I heard you say that Major Butler, a noble patriot and soldier, would be hung like a dog, and only because he dared defend his country against your invading blood-hounds! I won't condescend to hold further parley with you; here! [*takes from his hat a slip of writing-paper, and pencil from his pockets*] write as I shall dictate.

ENSIGN. What shall I write?

ROBINSON. Major Butler, who's in your brother's power, is a dear friend of mine: write then, and say to Colonel St. Jermyn, that you are held a prisoner by them as wouldn't hesitate to blow out your brains, if the least harm should fall on Major Butler, and that you'll be held in pawn till the aforesaid Major has had a fair and impartial trial, as befits his rank and station.

ENSIGN. I will not—cannot write that!

ROBINSON. [*Sternly.*] Write, or as I am a true man, and a soldier, I'll brain you where you stand!

ENSIGN. Oh! spare me, sir! I am young, have a mother and sister in England——

ROBINSON. What American was ever spared by your tiger-like companions, because he had mother or sister? Write, or——

ENSIGN. Enough! I write, sir!—but on compulsion only.

[CHRIS *beckons trooper forward; makes him stand in stooping posture, while* ENSIGN *writes on his back.*

ROBINSON. Write fairly. Remember, sir, your life depends upon that letter!

CHRIS. [*Overlooking* ENSIGN.] Lootenant, make him cross his T's. He doesn't dot his I's. I wish I had the dotting of 'em. [*Threateningly.*

ROBINSON. [*Taking letter.*] Chris, my lad, I must trust the delivery of this letter to you, while I take the Ensign to a spot whar he won't be likely to suffer from any interruption of the red-coats.

[*English quick-step played by brass instruments behind scenes.*]

ENSIGN. Ah! 'Tis English music! Shout, boys!

[ROBINSON *and* CHRIS *both level guns.*

ROBINSON. Another whisper, and you're a dead man! Look out, Chris, and see what it is.

CHRIS *backs up to window—looks hastily out.*

CHRIS. [*Whispering.*] A party of red-coats coming up the road! I can see 'em through the trees!

ROBINSON. Fall in! [*To* ENGLISH.] Fall in, I say! Now push for the woods—not a word! Your lives hang on a whisper!

[ROBINSON *leads the way, followed by* ENGLISH, CHRIS *bringing up the rear. Exeunt through door.*

SCENE IV.—*Front Wood.*

Enter ROBINSON *and party, in order of previous exit.*

ROBINSON. On! on! if we're overtaken, Ensign, you'll be the fust man shot.

CHRIS. Quick step, you rapscallions! or I'll jam this bayonet into a vital part. [*Looks back.*] They're a-comin', Captain. Push a-head! Go it—cripples and all!

[*Exeunt—English* SOLDIERS *get behind to be discovered.*

SCENE V.—*Landscape and Military Encampment—Set tents—Flagstaff with English colors, arranged to come down by the run—On either side of staff stack of arms, and a drum, upon which small English flags are laid transversely—Flourish.*

SENTRY *pacing stage, at back—*SOLDIERS *range with reversed arms—Table at the head of which,* ST. JERMYN *discovered —*DU POISTRE *to the left—*OFFICERS *grouped around—* BUTLER *on one side—*ADAIR, HABERSHAW *and* CURRY *on the other.*

ST. JERMYN, *or* TYRRELL. Major Butler, be seated, sir.

BUTLER. I prefer standing. It is my pleasure to hear the behests of my country's enemies in the attitude a soldier would choose to meet his foe in the field.

TYRRELL. [*Rising.*] The charges advanced against you are contained in this paper, which you have declined reading. First, *That you have violated your pledged word of honour* as expressed at the capitulation of Charleston. Secondly, Insinuating yourself, as a spy, into territory conquered by the royal troops, and endeavouring to win, by bribery, intelligence, which you designed using against the peace of his Majesty's government. Thirdly, That, with a confederate, you attempted to seize upon a subject of his Majesty's government, of great esteem and consideration, a Mr. Lindsay. The offense of treason and forfeiture of your plighted word——

BUTLER. He lies in his throat, who charges me with forfeiture of my plighted word! True, I have arrayed myself against what you are pleased to term "his Majesty's government," and I am proud to confess it here, in the midst of your band—but if aught be said which could attaint my honour, I throw the lie in the teeth of my foul accuser, and will make good my word whenever and wherever I may be permitted to meet the slanderer.

TYRRELL. A milder tone would better become you, Sir Rebel, in my presence. You are a native of Carolina?

BUTLER. I can scarcely deny that before one whom, I recently learned, has, during my absence, been busy in the investigation of my affairs.

TYRRELL. [*Starting.*] Insolent rebel! I understand the taunt. Your estates *have* been the subject of consideration, and, if my advice be listened to, the process will be a short one. Speak, sir! what say you, in reply to the allegations you have heard?

BUTLER. What should an honest man say to charges of dishonesty? They are each and all contemptibly false!—the evident efforts of a concealed enemy. Confront me with that man, and if I do not prove him an atrocious slanderer, I will tamely submit to whatever penalties the most exasperated of my enemies may invent.

CHRIS SHAW *enters, accompanied by* MARY, *bearing a basket of apples.*

MARY. [*Passing among* OFFICERS.] Buy my apples, gentlemen?—only three for a penny! They are very mellow! [TYRRELL *purchases*—MARY *crosses to* BUTLER, *and curtseying, offers him fruit. Whispering.*] Friends are about! Horseshoe Robinson is doing all he can for you!

[*Retires up.*

CHRIS. [*Apart.*] I feel my blood simmerin'—it'll bile over directly, and I'll be sure to tell the cut-throats all I think of 'em!

TYRRELL. Let the trial proceed. [*Calls.*] James Curry!

CURRY *advances.*

The court is prepared to hear your evidence.

CURRY. Please the court, I was present at the siege and final capture of Charleston, and have frequently seen the prisoner among the rebel officers, who were subsequently released on parole. A month or two ago, I accompanied my superior officer to the Dove-cote, in Virginia, the residence of Mr. Phillip Lindsay; and one day, whilst strolling through the woods in its vicinity, I accidentally overheard the prisoner and a notorious bully named Horseshoe Robinson——

CHRIS. [*Apart.*] You'll git your fifth rib stove in for that.

CURRY. Concoct a plan to seize upon Mr. Lindsay. Urged by indignation, I rushed from my hiding-place, and taxed them with their perfidy. I was thereupon violently assaulted by both, and with difficulty escaped with my life. They, the same night, departed for the rebels' headquarters South.

[*Bows and retires.*

CHRIS. [*Apart.*] That's a wholesale rotten lie!

MARY. Now do, Chris, keep your temper.

TYRRELL. [*Calling.*] Wat Adair!

ADAIR *advances.*

ADAIR. Please your worships, I had private word given me that a Continental officer, named Butler, accompanied by a desperate bully, named Horseshoe Robinson, would pass my cabin on their way South, at a certain time. Sure enough, in good time, they did come; and arter eating and drinking all they could force me to set afore 'em, this chap, Major Butler, said, if I'd give him some information concerning of the road to Ninety-Six and how it mought easily be took, he'd pay me handsomely. Of course, I refused the money——

CHRIS. [*Apart.*] Oh, of course, not the remotest doubt of it.

ADAIR. And declined givin' 'em any information; where-upon they both got cantankerous, and if my wife hadn't doc-tored the primin' of their guns—for she didn't like the looks of 'em from the fust—there's no tellin' whar I'd now be.

CHRIS. [*Apart.*] You'd be holdin' a confidential chat with the devil, or there ain't no sich chap!

MARY. [*Advancing to table, curtseying.*] Oh! please, gentlemen, hear me. Uncle Wat has told a great big story!

CHRIS. [*Interrupting.*] In point of fact, a damned big whopping lie!

HABERSHAW. Order! order!

MARY. I was at Walter Adair's the night Major Butler stopped there, and, I declare, he merely asked the road to the ford, offering to pay Uncle Wat for his trouble if he'd guide him. And so far from this gentleman being violent, it was Uncle Wat who first insulted them. They only beat him when he tried to hurt me. This is the truth, gentlemen. I couldn't tell a lie to save my own life!

CHRIS. And dash my old hat, if she'd tell one to save any-body else's! [TYRRELL *whispers to* CURRY, *who exits.*

HABERSHAW. Silence! you dog!

TYRRELL. [*Annoyed, to* MARY.] Who are you?

MARY. I am Mary Musgrove, sir, the miller's daughter.

CHRIS. Yes, and I'm his nephy; and if anybody here says I ain't, let 'em come out—that's all!

[*Throwing off his cap, and squaring.*

TYRRELL. Be silent, sir, or I'll have you placed under arrest. [*To* MARY.] You are an innocent girl, and easily imposed upon. Your uncle's testimony is capable of the fullest confirmation. [*Calls.*] Hugh Habershaw!

HABERSHAW. [*Advancing pompously.*] Your worship, I can fully corroborate all that my esteemed and veracious friend, Adair, has said. I was at Grindall's Ford with my brave squad, innocently enjoying myself, when this rebel Major, and his bully, came riding up. No sooner did they spy us, than whiz went a bullet by my ear, and they came pelting up full tilt. They soon found the work too hot, however, and the chap called Horseshoe Robinson made tracks. I followed him, but, cuss the devil, he had a grip like a blacksmith's vice, and by some sleight of hand, he capsized me down an embankment, where he left me, up to my waist-belt in mud—and saying he had an engagement which prevented his keeping my company, and wishing me all manner of ill-luck, rode out of sight. [*Retires up.*

TYRRELL. [*Rising.*] Major Butler, a fair and impartial trial has been granted you, and the evidence against you has been full and conclusive; nor have you been able to offer any rebutting testimony. You stand, accordingly, convicted of the three charges advanced against you; yet, ere we proceed to pass sentence, let us remind you that there are means at your disposal to avert the doom which will otherwise assuredly fall upon you. If—— [*Pause.*

BUTLER. Aye, speak it! Speak out the base thought that is rising to your lips! and, prisoner though I am, I will resent the insult! You would have me renounce the cause to which I have consecrated my life, and take shelter amongst the coward recreants that have crowded beneath the blood-stained banner of England. Spare yourself the trouble, sir. Death, to me, is a thousand times preferable to a life of shame!

CHRIS. Hurrah! I can't help it, Mary! I must, or I'll explode again. Please, your honour—no, burn me if I'll call him that!—your excellency—I mean Squire—respectin' this 'ere case, I want to give my opinion, though you hain't asked it. Now, my opinion is—and I charge you nothin' for it— that when an open-hearted, gentlemanly American is on one side of the question, and a set of damned cut-throats—present company excepted—on the other, why, dang me, I'd take the Major's word agin a whole army of 'em!

TYRRELL. Remove this clodpole from the camp!

[HABERSHAW *and* ADAIR *seize* CHRIS, *and bear him off*.

CHRIS. [*As he is borne off*.] Say, Quartermaster—them's my sentiments!

MARY. [*Following to wing*.] Oh! gentlemen, please don't hurt Chris!

[*Volley of musketry. Drum and flourish.* TYRRELL *starts, and comes forward, followed by* OFFICERS. MARY, *unseen, places letter on table. Enter* CURRY. HABERSHAW *and* ADAIR *re-enter*.

TYRRELL. Ha! Sergeant, what means this firing?

CURRY. Important news, sir, has arrived from Camden. Two days ago Lord Cornwallis defeated Gates, and cut his army entirely to pieces! [SOLDIERS *on stage give three cheers*.

BUTLER. God knows I feared this! Oh! my poor country, now commences thy reign of blood!

TYRRELL. Good news indeed! Sergeant, see that the victory be properly celebrated.   [CURRY *exits*.

DU POISTRE. Here is a letter, sir, addressed to you, I found upon the table.

TYRRELL. [*Reading written paper*.] "To Colonel St. Jermyn:—By ill luck I have fallen into the power of the Whigs. They have received tidings of the capture of Major Butler, and, apprehending that some mischief may befall him, have constrained me to inform you that my life will be made answerable for any harsh treatment he may receive at the hands of our friends. They are resolute men, and will certainly make me the victim of their retaliation.

"EDGAR ST. JERMYN."

A forgery—a shallow trick to aid the rebel! But the artifice shall not avail. What ho! Frazer, lead out the prisoner, and shoot him without delay! [*Apart to* BUTLER.] Now, Sir

Rebel, your time has come! [*Gives paper to* HABERSHAW, *who exits with* ADAIR.

BUTLER. I am ready, sir! I am glad I am, at least, permitted to die a soldier's death, and from my country's enemies. I shall face them, sir, as proudly as I have ever done upon the field of battle! My chief regret is, that I have but one life with which to attest my devotion to my country, and to her sacred cause!

TYRRELL. [*Standing down, front, apart from, and unheard by other characters on the scene.*] Indeed! Boasting rebel, now learn that your death removes the only bar to the realization of my dearest hopes! and when the corroding hand of time shall have blotted out the name and memory of Arthur Butler, Mildred Lindsay shall then be the wife of——

BUTLER. [*With sudden comprehension.*] Tyrrell?

TYRRELL. Ay, of Tyrrell! Have you no dying request you would convey to her?

BUTLER. Dastard! But I have no fear of your anticipated triumph;—for when I fall, be assured, she will receive—ay, and respect my last legacy—a freeman's scorn and hatred of his country's oppressors. [*To* OFFICER.] Conduct me to my fate!

TYRRELL. [*Vehemently.*] Ay, lead him to his doom! but be it no soldier's death! Let him perish like a rebel spy! Let him swing till the buzzards fatten on his corse!

MARY. Cruel man! Oh! heaven, if the prayer of youth and innocence can sway thy power, oh! suffer not this murder, but smite the oppressor with thy wrath!

TYRRELL. Silence, insolent wench! To the death with him!

[*Dead march*—SOLDIERS *march down, with reversed arms, and form across stage*—BUTLER *takes an affectionate leave of* MARY, *to whom he, unseen, gives a letter, kisses locket, and takes his position in centre of file of* SOLDIERS, *who march off to music of Dead March, and followed by* MARY.

TYRRELL. [*Exultingly.*] Mildred Lindsay, you are mine! Who, now, will interpose between us?

[*Sudden volley of musketry, commingled with clash of swords and the shouts of general combat*—*Drums*—

COLONEL WILLIAMS *enters, engages with, and drives* TYRRELL *off—English* SOLDIERS, *pursued by* AMERICANS, *fight across stage*—CURRY *enters, desperately defending himself against* ROBINSON—*They exit*—CHRIS *enters, driving* HABERSHAW *before him with stick—and out*—SOLDIERS *appear, and fight indiscriminately—Flourish*—ROBINSON *returns, tears British ensign from staff, and tramples it under foot*—ENGLISH *overpowered—Music, "Yankee Doodle," in orchestra till curtain descends.*

END OF ACT II.

ACT III.

SCENE I.—*Lawn in Front of* MR. LINDSAY'S *Mansion.*

Enter HENRY *and* MILDRED.

HENRY. You have risen early, sister.

MILDRED. Yes, Henry; the uncertainty of the times, and rumours of disasters to our cause, have filled my heart with dreadful imaginings of evil. Where is Steve?

HENRY. I saw him a moment since, preparing for his journey. Yonder he comes in his new regimentals.

Enter STEVE, *with soldier's hat and coat on.*

Well, Steve, are you prepared for a start?

STEVE. Indeed I is, Massa Henry. I bought dis coat from a diseased German granny dear 'specially for de journey.

HENRY. *Deceased,* I presume you mean.

STEVE. Well, it's pooty much de same. A feller's got to be *diseased* before he can be *deceased.*

MILDRED. Remember, Steve, it is a perilous enterprise you have undertaken, and, though I repose the utmost confidence in your fidelity and sagacity, yet you must necessarily encounter many shrewd enemies before you can safely accomplish your mission. The letter, mind you, must be delivered only into the hands of Major Butler, who is, I think, in the neighborhood of Ninety-Six.

STEVE. I'll deliver it, Miss Milly, if I have to crawl to him on my knees.

MILDRED. My father has consented to your taking as much time as may add to the success of my wishes.

STEVE. I won't stay longer dan I can help, Miss Milly, unless dere's any scrimmaging goin' on; in which case, I'd like to have an independent shot at dem Britishers, on my own hook.

HENRY. [*Looking off.*] I see father coming; let us leave, Steve.

STEVE. Come in de barn, Massa Henry, and finish teaching me dem military tactics afore I start dis arternoon.

[*Exeunt* HENRY *and* STEVE.

Enter MR. LINDSAY.

LINDSAY. Mildred, I have sought you to hold earnest conversation with you. Arthur Butler has been here—here, within the confines of my own dwelling—and you have concealed it from me. Have I not forbade all intercourse with him?—a base wretch, who would murder my peace, and steal its treasure from my heart.

MILDRED. Arthur Butler is one, father, who would scorn a base or dishonourable act, under whatever guise it might present itself. He was in this neighbourhood but for a single hour, attended by a single person, and left southward in the performance of his duties on the same evening. We met but for a few moments.

LINDSAY. My child, thou art innocent in thy nature, and know not the evil imaginings of this world. If he told you he came hither casually, he wickedly lied. I have here a letter assuring me Butler's visit in this neighbourhood was, with his wicked confederate, to seize upon my person, and compel me to the sacrifice of my dearest hopes.

MILDRED. It is false, father! He is not your enemy, and would sooner lay down his life than indulge a thought of harm to you. They falsely slander him who attribute to him aught than the purest motives; and if Mr. Tyrrell has such accusations to make, they should be made face to face with the man he would slander, rather than in my father's ear.

LINDSAY. This earnestness assures me you love him still— outlawed traitor and beggar as he is.

MILDRED. I loved him in his happier and bright days—I will not desert him in his adversity.

LINDSAY. And will neither time nor reflection root from your heart its fatal passion for that rebel?

MILDRED. Never! Call it infatuation, say it befits not my womanly reserve to acknowledge it; but if misfortune or death should fall upon Arthur Butler, there is that bond between us that I also must die.

Enter ROBINSON.

ROBINSON. If I mought be so bold, ma'am, as to ax, how fur am I from a place they call the Dove Cote?

LINDSAY. Does business take you there?

MILDRED. [*Eagerly.*] Are you from the army?

ROBINSON. Beg pardon, ma'am, but I'm an old soldier, and rather wary 'bout answering questions which consarn myself. I suppose it's likely I mought see a Mr. Lindsay there?

LINDSAY. 'Tis he who now addresses you.

ROBINSON. [*Crossing.*] Mayhap then you've hearn tell of Major Butler?

MILDRED. [*Eagerly.*] Oh, yes, sir! If you've any news from him, pray speak it quickly.

ROBINSON. By that sparkling of your eye, miss, 'tis no fool's guess that you are the identical lady I've ridden nigh on to three hundred miles to see. Major Butler, who has fallen into the power of the Philistines——

MILDRED. He has fallen into the enemy's hands!—he is wounded! Oh! quickly tell me all, or I shall die! Is he wounded?

ROBINSON. Not in body, ma'am; but he must be sore cut up in *sperit,* being prisoner to a heartless chap—you mought remember—called Tyrrell.

MILDRED. Tyrrell! Oh! my heart feared this.

ROBINSON. We were ambuscaded by a set of human bloodhounds, and the Major taken prisoner; I escaped, and—— Howsomever, ma'am, as I ain't no fust-rate hand at speechifying, I'll let the Major talk for himself. I've got some letters which he sent me through a little petticoat soger, for yourself and father.

MILDRED. Letters! Oh! quick, my good man, let me have them. Where are they?

ROBINSON. [*Seating himself.*] Do you see that foot, ma'am? It ain't so small but that I could put a letter crossways atwixt its upper and lower soles; correspondently, I stitched 'em in, and here they are.

[*Handing a letter to* MILDRED *and one to* MR. LINDSAY.

MILDRED. [*Hastily reading.*] 'Tis too true, dear father. Arthur has fallen into the power of Tyrrell, and his life is endangered upon the false and frivolous charge of attempting to seize your person.

LINDSAY. My letter states he had been tried by a court-martial and doomed to death, when his fate was averted by a sudden attack of the Whigs.

MILDRED. Where is he now?

ROBINSON. At present he's confined at Allen Musgrove's mill, under strict guard; but from the nature of those having him in charge, it ain't wise to calculate on his perfect safety. Mebbe he'll be shot without law.

LINDSAY. Those are the chances of war, sir.

ROBINSON. But not of fair or honourable war. This ambuscading an enemy's officers by cut-throats; murdering, by court-martial, them as fought fairly and openly agin you; this killing of women and children, and the burning down of peaceful homes, is a sorry business to tell of a Christian people, and a *cowardly* business for a nation like England, that's always boasting of its bravery. I trust, sir, you'll justify Major Butler's confidence in your generosity, and, as you have the influence, will go forrad, and, with one word of truth, save him from the lion's, or rather from the *tiger's* claws.

MILDRED. [*Crossing.*] Oh! go, dear father, and permit me to accompany you. You know the charge against him to be false, and your heart is too noble to tacitly lend itself to so infamous an attempt against the life of a brave man, and he—your daughter's husband.

LINDSAY. Your husband!

MILDRED. Yes, I need not blush to own, that for nearly a year have I been the wife of Arthur Butler.

ROBINSON. Hang me if I didn't think so! Well, the best wife a man can have, is the woman that takes to him through fire and water.

LINDSAY. Well, my child, heaven disposes of all events

for the best, and I will not murmur at the destruction of my dearest hopes. Come, let us prepare for this journey; my private animosities and deep-seated prejudices shall all be sacrificed upon the shrine of truth and justice.

ROBINSON. Spoken like a brave man, squire. But we've no time to spare; so drive ahead, and huzza for the volunteers of Dove Cote! [*Exeunt.*

SCENE II.—*Room at* MUSGROVE'S—*a very plain chamber.*

SENTINEL *pacing to and fro behind centre door*—BUTLER *seated right of table.*

BUTLER. This suspense and inaction is terrible in the extreme. To know that friends encompass me, whose brave hearts are hourly accomplishing the destiny of our country, while I, by this mortifying captivity, am debarred all participation in their glorious efforts. Dear Mildred, if Robinson has not forgotten me——

MARY MUSGROVE *enters centre door with basket—she places her fingers on her lips to express caution.*

MARY. [*Ostentatiously for* SENTRY'S *ear.*] My father thinks, sir, it belongs to a Christian people to do all we can for those Providence has placed under us; and I've gathered you some blackberries, thinking you might like them.

BUTLER. [*Going forward.*] You are a considerate girl, and I thank you.

MARY. [*Whispering.*] Father has arranged all for your escape to-night; he's being assisted by a colored man from Virginia, named Steve Foster.

BUTLER. Ah!

MARY. Who says he has a message and a letter for you, he'll deliver to no one else. He says the Whigs are rising in Virginia and in Carolina, and that a great battle is expected shortly.

BUTLER. Brave hearts! God prosper them! I feel inspired with fresh hopes of life.

Enter CHRIS *through centre door.*

CHRIS. [*Whispering.*] Major, it's all settled; you're to escape from the lobsters to-night.

BUTLER. Is the opportunity favourable?

CHRIS. Anything better wouldn't do as well. That dratted lynx-eyed Jeems Curry is going over to Ninety-Six to-night, on important business, and 'tain't likely he'll be back afore morning. I pumped from the drunken cut-throats that to-morrow they intend joining Ferguson's camp at Gilbert Town; but they won't stop there long, for Williams, Campbell, Shelly, and several other never-say-die southern true-blues are arter them fast and strong.

BUTLER. How will you dispose of the sentry?

CHRIS. Oh! leave him to me. If he should get obstropo-lous, I'll take him by the throat and strangle him as genteelly as it could be done. [*Loud laughter outside.*

MARY. Oh! if they should grow quarrelsome and get to fighting among themselves!

CHRIS. I wish they would, and make a Kilkenny cat affair of it. Steve Foster—and he's a good un—is down in the woods ready to *fersilitate* your escape.

BUTLER. Depend upon it, if the attempt does not succeed, it shall not fail through want of effort on my part.

CHRIS. I've our old mill-horse ready-saddled, and though "Wall Eye" ain't the most gracefullest critter to look at, he's a real good 'un to go.

[SENTINEL *stops and listens suspiciously.*

MARY. The sentry seems to grow suspicious at our whispering. We'd better leave you now, sir.

CHRIS. Remember, Major, when I whistle, get out of the windy.

[*Exit* MARY *and* CHRIS. BUTLER *resumes his seat at table, gazing at miniature.*

HABERSHAW. [*Outside.*] Hello! hello! pooty carrying on's this. Why ain't you watchin' your Yankee Doodle prisoner? I'll have you court-martialed for neglect of duty! [*Enters, slightly intoxicated.*] What are you setting down there for, you lazy rebel? Stand up! and thank your stars you haven't your arms tied behind you like a horse-thief.

BUTLER. [*Starting up.*] Insolent ruffian! leave this room, or, by heaven, I'll hurl you from the window!

HABERSHAW. Dare you speak thus to Hugh Habershaw? I'll cleave your skull! [*Advances with uplifted saber— MAJOR hurls him to the floor with the stroke of a chair—is*

about to repeat the blow, HABERSHAW *attempting to rise.*]
Help! Murder!

[SENTINEL *appears and levels his piece. Tableau.*

SCENE III.—*Very plain Front Chamber.*

HABERSHAW *heard exclaiming, outside. Enter* CURRY, *followed by* HABERSHAW.

CURRY.   Silence, you bully! Stop that infernal yelping!

HABERSHAW.   But damn it, Peppercorn, would you have me suck my thumbs while a traitorous and rebellious Yankee Doodle was beating a reveille on my skull?

CURRY.   You received your deserts, old bully.

HABERSHAW.   Bombs and bullets! I'll be revenged, by the everlastingly immortal Phœnix of eternity, I'll have revenge!
[*Half drawing sword.*

CURRY.   Come, Mr. Bragger, put up your cheese-knife till you know how to use it.

HABERSHAW.   Damn it, Peppercorn! don't irritate me—there's fighting blood in me.

CURRY.   Then it must have been let out long ago—damn it, when the rebels lately attacked our camp, you were the first to run like a frightened deer.

HABERSHAW.   All my superior tactics; and if they'd only kept on following me——

CURRY.   They would probably be following you yet. In my absence, keep an eye on the prisoner; and no more worrying him, or you may be helped to a taste of your favorite remedy, the court-martial.   [*Exit.*

HABERSHAW.   Damn it, Peppercorn! this is a breach of discipline. I'll resign.   [*Exit.*

SCENE IV.—*Exterior of* MUSGROVE'S *Mill, same as Act II, Scene I. Stage three-quarters dark.*

SENTRY *discovered, pacing stage, disappearing off stage at each round.* MARY *enters, cautiously, from house, and looks expectantly off. Enter* HABERSHAW, *from house.* CHRIS SHAW *and* STEVE *enter quickly, and conceal themselves behind tree.*

HABERSHAW.   Devil's bird! he shall be hung to-morrow!

Here, Clapper-claw! [*To* SENTRY.] Go in; I'll keep watch myself. [SENTINEL *exits into house. Seeing* MARY.] Ah! my lass, what are you peering at the moon for? An appointment, eh? Sly young puss! [*Chucks her under the chin.* CHRIS *starts forward, threateningly—is pulled back by* STEVE.] Eh! who's that? By my honour, I heard something. [*Drawing pistol.*] We'll see.

MARY. Oh! 'tain't worth your while, sir, to look. It's only Adam Gordon—he's half-witted, and about the only thing he does for a living is to come down here and bob for eels.

HABERSHAW. Oh! bobs for eels, does he? Well, Mister Adam Gordon must find some other time than night to come bobbing for eels. [*Producing flask.*] Won't you drink, lass? Well, here's your eternal good health. [*Attempts to chuck her under chin.* CHRIS *again starts forward, restrained by* STEVE.

MARY. [*Crossing.*] It's getting late, sir, and I'll leave you to your watch. But if you should hear anybody, please, sir, don't shoot—it will most surely be Adam Gordon taking his eels home.

[*Gives* CHRIS *a glance of intelligence, and exits into house.*

HABERSHAW. Bobbing for eels, eh? Ha! ha! ha! [*Yawns, and seats himself against portico.*] Curse it! how heavily the dews fall. [*Drinks.*] Bobbing for eels, eh? I must be on the lookout. [*Nods, dosingly.*] Catch a weasel asleep, and maybe you'll catch Captain Habershaw in a like predicament. [*Yawns and drinks.*] Damn this brandy! it's strong enough to make a statue wink. [*Falls murmuringly to sleep.* CHRIS *and* STEVE *come cautiously forward.*

STEVE. He's off, sure enough.

CHRIS. [*Flourishing stick.*] I'd like to wake him up, suddenly.

STEVE. Don't, Massa Chris, you might hurt his feelings.

CHRIS. Let's make sure of the old Belzebub. Tie him up in a meal bag, and throw him in the mill-dam; that's the easiest way of washing away his iniquities.

STEVE. We can do that arterwards; let's tie him now where he sits.

CHRIS. Good!   [*They proceed to bind him.*

HABERSHAW. [*Asleep.*] Bobbing for eels, eh?

CHRIS. Mebbe you'll go bobbing next.

HABERSHAW. [*Asleep.*] That's right; tie up the scoundrel. Tighter!

CHRIS. [*Pulling cord tightly.*] Oh! tighter, eh? Well, I like to oblige you.

STEVE. Dat's it! Now whistle for de Major.

[CHRIS *whistles peculiarly.* BUTLER *appears at window and commences descent.* STEVE *keeps watch over* HABERSHAW.

HABERSHAW. Damn it, Peppercorn! that's a breach of discipline. [BUTLER *reaches ground*—CHRIS *gives him sword.*

ADAIR *Enters.*

ADAIR. [*Firing pistol at* BUTLER.] What ho! Treachery! Escape! [*Engages with* BUTLER.

[STEVE *belabours* HABERSHAW, *who awakes.* BUTLER *cuts down* ADAIR, *as* CURRY *enters and attacks him.* ROBINSON *enters and engages with* ADAIR, *whom he finally cuts down.* CHRIS, *meantime, belabours the* SENTINEL, *who runs on from house at first alarm. Red fire in house.* CURRY *and* BUTLER *are still fighting, when scene quickly closes. The whole action brief and spirited.*

SCENE V.—*Front Wood.*

Enter COL. WILLIAMS *and the Carolinian partisan* SOLDIERS, *with* CAMPBELL.

CAMPBELL. So Ferguson is on the retreat, eh?

WILLIAMS. The fellow has a good deal of the bulldog about him, and stops to snarl and growl as if he'd defy us to follow him.

Shouts. [*Outside.*] Hurrah for Butler! Hurrah for Horseshoe Robinson!

Enter BUTLER, *followed by* ROBINSON, STEVE, *and* MUSGROVE.

WILLIAMS. [*Grasping* BUTLER'S *hand.*] 'Tis my old comrade, Butler.

ROBINSON. Fresh from the hands of the ongodly Philistians. We had a regular scrimmage at Musgrove's, when I arrived from Virginny, just in time to lend the Major here a helpin' hand. Out of spite, the varmints fired the mill; so we've brought Musgrove and his family along.

BUTLER. I have come to solicit a place in your ranks, where I trust the chances of battle may enable me to atone for my long enforced and miserable inactivity.

WILLIAMS. Welcome, comrade; you shall fight my equal in command. [SOLDIERS *all shout.*

ROBINSON. Ah! that's sweeter music than any piannyforty I ever heerd. But Major, I can't permit my Dove Cote Volunteers to be neglected in this 'ere awful way; so, if you won't introduce them, I must. [*Exit.*

BUTLER. True, gentlemen, I must claim your protection for a lady friend, who, to save my life and refute a falsehood, has traveled hither from Virginia, accompanied by her father and brother.

Re-enter ROBINSON, *conducting* MILDRED, *and followed by* MARY, LINDSAY *and* HENRY LINDSAY. MILDRED *crosses to* BUTLER.

WILLIAMS. Our friend, Major Butler, has acquainted us, Madam, with the motive of your presence in our camp. As soldiers and men, we will do all we can to serve and protect you; and if you will risk the perils of a camp——

MILDRED. I have tempted the dangers of flood and of storm for *his* safety, and I would not now blench, though the worst of dangers should present themselves.

LINDSAY. For myself, sir, I should prefer seeking the English camp. Conceiving that to be impossible, I will content myself with saying that I have accompanied my daughter hither through a sense of duty; and, however greatly recent circumstances have tended to alter my views respecting the justice of this quarrel, I must, for the present, beg permission to withdraw from your councils.

WILLIAMS. Assuredly, sir; our expedition requiring speed, we leave behind us all our infantry. With those, yourself and daughter can remain until the battle is decided. [*To* SOLDIER.] Conduct this gentleman to our camp.

[SOLDIER *exits, followed by* LINDSAY.

Shouts outside. Enter CHRIS, *waving folded paper.*

CHRIS. [*Crossing to* WILLIAMS.] Here's a paper, Lieutenant, which the red-coat I took it from, arter thrashing him, said was a dispatch from Ferguson to Cornwallis.

WILLIAMS. [*Taking and reading it.*] 'Tis, indeed. Ferguson says: "I have fortified myself on a mountain which, in honour of his Majesty, I have called 'King's Mountain'; and all the rebels out of hell cannot drive me from it."

ROBINSON. I ain't much of a prophet; but pound me into mincemeat, to feed hogs, if I don't think that barking dog will yelp for marcy afore sundown. Say, Major, can't you tip 'em a bit of speech, just to warm up their sensibilities a little?

BUTLER. Ah, Robinson! if the sacred sentiments of resistance to oppression animates their hearts, as I am sure it does, there will need no words of mine to incite them on to such deeds of heroism as Thermopylæ alone can parallel. [*Crossing to corner.*] Up, brothers of the holy cause! Before us is the enemy, that so long has gorged upon the best blood of our country—will you hesitate to rush upon and crush him? Is there a man amongst you who does not hail with eager joy this opportunity of revenging his murdered and fallen comrades?

CHRIS. Whoop! Stand off! I'm cantankerous, and mought bite.

BUTLER. Up, then! in the reverenced name of liberty!— by the memory of the martyred dead, whose sacred blood has consecrated our cause, and whose spirits now look smilingly down upon our enterprise from their abodes of bliss—in the name of your wives, your children, and your country!— strike! and strike deeply!

ROBINSON. That's the talk! By gum!

BUTLER. Come, then, comrades! Upon the high and holy altars of liberty, we'll once more offer our libation of blood; and, fail or triumph, our purpose, our names, and our this-day's deeds, will be forever registered among the most sacred memories of a grateful people.   [SOLDIERS *shout.*

ROBINSON. Forward, brothers! To King's Mountain!

OMNES. Aye, to King's Mountain! to King's Mountain!

[*Exeunt all but* BUTLER, MILDRED, *and* MARY.

MILDRED. Brave hearts! Oh! may the God of justice give success to your terrible sacrifices! Look, Arthur! see how beautifully bright the sun smiles down upon them, kissing their rifles with his golden rays, as if sanctifying them to the cause of freedom! May the omen prove auspicious, and its brightness typify the smiles of liberty shed upon her successful defenders!

BUTLER. My brave Mildred! the hour for action has come.

MILDRED. Go, Arthur—go, dear husband—I know your heart throbs to participate in this struggle for freedom, and I will not detain you. Yet—oh! coward that I am—my soul is chilled with apprehensions for your safety. Should you fall—oh! go, go, Arthur! 'twere madness now to think of that. Go, my husband, and may God protect you! [*Vehement shout to the right. Throws herself, weeping, upon his breast.*

BUTLER. [*Crossing to right.*] They have reached the hill; I must no longer delay. Adieu, Mildred! Should I fall, your true heart will find a solace for its grief in the consciousness that I fell where manhood and duty called me—battling on my country's soil, beneath my country's flag, and in defense of my country's liberty. Farewell. God bless you! [*Rushes out.*

MARY. They are all gone, and how lonesome it does feel, to be sure. Oh! I do wish I was a man—if only a little one—I would rush to encounter these invaders as eagerly as a bride rushes to meet her husband. I think I see my Chris rushing into all sorts of dangers. I wish they could fight without hurting or killing each other. Don't you think, ma'am, we could creep near enough to see what was going on?

MILDRED. Any danger were preferable to remaining here in this terrible suspense. I cannot endure it. Come, Mary, we'll follow them, and enjoy at least the sweet consciousness of being near those dear ones whom danger threatens. The same Great Power that has endowed woman's heart with an instinct of love, no time can weaken, nor danger appal, will protect us and those loved ones for whose safety we pray. [*Exeunt.*

SCENE VI.—*Interior of* ST. JERMYN'S *Tent, King's Mountain.*

Enter TYRRELL *and* CURRY.

TYRRELL. Curses on the swaggering upland bullies! They are for turning the tables on us, eh? Any later news of the rebels?

CURRY. They have left Gilbert Town with a picked force of nine hundred Virginians and Carolinians, and are rapidly approaching our position.

TYRRELL. Let 'em come! The skulking dogs! We'll send 'em yelping back to their kennels. I hold a position here impregnable to all the rebels the country contains.

Enter HABERSHAW, *quickly.*

What the devil's the matter, Sir Cut-throat?

HABERSHAW. The ventur'some Yankee Doodles are upon us. The rascals mean mischief, for they march as silently as Quakers to a prayer meetin'.

TYRRELL. We must enliven 'em a little. Give orders for an immediate charge of bayonets. [*Alarms.*

Enter ENSIGN ST. JERMYN.

ENSIGN. The rebels are closing round the hill. Among the foremost, I distinguish Butler and Robinson.

TYRRELL. Ah! then my triumph is near. [*Crossing.*] On 'em! Remember, 'tis war to the knife! *"Crush the damned rebels into the earth!"* [*Exeunt.*

SCENE VII.—*The Base of King's Mountain. English banner on apex of mount. Alarms.*

Musketry—noise of combat. English and American SOLDIERS *engage up hill, with alternate success.* BUTLER *drives* CURRY *across stage—* ROBINSON *drives* TYRRELL *in same direction—* WILLIAMS *drives* ENSIGN *across—* STEVE FOSTER, WAT ADAIR—CHRIS SHAW *finally beating* HABERSHAW *across. Re-enter* CURRY, *fighting with* WILLIAMS.

CURRY. Die, dog! [*Kills* WILLIAMS, *who falls off stage.*

Enter ROBINSON.

ROBINSON.   But not unrevenged!

[*Combat*—CURRY *is killed.* BUTLER *slays* TYRRELL *after set fight. Other characters and soldiery contending up mountain side.* CHRIS *enters, pursuing* HABERSHAW, *whom he shoots, and, at descent of curtain, bestrides, endeavoring to behead him.* STEVE *shoots* ADAIR. *Enter* LINDSAY, *conducting* MILDRED, *bearing American flag.* MARY, ALLEN MUSGROVE, *all the characters on.*

THE END.